THE OXFORD HANI

ENVIRONMENTAL POLITICAL THEORY

Set at the intersection of political theory and environmental politics, yet with broad engagement across the environmental social sciences and humanities, *The Oxford Handbook of Environmental Political Theory* defines, illustrates, and challenges the field of environmental political theory (EPT).

Featuring contributions from distinguished political scientists and scholars in related fields, this volume addresses canonical theorists and contemporary environmental problems with a diversity of theoretical approaches. The initial section focuses on EPT as a field of inquiry, engaging both traditions of political thought and the academy. In the second section, the handbook explores conceptualizations of nature and the environment, as well as the nature of political subjects, communities, and boundaries within our environments. A third section addresses the values that motivate environmental theorists—including justice, responsibility, rights, limits, and flourishing—and the potential conflicts that can emerge within, between, and against these ideals. The final section examines the primary structures that constrain or enable the achievement of environmental ends, as well as theorizations of environmental movements, citizenship, and the potential for on-going environmental action and change.

Teena Gabrielson is Associate Professor of Political Science and Associate Dean of the College of Arts and Sciences at the University of Wyoming. Her work on environmental citizenship, justice, and toxics discourse has been published in distinguished scholarly journals such as *Environmental Politics*, *Theory & Event*, and *Citizenship Studies*.

Cheryl Hall is Associate Professor of political theory in the School of Interdisciplinary Global Studies at the University of South Florida. She is the author of *The Trouble with Passion: Political Theory Beyond the Reign of Reason* and other work exploring the roles that emotions, values, imagination, deliberation, stories, and structures play in encouraging or discouraging more just and sustainable ways of life.

John M. Meyer is Professor in the Department of Politics, in Environmental Studies, and in the Environment and Community program at Humboldt State University in Arcata, California. He is the author of *Engaging the Everyday: Environmental Social Criticism and the Resonance Dilemma* (MIT Press, 2015), as well as other books and articles in environmental political theory.

David Schlosberg is Professor of Environmental Politics in the Department of Government and International Relations, and the Director of the Sydney Environment Institute at the University of Sydney. He is the author of *Defining Environmental Justice*, co-author of *Sustainable Materialism* and *Climate Challenged Society*, and co-editor of *The Oxford Handbook of Climate Change and Society*, all with Oxford University Press.

THE OXFORD HANDBOOK OF

ENVIRONMENTAL POLITICAL THEORY

Edited by
TEENA GABRIELSON,
CHERYL HALL, JOHN M. MEYER,
and
DAVID SCHLOSBERG

OXFORD
UNIVERSITY PRESS

OXFORD
UNIVERSITY PRESS

Great Clarendon Street, Oxford, OX2 6DP,
United Kingdom

Oxford University Press is a department of the University of Oxford.
It furthers the University's objective of excellence in research, scholarship,
and education by publishing worldwide. Oxford is a registered trade mark of
Oxford University Press in the UK and in certain other countries

First published 2016
First published in paperback 2019

Published in the United States of America by Oxford University Press
198 Madison Avenue, New York, NY 10016, United States of America

British Library Cataloguing in Publication Data
Data available

Library of Congress Cataloging in Publication Data
Data available

ISBN 978–0–19–968527–1 (Hbk.)
ISBN 978–0–19–882386–5 (Pbk.)

Cover illustration: © niyazz/123 RF

Acknowledgments

FIRST and foremost, we thank the collective wisdom of the participants in the environmental political theory workshop, held in Portland, Oregon, in March of 2012. More than 50 scholars there brainstormed the themes and contours of a handbook on this topic, and ensured a breadth of understanding that no single editor or editorial team could have matched.

Second, we thank Sam Gomes. Now a graduate of Humboldt State University with a major in philosophy, Sam reviewed and edited every chapter for consistency with Oxford's editorial standards, created systems to track the progress of all chapters through the revision process, and generally gave us the confidence that nothing was slipping through the cracks in the final stages of the unwieldy process of bringing this *Handbook* to completion.

Third, we thank Dominic Byatt and the entire team at Oxford University Press for supporting this project and shepherding the manuscript from proposal through to the final page proofs.

Finally, we thank each other. Some had suggested to us that four co-editors might become more cumbersome than helpful, but our experience proved otherwise. The range of our academic interests and skills proved complementary, and as a team we've been able to keep the *Handbook* moving forward whenever one or more of us faced professional or personal obstacles. Overall, it has been an incredibly productive, collaborative, and engaging partnership from which we have each learned and grown.

Contents

ENGAGING THE ACADEMY

PART III RETHINKING NATURE AND POLITICAL SUBJECTS

NATURE, ENVIRONMENT, AND THE POLITICAL

ENVIRONMENT, COMMUNITY, AND BOUNDARIES

PART IV ENDS, GOALS, IDEALS

SUSTAINABILITY

JUSTICE, RIGHTS, AND RESPONSIBILITY

FREEDOM, AGENCY, AND FLOURISHING

PART V POWER, STRUCTURES, AND CHANGE

IDENTIFYING STRUCTURAL CONSTRAINTS AND POSSIBILITIES

THEORIZING CITIZENSHIP, MOVEMENTS, AND ACTION

List of Illustrations

Figure

Tables

List of Contributors

John Barry is Professor of Green Political Economy in the School of History, Anthropology, Philosophy and Politics, Queen's University Belfast.

Mark Beeson is Professor of International Politics, University of Western Australia.

Andrew Biro is Professor in the Department of Politics, Acadia University.

Ingolfur Blühdorn is Professor of Social Sustainability at the WU Vienna University of Economics and Business and Head of the Institute of Social Change and Sustainability.

Mark B. Brown is Professor in the Department of Government, California State University, Sacramento.

Simon Caney is Professor in Political Theory, University of Warwick.

Peter F. Cannavò is Professor in the Department of Government, Hamilton College.

Romand Coles is Professor in the Institute for Social Justice, Australian Catholic University.

Diana Coole is Professor Emerita of Political and Social Theory in the Department of Politics, Birbeck College, University of London.

Giovanna Di Chiro is Professor of Environmental Studies at Swarthmore College.

Lisa Disch is Professor in the Department of Political Science, University of Michigan.

Andrew Dobson was Professor of Politics in the Department of Politics, International Relations, and Philosophy at Keele University.

John S. Dryzek is Professor in the Institute for Governance and Policy Analysis, University of Canberra.

Robyn Eckersley is Professor in the School of Social and Political Sciences, University of Melbourne.

Elisabeth Ellis is Professor of Philosophy and Politics, and Director of the Philosophy, Politics, and Economics Programme at the University of Otago.

Samantha Frost is Professor in the Department of Political Science and the Department of Gender and Women's Studies, University of Illinois.

Teena Gabrielson is Associate Professor of Political Science and an Associate Dean of the College of Arts and Sciences at the University of Wyoming.

Farah Godrej is Associate Professor in the Department of Political Science, University of California-Riverside.

Cheryl Hall is Associate Professor of political theory in the School of Interdisciplinary Global Studies at the University of South Florida.

Breena Holland is Associate Professor in the Department of Political Science and The Environmental Initiative, Lehigh University.

Paul Knights is a Postdoctoral Fellow in the Department of Philosophy, University of Manchester.

Jason Lambacher received his Ph.D. from the University of Washington-Seattle and currently teaches at University of Washington-Bothell.

Amy Linch is Lecturer in the Department of Political Science, Pennsylvania State University.

Timothy W. Luke is University Distinguished Professor in the Department of Political Science, Virginia Polytechnic Institute and State University.

Sherilyn MacGregor is Reader in Environmental Politics, joint-appointed to the Sustainable Consumption Institute and Politics Department at the University of Manchester, UK.

Joan Martinez-Alier is Professor, ICTA-Universitat Autònoma de Barcelona.

John M. Meyer is Professor in the Department of Politics, and programs in Environmental Studies and in Environment and Community, Humboldt State University.

John O'Neill is Hallsworth Chair in Political Economy, University of Manchester.

Adrian Parr is Dean and Professor at the College of Architecture, Planning and Public Affairs at the University of Texas at Arlington, and the UNESCO Chair on Water and Human Settlements.

Sean Parson is Associate Professor in the Department of Politics and International Affairs, Northern Arizona University.

Matthew Paterson is Professor of International Politics at the University of Manchester.

Emily Ray is Assistant Professor in the Political Science Department, Sonoma State University.

Catriona A. H. Sandilands is a Professor in the Faculty of Environmental Studies at York University and a 2016 Pierre Elliott Trudeau Foundation Fellow.

David Schlosberg is Professor of Environmental Politics in the Department of Government and International Relations, and the Director of the Sydney Environment Institute at the University of Sydney.

Kimberly K. Smith is Professor in the Departments of Environmental Studies and Political Science, Carleton College.

Piers H. G. Stephens is Associate Professor in the Department of Philosophy, University of Georgia.

Seaton Patrick Tarrant is Assistant Professor of Political Science and Sustainability Studies at the Oregon Extension in Ashland, Oregon.

Leslie Paul Thiele is Professor in the Department of Political Science and the Director of Sustainability Studies, University of Florida.

Steve Vanderheiden is Associate Professor, Department of Political Science, University of Colorado.

Steven Vogel is Professor in the Department of Philosophy, Denison University.

Kyle Whyte is Associate Professor and Timnick Chair in the Humanities in the Department of Philosophy, Michigan State University.

Justin Williams is a Ph.D. student in the Department of Political Science, University of Michigan.

Harlan Wilson is Emeritus Professor in the Department of Politics, Oberlin College.

Kerri Woods is Lecturer in the School of Politics and International Studies, University of Leeds.

Rafi Youatt is Associate Professor in the Department of Politics, New School for Social Research.

PART I

INTRODUCTION

CHAPTER 1

INTRODUCING ENVIRONMENTAL POLITICAL THEORY

TEENA GABRIELSON, CHERYL HALL, JOHN M. MEYER, AND DAVID SCHLOSBERG

What Is Environmental Political Theory?

What is "environmental political theory?" No doubt many readers begin this handbook reasonably confident that they have a sense of what the field addresses or entails. Yet for many others the contours of the field are likely quite opaque. In both cases, we are confident that the essays collected here will challenge and intrigue readers with their diverse subject matter, their fresh approaches to complex challenges related to the environment and sustainability, their insightful analyses, and their effective modeling of engaged and problem-centered political theorizing. Nonetheless, the question remains: what is environmental political theory (EPT)? We begin by sketching a preliminary answer, with the understanding that many of these points are developed more fully later in this introduction. Of course, the more adequate answer only unfolds throughout the handbook in its entirety.

As we and many contributors to this volume understand it, EPT is a broad field of inquiry in which some of the tools and techniques honed by political theorists—conceptual critique; normative analysis of structures of power; close reading of texts; nuanced and multifaceted understandings of political values including democracy, justice, and freedom; and eclectic methodologies drawing upon diverse disciplines—are utilized to develop insight into contemporary environmental challenges. EPT, then, is best understood as a broad field of inquiry rather than a rigid ideological position or a partisan allegiance to a particular political agenda. It is, however, characterized by the conviction that massive, often global concerns regarding climate change, species extinction, toxic pollution, and many others pose a broad and deep challenge to both political thinking and political communities, today and in the future.

At least since Aristotle, political theorists have paid normative and critical attention to the role that the non-human world plays in political community and political change (see the chapters in this handbook by Harlan Wilson and Peter Cannavò). Yet such attention has often remained at the periphery of their theories. Moreover, while some political theorists have attended to the human relationship with nature or the non-human, this relationship has by no means been consistently valued. EPT moves it to the center of its inquiry. Beyond this, it seems clear that although EPT theorists differ in their normative assessments, they are motivated not only to theorize about the human relationship to nature but also to theorize about ways to reverse, mitigate, and/or adapt to ecological threats and devastation.

Alongside its normative and critical attention to the non-human, environmental political theory also attends to structures of power within the human world. In this sense, EPT doesn't simply ask what we should do to address human impacts on the non-human world. Such a question can posit an abstract "view from nowhere," and, in neglecting to address explicitly how normative prescriptions can be adopted and implemented in society, can be read as presupposing that such prescriptions will be imposed by some sort of philosopher-king . . . or perhaps scientist-king. Work in EPT is often self-conscious in challenging this sort of presupposition. It explores how normative prescriptions become refracted through systems of power and privilege in political decision-making and in society (see, for example, Tim Luke's chapter). Along these lines, EPT also often poses questions about the implications of the arguments and rhetoric advanced by activists and policymakers involved on all sides of contemporary political discourse about environmental concerns.

EPT follows the work of many other political theorists in attending to the nature and meaning of long-central—and contested—political concepts, including justice, democracy, and freedom (see, for example, the chapters by Steve Vanderheiden, Elisabeth Ellis, and Jason Lambacher, respectively). These concepts permeate political discourse surrounding environmental concerns, yet their meaning is often left curiously unexamined. Examining them now is especially crucial given that many of these political concepts were developed in very different environmental contexts. How, for example, might a conception of democracy be altered by the realization of the value of the non-human realm, or the qualities of individual non-human entities? Moreover, new terms and concepts, including the Anthropocene, biodiversity, and—perhaps most visibly and influentially—sustainability, have come to play an important role in relation to environmental concerns. These concepts, too, have become subject matter for inquiry in EPT (and are addressed, for example, in the chapters by Giovanna Di Chiro, David Schlosberg, and Ingolfur Blühdorn).

EPT can be described directly, but another way to appreciate its contours is to notice that which it seems positioned against. In all their diversity, environmental political theorists nonetheless share a critique of those who—explicitly or implicitly—view environmental challenges as something that can be contained in the box of a particular "issue area" for government policy and civil society action. And against the longstanding practice of political theorizing narrowly focused upon a rational, liberal, individual human, the field is also premised on the recognition that political action exists within an ecological context, and often articulates the need to recognize non-human as well as human agency (as, for instance, can be seen in the chapters by Rafi Youatt, Justin Williams, and Lisa Disch).

Finally, while it seems wholly compatible with the pursuit of EPT to make use of scientific work to identify, document, model, and predict the character of major challenges such as climate change, species extinction, and other manifestations of ecological devastation, EPT is positioned against the temptation to move beyond science to scientism. That is, it rejects the notion that scientists should not only provide empirical understanding but normative authority as well. In response to this move, EPT raises a red flag, drawing attention to the processes of interpretation, contestation, and value-based judgment that necessarily mediate between scientific insight and political authority. In other words, EPT sees science and scientists as necessary but not sufficient in the effort to address environmental challenges. As Mark B. Brown's chapter in this handbook demonstrates, the precise character of the contribution by scientists (and science) makes all the difference.

The Emergence of Environmental Political Theory

As the discussion up to this point illustrates, to understand what EPT is, it is most important to understand its substantive interests and orientations. Yet one can also gain insight into both the contours and limitations of this field of inquiry by noticing its institutional and disciplinary locations. While work that might be labeled "environmental political theory" has been authored by scholars in philosophy, history, environmental studies, and other disciplines—as well as by authors from outside the academy—the field as such emerged in the 1980s and 1990s largely from the work of political theorists who were located within the discipline of political science. For those outside of this disciplinary location, a bit of explanation may be in order. For better or (and?) for worse, since at least the 1960s, political theory has been located *in* the discipline of political science, but has not been positioned as exactly part *of* this discipline. In part, this is a reflection of the tension between political theory's normative approach and the largely empirical approach of the rest of the discipline. More particularly, it reflects political theory's resistance to influential strands of the discipline that are committed to a positivist methodology. In an earlier generation this narrow methodological focus was manifest in a commitment to behaviorism; more recently this commitment has been superseded by the influence of rational choice theorizing (for further analysis of political theory's relationship to political science, see the chapter by Kimberly Smith).

Regardless of the explanation, one consequence of the rather loose connection between political theory and political science has been a notable degree of freedom for political theorists. Michael Walzer has referred to this freedom as a political theory "license" that has allowed practitioners to transgress usual disciplinary boundaries and schools of thought (Walzer 2013). In the field of political theory in general, transgression has often meant drawing upon work and influences from other fields, including philosophy, intellectual history, and cultural studies. Yet EPT presses the interdisciplinary borrowings far more widely, drawing from ecological science, science and technology studies, geographic thought, environmental history, and many other fields that can inform our understanding of the relationship of humans to non-human and more-than-human phenomena.

EPT shares other conventions with contemporary political theory besides transgression. Holding relatively loose obligations to the discipline of political science, political theorists have often treated the history of Western political thought as a resource for critical engagement; theorists have been regarded as sources that might illuminate contemporary political dilemmas, offer critical distance on contemporary political conceptions, and provide context for understanding some of the silences and blind-spots in contemporary social and political discourse. Of course critical engagement with this tradition is quite distinct from normative embrace of it. Many environmental political theorists share the sense that contemporary dilemmas might be better understood by working through the ideas of long-dead Western thinkers, a sense that often distinguishes them from environmental writers emerging from other locations in or out of the academy. But EPT has also become much more than a reinterpretation of past thinkers.

The foundations for EPT as a self-aware field were laid in the late 1980s and early 1990s, with the publication of works including John Dryzek's *Rational Ecology*, Robyn Eckersley's *Environmentalism and Political Theory*, Val Plumwood's *Feminism and the Mastery of Nature*, and Andrew Dobson's *Green Political Thought* (Dryzek 1987; Dobson 1990; Eckersley 1992; Plumwood 1993). Of course, these works did not appear out of the blue. They emerged from an interest in making political theory relevant to a key and growing set of political concerns made evident by decades of fervent and diverse forms of environmental activism. This activism included the obvious efforts to protect wild places, endangered species, and habitats. But it also included movements against nuclear energy and for demilitarization, for more appropriate development paths in non-industrialized societies, for ecological restoration, for public health, and (by the 1990s) for environmental justice, among others.

EPT also emerged in the shadow of the institutionalization of new environmental policies in many industrialized societies during the 1970s. Both the promise and the performance of these institutions could thus be evaluated in the years that followed, and many people concluded that earlier hopes had proven hollow or gone unrealized. A variety of critics—both inside and outside the academy—began to develop bodies of explicitly normative environmental thought, including environmental ethics, eco-feminism, and so-called deep ecology. Strikingly, relatively few of the early works in these literatures focused on the significance of political structures and ideas. Among the exceptions were William Ophuls' *Ecology and the Politics of Scarcity* and Murray Bookchin's *Ecology and*

Freedom, each of which was critically engaged by the environmental political theorists who followed (Ophuls 1977; Bookchin 1982).

It seems fair to say that, as it has emerged since these earlier decades, EPT as a specific field has been largely an Anglo-American academic dialogue. More precisely, it has been writers in and from Australia, Canada, the United Kingdom, and the United States who have been most visible in the construction of the field, though thinkers from continental Europe have also made important contributions. To be clear, though, this description of the field of EPT only refers to the primary centers of self-identified scholarship and teaching activity. Many of those involved draw upon the work and ideas of other scholars, intellectuals, and activists from the Global South and other parts of the world, though the latter do not—at least at present—usually characterize their work as EPT per se.

Having attempted to define and situate EPT in this introduction, we hasten to add that the field remains inchoate and its boundaries porous (for more developed accounts of EPT's emergence and contours, see Meyer 2006 and Luke 2015). By no means would everyone whom we have identified as an environmental political theorist—including some contributors to this volume—self-consciously adopt the label for themselves.

Labeling the Field

Finally, no attempt to answer the question "what is environmental political theory?" can end without some consideration of the very name of the field (and hence the title of this volume!). A number of different labels have been—or might be—applied: among others, "green political thought," "political ecology," and "political theory of sustainability." As editors of this handbook, we considered all of the above and more as potential titles. Yet in the end, despite the fact that EPT is far from a perfect name, no other title seemed to have the sort of broad acceptance necessary to supplant it.

"Green" political thought (or theory), widely used especially throughout the 1990s and early 2000s, is perhaps the most obvious alternative. Some have argued that "green" is a broader label than "environmental": specifically, that it more effectively flags the field's expansive interest in the intersection of environmental concerns with those of social justice, nonviolence, and the valuation of the non-human world for more than instrumental purposes. By contrast, according to this argument, "environmental" political theory appears to connote the mere application of already formed political theories to the "issue" of "the environment." While this argument raises important criticisms, and a number of theorists have continued to use this moniker as a result, other theorists worry that the "green" label is too readily identified with green political parties, and that work in the field will thus be construed as necessarily aligned with these parties or their ideology. A more inclusive or less partisan label seems needed.

"Political ecology" might serve the purpose. The term "ecology" has the advantage of connoting a more holistic and interconnected system, whereas "environment" often just connotes our "surroundings." Adding the adjective "political" to "ecology" could draw many elements of the field together. Yet there is an academic reason to shy away from this name, as it is already widely identified with the established work of a generation of scholars in anthropology, geography, and related fields, whose work often focuses upon the commons, resource use, and management issues, especially in rural communities. While work by these political ecologists has often greatly influenced that of environmental political theorists, it is in no way identical to it.

As with "green" and "ecology," the term "sustainability" is also understood by many as a more encompassing term than "environmental." Sustainability is often said to be premised on a foundational interconnection of three elements: the "3 Es" of ecology, economy, and equity. Thus, sustainability might be used to describe political theory in this area. The reality, however, is that relatively few have done so. In this handbook, we examine sustainability as a singular concept within a broader field of potential issues, interactions, and actors in the environmental space.

Our ambivalent conclusion, then, is that, despite its inelegance, "environmental political theory" is currently both the most recognizable, distinctive descriptor of this field and the least inadequate one. It is for these practical reasons more than any more principled ones that we have adopted it in the title, and throughout the contents, of this handbook.

The Vision for the Volume

As EPT has developed as a field of inquiry, so too have its practitioners developed as an academic community. Those interested in the intersection of political theory and the topic of environment aimed to differentiate their subject from both traditional foci within the field of political theory and the standard understanding of environmental politics as solely concerned with environmental *policy*. As is the case with many new cross-field efforts, this differentiation was initially difficult in the everyday life of political science conferences. While the main conferences of political scientists were not particularly receptive places for environmental theory (something that has begun to change in recent years), the annual meeting of the Western Political Science Association (WPSA) in the United States, with its reputation for excellent panels and participants in both political theory and environmental politics, became a place where those interested in the intersection came together. The "Environmental Politics and Policy" section, with its growing panels in science and technology policy and theory, environmental movements, and, importantly, "New Books in Environmental Politics," became a place for EPT and engagement with key books and authors. The WPSA has been supportive of the development of communities, as demonstrated by the various groups it has encouraged to host annual pre-conference workshops, including on feminist political theory and Latino/a politics. With this support, the EPT community grew. It began to host its own workshop in 2002, at times including over 60 scholars ranging from senior faculty to new Ph.D. students. And in 2004, EPT gained its own section in the Association's annual conference; the section currently averages approximately 14 panels with some 50 papers presented each year.

When the idea of a handbook on EPT first came up in 2012, the possibility was presented to the attendees at the WPSA pre-conference workshop in Portland, Oregon, who discussed it as a group. The goal of the discussion was to collectively develop general categories and specific topics to cover, a basic structure for the endeavor, and a list of potential contributors and editors. Over 50 people participated in a lively conversation about the field and its representation, leading to an initial list of 60 potential topics to address. Looking back on that crowd-sourced listing of ideas, we are pleased to note that the current collection covers all but seven of those suggestions. This process of engagement with the EPT community allowed for a broader conception of the field than any small set of editors could provide, generating suggestions for chapters and topics broadly intersecting with both other political science subfields and environmental subfields of related disciplines, including sociology, geography, economics, women's studies, and philosophy. At the conclusion of this discussion, the current team volunteered to serve as editors of the handbook.

Goals

Our primary goals in constructing this *Handbook of Environmental Political Theory* have been to respect past work in the field, represent the broad landscape of present concerns and scholarship, and point to new directions. Wherever possible, we have sought to be forward looking, engaging a variety of ideas about where the field may go in the coming years and even decades. Our task, as we see it, has not just been to identify foundational ideas and arguments in the field, but also to press outward to highlight key new ontologies, directions, foci, movements, pedagogies, and more.

We commissioned a number of chapters that illustrate these new directions, and explore areas not yet familiar to some—perhaps even many—who are familiar with the field of EPT. EPT has always been an inclusive endeavor, open to a wide range of approaches to the intersection of politics, theory, and the environment in which we are immersed. In this light, we have included a number of chapters from authors in disciplines other than political science whose work is nevertheless crucial to this mission; this includes philosophers such as Steven Vogel, Kyle Whyte, Paul Knights, and John O'Neill, and political economists such as Joan Martinez-Alier. We have also included many from political science who do not necessarily self-identify as environmental political theorists, though it is our conviction that their interests fit squarely within this field of inquiry; this includes Mark Beeson, Diana Coole, and Matthew Paterson. Overall, we believe the current collection represents how far the field has come, illustrates its broad base of material and appeal, and offers some sparks for new conversations—and, hopefully, some controversy.

Audience

Given the broad conceptual base of EPT, and as is evident in our wider than usual casting of the net for authors in a handbook of this type, we aim to appeal to an expansive readership. Clearly, one key audience is the range of existing scholars in the self-identified EPT community. Another key audience is students—both undergraduate and graduate—interested in learning about and potentially joining this engaged (and inviting) field. But we also hope to appeal to the growing number of political theorists and political scientists reflecting on the questions at the heart of our endeavor, perhaps as a result of frustration with the limits of attention to the non-human world in their own fields. And we aim to bring EPT to a range of environmental thinkers in other disciplines, and interdisciplinary fields such as environmental studies, who wish to explore a broader interdisciplinary conversation on the political change necessary to address the vast environmental challenges we face today.

The Organization of the Volume

Environmental Political Theory as a Field of Inquiry

While we understand the field of inquiry of EPT to be shaped by lively engagement with a broad and interdisciplinary array of scholarly work, we begin with a section that acknowledges EPT's indebtedness to and deep roots in the field of political theory. With chapters dedicated to the traditions of liberalism, republicanism, and critical theory (by Piers Stephens, Peter Cannavò, and Andrew Biro, respectively), this section both explores Western political thought as a rich resource for environmental political theorists and probes its limits for understanding, unpacking, and explaining a host of current political problems related to nature, non-humans, and the environment. As Harlan Wilson explains in his opening chapter, through close readings of Western thinkers, environmental political theorists have both appropriated and critiqued the approaches, concepts, and logics of past political theorists so as to explicate the politics that have contributed to our current ecological crises and to imagine more just and sustainable alternatives. Complementing these chapters, Farah Godrej's essay examines the potential of non-Western approaches for conceptualizing environmental issues. As a whole, the essays in this first section engage the past as a source for contemporary theorizing and revitalize our understandings of influential texts by considering how they respond to new orientations and concerns. Initiating a conversation that is sustained over the entire volume, they reflect on how we might best bring our normative commitments and critical theorizing to bear on contemporary material practices that, in many instances, threaten the future of humans and non-humans alike. The next set of essays turns to EPT's place in the academy in order to distinguish EPT from adjacent fields such as political science and environmental ethics and to convey its unique contribution to emerging disciplines such as sustainability and environmental studies. Focusing on the student, these essays pull the reader into the classroom by detailing the role of experiential learning, action research, and practically engaged political theory in the pedagogy of many EPT courses (chapters by Romand Coles, and Seaton Tarrant and Leslie Thiele).

Rethinking Nature and Political Subjects

The chapters in this section address two fundamental questions: "What is the environment?" and "Who or what is included in the political community?" These chapters are positioned less directly with respect to the historical texts of political theory; instead, they engage more closely with a Euro-American lineage of environmental thinkers that includes conservationists, preservationists, social constructionists, and, most recently, new materialists. Essays under the subheading "Nature, Environment, and the Political" each draw out the implications of different conceptualizations of the environment for our ability to address large-scale socio-political-ecological problems such as global climate change, environmental management, and human–non-human relations. From Steven Vogel's identification of the processes that tend to reify the built environment to Samantha Frost's discussion of the challenges that posthumanism presents to the human/environment dualism, this section offers insights for how we might think more productively about environment. The next set of chapters, gathered under the subheading "Environment, Community, and Boundaries," investigates questions of inclusion and exclusion as they inform our understandings of key political concepts such as sovereignty, power, justice, and obligation. The reach of these chapters is broad, including well-established topics such as cosmopolitanism in Simon Caney's essay as well as much more recent areas of inquiry such as the sensory powers of plants in Catriona Sandilands' essay. As a whole, the section demonstrates EPT's interdisciplinary character through chapters that engage with scholarship in geography, philosophy, animal studies, feminist theory, science and technology studies, and postcolonialism. The section is populated by plants, buildings, humans, animals, nation-states, networks, global processes, and habitats . . . all toward the end of better understanding how already existing interspecies relations, biopolitics, and conceptions of the environment and political community inform our ability to address environmental challenges in the age of what some have come to call "the Anthropocene."

Ends, Goals, Ideals

From the more phenomenologically minded section focused on *who* and *what* is explored in EPT, in this section we turn to the question of *why*. What values motivate both environmentalists and EPT scholarship? Echoing the concerns of many other political theorists, authors in this section illuminate core political ideals including justice

(Giovanna Di Chiro), responsibility (Robyn Eckersley), and rights (Kerri Woods). But several of the chapters in this section also demonstrate EPT's engagement with values inspired by environmental movements of the twentieth and twenty-first centuries, including sustainability and environmental justice, or reorient political concepts such as "limits" (Andrew Dobson) and "human flourishing" (Breena Holland and Amy Linch) to address the non-human as well. As a whole, these essays consider both how environmental political theorists have made use of traditional political ideals and norms such as justice and rights, and how environmental concerns have inspired re-conceptualizations of these ideals. At root, these chapters offer responses to the classic question of political theory, "What does the (or a) good life entail?," while taking into consideration some combination of the major factors that characterize our time, including capitalist logics of growth (John Barry), climate change, the pleasures of consumer society, the practices of neo-liberal forms of governance, the pressures of population growth (Diana Coole), the structures of racial, gender, and class inequalities, and widespread and growing environmental degradation. Tensions proliferate within and across these essays as the authors grapple with the conflicts that emerge among and between environmental and political values, collective and individual ends, and contemporary needs that bump into long-standing discursive formulations and institutional structures.

Power, Structures, and Change

The final section of our volume, dedicated to the question of *how* we might move forward, encompasses a great deal of territory. The first seven chapters examine some of the primary structures that constrain and/or enable the institutionalization of environmental ends. Together these chapters question and reflect on current relations among the state, citizens, the environment, and the economy. They draw our attention to the discourses and concepts that inform our understandings of these roles and the mechanisms through which power is articulated. Adrian Parr's analysis of neo-liberal forms of governance is followed by chapters that examine governmentality, the "green" state, scientific expertise, democratic action, authoritarianism, and global systems. They also parse contemporary systems of power to expose those affordances that might be amplified or reworked to produce positive environmental and social change. While most of these investigations revolve around the Western state, Mark Beeson's chapter examines the emerging "environmental authoritarianism" of China and John Dryzek's treats the larger system of global environmental governance. The final six chapters of this volume, collected under the subheading "Theorizing Citizenship, Movements, and Action," consider two interrelated questions: First, how do organizations, activists, and other actors themselves represent or embody environmental theorizing, and second, how does EPT understand the range of methods for bringing about change, including social and political organizations, movements, and other strategies? In response to the first question, chapters by Joan Martinez-Alier, Kyle Whyte, and Sean Parson and Emily Ray offer analyses of the power of environmental movements to affect conceptual vocabulary and the function of governance institutions; in response to the second question, chapters by Cheryl Hall, Sherilyn MacGregor, and Lisa Disch offer varying perspectives on how we might both green and democratize political action. Demonstrating the prominent place of praxis in EPT, these chapters illuminate the confluence of discourse, framing, nudging, democratic space, and embodiment in political action. And they draw from diverse intellectual resources—including actor-network theory, feminist theory, Marxism, postcolonial studies, radical environmentalism, the environmentalisms of the poor, and indigenous environmental movements—to both expose the limitations of contemporary thinking and push toward more just and sustainable futures.

Challenges for the Future

In collections of this scope, there are always unforeseen circumstances that interfere with the realization of the ideal. The essays collected in this handbook reflect a wide and diverse range of topics, insights, and viewpoints within EPT today. We are proud of the final set, but we recognize that inevitably the handbook has not been able to include all things that it might, equally well. We thus end this introduction by noting a few areas where more needs to be said.

Not surprisingly, some of the limits of the volume—and future opportunities for exploration—are topics of interest that were raised in the initial discussion of this handbook at the EPT workshop but that we were unable to address in full. Some of these topics are issues deeply constitutive of the idea of environmental theory itself, such as a thorough engagement with the romantic or transcendentalist tradition—especially in the history of American environmental thought. While much of that tradition would be considered conservative in the current academic climate, there has also been an increasing interest in rethinking contemporary conservative justifications for environmental ethics, action, and politics; this, again, was identified at our initial session and yet we were unsuccessful in commissioning a piece on the issue. The largest absence, however, is the participation of scholars representing perspectives outside of the Anglo-American world, and especially those who approach these questions from a non-Western perspective. As noted earlier, EPT has to date been taken up as a distinct field of study in the United States, the United Kingdom, Canada, and Australia, and is addressed by a range of contributors across Europe in numerous languages. But the field needs to reach out to audiences beyond these familiar academic geographic boundaries. Across Asia, Southeast Asia, Latin America, and Africa, scholars are addressing the human/politics/environment intersection in engaging, creative, and productive ways. It will be a key task of the field to establish relationships with a new generation of environmental scholars, and to break down existing boundaries to establish a broader and more inclusive EPT community. We wrap up this handbook convinced that this cross-national, cross-cultural, and often cross-ontological engagement will be one of the key directions for future research, and relationships, in the field.

References

Bookchin, Murray. (1982). *The Ecology of Freedom: The Emergence and Dissolution of Hierarchy* (Palo Alto: Cheshire Books).

Dobson, Andrew. (1990). *Green Political Thought* (London: Unwin Hyman).

Dryzek, John. (1987). *Rational Ecology: Environment and Political Economy* (New York: Basil Blackwell).

Eckersley, Robyn. (1992). *Environmentalism and Political Theory: Toward an Ecocentric Approach* (Albany: S.U.N.Y. Press).

Luke, Timothy W. (2015). "Environmental Political Theory." In *Encyclopedia of Political Thought*, edited by Michael T. Gibbons (Chichester, West Sussex, UK; Malden, MA, US: Wiley Blackwell), 1096–1103.

Meyer, John M. (2006). "Political Theory and the Environment." In *Oxford Handbook of Political Theory*, edited by John Dryzek, Bonnie Honig, and Anne Phillips (Oxford: Oxford University Press), 773–791.

Ophuls, William. (1977). *Ecology and the Politics of Scarcity: Prologue to a Political Theory of the Steady State* (San Francisco: W. H. Freeman).

Plumwood, Val. (1993). *Feminism and the Mastery of Nature* (London: Routledge).

Walzer, Michael. (2013). "The Political Theory License." *Annual Review of Political Science* 16(1): 1–9. doi:10.1146/annurev-polisci-032211-214411.

PART II

ENVIRONMENTAL POLITICAL THEORY AS A FIELD OF INQUIRY

ENGAGING TRADITIONS OF POLITICAL THOUGHT

CHAPTER 2

ENVIRONMENTAL POLITICAL THEORY AND THE HISTORY OF WESTERN POLITICAL THEORY

HARLAN WILSON

Introduction: Environmental Political Theory and "the Mainstream" of Political Theory

This chapter discusses several ways in which "classic" or "canonical" texts in the history of Western political theory, from Plato through the twentieth century, are treated in recent environmental political theory (EPT). I attempt to show how older texts are treated by scholars in EPT and why the "canon" should continue to be a significant source of political ideas in EPT.[1]

Western political theory is a very old activity, dating back to the ancient Greeks. Yet "the environment," in the sense of non-human (and sometimes human) nature, is a twentieth-century construct. The term "environmentalist," in its current meaning, dates only from the 1970s. Environmental political theory is an even newer field of activity, bringing together environmental concerns with the much longer and contested "tradition" of "classic" political theory. The marriage between the old and the new is not merely one of convenience; it helps to define EPT as an activity.

Dobson and Eckersley define EPT as the "interrogation of traditional political concepts from an environmental point of view—reflections on democracy, freedom and rights, distributive justice, the state, political space, security and citizenship" (2006: 2).

Environmental political theories, as well, interrogate common environmental notions such as sustainability and "nature."

EPT should not be confused with environmental ethics, personal expressions of eco-consciousness, environmental policy, environmental movements, or expressions of group interests or issue areas (Meyer 2006). Environmental ethics, for instance, is distinct from EPT insofar as it treats political ideas and institutions as well as collective decision-making and power as "of secondary importance" (Meyer 2001: ix). Moreover, terms such as "the environment" or even "ecology" should not be regarded as primarily "scientific" or "economic," so that the task of political thinkers is merely to accept derivatively the formulations of natural science and translate them into political policy. Most EPT writers think of "the environment" as always already political, both diagnostically and normatively. That is to say, diagnoses of the sources of environmental problems and proposed solutions inherently involve politics.

Political theory is conventionally a field of political science. Rather than a "subdiscipline," however, political theory might be described as an "undiscipline." There are, however, common tendencies and trends in the field. A significant component of the activity of political theorists consists in the close study, interpretation, commentary, and critique of classic texts. Many political theorists seek to draw upon classic texts to develop diagnoses, critiques, and visions of contemporary political life. As a subfield of political theory generally, EPT scholars build upon older texts as they work out diagnoses and critiques of the present as well as visions of a sustainable or greener world of the future.

Although this chapter refers to "classic" or "canonical" texts in political theory, the "canon" is contested and constantly being expanded.[2] However one defines the "canon," central to the activity of political theory from Plato and Augustine through Hobbes and Marx to Arendt and Habermas has been the diagnosis and critique of public crisis (see Wolin 1968: 318). Today the relation between humans and the non-human (and human) environment, especially climate change, constitutes perhaps the most intractable and challenging crisis humans have ever faced. It raises fundamental issues about leadership, democracy, justice, community, and the other "traditional" concepts central to political theory that have been debated from Plato's *Republic* and Thucydides' *History* to the present. Contemporary theorists puzzling over present-day environmental problems might be expected to take great interest in older texts that focus on crises of the past.

Moreover, canonical texts, beginning with Plato and Aristotle, sought to understand and theorize "nature," although their conceptions of "nature" and "the natural" were often quite different from those of later thinkers. Although twentieth-century theory has generally been more skeptical about categories such as "nature" and "the natural," twentieth-century political theorists such as Adorno, Marcuse, Habermas, and Arendt have all addressed themes of "nature." These themes include our economic relation with nature, the distribution of amenities, conflicts concerning distribution of resources, conceptions of place, and so forth. All of these point to "humanity's embeddedness in the natural world" (Cannavò and Lane 2014a: 9). EPT is deeply indebted to past thinkers who addressed these themes and issues.

Environmental political theory is a relatively recent enterprise, dating from the 1960s and 1970s. EPT writers have made use of the classical works since that time. The first text in EPT to appropriate and critique a range of canonical political theory texts about "nature" was probably the pioneering work of William Ophuls, *Ecology and the Politics of Scarcity* (Ophuls 1977). Several other writers, such as Mulford Sibley, Murray Bookchin, and Carolyn Merchant, also mined older texts for ecological content (Bookchin 1971; Sibley 1973, 1977; Merchant 1980). Garrett Hardin's *Tragedy of the Commons* (Hardin 1968), though based in population biology, was a restatement and unacknowledged application of Hobbesian theory. Since the early 1980s, and especially since the 1990s, EPT scholarship about historical texts has flourished.

Excavating and Interpreting Classic Texts

EPT's treatment of classic texts tends to be both selective and instrumental. Although environmental political theorists sometimes do engage in scholarly interpretation for its own sake, seeking to advance understanding of particular writers and texts, for the most part they tend to look at the canon of political theory in terms of its value for contemporary discourse about environmental issues.

The instrumental use of older texts for contemporary conversations may involve various agendas, purposes, and approaches. Daniel Sabia (1984) has identified three models through which the history of political thought can be interpreted and taught. I will briefly characterize Sabia's three models, showing how they may be applied to the study and deployment of canonical texts in EPT literature. Although interpretation of classic texts typically involves a mixture of models, the prevalent one in EPT is the third, Sabia's "perennial issues" model.

a) Historical. The first of the three models posited by Sabia, the "historical," treats political thought in terms of a more or less continuous historical progression of ideas and practice. The most familiar example of the use of this model is George Sabine's classic *A History of Political Theory* (1937), which emphasizes the contexts as well as influences of particular theory texts in a continuous progression from Plato to twentieth-century communism and fascism. For example, Plato's *Republic* is situated in terms of previous Greek philosophy and politics, and its influences on later thinkers are analyzed. An aggressive variant of the "historical" approach is that of Quentin Skinner, J. G. A. Pocock, John Dunn, and others (the "Cambridge school"), according to which it cannot be assumed that there is any continuous historical progression of ideas because texts consist only of particular linguistic acts in particular historical circumstances, hence ideas about coherent traditions or perennial issues in the history of political thought have no substance (see Pocock 2006 as well as discussions in Gunnell 1987 and Sabia 1994).

Applying Sabine's historical model to EPT uses of classic texts, we may say that an important purpose of reading older texts is to cultivate an historical sense and to show influences or factors that have affected contemporary environmental deterioration or political movements. Environmental discourse is undoubtedly influenced by past theory even when the influences are not readily apparent. A classic example is Garrett Hardin's restatement of Hobbes' diagnostic logic, already referenced. Locke's theory of property is often charged with having had a profound influence on environmental deterioration, while deep ecology is influenced by Rousseau in ways not often acknowledged (see Lane and Clark 2006). Many other examples could be cited of intellectual influences of this sort.

The restrictive Skinner–Pocock historical approach appears to be a dead end so far as EPT is concerned. If Skinner and Pocock are correct that there can be no trans-historical linguistic meanings and that all texts must be read only in terms of specific historical contexts, older texts would be of antiquarian interest only. Sabine's approach, however, together with more recent historical scholarship provides an understanding of historical connections that helps us grasp the sources for contemporary politics and environmental practices.

b) Traditional. Sabia's second model involves treating political theories as parts of a coherent tradition (not just a progression) of political thought, again comprising the so-called Great Books of the past from Plato to Marx or Nietzsche. Probably the best-known example of this model is the Straussian narrative of decline according to which the "tradition" of political theory has degenerated from the ancients to the moderns (Strauss 1953). Another version of the "tradition" was offered by Sheldon Wolin (1968, 1969), tracing the decline of the "political" in late modernity. Both Strauss and Wolin adopted the norm of the "tradition" partly as a counterpoint to the hegemonic behavioral political science of the postwar period in the United States. Wolin's version, however, unlike that of Strauss, ironically justified intellectual conservatism (the "tradition") on the ground that it could inspire contemporary political radicalism and social change.

The so-called "traditional" approach was critiqued by John Gunnell (1987), who pointed out that the "tradition" was largely a "myth" and a *post hoc* construction. Because the normative authority of the "myth" was generated largely as a reaction to behavioralist political science, it retains little interest for most environmental political theorists. The appeal to a mythic "tradition" hardly makes sense for people interested in contemporary environmental problems (of course some green thinkers, especially deep ecologists, offer their own narratives of decline). On the other hand, many EPT writers might, like Wolin, think of the activity of reading past theories as liberating and as envisioning radical change, especially in contrast with the standard social science and policy literatures.

c) Perennial issues. According to the third model proposed by Sabia, past political theories are relevant to contemporary life insofar as the political and philosophical questions raised in the past are similar, if not exactly equivalent, to contemporary issues in political theory and practice (for example, Plamenatz 1963). Sabia actually uses an environmental example to illustrate the model: "Although the current problems of conservation and resource management are indeed contemporary, the problematic relationship between man (*sic*) and nature has been a persistent concern throughout human history." We can thus call attention to those features of thought that "remind us" of these problems (1984: 997–8).

Although all three models are often combined in treatments of the history of political thought by EPT, the "perennial issues" model is the one most often implied. In order to regard older texts as relevant for contemporary environmental discourse it must be presumed that the basic sources of problems of human relations with "nature" persist through time. Only if ancient, modern, and contemporary writers are assumed to share a sufficiently common universe of meaning can the appropriation or critique of older texts make sense. When Meyer (2001: 11) writes in his study of Aristotle and Hobbes that, although we should not wrench these authors completely out of their historical contexts, we can still "explore a relationship that was central to [them]" and also to us, he is assuming a common, if shifting, universe of meaning over many centuries.

In order to elucidate further this "perennial issues" model as it applies to EPT, I will show how older texts are (i) appropriated, (ii) critiqued, and (iii) extended conceptually. Detailed consideration of these categories will then be laid out in the following two sections. It should be emphasized again that these three different ways of deploying older texts for contemporary purposes are seldom completely separable in practice.

i. *Appropriation:* Many EPT scholars actively seek to appropriate past texts for contemporary theory, often through close textual readings. Although classic texts can be treated uncritically as intellectual "authorities," such as in Ophuls' use of Plato (Ophuls 2011 or in appeals to Marxist orthodoxy (see Parsons, ed. 1977), most EPT writers maintain some intellectual distance from the texts they deploy. Many illustrations of appropriation will be found in the following section of this chapter.
ii. *Critique:* Textual interpretation also frequently aims at critique. Texts can be critiqued in order to exhibit the problematic character of historically important ideas for the non-human environment or for environmental politics. Critiques are mostly external rather than internal: in other words, they tend to question the theoretical construct itself rather than logical inconsistencies or ambiguities in the text. Some critiques are hostile—ironically pointing up the critics' belief in the lasting importance of these texts. More often, perhaps, critique and appropriation are inseparable, as scholars use texts to drive a debate forward or to develop new forms of green politics. Again, examples are provided in the next section.
iii. *Conceptual extensions:* The meanings attached to commonly used concepts such as justice, democracy, community, authority, and power are often extended in EPT. Discourse about environmental justice is an excellent example. Some writers have even sought to extend political concepts to non-human "nature." The assumption still remains that these terms and concepts have recognizable, if historically shifting, meanings, and that older texts provide paradigmatic understandings of these perennially familiar terms. Conceptual extensions in EPT will be discussed in the fourth section on "Conceptual Extensions."

The application of older texts in contemporary environmental discourse raises important and controversial general issues concerning the interpretation of texts. The general controversies about textual interpretation raised by such writers as Strauss, Wolin, Skinner, and Foucault should not be ignored. Although environmental political theorists who utilize older texts for various purposes do not always pay great attention to these problems of interpretation, it can at least be said that most EPT interpreters do attempt close readings of these texts. One EPT scholar who has explicitly attended to questions of interpretation is John Meyer, in *Political Nature*, a commentary on Hobbes' and Aristotle's conceptions about politics and nature. At one point he argues that these authors' claims about the relation between nature and politics can be "contrary to the nature–politics relationship actually present within the theory discussed" (Meyer 2001: 11). Thus Hobbes appears to claim to derive politics from his conception of nature, but in Meyer's reading really doesn't do this. Although Meyer acknowledges that there are dangers of forcing Hobbes and Aristotle into a world of contemporary concerns, he still thinks they help us see how deeply rooted and even universal some problems are, such as a failure to take politics seriously (Meyer 2001: 10–12).

EPT writers using canonical texts are reasonably circumspect about avoiding errors of ahistorical "presentism," such as imagining what Plato would say about climate change—a nonsensical question. Arlene Saxonhouse is surely right to caution against the use of old texts to guess "what would X think about Y?" (2006). Epistemological questions concerning the understanding of authors far removed in space and time are also of obvious importance.

Appropriations and Critiques: Examples

In the preceding section I noted that the appropriation and critique of classic or canonical texts are prominent features of EPT, and that these activities typically assume some version of the "perennial ideas" approach to the history of political theory. In this section I discuss some of the most important appropriations and critiques of classic or canonical texts/writers by EPT scholars.

The classical tradition of Plato and Aristotle has been a source of both appropriation and critique by recent EPT scholars. Forty years ago, the political theorist Mulford Q. Sibley (1973) sought to appropriate Plato's and Aristotle's notions of limit and *pleonexia* (wanting more than your share) for a sustainable socialist democracy. Melissa Lane (2011) has recently formulated a rather similar defense of Plato, arguing that Plato illustrates the dangers of *pleonexia* and *hubris* to the environment and that the Platonic insistence that citizens be educated for virtue should be recovered. Sibley and Susan Leeson (1979) a few decades ago, and Melissa Lane more recently, have argued that classical (Platonic and Aristotelian) insights into human nature and politics can temper the anti-environmental excesses of liberalism without turning to authoritarian alternatives. Similarly, too, John O'Neill (1993) has sought to show how Aristotle's ideas of character ethics can help one develop a notion of environmental authority (see also Orhan 2014). On the other hand, Plato is charged by Val Plumwood (1994) and Sheryl Breen (2014) with reinforcing dualisms, including the division between external nature and politics. Plumwood's critique of Plato is part of her general eco-feminist critical analysis. Aristotle largely seems to escape eco-critique, despite his conception of *phusis* (loosely, essential nature), so at odds with contemporary historical and constructionist ideas about nature. John Meyer's analysis of Aristotle's views of nature addresses these problems, balancing appropriation with critique (Meyer 2001).

Early modern theory from Hobbes to the nineteenth century remains a dominant source of interpretation by EPT scholars. Ophuls appropriates ideas of Plato, Hobbes, Rousseau, Burke, Jefferson, and Thoreau, passing over their fundamental inconsistencies with each other, in his attempt to articulate a green vision (Ophuls 1977, 1997, 2011). Thomas Hobbes, the great theorist of disastrous chaos, has had his defenders on occasion, mainly in the form of survivalists who think democracy inadequate to deal with the scope of environmental crisis (for example, Shearman and Smith 2007; and in part Ophuls 1977). More frequently, Hobbes comes under attack, as for example by feminist writers such as Carolyn Merchant (1980), for cultivating, in contrast with the ancients, an extreme and highly gendered individualism that allows free play to the most (environmentally) destructive appetites. Frank Coleman (1996) sees the "exposure" of Hobbes to the "terrors of deconstruction" as necessary to understanding the environmentally devastating material conditions of modernity itself. A more sympathetic approach is evident in John Meyer's (2001, 2014) already referenced treatment of Hobbes, which seeks to defend that author against charges of "dualism" and "derivatism," arguing that he saw nature and politics as bound up together in complex ways.

John Locke has been an even more popular object of EPT critics. His justification of property as originating in God's command to "subdue the earth," his apparent defense of unlimited property rights (that is, following upon the hypothetical invention of money), and his defense of the enclosure of common lands at the expense of English peasants and native Americans, all mark a target on his back. Yet Locke has his defenders too. An interesting contemporary argument is whether Locke or Mill is a better source of contemporary green liberalism. Locke, of course, was the great champion of natural rights, Mill of utility broadly conceived (and of the "stationary state"); yet that distinction does not fully capture the controversy. Zev Trachtenberg (2014) views Locke as having shown the human implications of the transformation of the natural world as well as having set forth a principle of stewardship. Susan Liebell (2011) has gone further, arguing that Locke's famous proviso requiring property appropriation to leave "enough and as good" for others might actually lead to environmental justifications for restrictions on property accumulation. Vanderheiden (2008a) invokes Locke's proviso on behalf of global climate justice. On the other hand, Mill, with his notion of a stationary state and his skepticism about a strictly material lifestyle, has his ardent defenders as well. Piers Stephens (2001, 2014), for one, argues vigorously that J. S. Mill, far more than Locke, is a "remarkably congenial fit" with contemporary environmental values, including a vision of a sustainable society.

Some noted scholars defend the liberal tradition of political theory, and especially "reform" liberalism dating from the end of the nineteenth century, as most likely to support sustainability objectives. Thus Marcel Wissenburg (1998, 2001, 2006) has developed and extended "green" ideas from Locke and subsequent liberals in order to show that the liberal tradition as a whole is broader and more inclusive than often caricatured, and therefore can accommodate most, though not all, arguments for sustainability and even social transformation. Richard Dagger (2006), Trachtenberg, and Stephens have all appropriated ideas from Locke and/or J. S. Mill in the hope of developing a greener (and less corporate-friendly) form of liberalism. Dagger especially has sought to enlarge liberal conceptions of freedom in environmental sustainability in the direction of T. H. Green's notions of positive liberty and rights (see also Barry 1998). Dobson and Eckersley (2006) remark that environmental political theory today generally has largely accommodated itself to some form of liberalism. Whether or not this is true, few EPT writers accept market fundamentalism or neo-liberalism, seeking instead to articulate a kinder, gentler, greener liberalism.

Thomas Malthus' population theory has long been a favorite target of critics, especially from the left, beginning with Marx himself and continuing with Bookchin (1991), Mellos (1988), Kovel (2007), and many others. The epithet "neo-Malthusian" is often applied, with some justice, to Garrett Hardin (1968) and William Ophuls (1977) for ascribing the causes of material scarcity to "human nature" in the form of inevitable population increase and lack of social resilience. For political theorists especially, to invoke favorably the name of Malthus is to invite immediate controversy. The unhistorical quality of Malthusian and neo-Malthusian theory is problematic, especially when combined with neo-Hobbesian authoritarian political suggestions.

Rousseau, too, is an author of great interest to EPT. Joseph Lane (2014) remarks that environmentalists "almost all begin from a perspective derived from Rousseau" as a key figure in the narratives of modernity. Although Lane is thinking especially of deep ecology, his analysis of Rousseau shows how that author can be held responsible for a whole set of notions that have inspired and bedeviled contemporary environmental thought and practice, such as the essentialization of "nature" as a principle of value, the nature/convention binary, and the dangers of political homogeneity (see also LaFreniere 1990; Whiteside 2002; Biro 2005; Lane 2006; Lane and Clark 2006).

The ideas of Edmund Burke have occasionally been recovered by conservative writers such as John Gray (1993) and Roger Scruton (2012) for green purposes. They appreciate his aesthetic values, hereditary principle, critique of utopianism, notion of intergenerational continuity and preservation, and his premonition of the "precautionary principle." Yet Burke has also been critiqued for having inspired a conservative environmentalism that, while theorizing aesthetically inspired politics, intergenerational obligation, and a sort of precautionary principle, exhibits surprising enthusiasm for unfettered markets without consideration of distributive justice or democratic equality (for example, Wilson 2014).

The canonical author whose texts are most commonly appropriated in contemporary EPT is doubtless Karl Marx. This is hardly surprising insofar as Marx developed a diagnosis of late-stage capitalism that still has great explanatory power. At one time Marx was invoked mainly by Marxists who sought to taint environmentalism as bourgeois ideology (see Benton, ed. 1996). But this has changed, as Marxists have mostly come to understand, not only that Marx was centrally concerned with human–nature interactions, but also that capitalist depletion of resources has to be a part of any critique of capitalism and discussion of the prospects of socialism. Tim Luke prefaces his exposition of Marx as a green thinker by proclaiming that Marxian theory is still "essential in any consideration of environmental political theory today" (Luke 2014: 203). Writers such as Koula Mellos (1988), Benton (1996), Luke (1999), Paul Burkett (1999), John Bellamy Foster (2000), Joel Kovel (2007), and many others have defended Marx's critique of capitalism as highly relevant to contemporary environmental thought and practice—sometimes while focusing on Marx's early writings, more often in relation to his mature emphasis on political economy.

Much work by eco-Marxists does not simply restate Marx and Engels but, in the spirit of Marx, drives his analysis forward by applying it to changing circumstances and reshaping the theory dialectically in light of those changing circumstances. James O'Connor's work (1998) stands out for its appropriation of Marx's fundamental contradiction between forces and relations of production and the elaboration of a "second contradiction" which Marx did not foresee, between the forces/relations of production and the conditions of production (that is, between unlimited capitalist growth and resource depletion). Of course, Marx and Marxism have frequently been the objects of green critique too, focusing on Marx's "anthropocentrism" and his alleged indifference to the costs of industrial and technological progress for the sake of socialism (for example, Eckersley 1992).

Critical theorists from Adorno to Marcuse and Habermas have often been appropriated by green theorists on the left (Vogel 1996; Luke 1997; Brulle 2000; Buck 2013; and others). Indeed, one might even regard Adorno, Horkheimer, and Marcuse, as well as André Gorz, as pioneering green or environmental thinkers in their own right. Although Jürgen Habermas has been roundly criticized for relegating the environment to the realm of instrumental rationality (for example, Scheuerman 2006), his work has also been selectively appropriated by theorists such as John Dryzek (1996, 2002), Doug Torgerson (2002), and Robyn Eckersley (2004) as well. Dryzek finds Habermas' notion of democratic communication applicable to his own notion of deliberative democracy, though not without revision. Torgerson appropriates Habermas' (and Arendt's) notion of the public sphere; and Eckersley critically appropriates, for green purposes, Habermas on state legitimacy and social movements. Andrew Biro's work (2005) on Rousseau, Marx, Adorno, and Marcuse is another close reading of critical theory with the aim of "denaturalizing ecological politics," that is, to try to imagine ecological politics without essentializing "nature." Biro seeks to appropriate critical theories for the aim of providing possible foundations of a new ecological political thought and movement (Biro 2005: 5; see also Biro, ed. 2011, arguing that Marcuse's mode of critical theory is superior to that of Adorno for the goal of social transformation). Biro's project seems very much in the spirit of Dobson and Eckersley's idea of "demonstrating unexpected possibilities" within the texts through both appropriation and critique in order to construct new theory, while remaining textually rigorous.

Of other twentieth-century theorists, Hannah Arendt and Michel Foucault are frequently appropriated and critiqued. Arendt is a particularly intriguing resource, the more so because she viewed nature as associated with the inferior "social realm" and with "labour" rather than political action. Nevertheless, many scholars (for example, Whiteside 1994 and 1998; Macauley 1996; Chapman 2007; Ott 2009) have found green resources and inspiration in Arendt's theory. Her conceptions of worldly home and political space (Cannavò 2007 and 2014), her notion of political action as performance (Torgerson 1999), and her conception of political plurality as an inspiration for the politics of environment and gender (Sandilands 1999), have attracted particular attention by EPT scholars.

Michel Foucault, an author with little apparent interest in environmental problems as such, and none whatsoever in the aesthetics of physical nature, has nevertheless found many admirers as well as a few critics in EPT. Foucault's perceived usefulness comes from his accounts of the complexity and hiddenness of power relationships, including those inherent in environmental regulation as governability or "environmentality" as Luke calls it (1999). Chaloupka and Cawley (1993) regard Foucault's ideas of power/knowledge as useful tools for exposing the anti-political qualities of mainstream environmentalism. Eric Darier's edited volume (1999) is entirely devoted to the significance of Foucault's work for one or another aspect of environmental politics. Biro (2005: 43–58) contains a well-balanced discussion of the pertinent issues. On the other hand, Murray Bookchin (1995), remained utterly hostile to Foucault and for that matter to any form of postmodernism. John Barry, as well, has offered a trenchant critique of the bearing of Foucault on environmental theory (2006: 262ff).

The work of John Dewey, the preeminent American democratic theorist, has not invited the attention by EPT scholars one might expect, though there are exceptions (Chaloupka 1987; Taylor 1990; Minteer 2002). Eckersley (2002) offers a critique of Dewey's pragmatist approach. There is still ample opportunity for further work by EPT scholars on Dewey, especially his analysis of scientific democracy in relation to public action in a world in which both are under duress.

Regrettably, minority and non-Western writers and texts have attracted limited attention among EPT scholars. Kimberly Smith's (2007) work on African–American environmental thought, especially W. E. B. DuBois, is an important exception. Joel Kassiola (2014) has appropriated elements of Confucius' thought as successfully exposing tensions of modernity and providing a critical vision through leverage against the dominant Western traditions. Vandana Shiva's work (for example, 1989, 2005) is quite influential, especially in feminist and postcolonialist thought; more than with Merchant her point of departure is material and cultural history more than canonical political theory (see also Salleh 1997). And Fareh Godrej has recently written on Gandhi and his relevance to EPT and the problem of citizenship (2012). In any case, much more remains to be done in this domain.

Conceptual Extensions

As I noted earlier, certain terms of political discourse such as justice, democracy, community, authority, and power are frequently reworked by environmental political theorists. In this section I will give some examples of how this reworking of past concepts takes place. It should be evident that this activity implies a continuity, if not total identity, of political issues between past and present.

The two most central concepts explored in contemporary EPT writing are surely justice and democracy. Justice and injustice have been themes in political theory since Thucydides, the Greek tragedians, Plato, and Aristotle. In recent years John Rawls' theory has situated much of the current debate about distributive justice. Iris Young (1990) and others, drawing from feminist discourses, have argued that notions of distributive justice fail to capture much of the sense of contemporary discourse about justice. These debates about the meaning of justice have been further extended in environmental political theory. One reason for this is that what is called "environmental justice" is as much a movement as a theory. Hence environmental justice becomes theorized empirically as much as normatively, as is particularly evident in David Schlosberg's work (2002, 2009). Schlosberg, building on the work of Young, Amartya Sen (1999), and Martha Nussbaum (2000), has further extended notions of justice to take into account such values as recognition and capabilities, reflecting how environmental justice movements actually conceive of justice. Climate change is increasingly recognized as a site for justice and injustice as well (Schlosberg 2009).

Environmental democracy and citizenship also are central themes in much contemporary EPT writing. Dryzek (for example, 2002) has been probably the most influential writer on environmental democracy; but Torgerson (1999), Dobson (2003), Eckersley (2004), Ball (2006), John Barry (2006, 2008), and others have each attempted to reimagine the meaning of state-centered democracy in a sustainable global world, as well as of democratic movements outside and even against the state (see Wilson 2006). In some of this work, interpretations of canonical political theory have little place. Of course, very much of political theory from Plato to Nietzsche is profoundly antidemocratic and difficult to appropriate by contemporary democrats; even Rousseau's politics of the general will and Dewey's notions of scientific democracy do not map well onto much current thinking about power and difference. The classical republican tradition of decentralist politics has been appropriated and critiqued as well (Barry 2006 and 2012; Cannavo 2007). Contemporary concerns about difference and diversity, and about global environmental problems such as climate change, make small-scale republicanism problematic. Yet, Hannah Arendt's republican notion of public, political space is occasionally invoked (Torgerson 1999; Cannavò 2007), as is Habermas' notion of communicative politics (Dryzek 2002; Eckersley 2004).

Ideas of authority, freedom, community, pluralism, and rights frequently surface in contemporary EPT. As mentioned, notions of positive freedom and positive rights (Dagger 2006) have been put forth as ways to transcend the conceptions of negative freedom and rights that are often identified with environmentally damaging practices. Yet environmental thinkers have generally not challenged prevailing ways of thinking about freedom, liberty, and agency. Rather, EPT has mostly accepted the approaches to these topics that are rooted in liberal political theory of the seventeenth through nineteenth centuries. Two chapters in this *Handbook* do, however, explore this terrain further (Gabrielson 2015; Lambacher 2015).

As previously noted, several EPT scholars have advocated a sort of "political extensionism," akin to the moral extensionism familiar in environmental ethics. The extension of moral and legal rights to non-human species is an occasional theme in EPT as well as environmental ethics and animal rights theory (Eckersley 1996). "Political extensionism" argues that political notions of order, community, justice, rights, and even democracy be extended to the non-human world. Examples are Schlosberg's (2006) attempt to expand the world of justice to include non-human entities and Dryzek's (1996, 2002) similar expansion of the notion of democracy to the non-human. Such moves are, of course, controversial; as far back as Aristotle's *Politics* it was argued that justice can exist only among humans because only they can speak and are capable of politics.

Environmental problems today demand a global intellectual reach for which the "traditional" canon of political theory does not always prepare us (see Meyer 2006: 12). Most of the canonical authors view political problems in terms of the *polis* or nation-state. There are exceptions within the canon—Machiavelli and Grotius are obvious, and Kant, Hegel, Hume, and Marx all contain elements of global thinking as well. EPT today is certainly tending towards a more global theory, utilizing canonical texts where they are pertinent. Some leading thinkers here are Dobson 2003, Eckersley 2004, Vanderheiden 2008a, 2008b, and Schlosberg 2009; Richard Howarth's work appropriating classical utilitarianism to diagnose the politics of climate change is another example. (See also Dryzek's chapter in this *Handbook*.)

Conclusion: The History of Political Theory, Environmental Political Theory, and Political Education

Environmental political theorists, perhaps more than "mainstream" theorists, engage with discourses as varied as scientific ecology, public policy, comparative political science, environmental ethics, and the study of environmental movements. Environmental political theorists also learn from activists' discourses and strategies at the same time as they often challenge them (Cannavò and Lane 2014a: 4). Nevertheless, interpretation and use of the canon of political theory should remain a very significant element of EPT.

Classic texts should not be presented as authorities that provide "answers" that save us the trouble of thinking through our own problems. Texts are never immediately "applicable;" their significance and meaning are always filtered through experiences and concerns and purposes. Nevertheless, the activity of understanding, appropriating, and critiquing canonical political theory texts should still matter for EPT and for environmental discourse more generally. Indeed, the argument that environmental thinkers or environmentalists should take seriously old political theory books is not too different from the argument that scholars, politicians, and ordinary citizens should do so.

Classic texts convey a "richness" of perspective that matters even when the aim is to problematize their specific arguments (Cannavò and Lane 2014a: 6–7). Close readings and critiques of classic texts can inspire a rethinking of the meaning of our political world and of crisis in that world. Ultimately, then, the "authority" of the canon is not restrictive but potentially liberating. As Meyer suggests, canonical thinkers "offer works of a depth and complexity" that present us with an "uncommon opportunity" to question our own assumptions (2001, 122). And as Dobson and Eckersley maintain, reflection on traditional political concepts such as rights, freedom, democracy, and the state, "have enriched these concepts by demonstrating unexpected possibilities within them" and within the texts that contain them (2006: 2).

An important additional justification for reading older texts has to do with the status of politics itself. As Bill Chaloupka has repeatedly reminded us (e.g. Chaloupka and Cawley 1993), it is crucially important that practitioners of environmental politics, especially those in social movements, be aware of the centrality of politics, the importance of not subordinating politics to ethics, economics, or "paradigm shifts." Many canonical texts in political theory, such as Aristotle, Machiavelli, Rousseau, Tocqueville, Mill, Marx, Weber, Dewey, and Arendt, are indispensable for encouraging us to reflect upon the political realm in ways that do not reduce politics to the non-political.

My discussion thus far has been directed towards showing why environmental discourse benefits from the interpretation and appropriation/critique of old books. Yet, equally important is the question of why "mainstream" political theorists should take EPT scholarship seriously. It appears as though many "mainstream" political theorists do not think of EPT as contributing much to the field of political theory. Though Dobson and Eckersley (2006: 3) claim to see a "palpable rise in interest in EPT among mainstream political theorists," the evidence for this is unclear. When "mainstream" political theory considers environmental matters at all, they are usually framed in terms of social and political movements, ideologies, or group interests, or else "the environment" is seen as a technical and scientific or economic or policy domain that is outside the interests and expertise of political theorists. The misperception that all environmental discourse focuses on "sacrifice" or merely reacts to disaster, rather than reimagining a progressive future, may also discourage some on the left.

As we have seen, most of the classic theorists do prefigure what we would call "environmental" concerns. Furthermore, contemporary EPT is arguably more representative of "traditional" concerns of political theory than much of what is published in contemporary political theory journals. EPT retains an interest in institutional forms, strategies for change, social composition, and relations to the non-human natural world that until recently has been missing in much work published in the most prominent political theory journals or presented at conferences. EPT writers must continue their efforts to demonstrate to others in the field of political theory how the "canon" in political theory helps generate crucial questions about human relations with the "environment" that, in turn, should be central to contemporary political theory. Unconventional green readings of older texts can help drive scholarship on those texts as well.

Environmental political theory can also reinvigorate and challenge "mainstream" political theory by reinforcing the importance of politics and the political. This includes not only the politics of gender, race, and class, but of older notions of power, freedom, democracy, justice, indeed politics itself, as they are inevitably transformed as a consequence of environmental crisis. Political theorists must pay attention to how core collective values such as freedom and democracy and justice can shift meaning in a condition of environmental crisis. Authority to frame such questions should not be bestowed on natural science or economics, because collective questions are inherently political. Environmental crisis will surely threaten core values and practices of freedom, democracy, and community: a town, or a planet, that is severely impacted by environmental crisis will not be congenial to values of democracy, justice, and civil liberties. Political theorists, not just those who write on environmental topics, need to understand these connections.

In the end, the best argument for the interpretation, appropriation, and critique of canonical texts—even with a constantly expanding "canon"—involves the possibilities of political education, not only for university students and environmental policy analysts but for the literate public. Reading older political theory texts yields new insights into the politics of our environmental problems, and reading them with environmental crises in mind yields new insights about these texts.

All this does not entail one right way of thinking, but rather a pluralistic appreciation of the value of an ongoing conversation. As John Barry has remarked, social theory should be more green, but not all in the same way! (2006: 262). Overall coherence is not to be expected. What should be expected instead is the posing of deep and interesting questions, the giving of diverse answers, and the facilitation of a more vigorous green public sphere. The activity of environmental political theory, rooted in the history of political theory generally, can contribute greatly to these aims.

Acknowledgments

I wish to acknowledge the very helpful editorial comments of Cheryl Hall and John M. Meyer on an earlier draft of this chapter, and also the comments of Wendy Sarvasy on my related conference paper at the 2014 meetings of the Western Political Science Association.

Notes

1. Although I have tried in this chapter to reference scholarly work that makes use of older texts in EPT, I will certainly have made important omissions that I regret and for which I apologize in advance.
2. For accounts of the history of political theory as a field, see Wolin 1968; Farr 2006: 225–42; Connolly 2006, 827–43; and Saxonhouse 2006: 844–58.

References

NOTE: This chapter relies heavily on the volume *Engaging Nature*, edited by Peter F. Cannavò and Joseph H. Lane Jr. and published in 2014. I have cited several papers in that collection, including the editors' introduction and concluding chapter. The volume consists of a number of contributions that treat political theorists from Plato to the present as sources of appropriations and critiques for environmental political theory. Along with the 2006 volume, *Oxford Handbook of Political Theory*, edited by John Dryzek, Bonnie Honig, and Anne Phillips, the Cannavò and Lane collection will be an indispensable source for those wishing to explore the area discussed in the present chapter.

Ball, T. (2006). "Democracy." In *Political Theory and the Ecological Challenge*, edited by Dobson and Eckersley (Cambridge: Cambridge University Press), 131–47.

Barry, J. (1998). *Rethinking Green Politics* (London: SAGE Publications).

Barry, J. (2006). *Environment and Social Theory*, 2nd edn. (London: Routledge).

Barry, J. (2008). "Towards a Green Republicanism: Constitutionalism, Political Economy, and the Green State." *The Good Society* 17(2): 3–11 .

Barry, J. (2012). *The Politics of Actually Existing Unsustainability* (Oxford: Oxford University Press).

Benton, T., ed. (1996). *The Greening of Marxism* (New York: Guilford).

Biro, A. (2005). *Denaturalizing Environmental Politics: Alienation from Nature from Rousseau to the Frankfurt School and Beyond* (Toronto: University of Toronto Press).

Biro, A., ed. (2011). *Critical Ecologies: The Frankfurt School and Contemporary Environmental Crises* (Toronto: University of Toronto Press).

Bookchin, M. (1971). *Post-Scarcity Anarchism* (Berkeley: Ramparts Press).

Bookchin, M. (1991). *Ecology of Freedom: The Emergence and Dissolution of Hierarchy*, rev. edn. (Montreal: Black Rose Books).

Bookchin, M. (1995). *The Reenchantment of Humanity* (London: Caswell).
Breen, S. (2014). "Plato: Private Property and Agriculture for the Commoners—Humans and the Natural World in *The Republic*." In *Engaging Nature*, edited by J. Cannavò and J. H. Lane Jr. (Cambridge, MA: MIT Press), 29–44.
Brulle, R. (2000). *Agency, Democracy and Nature: The U.S. Environmental Movement from a Critical Theory Perspective* (Cambridge, MA: MIT Press).
Burkett, P. (1999). *Marx and Nature: A Red and Green Perspective* (Basingstoke: Palgrave Macmillan).
Buck, C. (2013). "The Utopian Content of Reification: Adorno's Critical Social Theory of Nature." In *Second Nature: Rethinking the Natural Through Politics*, edited by C. Archer, L. Ephraim, and L. Maxwell (New York: Fordham University Press), 127–48.
Cannavò, P. (2007), *The Working Landscape: Founding, Preservation and the Politics of Place* (Cambridge, MA: MIT Press).
Cannavò, P. (2014). "Hannah Arendt: Place, World, and Earthly Nature." In *Engaging Nature*, edited by P. Cannavò and J. H. Lane Jr. (Cambridge, MA: MIT Press), 253–69.
Cannavò, P., and Lane, J. H. Jr. (2014a). "Introduction: How We Got Here." In *Engaging Nature*, edited by P. Cannavò and J. H. Lane Jr. Cambridge, MA: MIT Press, 1–27.
Cannavò, P. and Lane, J. H. Jr. (2014b, "Conclusion: The Western Political Theory Canon, Nature, and a Broader Dialogue." In *Engaging Nature*, edited by P. Cannavò and J. H. Lane Jr. (Cambridge, MA: MIT Press), 287–92.
Chaloupka, W. (1987). "John Dewey's Social Aesthetics as a Precedent for Environmental Thought." *Environmental Ethics* 9(3): 243–60.
Chaloupka, W. and Cawley, R. McG. (1993). "The Great Wild Hope: Nature, Environmentalism, and the Open Secret." In *In the Nature of Things: Language, Politics, and the Environment*, edited by J. Bennett and W. Chaloupka (Minneapolis: University of Minnesota Press), 3–23.
Chapman, A. (2007). "The Ways that Nature Matters: The World and the Earth in the Thought of Hannah Arendt." *Environmental Values* 16(4): 433–45.
Coleman, F. (1996). "Thomas Hobbes, the Bible, and Modernity." In *Minding Nature: The Philosophers of Ecology*, edited by D. Macauley (New York: Guilford), 24–42.
Connolly, W. (2006). "Then and Now: Participant-Observation in Political Theory." In *Oxford Handbook of Political Theory*, edited by J. Dryzek, B. Honig, and A. Phillips (Oxford: Oxford University Press), 827–43.
Dagger, R. (2006). "Freedom and Rights." In *Political Theory and the Ecological Challenge*, edited by A. Dobson and R. Eckersley (Cambridge: Cambridge University Press), 200–16.
Darier, E. (1999). "Foucault and the Environment: An Introduction." In *Discourses of the Environment*, edited by E. Darier (Oxford: Blackwell), 1–33.
Dobson, A. (2003). *Citizenship and the Environment* (Oxford: Oxford University Press).
Dobson, A., and Eckersley, R. (2006). "Introduction." In *Political Theory and the Ecological Challenge*, edited by A. Dobson and R. Eckersley (Cambridge: Cambridge University Press), 1–4.
Dryzek, J. (1996). "Political and Ecological Communication." In *Ecology and Democracy*, edited by F. Mathews (London: Cass), 13–30.
Dryzek, J. (2002). *Deliberative Democracy and Beyond: Liberals, Critics, Contestations*. (Oxford: Oxford University Press).
Dryzek, J. (2015, forthcoming). "Global Environmental Governance." In *Oxford Handbook of Environmental Political Theory*, edited by T. Gabrielson, C. Hall, J. M. Meyer, and D. Schlosberg (Oxford: Oxford University Press).

Dryzek, J., Honig, B., and Phillips, A. (2006). "Introduction." In *The Oxford Handbook of Political Theory*, edited by J. Dryzek, B. Honig, and A. Phillips (Oxford: Oxford University Press), 3–41.

Eckersley, R. (1992). *Environmentalism and Political Theory: Towards an Ecocentric Approach* (Albany: SUNY Press).

Eckersley, R. (1996). "Liberal Democracy and the Rights of Nature: The Struggle for Inclusion." In *Ecology and Democracy*, edited by F. Mathews (London: Cass), 169–98.

Eckersley, R. (2002). "Environmental Pragmatism: Ecocentrism and Deliberative Democracy." In *Democracy and the Claims of Nature: Critical Perspectives for a New Century*, edited by B. Minteer and B. P. Taylor (Lanham, MD: Rowman and Littlefield), 49–69.

Eckersley, R. (2004). *The Green State: Rethinking Democracy and Sovereignty* (Cambridge, MA: MIT Press).

Farr, J. (2006). "The History of Political Thought as Disciplinary Genre." In *The Oxford Handbook of Political Theory*, edited by J. Dryzek, B. Honig, and A. Phillips (Oxford: Oxford University Press), 225–42.

Foster, J. B. (2000). *Marx's Ecology: Materialism and Nature* (New York: Monthly Review Press).

Gabrielson, T. (2015, forthcoming). "Agency." In *Oxford Handbook of Environmental Political Theory*, edited by T. Gabrielson, C. Hall, J. M. Meyer, and D. Schlosberg (Oxford: Oxford University Press).

Godrej, F. (2012). "Ascetics, Warriors and a Gandhian Ecological Citizenship." *Political Theory* 40(4): 437–65.

Gray, J. (1993). "An Agenda for Green Conservatism." In *Beyond the New Right: Markets, Government and the Common Environment*, edited by J. Gray (London: Routledge), 124–77.

Gunnell, J. (1987). *Political Theory: Tradition and Interpretation*, 3rd edn. (Lanham, MD: University Press of America).

Hardin, G. (1968). "The Tragedy of the Commons." *Science* 162: 1243–8.

Howarth, R. B. (2011). "Intergenerational Justice." In *Oxford Handbook of Climate Change and Society*, edited by J. Dryzek, R. Norgaard, and D. Schlosberg (Oxford: Oxford University Press), 338–52.

Kassiola, J. (2014). "Confucius: How Non-Western Political Theory Contributes to Understanding the Environmental Crisis." In *Engaging Nature*, edited by P. Cannavò and J. H. Lane Jr. (Cambridge MA: MIT Press), 271–86.

Kovel, J. (2007). *The Enemy of Nature: The End of Capitalism or the End of the World?* (London: Zed Books).

LaFreniere, G. (1990). "Rousseau and the European Roots of Environmentalism." *Environmental History Review* 14(4): 41–72.

Lambacher, J. (2015). "Freedom." In *Oxford Handbook of Environmental Political Theory*, edited by T. Gabrielson, C. Hall, J. M. Meyer, and D. Schlosberg (Oxford: Oxford University Press).

Lane, J. H. Jr. (2006). "Reverie as Political Argument: Rousseau and the Experience of Convergence in Environmental Political Theory." *Review of Politics* 68(3): 474–99.

Lane, J. H. Jr. (2014). "Jean-Jacques Rousseau: The Disentangling of Green Paradoxes." In *Engaging Nature*, edited by P. Cannavò and J. H. Lane Jr. (Cambridge MA: MIT Press), 133–52.

Lane, J. H. Jr. and Clark, R. (2006). "The Solitary Walker in the Political World: The Paradoxes of Rousseau and Deep Ecology." *Political Theory* 34(1): 62–94.

Lane, M. (2011). *Eco-Republic: What the Ancients can Teach Us About Ethics, Virtue, and Citizenship* (Princeton: Princeton University Press).
Leeson, S. (1979). "Philosophic Implications of the Ecological Crisis: The Authoritarian Challenge to Liberalism." *Polity* 11(3): 303–18.
Liebell, S. (2011). "The Text and Context of 'Enough and as Good': John Locke as the Foundation of an Environmental Liberalism." *Polity* 43(2): 210–41.
Luke, T. W. (1997). *Ecocritique: Contesting the Politics of Nature, Economy, and Culture* (Minneapolis: University of Minnesota Press).
Luke, T. W. (1999). *Capitalism, Democracy and Ecology: Departing from Marx* (Urbana: University of Illinois Press).
Luke, T. W. (2014). "Karl Marx: Critique of Political Economy as Environmental Political Theory." In *Engaging Nature*, edited by P. Cannavò and J. H. Lane Jr. (Cambridge MA: MIT Press), 205–21.
Macauley, D. (1996). "Hannah Arendt and the Politics of Place: From Earth Alienation to *Oikos*." In *Minding Nature: The Philosophers of Ecology*, edited by D. Macauley (New York: Guilford), 102–33.
Mellos, K. (1988). *Perspectives on Ecology: A Critical Essay* (New York: St Martins).
Merchant, C. (1980). *The Death of Nature: Women, Ecology, and the Scientific Revolution* (San Francisco: Harper and Row).
Meyer, J. M. (2001). *Political Nature: Environmentalism and the Interpretation of Western Thought* (Cambridge, MA: MIT Press).
Meyer, J. M. (2006). "The Environment and Political Theory." In *The Oxford Handbook of Political Theory*, edited by J. Dryzek, B. Honig, and A. Phillips (Oxford: Oxford University Press), 773–91.
Meyer, J. M. (2014). "Thomas Hobbes: Relating Nature and Politics." In *Engaging Nature*, edited by P. Cannavò and J. H. Lane Jr. (Cambridge, MA: MIT Press), 83–98.
Minteer, B. (2002). "Deweyan Democracy and Environmental Ethics." In *Democracy and the Claims of Nature: Critical Perspectives for a New Century*, edited by B. Minteer and B. P. Taylor (Lanham, MD: Rowman and Littlefield), 33–48.
Nussbaum, M. (2000). *Women and Human Development: The Capabilities Approach* (Cambridge: Cambridge University Press).
O'Connor, J. (1998). *Natural Causes: Essays in Ecological Marxism* (New York: Guilford).
O'Neill, J. (1993). *Ecology, Policy and Politics: Human Well-Being and the Natural World* (London: Routledge).
Ophuls, W. (1977). *Ecology and the Politics of Scarcity* (San Francisco: W. H. Freeman).
Ophuls, W. (1997). *Requiem for Modern Politics: The Tragedy of the Enlightenment and the Challenge of the New Millenium* (Boulder: Westview Press).
Ophuls, W. (2011). *Plato's Revenge: Politics in the Age of Ecology* (Cambridge, MA: MIT Press).
Orhan, Ö. (2014). "Aristotle: Physis, Praxis, and the Good." In *Engaging Nature*, edited by P. Cannavò and J. H. Lane Jr. (Cambridge, MA: MIT Press), 45–63.
Ott, P. (2009). "World and Earth: Hannah Arendt and the Human Relationship to Nature." *Ethics, Place and Environment*, 12(1): 1–16.
Parsons, H., ed. (1977). *Marx and Engels on Ecology* (Westport, CT: Greenwood).
Plamenatz, John. (1963). *Man and Society*, vol. I. New York: McGraw-Hill.
Plumwood, V. (1994). *Feminism and the Mastery of Nature* (London: Routledge).
Plumwood, V. (2001). *Environmental Culture: The Ecological Crisis of Reason* (London: Routledge).

Pocock, J. G. A. (2006). "Theory in History: Problems of Context and Narrative." In *The Oxford Handbook of Political Theory*, edited by J. Dryzek, B. Honig, and A. Phillips (Oxford: Oxford University Press), 163–74.

Sabia, Daniel R., Jr. (1984). "Political Education and the History of Political Thought." *American Political Science Review*, 78(4): 985–99.

Sabine, George H. (1937). *A History of Political Theory* (New York: Holt, Rinehart and Winston).

Salleh, A. (1997). *Ecofeminism as Politics: Nature, Marx and the Postmodern* (London: Zed Books).

Sandilands, C. (1999). *The Good Natured Feminist: Ecofeminism and the Quest for Democracy* (Minneapolis: University of Minnesota Press).

Saxonhouse, A. (2006). "Exile and Re-Entry: Political Theory Yesterday and Tomorrow." In *The Oxford Handbook of Political Theory*, edited by J. Dryzek, B. Honig, and A. Phillips (Oxford: Oxford University Press), 844–58.

Scheuerman, W. (2006). "Critical Theory Beyond Habermas." In *The Oxford Handbook of Political Theory*, edited by J. Dryzek, B. Honig, and A. Phillips (Oxford: Oxford University Press), 85–105.

Schlosberg, D. (2002). *Environmental Justice and the New Pluralism: The Challenge of Difference* (Oxford: Oxford University Press).

Schlosberg, D. (2009). *Defining Environmental Justice* (Oxford: Oxford University Press).

Scruton, R. (2012). *Green Philosophy: How to Think Seriously About the Planet* (London: Atlantic Books).

Sen, A. (1999). *Development as Freedom* (Oxford: Oxford University Press).

Shearman, D. and Smith, W. J. (2007). *The Climate Change Challenge and the Future of Democracy* (London: Praeger), 139–52.

Shiva, V. (1989). *Staying Alive: Women, Ecology, and Development* (London: Zed Books).

Shiva, V. (2005). *Earth Democracy: Justice, Sustainability, and Peace* (Cambridge, MA: South End Press).

Sibley, M. Q. (1973). "The Relevance of Classical Political Theory for Economy, Technology, and Ecology." *Alternatives: Perspectives on Society and Environment* 2(2): 14–35.

Sibley, M. Q. (1977). *Nature and Civilization: Some Implications for Politics* (Itasca, IL: Peacock).

Smith, K. (2007). *African-American Environmental Thought: Foundations* (Lawrence: University Press of Kansas).

Stephens, P. H. G. (2001). "Green Liberalisms: Nature, Agency and the Good." *Environmental Politics* 10(3): 1–22.

Stephens, P. H. G. (2014). "John Stuart Mill: The Greening of the Liberal Heritage." In *Engaging Nature*, edited by P. Cannavò and J. H. Lane Jr. (Cambridge, MA: MIT Press), 189–204.

Strauss, L. (1953). *Natural Right and History* (Chicago: University of Chicago Press).

Taylor, B. P. (1990). "John Dewey and Environmental Thought: A Response to Chaloupka." *Environmental Ethics* 12(2): 175–84.

Torgerson, D. (1999). *The Promise of Green Politics* (Durham, NC: Duke University Press).

Trachtenberg, Z. (2014). "John Locke: This Habitable Earth of Ours." In *Engaging Nature*, edited by P. Cannavò and J. H. Lane Jr. (Cambridge, MA: MIT Press), 99–116.

Vanderheiden, S. (2008a). *Atmospheric Justice: A Political Theory of Climate Change* (Oxford: Oxford University Press).

Vanderheiden, S., ed. (2008b). *Political Theory and Global Climate Change* (Cambridge, MA: MIT Press).

Vogel, S. (1996). *Against Nature: The Concept of Nature in Critical Theory* (Albany: SUNY Press).
Whiteside, K. (1994). "Hannah Arendt and Ecological Politics." *Environmental Ethics* 16(4): 339–58.
Whiteside, K. (1998). "Worldliness and Respect for Nature: An Ecological Application of Hannah Arendt's Conception of Culture." *Ecological Values* 7(1): 25–40.
Whiteside, K. (2002). *Divided Natures: French Contributions to Political Ecology* (Cambridge, MA: MIT Press).
Wilson, H. (2006). "Environmental Democracy and the Green State." *Polity* 38(2): 276–94.
Wilson, H. (2014). "Edmund Burke: The Nature of Politics." In *Engaging Nature*, edited by P. Cannavò and J. H. Lane Jr. (Cambridge, MA: MIT Press), 153–71.
Wissenburg, M. (1998). *Green Liberalism: The Free and the Green Society* (London: Routledge).
Wissenburg, M. (2001). "Sustainability and the Limits of Liberalism." In *Sustaining Liberal Democracy*, edited by M. Wissenburg and J. Barry (London: Palgrave), 192–204.
Wissenburg, M. (2006). "Liberalism." In *Political Theory and the Ecological Challenge*, edited by A. Dobson and R. Eckersley (Cambridge: Cambridge University Press), 20–34.
Wolin, S. S. (1968). "Political Theory: Trends and Goals." In *International Encyclopedia of the Social Sciences*, vol. 12, edited by David L. Sills (New York: Macmillan), 318–31.
Wolin, S. S. (1969). "Political Theory as a Vocation." *American Political Science Review* 63(4): 1062–82.
Young, I. M. (1990). *Justice and the Politics of Difference* (Princeton: Princeton University Press).

CHAPTER 3

CULTURE AND DIFFERENCE

Non-Western Approaches to Defining Environmental Issues

FARAH GODREJ

How have human relationships to the non-human world been conceived of in different cultural traditions? In an attempt to discover intellectual resources for addressing the environmental crisis, much scholarship has sought to ask whether alternative ethical understandings of the relationship between humans and the non-human or natural world can be found in "non-Western" traditions. Could these traditions offer the West new ways to conceptualize the human–nature relationship? If so, would they provide resources with which to transform our ethical relationship to the natural world and address the environmental crisis? In what follows, I first identify what I characterize as a "civilizational" set of approaches to this question. These approaches are explicitly normative, emerging from studies of non-Western religions, philosophies, and cultures. These "civilizational" approaches follow the logic inherent in critiques of Western anthropocentrism and instrumentalism, which trace such tendencies back to the metaphysical or philosophical foundations of Western science and culture, and suggest that alternative philosophical foundations may produce different cultural attitudes toward nature. After problematizing these approaches, I describe a different approach to environmental issues which continues to rely on a non-Western intellectual tradition, but does so in a more sophisticated way, without reproducing the binaries and dichotomies to which the "civilizational" approach seems indebted. Because it is based on the moral and political thinking of M. K. Gandhi, I will term this a "neo-Gandhian" approach or method, highlighting how specific thinkers and communities in contemporary India have taken up Gandhi's conception of environmental issues as irreducibly linked to questions of everyday material needs and socio-economic justice. I will demonstrate how the method begins by turning outside the West for answers to environmental problems, but does not simply see other traditions as repositories of ethical knowledge, or rest with the question of ethics. Rather, it goes further than "civilizational" approaches do, by marrying normative environmental concerns with practical, material concerns and explicitly political critique and action, thus serving as an exemplar of an ethically- *and* materially-oriented environmental political thought. As such, the method can also be inspirational to many contemporary environmental justice movements outside India such as the food justice movement, and can serve to further the project of comparative environmental theorizing, in which ideas and practice from different cultural traditions can inform one another.

Philosophical and Ethical Foundations

As the extent of the environmental crisis began to become clear in the latter half of the twentieth century, scholars across a variety of disciplines began to examine the role that components of the West's civilizational heritage—religious, social, political, cultural, or scientific—may have played in this outcome. Variously characterized as environmentally destructive, rapacious, acquisitive, or anthropocentric, the Western intellectual tradition, along with its philosophical and even metaphysical foundations, was brought under scrutiny for the instrumental and utilitarian relationship with nature it had ostensibly encouraged. Perhaps the most common target of this critique was the Enlightenment view of scientific rationality. The Enlightenment's confidence in the capacity of human beings to assert control over the natural environment, to classify, quantify, categorize, and use it for their sustenance, was variously attributed to a combination of Judeo-Christian, Cartesian, and scientific worldviews, all of which were said to have alienated modern humans from nature. Carolyn Merchant famously argued that the achievements of the Scientific Revolution in the seventeenth century were deeply implicated in human dominion over nature, and in the ecological crisis that has since unfolded (Merchant 1983). While Merchant and others have acknowledged that the idea of dominion over the earth had existed in both Greek philosophy and Christian religion (Merchant 1983: 3), the detached observation, mastery, control, and manipulation of nature for the satisfaction of human economic utility that emerged in the modern era was a product of the Scientific Revolution view of nature as "brute," inert, and available for conquest (Passmore 1995; Bilgrami 2006). Such a notion of mastery and control was necessarily wedded to a Cartesian dualism in which the "human" person, "conjoining mind and body, could be set in total opposition to the non-human world" (Passmore 1995: 133). For Descartes, it was man's task therefore to make himself master and possessor of nature (Passmore 1995: 134). Val Plumwood points out that such dualism explains many of Western culture's most problematic features in its treatment of nature, producing in turn further dualisms that cast the very conception of the "human" as not only anthropocentric but masculinist, agentic, and rational, in contrast to the feminine, construed as inert, passive, and emotive, thus less than fully human, closer to nature, and hence subject to rule (Plumwood 1993: 38–9). For Merchant, Bilgrami, Passmore, Plumwood, and many others, the history of Western philosophy can be characterized by the steady victory of its rationalist, scientific, mechanistic, anthropocentric, mercantile, and instrumental elements over its holistic, affective, feminine, organismic, or paganistic ones.

Particularly controversial was an earlier argument made by historian of science Lynn White, who had gone even further, positing that this anthropocentric scientific rationality was directly linked to the earliest metaphysical foundations in Christian scripture, wherein human dominion over nature was explicitly mandated by the Creator (White 1967). White attributed Western civilization's anthropocentrism to Christianity, and specifically to the Western/Roman interpretation of Christianity, in contrast to its Eastern Orthodox one: God makes everything for man's benefit and dominion, man shares God's transcendence over nature, and it is God's will that man exploit nature for his own sustenance. By destroying pagan animism, Christianity desacralized natural objects, making it possible to exploit them in a mood of indifference to their spirit (Passmore 1985: 132). Perhaps counterintuitively, White argued that modern science and technology, rather than representing a secularized departure from Christianity, were in fact the progressive realization of the Christian dogma of man's transcendence and mastery over nature, for every major figure of the Scientific Revolution from Bacon to Newton explained their motivation in religious terms: namely, understanding the mind of God by learning how creation operates (White 1967).

White's provocative thesis predictably created a furor (see, among others, Dobel 2008). Indeed, though his thesis was by no means uncontroversial, its influence has been tremendous. At least two different edited collections of texts on environmental ethics include his now-classic article as the lead piece in the very first sections of their respective volumes, suggesting openly that the ecological crisis was rooted in the metaphysical foundations of the Western tradition (Pojman and Pojman 2001; Van De Veer and Pierce 1998). On the heels of such discourses linking the ecological crisis to the intellectual and metaphysical foundations of the Western tradition, many scholars—most notably, the thinkers of eco-centrism or biocentrism—began proposing alternative ethical and philosophical foundations for non-anthropocentric relations with nature (Leopold 1949; Naess 1984, 1986; Devall and Sessions 1985; Callicott 1987). If White was indeed right that "more science and more technology are not going to get us out of the present ecologic crisis until we find a new religion, or rethink our old one," then perhaps alternative foundations were indeed required. Thus, scholars began to ask the question of whether religious or philosophical traditions outside the West could provide intellectual foundations for such an alternative view. Perhaps most famously, Arne Naess, the thinker credited with articulating the "deep ecology" alternative to Western anthropocentrism, explicitly cited Hindu metaphysics as inspirational for his own particular version of biocentrism (Naess 1986: 24). Naess was motivated by Hindu metaphysics when calling for a "biocentric" egalitarianism in which all things in the biosphere should be accorded equal rights to live, while non-human life is to be accorded intrinsic rather than instrumental value. For Naess, realizing our identity as one with all living beings calls for us to recognize that violence against any living being is violence against the self (Naess 1984; Jacobsen 1996).

Indeed, as early as the 1960s, the indigenous Other—and particularly the Native American—had become a "symbol in the ecology movement's search for alternatives to Western exploitative attitudes. The Native animistic belief-system and reverence for the Earth as mother were contrasted with Judeo-Christian heritage of dominion over nature" (Merchant 1983: 28). Since then, there has been a flood of scholarship casting indigenous approaches to nature as more environmentally conscious and thus ethically exemplary (Booth 2003: 348–9). Subsequently, many scholars of non-Western religions and philosophies began to posit that alternative understandings of the human relationship to nature might be found within the metaphysics, ethics, and practices of non-Western civilizations such as Hinduism, Buddhism, Confucianism, and so on. In these works, both White's provocative thesis as well as the general sense of anthropocentrism in the worldviews and cultures associated with Abrahamic religions are often cited as motivations for such exploration (Tucker and Grim 2000: xxiv–xxv; Chapple 2000: xliii; Tucker and Grim 2002: xxii–xxiii).

Civilizational Approaches

Such scholarship tended mainly to cast ethical behavior as linked to metaphysical precepts contained in scriptural and/or philosophical texts and therefore to the wider cultural soil in which such behavior is rooted. I term these approaches "civilizational," for they implicitly or explicitly link attitudes and behavior toward nature with the intellectual, philosophical, and metaphysical foundations of a civilization, as reflected in the wider socio-cultural environment. Some scholars seem to be following the intuition that philosophical or religious foundations of a culture—in other words, broad "civilizational" influences—can explain something about human relations with nature in that culture (Cort 2001; Selin 2003). These works tend to be interdisciplinary, emerging from disciplines such as religious studies, philosophy, ethics, and Asian studies, reflecting the fact that these disciplines, considered disparate in the modern West, are often inseparable in the study of many non-Western traditions. This set of discourses is a curious mix of two antithetical tendencies: one strain tends to emphasize the radical contrast of non-Western holism with Western anthropocentrism, while a second strain insists on casting doubt on such stark contrasts as essentializing or falsely dichotomizing.

The first strain tends to emphasize those aspects of non-Western traditions—particularly South Asian and East Asian ones—that are considered more gentle, less violent, and more holistic in their cosmologies, that is, more aware of the continuities between the human and non-human worlds (Selin 2003: xix). In particular, South Asian religious traditions such as Hinduism, Buddhism, and Jainism are often cited as exemplars. Hinduism, for instance, it is said, has a more pronounced ontological continuity between divine and particular living beings than the Abrahamic traditions. Vedic accounts of creation set forth the oneness of the divine reality and the material world, and an examination of the multitude of Hindu cosmogonic myths demonstrates an organic and biological vision in which the completed universe is imagined as a living organism, in which everything belongs to the living pattern of the whole. Where the Abrahamic faiths are said to be God-centric, in that the divine Creator is above all else, including nature, and the worship of anything in nature as "divine" is considered sacrilegious, no such prohibition is found in Hinduism, where divinity is routinely manifested in the form of the natural elements and non-human life, often sacralized and worshipped as such (Coward 2003; Chattopadhyaya 2003).

Both Jainism and Buddhism, South Asian religions which originate in a rejection of Hinduism, are also characterized in this strain as demonstrating little or no discontinuity between human beings and other forms of life. Rather, karmic theory, which both of these theologies retain from their Hindu roots, includes living creatures of all kinds, and on this view, we travel endlessly through the cycle of birth and death, until liberation from rebirth is achieved. While liberation can ultimately only be achieved from a human birth, there is no difference in the essence of a human being, an animal, or a tree: each of these species can transform into the other over the course of multiple births. All beings are subject to the law of karma, and are mutually dependent upon one another, for any living being could be a relative, a loved one, or great sage in another life (Sahni 2008; Chattopadhyaya 2003; Sponsel and Natadecha-Sponsel 2003). In turn, this sense of mutual interdependence and connectedness gives rise to the notion of *ahimsa* or nonviolence toward all living beings, human or otherwise. It is important to note that this concept of *ahimsa* was particularly influential on Naess' articulation of deep ecology (Naess 1986).

As mentioned earlier, a second strain within these explorations of non-Western texts criticizes the strict examination of differences between the cosmological assumptions of different traditions, if it tends to essentialize or romanticize non-Western traditions, or emphasize only their otherness. No tradition is monolithic, this strain asserts, and the wholesale characterization of many non-Western traditions as gentle and holistic is also often acknowledged as a caricature. While there may be significant differences in cosmologies between certain traditions, the unselfconscious association of "non-Western" or "indigenous" spiritual traditions with a nonviolent and reverent attitude toward nature may rely in an uncritical way on the archetype of the "noble savage," often depicted as living closer to nature without being imprisoned in the artificial cultural constructs so prevalent in modern Western civilization (Kalland 2003). Some thinkers warn against this stereotype in environmental discourse, where it has served to romanticize or idealize the non-Western Other as the polar opposite of our industrialized, modernized and artificial Western selves. Non-Western or indigenous peoples and cultures are sometimes portrayed as static, untouched by history, eternally savage and wild, as required for them to serve as the Other of our anthropocentric, acquisitive selves. In other words, only by being "authentic" that is, uncontaminated by our "modern" ways, can these non-Western Others be noble and worthy of our consideration (Ray 2013). But to insist on idealizing all non-Western people as more connected to their ancient heritage, and as thus more noble and altruistic in their interactions with nature, creates a false dichotomy that reduces them to our antithesis, instead of exploring the continuities between "our" worldviews or practices and theirs (Kalland 2003).

Empirical examinations of specific practices of particular communities and subgroups within a tradition repeatedly demonstrate that the myth of the ecologically noble Other barely holds up to scrutiny, for non-Western or indigenous practices can be environmentally rapacious or destructive (Kalland 2003). Moreover, traditional ecological knowledge has rarely been static or untouched by change. But in insisting on romanticizing an Other forever locked into an ecologically friendly and exotic past, stereotypes of the noble savage deny non-Western peoples the right to engage with history, to evolve, develop, and to pick and choose the elements of modernity they may wish to incorporate into the evolution of their traditional practices. Critiquing deep ecology's invocation of Eastern spiritual traditions, the Indian historian Ramachandra Guha has famously asserted that "modern Western man has no monopoly on ecological disasters," rejecting the discourse in which the East is defined by a uniquely spiritual and non-rational "essence," denied agency and reason, serving merely as a vehicle for Western projections (Guha 1989).

Thus, while some scholars insist on drawing contrasts between Abrahamic/Western and non-Abrahamic/non-Western religions and philosophical traditions, others are attentive to the dangers of characterizing traditions in essentialist or romanticizing terms (for examples of the latter, see Patton 2000; Chapple 2001; Cort 2001). Often, these two strains appear in the same piece of writing, or within the same edited volume, suggesting the difficulty of undertaking such comparison while walking the fine line between recognizing and over-emphasizing distinctions among traditions. It should be noted that the more nuanced scholars are appropriately cautious in reflecting the dissent and internal plurality *within* non-Western traditions, often pointing out the environmentally destructive potentials inherent in traditions that are otherwise uncritically characterized as "biocentric." For instance, they point out, in both Hinduism and South Asian Buddhism, there is a tension between withdrawal from the world and affirmation of it. That is, there is a tension between those texts, myths, and practices which suggest that material reality is itself a creative manifestation of the divine, and should therefore be worshipped or at least treated with care; and those which suggest that material reality is ultimately insignificant, because all that matters is human liberation from the illusion of material life. Nature is matter (*prakriti*), while spirit (*purusha*) is timeless and eternal. The eighth-century Hindu philosopher Sankara argues that there is a radical separation between the ultimately reality, which is divine consciousness, and everything else in the phenomenal world, including nature. The realm of the world of nature is called by Sankara *maya* or illusion, in the sense that we take it to be real due to our sense perception, but it is not what is ultimately real (Chapple 2000: xliii; Nelson 2000: 136). So on this view, nature is simply part of the illusory material world that ceases to exist once we realize the ultimate truth in the enlightened state. This might lead to a disregard for the natural world as irrelevant to the task of spiritual liberation: why care about the destiny of a tree or a forest or even the entire planet, if the main goal of human life is to transcend the material world?

Meanwhile, more nuanced interpretations of Western traditions also continue to recognize that it is hardly univocal on questions pertaining to nature. Akeel Bilgrami reminds us for instance that the zeal to control, use, and manipulate nature which emerged from the new scientific outlook of the Enlightenment was hardly unanimous. Rather, it gave rise to a fierce philosophical critique which articulated the threatening consequences of seeing nature as inert or passive. These dissenting thinkers of the Enlightenment era were openly pantheistic, insisting that the natural world was suffused with divine value. To simply contrast scientific rationality with religion would be an oversimplification of Western intellectual history, for these dissenters did not deny or oppose the achievements of scientific rationality. Instead, they were deeply concerned about the cultural and political consequences of marrying such scientific rationality to a view of brute, desacralized nature available for conquest, domination, exploitation, and control (Bilgrami 2006). In much of pre-Enlightenment Europe, Merchant tells us, animism, the sacralization of nature, and the notion of earth as living organism and nurturing mother acted as a cultural constraint on the use of nature for technological and commercial purposes. European culture, as Merchant thus reminds us at length, "was far more complex and varied," scarcely reducible to the monolithic voice of scientific rationality married to the desire for dominion over nature (Merchant 1983: 29). More recently, instrumentalist, utilitarian attitudes toward nature have also been challenged by romantic strains of thought throughout modernity (including Transcendentalists such as Thoreau), and the modern quest to dominate nature has been thoroughly subjected to criticism by the first generation of critical theorists, particularly Adorno and Horkheimer in *Dialectic of Enlightenment*, not to mention more recent "green" thinking spanning a variety of perspectives from liberalism to pragmatism, Marxism, eco-feminism, biocentrism, and a whole host of others (Coole 2013; Lambacher, Biro, Stephens, all this volume).

To seek resources for environmental ethics in non-Western traditions is thus a fertile yet fraught endeavor. Those who do so seem to take their cue from critiques of the wider culture of anthropocentrism, mercantilism, domination, and instrumentalism supposedly rooted in the intellectual history of the West. I have cast this kind of scholarship as "civilizational" because it seems to draw a line of causal connection between a civilization's intellectual, philosophical, or metaphysical foundations, and the attitude of its adherents toward nature. Such scholarship is also ethically-oriented, for it suggests that the question of relations between the human and non-human world is one of normative import, both because its roots emerge from textual resources that are utterly normative in their thrust, and because it can have a discernible impact on the decline of the natural environment, seen as a good to be preserved. While a general exploration of the theoretical or philosophical underpinnings of a given civilization may be a useful way to begin exploring attitudes toward nature across traditions, in the remainder of this essay, I demonstrate an alternative way of approaching this question.

I go on to describe an approach that marries broad philosophical or metaphysical exploration with an emphasis on specific questions of political justice. Here, I describe a more practical and existential approach, and term it a "neo-Gandhian" approach or method, inspired by the work of M. K. Gandhi. Such an approach would ask how a particular thinker, community, or movement takes inspiration from a civilization's unique philosophical foundations, but would also put such foundations into practice within the context of specifically political questions and dilemmas. As Diana Coole notes, the ethical project alone in environmental thinking is deficient if it is not accompanied by "a critical analysis of the social structures that ethical beings inhabit," of the "systemic obstacles" such systems engender as a consequence of "politically invested institutions" and of those who "benefit materially and disproportionately from them" (Coole 2013: 463). In other words, while the "civilizational" approaches attempted to search solely for ethical or normative resolutions to the environmental crisis, the "neo-Gandhian" approach I detail here combines this attention to ethics with explicitly political critique and attention to systemic forms of injustice, and as such, incorporates both ethics and environmental political thought.

A Case Study: Contemporary Gandhian Environmental Thought and Practice in India

Contemporary Indian environmental practice provides perhaps one of the most fertile illustrations of a "neo-Gandhian" approach. Not only is India home to a plurality of spiritual traditions, as we have seen, the vast majority of these traditions are characterized by non-Western or non-Abrahamic ontological, philosophical, scriptural, and theological assumptions. More saliently, however, contemporary Indian thinking and practice around environmental issues presents a diverse mix of political commitments, discourses, and practices. And, while it is impossible to characterize the depth and diversity of India's countless environmental struggles monolithically, we see across a variety of cases that some of India's most prominent environmental advocates and thinkers explicitly appropriate the terminology, political commitments, and methodological approaches of M. K. Gandhi. Thus, the South Asian tradition is an ideal way to explore the intersection between broad philosophical approaches and concrete, specific practices, as well as that between ethical commitments and political critique.

Most scholars of the political thought of M. K. Gandhi see him as an idealist committed to moral principles in politics. Yet, despite his well-known principled commitments to *satya* (truth) and *ahimsa* (nonviolence), both taken from ancient Vedic metaphysics (Godrej 2006), political questions for Gandhi were not to be seen in the abstract, and could not be contemplated independently of everyday human needs and concerns. Gandhi famously claimed that "even God dare not appear to the poor man except in the form of bread." This emphasis on the political importance of fulfilling daily needs is particularly salient when examining his approach to environmental questions. Gandhi often expressed the idea that nature is valuable, but refuses to consider it an object of divine worship. While some scholars wish to read Gandhi as expressing a Vedic or Hindu reverence for nature, I have argued that Gandhi's approach to nature can be characterized as an ultimately anthropocentric position, in that nature is subordinate to the importance of human goals, needs, and desires (Godrej 2012).

In particular, questions of truth and justice for Gandhi were intimately connected to how human beings were able to produce, reproduce, consume, or otherwise stand in relation to their material environment. Gandhi was deeply concerned with truth-seeking as a matter of daily, bodily activity. Truth for Gandhi was not to be manifested simply through abstract commitments to moral knowledge, but rather through daily struggles with bodily, material life and the fulfillment of these needs. For Gandhi, *swaraj* (self-rule) and *swadeshi* (self-reliance or indigenous production) were not simply philosophical concepts emerging from India's rich Vedic tradition, or pertaining to India's independence from colonial rule; they were questions of access to material resources, and to specific modes of daily engagement with one's material environment (Gandhi 1949, 1958–94, 1962, 1955, 1993). The search for self-rule included autonomous decision-making regarding the specific conditions under which human beings were able to eat, drink, produce their own food and clothing, eliminate their waste, engage in sexual/reproductive relations, and otherwise engage with the world of material/natural resources. It is this commitment to self-rule and self-reliance understood as access to and autonomy over material resources that explains Gandhi's preoccupation with everyday, mundane aspects of material life, such as bodily functions, reproductive relations, dietary habits, waste disposal, and sexuality (Gandhi 1993; Parekh 2003; Rudolph and Rudolph 1967; Alter 2000; Mehta 1993). One could not contemplate questions of power, politics, justice, or equity without also thinking carefully about—and struggling with—bodily, material existence, and how one went about fulfilling material needs and desires. Gandhi insisted that human existence depended ineluctably on the socio-economic structures that produce and reproduce the conditions of our everyday lives; in other words, that everyday materiality mattered. Thus, he reinstated the material conditions of the production and reproduction of human life at the center of principled discussions about ideals in political life. In so doing, he anticipated the contemporary insistence of "new materialist" thinkers on recognizing the crucial political import of embodied humans in a material world and centering the fulfillment of everyday corporeal needs and material sustenance as the locus of a moral politics (Coole and Frost 2010).

For a comparative perspective, it is worth contrasting Gandhi's view to that of his contemporary and fellow nationalist Rabindranath Tagore, for whom the human interaction with the natural world was an abiding concern, appearing with regularity across his vast *corpus* of essays, books, plays, and poetry. Yet, Tagore's approach to nature is far closer to the philosophical commitments of the Hindu tradition in which nature is seen a manifestation of the divine. Tagore's evocative writings are filled with a longing for mystical union with the divine, often represented as nature, which evokes the same awe and wonder as the divine itself. Nature is never entirely inanimate, for it represents the vastness of cosmic creation itself. While Tagore does not ignore the crucial role of human–nature interaction in material sustenance, the dominant emphasis in his writings is on the deification or sacralization of nature, and its contemplation as a kind of spiritual practice (Tagore 1928, 1931, 1986, 1996).

Environmental thinkers and practitioners in contemporary India have been inspired far more by Gandhi's pragmatic, human-centered, and justice-oriented view of nature, rather than by Tagore's mystical, Vedic vision (Peritore 1993). Political debates surrounding the environment in India tend to pertain primarily to just living arrangements for daily life. Just as questions of truth, justice, and power for Gandhi required an engagement with the conditions under which humans could use material resources, environmental discourses in India keep their claims and demands interwoven with questions of access to and control over the conditions of everyday material sustenance. Their main concern, Ramachandra Guha reminds us, is about "the use of the environment and who should benefit from it," linking environmental demands to those of social justice, equity, and economic and political redistribution (Guha 1989, 1999).

Perhaps the most well-known such discourse is that of food security and food sovereignty, spearheaded by the activist and political philosopher Vandana Shiva. In her prolific and wide-ranging writings, Shiva cites Gandhian notions of self-sufficiency and self-reliance as inspiration for a uniquely Indian discourse about food sovereignty and food democracy (Shiva 1991, 2000, 2005, 2008). Shiva critiques the global industrial food production system for denying food producers in non-Western countries control over the production of food and over their own agricultural operations. She focuses on the pressure exerted by global, most often Western, political and economic formations on traditional forms of agriculture and other livelihoods to conform to a global system of production, often at disastrous cost to indigenous modes of production and ways of life. She is best known for criticizing the pressure applied by global agricultural firms such as Monsanto in compelling Indian farmers to use their seeds, along with the destruction that monocultures, industrial inputs, and other Western methods of farming have wrought on Indian agriculture. With the corporatization of agriculture, Western inputs such as seeds and agrochemicals are forced on Indian farmers, high costs push up production costs, while trade liberalization pushes down crop prices. The result is that farmers are often left facing crippling debt; since 1997, more than 250,000 farmers have committed suicide in India (Shiva 2008: 38–9). Shiva and others "consciously reject a narrative of progress that privileges centralization of knowledge and power and increases reliance on expensive technologies. The narrative of contemporary agriculture... emphasizes productivity, that is, high yields (an arbitrary standard), as the sole measure of value, and progress in the form of improved seeds and inputs such as fertilizers that are priced beyond the range of most farmers" (Sanford 2013).

The term that Shiva often employs is *beej swaraj* or "seed sovereignty," making explicit the linkage between contemporary Indian discourses of food production and Gandhi's ideals of self-reliance and democracy in everyday food production. Rather than being subject to fluctuating prices of foreign food controlled by foreign corporations, Shiva calls for a concept of food security that rejuvenates local farms in order to develop independence from the global economy (Shiva 2008: 39). Most importantly, these critiques are by no means simply theoretical; countless local communities of neo-Gandhians in India practice ideals of self-reliance through alternative—that is, traditional or non-Western—agriculture in their daily lives, staunchly insisting on self-reliance and sovereignty as it pertains to food production and access (Klenk 2010; Sanford 2013). In so doing, most of these communities employ the very same conceptual framework of self-rule, self-reliance, and self-sufficiency that Gandhi first articulated during the nationalist movement against empire.

Shiva, along with other Gandhian environmentalists such as Medha Patkar, also links environmental claims to those of social justice more broadly. These discourses highlight the importance of access to natural resources and opportunities to engage in traditional livelihoods as matters in which environmental and socio-economic justice are irreducibly intertwined. They point out that the forced reliance on the external inputs and foreign technologies of global capital removes natural resources from the traditional control of indigenous communities (Shiva 2008). For peasants, tribals, and other indigenous peoples in developing countries, the land and resources that global capital industrial regimes seek to appropriate have long performed life-support and livelihood functions. These communities rely on natural resources for needs such as nutrition, health care, energy, housing, and so forth. The shift toward global, industrial, capitalist modes of production causes dispossession of farmers and tribals, as biodiversity is transformed from a renewable to a non-renewable resource through modern technology (Shiva 1991: 52). As societies which were traditionally based on renewable resources have been pushed into fossil fuel dependence, we see the large-scale displacement and dispossession of women, peasants, tribals, and indigenous communities (Shiva 1989, 2008: 30). By appropriating natural resources, destroying biodiversity, and causing fossil-fuel dependence, the global industrial model of development threatens the life-support systems and livelihoods of millions of non-urbanized people outside the developed West. Patkar's work with the Narmada Bachao Andolan has also brought to the fore the issue of the displacement and dispossession of indigenous peoples and livelihoods as a result of the construction of the Sardar Sarovar dam on the river Narmada (Roy 1999; D'Souza 2002). Initially funded by the World Bank which later withdrew its support, plans to build the dam inspired one of India's largest and most wide-ranging environmental coalitions, consisting of tribal people, farmers, environmentalists and human rights activists, all collaborating to protest the environmental and livelihood impact of the project through hunger strikes, protest marches, and other forms of Gandhian nonviolent activism.

It is also worth noting that in resisting global appropriations of indigenous biological resources, these communities explicitly rely on combative and activist forms of Gandhian nonviolence. Despite his commitment to nonviolence, Gandhi repeatedly insisted that such nonviolence was not to be confused with passivity, instead articulating a nonviolence based on confrontational, warriorlike defiance in which the truth-seeker was duty-bound to confront injustice by breaking laws and disrupting the everyday workings of unjust political systems. Accepting the penalties and punitive consequences following from these disruptive, confrontational actions, and thus suffering in order to demonstrate the strength of one's convictions, was the very pillar upon which the moral logic of his nonviolence was founded (Godrej 2006, 2012). Such suffering was often highly public and physically painful in nature, intended to draw attention to the willingness to sacrifice one's physical wellbeing for the sake of the truth. In many of the above-described movements, Indian activists have conducted public, sacrificial acts of physically painful political disruption. Well-known examples are India's Chipko Andolan ("Hug the Tree Movement"), and the Narmada Bachao Andolan ("Save the Narmada Valley Movement"). In these and countless other instances, environmental activists have acted to protect trees in the Himalayas or to demand justice for the citizens of the Narmada River Valley through nonviolent physical confrontations such as tree-hugging, sit-ins, protest marches, and hunger strikes (Mishra and Tripathi 1978). As such, these contemporary movements and discourses underscore Gandhi's insight that matters of everyday material sustenance cannot be disentangled from questions of truth or justice, *and* that such truth-seeking must be accompanied by the willingness to actively disrupt political formations and organizations, while publicly paying the penalty for such disruption (Shiva 1998).[1] More importantly, they marry ethical questions of human–nature relations with explicitly political questions of justice and equity, insisting that normative ideals culled from the metaphysical foundations of South Asian religions be put into practice in service of just political outcomes and everyday political arrangements.

Conclusion

In the same way that Gandhian ideals were deeply interwoven with questions of everyday practical existence and sustenance, environmental discourses in India cast their claims as questions of basic justice. In the above Indian discourses, rather than a mystical awe and wonder at a sacralized nature articulated by Tagore, we see a practical and everyday Gandhian concern with nature as the crucial pillar of basic sustenance. Much of what we see in contemporary Indian environmental thought and practice is motivated by Gandhian ideals of self-sufficiency and self-reliance, which combine to form a notion of justice that is intrinsically wedded to autonomy over daily sustenance.

In concluding, I offer the suggestion that this neo-Gandhian approach offers a more insightful model for conceptualizing the human–nature relationship than that offered by the scholarship I earlier characterized as "civilizational." "Civilizational" approaches to environmental thought are not only forced to grapple with the problematic and essentialist characterizations of "West" and "non-West," but may also layer such characterizations onto other equally problematic dichotomies such as anthropocentrism and biocentrism. Perhaps because it emerged so clearly in response to critiques of the Western tradition's ostensibly anthropocentric philosophical foundations, what I call "civilizational" scholarship is bound up with casting the Other as the antithesis of such anthropocentrism, and, as such, may unwittingly lend itself to ultimately misleading dichotomies. In contrast, a Gandhian reconception of environmental issues as questions of truth, specifically cast in the language of access to resources and livelihoods, allows us to reject dichotomies such as anthropocentrism/biocentrism and humans/nature. On such a view, there is no contradiction between allowing the flourishing of human beings, and preserving nature. Nature is not something apart from humans, but rather a crucial entity with which the human struggle for justice is intimately connected.

It should be noted that a neo-Gandhian approach to nature, despite its emphasis on the use of natural resources by humans, should not ignore entirely the question of nonviolence toward nature. Deeply grounded in both the Hindu and Jain traditions, Gandhi was almost unconditionally wedded to *ahimsa* or nonviolence as the foundation of his political thinking. His staunch lifelong commitment to vegetarianism and his aversion to eating meat are often seen as a manifestation of this commitment to *ahimsa*. Indeed, it is precisely this concept of *ahimsa* that inspired "biocentric" deep ecologists such as Naess. Yet, Gandhi's insistence on nonviolence at no point required an insistence on leaving nature pristine or untouched. Rather, the use of the natural environment in generating everyday material sustenance is, for Gandhi, a foundational condition of human existence.

Such a non-dichotomous view of humans and nature has recently become more apparent in Western thinking about the environment. Perhaps because global capitalism has cast the flourishing of humans in terms of economic or technical progress and consumer access to goods, both of which require the excavation of natural resources, "humans versus nature" and "anthropocentrism versus biocentrism" have until recently been relatively common frameworks in thinking about environmental issues in the West. Indeed, there is still a significant pressure in Western discourse to cast environmental protection as coming at a cost or sacrifice to the pursuit of human consumption and pleasure as a whole, suggesting simplistically that humans and nature are in a zero-sum relationship (Beavan 2009; Leonard 2010). As Ramachandra Guha noted, the emphasis on the dichotomy between anthropocentrism and biocentrism, often accompanied by the preoccupation with the preservation of unspoilt wilderness, obfuscates the fact that it is not the human *use* of nature, but the overconsumption of material resources by some in the industrialized world that presents the gravest threat (Guha 1989: 273). In other words, it is not that we use nature at all to satisfy basic needs that constitutes the problem; rather, it is that we do not question the deeply inequitable use of nature by some, and the lack of opportunity this causes for others. Fortunately, recent environmental discourses and movements in the West have begun to offer more nuanced understandings of "nature" which see human beings as always already embedded within nature and drawing upon it for everyday sustenance. The dichotomous notion of leaving nature "apart" from humans in order to protect it from human intervention has begun to recede as a model for environmental thinking, with emphasis shifting instead toward the questions of *who* has greater access to these natural resources, and *how* such access could be more equitably distributed. Indeed, the discourses of "environmental justice," which include questions of "environmental racism" and "food justice," provide splendid examples of this.

For instance, "food justice" thinkers and activists are providing a challenge to industrial food systems by articulating questions of access to good and healthy food as questions of truth and justice intimately connected to power over material resources, while rejecting models of global industrial agriculture and capitalism as means for generating everyday sustenance (Alkon and Agyeman 2011; Guthman 2008; Gottlieb and Joshi 2013). In this emphasis on justice, the movement follows Gandhian concerns with self-sufficiency and self-reliance. Like Shiva and other neo-Gandhians, this discourse assumes that human life requires intervention within the natural world for the purpose of sustenance. Rather than positing human needs as dichotomously opposed to the protection of nature, these thinkers center the question of justice in how access to resources for such sustenance is structured, who controls such resources, who loses and who benefits from the existing patterns of access/distribution, and finally, what alternative patterns of access, production, and distribution might be more just. In so doing, they reflect the influence of a post-Gandhian discourse which seeks to highlight the configurations of power embedded in matters of everyday existence. They illustrate a neo-Gandhian approach to environmental questions, reminding us that as long as the struggle for human dignity remains tied to the struggle for access to resources, our conceptions of the human–nature relationship may need to remain equally yoked to questions of control over the fulfillment of basic material sustenance.

Finally, a Gandhian approach suggests that comparative theorizing which seeks resources for global environmental problems within the intellectual or metaphysical foundations of non-Western traditions need not adhere uncritically to dichotomies requiring others to be presented in stark contrast to the West. Neo-Gandhian environmental approaches may take inspiration from the metaphysical concepts and explicitly ethical ideals of the Vedic tradition, such as, for instance, *satya* (truth) and *ahimsa* (nonviolence), or use the indigenous ethical categories of *swaraj* (self-rule) and *swadeshi* (self-reliance) as Gandhi did. They may call upon such non-Western categories in order to inspire political action on questions of food sovereignty, food justice, fair wages and working conditions, just distribution of environmental outcomes, or any number of other contemporary problems of justice. In so doing, they need not cast adherents of the Indian tradition as gentle, holistic, "biocentric" Others who live in harmony with nature, or contrast them with acquisitive, mercantile, anthropocentric Western modes of being. They need not see these Others simply as wise repositories of environmental ethics and moral knowledge. Rather, they can combine the normative commitments that Gandhi acquired from the Indian tradition with his materialist and activist political sensibility, in order to envision a way of human "being" in relation to nature that is practical in its materialism (that is, acknowledges the necessity of using natural resources in order to fulfill material needs), as well as explicitly political in service of truth and justice (that is, engaged in questions of just political outcomes in the distribution of natural resources, using nonviolent activist methods). Such a neo-Gandhian approach may provide a promising avenue for the future of a "comparative" environmental political thought.

Note

1. See also Vandana Shiva, "Fortnight of Action for Seed Freedom and Food Freedom," posted at http://seedfreedom.in/fortnight-of-actions-letter-from-vandana-shiva/, Navdanya page on "Earth Democracy," posted at http://www.navdanya.org/earth-democracy

References

Alkon, Alison Hope and Julian Agyeman. (2011). *Cultivating Food Justice: Race, Class, and Sustainability* (Cambridge, MA: MIT Press).

Alter, Joseph S. (2000). *Gandhi's Body: Sex, Diet and the Politics of Nationalism* (Philadelphia: University of Pennsylvania Press).

Barsamian, David. (2009). "Vandana Shiva: Gandhi's Three Pillars of Freedom are Now the Key to our Survival." *Yes!* 50:12.

Beavan, Colin. (2009). No Impact Man: The Adventures of a Guilty Liberal Who Attempts to Save the Planet, and the Discoveries He Makes About Himself and Our Way of Life in the Process (New York: Farrar, Strauss, Giroux).

Bilgrami, Akeel. (2006). "Gandhi, Newton and the Enlightenment." *Social Scientist* 34(5/6): 17–35.

Booth, Annie L. (2003). "We Are the Land: Native American Views of Nature." In *Nature Across Cultures: Views of Nature and the Environment in Non-Western Cultures*, edited by Helaine Selin (Dordrecht/Boston/London: Kluwer, 2003), 329–50.

Callicott, J. Baird. (1987). *Companion to a Sand County Almanac* (Madison, WI: University of Wisconsin Press).

Chapple, Christopher Key. (2000). "Introduction." In *Hinduism and Ecology: The Intersection of Earth, Sky, and Water*, edited by Christopher Key Chapple and Mary Evelyn Tucker (Cambridge, MA: Harvard University Press), xxxiii–xlix.

Chapple, Christopher Key. (2001). "Hinduism and Deep Ecology." In *Deep Ecology and World Religions: New Essays on Sacred Ground*, edited by David Landis Barnhill and Roger S. Gottlieb (Albany, NY: SUNY Press), 59–76.

Chattopadhyaya, D. P. (2003). "Indian Perspectives on Naturalism." In *Nature Across Cultures: Views of Nature and the Environment in Non-Western Cultures*, edited by Helaine Selin (Dordrecht/Boston/London: Kluwer), 147–60.

Coole, Diana. (2013). "Agentic Capacities and Capacious Historical Materialism: Thinking with New Materialisms in the Political Sciences." *Millenium: Journal of International Studies* 41(3): 451–69.

Coole, Diana and Frost, Samantha, eds. (2010). *New Materialisms: Ontology, Agency and Politics* (Durham, NC: Duke University Press).

Cort, John E. (2001). "Green Jainism? Notes and Queries toward a Possible Jain Environmental Ethic." In *Jainism and Ecology: Nonviolence in the Web of Life*, edited by Christopher Key Chapple (Cambridge, MA: Harvard University Press), 63–94.

Coward, Harold. (2003). "Hindu Views of Nature and the Environment." In *Nature Across Cultures: Views of Nature and the Environment in Non-Western Cultures*, edited by Helaine Selin (Dordrecht/Boston/London: Kluwer), 411–20.

Devall, Bill and Sessions, George. (1985). *Deep Ecology: Living as if Nature Mattered* (Salt Lake City: Peregrine Smith Books).

D'Souza, Dilip. (2002). *Narmada Dammed: An Inquiry into the Politics of Development* (Gurgaon: Penguin Books, India).
Merchant, Carolyn. (1983). *Death of Nature: Women, Ecology and the Scientific Revolution* (New York: Harper & Row).
Dobel, Patrick. "The Judeo-Christian Stewardship Attitude to Nature." In *Environmental Ethics: Readings in Theory and Application*, edited by Louis P. Pojman and Paul Pojman (Belmont, CA: Wadsworth), 28–33.
Gandhi, M. K. (1958–94). *The Collected Works of Mahatma Gandhi*. 100 vols. (Delhi: Publication Division, Ministry of Information and Broadcasting, Government of India).
Gandhi, M. K. (1962). *Village Swaraj* (Ahmedabad: Navajivan Publishing House).
Gandhi, M. K. (1949). *Diet and Diet Reform* (Ahmedabad: Navajivan Publishing House).
Gandhi, M. K. (1955). *Ashram Observances in Action*. Translated by Valji Govindji Desai (Ahmedabad: Navajivan Publishing House).
Gandhi, M. K. (1993). *Nature Cure*. Edited by Bharatan Kumarappa (Ahmedabad: Navajivan Publishing House).
Gandhi, M. K. (1993). *An Autobiography: The Story of My Experiments with Truth* (Boston: Beacon Press).
Godrej, Farah. (2006). "Nonviolence and Gandhi's Truth: A Method for Moral and Political Arbitration." *Review of Politics* 68(2): 287–312.
Godrej, Farah. (2012). "Ascetics, Warriors and a Gandhian Ecological Citizenship." *Political Theory* 40(4): 437–65.
Gottlieb, Robert and Anupama Joshi. (2013). *Food Justice (Food, Health and the Environment)* (Cambridge, MA: MIT Press).
Guha, Ramachandra. (1989). "Radical Environmentalism and Wilderness Preservation: A Third World Critique." *Environmental Ethics* 11(1): 71–83.
Guthman, Julie. (2008). "Neoliberalism and The Making of Food Politics in California." *Geoforum* 39: 1171–83.
Guha, Ramachandra. (1999). *Environmentalism: A Global History* (Upper Saddle River, NJ: Pearson).
Jacobsen, Knut A. (1996). "Bhagavadgita, Ecosophy T, and Deep Ecology." *Inquiry* 39(2): 219–38.
Kalland, Arne. (2003). "Environmentalism and Images of the Other." In *Nature Across Cultures: Views of Nature and the Environment in Non-Western Cultures*, edited by Helaine Selin (Dordrecht/Boston/London: Kluwer), 1–18.
Klenk, Rebecca. (2010). *Educating Activists: Development and Gender in the Making of Modern Gandhians* (Lanham, MD: Lexington Books).
Lambacher, Jason. (2015, forthcoming). "Limits of Freedom and the Freedom of Limits." In *Oxford Handbook of Environmental Political Theory*, edited by T. Gabrielson, C. Hall, J. M. Meyer, and D. Schlosberg (Oxford: Oxford University Press).
Leonard, Annie. (2010). The Story of Stuff: How Our Obsession with Stuff is Trashing the Planet, Our Communities, and our Health—and a Vision for Change (New York: Free Press).
Leopold, Aldo. (1949). *A Sand County Almanac: And Essays on Conservation from Round River* (New York: Oxford University Press).
Mehta, Ved. (1993). *Mahatma Gandhi and His Apostles* (New Haven: Yale University Press).
Mishra, Anupam and Tripathi, Satyendra. (1978). *Chipko Movement: Uttarakhand Women's Bid to Save Forest Wealth* (New Delhi: People's Action for Development with Justice).

Naess, Arne. (1984). "Identification as a Source of Deep Ecological Attitudes." In *Deep Ecology*, edited by Michael Tobias (San Diego: Avant Books), 256–70.

Naess, Arne. (1986). *Self-Realisation: An Ecological Approach to Being in the World*. (Perth: Murdoch University Press).

Nelson, Lance E. (2000). "Reading the Bhagavadgita from an Ecological Perspective." In *Hinduism and Ecology: The Intersection of Earth, Sky, and Water*, edited by Christopher Key Chapple and Mary Evelyn Tucker (Cambridge, MA: Harvard University Press), 129–64.

Parekh, Bhikhu. (2003). *Colonialism, Tradition and Reform: An Analysis of Gandhi's Political Discourse* (Thousand Oaks, CA: Sage).

Passmore, John. (1995). "Attitudes to Nature." In *Environmental Ethics*, edited by Robert Elliot (New York: Oxford University Press), 129–41.

Patton, Laurie L. (2000). "Nature Romanticism and Sacrifice in *Rgvedic* Interpretation." In *Hinduism and Ecology: The Intersection of Earth, Sky, and Water*, edited by Christopher Key Chapple and Mary Evelyn Tucker (Cambridge, MA: Harvard University Press).

Peritore, N. Patrick. (1993). "Environmental Attitudes of Indian Elites: Challenging Western Postmodernist Models." *Asian Survey* 33: 804–18.

Plumwood, Val. (1993). *Feminism and the Mastery of Nature* (New York: Routledge).

White, Lynn. "The Historical Roots of Our Ecological Crisis." *Science* 155(1967): 1203–7.

Pojman, Louis P. and Pojman, Paul, eds. (2001). *Environmental Ethics: Readings in Theory and Application* (Belmont, CA: Wadsworth).

Ray, Sarah Jaquette. (2013). *The Ecological Other: Environmental Exclusion in American Culture* (Tucson, AZ: University of Arizona Press).

Roy, Arundhati. (1999). *The Cost of Living* (New York: Modern Library Paperbacks).

Rudolph, Lloyd I. and Rudolph, Susanne Hoeber. (1967). *The Modernity of Tradition: Political Development in India* (Chicago: University of Chicago Press).

Sahni, Pragati. (2008). *Environmental Ethics in Buddhism: A Virtues Approach* (London and New York: Routledge).

Sanford, Whitney. (2013). "Gandhi's Agrarian Legacy: Practicing Food, Justice, and Sustainability in India." *Journal for the Study of Religion, Nature and Culture* 7(1): 65–87.

Sanford, Whitney. (2012). *Growing Stories from India: Religion and the Fate of Agriculture* (Lexington, KY: University Press of Kentucky).

Selin, Helaine. (2003). "Introduction." In *Nature Across Cultures: Views of Nature and the Environment in Non-Western Cultures*, edited by Helaine Selin (Dordrecht/Boston/London: Kluwer), xix–xxiii.

Shiva, Vandana. (1989). *Staying Alive: Women, Ecology and Development* (London: Zed Books).

Shiva, Vandana. (1991). "Biodiversity, Biotechnology and Profits." In Vandana Shiva, Patrick Anderson, Heffa Schücking, Andrew Gray, Larry Lohmann, and David Cooper. *Biodiversity: Social and Ecological Perspectives* (London: Zed Books), 43–58.

Shiva, Vandana. (1998). *Globalisation, Gandhi and Swadeshi: What is Economic Freedom? Whose Economic Freedom?* (New Delhi, India: Research Foundation for Science, Technology and Ecology).

Shiva, Vandana. (2000). *Stolen Harvest: The Hijacking of the Global Food Supply* (Boston: South End Press).

Shiva, Vandana. (2005). *Earth Democracy: Justice, Sustainability and Peace* (Boston: South End Press).

Shiva, Vandana. (2008). *Soil Not Oil: Environmental Justice in an Age of Climate Crisis* (Boston: South End Press).

Sponsel, Leslie and Natadecha-Sponsel, Poranee. (2003). "Buddhist Views of Nature and the Environment." In *Nature Across Cultures: Views of Nature and the Environment in Non-Western Cultures*, edited by Helaine Selin (Dordrecht/Boston/London: Kluwer), 351–72.
Tagore, Rabindranth. (1928). *Prakritir Pratisodh* (Kolkata: Visva-Bharati).
Tagore, Rabindranth. (1931). *The Religion of Man* (London: Allen & Unwin).
Tagore, Rabindranth. (1986). *Rabindra Rachanavali, Sulabh Sanskaran* (Kolkata: Visva-Bharati).
Tagore, Rabindranth. (1996). "The Robbery of the Soil." In *The English Writings of Rabindranath Tagore: Vol. 3*, edited by Sisir Kumar Das (New Delhi: Sahitya Akademi), 866–71.
Tucker, Mary Evelyn and Grim, John. (2000). "Series Foreword." In *Hinduism and Ecology: The Intersection of Earth, Sky, and Water*, edited by Christopher Key Chapple, and Mary Evelyn Tucker (Cambridge, MA: Harvard University Press), xv–xxxii.
Tucker, Mary Evelyn and Grim, John. (2002). "Series Foreword." In *Jainism and Ecology: Nonviolence in the Web of Life*, edited by Christopher Key Chapple (Cambridge, MA: Harvard University Press), xiii–xxx.
Van De Veer, Donald and Pierce, Christine. (1998). *The Environmental Ethics and Policy Book* (Belmont, CA: Wadsworth).

CHAPTER 4

ENVIRONMENTAL POLITICAL THEORY AND THE LIBERAL TRADITION

PIERS H. G. STEPHENS

Liberalisms Old and New

"The Green movement," declared Andrew Dobson in 1990, "is in a position more akin to that of the early liberals than that of the early socialists—it is self-consciously seeking to call into question an entire world view rather than tinker with one that already exists" (Dobson 1990: 8). Dobson's view reflected the received wisdom of the time by defining the green movement *against* the presuppositions of contemporary liberal democratic societies, but more recent scholarship has examined both the oppositions and the compatibilities, examining ways in which environmentalism may be consistent with at least some liberal values and traditions. Accordingly, in this chapter I initially clarify key terms and note aspects of the liberal tradition that might both prefigure green politics and suggest possible points of fusion. With the historical material's significance clarified, I shall give an overview of positions in the current debate over the green–liberal relationship. Finally, I shall sketch an argument of my own aimed at connecting a key aspect of green politics to liberalism by invoking the significance of nature experience to the core liberal value of individual freedom.

I begin by sketching liberalism's scope, a loose exercise because there "is no definitively bound 'authentic liberalism' constituting, as it does, a variety of ideas and conflicting impulses" (Paton 2011: 9). However, the unifying ingredient is expressed by Maurice Cranston, that "a liberal is a man [i.e. person] who believes in liberty" (Cranston 1967: 459), to which we must add that the liberty in question is primarily that of the individual human agent, and that conceptions both of individual agency and of liberty itself are disputed within liberalism. Liberal prioritization of liberty as a political value means justifications are needed for restricting it, and in diverse ways liberals regard the equal liberty and equal moral worth of citizens as foundational. Thus liberalism's historic origins intertwined with social contract theories, in that both attempted to explain legitimate political authority in terms of consent; liberal assumptions about human liberty and equality in the state of nature opposed theories which assumed valid political authority arose through custom, natural hierarchy, or divine dispensation. Though not all contractarians were liberal—the legislative absolutisms of both Hobbes and Rousseau appear illiberal—one can reasonably see the first liberalism as being that of John Locke's *Two Treatises of Government* (1689), wherein pre-political natural rights to life, liberty, and property constrain legitimate boundaries of government activity. These are negative rights against interference, manifesting an emphasis on negative liberty in Berlin's sense: the absence of coercive interference by humans (Berlin 1969). This Lockean emphasis on negative liberty is found throughout the "old" or "classical" liberalism of Francis Hutcheson, Adam Smith, and their successors, through to contemporary figures such as F. A. Hayek. It intertwines with an emphasis on private property rights and a market order resultant from them as manifesting, protecting, and enabling liberty in various respects. The boundaries, applications, and goals of particular private property regimes may be constructed and interpreted in diverse ways, and the relationship between private ownership and the public good can be variously conceived accordingly. But this Lockean line of thought emphasizes the importance of the individual's relationship to their property, so it may loosely be associated with the tradition C. B. Macpherson critically names "possessive individualism" (Macpherson 1962), and I shall accordingly refer to it as "old liberalism" or "neo-Lockean liberalism" in what follows.

A second strand, the "social liberalism" or (as I shall call it) "new liberalism" that emerged in the nineteenth century, contests both the negative liberty emphasis and the neo-Lockean stress on private property rights. Though earlier inspirations are present in Romanticism, "new liberalism" most clearly emerges into the tradition through John Stuart Mill's work, especially *On Liberty*. Here we see a conception of positive liberty—that is, liberty as self-rule, in which the freedom of an agent's actions is manifested through the individual being able to exercise her will *authentically*, attaining goals and demonstrating command of her own life rather than obedience to custom or compulsion—emerge to sit alongside negative liberty. Mill's new liberalism, as Wendy Donner observes, "does not embrace possessive individualism" and does not "assume isolated individuals lacking social bonds" but rather is "centered around the value he places on the individual as the generator, focus, and appraiser of value," is "developmental to its core," and shows an emphasis on being "in control or possession of one's own life and powers" and having "one's ideas and activities and projects be an expression of one's own particularity" (Donner 1991: 148–9). Mill's innovations, both in *On Liberty* and elsewhere, helped initiate new emphases on autonomy and a new liberal awareness of the ways in which market inequality and private property might undermine liberty instead of promote it. These new emphases, which increasingly extended towards countenancing increased state regulation, economic planning, and redistribution, were steadily developed through the later nineteenth and twentieth centuries. Whilst Mill's initial moves were inspired by ancient Greek and Romantic notions of agency, his resultant rethinking was so influential that John Skorupski sees this "notion of human good as the balanced development of human powers of both rational will and feeling, together with a wish to give all human beings equitable access to this good" as being "liberalism's *ethical* idea" in this period (Skorupski 1999: 215). The emphasis on autonomy was developed by T. H. Green and others in the late nineteenth century, and was sometimes later blended with the socialist idea that freedom means an effective power to act (Tawney 1931). This created a fuzzy boundary between the new liberalism and democratic socialism, as both espoused welfare state measures and economic interventionism in the first half of the twentieth century in Western Europe. In the United States, Deweyan pragmatism and social experimentation—America's home grown new liberalism—served a similar function during the New Deal era.

It is from these developments that our last components emerge, the emphases on social justice and state neutrality. Though distributive justice was part of new liberalism's lexicon, it was thrust into the forefront of liberal discourse with publication of John Rawls' *A Theory of Justice* (1971), which in turn strongly influenced contemporary new liberals such as Ronald Dworkin and Bruce Ackerman. (In contrast, contemporary representatives of old liberalism, such as F. A. Hayek (1976) and Robert Nozick (1974), have argued that such a focus on distributive patterns represents an illusion or even a threat to individual liberties.) State neutrality, the idea that the liberal state may be defined by its being neutral between competing conceptions of the good, is more contentious in its significance and emergence within liberal political thought. Several figures in the green–liberal debate, most prominently Marcel Wissenburg (1998) and Simon Hailwood (2004), characterize liberalism paradigmatically along these lines, but whilst some liberals (such as Dworkin (1985)) espouse this definition, it is dubious whether this neutralism can be applied to the full tradition without distortion. Jeremy Waldron sees no formulation in these terms before 1974 (Waldron 1989: 62), and historically minded critics such as Skorupski (1999: 220–4) and John Zvesper (1993) reject both the historical accuracy and political desirability of contemporary neutralist accounts of liberalism. I support their repudiations (Stephens 1996, 2001), but awareness of neutralism's current pervasiveness is necessary to understand contemporary liberal political philosophy.

Defining environmental political theory is also thorny and I shall not attempt a comprehensive definition here. Rather I espouse an inclusive approach that sees the divisions within environmental political theory most relevant to this discussion as themselves emanating from green politics and environmental ethics, and am here explaining my conception of those divisions. Green politics and environmental ethics are haunted by dichotomies between reformism, usually anthropocentric, and radicalism, usually non-anthropocentric. One can easily draw a division like Dobson's between environmentalism, taken as a human-centered piecemeal reformist approach, and ecologism, which demands radical moral, political, and economic changes (Dobson 1990: 13–36). I believe, however, that green politics is better viewed on a spectrum ranging from reformism to ecological radicalism, and moreover that the division may be less straightforward than Dobson believes: as Bryan Norton argues, an enlightened anthropocentrism might converge with non-anthropocentrism in practical policy terms (Norton 1991).

Adopting an inclusive approach also enables us to see historic linkages between green politics and liberalism in a way that is impossible if one focuses on ecologism as a post-1960s phenomenon, and whilst Dobson's more recent assertion that "environmentalism and liberalism are compatible but ecologism and liberalism are not" (Dobson 2000: 165) contains some truth, I shall later conclude by suggesting how a key value of ecologism, the stress on nature experience, can actually enrich the liberal focus on freedom. But first we turn to historic aspects of the liberal tradition that can be seen as connecting to current environmental politics.

Liberalism's Environmental Heritage

The radical character of most 1970s and 1980s' ecological activism, much of it based around the idea of natural limits to economic growth, alongside the political resurgence of a neo-Lockean liberalism aimed at increasing such growth, served to minimize scholarly interest in the possibilities of green–liberal compatibility. In particular, the confusion of liberalism with so called neo-liberalism, an ideology which actually "derives, in part, from radical nineteenth century libertarianism on the one hand and a resurgent socio-political conservatism on the other" (Paton 2011: 6) and which draws from the old liberal tradition merely in terms of economic anti-statism, has caused much reflexive rejection of liberalism. As a result, interest in green–liberal rapprochement did not really take off until the later 1990s. Most such interest before then came from philosophers rather than political theorists; in particular, various attempts were made to rescue Lockean property theory from the charge that it manifested a destructive Christian dominion orientation (Squadrito 1979; Attfield 1983: 107–10; Shrader-Frechette 1993). All of these represented attempts to excavate environmental positives from liberalism's history and anticipated later disputes, but as the backdrop was the debate over Christianity's role in environmental destruction, a wider examination of liberalism's environmental credentials was not triggered. Still, these efforts point to potentialities within the tradition, and I shall now develop the picture further.

To begin at the beginning, it is indeed possible to read elements of Lockean property theory as mandating some intergenerationally orientated restriction upon economic exploitation of nature. Though Locke notoriously claims that 99 percent of the value of goods made from natural resources comes from the human labor deployed in production, Kristin Shrader-Frechette suggests that the remaining 1 percent of value attributed by Locke to nature could be used to suggest an idea of moral restraint on human dealings with the natural world. But Shrader-Frechette's idea has had little support, perhaps because a better explanation of the 1 percent value might be that Locke was trying to avoid the implication that God's creation was valueless without human input. Attfield's invocation of the restrictive provisos in Locke's property theory has proved more fertile. At least one great liberal, Jefferson, may have read Locke this way, and some scholarship has attempted to create accounts of environmental liberalism on neo-Lockean lines. There are in fact two provisos in Locke's property theory in Chapter V of the *Second Treatise*, both of which are portrayed as operating in the state of nature. The first is the spoilage proviso in Section 31 whereby "nothing was made by God for man to spoil or destroy" and the second occurs in Section 33, where private property is gained from the commons by mixing one's labor with the item "at least where there is enough, and as good, left in common for others" (Locke 1988: 290–1). Both of these provisos may restrain the legitimate extent of acquisition rights. However, significant controversy exists over whether or not the arrival of imperishable money, which could enable surpluses of perishable goods to be built up for sale without violating the spoilage proviso, actually renders the first proviso inoperative; indeed, it might join with the increased productivity generated by private land ownership to also obviate the second proviso if one accepts Macpherson's portrait of Locke as a proto-capitalist, or even if one simply reads such expansion as mandated by God having "bid Mankind increase and multiply" as "the main intention of Nature" according to Locke's words in the *First Treatise* (Macpherson 1962: 203–20; Locke 1988: 169, 183). It seems likely, however, that Locke's admirer Thomas Jefferson did not regard either proviso as being transcended by the arrival of money or civil government, as these provisos could explain Jefferson's apparent suggestion of usufruct (that is, without rights of destruction) land ownership in his 1789 letter to James Madison on intergenerational obligations. For as Luigi Marco Bassani maintains, ongoing usufruct restraints would embody the Lockean provisos so as to grant each generation "the right to receive a world in which the present has not been mortgaged by the ancestors" and to do so because "their relations are regulated by the law of nature" which demands "to leave land enough and as good for the following generations" (Bassani 2004: 74). Jefferson's proposals, which attempted to calculate each generation's longevity to help evaluate their obligations to each other, were convincingly refuted by Madison's reply and Jefferson never raised the question again, but it may stand as an early liberal effort to grapple with intergenerational justice. The core principle is that "an earlier generation cannot bind or obligate a later one" but "each generation is obligated or bound to leave succeeding generations free to act as they decide" (Ball 2000: 72), a view with recent echoes. These echoes include attempts to interpret Locke's intentions along Jeffersonian lines, and a division exists between greens who regard Locke's philosophy as offering means to a reformist liberal environmentalism as against those who see Locke as legitimating proto-capitalist economic expansionism and thus as anti-green.

Our next liberal call, however, is to utilitarian philosopher Jeremy Bentham's work (1748–1832). Bentham's significance is threefold. First, and least environmentally acknowledged, he inspired his supporter Edwin Chadwick to promote the greater happiness through such measures as improving sanitation and minimizing waste disposal problems. Chadwick's 1842 report on the Sanitary Condition of the Labouring Population led to Britain's 1848 Public Health Act and the creation of the Central Board of Health, with powers to ensure clean streets and improve water and sewage systems—arguably the first big modern environmental health initiative (Lewis 1952). Secondly, Bentham's utilitarianism has inspired the animal liberation movement to advocate rethinking our relationship to non-human animals, thanks greatly to Peter Singer's work emphasizing sentience as the proper boundary line for moral considerability (Singer 1975). Bentham's comment from his 1789 *Introduction to the Principles of Morals and Legislation* that "the question is not Can they *reason*? nor Can they *talk*? But Can they *suffer*?" was popularized as a vegetarian slogan by Singer, though as Warwick Fox notes, Singer takes the quotation out of context since Bentham actually "argues that nonhuman animals are generally *better off* being killed and eaten ... by us" in traditional agriculture than they would have been facing a more painful and difficult life in nature (Bentham 1970: 283; Fox 2006: 286). However, Singer's utilitarian adoption of liberation language beyond the species barrier illustrates a common environmentalist motif that draws on liberal precedents: the idea that consistency may require us to expand the circle of moral considerability beyond its present boundaries, just as it was previously extended to other oppressed groups such as slaves, women, and people of color. The attempt to extend such consideration to diverse natural items—animals, living things, ecosystems, etc—is a vital element in green thought, but using liberal reformist extensionism is problematic for more radical ends. Though rights theory can plausibly be extended to animals, some efforts have been made to extend animal rights into liberal justice theory (Regan 1983; Garner 2013), and it is at least possible to indirectly argue for strong systemic environmental protections on such individualist lines (Varner 1998), moral extensionism moves beyond the gamut of the existing liberal tradition once it goes past the sentience criterion for considerability. Similarly, extending considerability to collectivities per se, as with species, ecosystems or Leopold's "land community" (Leopold 1987: 204), is problematic given liberalism's individualism and the difficulties of ascribing interests to these groupings. Accordingly, though environmentalist efforts to extend moral considerability's boundaries follow a liberal strategy, they often do so in ways that are of questionable compatibility with liberalism itself.

The third area of Benthamite liberal influence exists via intellectual cross-pollination. The English clergyman Thomas Malthus' work *An Essay on the Principle of Population* (Malthus 1992), which went through six editions between 1798 and 1826, attempted to argue that unchecked population increases geometrically (for example, 1, 2, 4, 8) whereas food supply increases only arithmetically (for example, 1, 2, 3, 4) and so there is a continuous tendency for demand to outstrip the supply of necessities when population rises, as well as a permanent likelihood of poverty for some section of the populace. Malthus intended his arguments as a conservative refutation of perfectibility doctrines, but utilitarian liberal reformists accepted some of his ideas and modified them for more optimistic ends. The most significant such reformer was John Stuart Mill. Mill accepted Malthus' notion of tense disparity between rapid population growth and a crawling resource base, but supported the use of working class birth control to reduce the spare labor pool, thus increasing wages and social improvement opportunities. As against Malthus' population emphasis, Mill also recognized the roles of wealth differentials and consumption, arguing in the *Principles of Political Economy* (1848) that a future "stationary state" of zero economic growth was both inevitable and compatible with progress; indeed, he even suggested that a more egalitarian wealth distribution and a reduction in economic competition could promote general intellectual improvement and improve human moral and emotional progress. Accordingly, Mill was the first philosopher to advocate a sustainable economy of the type contemporary greens support. Moreover, he embedded his political economy within terrestrial nature and connected it to social dynamics of improvement, praising Wordsworthian peasant agriculture, and argued for his views partly on Romantic grounds, namely the effect of immersion in nature on human character, thus purging Malthusian joylessness. Mill later connected such peasant agriculture to his support for local collective cooperationism in a perspective that John Parham maintains "broadly corresponds to the emphasis on sustainable, decentralized governance in contemporary ecological social philosophy" (Parham 2007: 46–7). To this we should add that Mill, on liberal grounds, repudiated Comte's call for eliminating all animals and plants without a human use, protesting that the "power of the whole human race cannot reproduce a species once eradicated" and condemning the "rule of one who assumes that he knows all there is to be known" (Mill 1969: 357–8; Winch 2004: 116). Mill also supported the new Commons Preservation Society in 1865 and made three separate parliamentary interventions from 1866 to 1868 to protect urban trees in London (Capaldi 2004: 325)—a significant use of time for an MP who served for only three years, and before the word "environmentalism" existed. For these reasons, amongst others, I have argued that Millian new liberalism is the variant best suited to synthesis with environmentalist goals and values (Stephens 1996, 2001, 2014), and it is to such contemporary debates I now turn.

Liberalism and Environmental Political Theory: The Contemporary Situation

Though the liberal tradition furnishes some inspiration to environmentalism, the modern green movement's Western genesis is usually tracked to Rachel Carson's *Silent Spring* (1962) and subsequent concerns over pesticides and overpopulation, followed by the defining moment of the *Limits to Growth* report in 1972 (Carson 1962; Meadows and Meadows 1972) and the forming of various green political parties. The only theorist to seriously examine the green–liberal interface immediately after this period was John Rodman. As early as 1973, Rodman suggested that T. H. Green's new liberalism might lend itself to ethical extensionism toward nature, and explored liberalism's connections to ecological concern in path-breaking papers that drew little initial attention but anticipated today's discussion (Rodman 1973, 1977, 1979).

The wider political theory debate, however, began only in the 1990s, as a few scholars began to examine the issues involved, culminating in the first book attempting a full synthesis, Marcel Wissenburg's *Green Liberalism* (Achterberg 1993; diZerega 1996; Eckersley

1996; Stephens 1996; Dobson 1998; Vincent 1998; Wissenburg 1998). Wissenburg, like most advocates of greening liberalism, accepts the neutralist characterization of liberalism and argues that much of the green agenda can be captured in a liberal democratic setting. Rejecting intrinsic value arguments, Wissenburg's project is weakly anthropocentric and develops a variant of Rawls' just savings principle of intergenerational justice, the "restraint principle," a liberal side-constraint aimed at sustainability by protecting nature against needless destruction. Wissenburg's Rawlsian credentials anticipated much subsequent green liberal work, but the primary questions asked in the most sustained discussion of the book, the *Environmental Politics* debate that he and I had in 2001, were of whether neutralism was an accurate or helpful representation of liberalism and whether Wissenburg's model of human agency, value, and motivation could practically generate room for liberalism to be greened (Stephens 2001a, 2001b; Wissenburg 2001). The criticism that a neutralist liberalism cannot *in practice* motivate green change or oppose runaway instrumentalization because of its refusal to examine preference formation mechanisms does not seem to me to have yet been adequately answered, whilst my view that Millian liberalism offers better grounds for green liberal synthesis has sympathizers yet remains a minority perspective (de Geus 2001, 2003; Winch 2004; Parham 2007; Donner 2009, 2014). The suspicion that a non-neutralist liberalism would better suit environmentalism is probably more widely held than the relatively small number of these sources would suggest, but no full monograph treatment of such a green liberalism has been produced. Some worries were tackled by Derek Bell's invocation of Rawls' later works to argue that "neutralist liberalism . . . is able to accommodate more of environmentalists' concerns than might have been supposed," but arguments over neutralism and *motivating* green change are largely ignored in Bell's treatment, and even after demonstrating the validity of sustainability on neutralist grounds, he admits that "Rawlsian liberalism is a 'contingently green liberalism' rather than an 'intrinsically green liberalism' " (Bell 2002: 705, 721).

Bell's defense, however, indicates the debate's direction in the early 2000s, with Rawlsian neutralist styles of liberalism being extensively mined for potential to encapsulate core green concerns, especially sustainability. Indeed, so quickly did this idea of liberalism capturing environmentalism's core goals become prominent that talk of the "end of environmentalism" emerged by 2004 (Wissenburg and Levy 2004), alongside development of two more syntheses, Simon Hailwood's *How to Be A Green Liberal* (2004) and Brian Baxter's *A Theory of Ecological Justice* (2005). Hailwood's work takes Rawls as its representative liberal and argues for respect for nature precisely on neutralist grounds whilst espousing a non-instrumental view of nature's value. For Hailwood, the value of nature's "otherness"—its being "not the expression of any prior human purpose, design or conception of the good"—should be appreciated non-instrumentally by neutralist liberals because it resonates with a repudiation of expressivism on the part of the state, that a liberal government should not express a comprehensive moral ideal. As such, "there is a deep congruence between reasonable respect for nature as other, and the stance of political 'reasonableness' " (Hailwood 2004: 22, 90) which liberals should recognize. Similarly, Baxter adopts Brian Barry's theory of justice as impartiality and attempts to expand its primary constituency to argue that "the liberal theory of justice . . . is capable of encompassing justice towards the non-human and of justifying some constitutional provisions to secure the claims of the non-human to their fair share of environmental resources" (Baxter 2005: 126). Yet these works attracted relatively little commentary, perhaps because the debate shifted focus to the importance of citizenship and justice concerns: with arguments made for broadly naturalist Millian perfectionist liberalism and for a non-naturalist neutralist liberalism, two camps exist for synthesizing environmentalism with new liberalism, but both acknowledge the importance of citizenship and justice concerns and subsequent scholarship has moved in these directions (Dobson 2003; Dobson and Bell 2006; Nussbaum 2006; Gabrielson 2008). Meanwhile, efforts to repudiate environmentalist criticism of neo-Lockean old liberalism and to resurrect a Jeffersonian green liberalism have generated little environmentalist support and may be misguided (Peter 2007; Liebell 2011; Thompson 2014).

Concluding Thoughts: Nature as Stimulus to Liberty

As should now be clear, some notion of sustainability is present in all the greened liberalisms discussed—Lockean/Jeffersonian, Millian, and neutralist—but details vary as to what this means. In contemporary discussions sustainability has multiple forms, but as Norton explains, two basic defining options are available: weak sustainability, defined by intergenerational utility comparison (UC) over time whereby sustainability is defined by a steady non-declining standard of welfare (utility), and strong sustainability, his variant of which is defined by listing stuff (LS) that should be saved for future generations. The "stuff" in the latter consists of natural items whose loss would "result in the diminution of the quality of future lives, *regardless of the amount of compensation/wealth that is provided as a substitute for the lost features* (emphasis in the original)." Norton argues that we may be obliged "not to unduly narrow the range of options and opportunities open to future people" (Norton 1999: 130–1) and makes the analogy with a rich sexist widower who bequeathes his daughters an excellent income for life on condition that they not seek an education: though they are financially affluent, harm is done through narrowing the range of developmental opportunities. With its view that "what is value*able* for human enrichment, has to be expanded. . . . in terms of a greatly extended notion of human interest" (Rosenthal and Buchholz 1996: 43), Norton's suggestion resonates with ideals of development in both Millian liberalism and American pragmatism, for he then argues that strong sustainability should specify certain features of the natural world, associate them with measurable indicators, and protect them as representing options and opportunities that future people would be worse off without. Drawing on the notion of natural areas representing human developmental opportunities, I now want to argue for nature's significance in enabling and expanding human liberty. The question "why should liberals protect nature?" will be answered by saying "because they protect developmental liberties by doing so."

To initially give ontological grip, I here invoke earlier work arguing that nature should be defined across a tripartite spectrum in which naturalness is defined by the extent to which an item or area is *untransformed* and *not instrumentalized according to the dictates of particular historically specific types of anti-naturalistic instrumental rationality*, with the spectrum itself derived from William James' model of the human cognitive faculties in their perceptual operations of truth-seeking (Stephens 2000).[1] Briefly, the types of instrumental rationality that I have in mind derive from the Enlightenment and reject earlier traditions of thought in which nature was thought of as a guide to ethical reflection and a touchstone of liberty. These modern types of instrumental rationality are anti-naturalistic in that they (i) primordially separate subject from object in felt epistemological relationship, (ii) are informed by a clear duality between reason and the passions that associates nature with the latter and with impurity, and (iii) regard the technological conquest and reduction of nature to mere economic resource as a paradigmatically rational activity. Accordingly, it is the processes of instrumentalization and artifacticity that are the antitheses of the natural; the mere presence of human input, as with a ship in the ocean deeps, does not of itself eliminate naturalness unless we wrongly assume an absolutistic dualism in which *any* human input is seen as utterly transformative.

The absence of these instrumentalizing elements is critical for what is vital in nature experiences: the extent to which they grant possibilities of new perception through non-instrumentalized immediate experience. As known since William James's pragmatism, consciousness is selective and instrumental, reinforcing attention to already existing interests, goals, and associations, building up habitual patterns and excluding extraneous information. But as these patterns of awareness guide us in our customary orientations, they are necessarily committed to the existing framework of ends, functioning to streamline our awareness and edit out novelty as irrelevant unless it impacts existing goals and interests. What is reduced in such instrumentally dominated awareness, and reduced ever more strongly as habitual thinking grows over a lifetime, is *the capacity to step outside the existing framework of priorities*, to question the existing instrumental framework so as to view issues afresh, to gain openness, to perceive novelties that might make us revise our views. We thus steadily build a shell of habitual perceptions and pre-set means-end reasoning, but at the cost of flexibility, sensory vividness, the capacity to learn afresh, and some restriction of the imagination.

However, as I have argued elsewhere (Stephens 2009), there is a pragmatic naturalist antidote to this limiting tendency, a way in which we may continue to protect and grow our freedom. It lies in types of experiences in which we are more receptive to direct sensation with minimal overlay from ready-made descriptions and pre-set instrumental purposes: quiet attention to snowflakes falling outside, the sudden glimpse of a kestrel above, calm perception of a spider's web-work bridging two shrubs. These experiences draw us out of habitual instrumentalizing consciousness because they are *radically* non-instrumental, being neither means nor ends. They require from us a certain willingness to receive attentively without rushing to judgment and to engage reflectively with the impression thereafter, thus demanding a certain posture from the agent. But availability of such possibilities for growth also has a significant external component, for they are noted to occur in one context especially often: nature experience.

Both Mill and William James found value in nature experience of the type described, James noting "the intense interest that life can assume when brought down to the . . . level of pure sensorial experience" and that such interest "starts upon us often from non-human natural things" (James 1929: 18–19, 9). There is, one might infer, a resonance between our primal inner nature—relatively unverbalized direct sensation—and the outer nature we encounter, a resonance that gives novelty and freshness to experience and thus allows new perspectives to be developed. I suggest that this is indeed the case, and supporting argument comes from the implications of certain creativity tests. In these, a person is shown artifacts and asked to think of as many possible uses for them beyond their design function, with highest creativity given to the largest number of alternative uses. This is a test precisely because artifacts contain embedded purposes that immediately spring to mind, and they thus encourage thinking instrumentally but *against* originality of application. The point of the test is that constant association of items with pre-set goals makes it hard to envision the items otherwise, and taking this logic to its conclusion, an individual surrounded wholly by instrumental reasoning and its products comes to lack the capacity to see outside such a framework, to engage with spontaneous experience and learn. We are already seeing something like this in the internet phenomenon of epistemic closure, whereby people become both enframed by screen technology and unwilling to look outside a small range of goals, sites, and values as they need not be exposed to novelty or disagreement. Similarly, the dystopias of Zamyatin, Orwell, and Huxley feature inhabitants enframed by instrumentality, the politics and technology of management excluding natural novelty.

Nature experience contrasts with this because it lacks such pre-set human ends. Paradoxically, the "usefulness" of nature thus lies partly in its lying outside predefined use categories and thus its capacity to evoke open possibilities, stimulating wonder, spontaneity, and non-instrumental relationship. Evidence for my claim that nature experience psychologically assists freedom by countering internalized instrumentalism is culturally abundant in the traditions that counterpose natural vitality to urban artifice: the classical notion of *kosmos* as a spontaneous, unfolding, and beautifully harmonious process distinct from the manipulations of city life, the associations of virtue with agrarian life from antiquity to Wendell Berry, the tales of sylvan liberty involving persistent association of forests with freedom, wildness, and corrective transformation (Harrison 1992). I suggest that the historic persistence of such associations indicates their deep significance. The repudiation of instrumentalism, politicking, and fashion in favor of nature's spontaneous novelty and authenticity suggests a further move: the highlighting of imagination as stimulated by nature experience and as a transformative agent in actualizing liberalism's core value, liberty. For imagination can operate not merely to envision alternatives but to concretize freedom by doing so. It can, for instance, shift an agent from possessing negative freedom, an absence of coercive blockage, to manifesting positive freedom—actually attaining what was previously only a potentiality—through coming to possess the ability to envision. Imagination is thus connected to practical liberty, rendering abstract freedom into concreteness, and is psychologically fostered and encouraged by the continued presence and experience of maximally natural environments. A natureless world, like the life lived by Norton's uneducated affluent heiresses, would be one in which we had been deprived of vital options for transformative growth.

Thus it is, I suggest, that liberalism's core value of liberty is protected through nature experience, and thus also why non-human nature should be protected by liberalism. Though my argument bridges the Millian and Jamesian pragmatist traditions, eschewing Rawls, my suggestion is that non-human nature should be viewed like a Rawlsian liberal's primary good—something that we must sensibly want, whatever else we may come to want. In this respect, my argument supports my fellow contributor Jason Lambacher's view that greens have to show themselves to favor liberty, but also builds upon the overview given. As we have seen, significant attempts have been made to demonstrate the compatibility of environmentalist ideals with liberalism, and two types of new liberalism especially—Millian and neutralist—have shown promise. Just as new liberalism sought to go beyond old liberalism, in part by recognizing the value of self-development to meaningful human freedom, so my argument here tries to show that such new liberal freedom may itself require nature experience as a background condition. As such, the argument suggests not merely that liberal political theory may be greened, but that in an increasingly technologized world, the green ideals of nature experience may be precisely what fulfilling the liberal value of liberty demands.

Note

1. The basic threefold categories are (i) untransformed nature, (ii) borderline places (e.g. farms and cultural products as "cultus," produced with respect for existing natural dynamics), and (iii) artifacts, themselves further subdivided into completed "cultus" artifacts and artificial products.

References

Achterberg, Wouter. (1993). "Can Liberal Democracy Survive the Environmental Crisis? Sustainability, Liberal Neutrality and Overlapping Consensus." In *The Politics of Nature*, edited by Andrew Dobson and Paul Lucardie (London: Routledge), 81–101.

Attfield, Robin. (1983). *The Ethics of Environmental Concern* (Oxford: Basil Blackwell).

Ball, Terence. (2000). "'The Earth Belong to the Living': Thomas Jefferson and the Problem of Intergenerational Relations." *Environmental Politics* 9(2): 61–77.

Bassani, Luigi Marco. (2004). "Life, Liberty and . . .: Jefferson on Property Rights." *Journal of Libertarian Studies* 18(1): 31–87.

Baxter, Brian. (2005). *A Theory of Ecological Justice* (New York: Routledge).

Bell, Derek. (2002). "How can Political Liberals be Environmentalists?" *Political Studies* 50(4): 703–24.
Bentham, Jeremy. (1970). *An Introduction to the Principles of Morals and Legislation* (London: The Athlone Press).
Berlin, Isaiah. (1969). *Four Essays on Liberty* (Oxford: Oxford University Press).
Capaldi, Nicholas. (2004). *John Stuart Mill: A Biography* (New York: Cambridge University Press).
Carson, Rachel. (1962). *Silent Spring* (Boston, MA: Houghton Mifflin).
Cranston, Maurice. (1967). "Liberalism." In *The Encyclopaedia of Philosophy*, edited by Paul Edwards (New York: Macmillan and the Free Press), 458–61.
diZerega, Gus. (1996). "Deep Ecology and Liberalism: The Greener Implications of Evolutionary Liberal Theory." *Review of Politics* 58(4): 699–734.
Dobson, Andrew. (1990). *Green Political Thought*, 1st edn. (London: HarperCollins).
Dobson, Andrew. (1998). *Justice and the Environment: Conceptions of Environmental Sustainability and Theories of Distributive Justice* (Oxford: Oxford University Press).
Dobson, Andrew. (2000). *Green Political Thought*, 3rd edn. (London: Routledge).
Dobson, Andrew. (2003). *Citizenship and the Environment* (Oxford: Oxford University Press).
Dobson, Andrew and Bell, Derek, eds. (2006). *Environmental Citizenship* (Cambridge, MA: MIT Press).
Donner, Wendy. (1991). *The Liberal Self: John Stuart Mill's Moral and Political Philosophy* (London: Cornell University Press).
Donner, Wendy. (2014). "John Stuart Mill's Green Liberalism and Ecofeminism." In *Consequentialism and Environmental Ethics*, edited by Avram Hiller, Ramona Ilea, and Leonard Kahn (New York: Routledge), 174–89.
Donner, Wendy and Fumerton, Richard. (2009). *Mill* (Chichester, Sussex: Wiley-Blackwell).
Dworkin, Ronald. (1985). *A Matter of Principle* (Cambridge, MA: Harvard University Press).
Eckersley, Robyn. (1996). "Greening Liberal Democracy: The Rights Discourse Revisited." In *Democracy and Green Political Thought*, edited by Brian Doherty and Marius de Geus (London: Routledge), 212–36.
Fox, Warwick. (2006). *A Theory of General Ethics: Human Relationships, Nature, and the Built Environment* (Cambridge, MA: MIT Press).
Gabrielson, Teena. (2008). "Green Citizenship: A Review and Critique." *Citizenship Studies* 12(4): 429–46.
Garner, Robert. (2013). *A Theory of Justice for Animals* (Oxford: Oxford University Press).
de Geus, Marius. (2001). "Sustainability, Liberal Democracy, Liberalism." In *Sustaining Liberal Democracy: Ecological Challenges and Opportunities*, edited by John Barry and Marcel Wissenburg (Basingstoke: Palgrave), 19–36.
de Geus, Marius. (2003). *The End of Overconsumption: Towards a Lifestyle of Moderation and Self-Restraint* (Utrecht: International Books).
Hailwood, Simon. (2004). *How to Be a Green Liberal: Nature, Value and Liberal Philosophy* (Chesham, Bucks, UK: Acumen).
Harrison, Robert Pogue. (1992). *Forests: The Shadow of Civilisation* (Chicago: University of Chicago Press).
Hayek, F. A. (1976). *The Mirage of Social Justice* (Chicago: University of Chicago Press).
James, William. (1929). "On a Certain Blindness in Human Beings." In *Selected Papers in Philosophy*. Edited by Ernest Rhys (London: Everyman), 1–21.

Leopold, Aldo. (1987). *A Sand County Almanac, and Sketches Here and There* (Oxford: Oxford University Press).
Lewis, R. A. (1952). *Edwin Chadwick and the Public Health Movement 1832–1854* (London: Longmans Green & Co).
Liebell, Susan P. (2011). "The Text and Context of 'Enough and As Good': John Locke as the Foundation of an Environmental Liberalism." *Polity* 43(2): 210–41.
Locke, John. (1988). *Two Treatises of Government* (Cambridge: Cambridge University Press).
Macpherson, C. B. (1962). *The Political Theory of Possessive Individualism: From Hobbes to Locke* (Oxford: Clarendon Press).
Malthus, Thomas. (1992). *Essay on the Principle of Population* (Cambridge: Cambridge University Press).
Meadows, Donella. H and Meadows, Dennis L., et al. (1972). *The Limits to Growth* (London: Universe Books).
Mill, John Stuart. (1848). *The Principles of Political Economy*. 2 vols. (Boston: Charles C. Little & James Brown).
Mill, John Stuart. (1969). *The Collected Works of John Stuart Mill: Essays on Ethics, Religion and Society*. Edited by J. M. Robson. Vol. 10 (Toronto: University of Toronto Press).
Norton, Bryan G. (1991). *Toward Unity Among Environmentalists* (Oxford: Oxford University Press).
Norton, Bryan G. (1999). "Ecology and Opportunity: Intergenerational Equity and Sustainable Options." In *Fairness and Futurity: Essays on Environmental Sustainability and Social Justice*, edited by Andrew Dobson (Oxford: Oxford University Press), 118–50.
Nozick, Robert. (1974). *Anarchy, State and Utopia* (New York: Basic Books).
Nussbaum, Martha C. (2006). *Frontiers of Justice: Disability, Nationality, Species Membership* (Cambridge, MA: Harvard University Press).
Parham, John. (2007). "What is (Ecological) 'Nature'? John Stuart Mill and the Victorian Perspective." In *Culture, Creativity and Environment: New Environmentalist Criticism*, edited by Fiona Becket and Terry Gifford (New York: Rodopi), 37–54.
Paton, G. J. (2011). *Seeking Sustainability: On the Prospects of an Ecological Liberalism* (Abingdon, Oxon: Routledge).
Peter, Kenneth P. (2007). "Jefferson and the Independence of Generations." *Environmental Ethics* 24(1): 61–77.
Regan, Tom. (1983). *The Case for Animal Rights* (Berkeley: University of California Press).
Rodman, John. (1973). "What is Living and What is Dead in the Political Philosophy of T.H. Green?" *Western Political Quarterly* 26(3): 566–86.
Rodman, John. (1977). "The Liberation of Nature?" *Inquiry* 20: 83–145.
Rodman, John. (1979). "Animal Justice: The Counter-Revolution in Natural Right and Law." *Inquiry* 22: 3–22.
Rosenthal, Sandra B. and Buchholz, Rogene A. (1996). "How Pragmatism *is* An Environmental Ethic." In *Environmental Pragmatism*, edited by Andrew Light and Eric Katz (London: Routledge), 38–49.
Shrader-Frechette, Kristin. (1993). "Locke and Limits on Land Ownership." In *Policy for Land: Law and Ethics*, edited by Lynton Keith Caldwell and Kristin Shrader-Frechette (Lanham, Maryland: Rowman & Littlefield), 65–84.
Singer, Peter. (1975). *Animal Liberation* (London: HarperCollins).
Skorupski, John. (1999). *Ethical Explanations* (Oxford: Oxford University Press).
Squadrito, Kathleen M. (1979). "Locke's View of Dominion." *Environmental Ethics* 1(3): 255–62.

Stephens, Piers H. G. (1996). "Plural Pluralisms: Towards a More Liberal Green Political Theory." In *Contemporary Political Studies 1996*, Vol. 1, edited by Iain Hampsher-Monk and Jeffrey Stanyer (Oxford: Political Studies Association), 369–80.
Stephens, Piers H. G. (2000). "Nature, Purity, Ontology." *Environmental Values* 9(3): 267–94.
Stephens, Piers H. G. (2001a). "Green Liberalisms: Nature, Agency and the Good." *Environmental Politics* 10(3): 1–22.
Stephens, Piers H. G. (2001b). "The Green only Blooms amid the Millian Flowers: A Reply to Marcel Wissenburg." *Environmental Politics* 10(3): 43–7.
Stephens, Piers H. G. (2009). "Toward a Jamesian Environmental Philosophy." *Environmental Ethics* 31(3): 227–44.
Tawney, R. H. (1931). *Equality* (New York: Harcourt, Brace).
Thompson, Paul B. (2014). "Thomas Jefferson's Land Ethics." In *Thomas Jefferson and Philosophy: Essays on the Philosophical Cast of Thomas Jefferson's Writings*, edited by M. Andrew Holowchak (Lanham MD: Lexington Books), 79–90.
Varner, Gary. (1998). *In Nature's Interests? Interests, Animal Rights and Environmental Ethics* (Oxford: Oxford University Press).
Vincent, Andrew. (1998). "Liberalism and the Environment." *Environmental Values* 7(4): 443–59.
Waldron, Jeremy. (1989). "Legislation and Moral Neutrality." In *Liberal Neutrality*, edited by Robert E. Goodin and Andrew Reeve (London: Routledge), 61–83.
Winch, Donald. (2004). "Thinking Green, Nineteenth Century Style: John Stuart Mill and John Ruskin." In *Markets in Historical Contexts: Ideas and Politics in the Modern World*, edited by Mark Bevir and Frank Trentmann (Cambridge: Cambridge University Press), 105–28.
Wissenburg, Marcel. (1998). *Green Liberalism: The Free and the Green Society* (London: UCL Press).
Wissenburg, Marcel. (2001). "Liberalism is Always Greener on the Other Side of Mill: A Reply to Piers Stephens." *Environmental Politics* 10(3): 23–42.
Wissenburg, Marcel and Levy, Yoram, eds. (2004). *Liberal Democracy and Environmentalism: The End of Environmentalism?* (London: Routledge).
Zvesper, John. (1993). *Nature and Liberty* (London: Routledge).

CHAPTER 5

ENVIRONMENTAL POLITICAL THEORY AND REPUBLICANISM

PETER F. CANNAVÒ

Introduction

Environmentalism and civic republicanism have important historical and conceptual connections. Yet only recently has environmental political thought begun to engage civic republicanism (see Curry 2000; Barry 2008, 2012; Barry and Smith 2008; Williamson 2010; Cannavò 2010a, 2010b, 2012a, 2012b). This chapter attempts to broaden our understanding of the connection between republican and green perspectives and consider the implications of this connection for environmental politics, particularly climate change.

Engagement with republicanism is important for environmental political theory (EPT). First of all, environmental values may have partly emerged from civic republicanism, especially in the United States (Cannavò 2010a, 2012a, 2012b), so any understanding of the history of green thought must engage with republicanism. Moreover, contemporary environmentalism shows striking similarities with republicanism: non-neutrality with respect to the good; an emphasis on participatory democracy and decentralization; a critical stance toward capitalism and economic growth; a quest for stability and/or sustainability; and, finally, a tension between communitarianism and a more "contestatory" democratic politics. By investigating these similarities, environmental political theorists can better grasp environmentalism's political implications and internal tensions. Moreover, engagement with republicanism can also yield insight into how we might address ecological threats, including climate change. Republican conceptions of dispersed sovereignty, civic virtue, and even the proper use of nature can help guide us to a more ecologically sustainable society.

First, a disclaimer: For simplicity, I often refer simply to "republicanism" or "environmentalism." However, I am not trying to characterize either republicanism or environmentalism *in toto*. Both are diverse traditions. With regard to environmentalism, some green version has been proposed for perhaps every political perspective. Moreover, much environmentalism involves a reformism or conservationism focused on working within existing political and economic structures and values, including industrial capitalism, to protect natural resources, ecosystem services, and scenic areas from excessive degradation. There are few similarities with republicanism here. However, commonalities exist between republicanism and more radical environmental perspectives that articulate a social and political program beyond reformist or conservationist goals.

Defining Republicanism

Civic republicanism emphasizes citizens' active participation in deliberating on, crafting, and pursuing their community's common good or, more accurately, common goods (Honohan 2002). Republican liberty is not so much about freedom *from* government, but about collective *self-government* and virtues that enable citizens to be self-governing. Williamson notes, "The most fundamental claim of contemporary civic republican thought is that freedom should be centrally understood as the ability to influence, through participation in collective action, the social forces that shape the life of both individuals and communities: self-governance, in short, is coextensive with freedom" (2010: 188–9). Iseult Honohan says, "Republican political autonomy means that citizens ... follow purposes that they can endorse as theirs, in so far as they have a say in shaping and sustaining them." Citizens must have "some ability to control the conditions of their collective life" (2002: 188). Republicans would extend such self-government not only to political institutions, but also to the economy, civil society, and even the family. Republican freedom is not just about being left alone by government or choosing private ends under given societal conditions, but is about using political processes and deliberating with other citizens to actually shape those very conditions. Republican citizens pursue not just individual ends or conceptions of the good, but collective ends, including common goods that animate a community's life.

Civic republicanism has roots in Aristotle and Cicero and the historical experience of the Greek city-states and the Roman Republic. Civic republican ideas flourished in Renaissance Florence and early modern Poland, Holland, and England, and in the writings of Niccolò Machiavelli, Montesquieu, and Jean-Jacques Rousseau, among others (Pocock 1975, 1989: 80–103; Pettit 2012: 6–7). In the United States, civic republicanism was prominent during the Revolutionary and Founding eras (1763–1824), but lost influence to liberalism (Wood 1969; McCoy 1980; Bailyn 1992; Sandel 1996). Republican themes persisted in the American labor, Civil Rights, and community organizing movements (Sandel 1996), and, as noted earlier, in the environmental movement. In recent decades, some theorists have adopted republicanism as a more communitarian, egalitarian, and/or participatory alternative to liberalism (Sandel 1996; Pettit 1997; Honohan 2002; Maynor 2003).

Community and Contestation in Republicanism

The twin emphases on the common good and self-government points to a tension in republican thought between a strong, a priori sense of an overriding collective good, which would tend to constrain political deliberation, and a focus on meaningful, open-ended participation and deliberation. In line with this tension, some strains of republicanism, going back to Aristotle, identify active citizenship, including political participation, and the associated virtues, with the human good itself (Aristotle 1984: 37; Pocock 1989: 85). Any unitary, predetermined conception of the human good and of human virtue, or even any predetermined conception of the good of a particular community, prejudges citizens' collective ends and limits the scope of politics. Perhaps the most striking example is Rousseau's concept of the general will, from *The Social Contract*. The general will, or the common good of the community, is established in advance by a founding Legislator (Rousseau 1978: 67–70). The Legislator determines the character and good of the community, including how it adapts, in terms of population size and distribution and economic activity, to its physical environment (1978: 73). Subsequent political life presupposes conformity to the general will. Indeed, Rousseau suggests that pursuit of the general will actually precludes true collective discussion: "If, when an adequately informed people deliberates, the citizens were to have no communication among themselves," factions would not arise, only small differences in perspective would emerge among the populace, "and the deliberation would always be good" (1978: 61).

Other republican approaches are agnostic regarding the most important good (Barry 2012: 270), whether for humanity or for a particular community. For them, self-government is not explicitly tied to some conception of the human or communal good, but has instrumental value in preventing citizens from subordinating one another. Drawing on Roman republicanism as well as Machiavelli's writings, Philip Pettit (1997, 2012), Quentin Skinner (1990), and John Maynor (2003) emphasize *non-domination*, the idea that no one citizen should be fundamentally subject to the power and whim of another. Michael Sandel thus speaks of "more modest versions of the republican ideal [that] see civic virtue and public service as *instrumental* to liberty" (1996: 26; emphasis in original). Such an approach presents fewer a priori constraints on contestation about the common good and thus offers a "republican politics [that] . . . is more clamorous than consensual" (Sandel 1996: 320). Politics avoids final, irrevocable answers, but is more oriented to provisional decisions and experimentation.

If the good were to be defined in advance, that would suggest more of a predetermined conception of community. A more open, provisional sense of the common good would make conceptions and ties of community more fluid and more subject to debate and contestation.

Though there are different versions of republicanism, I would also maintain that an overall tension between community and contestation runs throughout republicanism, though in varying weights or degrees. This tension pits communitarianism, virtue, and predetermined constraints on the good against political contestation and a more open-ended approach to deliberation.

Moreover, republicans' emphasis on self-government and deliberation itself involves a strong notion of civic virtue and character formation, thus presenting further constraints on contestation. Republicanism pursues a "formative politics" (Sandel 1996: 6) of inculcating virtues conducive to civic engagement, self-government, and pursuit of the common good through deliberation. These virtues may include a strong sense of civic responsibility; a cooperative attitude toward fellow citizens; appreciation of social interdependence; a willingness to put the common good ahead of private interests and the ability to distinguish between the two; moderation with regard to consumption and wealth; a critical, vigilant attitude toward social and political power structures; courage in the face of internal and external challenges to the political community; pursuit of stability or sustainability in the face of degenerative change; and practical wisdom and courage to think independently, critically, and deliberatively regarding matters of common concern. These virtues may be cultivated through public education, opportunities for political participation, and policies that restrain the morally corrosive impacts of the market.

A Politics of the Common Good(s)

One way of somewhat relaxing the tension between community and contestation is to abandon the idea of single common good and instead see politics in terms of the pursuit of multiple common *goods*, emerging from, rather than being antecedent to, political life (Honohan 2002). A common good is a set of related practices, meanings, institutions, and objects that "can be realized only in interaction with others" (152), that is, through collective undertakings, "participated in *with* others" (153; emphasis in original). Honohan sees a shared political life—including collective participation, self-government, and deliberation—as a key common good in a republican society. However, as Honohan notes, a republican political community would sustain other common goods as well. These might include a collective system of shared risk and mutual assistance on social welfare issues (such as health care); a common experience of national service; an inclusive, diverse, tolerant, and egalitarian civic life; quality educational institutions; an economy based on small businesses or workplace cooperatives; widespread participation in urban gardens and community-supported and other local or regional agriculture; pedestrian-friendly urban, suburban, and village life; vibrant civic associations; community-based economic development; flourishing arts and other cultural institutions; and a shared commitment to and identification with the natural and built landscape. A plurality of common goods emerging from social and political interaction would open up more scope for deliberation and contestation regarding which goods besides those directly connected with republican citizenship the political community ought to prioritize.

Whether or not it advances a unitary conception of the good, republicanism, with its communitarian elements and formative politics, is not neutral regarding the good, particularly in contrast to liberalism. A focus on common goods privileges sociality and human flourishing through collective endeavors. Even a focus simply on non-domination would necessitate a highly participatory, engaged, deliberative political culture; cultivation of relevant civic virtues; and pursuit of a non-dominating way of life not only in politics, but also in economics, workplaces, families, and civil society (Pettit 1997: 138–43, 245, 2012: 9; Maynor 2003; Williamson 2010: 182; Barry 2012: 239–40). Moreover, central to republicanism is elevation of a community's common good or goods over and above the pursuit or protection of private interests (Wood 1969: 68). Citizens, whatever their particular loyalties and attachments, must have a strong sense of civic identity and see in deliberation a common enterprise to further shared ends. Sandel (1996: 274) notes that republican "[s]elf-government... requires... citizens who sufficiently identify with their communities to think and act with a view to the common good."

In line with the underlying tension between community and contestation, republicanism must balance any determination of the good and of civic virtue with meaningful self-government and deliberation. Indeed, republicans argue that pursuit of the common good means giving the people—rather than concentrated economic and political special interests—collective governance of society (Wood 1969: 56; Pettit 2012: 22).

Collective self-government in turn suggests some degree of political and economic decentralization. This can involve actual local governance and/or the dispersal of political participation and authority throughout civil society.[1] One need not abolish the nation-state or international organizations, but there must be significant scope for more direct, local participation. Sandel (1996: 345), for example, talks about "dispersing sovereignty" across various levels of governance to create "a multiplicity of communities and political bodies." In terms of relocalizing the economy, Sandel favors citizens' groups geared toward local community organizing and development, policies to protect local businesses from chain-store competition, and global, national, and local institutions to regulate trade (333–46).

Republican Independence and Political Economy

A key republican virtue is the ability to think independently when deliberating with others. Though seeking the public good, an independent citizen is self-determining, or autonomous, and self-motivated in pursuing that good (Pocock 1989: 87). Related is Pettit's view that the republican citizen is not dominated by others and does not exercise freedom at their sufferance (1997, 2012).

This emphasis on independence has egalitarian distributive implications. Citizens who are dependent on individuals with disproportionate economic or political power will seek not the common good, but the particular good of those on whom they depend.

Inequality thus undermines meaningful deliberation and self-government. Moreover, republicans see significant economic inequalities as dividing a community and undermining its pursuit of the common good (Sandel 1996). Consequently, republicanism opposes heavy concentrations of corporate or political power and great inequalities in wealth (Wood 1969: 73; Pocock 1975: 208–11; McCoy 1980: 54–7, 66–70; Pettit 1997: 117; Dagger 2006). In Rousseau's words, "[W]ith regard to wealth, no citizen should be so opulent that he can buy another, and none so poor that he is constrained to sell himself" (1978: 75).

Republican independence and egalitarianism provide an argument for private property. Historically, republicans celebrated those having an independent economic base, such as the small, individual landowner and the self-employed artisan.[2] Importantly, such independence "permitted a citizen to participate responsibly in the political process" and was not meant to foster "selfish privatism," but instead provide "the necessary basis for a committed republican citizenry" (McCoy 1980: 68).

When some citizens become dependent on others rather than independent and self-governing, society becomes *corrupt*. Corruption also arises when individuals, particularly powerful ones, put private interest before the common good (Pocock 1989: 88).[3] A society focused on economic growth and material consumption is especially susceptible to corruption (Sandel 1996: 224). Economic growth and development can generate large governmental or corporate power structures to which individuals may become subordinate. Moreover, the emphasis on material consumption that accompanies economic growth entails citizens' greater subservience to market forces and makes people "increasingly, selfish, greedy, and hedonistic, concerned more with their own personal wealth and comfort than with the welfare of society as a whole" (McCoy 1980: 23).

Rather than evaluating economic practices in terms of growth and prosperity, republicanism thus focuses on the impact on citizens' civic characters (McCoy 1980: 8; Sandel 1996: 123–200; Dagger 2006). Thus, for example, republicans would reject the high consumption way of life associated with suburban sprawl, even if it promotes growth, and instead favor forms of urban design more likely to foster community (Williamson 2010: 179–216). Relatedly, republicans critique the commodifying invasion of market relations into a myriad facets of contemporary life and the associated corrosion of the public realm, for example as seen with for-profit schools, hospitals, and prisons; private military contractors and police forces; omnipresent branding; and the influence of money on politics (Sandel 2012). In short, republicanism is fairly suspicious of capitalism.

Republican Stability and its Relationship to Nature

Corruption can be avoided and the republic stabilized, at least for a time, through cultivation of civic virtue (Pocock 1975: 183–4). This republican emphasis on stability is similar to green notions of sustainability (Barry 2012), a point I address later. Moreover, the emphasis on stability bolsters the communitarian side of the republican tradition. Stability means privileging existing collective identities, norms, and practices and favoring less of an open-ended political process.

In the eighteenth century, republican concerns about the corrupting, destabilizing effects of emerging capitalism translated into a critique of modernity and "progress" (McCoy 1980; Lienesch 1988; Cannavò 2010a). In his 1755 *Discourse on the Origin of Inequality*, Rousseau critiqued modernity as degeneration into vanity and misery. With remarkable prescience, he also detailed the degree to which nature has been transformed by the arts and sciences and questioned whether all this has promoted genuine happiness (1964: 193). In the United States, republicans, most notably Thomas Jefferson and his followers, believed that corruption could be forestalled by avoiding industrialization and urbanization and instead maintaining an agrarian society of small, independent yeoman farmers, artisans, and mechanics, living frugally and self-sufficiently and eschewing commercial values (Jefferson 1975; Cannavò 2010a). Indeed, commentators on both sides of the Atlantic saw in America the promise of a virtuous, pastoral middle ground between savage wilderness and corrupt, urbanized civilization (Marx 1964).

With explosive industrialization and urbanization in the United States, the Jeffersonian vision failed. As I have argued elsewhere, this failure, plus the clearing of the American wilderness, may have turned US republicanism toward an environmentalist path (Cannavò 2010a). Early green thinkers, especially Henry David Thoreau, critiqued the corrupting effects of capitalism. They lamented the loss of the wilderness and sought a virtuous society not through agrarianism but through harmony with untamed nature (Cannavò 2012a). Wilderness became the new repository of virtue and haven from corruption (Nash 1982: 44–83, 96–107; Cronon 1995). However, it is beyond the scope of this chapter to determine the actual degree to which contemporary environmental values trace their origins to republicanism.

Similarities Between Republicanism and Environmentalism

Republicanism has not always had green implications. Jeffersonian republicanism was predicated on clearing the American wilderness for farms (Cannavò 2010a), and the notion of human control over nature is a recurring theme in republicanism (Barry 2012: 219). The struggle against corruption is related to struggle against non-human nature. Corruption, as Pocock (1975: 211) says, is "part of the mutability and entropy of sublunary things." Part of the republic's impermanence arises from its materiality and its vulnerability to the vagaries of fortune: "The republic attempted to realize a totality of virtue in the relations of its citizens with one another, but did so on a footing that was temporally and spatially limited" (1975: 185). In Chapter XXV of *The Prince*, Machiavelli (1985: 98–9) thus presents fortune in terms of natural destructiveness, specifically a violent river that must be controlled with dikes, dams, and canals.

Yet, whether correlation or causation, there are striking similarities between republican and green perspectives. Like republicanism, environmentalism tends to be non-neutral regarding the good and has strong communitarian overtones. Environmental issues are not just about pollution, public health, or even human survival, but also about how ecologically-oriented practices and policies can promote key human values or human flourishing and/or the flourishing of non-human nature. Environmentalists often go well beyond the reformism cited earlier. They variously champion aesthetic, recreational, and spiritual goods provided by non-human nature; a strong sense of place; the superiority of qualitative over quantitative measures of wellbeing and of material simplicity or sufficiency over limitless consumption and economic growth; and the moral worth of non-human organisms and/or natural ecosystems. They often pursue these values through public policy and privilege them over other ways of life. Williamson's remarks about green theory thus apply to many environmentalists: "green political theorists reject any implication that the state should be value-neutral; indeed, green political theorists seek to politicize and subject to critical scrutiny a whole range of practices regarding consumption, travel patterns, and the like, which are now regarded in liberal democracies as matters of private choice" (2010: 264).

Though many environmentalists prize solitary wilderness experiences, green politics is in fact about goods—whether wilderness protection, ecosystem preservation, clean air and water, a stable climate, liveable cities, secure places, or a sustainable food system—that can only be secured or enjoyed collectively. Williamson notes, regarding suburban sprawl, "The question with regard to land use is not if public policies will favor one particular version of the good life rather than another, but which *kind* of community and social life public policy should aim to enhance as it shapes and reshapes the landscape and the built environment" (2010: 195; emphasis in original).

Consequently, like republicans, many environmentalists emphasize the common good or common goods and self-sacrifice over negative liberty and private interest. Green politics is a collective enterprise oriented to the flourishing of not only the individual but also the larger community. Furthermore, that larger community may be social *and* ecological (Di Chiro 1995; Eckersley 2006). For example, Aldo Leopold's land ethic, which articulates humanity's ecological role in terms of citizenship, combines republican notions of civic obligation with environmental responsibility (Cannavò 2012b). The land ethic embodies an ecological common good that entails communal obligations on the part of nature's human citizens. Respect for nature goes beyond enlightened self-interest to considerations of "right or wrong," "obligation," and "sacrifice" (1949: 207–8).

Participatory Democracy and Decentralization

Like republicans, many environmentalists see civic participation as upholding the common good against special interests. Robert Paehlke (1989: 144, 174–5) notes that "nearly every piece of important environmental legislation in the United States has contained provisions for the expansion of openness and participation." These provisions include public hearings, public comment, citizens' advisory boards, and public access to information about companies' toxic inventories and releases.

Though reformist environmentalists might support centralized regulation and top-down ecological management, more radical green activists distrust governmental or corporate bureaucracies. They share republicans' preference for political decentralization and local self-government. Notable examples include the bioregional vision of small polities organized around local ecosystems (Sale 1985; Berg 2014); social ecology's "libertarian municipalism" (Bookchin 1982; Biehl 1998); the international Green Party movement's emphasis on small-scale, participatory democracy (Spretnak and Capra 1986); watershed-based collaborative conservation efforts involving environmentalists and resource interests (Shutkin 2000; Brick, Snow, and Van De Wetering 2001); civic agriculture, an emerging movement that opposes globalized, centralized, agribusiness and sees local food systems as key components of active citizenship and self-government (Lyson 2004; Travaline and Hunold 2010); and the environmental justice movement (and related anti-toxics movement), which empowers minority and lower-income neighborhoods to resist the siting of environmental hazards, to create green space, and to take control of their economic development (Bullard 1993; Schlosberg 1999; Shutkin 2000).

For many environmentalists, the basis for this participatory, decentralist, democratic orientation seems twofold. First, democratic decentralization can give political voice to local community ties, place-attachments, and environmental knowledge and consciousness. Second, democracy and decentralization enable resistance to powerful special interests—polluters, builders, resource management or development agencies—who exercise domination over individuals, communities, and non-human nature. In fact, Pettit explicitly ties environmental protection to non-domination: "The republican state that . . . is dedicated to promoting freedom as non-domination, is bound to espouse what we may loosely describe as the environmental cause" (1997: 138).

However, as with republicanism, a tension between community and contestation arises here. Though many environmentalists may naïvely believe otherwise, local democratic empowerment may not necessarily yield green communal values. Residents of a particular community may, for example, support oil and gas drilling, unsustainable levels of logging, or construction of suburban subdivisions. I return to this issue later.

Political Economy and Private Property

Like republicans, more radical environmentalists criticize capitalism and limitless growth and favor material simplicity over luxury and consumption. We saw how republicanism associates capitalism with corruption. Many greens see similar problems: capitalism enables special interests, such as polluters and developers, to profit from environmental abuse; it makes economically dependent workers, such as coal miners, oppose sustainability; it commodifies nature and place; its focus on consumption and growth violates ecological limits, promotes pollution and environmental destruction, fosters materialism and greed, and discourages sacrifice for the ecological good. Williamson (2010: 179–216) thus critiques sprawl from both republican and environmentalist perspectives as fostering excessive consumption, privatism, and inequality; undermining local ways of life; and ruining the environment.

Environmentalists support regulation of the economy and private property, as do republicans (Sandel 1996; Dagger 2006). Even resource conservationism, the most limited form of environmentalism, has significant regulatory implications regarding resource extraction. And though republicans see private property as promoting civic virtue, Barry argues that republican theory, when infused with green values, is ultimately suspicious of property rights and more willing to prioritize the community's common good (2012: 242–7).

This communal, ecological reading, Barry (2012: 220) acknowledges, seems in tension with republicans' emphasis on economic independence. However, republican independence has always been situated in a communitarian context. The Jeffersonian yeoman "[was] not [an] isolated frontiersman . . . but a Virginia husbandman bound to neighbors and friends for mutual assistance and cooperation" (Yarbrough 1998: 68). The nineteenth-century US labor organization, the Knights of Labor, used the independence ideal to oppose capitalist wage labor and advocate workplace cooperatives (Sandel 1996: 168–200). The contemporary civic agriculture movement advances a neo-Jeffersonian ideal of individual producer independence from corporate agriculture, but also aims to rebuild local community and civic consciousness around farming and food (Berry 1996; Lyson 2004).

Republican Stability and Environmental Sustainability

In the face of moral or ecological corruption or degradation, both republicanism and environmentalism seek stability or sustainability. Yet, in both Machiavelli's thought and

Jeffersonian republicanism, political stability depended on the subordination, or at least the domestication, of nature. However, following Barry (2012), I do not believe that this reflects a fundamental conflict between republicanism and environmentalism.

First, the need to restrain potentially destructive natural forces—such as Machiavelli's flood-prone river—is inescapable for any viable political theory. Here, in fact, republicans can offer a corrective to what Barry (1999) calls the "submissive quietism" espoused by environmentalists (259) who have "unreflective sentimental or romantic views of human–nature relations" (33) and do not acknowledge the need for an "ethics of use" (8) in relation to nature. At the same time, republican political economy, with its emphasis on civic virtue and material simplicity, presents a model of a restrained use of nature that also opposes capitalism's paradigm of endless growth.

Second, despite Machiavelli's imagery and Jefferson's program of wilderness conquest, the republican tradition has also often questioned the domination of nature. Earlier, I noted Rousseau's connection between the subordination of nature and the degeneration and corruption of human character (see also Lane 2014). Similarly, Thoreau used republican language in critiquing the social and moral failings of emerging industrial capitalism and he connected these problems to mistreatment of, and alienation from, nature (Cannavò 2012a).

Moreover, in an era of ecological crisis and limits, the sustenance of political communities and ecological systems is much more clearly interconnected. A political community relies upon relatively stable ecological conditions (Curry 2000: 3, 8). Environmental problems threaten communities' public health, livelihoods, and/or physical security and integrity. Barry (2012: 218–19, 222–6) in fact argues that the republic's determinate existence in space and time, and the associated concerns about eventual corruption give republicanism an appreciation of limits, of human dependence on and vulnerability to external forces, and even of the ecological conditions and specificities of place. The threat of corruption makes sustainability "a central value for republicans" (Barry 2012: 227) and adds a further moral dimension to green politics.

Green Republicanism and Climate Change

Based on the foregoing, one might conceive of a green republicanism that advances a politics of the common good centered on civic engagement, a strong sense of community and place, and pursuit of environmental quality; that advocates decentralization and democratic participation; that regulates private property and the market to foster environmental protection; and that promotes ecological sustainability as a foundation of political stability.

Such a green republicanism faces both opportunities and challenges as we confront the threat of climate change. This crisis requires a sense of planetary responsibility and citizenship that goes beyond traditional political boundaries and allegiances (Hirsch and Norton 2012). This has mixed implications for republicans and the many environmentalists who also emphasize smaller-scale political communities.

The tension between community and contestation re-emerges here. The exigencies of the climate crisis would seem to demand that scientific conceptions of nature provide a thick set of a priori, substantive constraints and ends for politics, even a coercive green communitarianism and an overriding conception of the common good. Climate change also presents a planetary challenge that seemingly forecloses local autonomy and action. The climate crisis thus seems to greatly narrow the scope of deliberation and contestation and to dictate an ecological agenda to politics. Indeed, environmentalists' faith in participatory democratic values is often predicated on this sort of depoliticization, on an assumption that democratically empowered communities will simply derive political programs directly from ecological principles or other foundational conceptions of nature (Meyer 2001).

Indeed, it would be ecologically suicidal to deny that climate change and other environmental challenges demand aggressive mitigation and adaptation and necessarily foreclose certain political and economic choices. In the face of this crisis, politics can only be open-ended to a certain degree. As noted earlier, a decentralized, democratic politics in no way guarantees ecologically viable outcomes. Moreover, local autonomy and decentralization would seem to exacerbate the kinds of collective action and coordination problems that have dogged efforts to address climate change.

Republicanism offers useful resources here. First, regarding centralization versus decentralization, one might turn to dispersed sovereignty. As noted earlier, Sandel (1996) warns against a cosmopolitan, globalized perspective that erases local communal attachments and self-government, but instead calls for dispersed sovereignty across a variety of communities and jurisdictions at different levels of scale and governance. Such a republican approach could involve global- or national-level authorities setting emissions targets or taxes and providing funding for mitigation and adaptation, with actual formulation and implementation of specific measures at a local (for example, municipality or town) or regional (for example, metropolitan or watershed) scale. Implementation policies could involve renewable energy portfolios, solar and wind power development, local agriculture, green buildings, planning and construction of hard (for example, sea walls, levees, and floating structures) and soft (for example, wetlands) infrastructure to protect against rising seas, managed retreat from vulnerable areas, and higher density alternatives to sprawl. Local implementation could enable the sort of flexibility and experimentation that are essential in addressing a radically changing climate (Dryzek, Norgaard, and Schlosberg 2013) and also foster pursuit of a variety of locally based common goods.

Paul Hirsch and Bryan Norton (2012) present this kind of approach. They call on us to "think like a planet" in coming to grips with climate change. Yet they acknowledge that such an expansion of the scale of political action could lead to excessive political centralization. Their solution is not to replace existing political communities, but to add additional, complementary institutions concerned with climate and other environmental matters and so create a set of overlapping political entities or centers (329).

Similarly, Barry (2012) sees the international Transition Towns movement as exemplifying green republicanism. The Transition movement addresses climate change, resource shortages, and global economic crises through local community measures to promote sustainability, flexibility, and resiliency (89–108). These measures also emphasize local or regional autonomy, democracy, and social solidarity and community. They include reducing energy consumption; switching to locally sourced, renewable energy; promoting local food production; establishing community-owned utilities and other enterprises; and even creating local currencies (see http://www.transitionnetwork.org/). Barry sees Transition as involving an open-ended, creative, pluralist, multi-level approach to climate change rather than a uniform, top-down set of solutions (95). Transition hearkens back to republican notions of independence, but on a more communal level (107, 115). It also involves an ethic of responsibly using nature—for example, through local food production—to promote local autonomy and community, a sense of place, and sustainable ecological practices. And, its cultivation of locally based institutions and practices enables a plurality of common goods.

Second, there are ways of addressing, though not entirely resolving, the tension between community and contestation in confronting environmental problems. Here, republicanism contributes a formative politics of virtue cultivation. A preconceived conception of virtue necessarily limits the scope of a vibrant, contestatory politics, by shaping citizens' characters from the outset, yet it also ensures some continuity in a community's core principles, even as these principles and the virtues that sustain them might evolve over time. For a democratic, decentralized politics to reliably tackle climate change and other environmental problems rather than pursue local economic self-interest would require a certain type of citizen and public culture. Ecological citizenship in an era of climate change would require a strong sense of collective action and a number of green virtues (Sandler and Cafaro 2005; Thompson and Bendik-Keymer 2012). Such virtues would allow us to meet the challenge of global warming through both mitigation of future climate change and adaptation to changes that are now inevitable. The republican virtues I listed earlier would certainly be useful. More specifically green virtues could include a sense of place; an appreciation of ecological complexity and interdependence; sensitivity to ecological impacts; scientific literacy; caution and humility regarding human relations with nature; care and respect for nature and also for the existing built environment; a broadened spatial and temporal perspective; flexibility, courage, resilience, creativity, and hope in the face of ecological change; the ability to adapt existing goods and values of the past to radically changed ecological conditions; a strong sense of international, intergenerational, and interspecies justice; and a sense of collective responsibility for the planet (Sandler 2012; Thompson 2012; Hirsch and Norton 2012; Williamson 2010: 195–6, 206; Barry 2012: 78–89, 96–101). Cultivation of these green virtues would involve policies to promote environmental education, to protect or expand opportunities for direct interaction with non-human nature (most obviously through preservation or creation of wilderness areas, parks, and other open spaces), and to enable citizens to directly participate in environmental decision-making and management. Moreover, there would be a need for further policies to restrain the influence and demands of markets and so open up space for alternative economic and social values.

However, any balance achieved between the more communitarian and the more contestatory elements of republicanism will never be perfect or final. The sorts of policies outlined above would, if anything, bring this tension to the fore by explicitly acknowledging it. Green republicanism could in fact make the proper balance between communitarian and democratic values itself a matter of deliberation. And this explicit acknowledgment may be perhaps the most important contribution republicanism can provide environmental politics. Environmentalism, while often proclaiming democratic values, is vulnerable to depoliticized notions of community based on ecological imperatives. In simultaneously prioritizing both community and contestation, republicans force us to consider how we may best secure both. Republicanism also alerts us to the need for character virtues requisite for both. At the same time, environmentalism emphasizes the ecological basis for a stable political community. It can thus provide a stabilizing influence on a deliberative, contestatory politics. In the end, environmentalism and republicanism can inform one another and also help guide a more sustainable, ecological, politically engaged society.

Notes

1. Though the republican tradition is divided here. See Seijo (2014) on Machiavelli's warnings about dangers facing small republics.
2. Historically, republicans saw such figures as male, and not simply because the economic roles in question largely excluded women. In the past, republicanism was highly gendered (see Phillips 1991: 45–6). One might cite Machiavelli's notorious feminine characterization of fortune and his association between *virtù* and rape in *The Prince*. (His accompanying comparison of fortune to a violent river that must be tamed links gender subordination to the domination of nature.) Republicanism also emphasized the martial virtues of the male citizen-soldier (Pocock 1975: 201). Aristotle (1984) consigned women to a subordinate, domestic status outside of politics. Thomas Jefferson, one of the most prominent US republicans, similarly rejected any political role for women and stressed their domestic and sexual servitude. See, for example, his letters to Anne Willing Bingham (May 11, 1788), George Washington (December 4, 1788), Albert Gallatin (January 13, 1807), and Thomas Appleton (July 18, 1816). Though a fuller discussion of republicanism's gendered aspects is beyond the scope of this chapter, I believe that neither a martial nor a gendered orientation is essential to republicanism. For example, Mary Wollstonecraft and Jane Addams both drew on republican themes in advancing gender equality and, in Addams' case, pacifism (Sarvasy 2010). Contemporary republican notions of civic engagement, self-government, and non-domination can all promote gender equality and the redefinition of gender roles, within both the public and private spheres (Pettit 1997: 138–40).
3. The republican notion of corruption was developed perhaps most influentially in Machiavelli's 1517 *Discourses on Livy*.

REFERENCES

Aristotle. (1984). *Politics*. Translated by C. Lord (Chicago: University of Chicago Press).
Bailyn, B. (1992). *The Ideological Origins of the American Revolution* (Cambridge: Harvard University Press).
Barry, J. (1999). *Rethinking Green Politics* (London: Sage).
Barry, J. (2008). "Towards a Green Republicanism." *The Good Society* 17(2): 1–12.
Barry, J. (2012). *The Politics of Actually Existing Unsustainability* (Oxford: Oxford University Press).
Barry, J. and Smith, K. (2008). "Civic Republicanism and Green Politics." In *Building a Citizen Society*, edited by D. Leighton and S. White (London: Lawrence and Wishart), 137–47.
Berg, P. (2014). *The Biosphere and the Bioregion*. Edited by C. Glotfelty and E. Quesnel (New York: Routledge).
Berry, W. (1996). *The Unsettling of America* (San Francisco: Sierra Club).
Biehl, J. (1998). *The Politics of Social Ecology* (Montreal: Black Rose).
Bookchin, M. (1982). *The Ecology of Freedom* (Palo Alto: Cheshire).
Brick, P., Snow, D., and Van De Wetering, S., eds. (2001). *Across the Great Divide* (Washington: Island Press).
Bullard, R., ed. (1993). *Confronting Environmental Racism* (Cambridge: South End Press).
Cannavò, P. F. (2007). *The Working Landscape* (Cambridge: MIT Press).
Cannavò, P. F. (2010a). "To the Thousandth Generation." *Environmental Politics* 19(3): 356–73.
Cannavò, P. F. (2010b). "Civic Virtue and Sacrifice in a Suburban Nation." In *The Environmental Politics of Sacrifice*, edited by M. Maniates and J. M. Meyer (Cambridge: MIT Press), 217–46.
Cannavò, P. F. (2012a). "The Half-Cultivated Citizen." *Environmental Values* 21(2): 101–24.
Cannavò, P. F. (2012b). "Ecological Citizenship, Time, and Corruption." *Environmental Politics* 21(6): 864–81.
Cronon, W. (1995). "The Trouble with Wilderness." In *Uncommon Ground*, edited by W. Cronon (New York: W.W. Norton), 69–90.
Curry, P. (2000). "Redefining Community." *Biodiversity and Conservation* 9(8): 1059–71.
Dagger, R. (2006). "Neo-Republicanism and the Civic Economy." *Politics, Philosophy and Economics* 5(2): 151–73.
Di Chiro, G. (1995). "Nature as Community." In *Uncommon Ground*, edited by W. Cronon (New York: W.W. Norton), 298–320.
Dryzek, J. S., Norgaard, R. B., and Schlosberg, D. (2013). *Climate-Challenged Society* (Oxford: Oxford University Press).
Eckersley, R. (2006). "Communitarianism." In *Political Theory and the Ecological Challenge*, edited by A. Dobson and R. Eckersley (Cambridge: Cambridge University Press), 91–108.
Hirsch, P. D. and Norton, B. G. (2012). "Thinking Like a Planet." In *Ethical Adaptation to Climate Change*, edited by A. Thompson, and J. Bendik-Keymer (Cambridge: MIT Press), 317–34.
Honohan, I. (2002). *Civic Republicanism* (London: Routledge).
Jefferson, T. (1975). "Notes on the State of Virginia." In *The Portable Thomas Jefferson*, edited by M. D. Peterson (New York: Penguin), 23–232.
Lane, J. H., Jr. (2014). "Jean-Jacques Rousseau: The Disentangling of Green Paradoxes." In *Engaging Nature*, edited by P. F. Cannavò and J. H. Lane, Jr. (Cambridge: MIT Press), 133–52.
Leopold, A. (1949). *A Sand County Almanac* (Oxford: Oxford University Press).

Lienesch, M. (1988). *New Order of the Ages* (Princeton: Princeton University Press).
Lyson, T.A. (2004). *Civic Agriculture* (Lebanon, NH: University Press of New England).
Machiavelli, N. (1985). *The Prince*. Translated by H. C. Mansfield, Jr. (Chicago: University of Chicago Press).
Marx, L. (1964). *The Machine in the Garden* (New York: Oxford University Press).
Maynor, J. W. (2003). *Republicanism in the Modern World* (Cambridge: Polity Press).
McCoy, D. (1980). *The Elusive Republic* (Chapel Hill: University of North Carolina Press).
Meyer, J. M. (2001). *Political Nature* (Cambridge: The MIT Press).
Nash, R. (1982). *Wilderness and the American Mind* (New Haven: Yale University Press).
Paehlke, R. C. (1989). *Environmentalism and the Future of Progressive Politics* (New Haven: Yale University Press).
Pettit, P. (1997). *Civic Republicanism* (Oxford: Oxford University Press).
Pettit, P. (2012). *On the People's Terms* (Cambridge: Cambridge University Press).
Phillips, A. (1991). *Engendering Democracy* (University Park: Pennsylvania State University Press).
Pocock, J. G. A. (1975). *The Machiavellian Moment* (Princeton: Princeton University Press).
Pocock, J. G. A. (1989). *Politics, Language, and Time* (Chicago: University of Chicago Press).
Rousseau, J. J. (1964). *The First and Second Discourses*. Translated by D. D. and J. R. Masters (New York: St. Martin's Press).
Rousseau, J. J. (1978). *On the Social Contract*. Translated by J. R. Masters (New York: St. Martin's Press).
Sale, K. (1985). *Dwellers in the Land* (San Francisco: Sierra Club).
Sandel, M. J. (1996). *Democracy's Discontent* (Cambridge: Harvard University Press).
Sandel, M. J. (2012). *What Money Can't Buy* (New York: Farrar, Straus and Giroux).
Sandler R. (2012). "Global Warming and the Virtues of Ecological Restoration." In *Ethical Adaptation to Climate Change*, edited by A. Thompson, and J. Bendik-Keymer, J. (Cambridge: MIT Press), 63–79.
Sandler R. and Cafaro, P., eds. (2005). *Environmental Virtue Ethics* (Lanham: Rowman and Littlefield).
Sarvasy, W. (2010). "Engendering Democracy by Socializing It." In *Feminist Interpretations of Jane Addams*, edited by M. Hamington (University Park: Pennsylvania State University Press), 293–310.
Schlosberg, D. (1999). *Environmental Justice and the New Pluralism* (Oxford: Oxford University Press).
Seijo, F. (2014). "Niccolò Machiavelli: Rethinking Decentralization's Role in Green Theory." In *Engaging Nature*, edited by P. F. Cannavò and J. H. Lane, Jr. (Cambridge: MIT Press), 65–81.
Shutkin, W. (2000). *The Land that Could Be* (Cambridge: MIT Press).
Skinner, Q. (1990). "The Republican Ideal of Political Liberty." In *Machiavelli and Republicanism*, edited by G. Bock, Q. Skinner, and M. Viroli (Cambridge: Cambridge University Press), 293–309.
Spretnak, C. and Capra, F. (1986). *Green Politics* (Santa Fe: Bear & Company).
Thompson, A. (2012). "The Virtue of Responsibility for the Global Climate." In *Ethical Adaptation to Climate Change*, edited by A. Thompson, and J. Bendik-Keymer (Cambridge: MIT Press), 203–21.
Thompson, A. and Bendik-Keymer, J., eds. (2012). *Ethical Adaptation to Climate Change*. (Cambridge: MIT Press).

Travaline, K. and Hunold, C. (2010). "Urban Agriculture and Ecological Citizenship in Philadelphia." *Local Environment* 15(6): 581–90.

Williamson, T. (2010). *Sprawl, Justice, and Citizenship* (Oxford: Oxford University Press).

Wood, G. S. (1969). *The Creation of the American Republic, 1776–1787* (New York: W. W. Norton).

Yarbrough, J. M. (1998). *American Virtues* (Lawrence: University of Kansas Press).

CHAPTER 6

HUMAN NATURE, NON-HUMAN NATURE, AND NEEDS

Environmental Political Theory and Critical Theory

ANDREW BIRO

CRITICAL theory can be understood as a political–intellectual project oriented around a critique of domination. Stated more positively, it is a project with a goal of emancipation, understood as the capacity for the autonomous definition of needs. Karl Marx, who would later define the ideal social system as one in which each member of society receives "according to their needs" (Marx 1978: 531), defined the task of the critical theorist as "the self-clarification (critical philosophy) of the struggles and wishes of the age" (Marx 1975: 209). The human relationship with the non-human world—climate change, resource scarcity, biodiversity loss, and so on—is often regarded as one of the most important challenges facing contemporary society. Moreover, particularly in the context of the Global North, this challenge is often defined as a problem of overconsumption: we are taking or using more than we *need*.

This suggests at least two problems (or "struggles and wishes") that require clarification. The first is defining what we need: on what basis are environmentalists able to claim that (some) people are overconsuming resources? Defining what is a "need" for the kinds of beings that are as deeply socially conditioned as *homo sapiens* are turns out not to be an easy task (Xenos 1989; Panayotakis 2011). Indeed, from a critical theoretical perspective, such definitions cannot be externally imposed (hence, for Marx, "*self*-clarification"). Human emancipation (liberation, autonomy) is about having the capacity to fulfill one's needs, including the need to express or articulate one's needs for oneself.

This brings us to the second problem that is raised for critical theory in an era of environmental concerns: the status of the other-than-human world. Members of the Frankfurt School, which is often regarded as the epitome of critical theory (the entry in one reference text for "Critical Theory" reads simply: "See Frankfurt School" (Bottomore 1983: 122)), often discussed the target of critique as "the domination of nature." This concept, deployed quite broadly, remained underspecified, referring to the capacity of the human subject to objectify and dominate anything outside of or other than itself (Leiss 1994). Frankfurt School member Herbert Marcuse wrote, again in somewhat elusive terms, about the "liberation of nature" (Marcuse 1972). But how can "we" (human beings) know what (non-human) nature wants? To what extent can we determine if non-humans are being given "according to their needs"? Who articulates the needs of the non-human world, and how?

The chapter first provides a brief discussion of the "domination of nature" and "instrumental rationality": key themes for at least the first generation of the Frankfurt School, a multidisciplinary group of intellectuals associated with the Institute for Social Research, founded in Frankfurt in 1923. It then examines Jürgen Habermas's "communicative turn": a decisive (though not universally acclaimed) transformation in Frankfurt School critical theory. Habermas's innovation is assessed in terms of both its positive and negative implications for environmental theorizing. The most important of these negative implications for environmental political theory is a renewed and strengthened commitment to anthropocentrism. The chapter goes on to explore some possibilities for transcending the anthropocentric limitations of the Habermasian worldview. The last section turns finally to consider some of the thematics of the first-generation critical theorists, particularly their emphasis on the issue of subject-formation (what makes people who they are, with the particular needs that they have), in light of recent developments that are of particular interest to environmentalists and environmental political theorists.

Critical Theory, Instrumental Rationality, and the "Domination of Nature"

Arguably the most important work of the Frankfurt School was Max Horkheimer and Theodor Adorno's *Dialectic of Enlightenment* (1987). Horkheimer and Adorno develop a critique of "instrumental rationality." This term refers to means-oriented thinking, figuring out how to most efficiently achieve ends or goals, bracketing the substantive evaluation of those ends or goals themselves. For Horkheimer and Adorno, the development of Western modernity is one where instrumental rationality has grown in its influence, to the point of becoming our understanding of rationality as a whole. We are increasingly incapable of evaluating our ends, except in the barest terms of sheer survival. The process of modernization involves subjecting premodern value systems, such as religion, to rational critique. But instrumental reason, which is focused solely on questions of efficiency, finds itself insufficient to the task of providing a guide for human behavior. Once reason has shattered the myths that structured our worldview and guided our actions, how do we know what to do?

For the Frankfurt School, the developments of the first half of the twentieth century showed clearly our collective inability to answer that question in a humane way. The liberal capitalism of the Anglo-American world was being transformed into "monopoly capitalism" in which large corporations and their logics (simultaneously bureaucratic and competitive) dominated economic life. Moreover, economic life dominated social life more generally, as the logic of market competition and the commodity form colonized leisure time and the aesthetic realm (the industrialization of culture), right down to the psychic constitution of individuals. Meanwhile, in Russia, the Communist revolution, which promised workers' liberation, delivered unprecedented bureaucratic intrusion and control. Rather than "withering away" as Marx promised, the state under Stalin metastasized. And in the case of fascism in Central Europe, the "liquidation of the individual" was literally programmed into the regime's basic functioning. While not identical, for members of the Frankfurt School these developments are part of a continuum, and all emerge out of the progressive triumph of instrumental rationality. In all cases, while traditional ways of doing things were swept aside in the name of progress, the forces unleashed were not subject to conscious rational control, but were experienced as a "second nature."

Just as traditional ways of life were cast as "irrational" from the perspective of modern instrumental reason, nature itself was subjected to the same logic. Non-human nature is increasingly only conceivable as a means to human ends. Thus for members of the Frankfurt School, the "domination of nature" referred to the capacity of the human subject to objectify and dominate anything outside of or other than itself. "Enlightenment," for Horkheimer and Adorno, involves the "mastery of nature," and thus the conceptual and practical reduction of "nature" to limited terms that are comprehensible and useful for the rational subject.

Thus while instrumental rationality is obviously useful, it also has some disturbing implications: the process of reification that abstracts from things only what is useful to the task at hand, ignoring or repressing everything else, can be seen in how we treat non-human nature, other humans, and our own selves. For Adorno in particular, the belief that we can separate "human" or "social" from "natural"—or in other words that we can insulate ourselves from the reifying logic of instrumental rationality—is false. As Deborah Cook puts it, "showing that human history is always also natural history and that non-human nature is entwined with history" informed Adorno's work from beginning to end (Cook 2011: 1). In one of his earliest works, Adorno insists that we must "comprehend historical being in its most extreme historical determinacy, where it is most historical, as natural being, [and] comprehend nature as an historical being where it seems to rest most deeply in itself as nature" (1984: 117). The mutual implication of the natural and the social is central to Adorno's philosophy. Deeply influenced by Freudian psychology, for the Frankfurt School the "domination of nature" thus referred as much to the domination of *internal* nature (the (de)formation of human subjectivity) as to the domination of *external* nature. Indeed, psychic interiority itself functions as a kind of "untamed wilderness."

The result is both suggestive and limited. On the one hand, the resonances between systems of social domination and the domination of nature is a point that is later taken up in the "social ecology" of Murray Bookchin and some strands of eco-feminism. At the same time, however, with the exception of some of Marcuse's very last works (Marcuse 1992), references to the domination of non-human nature remain scattered and unsystematized: what Robyn Eckersley characterizes as an unredeemed "promise" (Eckersley 1992: 97–117). Some more recent attempts to cash in this promise are discussed in the latter parts of this chapter. But before turning to those, I will examine the turn in Frankfurt School critical theory effected by Jürgen Habermas, which at least in some ways has short-circuited the possibility of redeeming the original promise.

The Habermasian Turn

One of the key points in the development of Frankfurt School critical theory more generally is the Habermasian "communicative turn." Habermas begins with the claim that the critique of enlightenment, laid out programmatically in Horkheimer and Adorno's *Dialectic of Enlightenment*, leads to a dead end. The critique of instrumental rationality becomes totalizing, as even the basis for critique itself is undermined. Once "the critique of ideology has lost its foundations," then "critique becomes total: it turns against reason as the foundation of its own analysis" (Habermas 1982: 21–2).

Habermas tries to avoid the fatalism—the truly totalizing critique of reason—that he argues is found in Nietzschean post-structuralists such as Foucault, Derrida, and Deleuze. At the same time, he is aware of the impossibility of reimposing a transcendent standard of rationality that is capable of withstanding the critique of enlightenment articulated by Horkheimer and Adorno. Or, at least, a transcendent standard of rationality, *tout court*. Habermas's response to the dilemma posed by the *Dialectic of Enlightenment* is to argue that Horkheimer and Adorno's account wrongly assumes that instrumental reason is in fact capable of completely devouring other forms of rationality. Instead, Habermas argues, communicative rationality is an essential component of our species-being, as social and flexible (or "biologically underdetermined") beings. Communicative rationality—a mode of reason grounded in the need to express oneself and have that self-expression be understood, and to understand the self-expression of others—is both part of the human condition and fundamentally different from the instrumental rationality that is also essential to human survival. The result is what Lenny Moss and Vida Pavesich describe as "a kind of theoretical ju-jitsu ... [in which] the march toward a fully instrumentalized world is vitiated by transcendentally conceding an aspect of it while putatively emancipating the remainder" (Moss and Pavesich 2011: 148–9).

For environmental political theory, Habermas's "communicative turn" both provides new openings and forecloses certain possibilities. One opening has been a renewed attention to the theoretical and practical underpinnings of deliberative democracy. From a Habermasian perspective, the communicative turn blocks the possibility of a "fully instrumentalized world," feared by Horkheimer and Adorno. For Horkheimer and Adorno, the only bulwark against instrumental reason is reason's critical self-reflection: thinking about what our thinking is doing. As they say in the opening pages of *Dialectic of Enlightenment*, "the Enlightenment *must consider itself*, if men are not to be wholly betrayed" (Horkheimer and Adorno 1987: xv; emphasis in original). By contrast, for Habermas, communicative rationality, an inherently separate form of rationality from instrumental reason, can serve to contain the latter. A Habermasian approach thus at least opens the possibility of environmental issues being governed by communicative rationality, rather than being simply problems of managing or administering nature (as Horkheimer & Adorno's *Dialectic of Enlightenment* might suggest). From this perspective, dealing with environmental problems not only requires the effective administration of the non-human world (instrumental rationality), it also requires an attentiveness to the differing values, goals, and identities of the various humans associated with that environment. Human needs are flexible and must be articulated for social cooperation to occur: they are not merely biological, pre-given, or comprehensible in strictly objective terms. As a result, attention ought to be paid to different groups and how their needs (or interests) are articulated.

Habermas's proposal for a "principle of discourse ethics" (Habermas 1990: 43–115), in which rational argument is unimpeded by unequal power relations, can thus provide a template for a variety of participatory approaches to environmental management, ranging from stakeholder participation groups and integrated resource management to citizen juries and the extended peer communities of post-normal science. What all of these approaches share is a commitment to seeing environmental issues not simply as technical problems of how to manage (non-human) nature, but also as material expressions of conflicts between different modes of life. Despite the often highly analytic tone of Habermas's philosophical work, and the rationalist formalism that it might imply, the point of a focus on communication as an activity that is not strictly instrumental is to highlight the ways in which human activity is never merely reducible to instrumentalism. The essence of human *communicative* action—differentiated from *instrumental* action—is that it is about the expression of human needs, which are, by definition, flexible and culturally constituted rather than biologically given. A key Habermasian term is the "lifeworld": "the web of everyday interactions and communication surrounding 'our' cognitive achievements. The latter are intrinsically intersubjective and cooperative" (Habermas 1990: 9). Thus, managing river flows, for example, is not just a matter of meeting some singular objectively acceptable volume or chemical composition of water, but of negotiating the needs of diverse groups (fishermen, tourism operators, farmers, etc.) who "need" different amounts and kinds of water in different ways, at different times, and so on. Andrew Light's work on ecological restoration offers another example, albeit not explicitly grounded in Habermasian discourse ethics (and perhaps more clearly linked with Deweyan pragmatism). For Light, seeing ecological restoration as a site for the expression and cultivation of ecological citizenship emphasizes the extent to which claims about ecological management must always be grounded in a particular shared lifeworld rather than scientific abstractions (Light 2002, 2012). A case for ecological restoration, which is always about choosing to restore some things but not others, is made by "our ability to identify a compelling narrative about the continuity from the past to the future in any place" (Light 2012: 117).

In practice, of course, discursive democratic modes of governance cannot fully live up to the principle of discourse ethics or "ideal speech situation," and must inevitably find a balance or tension between allowing for the genuine expression of the needs of subordinate groups and legitimating existing power imbalances crystallized in the state and other institutions of representation. For first-generation critical theorists such as Marcuse, the dominance of instrumental rationality increasingly foreclosed the possibility of such needs being expressed and understood as such. An aspect of what Marcuse called "one-dimensional society" was its "rationalized irrationality": needs that were not already met by the system could only be perceived as "irrational" complaints (Marcuse 1964). Similarly, for post-structuralists such as Foucault, even needs themselves are constituted in and through power relations (Foucault 1978). In this sense the very viability of the Habermasian edifice as political theory—whether one finds it persuasive or not—thus depends on the capacity to effect this separation between communicative and instrumental action.

In a critical yet sympathetic account of Habermasian critical theory, Nancy Fraser notes that this distinction between communicative and instrumental action is best understood "as registering a difference in degree... In few if any human action contexts are human actions coordinated absolutely nonconsensually and absolutely nonnormatively" (Fraser 1987: 35). Habermas emphasizes their separation because for him the process of modernization involves precisely the differentiation of "system" and "lifeworld" and thus the emergence of a genuine public sphere. For Fraser, what is problematic here are the gendered assumptions that are not only unexamined but actually reinforced in, for example, the separation of public and private spheres. Hence, certain gendered forms of domination are not holdovers of premodern society, but "intrinsically modern in Habermas's sense" insofar as Habermas's very conception of modernization legitimizes "the modern institutional separation of family and official economy" (Fraser 1987: 46 and 39).

As Fraser shifts from more abstract considerations of gender politics to a discussion of welfare capitalism, a definition of freedom from domination becomes clear: it is about subjects' "capacities to interpret their own needs, experiences and life-problems" (Fraser 1987: 46–7). The relevance of the contours of modernity's public–private distinction is that it reinforces a set of gendered relations of domination, insofar as women's work (for example, domestic reproduction) is consigned to a private sphere where "socially integrated action" is "normatively secured." Action here is coordinated by convention or tradition, and in fact is categorically separated from the social reproduction that requires "communicatively achieved forms of socially integrated action" (the communicative action found in the market and the state). Where social cooperation is undertaken without communicative action (that is, by convention or tradition), then the principle of discourse ethics is not in play. Shut out of the public sphere, unable to engage in political speech, and more specifically to provide or withhold consent, women are afforded fewer opportunities to use communicative rationality, and develop their "capacities to interpret their own needs, experiences and life-problems."

Fraser's essay begins with Marx's definition of critical theory cited at the outset of this chapter: "the self-clarification of the struggles and wishes of the age" (Fraser 1987: 35). The emphasis here—what makes a theory a *critical* theory—is attention to the capacity for the expression of needs, which are not taken as immutable and pregiven, but always need to be "clarified" or "interpreted." For environmental political theory, a question can be raised about the extent to which non-human beings—the subject of environmentalism—have those capacities for need-interpretation. If so, then what does a critique of domination entail in terms of how humans relate to non-human beings with similar interpretive capacities? Is it mere convention or tradition that relegates human–non-human relations to a realm outside of politics? And if we allow that non-humans might be able to interpret their own needs, how might these be articulated in ways that humans can understand?

The capacity to know and articulate one's own (genuine) needs as an index of liberation is a thread that connects Habermas with earlier critical theorists such as Marcuse. The question is whether something like Habermas's ideal speech situation is a sufficient condition for the articulation of genuine needs, whether needs are just there, self-evident to the subject, and waiting to be expressed, or whether, as Marcuse argued, human needs are the product of a more complex historical dynamic (Marcuse 1964: 1–18). We shall return to the theme of the expression of needs momentarily.

Before doing so, we might first pursue a bit further the argument of those critical theorists who reject the Habermasian turn and its hard separation between communicative and instrumental rationality. Moss and Pavesich, cited earlier, provide a synopsis of this critique that perhaps most clearly opens up implications for environmental thinking, although similar critiques are developed by others as well.

As suggested earlier, Moss and Pavesich describe Habermas's foundational theoretical move as the grounding of "flexible, normatively structured, social cooperativity" in "a *non-instrumental* orientation toward mutual understanding" (Moss and Pavesich 2011: 149; my emphasis). For Habermas, language carves out a distinct sphere of human activity, and that distinction allows for a crucial separation, variously cast as a separation between interaction and labor, between symbolic and material reproduction, between "lifeworld" and "system," or between intersubjective and subject–object relations. In each case, human emancipation for Habermas depends on not letting the instrumental rationality inherent in the realm of the latter term infect the realm of the former. As C. Fred Alford succinctly summarizes Habermas's project: the goal is "to prevent social relations from becoming like our relations with the natural world" (quoted in Eckersley 1992: 108).

Habermas's project is thus unapologetically anthropocentric. To return to the examples of environmental issues being governed by communicative rationality mentioned above, we can see that in such cases, the problematics of domination and reification are only avoidable with respect to the relations between the humans who have different views of how the environment ought to be treated. The normative principles of non-domination in fact apply only to those human actors, and not to the aspects of the non-human environment that happen to be the object of their attention. Non-instrumental rationality is grounded strongly in linguistic communication, as *the* form of human social interaction par excellence. As a result, the hope for something like a non-dominating relationship with the non-human world, which animated the works of earlier critical theorists such as Adorno and Marcuse (Vogel 1996; Biro 2005; Cook 2011), appears for Habermas to be something like a category mistake.

Can Non-human Nature Speak?

But what if Habermas's communicative turn could be pried out of its particular anthropocentric presuppositions? In other words, is a greening of the communicative turn conceivable through an expansion of the subjects of communicative rationality? While Habermas's notion of communicative rationality is clearly grounded in a specifically *human* capacity and need for intersubjective communication, it might be possible to maintain his emphasis on communication and intersubjectivity, while jettisoning its anthropocentric presuppositions.

Indeed, the roots of such a project can be seen to stretch back at least as far as Aldo Leopold's famous exploration of the possibility of "thinking like a mountain," and his injunction that human beings ought to shift their self-understanding from "conqueror of the land community to plain member and citizen of it" (Leopold 1966: 240). Bringing the non-human into the political sphere of course raises difficult problems of representation. A number of pragmatic solutions have been developed to the problem of how to represent the interests or rights of non-humans. But from a Habermasian perspective, the issue must go beyond the negative liberty of rights, or a static or objective conception of interests. The sphere of communicative action is intended to be the space that can provide a passage to freedom understood in the particular context of social beings capable of conscious self-governance. The ticket to entry therefore is not merely having interests, but more specifically having the capacities to communicate one's needs and to act based on a reflexive consideration of those needs and the articulated needs of others. It is precisely because, for Habermas, non-humans are not biologically constituted in such a way that their "needs" are flexible and culturally or discursively shaped, that their needs are incapable of being expressed intersubjectively in a meaningful way. A dog may sit by her dish with a certain look, and making a certain noise, that may effectively communicate "I need food." And I may well understand that message. But what is ruled out, for Habermas, is the possibility of intersubjective communication that allows us to negotiate the terms of satisfaction of those needs, and particularly for that negotiation to be based on the "unforced force" of rational argument.

More recently, the problem of representing the non-human in the political realm has been given new life by the "posthumanist" (or "new materialist") approach that is largely inspired by Bruno Latour's Actor-Network Theory. Jane Bennett's *Vibrant Matter*, for example, suggests: "The ethical task at hand here is to cultivate the ability to discern nonhuman vitality, to become perceptually open to it" (Bennett 2010: 14). "Agency" is expansively reinterpreted, and what had been seen as the specifically human capacity for agency is shown to be dependent on the actions of a whole host of non-human (and not always controllable by humans) actants, each "vital" in their own ways: bacteria, food, minerals, etc. For Bennett, the cultivation of this ability is similar to Adorno's negative dialectical project, which focuses on "nonidentity," or the ways in which things always exceed our conceptualizations: "objects do not go into their concepts without leaving a remainder" (Adorno 1973: 5). Immediately after Bennett defines the ethical task, she says: "In a parallel manner, Adorno's 'specific materialism' also recommends a set of practical techniques for training oneself to better detect and accept nonidentity" (Bennett 2010: 14). Bennett's book uses a variety of cases to pursue a "dogged resistance to anthropocentrism" (Bennett 2010: xvi), or to understand the ways in which non-human actants have a certain vitality. For Adorno, the negative dialectical method is intended to highlight the inadequacies of conceptual thinking, and thus the ways in which instrumental rationality necessarily entails violence: the domination of nature. Scientific progress, for Adorno (and Horkheimer), literally depends on the positing of "objects" capable of being studied, and this process of objectification (reification) necessarily entails a "forgetting" or obscuring as a being is objectified (Horkheimer and Adorno 1987: 230). New materialism, which for Bennett entails a focus on the "vitality of matter" similarly intends to draw attention to the ways in which non-human things have an agency or vitality that exceeds their human instrumentality.

Similarly, although somewhat critical of what he takes to be Adorno's "tragic or pessimistic" view (favoring a return to Marx), Steven Vogel argues for an ontology that accounts for the agency of non-humans even in "social construction[ist]" accounts of nature: "Construction—in the physical, literal sense—takes place in a real material world; it's hard work, takes effort, sometimes fails, and always turns out differently from what those who engage in it expect" (Vogel 2011: 198). While Vogel does not identify the source of this resistance or recalcitrance, and may not share Bennett or Latour's terminology, there is a similar concern with the ways in which human agency never tells the whole story. Thus one way to ask what critical theory can bring to environmental political theory (and vice versa), is to ask whether critical theory as it is currently constituted, provides the intellectual resources for the "interpret[ation] ... [of] needs, experiences and life-problems" beyond the human realm. Can we conceive of a non-dominating or non-instrumental relationship with the non-human world—a "perceptual openness" to use Bennett's term—that would allow the expression of the needs of non-humans to be heard? Even more strongly: can the Habermasian conception of communicative action be rewritten to account for the various ways in which the actions of human–non-human assemblages, and the needs of the various actants therein, are "negotiated"?

A number of attempts have been made to answer this sort of question. John Dryzek's notion of "ecological democracy" offers perhaps the most well-developed attempt to do so while remaining within a broadly Habermasian framework (Dryzek 1994). David Schlosberg develops a "systems- or community-based application," of Martha Nussbaum's "capabilities" approach to justice theorizing, grounded in the need for "integrity" (Schlosberg 2012: 174–8). Despite their differences, Schlosberg's project can be seen as an extension of Habermas's, at least insofar as it emphasizes the use of "deliberative tools" and is grounded in the discourses of environmental and climate justice movements. Latour's *Politics of Nature* (2004) uses actor-network theory to offer a different way to approach the problem of representation. Unlike Habermas, Latour does not ground ethical action in a particular—and particularly human—form of rationality. Instead, he asserts that "political ecology" (or the politics of nature) necessarily entails the mobilization of science*s* and nature*s* (plural), or "associations of beings that take complicated forms—rules, apparatuses, consumers, institutions, mores, calves, cows, pigs, broods," in inherently politicized discourses, or "matters of concern" (Latour 2004: 21–2).

Rethinking Human Nature

The risk of such an approach, however, is the potential for collapsing the distinction between human and non-human, or (living) being and (non-living) thing, completely. The flattening of those ontological distinctions, and the radical distribution of agency, risks throwing out the baby with the bathwater (Bennett 2010: 36–8).

A different path might be to take the basis for Habermas's distinction between human and non-human as important for certain political purposes, without endorsing the environmental conclusion that human–non-human relations are necessarily instrumental. The key here would be to emphasize the open-ended character of what it means to be human: a dialectical anthropology. In his Frankfurt School-inspired history of hydraulic manipulations in the American West, Donald Worster argues that the central question for environmental history should be "How, in the remaking of nature, do we remake ourselves?" (Worster 1985: 30).

If the previous section sought to ask whether the articulation of needs could be expanded beyond human beings, this section asks whether or to what extent human beings themselves can actually articulate their genuine needs. Central to the task of the critical theorist, in the quotation from Marx cited earlier, is the assumption that needs ("the struggles and wishes of the age") are not self-evident, but require clarification. Again, a central feature of first-generation Frankfurt School theorizing was an attempt to show how the totally administered societies of the mid-twentieth century (monopoly capitalism, Soviet communism, fascism) prevented the articulation of genuine needs. Trapped in a world in which societal irrationality is rationalized, in which desires are fulfilled in a way that only increases unfreedom (Marcuse's "repressive desublimation"

(Marcuse 1964: 56–83)), subjects are incapable of knowing what they really want. In the mid-twentieth century, for the Frankfurt School, perhaps the most prominent example was the working class in advanced capitalist societies. Transformations in everything from family structure to culture rendered people incapable of experiencing or desiring freedom, except in the limited form of commodity consumption. Subjectivity was "damaged" (Adorno 2005) and "cultural needs" (that is, the need for commodity consumption) "sunk down into the biological dimension" (Marcuse 1972: 20). Walter Benjamin put it most pointedly: humanity's "self-alienation has reached such a degree that it can experience its own destruction as an aesthetic pleasure of the first order" (Benjamin 1968: 242). The desire for the working class to become a "class for itself"—their need to free themselves by taking control of society's productive capacities for themselves—was dissipating in deference to authority and the shallow pleasures of mass commodity consumption. "Second nature" was so called because social forces prevented the fulfillment of more obviously immediate biological needs (despite unprecedented social wealth, the poor continued to go hungry), and because the inability to meet those needs was naturalized: not up for debate. To the extent that the remaking of nature is not seen as the remaking of ourselves, the capacity to shape who we are (including what we need) is closed off.

To be sure, compared to the mid-twentieth century, postmodern capitalism appears to offer greater choice (gone are the days of Henry Ford: "you can have any color as long as it's black"), and the Frankfurt School's Freudian psychological model has fallen out of favor. But it is far from clear that the problems identified by the Frankfurt School have been solved. Freedom is still largely confined to the ability to choose between pre-given commodities offered on the market, and between bureaucratic and ideologically similar political parties (metonymically condensed in their "leader") in periodic elections. Despite our tremendous productive capacity as a species (to the point where the geological impacts of human activity outstrip all other forces), our sense of autonomy remains highly circumscribed. This disjuncture is still maintained by obscuring our needs from ourselves.

Thus Ingolfur Blühdorn has argued that contemporary politics around issues of "sustainability" have involved "a practice of self-deception" in which we demand the "performance of seriousness" (rhetoric about "getting serious" but without actually taking serious action) (Blühdorn 2007: 267–8). This societal self-deception is necessary, Blühdorn argues, to maintain increasingly contradictory needs: the desire to reduce ecological impacts, such as greenhouse gas emissions, to sustain human civilization on the one hand, and the desire to maintain high-impact (high-emissions) forms of (consumerist) identities on the other hand. These identities are, at this point, not merely a "lifestyle choice," nor is material prosperity merely one value choice among many. Rather, these are strongly rooted cultural conceptions of the good life that, in Marcuse's terms, are effectively transformed from ("merely") cultural needs to biological ones (Marcuse 1964, 1972; see also Bauman 2000).

Somewhat similarly, Erik Swyngedouw has argued that current climate change politics represent a "post-democratic" and "post-political" consensus (Swyngedouw 2010).

For Swyngedouw (drawing on the work of Jacques Ranciere and Chantal Mouffe rather than the Frankfurt School), climate change politics are post-democratic and post-political to the extent that social cleavages are erased in the production of an elite consensus that "we are all in this together." On this view, precisely because it is a "global" threat, climate change is the kind of problem that can (and indeed, must) constitute a global society in order to be dealt with (Beck 1999). But in stark contrast to Habermas, Swyngedouw argues that "dialogical consensual practices" foreclose the possibility of "proper political choice as the agonistic confrontation of competing visions of a different socio-ecological order" (Swyngedouw 2010: 226). Political transformation on this agonistic view thus requires named subjects (for example, the proletariat for Marxism, women for feminism), whose needs are at odds with the given reality, and who are capable of articulating "great new fictions that create real possibilities for constructing different socio-environmental futures" (Swyngedouw 2010: 228).

Again, what can be seen as preventing the emergence of such a subject is an inability to articulate genuine needs that are not provided by the system as currently structured. Human needs may be flexible and malleable, but they are not infinitely plastic. But it is their evolution, and not just their fulfillment, that is in principle amenable to conscious, rational development. The promise of critical theory is that it maintains faith in the possibility, not that we can always get what we want, but that we can become the kinds of beings that we want. As Benjamin puts it, the task for human beings at this point in their evolution, is "not the mastery of nature, but the mastery of humans' relationship with nature."

Acknowledgments

Thanks to Cheryl Hall, Yogi Hendlin, Brad Mapes-Martin, and John Meyer for helpful comments on an earlier version of this chapter.

References

Adorno, Theodor W. (1973). *Negative Dialectics*. Translated by E. B. Ashton (New York: Continuum).

Adorno, Theodor W. (1984). "The Idea of Natural History." Translated by Robert Hullot-Kentor. *Telos* 60.

Adorno, Theodor W. (2005). *Minima Moralia: Reflections on a Damaged Life*. Translated by E. F. N. Jephcott (New York: Verso).

Bauman, Zygmunt. (2000). *Liquid Modernity* (Cambridge: Polity).

Beck, Ulrich. (1999). *World Risk Society* (Cambridge: Polity).

Benjamin, Walter (1968). "The Work of Art in an Age of Mechanical Reproduction." In *Illuminations*, edited by Hannah Arendt (New York: Schocken Books), 217–51.

Bennett, Jane. (2010). *Vibrant Matter: A Political Ecology of Things* (Durham, NC: Duke University Press).
Biro, Andrew. (2005). *Denaturalizing Ecological Politics: Alienation from Nature from Rousseau to the Frankfurt School and Beyond* (Toronto: University of Toronto Press).
Blühdorn, Ingolfur. (2007). "Sustaining the Unsustainable." *Environmental Politics* 16: 2.
Bottomore, Tom, ed. (1983). *A Dictionary of Marxist Thought*, 2nd edn. (Oxford: Blackwell).
Cook, Deborah. (2011). *Adorno on Nature* (Durham, UK: Acumen).
Dryzek, John S. (1994). *Discursive Democracy: Politics, Policy, and Political Science* (Cambridge: Cambridge University Press).
Eckersley, Robyn. (1992). *Environmentalism and Political Theory: Toward an Ecocentric Approach* (Albany: SUNY Press).
Foucault, Michel. (1978). *The History of Sexuality Volume 1: An Introduction*. Translated by Robert Hurley (New York: Random House).
Fraser, Nancy. (1987). "What's Critical about Critical Theory: The Case of Habermas and Gender." In *Feminism as Critique*, edited by Seyla Benhabib and Drucilla Cornell (Minneapolis: University of Minnesota Press), 31–56.
Habermas, Jürgen. (1982). "The Entwinement of Myth and Enlightenment: Re-Reading *Dialectic of Enlightenment*." *New German Critique* 26.
Habermas, Jürgen. (1990). *Moral Consciousness and Communicative Action*. Translated by Christian Lenhardt and Shierry Weber Nicholsen (Cambridge, MA: MIT Press).
Horkheimer, Max and Theodor W. Adorno. (1987). *Dialectic of Enlightenment*. Translated by John Cumming (New York: Continuum).
Latour, Bruno. (2004). *Politics of Nature: How to Bring the Sciences Into Democracy*. Translated by Catherine Porter (Cambridge, MA: Harvard University Press).
Leiss, William. (1994). *The Domination of Nature* (Montreal: McGill-Queens University Press).
Leopold, Aldo. (1966). *A Sand County Almanac* (New York: Ballantine).
Light, Andrew. (2002). "Restoring Ecological Citizenship." In *Democracy and the Claims of Nature: Critical Perspectives for a New Century*, edited by Ben Minteer and Bob Pepperman Taylor (Lanham, MD: Rowman & Littlefield), 153–72.
Light, Andrew. (2012). "The Death of Restoration?" In *Ethical Adaptation to Climate Change: Human Virtues of the Future*, edited by Allen Thompson and Jeremy Bendik-Keymer (Cambridge, MA: MIT Press), 105–21.
Marcuse, Herbert. (1964). *One-Dimensional Man* (Boston: Beacon Press).
Marcuse, Herbert. (1972). *An Essay on Liberation* (London: Penguin Books).
Marcuse, Herbert. (1992). "Ecology and the Critique of Modern Society." *Capitalism, Nature, Socialism* 3: 3.
Marx, Karl. (1975). "Letters from the *Franco-German Yearbooks*." In *Karl Marx Early Writings*. Translated by Rodney Livingstone and Gregor Benton (New York: Vintage Books), 199–209.
Marx, Karl. (1978). "Critique of the Gotha Program." In *The Marx-Engels Reader*, 2nd edn, edited by Robert C. Tucker (New York: W. W. Norton), 525–41.
Moss, Lenny and Vida Pavesich. (2011). "Science, Normativity, and Skill: Reviewing and Renewing the Anthropological Basis of Critical Theory." *Philosophy and Social Criticism* 37: 2.
Panayotakis, Costas. (2011). *Remaking Scarcity: From Capitalist Inefficiency to Economic Democracy* (London: Pluto).

Schlosberg, David. (2012). "Justice, Ecological Integrity, and Climate Change." In *Ethical Adaptation to Climate Change: Human Virtues of the Future*, edited by Allen Thompson and Jeremy Bendik-Keymer (Cambridge, MA: MIT Press), 165–83.

Swyngedouw, Erik. (2010). "Apocalypse Forever? Post-political Populism and the Spectre of Climate Change." *Theory, Culture & Society* 27(2/3): 213–32.

Vogel, Steven. (1996). *Against Nature: The Concept of Nature in Critical Theory* (Albany: SUNY Press).

Vogel, Steven. (2011). "On Nature and Alienation." In *Critical Ecologies: The Frankfurt School and Contemporary Environmental Crises*, edited by Andrew Biro (Toronto: University of Toronto Press), 187–205.

Worster, Donald. (1985). *Rivers of Empire* (Oxford: Oxford University Press).

Xenos, Nicholas. (1989). *Scarcity and Modernity* (New York: Routledge).

ENGAGING THE ACADEMY

CHAPTER 7

ENVIRONMENTAL POLITICAL THEORY, ENVIRONMENTAL ETHICS, AND POLITICAL SCIENCE

Bridging the Gap

KIMBERLY K. SMITH

ONE way to understand the field of environmental political theory (EPT) is that it attempts to bridge the gap between political science and environmental ethics. Specifically, EPT tries to correct for the limitations in both of those fields that prevent them from dealing effectively with environmental problems. On one hand, environmental ethics has made substantial progress in explaining and justifying our duties to non-human nature and expanding our conception of the moral community. But environmental ethics as a field has traditionally been limited by its focus on individual ethical choice. It doesn't have a wide range of tools for analyzing the larger social and political forces that shape environmental outcomes by structuring choice situations. On the other hand, political science is well-suited to analyzing structural forces that give rise to systems and patterns of injustice—but political scientists have had considerable difficulty in moving away from the field's anthropocentric foundations. Justice, for most political scientists, is still for humans only. Environmental political theory, in contrast, embraces the critique of anthropocentrism developed by environmental ethicists. It attempts to build theories of justice, citizenship, and political rights and duties on a more expansive understanding of the community of justice—an understanding that takes seriously our duties to non-human entities. This allows EPT to draw on concepts and theories that political scientists use to understand power, injustice, and freedom, and to apply those concepts and theories to our management of non-human entities and systems. As a result, EPT is well-positioned to foster a richer conversation between political scientists and environmental ethicists. Recent developments in environmental ethics suggest that ethicists, at least, are ready to take up that conversation. Whether political scientists will follow suit remains to be seen.

The Limits of Environmental Ethics

Environmental ethics as an academic field took shape from the early 1970s through the 1980s, when academic philosophers including Richard Sylvan, Holmes Rolston III, and J. Baird Callicott began exploring the failure of conventional ethics to account for the value of non-human entities (Sylvan 1973; Callicott 1987; Rolston 1988). Environmental ethicists drew on the work of animal liberation theorists (prominently Peter Singer (1975)) in arguing that non-human entities could have moral status, thus expanding dramatically our understanding of the moral community. In addition, philosophers such as Derek Parfit made significant contributions to this field by exploring the concept of duties to future generations (of humans or, presumably, non-humans) (Parfit 1984). The arguments developed by these ethicists inspired environmental activists and mapped much of the ethical terrain of contemporary environmental policy.

It is not too much of a generalization to say that environmental ethics in these early years largely followed conventional philosophy in focusing on individual ethical choice. One of the classic works, for example, is Richard (Routley) Sylvan's "Is There a Need for a New, an Environmental, Ethic?" (1973). Sylvan poses in that piece the famous "last man scenario": "The last man (or person) surviving the collapse of the world system lays about him, eliminating, as far as he can, every living thing, animal or plant (but painlessly, if you like, as at the best abattoirs)" (1973: 207). Sylvan uses the scenario to explore what grounds we have for thinking this man's action are wrong, even though no human is hurt by them. It's an effective way to explore our moral intuitions about our duties to non-humans. But notice also that the scenario conveniently eliminates the political, economic, and social systems in which moral choices are usually made. The last man is mysteriously empowered with vast destructive capacities that are (in the real world) characteristic of industrial systems, not individuals. To be sure, Sylvan does develop the scenario, asking next what the "last people" might do, and even inquiring about the duties of the "great entrepreneur" and "industrial society." But in doing so, he treats the community and the great entrepreneur as though they are morally responsible individuals (albeit with vastly greater power than actual individuals). The decision calculus, he implies, is the same whether it is an individual or community acting. But communities are not individuals, and "great entrepreneurs" are merely a fantasy: No single individual "runs a giant complex of automated factories and farms," as Sylvan's great entrepreneur does (208). Communities and industrial systems aren't comparable to individual moral agents, and individuals operating in these groups have very limited levels of moral agency.

Sylvan is hardly unusual among environmental ethicists in trying to "scale up" from an (artificial) individual choice situation to public policy. Derek Parfit's widely reprinted essay, "The Energy Problem and the Further Future" (1983) is also centrally concerned with how policy choices, not just individual decisions, affect future generations. Parfit, like Sylvan, begins with an individual: a nuclear technician whose laziness results in a radiation leak that kills thousands of people. That scenario in itself is problematic; if one person could cause such a catastrophe, surely the blame would lie on those who designed and ran the system. But Parfit (again like Sylvan) compounds the problem by comparing the technician's actions to the decision of a community to choose an energy policy. Indeed, Parfit and Sylvan are part of a long tradition in moral philosophy of deriving principles of public policy from individual-level ethical choices without attending to how social structures determine, limit, or facilitate moral agency. These early works in environmental ethics showed little interest in explaining why some people are in a position to make ethical choices and others are not. Nor did they explore issues of collective agency in much depth—that is, how, and how far, a group of individuals can come to bear moral responsibility for consequences resulting from group processes.

A major exception to this generalization is feminist environmental ethics (or eco-feminist ethics). Like other feminist scholars, environmental ethicists such as Ynestra King (1989), Val Plumwood (1993), and Karen Warren (2000) focus on *structural* injustice rather than simply individual choice. Of course, eco-feminism is too big and diverse a field to canvass here; suffice to say that eco-feminist scholars start from the premise that there are complex interconnections—causal, conceptual, theoretical, experiential, and political—between the domination of women and the domination of nature (Warren 2000). Under this view, environmental ethics (like feminist ethics) has an important political dimension; it aims at liberating both humans and non-humans from oppressive social practices and structures. Thus, many eco-feminists embrace a theory of social change that begins with personal transformation but manifests in political action aimed at opposing or supporting particular policies. King, for example, cites anti-military protests at the United States' Pentagon in the early 1980s as an example of eco-feminist praxis (1989: 25). As a result of this perspective, eco-feminists have had more to say about the traditional concerns of political scientists than did the early environmental ethicists.

Nevertheless, eco-feminist ethical analyses have not entirely bridged the gap between ethics and political science; they remain largely focused on individual-level ethical choice. One example will serve to illustrate the point: Deborah Slicer's excellent eco-feminist analysis of the issue of animal research shows that the utilitarian and Kantian approaches taken by Peter Singer and Tom Regan fail to appreciate the complexities of the issue; a feminist ethic of care would provide better guidance in navigating the competing values at risk in this policy area. But she, like Singer and Regan, still approaches the subject from an individual perspective, asking what an ethical individual should think about animal research (rather than what institutions and practices would help us better to attend to the morally relevant issues in animal research) (1991). Despite their interest in structural injustice, eco-feminists thus far have not given much attention to reforming specific institutional arrangements or to questions of collective agency. Thus, most eco-feminist as well as non-feminist environmental ethics are subject to the following two critiques:

First, individual ethics cannot simply be "scaled up" and turned into public laws. Public policy is not individual moral duty writ large. To take a simple example, you may have a duty not to lie to your friend, but this doesn't mean the government is justified in penalizing lying to one's friends. Similarly, you may have a private moral duty not to kill a whale or cut down an ancient forest, but that doesn't necessarily mean the government is justified in penalizing such departures from individual moral rectitude.

The proper extent of government power is of course a fundamental question in political theory. Whether the government is justified in enforcing individual moral obligations depends on one's theory of the proper role and function of the state. Liberal governments, for example, are supposed to be limited governments. Out of respect for individual moral autonomy, liberal governments are expected to leave the individual a substantial amount of freedom to make independent moral judgments. They therefore follow some version of the "harm principle": They penalize only individual behavior that interferes with or harms other (human) individuals. Of course, contemporary political scientists are right to point out that public policy does much more than that. It may not dictate individual moral choices in all cases, but it does structure the choice environment. All policy decisions end up making some choices easier and others harder. Traditional ethical analysis has an important role to play in informing policymakers' decisions about which choices to favor or disfavor. Nevertheless, the fact remains that ethicists usually analyze moral choice at the moment the individual faces an actual choice. Political scientists are more likely to focus on how larger political structures—institutions, laws, and practices—edit and organize choices for the individual, and how far that choice-editing function should go (Thaler, Sunstein, and Balz 2010; Sunstein 2013). Which moral principles can the government enforce, which ones should it simply encourage or make easy, and which ones should be left entirely to individuals' independent judgment?

Second, environmental ethicists traditionally don't give adequate attention to *collective* choice—mechanisms for aggregating individual decisions and organizing collectivities that are capable of making responsible choices. Political scientists don't assume that a community can simply be substituted for the individual in Sylvan's scenario. Rather, they would be interested in identifying who is actually determining policy in that community and how the people in power maintain control. Who is included in these collectivities, who has or should have power, and whose voices should be heard? And they are also interested in the implementation of collective choice: what practices and institutions are necessary for public choices to be carried out effectively and fairly? More generally, what sorts of arrangements are necessary for a community to "act" in a morally relevant way? These questions have important ethical dimensions, to be sure, but they are also questions of organizational design and administration.

In short, environmental ethicists know how to analyze a question like "what is a morally defensible individual choice concerning biodiversity preservation?" Political scientists know how to analyze a question like "under what conditions, with what civic education and institutional arrangements, will a political community come up with and carry out a morally defensible policy concerning biodiversity preservation?"

The Limits of Political Science

Among political scientists, it has been the role of political theorists to explore the second kind of question—call them "politico-ethical questions." One role of political theory is to develop theories of justice, freedom, representation, citizenship, and related concepts that will help political scientists answer such questions as what the government (and citizens) may do to realize moral values and how citizens' moral character and behavior is shaped by political institutions. Unfortunately, the theories of justice that dominate conventional political theory are not well-suited to answering questions about environmental policy. Their chief problem is that conventional political science relies on too simple a model of the non-human world. Generally, the theories used by political scientists follow economists in modeling non-human entities as a collection of inert resources that human actors can use, manipulate, and interpret at will. Humans are agents and the primary causal factors; nature is simply acted upon. This view is reflected in the widely used textbook by Tietenberg and Lewis, *Environmental Economics and Policy*: "In economics the environment is viewed as a composite asset that provides a variety of services" (2010: 15). The text remains true to that conceptualization: It teaches that natural resource policy should be based on general principles that apply in the same way to fisheries as they do to forests or cattle. It advises us to identify the human stakeholders with an interest in the resource; assume human actors will rationally pursue their economic interests; and design policy tools to put the proper incentives in place to get the behavioral outcome you want (from the humans involved). The leading political science texts on environmental policy take the same approach. For example, Norman Vig and Michael Kraft's *Environmental Policy* (now in its ninth edition), consistently treats the environment as a collection of natural resources. The essays in that text pay more attention than do Tietenberg and Lewis to how large-scale political systems shape individual resource extraction behavior (Vig and Kraft 2013). But all of these conventional analytic approaches fail to consider the possibility that humans may have different kinds of moral duties toward fish, forest, and cattle; that forests and fish behave very differently in response to human actions; or that these non-human entities may be actors in their own right.

The political scientists' oversimplified model of non-human nature is replicated in most conventional theories of justice. For example, Robert Nozick's subjects don't have to deal with the complexity of actual natural resources or the intransigence of non-human animals; they simply buy and sell "holdings" (1974). Bruce Ackerman similarly develops his theory of justice by imagining a world where the only natural resource is a substance he calls "manna"—an infinitely divisible and malleable substance that can be made into anything we want (1981). John Rawls also has little to say about how the characteristics of non-human nature might affect his theory of justice. Most famously, he declines to consider whether we may have duties of justice to non-human animals (2005: 21). Andrew Dobson notes that Amartya Sen also has spent a career studying poverty without developing any theoretical perspective at all on the natural environment (1998: 133).

This tendency to simplify the natural world isn't universal, of course. Dobson notes that Michael Walzer is an exception to this generalization; his theory of justice does posit that the social meaning of the things being distributed affect the principles governing their distribution (Walzer 1983; Dobson 1998: 76). Jeremy Waldron also suggests in his writings on property theory that property rights might be defined with reference to the thing that is owned—so that different rules might govern property in critical wetlands, in ideas, in the atmosphere, in the oceans, or in the Arctic (1988: 30). Those theories invite us to bring into view the actual physical and moral complexity of the natural world—but even these theories tend to model non-human nature as composed of discrete objects, passively awaiting our attention.

In contrast, the environmental sciences give us a much different model of non-human nature: For natural scientists, the planet is a collection of extremely dynamic and interrelated systems and stochastic processes. It is not simply acted upon; it acts upon us in return. When we combine that understanding with the view from environmental ethics, we see more complexity: Non-human nature also includes beings with varying kinds of moral status. Rather than modeling all of non-human nature as interchangeable, inert resources, environmental policy must account for the possibility that forests, cattle, and fish might have different moral statuses, which in turn might depend on cultural norms that develop in ecological context. Non-human entities also may be expected to behave in different ways in response to human actions. Some animals will develop relationships with humans; others will not. Forests, watersheds, and tornadoes may stubbornly refuse to act in any predictable way. Conventional political science doesn't even attempt to model these different responses, much less the dynamic interactions among cultural norms, social structures, and ecological systems. If environmental ethics and environmental science are to inform environmental policy, then the way political scientists model socio-ecological systems has to incorporate those understandings.

In short, as theorist Bruno Latour put it, political theory, in the environmental age, "abruptly finds itself confronted with the obligation to internalize the environment that it had viewed up to now as another world" (2004: 58). Instead of bracketing off non-human nature, we must consider how humans and non-humans are interconnected—and we must model those connections.

Environmental Political Theory

In fact, by the time Latour made that observation, environmental political theorists were already attempting to bridge the gap between environmental ethics and political science. I won't attempt to survey the whole history of environmental political theory here, but focus on a few examples.

One question environmental political theorists attend to is the relationship between eco-centrism and traditional anthropocentric political theories. For example, Robyn Eckersley's 1992 work *Environmentalism and Political Theory* focuses on how eco-centrism challenges the political theories contributing to Green ideology: Marxism, post-Marxist socialism, critical theory, and anarchism. This work engages broad philosophical questions—notably, Marx's conception of human nature and humans' relationship to the natural world—but Eckersley's immediate, practical objective is to elucidate how best to incorporate eco-centrism more centrally into Green politics—that is, to bridge the gap between eco-centric ethics and political practice. She concludes that the best strategy for doing so is to expand democratic socialism's traditional concern with respect for all persons to include non-human entities. She also points toward institutional reforms that would "democratize society at large by gradually breaking down excessive concentrations of political and economic power"—reforms that include both shifting power up to international democratic decision-making bodies and down to democratic local governments (1992: 182–3).

That attempt to consider what environmental ethics means for political practice is also a goal of Andrew Dobson's scholarship. For example, his 1998 work, *Justice and the Environment*, is offered as a guide to citizens and policymakers wondering how pursuing sustainability can be made compatible with the goal of social justice. His interest here is not merely philosophical consistency but political legitimacy: Policies that promote sustainability without attending to distributive justice may meet serious, and legitimate, resistance. His exploration of the relationship(s) between justice and sustainability thus occupies the "midrange" territory between abstract philosophical systems and specific policies—the territory traditionally occupied by political theorists.

Dobson argues that advocates for sustainability challenge traditional theories of distributive justice, first, by expanding our understanding of what is being distributed. In place of Ackerman's infinitely malleable manna, we must consider how to "distribute" environmental goods. Our theories of justice must come to grip with goods that cannot be physically distributed (like natural wonders), goods that are actually complex dynamic systems (like the climate system), and goods that have moral status (like animals). Different kinds of goods, he suggests, should be governed by different kinds of principles.

Second, advocates for sustainability attempt to expand the community of justice beyond its traditional bounds. They call for justice among a global (not just national) community; they call for justice to future generations; and many of them call for justice to non-human nature. All of these extensions create not only theoretical challenges but political and institutional challenges. Dobson, however, postpones investigating those challenges, concluding merely that the relationship between sustainability and social justice is a complex and contingent one, leading him to suggest a "long-term programme of empirical research aimed at clarifying the social, economic, and ecological circumstances under which social injustice is a cause of environmental unsustainability"

(1998: 244). Such a research agenda would go a long way toward bridging the gap between environmental ethicists' concern with our duties to future generations and political scientists' concern with building just institutions.

David Schlosberg's *Defining Environmental Justice* (2007), in contrast, has pursued a different empirical agenda: investigating the concept of "justice" being developed by advocates for environmental justice. Schlosberg, too, is concerned not only with theory in itself but its relation to political practice. Thus his question is: what conception of justice can bring together the environmental justice and the more traditional environmental protection movements? Schlosberg's analysis takes us beyond the conventional, anthropocentric theories of distributive justice that Dobson was focusing on. Drawing on the work of Nancy Fraser, Axel Honneth, Iris Young, and Martha Nussbaum, he offers an expanded conception of justice as involving not only distribution of goods but recognition of identity, participation in decision-making, and protection of capabilities—and his empirical findings show how this richer understanding of justice can apply (and is applied) to both humans and non-human entities. In short, he examines how anthropocentric theories of justice might be transformed to apply to a broader community of justice and also how such theories might be deployed effectively in environmental politics.

But what sort of political institutions would a more eco-centric concept of justice entail? That's the question taken up by Robyn Eckersley in *The Green State* (2004). Eckersley notes that the concept of the state used by political scientists has a normative foundation; it is typically grounded on the liberal value of individual autonomy, a value that determines the role and function of a legitimate state. Her question is what a "green state" would look like: What if we placed the state on a normative foundation informed by critical political ecology—that is, a normative theory that aims at the emancipation of the human and non-human world? (2004: 8–9). In making this move from eco-centric ethics to practical politics, she offers the following principle: "All those potentially affected by a risk should have some meaningful opportunity to participate or otherwise be represented in the making of the policies or decisions that generate the risk" (2004: 111). That principle, extended to include future generations and non-human entities, gives rise to political and institutional reforms aimed at better representation of the interests of those who cannot speak for themselves. Eckersley draws on the rich theoretical and empirical literature on deliberative democracy and on representation to imagine what an eco-centric politics might look like. Beyond simply expanding the variety of interests considered in policy deliberation, she suggests that these new practices would embody a new rationality and a new normative purpose for the state. The green state is imagined not merely as a means to realize individual autonomy but as an "ecological steward and facilitator of transboundary democracy" (2004: 3).

These examples demonstrate how environmental political theory aims to inform political practice and institutional reform, thus speaking directly to the central concerns of political scientists. Unfortunately, political science as a field has thus far proved resistant to these ideas—in spite of the fact that the field of EPT was developed primarily by political theorists. Within the United States, for example, the Western Political Science Association remains the only political science association with a section on environmental political theory. The *American Political Science Review* (APSR) (the flagship American political science journal) has not published a single article on environmental political theory; instead, the influence of EPT in the pages of that journal has been at best indirect. For example, John Dryzek—one of the leading environmental political theorists—has published twice in the APSR since 2000. His 2008 article on discursive representation has direct relevance to the EPT project of expanding our conceptual tools for reconceptualizing political institutions. Dryzek and his co-author Simon Niemeyer propose a "Chamber of Discourses" in which different discourses (as opposed to persons or interests) could find a hearing. Several of their examples make it clear that this sort of institution could help ensure that non-human interests are represented in public deliberation. But they carefully avoid centering the argument on those examples. Rather, this institutional innovation is offered as a solution to problems of representing human communities (Dryzek and Niemeyer 2008). The article illustrates how environmental political theory might influence mainstream political science, but it also evinces a healthy respect for the field's suspicion of eco-centric language. Indeed, Dryzek himself notes in his 2006 APSR article on the history of American political science, "many have tried to change the character of American political science, but few have succeeded" (2006: 487). His review of those attempts doesn't even mention environmental political theory, suggesting that it has had thus far very little influence in the United States.

The influence of EPT on political science outside the United States, however, may be greater, considering that many of the leading theorists in this subfield hail from Australia, Canada, Europe, and the United Kingdom. Stronger Green parties in those regions also provide a more promising political environment for theorizing about eco-centric political practice. But even outside of the United States, environmental political theorists seem inclined to avoid eco-centric language when speaking to mainstream political scientists. Robyn Eckersley, for example, published an article in the British *Review of International Studies* in 2007 that focused on how the political culture of democratic national communities might be transformed to generate wider loyalties that serve wider communities in space and time. That project clearly grows out of her argument for ecological democracy in *The Green State*—but, like Dryzek, she carefully avoids bringing eco-centric language into her argument. Aside from an unexpected reference to Mary Midgeley, there is nothing in the article that would mark Eckersley as an environmentalist. This stealth strategy may help open political science to new ways of thinking about political community and the role of government, but whether it will transform the foundational assumptions of the field remains to be seen.

Happily, the conversation between environmental ethics and environmental political theory has been more robust. Several environmental ethicists are beginning to take a closer look at questions of collective agency and responsibility. A good example is the 2012 collection by ethicists Allen Thompson and Jeremy Bendik-Keymer, *Ethical Adaptation to Climate Change* (2012). Allen and Bendik-Keymer argue in their introduction that the field (environmental ethics) must move beyond its "overly private or individualistic focus" and examine "the way our individual lives are enmeshed in and constrained by institutions, including the ways we organize our lives and our politics" ("Introduction," 2012: 11). Bendik-Keymer's essay "The Sixth Mass Extinction is Caused by Us" elaborates: "As a matter of virtue . . . we shouldn't expect people to be saints. My worry about focusing on the 'who we are' question . . . is that we risk moralism and miss morality's complex relation to its organizational context and to our human nature. Sometimes, the problem is not *who* we are, but *where* and *how* we are" (2012: 273). In particular, he points to the bureaucratically organized world whose economic and political systems make it hard to address issues such as mass extinction. Instead, he suggests, "We have to reorganize our institutions to enable human virtue" (2012: 276).

Similarly, Steven Vogel's essay "Alienation and the Commons" takes up the collective action problem inherent in reducing pollution--that is, the fact each individual actor might rationally conclude that her own efforts will have no significant impact on the problem. The solution, he concludes, does not lie in encouraging individual virtue, because the problem is not a failure of individual virtue. We are not greedy or wanton. We simply don't have political structures in place that help us to act together (2012: 310). He therefore turns to political theorist Iris Marion Young for a solution. He finds useful Young's argument that we need a common politics that allows us to share responsibility for environmental problems: a democratic, deliberative process that would allow us to develop a communal consensus about what we ought to do (2012: 311). These essays should not be taken as a sign that ethicists are abandoning their focus on individual moral choice, or that environmental ethics and EPT will eventually merge into one field. But they do open the door for a richer conversation between environmental ethics and environmental political theory.

We can only hope that political science will eventually take greater notice of these developments and begin a deeper conversation with environmental political theory. Global environmental issues call for not only new modes of ethical thinking but innovative political institutions and practices founded on a broad conception of the biotic community. EPT is well-positioned to lead that effort.

References

Ackerman, B. (1981). *Social Justice in the Liberal State* (New Haven: Yale University Press).

Bendik-Keymer, J. (2012). "The Sixth Mass Extinction is Caused by Us." In *Ethical Adaptation to Climate Change*, edited by A. Thompson and J. Bendik-Keymer (Cambridge: MIT Press), 263–80.

Callicott, J. B., ed. (1987). *Companion to a Sand County Almanac* (Madison: University of Wisconsin Press).

Dobson, A. (1998). *Justice and the Environment* (Oxford: Oxford University Press).

Dryzek, J. (2006). "Revolutions without Enemies: Key Transformations in Political Science." *American Political Science Review* 100(4): 487–92.

Dryzek, J. and Niemeyer, S. (2008). "Discursive Representation." *American Political Science Review* 102(4): 481–93.

Eckersley, R. (1992). *Environmentalism and Political Theory* (Albany: State University of New York Press).
Eckersley, R. (2004). *The Green State* (Cambridge: MIT Press).
Eckersley, R. (2007). "From Cosmopolitan Nationalism to Cosmopolitan Democracy." *Review of International Studies* 33(4): 675–91.
King, Y. (1989). "The Ecology of Feminism and the Feminism of Ecology." In *Radical Environmentalism*, edited by P. List (Belmont, CA: Wadsworth Publishing Co) (First published in *Healing the Wounds*, edited by J. Plant (Philadelphia, PA: New Society Publishers), 18–28.
Latour, B. (2004). *Politics of Nature* (Cambridge: Harvard University Press).
Nozick, R. (1974). *Anarchy, State, and Utopia* (New York: Basic Books).
Parfit, D. (1983). "Energy Policy and the Further Future: The Identity Problem." In *Energy and the Future*, edited by D. Maclean and P. Brown (Totowa, NJ: Rowman and Littlefield).
Parfit, D. (1984). *Reasons and Persons* (Oxford: Clarendon Press).
Plumwood, V. (1993) *Feminism and the Mastery of Nature* (London: Routledge Press).
Rawls, J. (2005). *Political Liberalism*, expanded edn. (New York: Columbia University Press).
Rolston, H. (1988). *Environmental Ethics* (Philadelphia: Temple University Press.)
Schlosberg, D. (2007). *Defining Environmental Justice* (Oxford: Oxford University Press).
Singer, P. (1975). *Animal Liberation* (New York: HarperCollins).
Slicer, D. (1991). "Your Daughter or Your Dog: A Feminist Assessment of the Animal Research Issue." *Hypatia* 6(1):108–24.
Sunstein, C. (2013) "Behavioral Economics, Consumption, and Environmental Protection." Regulatory Policy Program Working Paper RPP-2013-19. Cambridge, MA: Mossavar-Rahmani Center for Business and Government, Harvard Kennedy School, Harvard University.
Sylvan (Routley), R. (1973). "Is There a Need for a New, an Environmental Ethic?" *Proceedings of the 15th World Congress of Philosophy*, 1: 205–10 (Sophia: Sophia Press).
Thaler, R., Sunstein, C., and Balz, J. (2010) "Choice Architecture." Available at SSRN: http://ssrn.com/abstract=1583509 or http://dx.doi.org/10.2139/ssrn.1583509
Tietenberg, T. and Lewis, L. (2010). *Environmental Economics and Policy*, 6th edn. (Boston: Pearson Education).
Thompson, A. and Bendik-Keymer, J. (2012). "Introduction: Adapting Humanity." In *Ethical Adaptation to Climate Change*, edited by A. Thompson and J. Bendik-Keymer (Cambridge: MIT Press), 1–23.
Vogel, S. (2012). "Alienation and the Commons." In *Ethical Adaptation to Climate Change*, edited by A. Thompson and J. Bendik-Keymer (Cambridge: MIT Press), 299–315.
Vig, N. and Kraft, M., eds. (2013). *Environmental Policy: New Directions for the 21st Century* (Washington, DC: CQ Press).
Waldron, J. (1988). *The Right to Private Property* (Oxford: Clarendon Books).
Walzer, M. (1983). *Spheres of Justice* (New York: Basic Books).
Warren, K. (2000). *Ecofeminist Philosophy* (Lanham: Rowman and Littlefield Publishers).

CHAPTER 8

ENVIRONMENTAL POLITICAL THEORY'S CONTRIBUTION TO SUSTAINABILITY STUDIES

SEATON PATRICK TARRANT
AND LESLIE PAUL THIELE

INTRODUCTION

THE development of environmental political theory (EPT) and sustainability studies (SS) education were common reactions to the growing recognition of environmental limits and interdependence. In 1977 William Ophuls published his now classic challenge to liberal democratic responses to ecological problems. That same year, the delegates at the Tbilisi intergovernmental conference on environmental education (sponsored by UNESCO and the United Nations Environmental Program) refined the three primary goals of what became the basis of sustainability pedagogy:

- to foster clear awareness of, and concern about, economic, social, political, and ecological interdependence in urban and rural areas
- to provide every person with opportunities to acquire the knowledge, values, attitudes, commitment, and skills needed to protect and improve the environment
- to create new patterns of behavior of individuals, groups, and society as a whole toward the environment. (Monroe et al. 2007: 206)

Over the ensuing years, both the academic field of sustainability and public concern for sustainability saw considerable growth. To some degree, the increasing focus on sustainability displaced environmental discourse. By the mid-1990s Douglas Torgerson (1995: 10) could observe that "public discussion concerning the environment has become a discourse of sustainability." Likewise, in academia sustainability studies grew markedly and, to some degree, displaced established environmental studies curricula.

Today EPT remains relatively unknown in the public eye, a specialty subfield of political theory that also includes representatives from other social science and humanities disciplines. In contrast, sustainability is now a vibrant part of public discourse, and students increasingly seek out courses and degree programs focused on sustainability. Indeed, SS is one of the fastest growing curricular developments at US colleges and universities.[1]

Of course, the words *sustainable* or *sustainability* are deployed in sundry ways and have accumulated diverse meanings both in academia and the public realm. Their widespread use is not, in itself, a particularly positive development. Certainly it does not indicate an equally widespread set of meaningful practices. Moreover, vast amounts of corporate and governmental *greenwashing* occur under the cover of sustainability. In this respect, however, *sustainability* fares no better or worse than *democracy* or any of a number of terms that are germane to political theory. As John Dryzek (1997) reminds us, it is not unusual for important concepts to be contested politically, or to have multiple definitions and uses. Sustainability appears to merit the designation, along with democracy, as an "essentially contested concept." As William Connolly (1974) maintains, such concepts can facilitate productive dialogue amongst stakeholders, including those who see themselves as antagonists.

We conceptualize sustainability as adaptive art, wedded to science, in service to an ethical vision. It entails satisfying current needs without sacrificing future wellbeing through the balanced pursuit of ecological health, economic welfare, social empowerment, and cultural creativity. Sustainability involves managing the rate and scale of change within a system, defined by its interdependencies, in a manner that conserves core values and relationships (Thiele 2013).

And yet, to say that sustainability entails *managing* the rate and scale of change within social and ecological systems is not to suggest that it demands a heavy-handed approach. At times, and in certain places, the best management practice for a system—that is, the practice that best ensures its conservation—may be a hands-off orientation that leaves it to its own devices. Whatever the intrusiveness of the practice, the management of ecological, economic, and social interdependencies is necessarily tentative and adaptive, grounded both locally and globally in lived relationships of caretaking and "safe to fail" experimentation. This understanding of sustainability as an adaptive art, wedded to science, in service to an ethical vision bears on the issue of its pedagogy and its relationship to EPT.

What sort of impact has EPT had on sustainability studies? To answer this question we first performed a content analysis of 99 SS syllabi. All of these syllabi represent courses offered towards fulfillment of an undergraduate degree in sustainability or sustainable development.[2] These courses are diverse in their focus and discipline, and many are interdisciplinary. The plurality, about 43 percent, includes courses in the social sciences or humanities.[3] The syllabi were coded for assigned readings, and checked against our list of 136 EPT and EPT-related authors.[4] A total of 399 authors are cited in these SS syllabi, including nine EPT authors.[5] That is to say, despite the strong social science and humanities focus in these syllabi, only 2.25 percent of the authors that appear as required readings on sustainability syllabi are environmental political theorists.

The non-EPT authors that are most prominent are primarily associated (in order of decreasing frequency) with Journalism (for example, Michael Pollan, Bill McKibben, Richard Heinberg), English (for example, Wendell Berry), the Natural Sciences (for example, Garret Hardin, Rachel Carson, Will Steffen), and Systems Thinking (for example, Meadows et al.).

As environmental political theorists, we were surprised by these findings. How to account for them? It may be that much EPT simply goes unnoticed by educators in sustainability programs. Or, it may be that sustainability educators are aware of EPT, but seldom select it for their courses, deeming it inappropriate or unhelpful. As we did not conduct surveys or interviews of sustainability educators to determine their rationale for text selection, we cannot definitively address the reason for the relative neglect of EPT in SS. For now, we use our finding as an empirical point of departure from which to consider a practical question: Despite the relative absence of EPT authors within the assigned readings of these sustainability programs, to what extent do the pedagogical practices of EPT align with those of SS?

Obviously, the readings that sustainability educators assign, including those they write themselves, have a significant impact on students. But teachers are not only, or even primarily, public educators by way of their roles as authors and formulators of reading lists. Their strongest and most enduring impact on students likely occurs in the classroom. Here the skills of citizenship find their first opportunity for instantiation. That is to say, it is in the classroom and in the quality of the course assignments that sustainability *thought* has the greatest opportunity to be transformed into sustainability *practice*.

The UN-commissioned expert literature review of sustainability education for the Decade of Education for Sustainable Development (DESD 2005–14) highlights sustainability education's commitment to learning outcomes that include the gaining of a specific set of skills, in addition to a specific body of knowledge. These skills include the ability to a) ask critical questions, b) clarify one's own values, c) envision more positive and sustainable futures, d) think systematically, e) respond through applied learning, and e) explore the dialectic between tradition and innovation (Tillbury 2011: 8). Arjen Wals (2012: 10), professor and UNESCO chair in social learning and sustainable development, identifies four distinct lenses for this type of skills-based education: a) an integrative lens that allows for a holistic perspective, b) a critical lens that questions taken-for-granted patterns, c) a transformative lens that moves from simple awareness raising to empowering change, and d) a contextual lens that embeds the values of pluralism in learning.

With this in mind, we set out to discern the similarities and differences between a collection of EPT course syllabi and the SS syllabi we had already coded. We collected 102 syllabi from subscribers to a prominent EPT listserv, and from a list of syllabi posted on a prominent EPT website. We then coded these, alongside the 99 SS syllabi, for reference to skills-based, experiential education.

By skills-based, experiential education, we are not referring to the training of students for specific careers. It is not, in this respect, a technical training. Rather, we are referring

Table 8.1 Civic Skills Framework

Critical Thinking Skills	Communication and Collaboration Skills
The ability to assess the accuracy, relevance, and reliability of different types and sources of information and evidence	The ability to communicate effectively in diverse social situations
The ability to evaluate the clarity, consistency, and credibility of claims and arguments and the stated or unstated assumptions or convictions upon which they rest	The ability to cooperate and collaborate on shared tasks and engage in collective decision-making processes
The disposition of ongoing creative and curious interaction with information, evidence, and perspectives	The ability to create and learn through interactive engagement in the world

to the tradition of skill development that originates in Socrates' modeling of the critical and deliberative thinker, and is further developed in Aristotle's discussion on the discerning and participating citizen. John Dewey adapted this tradition of participative pedagogy for a modern, democratic age. We see sustainability educators as furthering the Deweyan project of democratic education, updated for an ecological age.

Skills-based education for sustainable societies, we suggest, is best viewed as emerging from the challenges and successes associated with civics education in an ecologically precarious world. It is aimed at the development of resilient societies grounded in adaptive learning. We endorse this pedagogy based on its prevalence in the contemporary sustainability education literature, its prominence within the liberal arts tradition, its democratic and Deweyan impulse, and our own positive experiences practicing such a pedagogy in and out of the classroom. Table 8.1 summarizes the basic skills.[6]

Students practice critical thinking when they interrogate the conceptual and normative foundations, assumptions, and implications of different arguments, perspectives, and actions, including their own. Critical thinking prepares students for cutting through faulty arguments, misleading rhetoric, and illegitimate assumptions, and for maintaining an inquisitive disposition (Facione 1990). We found that 23 percent of SS syllabi and 16 percent of EPT syllabi explicitly reference critical thinking. In both SS and EPT syllabi, critical thinking skills were primarily developed through student engagement with the literature, and also took the form of "critical thinking questions," assigned at various points in the semester. Critical thinking is often developed and deployed by way of textual analysis and the formulation of argumentative essays.

It is likely that many teachers who do not explicitly mention critical thinking in their syllabi value this skill highly and would claim to develop it in their students. However, research on critical thinking in college classrooms demonstrates that while the vast majority of professors assert the importance of critical thinking (89 percent), very few actually teach for it on any given day (9 percent) (Elder 2014, referencing Arum and Roska 2011 and Paul, Elder, and Bartell 1997). With this in mind, we assume that those teachers *most* committed to developing the skill of critical thinking in their classrooms also include reference to it in their syllabi.

Relatedly, communication and collaboration skills hold significant and ongoing roles within both EPT and SS. Twenty-nine percent of EPT syllabi and 34 percent of SS syllabi reference communication skills. Eleven percent of EPT syllabi and 31 percent of SS syllabi reference collaboration skills. The fact that EPT classrooms place more emphasis on communication skills than collaboration skills (compared to SS classrooms), suggests that many of the EPT student presentations are individual efforts, rather than the culmination of group collaboration. In the SS syllabi, collaboration and communication skills were more often linked via a small student group project that culminated in a presentation to the class.[7]

Environmental political theorists have long worked on expanding theories of democratic communication and action to address ecological interdependence (for example, Dryzek 1995; Dobson 2010). Also, the communication and collaboration skills required for managing the rate and scale of change of social and natural systems are prevalent in the literature that is common to both EPT and SS. For example, reacting to Garrett Hardin's (1968) work on the tragedy of the commons, Elinor Ostrom's (1990, 1998) Nobel Prize winning research concentrates on the processes by which common (pool) resources can be collectively sustained with the minimum impingement upon individual rights.

It must be assumed, however, that a student's critical reading of literature addressing the importance of collaboration and collective action does not on its own adequately develop the skills required for active citizenship. Aristotle affirmed that virtues are developed less through their conceptual understanding than their worldly practice. The same is true of skills. Educators who wish to give students the opportunity to develop sustainability skills must move beyond the discussion of required readings, toward opportunities for experiential education in the classroom and, through course assignments, on campus and in the local community.

This sort of skills development aligns with an understudied but vital component of sustainability: *adaptive learning* (Diduck 1999; Armitage et al. 2008; Diduck et al. 2012). Adaptive learning involves the cycle of experimenting in "safe to fail" ways, monitoring feedback, and adjusting before experimenting again. It entails navigating human relationships and designing built environments and socio-political systems with the recognition that change is inevitable in a dynamic environment. Pursuing sustainability in such environments is a matter of refining responsiveness and engaging in adaptive innovation. In this regard, a sustainable society is largely defined by its resilience.

Resilience is the capacity to respond to change not just flexibly, but with the benefits of learning, such that the intellectual and experiential capacity for adaptation is developed in real time (Lovins and Lovins 1982). Much the way Dewey described the democratic challenge so many years ago, citizens today are faced with the task of adaptive learning. Dewey emphasized deep engagement with one's environment, awareness of one's interdependence with that environment, and commitment to socially cultivating the greatest possible number of responses to a given situation. Dewey's (1898) reconciliation of ethics and evolution planted the seeds of what would become his democratic project of lifelong learning:

> [M]an is an organ of the cosmic process in effecting its *own* progress. This progress consists essentially in making over a part of the environment by relating it more intimately to the environment as a whole; not, once more, in man setting himself against that environment . . . The environment is now distinctly a social one, and the content of the term "fit" has to be made with reference to social adaptation . . . A part of his fitness will consist in that very flexibility which enables him to adjust himself without too much loss to sudden and unexpected changes in his surroundings. So far as the progressive varieties are concerned, it is not in the least true that they simply adapt themselves to current conditions; evolution is a continued development of new conditions which are better suited to the needs of organisms than the old. (Dewey 1975, vol. 5: 52)

While Dewey does not employ the language of sustainability, his focus on adaptive learning well captures its mandate of fostering social resilience.

For EPT and SS educators who are committed to something like Dewey's project, the lynchpin of skills education is experiential learning. In its most basic form, experiential learning might include an assignment that involves students keeping track of their personal food or energy consumption or waste production outside of class. Students might interview or otherwise interact with local non-profits or environmental activist groups, and local stakeholders or community leaders. Alternatively, they might collaborate via the Internet with students in another part of the world, or design educational materials for younger students that are specific to their community context. In such cases, students relate much of the literature they are reading to these practical experiences.[8]

While 32 percent of SS syllabi involve an experiential component, only 8 percent of the EPT syllabi indicate experiential learning. EPT's lack of experiential learning opportunities is mirrored in its lack of trandisciplinary pedagogy. The more familiar term, *interdisciplinary*, involves the inclusion and integration of concepts and methods from different academic disciplines. In contrast, *transdisciplinary* refers to the inclusion and integration through mutual learning processes of values and knowledge from various sectors of society at large into the production of knowledge (Posch and Scholtz 2005). In classroom practice, evidence of transdisciplinary learning includes the incorporation of off campus guest speakers, and students working with and interviewing experts and stakeholders from the local community. Similar to our findings regarding experiential learning, while 27 percent of SS syllabi exhibit transdisciplinary pedagogy only 7 percent of EPT syllabi do so.

Lastly, we coded syllabi for reference to systems thinking. Systems thinking is a basic capacity for recognizing and understanding complex adaptive systems in terms of their boundaries, drivers, adaptive processes, and the direct and indirect interactions of their component parts. It involves coordinating a diversity of knowledge forms to grapple with multi-variable cause and effect relationships, intricate feedback loops, and emergent behavior, as well as the "mental models" that guide our beliefs and assumptions about the systems with which we interact (Gunderson and Holling 2001). Examples of this adaptive skill at work include learners choosing the scale at which they define and investigate particular systems and problems, and group projects that work to find effective leverage points for change (Meadows 1999). For example, Bell and Morse (2010) have developed an exercise called Rich Picture Deliberation. This participatory exercise organizes students toward framing issues and brainstorming solutions for complex social-ecological problems by assigning student groups the collective task of visually mapping the components involved in various systems and their interrelationships.

Systems thinking might be viewed as a distant relative of the critical thinking that Socrates modeled 2500 years ago, which the liberal arts and sciences have been teaching for the last few centuries. In systems thinking, the interrogation of conceptual and normative foundations, assumptions, and implications of different arguments, perspectives, and actions that constitutes the hallmark of critical thinking gets placed within an ecological framework. This allows for the understanding of complex adaptive systems by coordinating a diversity of knowledge forms, self-reflectively analyzing the mental models that guide beliefs and assumptions about systems and their component parts, and engaging in an analytical exercise that relates the parts to the whole. Systems thinking is a key addition to the traditional skill set of citizenship for an ecologically, socially, and economically interdependent world. While 27 percent of SS syllabi referenced systems thinking, less than 1 percent of the EPT syllabi did so.[9]

In summary, as Figure 8.1 shows, EPT and SS hold a common set of core skills that builds upon the tradition of liberal arts, and today may be considered the skills of citizenship in democratic societies. These include critical thinking skills, communication skills, and collaboration skills. In turn, sustainability education also emphasizes experiential and transdisciplinary education, and promotes systems thinking as an important strategy for negotiating complexity.

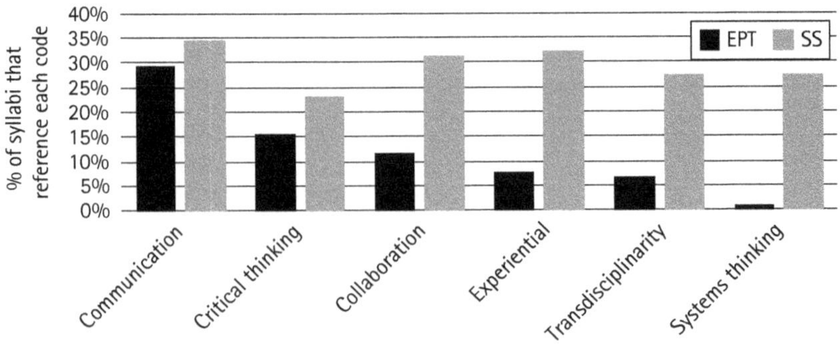

FIGURE 8.1 Skills, Experiential Education, and Sustainable Pedagogy.

Discussion

According to our content analysis, experiential education, broadly speaking, as well as transdisciplinary education and systems thinking, are well represented in the SS classroom, but are neglected in EPT courses. We argue that environmental political theorists are well positioned to incorporate these skills into their pedagogy.

Transdisciplinary education is based upon the inclusion of "non-expert" knowledge forms, supporting citizen deliberation processes and instilling the values of democratic pluralism. Political theorists are trained to be sensitive to the workings of power, the sociology of knowledge, and the impact of normative values and commitments. Most have (qualified) commitments to democracy and pluralism. Transdisciplinary education might be seen as an effective way for environmental political theorists to expose students experientially to the primacy of perspective, the impact of class, race, and gender roles, and the broader question of the social construction of reality.

As to the appropriateness of *systems thinking* in the classroom, we turn to John Dewey, whose prescient work on education and democracy grasped the importance of a systems perspective long before computerization had made modeling the complexity of our environment a realistic challenge. Dewey wrote that the adequacy of any given account of a situation is "found in the extent to which that account is based upon taking things in the widest and most complex scale of *associations* open to observation" (1986 3:42; italics added). Social phenomena, as well as physical scientific objects, should be understood as dynamic relational phenomena, and so "a transaction extending beyond the spatial limits of the organism" (1986 12:32). Recognizing and outlining the complexity of the modern and increasingly global situation, Dewey underlined the importance of cultivating judgment as a way of critically understanding a world that is rich with interrelated processes (1980 9:128). In short, Dewey advocated systems thinking *avant la lettre*, applying it primarily to the social and political realms. EPT is well positioned to promote this awareness of complexity and interdependence within the human and the natural environments.

In *Refounding Environmental Ethics* (2011), Ben Minteer documents the negligible impact that environmental ethicists have had on policymakers and the broader world of environmental politics. The reason, he argues, is that the field of environmental ethics has turned inward, "becoming an increasingly specialized and insular academic discourse," instead of "becoming a productive ally in the work of shaping critique and justifying sound environmental policy agendas and clarifying key debates and normative standards" (2011: 2). Such insularity, Minteer suggests, may well serve the academic field and the professional needs of the ethicists and philosophers who populate it. But it has proven to be of comparatively little value in addressing "real world" environmental issues. In light of this insularity and its worldly impact, Minteer advocates "a fundamental rethinking of the field's wider political and policy ambitions" (2011: 3).

Unlike Minteer, we are not advocating that environmental political theorists transform their field into a handmaiden of policy development. Our focus is not on the role theorists might play in the arena of practical politics, at least not directly. Rather, we suggest that environmental political theorists both strengthen and adapt their traditional roles as pedagogues. By cultivating sustainability skills, EPT can educate and empower students to grapple intellectually and practically with the interdependent social, environmental, and economic challenges that define their lived reality and future prospects.

John Dewey wrote that, "Philosophy recovers itself when it ceases to be a device for dealing with the problems of philosophers and becomes a method, cultivated by philosophers, for dealing with the problems of men" (1980, vol. 10: 46). This role of the theorist, and its embodiment in John Dewey, is captured in Sheldon Wolin's (2009: 504) seminal work, *Politics and Vision*:

> Paradoxically, although Dewey was educated in philosophy and associated with it throughout most of his life, he might be considered to have practiced political theory rather than political philosophy. Political theory might be described as the attempt to theorize the political by addressing the concerns of politics rather than of philosophers and using civic rather than professional forms of discourse.... that is, issues are addressed because of their public importance rather than their relevance to the ongoing controversies in the private world of philosophers.... Throughout a long life of engagement he [Dewey] kept steadily focused upon the implications or consequences of events as they affected the fortunes of democracy and especially the prospects for ordinary citizens to share in the fruits of scientific and economic progress.

Dewey's and Wolin's vision of political theory has important implications for educators who wish to contribute to the development of a democratic culture and a resilient citizenry. It is suggestive of the obligation of environmental political theorists creatively to adapt their classrooms for the cultivation of sustainability skills. To avoid the insular tendencies of "high" theorizing, EPT must not view itself solely or even primarily as a discursive, literary project rooted in the examination and production of critical texts. Rather, EPT can be practiced as an activist pedagogy amenable to experiential and transdisciplinary learning. Such pedagogy is aligned with what Julian Agyeman calls "action competence," which "has as a goal in mind, the resolution of the problem" (2006: 516). Education is best organized around meaningful problems, or as Dewey would say, situations, where student learning occurs through the development of opportunities to effect positive change.

In this respect, environmental political theorists might view themselves, with John Dewey, as activist pedagogues. Their mandate is to empower citizens in an age awakening to the realities of social, environmental, and economic interdependence. The practical challenge is to model this integrated approach to deep awareness and adaptive learning for our students, and to cultivate opportunities for students to practice these same strategies and skills. To the extent we take on this charge, environmental political theorists will be both *teaching* sustainability *to* students, and *doing* sustainability *with* students.

APPENDIX

Methods Overview

A cloud-based mixed methods content analysis program, *Dedoose*, was used for aggregating and measuring the data. Our content analysis of syllabi distinguished between the assignment of books, articles, and single chapters within books. When a topical reader or anthology was used, we counted the editor of the reader as having his or her book assigned, and we counted the individual chapters from the reader that were assigned in the class schedule for their respective authors. For obvious reasons, we eliminated those cases where instructors assigned their own works.

We composed our list of 136 environmental political theorists from those authors whose works appear on syllabi received through the EPT listserv or posted on the EPT website and from participants in EPT exchange. We tried to err on the side of inclusion. While some of the authors listed here may not self-identify as environmental political theorists, we wanted to ensure that no widely read EPT work was omitted.

Environmental political theorists included in our study (in alphabetical order):

Julian Agyeman
Bill Alexander
Susan Armstrong
Tom Athanasiou
John Barry
Dennis Becker
Mark Beeson
Todd Belt
Jane Bennett
Ted Benton
Andrew Biro
Ingolfur Bluhdorn
Murray Bookchin
Nadine Bopp
Magalie Bourblanc
Sheryl Breen
Steve Breyman
Mark Brown
Christopher Buck
John Bugge
Simon Caney
Peter Cannavò
William Chaloupka
Rom Coles
Diana Coole
Layne Coppock
Marius Cristen
Edward Davis
Jack Davis
Avner de-Shalit
Giovanna Di Chiro
Lisa Disch
Andrew Dobson
Brian Doherty
Heather Douglas
John Dryzek
Elisabeth Ellis
Robyn Eckersley
Anne Ferguson
Luc Ferry
Frank Fischer
Adrian Flint
Dan Freedman
Samantha Frost
Greta Gaard
Teena Gabrielson
Brian Gareau
Farah Godrej
Anderson Gold
Robert Goodin
Eduardo Gudynas
Arjun Guneratne
Cheryl Hall
Michael Hamilton
Kenneth Hansen
Susanna Hecht

Ray Heithus
Ronald Herring
Bryan Higgins
Sandy Hinchman
David Holdsworth
Breena Holland
Steven Hopp
David Hughes
Lori Hunter
Sheila Jasonoff
Simon Joss
Joel Kassiola
Eric Katz
Mike Kilgore
Jason Lambacher
Bruno Latour
Alex Latta
Jennifer Lawrence
Andrew Light
Ronny Lipschutz
Michael Lipscomb
Francis Longworth
Tim Luke
Sherilyn Macgregor
Mapes-Martin Brad
Juan Martinez-Alier
Kathleen McAffee
Bryan McDonald
John M. Meyer
Roberta Millstein
Ronald Mitchell
Catriona Mortimer-Sandilands
Arne Naess
Ted Nordhaus
John O'Neill
William Ophuls
David Orr
Kelly Parker
Adrian Parr
Sean Parsons
Mat Paterson
Devon Pena
Judith Perrolle
Laurel Pheonix
Val Plumwood
Emily Ray
David Robertson
Monty Roper
Alan Rudy
Mark Sagoff
Catriona Sandilands
Andrew Scerri
David Schlosberg
Kristin Shrader-Frechette
Kim Smith
Marvin Soroos
Piers Stephens
Demitris Stevis
Peter Stillman
Peter Taylor
Leslie Paul Thiele
Tom Thorton
Ted Toadvine
Doug Torgerson
Katherine Traveline
David Turkon
Bob Turner
Steve Vanderheiden
Steve Vogel
Lieske Voget-Kleschin
Paul Wapner
Karen Warren
Kyle Whyte
Justin Williams
Harlan Wilson
Marcel Wissenburg
Clark Wolf
Kerri Woods
Danielle Worth
Rafi Youatt

Five EPT books and five EPT articles/chapters were utilized in the sustainability studies courses we surveyed (see Tables 8.2 and 8.3). Each of these works appeared once, with the exception of the Shellenberger and Nordhaus (2004) essay, which appeared twice.

Table 8.2 Environmental Political Theorists With Articles or Chapters Assigned on Sustainability Syllabi

Environmental political theorists with articles or chapters assigned on sustainability syllabi	Work Assigned
Ramachandra Guha	(2000) *Environmentalism*
Michael Maniates	(2007) "Going Green: Easy Doesn't Do it."
William Ophuls	(1992) *Ecology and the Politics of Scarcity Revisited*
Robert Paehlke	(2005) "Democracy and Environmentalism"
Shellenberger and Nordhaus	(2004) "The Death of Environmentalism"

For more information on sustainability skills and pedagogical resources, see http://sustainability.clas.ufl.edu/handbook

Table 8.3 Environmental Political Theorists With Books Assigned on Sustainability Syllabi

Environmental political theorists with books assigned on sustainability syllabi	Work Assigned
Ramachandra Guha	(2006) *How Much Should a Person Consume?*
Robert Bullard	(2005) *The Quest for Environmental Justice*
Agyeman, Bullard and Evans	(2003) *Just Sustainabilities*
John Bellamy Foster	(1999) *The Vulnerable Planet*
Thomas Homer-Dixon	(2006) *The Upside of Down*

Notes

1. Nearly 700 American college and university leaders have signed a climate commitment agreeing to make sustainability a part of the educational experience of all their students (ACUPCC 2013). Three sustainability-related programs were added to US colleges and universities in 2005, 66 in 2008, and over 100 new programs in sustainability were added in 2009 (Schmitt 2009). As of December 2013, the Association for the Advancement of Sustainability in Higher Education (AASHE) maintains a list of over 1400 sustainability-focused academic programs in US states and Canadian provinces.
2. We acknowledge that there is considerable disagreement regarding the use of these terms, and specifically regarding the difference between sustainable development and sustainability. For the purposes of this study we used the derivatives of this same root, sustainable, to identify undergraduate programs from which to pull syllabi.
3. The breakdown of the syllabi is as follows: 6 percent agriculture, 9 percent humanities, 34 percent social sciences, 15 percent natural sciences, 9 percent business, and the

remainder comprised of a mix including capstone courses, courses rooted in the community, courses focused on sustainability skills, systems thinking, and green building. Roughly 15 percent of the courses were introductory courses, the rest spanned the four-year degree process.

4. See the appendix for more information on methodology, including how EPT authors were identified, and summary findings from the content analysis.
5. One author was mentioned twice, for a total of ten EPT works.
6. We found evidence of a focus on skill development primarily in the learning outcomes and course descriptions at the beginning of each syllabus; e.g. "The course advances critical thinking and professional skills, especially evidence-based written and verbal communications as well as collaborating with others in teams" (SS syllabus 68-320); and "[This course encourages students to] b) think logically, critically, and creatively; (c) communicate verbally and visually; (d) work cooperatively in teams or small groups; (e) respect inter-disciplinary diversity . . ." (EPT syllabus LC).
7. E.g. "Students are organized into small groups to work on a particular sustainability assessment project. With supervision of the instructor, each group will identify a place, collect data, choose a set of indicators, and carry out the sustainability assessment. A group report and a class presentation are required" (SS syllabus 68-404). Communication skills were sometimes referenced in the learning outcomes of the course, but there was no evidence of classroom activities that justified the stated outcome. We did not code for communication unless syllabi indicated that students were given an opportunity to deliver a presentation, run a class discussion, or present their ideas in some alternative media format. Likewise, we did not code for collaboration unless there was evidence of a group or team project, or cooperative projects involving community members or other classes.
8. The following excerpt from an SS syllabus exemplifies this type of experience: "You will be working with a 'community partner' or 'client' to solve a problem. The project incorporates a problem-based approach to community service learning. You will match learning objectives to community service in a way that enhances both your education and the community. By doing a problem-based service learning (PBSL) project, you are expected to gain a deeper and practical understanding of course content, enhance interpersonal and leadership skills, and deepen a sense of connection to your community" (SS syllabus 21-S).
9. The single EPT syllabus that referenced systems thinking introduced it as an important modification to Western thinking, explaining it thus: "Systems thinking provides a structure for viewing the world that is different from the reductionist paradigm that has dominated Western thought since the 1600s. The reductionist paradigm has proved very powerful, yet it appears to be ill suited for addressing many of today's most pressing problems. In other words, it is necessary but not sufficient for full understanding. A common emphasis will be the creation of links between social and ecological systems" (EPT syllabus RH-25). Among the SS syllabi, the most interesting case is Arizona State University, which has incorporated a framework for its school of sustainability that puts systems thinking and transdisciplinary education at the core of all its course offerings. The school's syllabi consistently state the following: "All courses in the School of Sustainability are designed to build and deepen your understanding of the following key concepts:

Systems Dynamics: Human systems and natural systems are linked. Changes in any part of any system have multiple consequences that reach far beyond the initial change.

Tradeoffs: Solving almost all problems related to sustainability involves tradeoffs. There are rarely perfect solutions with no costs, and there are often winners and losers.

Cascading Effects and Unintended Consequences: There are cascading effects (positive and negative, intended and unintended) of human policies, decisions and actions, all of which have implications for sustainability.

Scale: Problems of sustainability exist at multiple scales. Solving a problem at a local level is a very different thing than solving a problem across international boundaries.

Transdisciplinarity: There is no one 'solution' to address sustainability—no one person or field of study has the answer. We need scientists and social scientists from all disciplines, politicians, entrepreneurs, artists, farmers, business and community leaders, and you to work towards a sustainable future."

References

ACUPCC. (2013). *University Presidents Climate Commitment.* Retrieved from http://www.presidentsclimatecommitment.org/signatories/list/state

Agyeman, J. (2006). "Action, Experience, Behavior, and Technology." *Environmental Education Research* 12(3–4): 513–22.

Agyeman, J., Bullard, R. D., and Evans, B., eds. (2003). *Just Sustainabilities: Development in an Unequal World* (Cambridge: The MIT Press).

Armitage, D., Marschke, M., and Plummer, R. (2008). "Adaptive Co-Management and the Paradox of Learning." *Global Environmental Change* 18(1): 86–98.

Arum, R. and Roska, J. (2011). *Academically Adrift: Limited Learning on College Campuses* (Illinois: University of Chicago Press).

Connolly, W. E. (1974). *The Terms of Political Discourse* (Oxford: Blackwell Publishing).

Dewey, J. (1975). *The Early Works, 1882–1898* (Carbondale: Southern Illinois University Press).

Dewey, J. (1980). *The Middle Works, 1899–1924* (Carbondale: Southern Illinois University Press).

Dewey, J. (1986). *The Later Works, 1925–1953* (Carbondale: Southern Illinois University Press).

Diduck, A. (1999). "Critical Education in Resource and Environmental Management: Learning and Empowerment for a Sustainable Future." *Journal of Environmental Management* 57(2): 85–97.

Diduck, A., Hostetler, G. and Fitzpatrick, P. (2012). "Transformative Learning Theory, Public Involvement, and Natural Resource and Environmental Management." *Journal of Environmental Planning and Management* 55(10): 1–20.

Dobson, A. (2010). "Democracy and Nature: Speaking and Listening." *Political Studies* 58(4): 752–68.

Dryzek, J. S. (1995). "Political and Ecological Communication." *Environmental Politics* 4(4): 13–30.

Dryzek, J. S. (1997). *The Politics of the Earth: Environmental Discourses*, 2nd edn. (New York: Oxford University Press).

Elder, Linda. "Letter from the President of the Foundation for Critical Thinking," *email correspondence.* May 29, 2014.

Facione, P. A. (1990). Critical Thinking: A Statement of Expert Consensus for Purposes of Educational Assessment and Instruction. Research Findings and Recommendations. Retrieved from http://www.eric.ed.gov/ERICWebPortal/detail?accno=ED315423

Gunderson, L. H. and Holling, C. S. (2001). *Panarchy: Understanding Transformations In Human And Natural Systems* (Washington, DC: Island Press).

Hardin, G. (1968). "The Tragedy of the Commons." *Science* 162(3859): 1243–8.

Lovins, A. B. and Lovins. (1982). *Brittle Power: Energy Strategy for National Security* (Andover: Brick House Publishing).

Meadows, D. (1999). *Leverage Points: Places to Intervene in a System* (Hartland: The Sustainability Institute).

Minteer, B. A. (2012). *Refounding Environmental Ethics: Pragmatism, Principle, and Practice* (Philadelphia: Temple University Press).

Monroe, M. C., Andrews, E., and Biedenweg, K. (2007). "A Framework for Environmental Education Strategies." *Applied Environmental Education and Communication* 6: 205–16.

Ostrom, E. (1990). *Governing the Commons: The Evolution of Institutions for Collective Action* (Cambridge: Cambridge University Press).

Ostrom, E. (1998). "A Behavioral Approach to the Rational Choice Theory of Collective Action." *The American Political Science Review* 92(1): 1–22.

Paul, R., Elder, L., and Bartell, T. (1997). *California Teacher Preparation for Instruction in Critical Thinking* (Sacramento: California Commission on Teacher Credentialing).

Posch, A. and Scholz, R. W. (2006). "Transdisciplinary Case Studies for Sustainability Learning." *International Journal of Sustainability in Higher Education* 7(3): 226–51.

Schmitt, J. (2009). "As Colleges Add Green Majors and Minors, Classes Fill Up." *USA Today*, December 29.

Thiele, L. P. (2013). *Sustainability* (Cambridge, UK: Polity).

Tillbury, D. (2011). *Education for Sustainable Development: An Expert Review of Processes and Learning* (DESD Monitoring and Evaluation) (Paris: UNESCO).

Torgerson, D. (1995). "The Uncertain Quest for Sustainability: Public Discourse and the Politics of Environmentalism." In *Greening Environmental Policy: The Politics of a Sustainable Future*, edited by F. Fischer and M. Black (London: Palgrave Macmillan).

UNESCO. (1997). *Educating for a Sustainable Future*. Retrieved from http://www.unesco.org/education/tlsf/mods/theme_a/popups/mod01t05s01.html

Wals, A. E. J. (2012). *Shaping the Education of Tomorrow: 2012 Full-Length Report on the UN Decade of Education for Sutainable Development* (DESD Monitoring and Evaluation) (Paris: UNESCO).

Wolin, S. (2004). *Politics and Vision: Continuity and Innovation in Western Political Thought* (Princeton: Princeton University Press).

CHAPTER 9

ENVIRONMENTAL POLITICAL THEORY AND ENVIRONMENTAL ACTION RESEARCH TEAMS

ROMAND COLES

To inquire about the conditions under which pedagogies of environmental political theory might flourish is to inquire about the conditions for the flourishing of environmental political theory *as such*, if by the latter we mean not merely the scholarly activities of a small number of professional theorists, but also the widespread proliferation of profound reflection upon environmental politics that might contribute to changing the world. Transformative quotidian work and action is itself an indispensable condition for *both* stimulating *and* proliferating such reflection. In the absence of environmental action research pedagogies, rapidly developing neo-liberal political economic dynamics will increasingly undermine the spaces and possibilities in institutions of higher education that have been integral to the development of transformative environmental political theory.

Environmental action research is a mode of problem-based democratic pedagogy that integrates theory and practice in ways that promise to enrich both. That transformative theory and practice are immanent conditions of each other's possibility should not surprise environmental political theorists, for many of us have conducted much of our reflective work in proximity to social movements responding to urgent problems of our times. By engaging the critical and prefigurative horizons of "living theory" intertwined with a myriad practices of resistance and alternative enactment, environmental political theory has been informed and energized in ways that have enhanced the vitality of scholarship and enriched pedagogical opportunities.

A central thesis of action research is that our capacities to engage in transformative theory and action are profoundly entangled in the practices of our everyday lives. Pierre Bourdieu employed the term "habitus" to theorize the ways in which our perceptions, cognition, dispositions, and institutions came to be articulated with each other through daily practices (Bourdieu 1977). For Bourdieu our improvizational capacities were not "free," but profoundly animated, directed, and limited by the generative structures of a given habitus. In this essay, I sketch some of the dynamics of the neo-liberal habitus that are undermining our capacities for transformative environmental political thought and action. Contra Bourdieu, however, I suggest that it is possible to engender a radically democratic habitus that nurtures our capacities for "game-transformative practices," or practices that cultivate our abilities to interrogate and change basic dimensions of these practices themselves. Thus, working to co-create a radically democratic pedagogical habitus would be an integral condition for radical environmental political theory. I explore this possibility as it is developing in a movement for action research pedagogy at Northern Arizona University, which is reflective of broader trends.

* * *

Consider a few of the dynamics that are undermining planetary ecology, democracy, and educational institutions and must be engaged by environmental political thought. The first concerns dynamics of governmentality (Foucault 2009) at work in a *political economy of mega-circulations* that are uprooting a myriad forms of life and reconstituting them—capillary by capillary—to increase the magnitude of circulations moving through gargantuan channels controlled by fewer and fewer corporations. Michael Pollan analyzes the genetically engineered global "river of corn" flowing from a field twice the size of New York State, showing how this flow is managed by a corporate–political technocracy governed by several mega-firms that control the regulatory and subsidy environment, have differentiated corn into over 10,000 products, and manipulate everything from advertising, to sweetness, to caloric composition, and produce "industrial eaters" who desire and absorb ever-increasing volumes (Pollan 2007). Through the lens of corn, he traces the ways in which related mega-circulations of fertilizer, pesticides, energy, water, animals, finance, fast foods, pharmaceuticals, military, migrants, and institutional revolving doors are reconstituting and wreaking havoc on eco-systems, our communities, bodies, and political economy. Each circulatory system is entwined with and often intensifies the others, in ways that are lurching toward planetary ecological catastrophe, the dissolution of democracy, and the enclosure of the commons (including public education).

The second contemporary dynamic is what William Connolly (2008) calls a *resonance machine*: To an unprecedented degree, powers seek to govern the world through televisual practices (network news, televangelists, press conferences, TV and radio talk shows, Internet messaging, corporatized tele-education, infomercials, blogspheres, endless polling, inane political campaigning, cinema) that bombard us with resonant waves of light and sound (in our homes, classrooms, offices, waiting rooms, sporting events, churches, cars, airports, airplanes, shopping spaces, restaurants, gas stations) that mediate our experiences, dispositions, attention, inattention, feelings, and practices. Connolly argues that, in the United States, these techno practices amplify the reverberations among increasingly resentful, punitive, and dogmatically fundamentalist *forms* of both neo-liberal capitalism and Christianity in ways that drive anti-democratic and ecologically destructive dynamics around the world.

Taken together, these two dynamics contribute mightily to a form of contemporary capitalism that is spinning evermore wildly beyond ecological limits, engendering nearly unfathomable topographies of inequality, colonizing and reconstituting the state with hybrid and dynamic forms of corporatized power, and undermining a myriad efforts to respond to present and looming ecological disasters (for example, Wolin 2010). Intimately intertwined with these dynamics are increasingly fine-tuned arts of manufacturing and utilizing a host of economic, political, and "natural" crises, in ways that send surges of devastation through communities, polities, and public sector institutions. Naomi Klein (2007) coined this process "shock doctrine," which, analogous to electric shock treatment, seeks to uproot relationships and memory in ways that "wipe the slate clean" for neo-liberal reengineering. Sheldon Wolin powerfully analyzes the ways in which relentless change and perpetual mobility become engines that devastate individual and collective capacities for democratic citizenship.

To teach environmental political theory in the United States (and also in significant portions of the "developed" world) under these conditions means to teach students whose desires, aspirations, imaginations, and intellects have been profoundly oriented, truncated, and distracted by lives swept up in the capillaries of mega-circulations, bombarded by a multitude of unending corporatized audio-visual projections, and frequently uprooted from relational networks and places. They have typically been subject to educational systems that have been downsized by repeated shock politics and reconstituted according the test-driven "banking education" imperatives of neo-liberal capitalism that are putting tremendous pressure upon and frequently replacing broader liberal education tendencies associated with earlier democratic struggles. They have come of age at a time when the dynamics of global capitalism have become especially powerful and are often presented as inexorable, even as they generate suffering of unimaginable proportions. They live in a time when planetary climate catastrophe appears increasingly inevitable, even as powerful forces continue to deny anthropogenic climate change. They find themselves paying higher tuition, sinking into deeper debt that profoundly constrains their imagination of occupational futures, crammed into huge classes, taught by growing numbers of precarious, stressed, and overworked adjunct faculty members, and painfully aware that growing numbers of college graduates in the United States today are living near or in poverty.

Environmental political theory must address these dynamics if it is to articulate powerful insights into the driving forces of catastrophe in our times, as well as what we might do in response to them. Relatedly, efforts to do and teach radical environmental political thought under these conditions require that we fashion pedagogies that begin to respond and provide alternatives to this neo-liberal habitus that so powerfully undermines our capacities for thought and action. We must co-create new ways to attract and engage large numbers of students, on the one hand, and make potentially transformative in-roads into the conditions that are rapidly undermining the practices and institutions of our pedagogy. We must create a game-transformative practice that can resist the neo-liberalization of education, our polities, and the planet, and generate powerful alternatives. Democratic environmental action research is an effort to do so.

Democratic Environmental Action Research

Democratic environmental action research is a phrase I use here to refer an emergent movement in higher education that links theoretical, empirical, and historical scholarship on a broad range of sustainability issues with democratic pedagogies in which students collaborate with each other and members of broader communities in order to craft research, work, and action in response to mutually identified issues and problems. The phrase does not designate a settled practice, but rather a cluster of initiatives with several roots that are evolving on many campuses.

This pedagogy draws sustenance from an eclectic mix of sources. John Dewey's (1997) pragmatic pedagogical philosophy informs many in this movement, as do the innovative educational initiatives pioneered in civil rights struggles such as the Citizenship Schools founded by Septima Clark in the 1950s and the Freedom Schools formed by the Student Nonviolent Coordinating Committee in the 1960s (for example, Payne 1995). Paulo Freire's engaged theoretical work on critical pedagogy has also been a seminal inspiration for many (especially, Freire 2000). The environmental focus in many initiatives has been influenced by the "eco-literacy" movement in which David Orr has played an important role (Orr 1994). The broad-based community organizing movement has informed the evolving democratic practices at Northern Arizona University (NAU), as have eco-feminist approaches, and the civic engagement practices of Public Achievement.[1] Democratic environmental action research tends to address a wide range of problems manifest in everyday life, including environmental justice issues in urban areas (Gottlieb 2002, 2010). The trend is toward broad definitions of environment and sustainability, such that questions of community, immigration, health, food justice and food security, and economic justice, indigenous environmental justice, and environmental racism are frequently integral to such initiatives.

During the past five years Northern Arizona University's Action Research Teams (ARTs) initiative has become widely recognized as one of the leading initiatives in the United States in this area, both for developing innovative practices and for integrating transformative pedagogy across a wide range of topics, units, and sectors of campus and community life. Because several key faculty leaders in NAU's ARTs initiative are political and social theorists, environmental political thought and radical democratic theory have been integral to the evolving vision and practices of the ARTs. As I am a leader in this initiative I use it here as a case study to explore possibilities for enlivening environmental political theory and pedagogical practice through action research that responds to many of the key neo-liberal dynamics sketched earlier.

Yet first consider that conditions in Arizona are at the extreme right-wing of the neo-liberal assault just discussed. The vast majority of students at NAU are residents of Arizona, where they receive some of the worst and most under-funded, over-crowded, test-oriented rote education in the United States. Arizona politics is frequently at the leading edge of highly resonant and militaristic xenophobia, police-intensive "libertarianism," racism, aggressive anti-environmentalism (including one bill to protect tungsten filament incandescent light bulbs from purported federal regulations that would privilege compact flourescent lamps (CFLs) and another bill to prevent municipalities form passing new energy efficiency ordinances), and persistently hostile to education as evidenced by severe budget cuts and unrelenting culture war (as exemplified by the law banning ethnic studies, commonly known as HB 2281). Progressive social movements have made less of a mark on the history and contemporary political ecology of the state than they have in many other places. Arizona is also the location for some of the most intense impacts of climate change, social and environmental injustice to indigenous peoples, and Phoenix—arguably the least sustainable city in the United States (Ross 2011). In this context—highly conducive to ignorance, disengagement, despair, a sense of powerlessness, and narrowly channeled aspirations—the task of engaging 18-year-olds in democratic pedagogies focused on transformative ecological political theory and practice is challenging.

Nevertheless, we have made rapid and significant progress. The NAU ARTs initiative began in the Fall of 2009 as a collaboration between the Program for Community, Culture and Environment (CC&E), the First Year Seminar (FYS) Program, and the Masters of Arts in Sustainable Communities. Though the university has been struggling with increasing neo-liberal pressures, there were many faculty members who were supportive and who worked on a variety of environmental and social justice initiatives at NAU—not only from the programs mentioned above, but also from Environmental Studies, to Ethnic Studies, Women and Gender Studies, and so forth. Institutions are nearly always highly complex spaces with far more transformative potential than people realize. Students in a newly established residential learning community called SEED (Sustainable Environments and Engaged Democracy) enrolled in an FYS on "Democracy, Social Justice and the Environment," which pioneered several ARTs in which students were required to work three hours each week on teams such as AGWA (Action Group on Water Advocacy), WACBAT (Weatherization and Community Building Action Team), SSLUG (Students for Sustainable Living and Urban Gardening), Public Achievement (grassroots democracy education in K-12 schools), Sustainable Café, Immigration, and Foodlink. Graduate students in the Sustainable Communities core seminar (on philosophical, social, and political perspectives on sustainable communities) were required to mentor undergraduates and facilitate the work of an ART. Each ART collaborated on research, work, and action with a variety of community partners in Flagstaff's comparatively rich civic ecology—such as Friends of Flagstaff's Future, Northern Arizona Interfaith Council (NAIC, with Industrial Areas Foundation), Sustainable Economic Development Initiative, Killip Elementary School, Flagstaff Foodlink, and others. New ARTs emerge each year (often as a result of student initiatives), such as Velocomposting (campus composting with bicycle trailers), HEALTH, Queer and Ally, Total Liberation (exploring intersectionality around animal rights), SNAIL (Student Nurturing Alternatives in Landscaping), NE NAU (New Economy NAU), Indigenous Environmental Justice, and ARTs students have launched a chapter of Divest NAU (affiliated with 350.org). Several ARTs have expanded their work and developed subteams. The FYS program now hosts dozens of problem-focused ARTs-based seminars; growing numbers of faculty are participating; NAU has increased its funding each year for graduate student facilitators and undergraduate peer teaching assistants with the ARTs, hired several instructors and lecturers (non-tenure track), recently approved a Civic Engagement Minor, approved two new tenure-track lines in community-based sustainable economic development and community-based agriculture, while the number of first year students taking ARTs seminars grew to 450 during the Fall of 2013 and grew to 591 in the Fall of 2014.

In every ARTs-based first year seminar students study theories and practices of grassroots democracy—theories of self, community, power, history, critique, narrative, relationship, strategy, networks, action, public work, engaged pedagogy, political economy, alternative visions and practices, transformation, etc. Students also study scholarship on the seminar topic and all this comes together in action research in the affiliated ARTs.

The link between theory and practice is dynamic, as students frequently begin to awaken while working in and with the community—from their own experiences of how Arizona's political economy has damaged the environment and the poor, rather than from professors whom the state legislature accuses of brainwashing the youth. Students going door to door in impoverished neighborhoods to discuss a large community event on residential energy efficiency and community organizing discover themselves in the midst of houses that provide little shelter from the elements, facing people who are afraid that the knock on the door may be Immigration and Customs Enforcement (ICE). The next week some of these students whose participation had been lack-luster begin to enter into discussions of critical theories of environmental injustice with seriousness, urgency, specificity, and enthusiasm. Other students coaching K-12 youth on grassroots democracy and community stewardship discover that small teams of kids are capable of learning democratic theory and practice (that the coaches learn only a few weeks beforehand) and employing it in powerful ways in relation to co-created projects in their schools and neighborhoods. In a break-out discussion at a large symposium on the ARTs at the end of the semester, one of these students places his elbow on the table, forearm straight up in the air, and says: "You know, everywhere I wanted change before, I used to see walls." Lowering his forearm to the table he says: "After seeing what kids can do when they organize—now I'm starting to see pathways and possibilities." Alternative food systems and student–community agency become palpable as students work in community gardens or student-initiated campus composting projects. Alternative ecological and economic practices become less of a pipe dream as students form a composting cooperative, draw 100 community leaders into a workshop on creating sustainable commonwealth, and engage in sustainable social entrepreneurship initiatives with NE NAU.

As students begin exploring political and environmental scholarship and action, they are—from nearly the moment they arrive on campus—engaged in self-exploration in ways that enable them to make profound and evolving connections between their own lives, their academic and theoretical work, and their public work and political action. Many of the seminars begin by having students read Marshall Ganz's essays on "public narrative" (especially, Ganz 2011), then writing their own narratives of self, community, and urgency, sharing these with their colleagues in one–one conversations, and rewriting their public narratives as they grow in the conversations with their peers and professors. Ganz's essays ask readers to consider the deep experiential, traditional, familial, spiritual, and community roots of their sense of themselves in relation to the broader world of problems and possibilities, their sense of needed action, and their sense of urgency. Drawing on half a century of radical democratic organizing, he connects these narratives to the power of social movements—their orientation, capacities for motivation, endurance, ability to be compelling and attract others, their strategic resources and dexterity, their receptivity to differences, etc. In Ganz's terms, the work of transformation must deeply connect with and draw from the head (ideas), the hands (actions), and the heart (passionate sense of self, relationships, and commitments). Our pedagogies for democratic and environmental political theory in the ARTs seek to draw students to explore each of these dimensions and their profound implications for and immanent relationships with each other. Ganz's work is often used by environmental movements, such as 350.org's "fossil free" divestment campaign, and seminars often make use of these more ecologically inflected materials.

In addition to countless qualitative anecdotes, significant quantitative assessments are yielding highly positive results for the ARTs first year seminars. Forty percent of NAU students are among the first generation in their family to pursue higher education and a comparatively high percentage of the student body is Hispanic or Native American students. Overall, the retention rates (71 percent of NAU's first year students continue to the second year) for students who take one FYS-ARTs increased 7 percent, while the retention rates for minority students (59 percent for Native Americans, 64 percent for Hispanics/Latinos) increased 16 percent in aggregate, and women's rates (73.5 percent) rose 9 percent. Students who complete an FYS-ARTs reported very significant increases in engagement in learning activities related to course and Liberal Studies outcomes such as "analyzing the meaning and implications of diversity within society," "describing how language reflects ways of thinking, cultural heritage, larger cultural values, or aspects of society," "identifying the personal, family, and cultural influences that determine [their] world views," and "understanding different cultures of the world through the study of language, literature, religion, or artistic expression" (Michele Miller 2013).[2]

While additional interview, ethnographic, and quantitative research is underway to gain greater insight into learning implications of NAU's ARTs pedagogy, including questions focused on sustainability and environmental political thought, it is already clear that these are highly favorable and significant. ARTs pedagogy connects theory, broader scholarship, engagement, and students' own narratives in ways that are tangible, impactful, and sometimes even transformative. In these ways ARTs pedagogy facilitates affective, reflective, and active connections between cultures of higher education and students' life worlds prior to entering NAU—thereby easing a transition that is particularly challenging for first generation students. These connections are made in the midst of pedagogical process where students begin to cultivate themselves as change agents in ways that inspire, inform, and are informed by their more academic work (Coles and Scarnati 2015. The widespread hopelessness that tends to block inquiry into environmental catastrophes, movements for radical democratic and environmental transformation, and alternative horizons of possibility begins to erode in the process, freeing the mind, the imagination, and hearts frozen in fear-borne oblivion.

Now consider NAU's ARTs pedagogy from the vantage point of the environmentally and democratically catastrophic dynamics we sketched at the outset. In the context of a global political economy of governmentalized mega-circulations, the implications are radical insofar as the ARTs are designed around experience, theoretical reflection, and collaborative agency that explore practices and movements of counter-circulations and alternative circulations. In resistance to the massive circulations of the plutocratic carbon economy, students and community partners are involved in critical inquiry and practices that promote alternative flows associated with energy efficiency and renewable energy linked to widely distributed prosperity, mass transit, and human powered transportation. The ART that participated in convincing the Arizona Corporation Commission (ACC) to successfully pass a revolving loan fund for residential energy efficiency retrofits, created a regional flow of common finance to circulate among residents to promote a common good.[3] The students who collaborated with community groups to crowd source fund solar panels on a community center participated in imagining, propelling, and theorizing alternative political economic horizons based on community finance. To do this work, they moved their bodies, ears, voices, and receptive senses into neighborhoods most have been taught to fear or seek to leave, thereby initiating a habitus highly at odds with those that animate us according to mega-circulations of money and political power. This local work joins kindred flows to create larger streams with nationally and globally active groups like 350.org.

Similarly, students and community groups are countering the mega-circulations of corporate agriculture, by co-creating alternative flows in everyday life such as student and community gardening that involve finely honed attentiveness to microclimates, soil, and sunlight in permaculture designs; seed exchanges disseminating plants more suitable to semi-arid high elevation agriculture; potlucks where people recover slow food arts of convivium; political organizing for sustainable cooperative food systems that cultivate local and regional flows of food, finance, and networks. In contrast to the prevalent practices of heedless water misuse in a semi-arid environment, students are studying and promoting water harvesting that creatively gathers micro-flows for gardens, advocating for citywide water ordinances, and linking these micro-practices to broader questions and global movements around water rights and governance.

As governmental powers in Arizona and the United States turn their backs on young people—especially in poor and minority neighborhoods—NAU students working with the Public Achievement ART move receptively to work with K-12 students, facilitating the grassroots leadership around a myriad issues identified by children and youth. As a virulent mix of global corporations, NAFTA, climate change, and circulations of drugs and arms associated with gang violence and state corruption conspire to drive large flows of people from their communities south of the US border and northward across extremely dangerous US deserts and into a regime of privatized detention centers, "involuntary return," neo-fascist policing, and malignant xenophobia, NAU students involved in the Immigration ART work in solidarity with the immigrant community in Northern Arizona to educate and advocate for justice and hospitality on these issues. Dozens begin to learn about the extent of the problem for the first time as they move their bodies attentively to the border on field trips where they begin to see, listen, and reflect upon the situation for themselves. Some become active in No More Deaths to create micro-flows of water and emergency health supplies to harsh areas where crossings are frequent.

Increasingly, ARTs pedagogies that involve students in reconstituting our habitus around alternative circulations simultaneously link up with organizations and movements oriented toward advancing these modes of being and aspirations through trans-local, national, and global networks, organizations, and powers. This everyday politics draws students corporeally and sensually toward witness, reflection, and action that attenuate the aura of remoteness, irrelevance, hopeless abstraction, and impossibility that such larger scales often conjure up for many people today. In turn, learning about problems and promising work elsewhere connects with their own initiatives and infuses them with greater depth and expansive theoretical significance.

Depth and expansive significance are also enhanced by how the ARTs engage the dynamics of the mega-capitalist-fundamentalist resonance machine. As I suggest elsewhere, it is likely no exaggeration to suggest that this pedagogy is engendering an alternative habitus starting at the cellular level.[4] Contemporary neuroscience research on mirror neurons demonstrates that our capacities for perception and understanding are entangled with resonant inter-corporeal relationships with others. As infants, we come to sense our own smile through the experience of others smiling when our face evinces the beginnings of smiling, and this in turn is linked to our recognition of other peoples' smiles. When people converse with one another, their faces and corresponding mirror neurons fire ceaselessly in intervals consisting of small fractions of a second, without which our capacity to recognize—let alone understand—others is greatly impaired. When an audience is asked to interpret the emotions of faces on a screen, those who clench their jaws around a pencil are sluggish and incompetent compared to those whose faces are relaxed and firing in neurological resonance with the faces that appear. Similarly, mirror neurons of people who regularly engage in practices and games with others develop neurological resonances and capacities for perceptual recognition that are far greater and fire very differently than do those of people unfamiliar with these games and practices. Equally important, studies show that people who are typically deemed impertinent to a given situation or practice tend to occupy zones of dampened resonance in relation to those who are deemed to be engaged: the mirror neurons of the latter often do not fire in relation the presence of the former.

Though neuroscientists have yet to conduct studies of mirror neurons in relation to contemporary patterns of power and alternative grassroots democratic practice, the relevant research suggests that institutions, media projections, and inter-corporeal practices of power that render people (for example, of certain races, classes, genders, etc.) impertinent likely engender mirror neuronal patterns and (in)capacities for resonance and dampening that anchor and animate dominant resonance machines at the cellular level—and greatly impede our capacity to imagine, perceive, and cultivate alternatives. It appears likely that the attentive border-crossing movement, deeply relational work, and pedagogical–political practices of the ARTs may engender a distinct set of neurological capacities for receptive democratic resonance. Radical democracy, more than most practices, is a "game-transformative practice": it involves questioning, receptivity, provocations, and experimental interactions that repeatedly probe possibilities for transforming and further democratizing the basic conditions of the practice at any given point in time. The science of mirror neurons shows that our experiences and capacities in relation to any practice are profoundly biocultural: Our biological and cultural registers engender and impede each other in feedback loops that are immanent in each other. Just as the mirror neurons of people unfamiliar with soccer will fail to resonate in ways that facilitate their ability to perceptually follow the game, it is likely that those lacking experience with the interrogative, receptive, and transformative qualities of democracy will have more difficulty perceiving it, and may even be anxious, agitated, and angry in the presence of democratic action in ways that are easily amplified by the contemporary anti-democratic resonance machine. In contrast, the more we engage in the democratic game-transformative practices of the ARTs, the more we tend to engender biocultural capacities to experience—and act in—the world as a space of possibility that solicits radical democratic inquiry and artful co-action.

Just as the alternative circulations of the ARTs tend to connect with far vaster circulations, so too, alternative relationships and practices of local receptive resonance are pregnant with possibilities for participating in wider patterns of resonance with other practices and people nurturing similar world-transformative sensibilities. In the NAU ARTs initiative, students are urged to explore these possibilities through a variety of inter-ART collaborations, including an ARTs Symposium each semester in which students in the ARTs present and discuss their work and the broader ARTs movement—often with resonant enthusiasm. Growing numbers of students are extending this resonance into virtual spaces, participating in and contributing to multi-media televisual communications forums in a variety of national and transnational networks concerning climate change, water rights, sustainable food systems, Public Achievement, new economic initiatives, democratic transformation of higher education, and more. The contours of a radically democratic and ecological resonance machine are beginning to emerge.

Conclusion

In the midst of all this democratic environmental action research among students and community members, there are signs that a radical democratic habitus may be emerging, in which new dynamics among our perceptions, dispositions, theoretical abilities, practices, and institutions increasingly tend to nurture more than they impede democratic and transformative co-creation. As this happens, students' academic achievement is improving markedly, and this in turn is convincing the administration to direct increasing resources toward the democratic and environmental action research initiative. All of this is beginning (in modest but highly significant ways) to alter dynamics of institutional development and power at NAU. And these changes would appear to be widely replicable at institutions where there are people and programs with significant aspirations for democracy, social justice, and environmental change; where increasing student retention, achievement, and graduation rates is a priority; and where there are community partners such as schools, community centers, nonprofits, businesses with green aspirations, social movements, and so forth, with whom to collaborate.

As these dynamics develop, ARTs education at NAU is becoming "public" in new ways:[5] Increasingly it involves hundreds of community members in collaborative inquiry, deliberation, public work, ecological tending, and political action. As it does, the irrelevant, out of touch, anti-American, ivory tower image is beginning to wane. Beyond right-wing vilifications, for growing numbers, the university comes to be experienced instead as a collaborative institution in which they have co-ownership and relationships with (and support for) specific people co-creating energy efficiency, community gardens, coaching youth in community stewardship and grassroots democracy, advocating for hospitable, just, and livable communities with new immigrants, generating tangible community economy initiatives that are fostering widespread prosperity, and linking resistance to climate change to green economy developments. Interestingly, in this context "relevance" ceases to be a tool for constraining imagination and political action (as Wendy Brown rightly criticizes the term as it is deployed in other situations),[6] and becomes a generative location and condition for thinking and acting in an increasingly game-transformative pedagogical–political practice that exceeds the bounds of the given order.

Though the NAU ARTs initiative is still very new, its implications for environmental political theory appear very promising. In Flagstaff, as growing numbers of students opt to explore pedagogical practices where they can experience and investigate new relationships, receptivity, resonances, and agency with community partners and the more than human world, the habitus that is implicated in the rapid destruction of communities, democracies, and eco-systems is increasingly infused with alternative dynamics and emergent tendencies. Partly because of the intimate connection between scholarship and action in action research seminars, this change in quotidian inter-corporeal practices appears to be dynamically intertwined with enhanced capacities and desires for imagining and reflectively exploring modes of organizing, struggles, and alternative futures that are the integral to the possibility and proliferation of radical environmental political thought. It may be that without such ventures in alternative practices the habitus in which environmental thought might flourish will continue to wither. Yet from the vantage point of initiatives such as NAU's ARTs, it may be possible to craft a future in which students and community members strengthen their capacities for thinking and acting toward democratically and ecologically vital futures, reinvigorate a commons that includes institutions of higher education that support such futures, and erode and ultimately abolish those powers that seek to make even pedagogies that would theoretically investigate such possibilities a thing of the past.

Notes

1. For an overview of broad-based organizing, see Edward Chambers (2003). Starhawk (2011) distills insights gleaned from her decades of organizing in the eco-feminist and anti-globalization movements. Public Achievement is an international youth democratic pedagogy movement at work across the United States, Eastern Europe, Palestine, South Africa, and beyond that began in Minneapolis with the leadership of Harry Boyte and Dennis Donovan; see Robert Hildreth (1997).
2. The study carefully controlled its comparison sample in order to avoid "propensity biases," according to which those who self-selected into the FYS-ARTs might be expected to have higher rates of retention on this basis alone. To avoid such bias FYS and non-FYS student samples were matched and equivalent on the following characteristics: Ethnicity, Gender, AZ Residency, FAFSA/PELL Eligibility, Attended Previews, High School Deficiencies (Math, English, Lab Science), Declared College, ACT/SAT Scores, High School CORE GPA, and Student Success Inventory (Six Scales). NAU's retention rate data are available at http://www4.nau.edu/pair/RetentionAndGraduation/CohortRetention.asp
3. However, implementation of this unanimous decision made by the ACC with a moderate Republican majority has been stalled, due to the following election that tilted the leadership to the extreme right.
4. I develop this argument in relation to an extensive review of the neuroscience literature in (Coles 2012 and 2015, forthcoming). Here I provide only the briefest summary of some of this research. In *Visionary Pragmatism*, I discuss mimetic neurological relationships that are likely embedded in relationships between human and non-human beings. See too Iaccaboni (2009) and Rizzolatti and Sinigaglia (2008).
5. I have developed a more extensive discussion of institutional transformation and the publicness and power of higher education (Coles 2014).
6. See Wendy Brown's (2001) critique of "relevance." I discuss questions of relevance and vision in *Visionary Pragmatism*.

References

Bourdieu, P. (1977). *Outline of a Theory of Practice* (Cambridge: Cambridge University Press).
Brown, W. (2001). *Politics Out of History* (Princeton: Princeton University Press).

Chambers, E. T. (2003). *Roots for Radicals: Organizing for Power, Action, and Justice* (London: Bloomsbury Academic).

Coles, R. (2012). "The Neuropolitical Habitus of Resonant Receptive Democracy." In *Essays on Neuroscience and Political Theory: Thinking the Body Politic*, edited by F. Vander Valk (New York: Routledge Press), 178–98.

Coles, R. (2014). "Transforming the Game: Democratizing the Publicness of Higher Education and Commonwealth in Neoliberal Times." *New Political Science* 36(4): 622–39.

Coles, R. (2015). *Visionary Pragmatism: Radical and Ecological Democracy in Neo-Liberal Times* (Durham: Duke University Press).

Coles, R. and Scarnati, B. (2015). "Transformational Ecotones: The Craftsperson Ethos and Higher Education." In *Democracy's Education: Public Work, Citizenship, and the Future of Colleges and Universities*, edited by H. Boyte (Nashville: Vanderbilt University Press), 115–25.

Connolly, W. E. (2008). *Capitalism and Christianity, American Style* (Durham: Duke University Press).

Dewey, J. (1997). *Democracy and Education* (New York: Touchstone Press).

Foucault, M. (2009). *Security, Territory, Population: Lectures at the College de France 1077–1978* (New York: Picador Press)

Freire, P. (2000). *Pedagogy of the Oppressed* (London: Bloomsbury Academic).

Ganz, M. (2011). "What is Public Narrative," *Working Paper* http://marshallganz.com/publications/

Gottlieb, R. (2002). *Environmentalism Unbound: Exploring New Pathways for Change* (Cambridge: MIT Press).

Hildreth, R. (1997). *Building Worlds, Transforming Lives, Making History: A Coaches Guide for Public Achievement* (Minneapolis: Center for Democracy and Citizenship).

Iaccaboni, M. (2009). *Mirroring People: The Science of Empathy and How We Connect With Others* (New York: Picador)

Klein, N. (2007). *The Shock Doctrine: The Rise of Disaster Capitalism* (New York: Henry Holt and Co.).

Miller, M. (2013). "Assessment Report for AY 2012–2013 First Year Seminar/FYSeminar-ARTs" (Flagstaff: Northern Arizona University).

Orr, D. (1994). *Earth in Mind: On Education, Environment, and the Human Prospect* (Washington, DC: First Island Press).

Payne, C. (1995). *I've Got the Light of Freedom: The Organizing Tradition and the Mississippi Freedom Struggle* (Berkeley: University of California Press).

Pollan, M. (2007). *The Omnivores's Dilemma: A Natural History of Four Meals* (New York: Penguin Press).

Rizzolatti, G. and Sinigaglia, C. (2008). *Mirrors in the Brain: How our Minds Share Actions and Emotions* (Oxford: Oxford University Press).

Ross, A. (2011). *Bird on Fire: Lessons from the World's Least Sustainable City* (Oxford: Oxford University Press).

Starhawk (2011). *Empowerment Manual: A Guide for Collaborative Groups* (Gabriola Island, British Columbia: New Society Publishers).

Wolin, S. (2010). *Democracy Inc.: Managed Democracy and the Specter of Inverted Totalitarianism* (Princeton: Princeton University Press).

PART III

RETHINKING NATURE AND POLITICAL SUBJECTS

NATURE, ENVIRONMENT, AND THE POLITICAL

CHAPTER 10

"NATURE" AND THE (BUILT) ENVIRONMENT

STEVEN VOGEL

ENVIRONMENTALISTS, obviously, are concerned about the *environment*. They want to protect it from harm, they want us to appreciate its complexity and its beauty, they want to prevent it from being destroyed by the forces of modernity or neo-liberalism or technology or anthropocentrism. The environment, they say, is endangered by pollution, by toxic wastes and acid rain, by loss of habitat and extinction of species, and above all nowadays by the threat of global warming. Environmental scientists study the environment in order to understand the threats it faces and to find ways to avoid the damage to it that is already taking place, while environmental sociologists and economists attempt to grasp the social processes that have led to that damage and to propose alternatives to reduce or eliminate it. Environmental philosophers worry about what our moral obligations are to the environment; environmental historians look at the history of human interactions with it; environmental critics examine the way it is and has been portrayed in works of literature and art. And yet there is surprisingly little discussion, neither by environmental activists nor by environmental academics, about what the environment *is*, or even what the word "environment" itself means and what aspects of the world it is supposed to pick out.

Most typically the environment is treated as being identical with *nature*: it's nature we want to protect from damage, it's nature's complexity and beauty we want people to acknowledge, it's nature that modernity or technology threatens to destroy. Nature is in danger of being paved over, its untrammeled landscapes being replaced everywhere by the ugly concrete human world of buildings and factories and highways. When environmentalists talk of the environment they mean the climate, the seas, the rain forests, the mountains and deserts—the *natural world* within which or beneath which we humans live and build our homes, drive our cars, emit our greenhouse gases. The environment is the air we breathe, the water we drink, the sun that sustains us, the earth on which we walk, the natural processes that were at work millennia before we came on the scene and that will continue (we hope) to function for millennia to come. It also, surely, includes the other living creatures with whom we share the earth—the plants and animals, the insects and plankton and microbes whose numbers are immeasurable and whose existence goes beyond anything we are capable of knowing. *Environment* means *nature*; environmentalists are lovers and defenders of nature.

Yet the word "environment," strictly speaking, simply means "that which environs," which is to say that which surrounds us. In German the word is *Umwelt*, "the world around" or "the surrounding world"; in French it's *milieu*, something like "the place we're in the middle of." And if I look around at that which I'm in the middle of right now, that which surrounds me, it's not clear that what I find is nature. I'm in a room, looking at a computer screen, surrounded by file cabinets, bookcases, some tables and chairs. Below me is a floor, and below that a basement; above me is a ceiling and above that another story and a ceiling. The house I'm in was built in the 1920s; it's surrounded by, is in the middle of, a neighborhood that was developed from an area that was previously farmland. Behind the house is a yard with grass and bushes; in front of it is a lawn that I mowed last week and should probably mow again. Behind the yard is a paved alley and in front of the lawn is a sidewalk and paved street with automobiles parked on it. The town I live in is surrounded by a larger city, a state capital. Is any of this nature?

Perhaps it is. Much will depend on what's meant by "nature," a famously ambiguous term. John Stuart Mill had pointed out already in the nineteenth century that the word has at least two distinct meanings. In one quite ordinary sense it refers to what he described as "the sum of all phenomena," everything that exists in the physical world and operates subject to the ordinary physical forces described by what are called the "laws of nature" (Mill 1963: 373–5). The opposite of "natural" in this sense would be "supernatural." And in this sense everything just mentioned—the computer, the house, the street, the cars—are "natural" (they're surely not supernatural!): the laws of physics and chemistry and the other natural sciences all apply to them. They're natural, too, in the sense that human beings, who are surely themselves natural organisms, constructed them using various skills and capacities (like intelligence and reason) that themselves presumably evolved through natural selection just as the skills and capacities of other organisms did.

But of course that's not really what most environmentalists mean when they identify the environment with nature: they certainly don't have in mind the *built* environment that surrounds us most of the time, and that's because they seem not to have this first sense of the word in mind at all. Although they're usually willing to say that human beings themselves are natural organisms (and indeed often claim that humans ought to acknowledge more than they do their embeddedness in the natural world), the notion that things like computers or automobiles are "natural" seems ridiculous: they're not natural, they're man-made. Here the second sense of the word "nature" identified by Mill is being employed: a sense referring to those aspects of the world that are independent of human beings, unaffected by them, operating separately from them. The opposite of the natural in this second sense isn't the supernatural but the *artificial*, that which humans have built. And indeed the worry environmentalists feel about the environment is a worry that the artificial is taking over: that the natural world is being harmed or even destroyed as more and more of it is urbanized, paved, or otherwise transformed by human technologies.

But if *this* is what "nature" means—the part of the world that is independent of human beings and hasn't been affected by them—then it's a little hard to understand why it should be identified with the environment, or why a concern for its protection against human encroachment should be called environmentalism. For as I've just noted the environment surrounding us is *not* "nature" in this sense of the word—precisely because what human beings seem to do, quite thoroughly and impressively, is to transform the world that surrounds them and make it into one very different from what it "naturally" was before they came on the scene. Smart tool-users that we are, as soon as we show up in an area we start to change it, building shelters, hunting and developing agriculture, clearing land and domesticating animals (and thereby altering the flora and fauna around us), constructing villages and cities, eventually inventing steam engines and mining coal and using electricity and developing the Internet in a way that radically transforms the world that environs us so that it no longer looks like "nature" in the second sense of the word at all. Our activities in this sense don't seem to *harm* the environment but rather to *build* it, turning the nature humans originally found around them into an artificial or built environment perhaps easier for them to negotiate.

It's not even clear, I should add, that these world-transforming activities that humans engage in harm *nature*, except in a more or less tautological way. For if nature = the part of the world that humans have not changed, then it's true by definition that whenever humans do anything in the world, whatever nature was there before disappears—yet this is harm by definition, not by actually causing damage. (If paint is applied to a blank canvas, is the blankness *harmed*?) On this understanding of the word "nature" the danger humans pose to it follows from the word's meaning, and so there's no way it could be avoided. Living "in harmony" with nature is impossible, no more coherent a possibility than the paint on a canvas living in harmony with its previous blankness.

What's especially curious about the definition, though, is why it was ever made in the first place. We don't have a special word for that part of the world that insects haven't affected, or seagulls, or kudzu: why do we need one for that part that has escaped the human touch? We are perfectly happy to call spider webs and beaver dams natural, and see no reason to draw any significant distinction in terms of naturalness or anything else between those areas that have been affected by bee pollination (for instance) and those where bees aren't found. But when humans build something or transform some landscape we think of it as outside nature. It's hard to avoid the sense that a kind of anthropocentrism is at work here—*insects* don't change nature into something "unnatural" or "artificial" when they act, but only *we* are special enough to be able to do so. We're fascinated, it seems, by the difference between what is us (or has been changed by us) and what isn't; something about this fascination suggests a kind of reverse narcissism, as we try desperately to examine the reflection in the lake for what's beyond or behind our own image in a way that suggests we're still focused, if only negatively, on ourselves and what we do. Humans seem to be a unique species—*metaphysically* unique, one might be tempted to say—because only they are able to remove the property of "naturalness" from something just by working on it.

In any case, the simple identification of the environment with "nature," in *either* sense of the latter word, leads in unexpected directions. If "nature" means the world independent of humans, the identification just seems false: we're not environed by such a world, but rather by a world that humans have already built and transformed. The environment surely is *not* nature in this sense, but rather is the built world that actually surrounds us. And if "nature" means everything that exists subject to the ordinary forces of physics and chemistry and biology, then doubtless the environment *is* nature, but still turns out to be a world of artifacts built by humans that are nonetheless subject to those forces. The *environment*, that is, is a *built environment*, a humanly produced one. And if that is so, then environmentalism ought to be about *that* environment, the one we actually inhabit: not "nature" (in the sense of the non-human) but something that human beings have constructed through their social practices. (And *this* would be what it would mean to say that the environment—not nature!—is a "social construction." People built it!)

What would an environmentalism of the built environment look like? It would concern itself above all with *where we live*, with the actual spaces within which human beings find themselves: spaces which tend so often today to be ugly, to be dangerous, to be harmful both to humans and to the other creatures with whom we share such spaces. It would ask about cities and their livability; it would ask about suburbs and their impact on the people who live in them and also on those who live elsewhere but whose labor and liability to health and other harms make those suburbs possible; it would ask about the impact of consumption and population on the lands that humans inhabit. It would think about things like carbon footprints and fossil fuel use, worrying about the effect of human activity on the atmosphere and the harms it will cause to people (and others) distant from that activity both in space and in time. Its politics would be a democratic one, not one associated with the simplistic idea of "defending nature." Nature would not serve as an external normative standard determining how humans should act, but rather the question of how we should act would be understood as one for *us* to decide ourselves, and to decide democratically.

The claim that nowadays the environment we inhabit has become a fully man-made one has been offered before, but typically as something to be bemoaned. The *locus classicus* here is Bill McKibben's *The End of Nature*, which claimed that in addition to all the specific environmental harms human beings were producing in the world, something else was being destroyed: nature itself. Here "nature" of course was meant in the second sense discussed earlier: it was the world separate from human beings that was being lost, McKibben argued, and that loss was grounds for a deep sadness independent of whatever other damage was being done. For him the key phenomenon was global warming caused by the burning of fossil fuels, for it meant that the temperature at every spot on earth was different from what it would otherwise "naturally" have been. "We have changed the atmosphere and so we are changing the weather," McKibben wrote. "By changing the weather, we make every spot on earth man-made and artificial. We have deprived nature of its independence, and that is fatal to its meaning. Nature's independence *is* its meaning; without it there is nothing but us" (McKibben 1989: 58). Here the recognition that what environs us is (in part) our own product appears as a source of sorrow, and nostalgia. Nature has disappeared, and we have destroyed it. Instead the world is a human-made one, an unnatural artifact.

More recently an increasing number of thinkers have tried to consider the implications of this (supposedly recent) transformation of the world from something natural to something like a human creation but without McKibben's tone of regret and anger, treating it instead simply as another fact in the history of an earth whose fundamental character (geological, atmospheric, climatological) has frequently changed before, sometimes in response to changes in the living organisms who inhabit it. (That there is as much oxygen in the atmosphere as there is, for example, is the result of photosynthesis by living things; until what has come to be called the Oxygen Catastrophe that occurred some 2.3 billion years ago and resulted from the development by cyanobacteria of the ability to photosynthesize, almost no oxygen was to be found there, and what there was in fact was poisonous to most other organisms at that time. See, for example, Margulis 1984; Knoll 2003.) But of course that the scale and breadth (and especially the complexity and diversity) of the human impact on the earth is extraordinary, and perhaps unique in the planet's history, is hard to deny. Some (for example, Crutzen and Stoermer 2000; Zalasiewicz et. al 2008; Zalasiewicz, Williams, Steffen, and Crutzen 2010) have gone so far as to suggest that the earth has entered a new geological epoch, having passed from the Holocene that started with the end of the last ice age into what ought now to be called the Anthropocene, an epoch marked by permanent changes that will be visible in the geological record for millions of years to come and that are the result of human beings' transformative activities. Not only the rapid increase in CO_2 and other greenhouse gases into the atmosphere and the resulting changes in the climate, but the transformation of soils throughout the world, the introduction of "exotic" species into new environments, the loss of species on a scale unknown since at least the last mass extinction at the end of the Cretaceous, fundamental changes to ocean chemistry and to the geology of the polar regions, etc., have all altered the earth, they argue, at the kind of scale associated with previous epochal transformations.

Curiously, this sort of "discourse of the Anthropocene" has come in for significant criticism from those who might at first have been thought to agree with it—that is, those who see the transformation of the natural world into an artificial one as something to be condemned, and who might have been expected to appreciate the idea of an Anthropocene as a clear formulation of their greatest fear. A recent anthology (Wuerthner, Crist, and Butler 2014), for example, accuses authors who engage in such discourse of hubristically desiring human domination over nature, of failing to see the value of wilderness and wildness, and indeed of over-estimating the human ability to transform the world. This kind of criticism seems to want to have it both ways: both to bemoan the extent to which humans have destroyed nature or wilderness but at the same time to assert that nature is always somehow more powerful than humans and can never be entirely destroyed. Ned Hettinger, for instance, writes that the concept of the Anthropocene "is deeply insidious" and "threatens the key environmental values of 'naturalness' and respect for nature" (Hettinger 2014: 174). The focus on human transformation of the world, he says, is "the latest embodiment of human hubris," and "manifests a culpable failure to appreciate the profound role nonhuman nature continues to play on Earth and an arrogant overvaluation of humans' role and authority" (179). "It is true," he concedes, "that there is a decreasing extent of naturalness on the planet and thus there is less of it to value," but this only means "that what remains has become all the more precious" (177–8). The claim here seems to be that nature is threatened but not yet entirely extinct, and obviously here it is "nature" as the non-human world that is meant. Yet elsewhere in his article Hettinger writes that defenders of the idea of the Anthropocene "overstate . . . the extent to which humans have influenced nature . . . We are not responsible for the existence of sunlight, gravity, or water; nor for the photosynthetic capacity of plants, the biological process of predation, or the chemical bonds between molecules" (176), and now things start to get confused—"nature" *here* is being used in the *other* sense, as that which is subject to ordinary physical forces. Those forces, of course, are *not* things humans have produced—but they would continue to operate even in a fully humanized Anthropocene where nothing "natural" in the non-human sense would be left.

It's really nature as the non-human that Hettinger and similar thinkers are concerned about, of course; the trouble, though, is that if they admit that less and less of that nature exists the idea of "defending" or "protecting" it becomes less and less relevant. Once nature (in that sense) is gone, defending its value is something like rooting for the Brooklyn Dodgers—you can still do it, but it's not clear what the point is. In the case of the Dodgers, however, there was *once* something worth rooting for; in the case of non-human nature, though, it's really not clear that there ever was, for the reasons I've been trying to explain. Why should we place a special value on that part of the world unaffected (or relatively unaffected) by one particular species—unless, as I've already suggested, we think there's something metaphysically unique about that species, some special ability it has to escape nature? The anthropocentrism here is at the same time a misanthropy: the only way to avoid destroying nature would be for this species to stop doing what it does, stop affecting the world—and since one cannot live without affecting the world, that would mean somehow stopping living.

(And it won't do to say, as many who want to reject the idea that nature is gone or never was try to argue, that naturalness is a "relative" term, that naturalness and artificiality exist on a continuum rather than being a dichotomy, that although nothing nowadays is "purely" natural because humans have indeed affected everything to some extent, still we can protect those areas that are "more" natural than others. Relativizing a dualism like this doesn't render it any less of a dualism, and in particular it remains unexplained why the poles of the continuum are still humans on the one side and nature on the other. A racism that distinguishes Jews from Aryans isn't made less awful—or even less dichotomous—by the acknowledgment that various degrees of mixed races exist as well. Why not draw a continuum with butterflies on one end and the non-butterfly world on the other, ranking areas on the degree to which butterfly-aided pollination has affected their flora? That this seems silly suggests that the continuum drawn with respect to humans is a metaphysical, not a biological one: that humans are outside of nature is assumed in the latter case *before* the continuum is posited.)

However the debate about geological nomenclature resolves itself, the point remains that humans have indeed transformed the world in increasingly significant ways, but—if what I have been arguing is correct—this does not mean that anything *ontologically* or *metaphysically* unique has happened. A new species has turned out to be atmospherically and geologically decisive, that's all. There is no reason simply because of this fact either to bemoan what has taken place or to celebrate it. As *political* actors, though, we certainly have to cope with and respond to it. This raises the question of the politics of the Anthropocene, and I want to conclude my discussion by turning to that question. Here too the key step is to drop the notion that "environment" means "nature," or rather to recognize that even if it did mean nature still the nature that it means would be the nature of the Anthropocene—and so again we're driven to the conclusion that environmental political theory has to be a *political theory of the built environment.* Environmental thought has to deal with *where we live*—which is to say, the already humanized and urbanized world we actually inhabit—not with a "nature" understood as a place where (by definition) we cannot be (Cronon 1998; Light 2001).

The focus of such a theory, it seems to me, has to be on the practices human beings engage in through which they construct the environment they inhabit. Indeed, I would argue that it's not simply the built or humanized character of the environment that needs to be recognized: rather one has to pay attention to the *practices of building* through which that environment has come to be what it is. It's pretty clear to all of us that the world environing us is "human" in the sense that the objects in it have human meanings, satisfy human needs, play a role in human culture, have a market value, etc. But there is another fact about each of those objects that is harder to recognize or rather harder deeply to feel: the fact that each of them is *humanly built*, that every object in one's immediate environment required the active labor of many humans in order to produce. The desk I'm working at right now is made of wood; to build it trees had to be felled, transported, hewn; designs had to be drawn; pieces had to be measured, cut, fitted together; nails were used, which themselves had to be fashioned from pieces of metal mined from the earth, using machines that themselves had to be built, using other materials that had their own history of making; at each step records were kept, paper and ink and computers were employed, each of which themselves had to be fabricated; financing was needed for the process, and lawyers and bankers and office assistants had to work, themselves using other machines, other paper, other desks. It's *this* process that we lose sight of nowadays, failing to notice (and failing, I'd add, to feel grateful for) the enormous number of people and the enormous quantity of their effort needed for the fabrication of this simple desk which I am now relying upon to write these words. A good name for this process, and for the way it tends to be forgotten, might be *reification.* (See Lukács 1971.) The term would be intended to mean on the one hand simply the making of things, but on the other would point to the way in which the things we make appear as static fixed items, part of the ordinary furniture of the world, without recognition of the practices of building and the human builders needed to help them come into existence.

Of course other, non-human entities had roles to play in this process too: the trees themselves, the worms and microbes that transformed the soil, the billions dead who made possible the fuel that brought them from the forest. And not only living creatures: the sun had a crucial function, the rain and wind too, the veins of iron ore that helped produce the machines, the silicon from which the computer chips were fashioned. Human building takes place *in* "nature" (in Mill's first sense); the constructed world we live in isn't one we've constructed "by ourselves"—indeed, it's not even clear what that would mean: we're never by ourselves, we're always active in a world with other entities that themselves are active. To build is to co-build: no building can happen without the cooperation of thousands or millions of non-human entities in the world.

To overcome reification would be to acknowledge the built character of our environment and the work and effort of others needed to produce that "ordinary furniture" upon which we so profoundly depend. The built objects around us would appear, without reification, not simply as objects to be used but as indicators of our deep interconnections with each other, of a community upon which each of us necessarily depends and without which none of us would be able to do anything at all. And here it is the *human* co-makers who play a key role, because we (you and I, reader) are humans, and for us building inevitably introduces a *political* issue: we have to decide *what* to build, and *how*, and we need a procedure for making that decision. And so those built objects turn out to always have a political meaning, as each of them is the product of social practices of construction that had to be organized, that were normatively structured, and to which terms such as "legitimacy," "fairness," "equality," or "exploitation" and "injustice" could be applied.[1]

But in a social order determined by individual transactions in the marketplace, where consumption is a matter of private choice and production depends upon wage labor, reification seems hard to avoid. Both the processes of building and the communal character of those processes are hidden by such a mode of organization. In the marketplace neither the built nor the social nature of the objects we consume is evident; instead they seem to come fully formed from the marketplace (the Costco, the Ford dealer, the Apple Store) itself. But there is a further and even more significant reified consequence of individualized market transactions, for when aggregated they generate an entire system, an economy, that appears to the individuals who produce them *not* as a social product but rather, again, as a set of fixed, static, and unchangeable things. The GDP, the rate of inflation or unemployment, the price of fuel or of milk, the performance of the NASDAQ: all these things too are in fact the *product* of the myriad activities of all the individuals transacting with each other in the free marketplace—and yet to each of those individuals they appear as simple facts of the world ("natural facts," one might be inclined to say) to which those individuals must simply adjust themselves. Again, the reality that these things indeed are social "products"—although the sociality of their production is entirely implicit, since they simply result unconsciously from millions of actors making millions of private decisions—remains hidden in this reified structure.

An environmentalism of the built environment, it seems to me, should take reification seriously and think about its consequences for the environment we inhabit. For there's no question, as I've already said, that mostly that environment is a pretty terrible one: it's ugly, it's dehumanizing, it's harmful to life, and furthermore it is rapidly warming in a way whose effects look to be dire. *We* have built that world—we have "socially constructed" it—but only in a reified and unconscious manner. No individual has *chosen* that environment, and I doubt frankly that many individuals would; rather to each of us it appears as something we have to accept and within which we try to make the best life for ourselves that we can. (It's a built environment, but it almost seems as if it's nature!) Each of us faces, in the many decisions we make, something like Garrett Hardin's famous "tragedy of the commons," where a group of herdsmen each have to decide whether to add cows to their individual herd (Hardin 1968). If they each keep adding cows, the commons collapses, and yet for each individual there's an advantage to adding a cow (no matter what!)—and since (by hypothesis) there's no way for them to decide *together* how to use the commons each one is forced into behavior that each knows will end in tragedy for all. I know that my carbon footprint makes me complicit in harms that will take place in the future to people all over the world; and yet if I decrease that footprint those harms will take place nonetheless—and so it's hard to see how I can be expected to make my own life worse by giving up my car and my job and my air-conditioning. And yet it's all of us together making those (rational!) decisions that will absolutely cause that future harm. The reified social consequence of our actions is something we have no way of acknowledging and taking responsibility for as a society now.

Environmental problems, from this point of view, are not problems about "nature." They're problems that arise from our failure to grasp the social consequences of our actions—a failure, that is, to grasp their consequences for the world that environs us—and above all from our failure to find a way to *decide together* what actions we want to perform and what consequences we hope to produce. We don't solve environmental problems by living more in accordance with nature, or by doing what nature wants, or by trying to leave nature alone, we solve them by *acknowledging that the environment is built* and then by *deciding socially to build it better*. The environment we currently inhabit is as bad as it is—as dangerous, as toxic, as ugly—not because anyone decided to build it that way but because no *decision* was made at all: and so the shape of the environment is left as the outcome of the anarchic processes that result when millions of individuals engage in private transactions without any ability to decide publically and communally what they *want* that shape to be.

If this is so, then the identification of "environment" with "nature" I began this chapter by discussing—where "nature" is taken as meaning that which is other than the human, and hence as *not* the product of human acts of making—starts to look like a symptom of reification more than as the foundation of an environmentally progressive view of the world. It's the result of a failure to see the extent to which the world *is* in a certain sense our product, that we *do* live in the Anthropocene, and that the real problem is our failure to *choose consciously* what we do and what consequences we want our practices to have. The trouble with an environmentalism based on nature is that it treats nature as a normative standard determining how human beings should act. But it cannot serve as such a standard, for reasons that have been elucidated by Hume, Mill, Moore, and many others. Treating nature as such a standard, after defining it precisely as something independent of humans, is an attempt to avoid responsibility, treating the world around us as other than us and as something we cannot and should not affect. But we *do* affect it, and can't help doing so, as I have been arguing—just as we do affect the NASDAQ and the rate of inflation, and just as Hardin's herdsmen affect the commons. *We cannot avoid this responsibility, although we can fail to take it up consciously.*

To overcome reification, and to acknowledge our responsibility for the world our actions inevitably help produce, requires moving from the realm of the market to the realm of politics. The herdsmen in Hardin's story have to *talk together* and *decide together what to do*; left to their own individual choices the result will be catastrophe.[2] We too have to talk together and decide, entering into a realm of discursive democracy where a community can consciously choose what sorts of practices it wishes to engage in and, most importantly, what sort of environment it wishes to inhabit. *Environmental problems are not problems about nature*: they are social and political problems about how human practices ought to be organized and about the norms by which those practices ought to be guided. Those problems are not solved by appealing to nature, or to anything outside of the human realm; they are—perhaps unfortunately—problems only humans can solve, because only humans (it turns out) are the ones able to talk and choose together what they do.

Notes

1. Non-humans seem not to face this issue, because the question of choice seems not to arise for them and because they seem not to use language and hence normativity and justification seem to play no role in their behaviors. In this sense Latour (1993) is wrong to call for a "Parliament of Things": things seem not to be able to parley. (These are empirical claims, of course: if non-humans do have access to the realm of the political then they too deserve a voice within it.)
2. Hardin thinks there's another solution, which he prefers: to "privatize" the commons, which is to say to destroy its character as *common*. This is the reified solution characteristic of the ideology of free markets, in which an "invisible hand" turns the self-interested actions of private actors magically into a social good that none of them necessarily intended. (The social good, that is, is *built* by them but they do not recognize it as such.) Privatization requires the abolition of externalities; the trouble is that externalities are not so easily done away with.

References

Cronon, W. (1998). "The Trouble with Wilderness, or Getting Back to the Wrong Nature." In *The Great New Wilderness Debate*, edited by J. B. Callicott and M. P. Nelson (Athens, Ga.: University of Georgia Press), 471–99.

Crutzen, P. J. and Eugene F. Stoermer (2000). "The 'Anthropocene.'" *The IGB Newsletter* 41: 17–18.

Hardin, G. (1968). "The Tragedy of the Commons." *Science* 162(3859): 1243–8.
Hettinger, N. (2014). "Valuing Naturalness in the 'Anthropocene': Now More Than Ever." In *Keeping the Wild: Against the Domestication of Earth*, edited by G. Wuerthner, E. Crist, and T. Butler (Washington: Island Press), 174–82.
Knoll, A. H. (2003). *Life On a Young Planet* (Princeton: Princeton University Press).
Latour, B (1993). *We Have Never Been Modern* (Cambridge, Mass.: Harvard University Press).
Light, A. (2001). "The Urban Blind Spot in Environmental Ethics." *Environmental Politics* 10(1): 7–35.
Lukács, G. (1971). "Reification and the Consciousness of the Proletariat." In *History and Class Consciousness: Studies in Marxist Dialectics*. Translated by Rodney Livingstone (Cambridge, Mass.: MIT Press), 83–222.
Margulis, L. (1984). *Early Life* (Boston: Jones and Bartlett Publishers).
McKibben, B. (1989). *The End of Nature* (New York: Anchor), 58.
Mill, J. S. (1963). *Nature. Collected Works*, vol.10 (Toronto: University of Toronto Press), 373–402.
Wuerthner, G., Crist, E., and Butler, T., eds. (2014). *Keeping the Wild: Against the Domestication of Earth* (Washington: Island Press).
Zalasiewicz, J. et al. (2008). "Are We Now Living in the Anthropocene?" *GSA Today* 18(2): 4–8.
Zalasiewicz, J., Williams, M., Steffen, W., and Crutzen, P. (2010). "The New World of the Anthropocene." *Environmental Science and Technology* 44(7): 2228–31.

CHAPTER 11

THEORIZING THE NON-HUMAN THROUGH SPATIAL AND ENVIRONMENTAL THOUGHT

JUSTIN WILLIAMS

INTRODUCTION

WHAT is the relationship between "space" and "environment," and how might their relationship inform environmental political theory? Henri Lefebvre, one of the most celebrated spatial thinkers, answers the question this way: "Indeed, pollution, the environment, ecology and ecosystems, growth and its finality, all fragment and conceal the problems of space" (Lefebvre and Lebas 1996: 186). Here, Lefebvre imagines a difference in scale: ecology was one of many ways that scientists had attempted to grasp the much more general phenomenon of space. Ecology's particular corner of spatial science was knowledge of a *natural* space. For Lefebvre, this fragmentation of space led to the pursuit of wilderness leisure: like wilderness critics who would emerge in the 1980s and '90s, Lefebvre argued that wilderness was a politics that had fragmented the more general social category—space—into a commodified form, a fragmentation that undermined the possibility of a society-wide politics capable of addressing capitalism's crises (1996: 158). If Lefebvre is right, then one would scarcely need to pay attention to environment at all: being sufficiently attentive to space would reveal everything there was to know about ecology and environment.

Yet Lefebvre's depiction of ecology was premised on a particularly constrained vision of natural space, one that resembled an original wilderness (Lefebvre 1992: 29–30, 329). Environmental scholars, for their part, have increasingly distanced themselves from this kind of nature (Cronon 1995; Schlosberg 2013). Environment has come to encompass seemingly every corner of the world, and one could just as plausibly claim that Lefebvre's "space" is a rather arbitrary fragmentation of "environment:" second nature is everywhere, and referring to space is simply a way of hiding that fact. It seems that both concepts, at their outer margins, are capable of gobbling up the other.

Rather than following Lefebvre in assigning conceptual priority to space, I argue in this chapter that space and environment are two separate, but often complementary, analytic traditions for problematizing the relationship between humans and non-humans. I argue that they overlap insofar as they both offer what I call a *production* view of nature and space, which unsettles the presumed un-human character of both nature and space. I begin with a discussion of geographic space, to outline what it means to think spatially. I then argue that despite their shared interest in bringing non-humans into social life, scholars from these traditions diverge in two important respects: 1) they generally emphasize different sets of non-humans; 2) many spatial theorists are implicitly less amenable to analyzing the role of non-humans for constituting politics. Finally, I argue that spatial and environmental thinkers can improve each other's analyses: spatial thinkers offer a developed set of analytics that are especially powerful for environmental thinkers; environmental thinkers argue for a stronger form of embeddedness that spatial thinkers should both endorse and deploy.

Geographic Space

Although space is a term that is used regularly in everyday speech, geographers mean something perhaps counter-intuitive when they talk about it. In everyday speech, we often think of space as emptiness: I move to a big house in the suburbs so that I can get some more space, some emptiness in which to put my things. In this everyday sense, space is treated as a dimension in which things—not just my articles to be stored, but also social things (I always wanted a big dining room for hosting dinner parties)—exist and move. Spatial theorists often label this understanding of space *abstract space*. Abstract space is basically a container, a static and unchanging dimension that pre-exists the things that populate it. Rocks, trees, power plants, and people are distributed across a grid of latitude and longitude, in the emptiness that pre-exists those things. Abstract space is usually associated with mapping on a grid: one can project lines of latitude and longitude on top of the entire universe (or at least over the entire earth), and locate objects as they correspond to the points that occupy it. Many spatial theorists have attempted to unsettle this everyday view and moved toward a view of space as *relational* and *social* (Merriman et al. 2012: 4), in what Lefebvre has called a production of space.[1]

To understand why such a shift occurred, a brief discussion of its most proximate developments may be useful.[2] Geographers in academic departments were, until the 1930s, mainly concerned with *regions*: with how the areas of the earth became differentiated through, for example, geological processes. Beginning in the 1940s, positivist social scientists in geography critiqued this focus on particular regions, demanding instead a general "spatial science" that could accurately predict how and when towns would expand, why people move in the way they do, and other similarly "universal" features of geography. Although the mid-century turn to spatial science later fell out of favor with spatial theorists, it nonetheless focused the attention of geographers on *general characteristics of space* rather than descriptions of particular regions of the world.

Beginning in the late 1960s, two strains of geographic thought criticized this spatial science from separate standpoints. First, humanistic geographers urged a focus on closely related term, "place." If regional geographers described particular locations, humanistic geographers sought to focus on the general experience of inhabiting locations. Drawing on phenomenologists like Heidegger and Merleau-Ponty, these scholars theorized "a sense of place:" how do people become attached to locations? And how has modernity, with its corollary focus on a general and abstract space, unsettled those attachments? Humanistic geographers critiqued the abstract, universalizing, un-human space of spatial scientists, focusing instead on what it means to inhabit places (Casey 1996; Tuan 2001; Cresswell 2004).

Second, Marxist geographers critiqued how spatial scientists characterized space. Instead of turning to the experience of place (a feature of individuals and communities) and away from the abstractions of space, geographers inspired by Marx investigated how space itself is socially produced. Two figures were especially influential in this tradition: Henri Lefebvre and David Harvey.[3] In opposition to abstract space, space understood as an infinite, pre-social grid in which material processes occur, both Lefebvre and Harvey argued that space is *relational*: space is a shifting set of relations among bodies. In Lefebvre's words, "physical space has no 'reality' without the energy that is deployed within it" (Lefebvre 1992: 13), and, "a space is not a thing but rather a set of relations between things (objects and products)" (1992: 83). In this view, space is no longer understood as a dimension that pre-exists bodies; rather, space is made of the very relations among things. This latter, relational view of space characterizes much contemporary work in spatial theory (see also Harvey 1973, 1974, 1996, 2007; D. B. Massey 1994; E. Soja 1999; Merriman 2012).

The conceptual shift from abstract to relational space has two important implications for understanding space. First, relational space implies a dynamism: because space is made of relations among things that always shift, space itself is always shifting. Any given location in the universe is merely one moment in ongoing processes. This insight has been especially important for theoretical developments on place, which is no longer at odds with "space" as an intellectual category. No essential quality—either in terms of territorial boundaries or identity ("a sense of place")—defines, for instance, a shopping district in geographer Doreen Massey's north London neighborhood: "while Kilburn may have a character of its own, it is absolutely not a seamless, coherent identity" (1994: 153). Rather, the Kilburn shopping district is refashioned through the increasingly cosmopolitan relations that move through it: Kilburn is now characterized in part by Indian and Irish grocery stores. And so, too, with any place: as the flows of people, pollutants, wildlife, and consumer goods change, so too does Detroit, San Francisco, the Great Plains. In its dynamism, space is inextricably linked with time: space and time are really two sides of the same coin, such that it would be better (but analytically very difficult) to talk of space-time (D. Massey 1999).

Second, space is understood as being socially produced. Space, as we've already seen, is composed of relations among different sorts of things; to the extent some of those things are social in character, space is also social in character (Harvey 1973: 28). In a distinct break from abstract space, which treats geography as a natural phenomenon that precedes social production, theorists of relational space argue that understanding space requires that we understand all the different connections and processes that make locations. This was Lefebvre's point when he called for "a movement from *products . . .* to *production*" (1992: 26). Lefebvre wants to call attention to the social character of how geography comes into being. The influence of Marx is especially important here: what spatial scientists had taken to be universal geographic phenomena were instead the characteristics of a specifically capitalist geography. Where spatial scientists were interested in universal characteristics of "the city," David Harvey argues that "the self-same set of buildings will assume a different meaning under capitalism compared to feudalism or socialism" (2001: 75). The physical landscape is a product of human and non-human entities interacting within wider sets of social relations. Social action has an important role to play in producing what many geographers had assumed to be natural processes like the growth of cities.

If the fixed and static character of geography has been abandoned in favor of thinking of space as a production, a significant question has remained for spatial theorists: how is space produced, and through what processes? Spatial theorists tend to answer this question through four analytic perspectives: territory, place, scale, and network (Jessop, Brenner, and Jones 2008).[4] Territory refers to bounded entities, be they national, regional, or international. The focus, here, is on how borders are maintained and expanded, how regions are enclosed, and the political effects of that enclosure (P. J. Taylor 1994; Ballvé 2012). If scholars of territory tend to focus on making boundaries, those who focus on place tend to emphasize the experience of inhabiting geographic entities. As I argued earlier, place is often treated as particular, experienced, embodied geography, as opposed to the "abstract" space that Lefebvre and others criticized (Tuan 2001). Yet if place and space began as two divergent paths for understanding geography, they have more and more become complementary, with place-making becoming an important mode of producing space (D. B. Massey 1994; Harvey 1996; Pratt 1999; Castree 2004; Cresswell 2004; Qian, Qian, and Zhu 2012). Scholars of scale are interested in how space is produced as a hierarchy. Although there is significant debate surrounding the concept (Marston, Jones, and Woodward 2005), scale usually refers to the nested character of geographies: counties within states within nations within continents; meadows within cities within forests within watersheds. Scholars of scale are interested in how any given geography can be examined at all of these different registers: scale is a vertical organization of space (Delaney and Leitner 1997; Leitner 1997; Collinge 1999; Marston 2000; Brenner 2004: 9). Most recently, space has been investigated as a network: network scholars instead trace how geographies are made by economic, social, and material connections that move across boundaries (Amin 2002; Castells 2011).

Manuel Castells perhaps best captures the spirit of network analysis in geography: "Our society is constructed around flows: flows of capital, flows of information, flows of technology, flows of organizational interaction, flows of images, sounds, and symbols" (Castells 2011: 411). That is, space is produced through the interconnections among people and things, the networks among bodies that move across borders and long distances (Murdoch 1998; Beaverstock, Smith, and Taylor 2000; Whatmore and Thorne 2000; R. G. Smith 2003; Dicken 2004).

In practice, these four different analytic tendencies in spatial theory—territory, place, scale, and network—often overlap. For instance, territory can be viewed as a bordering strategy that creates certain experiences of place and produces a certain scaling of power (Jessop, Brenner, and Jones 2008: 396). In this way, territory can be seen as a factor that influences the production of place and scale. These four spatial analytics share the conviction that space is composed of relations (both human and non-human) that shift over time, a point of central importance for spatial theory.

Space and Environment

In the remainder of this essay, I argue that space and environment are two different intellectual and political traditions for problematizing the same concern: the role of non-humans in social and political life. One primary, shared trend characterizes their stance toward non-humans: both traditions more and more converge toward understanding humans as in an interactive exchange with the world around them, in what I will, borrowing from Lefebvre, characterize as a production. Two main differences characterize the lineages: they are focused on different kinds of non-humans and deploy different analytic tools; and environmental scholars have tended to admit a more active role for the non-humans they identify. I end with a brief discussion of Urban Political Ecology, an intellectual subfield that capitalizes on the insights of both traditions.

Lineages

Environmental thought and spatial theory emerge from two distinct intellectual and political lineages[5] Although environmentalism's history is often told as the history of a wilderness ethic, Robert Gottlieb argues that environmental thought emerged from diverse voices reacting to Progressive Era industrialization. On the one hand, a familiar strain of wilderness and leisure environmentalism of John Muir and Gifford Pinchot sought to limit and regulate the encroachment of an expanding industrial, urban society into the hinterlands. On the other hand, activists like Jane Addams and Alice Hamilton critiqued the influence of industrialization in cities, another site of industrialism's intensifying effects: pollution, the spread of disease, and sanitation were paramount concerns (Gottlieb 2005). These two related critiques of industrialization are still with us, represented both by an environmental ethic with the reverence and protection of nature at its forefront (Devall and Sessions 1985) and anti-toxics activism in environmental justice movements (D. E. Taylor 2000).

Spatial theory in its present form, as I discussed earlier, emerges in large measure from Marxist geographers rejecting abstract spatial science. Like environmentalists, Marxist geographers were grappling with their own set of political problems, and it was precisely the inability of spatial scientists to understand and explain such problems that led to the expansion of a relational theory of space: "There is an ecological problem, an urban problem, an international trade problem, and yet we seem incapable of saying anything of depth or profundity about any of them" (Harvey 1973: 129). Although Marx's presence is also obvious in environmental thought and activism (Bookchin 2005; Kovel 2007), and nature is of central importance to spatial thinkers (Harvey 1974; N. Smith 1984), the interest has emerged from different historical emphases.

Humans and Non-humans: Two Questions

Despite their different lineages, spatial and environmental thought share an important intellectual and conceptual concern: the role of non-humans in social and political life. I outline two general questions suggested by such an inquiry. The first question involves the effect of social action on nature and space: to what extent do humans come to actively produce environment and space? It is noteworthy that both environmental and spatial thinkers have moved toward a production view of their respective fields. Like "space," "environment" is increasingly viewed as dynamic and relational. This has been true both in the academy and in many of the concerns of environmental activists. In the academy, this move toward thinking about environment as socially and dynamically constituted appears in the critique of deep ecology and wilderness that emerged in the 1990s. Not long after Deep Ecologists embarked on their journey to systematize an ethics founded on a relatively untrammeled (in other words, fixed, static, original, and non-human) nature (Devall and Sessions 1985), wilderness environmentalism began to attract critics wary of their politics (Guha 1989; Cronon 1995). Perhaps best known among these, William Cronon argued that a troubling notion of wilderness—as distant, pristine, untouched, timeless—underpinned much environmental politics at the time. Cronon and others critiqued this nature as a historically specific ideal, and argued that humans have for a very long time helped to produce their environments. The wilderness critique is only one prominent line of thought that argues for understanding nature not as a static entity, but as something produced and dynamic, a second nature in part made by humans and their social configurations.

Outside the academy, political movements have likewise adopted a dynamic, social understanding of environment, a trend perhaps most visible in the increasingly important claims of environmental justice activists. As David Schlosberg noted, environmental justice activists offer a broad frame for social criticism that rethinks "environment" (Schlosberg 2013: 38). "Environment" is understood as the places where we "live, work, and play," such that every place—urban, suburban, rural, wilderness, park—is a site of environmental concern. The expanding scope of environmental justice is evident in analyses of not only "civil rights and anti-toxics movements, but also indigenous rights movements, the labour movement (including farm labour, occupational health and safety, and some industrial unions)", and also "transportation, access to countryside and green space, land use and smart growth policy, water quality and distribution, energy development and jobs, brownfields refurbishment, and food justice" (Schlosberg 2013: 41). This exhaustive list leaves little outside its borders: environment, it seems, now consists of nearly everywhere. Notably, environment has become increasingly social: where we "live, work, and play" is the complex product of ecological processes, economic activity, political contestation, and urban land use policy. The emphasis is not on protecting a natural realm that has fallen from grace, but instead on how localities are (often unjustly) produced.

Environmentalism's increasing embrace of the production of nature—expanding what counts as an environmental concern—marks an important convergence with spatial thought. As I argued in the first section, spatial thinkers have, at least since the 1970s, taken the social production of the non-human world to be an important intellectual consideration. Both environment and space—amalgamations of particular kinds of non-human entities—are more and more conceived of as produced, which marks perhaps the most important overlap between these two traditions.

A second question about the human–non-human relationship runs in the other direction: to what extent do non-humans shape political and social life? Environmental thinkers and activists have a long history of arguing for the active role of non-humans in political life. Whether in Thoreau's argument that encounters with the Wild are of fundamental importance for our personal and political health (B. P. Taylor 1994; Thoreau 2009), in the argument that global natural resources are a profound and limited, if often overlooked, pre-condition for economic growth and social action (Meadows, Randers, and Meadows 2004), or in the ever louder pleas to address how climate change will likely reforge political and social relations, environmental philosophy and activism has started from the premise that the non-human world actively re-configures political and social life.[6] There has, of course, been much debate about how to characterize and what to do about that fact. Still, an enduring feature of much environmental thought is an acknowledgment that non-humans are centrally important features of our politics and ethics, transcending the too-simple presumption that the non-human world is there for the taking, to be transformed and molded into whatever humans see fit.

Spatial thinkers, on the other hand, have been both more ambivalent and less attentive to the role of non-humans in forging political relations. To be sure, spatial thinkers have long wondered whether space—understood as a set of material relations—exerts some kind of productive power of its own (Castells 1979). Yet perhaps because of their desire to distance themselves from an abstract spatial science, spatial thinkers have been cautious to admit a strong role for non-humans in political life. Lefebvre is exemplary on this score: "Though a *product* to be used, to be consumed, it is also a *means of production*; networks of exchange and flows of raw materials and energy fashion space and are determined by it" (1992: 85). For Lefebvre, space was a commodity in the Marxist sense, an artifact that was socially produced. We may be tempted to view commodities as products isolated from the processes that gave them form, but Marx urges us to think of commodities instead as both having social histories (the labor, materials, and coordination involved in producing a commodity) and as serving also as inputs to other productive processes (yarn—an output from the woolen mill—is an input into production for the weaver). Much like any other commodity, space exhibits this twofold character of being both output of social processes and input into future production. Lefebvre leaves some room for the appearance of space in politics, but its appearance is mostly itself the outcome of primarily social processes. Both David Harvey and Manuel Castells likewise treat space as a commodity, although Castells, in particular, is deeply resistant to the claim that spatial relationships configured social and political ones. Edward Soja, on the other hand, later developed a stronger claim about the effects of the space on society, in what he called the "socio-spatial dialectic:" "the spatiality of whatever subject you are looking at is viewed as shaping social relations and societal development just as much as social processes configure and give meaning to the human geographies or spatialities in which we live" (E. W. Soja 2010: 4). A strong claim in this regard might involve how automobile infrastructure cuts up urban landscapes. Highways not only displace city residents, but also create barriers over which pedestrians and bicyclists must cross, thereby changing the city's geography. And this change to the city's geography very well may change who visits whom, how one gets to the grocery store, the siting of manufacturing, and the ability to participate in city council meetings. In turn, these changing social relations have effects on what the city becomes in the future: where highways move next, what kinds of city services are possible for different neighborhoods. In this way, spatial relations and social relations co-produce each other. Yet, as I later discuss, even Soja, while explicitly endorsing the productive power of spatial relations, has often implicitly treated those non-human, spatial relations as more passive receptacles than active constituents in political life.

Examples: Gentrification and Justice

The different way in which environmental and spatial thinkers treat the active participation of non-humans suggests one primary way in which, although the two traditions clearly overlap in their areas of study, they tend to diverge in their emphases. In the next subsection, I return to the theme of the active role of non-humans. Here, I focus on a second main difference between spatial and environmental thought: the non-humans on which they focus. In brief, spatial thinkers typically examine features of built environments, while environmental thinkers typically attend to relatively natural features of environments. I offer two examples: gentrification and justice.

Gentrification, the process of neighborhood transformation whereby typically white and affluent residents move into low income neighborhoods (and many scholars argue displace those low income residents), is a phenomenon studied widely by geographers, urban planners, and sociologists. This literature is primarily concerned with how and where people are displaced and the general social processes (and especially capitalism) and neighborhood revitalization attendant to the process (Marcuse 1985; N. Smith 1996; Vigdor 2002; Freeman and Braconi 2004; Lees, Slater, and Wyly 2007). Another approach to studying gentrification is through "eco-gentrification," which focuses on the production and consumption of natural resources that attends the gentrification process (Quastel 2009; Eckerd 2011). Quite clearly, eco-gentrification exhibits an overlap between spatial and environmental thinking: neighborhoods are transformed as far-flung goods and services enter and leave. Yet the whole point of developing an eco-gentrification analysis is to call attention to a particular aspect of that process: natural resources and environments, with strong connotations of nature. And, if one is concerned with these sorts of traditionally ecological categories, such an emphasis is probably necessary, because much of the gentrification literature is concerned with analyses of movement, displacement, and poverty, but rarely an explicitly natural resource or ecological analysis. So although these two approaches to gentrification share a concern with how gentrification produces unjust neighborhoods, they tend to emphasize different aspects of that injustice. Where many gentrification scholars ask "how does gentrification change how people relate to each other and their neighborhoods?," scholars of eco-gentrification ask "how does gentrification alter ecological flows?"

The point is not that gentrification is an exclusively spatial, while eco-gentrification is an exclusively environmental or ecological, analysis. I draw attention to these two ways of studying gentrification to demonstrate their different critical emphases on different kinds of non-humans. Eco-gentrification scholars deploy conceptual frameworks that are centrally important to spatial theorists. Yet there is a distinct critical emphasis implied by eco-gentrification: precisely the point of adding the prefix "eco" to gentrification is to call attention to the ecological implications—for water, air, waste disposal—often left unattended by gentrification scholars.

I turn now to justice, which I will approach from two directions. First, it's noteworthy that some geographers analyze the *space* of environmental justice, as it suggests the analytic differences for which I have argued. Gordon Walker (2009), for instance, argues that the "first wave" of environmental justice scholarship focused on proximity—how poor and minority residents were located close to toxic dumps—and the uneven distribution of pollutants. Beyond these early emphases on what resembles the cartographic and abstract space of the map, Walker argues that environmental justice activists have broadened their articulation of space to include considerations of responsibility (where pollutants come from, just as much as where they are sited), the production of toxic places (how certain locations become marked with "trash"), and mapping participation (how to draw boundaries around affected communities) (Walker 2009). To extend the framework I outlined in the first section of this essay, Walker investigates how issues of territory, place, scale, and network inform, frustrate, and produce a politics of environmental justice. Scale, in particular, has been a fruitful conceptual tool for thinking spatially about environmental justice (N. C. Heynen 2003; Bickerstaff and Agyeman 2009; Sze et al. 2009). Again, the point is not to draw firm borders around what can count as a spatial instead of environmental analysis; there is significant exchange among thinkers in both traditions. Rather, a spatial approach to the question of environmental justice provides a distinct set of analytic tools—focused on a particular set of non-humans—for problematizing environmental degradation.

As a second approach to space and justice, consider the emerging concept of "spatial justice." Although justice was a topic taken up by geographers as early as 1973 (Harvey 1973; Pirie 1983), the term spatial justice has recently emerged to more explicitly address the relationship between geography and justice. Geographer Edward Soja is most visible in this regard: "Guiding the exploration [of spatial justice] from the start is the idea that justice, however it might be defined, has a *consequential geography*, a spatial expression that is more than just a background reflection or set of physical attributes to be descriptively mapped" (E. W. Soja 2010: 1, emphasis in the original). In other words, spatial justice is an analytic framework that investigates how spatial relationships constitute justice relations. To return to the example of automobile infrastructure: highways cut up the metropolitan landscape, prohibiting certain kinds of movements (how and where one walks), enabling others (how and where one drives). This division of the urban landscape has provoked critiques of the injustice of this arrangement, both from activist and academic circles (Patterson 2007). The relevant question for such a framework is how the spatial features of territory, place, scale, and network produce just (or more often, unjust) relations among people.

Viewed from a distance, spatial justice appears quite similar to environmental justice. After all, they are both concerned with how material relations—well beyond merely economic materials—constitute relations of justice and injustice. Yet in practice, scholars in both traditions tend to be preoccupied with different non-humans. Although it is clearly not the case that environmental justice is preoccupied with nature conceived of as pristine, unchanging, and definitively not human, scholars often ground the core of the movement on either "ecology" or "environment." Schlosberg, for instance, argues than an important feature of environmental justice is its awareness of how humans are immersed in our environments and manipulate nature, and furthermore how a notion of justice might be extended to those natural services and features (2013: 43–4). Likewise, Sze and London define the basic orientation of environmental justice as "a critical analysis of power as it plays out in the (mal)distribution of harms and opportunities related to the environment with special attention to race and class" (Sze and London 2008: 1348). Although these scholars clearly acknowledge the exchange between humans and their environments, something particular to "the environment" unites struggles for environmental justice, a union that, in the case of the United States, seems to capture a specific set of non-humans: water, air, pesticides, soil erosion, fields of grain, elk migration. Environmental justice critiques how ecological systems are altered in a way that affects people in unequal ways. Spatial theory, on the other hand, has never looked to "nature" or "ecology" as its primary muse, instead focusing on how geography is socially produced. Spatial justice, too, has tended to focus on its own set of non-humans: transit routes, buildings, borders, the architecture of security, and public meeting places. To be sure, both approaches are compatible with each other: one might speak of the spatial injustice of climate change, for instance (Anguelovski and Roberts 2011). Yet environment and space offer two different starting points for incorporating non-humans into political life: spatial theory often begins from the priority of the built environment, and environmental theory often begins from ecologically produced things.

A Critical Exchange

Given their similarities and divergences, how, then, do spatial and environmental thought inform each other? One answer concerns the distinct analytic tools offered by spatial theory: a spatial approach can call explicit attention to an expanded range of non-humans and certain kinds of relations among them. Because of its emphases on issues of territories, places, scales, and networks, spatial theory offers some important tools for analyzing contemporary environmental politics. Environmental thinkers—sometimes explicitly, other times implicitly—use each of the four spatial analytics I outline above, and in particular place and scale.

Place, as I argued earlier, refers to meaningful locations. Scholars of place are interested in how geography, identity, and power produce each other through particular locational attachments (Cresswell 1996). For environmental scholars and activists, place is an important analytic and political category. Often, environmental scholars are interested in how a reinvigorated sense of place can enliven environmental ethics, politics, and resource management. Peter Cannavò, for example, has argued that land use practices in the United States pay too little heed to the preservation of places and instead over-emphasize their transformation. Thus, a loss of a sense of place now characterizes the experience of many Americans. Cannavò urges the cultivation of a practice of place, one that balances between transformation and preservation. Such a balance might help to mediate, for instance, contentious forest preservation politics (Cannavò 2007). The process of place-making has also been a central feature of environmental justice activism and scholarship. Associating places (and their residents) with trash—producing a spatial identity for a particular place—marks those places as the unproblematic site for further dumping. It should perhaps not be surprising that environmental justice activists seek to reclaim the identity of places made into dumps (Walker 2009: 626). Environmental justice critiques not only the distribution of dumps and their proximity to poor and minority communities, but also how certain places are made.

Scale, too, has been an important component of environmental scholarship, as any discussion of climate change will demonstrate. Scale refers to the different levels at which events occur (from the local to the global). Climate change is an event that demands reckoning at all possible scales. At its core, climate change is a global phenomenon: it describes an aggregate rise in global temperatures. Yet the effects of climate change will be experienced differently across continents, ecosystems, watersheds, cities, and regions. Further, any mitigation of or adaptation to climate change will involve political action at different scales: international regulations on carbon emissions may or may not ever come to pass, but in the meantime, national, state, and municipal governments are all offering regulations of their own. Adaptation to climate change will certainly require policy action at all of those scales (Neil Adger, Arnell, and Tompkins 2005). Climate change is one especially powerful example of how careful attention to scale—an analytic for which spatial thinkers have developed thoughtful conceptual vocabularies—will become increasingly important in assessing environmental politics.

Second, environmental thought calls more explicit attention to the unbuilt character of the non-human world (Vogel, this volume). That is, even while environmental thought and activism has moved away from a view of nature as deterministically fashioning social interaction, this line of thought as a whole is amenable to a strong claim that human embeddedness in natural systems reshapes social relations, and furthermore that humans are not the sole makers of the non-human world. On the other hand, when spatial theorists approach the question of justice, they often inadvertently treat space as almost entirely the product of social intention or action. For example, when Soja discusses unjust transit geographies, he implicitly characterizes the injustice as emerging in social practice: unjust transit geographies are seen as unjust insofar as they are the outcome of unjust planning decisions—social procedures that have been arrived at unfairly (E. W. Soja 2010: x). While planning decisions are quite obviously important for producing such an injustice, Soja's evaluation overlooks how bus routes actually refashion social relations among bus riders, for example. Instead, transit geographies become the mirror of unjust planning procedures. I bring up Soja's treatment of unjust transit geographies because it exhibits a tendency (hardly a universal, but a strong tendency all the same) running through much spatial theory: on the one hand, an explicit endorsement of the productive power of non-humans on political life; on the other hand, a tacit treatment of non-humans as passive receptacles for social action (Philippopoulos-Mihalopoulos 2011).[7] In other words, spatial theorists often overlook what Bruno Latour and others have called "the actancy of non-humans:" buildings, highways, parks, borders and other non-human features of built environments actually reconfigure social relations. Transit geographies are not simply a mirror for more general social processes, but can actively reshape how humans interact. And it is just here that environmental thinkers can make an important contribution to spatial thought.

If spatial and environmental thought can enrich each others' analyses, then one field of inquiry that explicitly emphasizes their complementary character is urban political ecology. Urban political ecology is a field that investigates "the interconnected economic, political, social and ecological processes that together form highly uneven urban sociophysical landscapes" (N. Heynen, Kaika, and Swyngedouw 2006: 16).[8] One noteworthy feature of this field is the way in which the city, long the focus of spatial thinkers like Lefebvre and David Harvey, is always taken to be in a metabolic relationship with ecological processes, such that "urban" and "nature" are constantly refashioned in relation to each other. To put this another way, urban political ecology studies the productive power of an expanded set of non-humans. Paul Robbins, for instance, has studied how the expansion of lawns in metropolitan areas remakes urban ecology, complete with new pollution problems (P. Robbins, Polderman, and Birkenholtz 2001; P. Robbins 2007). Similarly, Matthew Gandy investigates the way in which the remaking of New York City's urban nature was imperative for the city's rise to international powerhouse (Gandy 2002). The city developed a vast "'ecological frontier' of water technologies into upstate New York," transforming not only the city's water delivery infrastructure (including the development of aqueducts, plumbing, and monuments) but also landscapes in the Catskills (including dam and reservoir construction) (2002: 19). Both the city's geography and ecology were remade through diverting the flow of water—built and natural landscapes transformed each other. Geography was remade, for example, as settlers in the Catskills were displaced to make way for massive water infrastructure projects (2002: 46–7). Nature, too, was remade as water flowed plentifully into the city's homes. Gandy demonstrates how both the built and natural environments actively remade each other. More than simply social action infringing on the world, the remaking of those landscapes remade the social relations among both city dwellers and residents of the Catskills. Gandy incorporates both the spatial thinker's analytics—thinking across regional scales to examine the production of landscapes—and the environmental thinker's strong sense that remaking the non-human world has a profound influence on human politics and ethics.

Conclusion

What, then, is the relationship between space and environment? They are two distinct, yet often overlapping, intellectual traditions that are preoccupied with a similar question: what is the role of the non-human world in political and social life? They have both answered this question by arguing for the non-human world as produced, as in a dynamic exchange with humans. Yet they have tended to focus on different kinds of non-humans, and furthermore to implicitly argue for different levels of non-human influence on social relations. Their continued exchange, as represented in the field of urban political ecology, is fertile intellectual ground.

Notes

1. Readers familiar with environmental thought may be inclined to understand this conversation as the difference between "space" and a closely related term, "place." I say more about the relationship between those terms later.
2. In tracing the lineage of spatial theory, I draw on Tim Cresswell's excellent *Geographic Thought: A Critical Introduction* (2013).
3. Lefebvre's work was translated into English in the early 1990s; thus, his effect on English language geography was felt later than some of Harvey's early work. Still, Lefebvre's effect on the ensuing conversation among spatial thinkers cannot be overstated.
4. Jessop, Brenner, and Jones argue for a synthetic approach to studying space, and therefore discourage studying geography by narrowly focusing on any one of these analytics. My

purpose here is not to undermine that argument; rather, I find this typology useful for thinking about how scholars tend to approach the study of space.

5. In both cases, one could trace the origin of the concepts through long, rich histories. For instance, spatial thinkers often address (and critique) the conception of space developed by Descartes (Harvey 1973; Lefebvre 1992). Likewise, understandings of nature and environment have been examined in the work of Aristotle (Meyer 2001). Although the long histories of both concepts influence our present understandings, I limit myself here to the most proximate developments.
6. It is noteworthy that each of the three categories I outline—wilderness, limits to growth, and climate change—provoked their own critiques (Cole and University of Sussex 1973; Guha 1989). These critiques have stressed the unavoidably social character of each of these categories. I do not mean to overstate the unity of environmental thought in its attention to the power of non-humans to reshape politics. However, compared to spatial thinkers, environmental thinkers have, in general, been more instinctively amenable to such an analysis.
7. For a notable, but hardly isolated, exception, see Mitchell's (2002) *Rule of Experts*, which charts how Egypt's geography was an important component of its development policy.
8. See R. Keil (2003) and R. R. Keil (2005) for a two-part review of urban political ecology as a field of inquiry.

References

Amin, Ash. (2002). "Spatialities of Globalisation." *Environment and Planning A* 34(3): 385–99. doi:10.1068/a3439.

Anguelovski, Isabelle and Roberts, Debra. (2011). "Spatial Justice and Climate Change: Multiscale Impacts and Local Development in Durban, South Africa." In *Environmental Inequalities Beyond Borders: Local Perspectives on Global Injustices*, edited by JoAnn Carmin and Julian Agyeman (Cambridge, Mass: MIT Press), 19–44.

Ballvé, Teo. (2012). "Everyday State Formation: Territory, Decentralization, and the Narco Landgrab in Colombia." *Environment and Planning D: Society and Space* 30(4): 603–22. doi:10.1068/d4611.

Beaverstock, Jonathan V., Smith, Richard G., and Taylor, Peter J. (2000). "World-City Network: A New Metageography?" *Annals of the Association of American Geographers* 90(1) (March): 123–34. doi:10.1111/0004-5608.00188.

Bickerstaff, Karen and Agyeman, Julian. (2009). "Assembling Justice Spaces: The Scalar Politics of Environmental Justice in North-East England." *Antipode* 41(4) (September): 781–806. doi:10.1111/j.1467-8330.2009.00697.x.

Bookchin, Murray. (2005). *The Ecology Of Freedom: The Emergence And Dissolution Of Hierarchy* (Oakland, CA: AK Press).

Brenner, Neil. (2004). *New State Spaces Urban Governance and the Rescaling of Statehood* (Oxford; New York: Oxford University Press).

Cannavò, Peter F. (2007). *The Working Landscape: Founding, Preservation, and the Politics of Place* (Cambridge, Mass.: MIT Press).

Casey, Edward. (1996). "How to Get from Space to Place in a Fairly Short Stretch of Time: Phenomenological Prolegomena." In *Senses of Place*, edited by Steven Feld and Keith H. Basso (Santa Fe, NM: School of American Research Press), 13–52.

Castells, Manuel. (1979). *The Urban Question: A Marxist Approach* (Cambridge, Mass: MIT Press).
Castells, Manuel. (2011). *The Rise of the Network Society: The Information Age: Economy, Society, and Culture* (West Sussex, UK: John Wiley & Sons).
Castree, Noel. (2004). "Differential Geographies: Place, Indigenous Rights and 'local' Resources." *Political Geography* 23(2) (February): 133–67. doi:10.1016/j.polgeo.2003.09.010.
Cole, H. S. D. and University of Sussex. (1973). *Models of Doom; a Critique of the Limits to Growth* (New York: Universe Books). http://hdl.handle.net/2027/[u]: mdp.39015002141953
Collinge, Chris. (1999). "Self-Organisation of Society by Scale: A Spatial Reworking of Regulation Theory." *Environment and Planning D: Society and Space* 17(5): 557–74. doi:10.1068/d170557.
Cresswell, Tim. (1996). *In Place/Out of Place: Geography, Ideology, and Transgression*, Minnesota Archive Editions (Minneapolis: University Of Minnesota Press).
Cresswell, Tim. (2004). *Place: A Short Introduction* (Malden, MA: Blackwell Publishers).
Cresswell, Tim. (2013). *Geographic Thought: A Critical Introduction* (Malden, MA: Blackwell Publishers).
Cronon, William. (1995). "The Trouble with Wilderness; Or, Getting Back to the Wrong Nature." http://www.williamcronon.net/writing/Trouble_with_Wilderness_Main.html
Delaney, David and Leitner, Helga. (1997). "The Political Construction of Scale." *Political Geography* 16(2) (February): 93–7. doi:10.1016/S0962-6298(96)00045-5.
Devall, Bill and Sessions, George. (1985). *Deep Ecology* (Layton, UT: Gibbs Smith).
Dicken, Peter. (2004). "Geographers and 'Globalization': (Yet) Another Missed Boat?" *Transactions of the Institute of British Geographers* 29(1) (March): 5–26. doi:10.1111/j.0020-2754.2004.00111.x.
Eckerd, Adam. (2011). "Cleaning Up Without Clearing Out? A Spatial Assessment of Environmental Gentrification." *Urban Affairs Review* 47(1) (September 1): 31–59. doi:10.1177/1078087410379720.
Freeman, Lance and Braconi, Frank. (2004). "Gentrification and Displacement: New York City in the 1990s." *American Planning Association. Journal of the American Planning Association* 70(1) (February 1): 39.
Gandy, Matthew. (2002). *Concrete and Clay: Reworking Nature in New York City. Urban and Industrial Environments* (Cambridge, Mass.: MIT Press). http://mirlyn.lib.umich.edu/Record/004241734
Gottlieb, Robert. (2005). *Forcing the Spring: The Transformation of the American Environmental Movement* (Washington, DC: Island Press).
Guha, Ramachandra. (1989). "Radical American Environmentalism: A Third-World Critique." *Environmental Ethics* 11(1) (January 1): 71–83.
Harvey, David. (1973). *Social Justice and the City* (Athens, GA: University of Georgia Press).
Harvey, David. (1974). "Population, Resources, and the Ideology of Science." *Economic Geography* 50(3) (July 1): 256–77.
Harvey, David. (1996). *Justice, Nature and the Geography of Difference* (Cambridge, Mass.: Blackwell Publishers).
Harvey, David. (2001). *Spaces of Capital: Towards a Critical Geography* (New York: Routledge).
Harvey, David. (2007). *Limits to Capital* (London: Verso).
Heynen, Nik, Kaika, Maria, and Swyngedouw, E. (2006). *In the Nature of Cities: Urban Political Ecology and the Politics of Urban Metabolism* (New York: Routledge).

Heynen, Nikolas C. (2003). "The Scalar Production of Injustice within the Urban Forest." *Antipode* 35(5) (November): 980–98. doi:10.1111/j.1467-8330.2003.00367.x.
Jessop, Bob, Brenner, Neil, and Jones, Martin. (2008). "Theorizing Sociospatial Relations." *Environment and Planning D: Society and Space* 26(3): 389–401. doi:10.1068/d9107.
Keil, R. (2003). "Urban Political Ecology." *Urban Geography* 24(8) (November 1): 723–38.
Keil, Roger R. (2005). "Progress Report—Urban Political Ecology." *Urban Geography* 26(7): 640–51.
Kovel, Joel. (2007). *The Enemy of Nature: The End of Capitalism Or the End of the World?*, 2nd edn. (New York: Zed Books).
Lees, Loretta, Slater, Tom, and Wyly, Elvin. (2007). *Gentrification*, 1st edn (London: Routledge).
Lefebvre, Henri. (1992). *The Production of Space*. Edited by Donald Nicholson-Smith (Malden, MA: Blackwell).
Lefebvre, Henri and Lebas, Elizabeth. (1996). *Writings on Cities* (Cambridge, Mass.: Blackwell Publishers).
Leitner, Helga. (1997). "Reconfiguring the Spatiality of Power: The Construction of a Supranational Migration Framework for the European Union." *Political Geography* 16(2) (February): 123–43. doi:10.1016/S0962-6298(96)00047-9.
Marcuse, Peter. (1985). "Gentrification, Abandonment, and Displacement: Connections, Causes, and Policy Responses in New York City." *Washington University Journal of Urban and Contemporary Law* 28 (January 1): 195.
Marston, Sallie A. (2000). "The Social Construction of Scale." *Progress in Human Geography* 24(2) (June 1): 219–42. doi:10.1191/030913200674086272.
Marston, Sallie A., Jones, John Paul, and Woodward, Keith. (2005). "Human Geography Without Scale." *Transactions of the Institute of British Geographers* 30(4) (December): 416–32. doi:10.1111/j.1475-5661.2005.00180.x.
Massey, Doreen B. (1994). *Space, Place, and Gender* (Minneapolis: University of Minnesota Press).
Massey, Doreen. (1999). "Space-Time, 'Science' and the Relationship between Physical Geography and Human Geography." *Transactions of the Institute of British Geographers* 24(3) (September): 261–76. doi:10.1111/j.0020-2754.1999.00261.x.
Meadows, Donella H., Randers, Jorgen, and Meadows, Dennis L. (2004). *Limits to Growth: The 30-Year Update*, 3rd edn. (White River Junction, VT: Chelsea Green).
Merriman, Peter. (2012). "Human Geography Without Time-space1." *Transactions of the Institute of British Geographers* 37(1): 13–27. doi:10.1111/j.1475-5661.2011.00455.x.
Merriman, Peter, Jones, Martin, Olsson, Gunnar, Sheppard, Eric, Thrift, Nigel, and Tuan, Yi-Fu. (2012). "Space and Spatiality in Theory." *Dialogues in Human Geography* 2(1) (March 1): 3–22. doi:10.1177/2043820611434864.
Meyer, John M. (2001). *Political Nature: Environmentalism and the Interpretation of Western Thought* (Cambridge, Mass.: MIT Press).
Mitchell, Timothy. (2002). *Rule of Experts: Egypt, Techno-Politics, Modernity* (Berkeley: University of California Press).
Murdoch, Jonathan. (1998). "The Spaces of Actor-Network Theory." *Geoforum* 29(4) (November): 357–74. doi:10.1016/S0016-7185(98)00011-6.
Neil Adger, W., Arnell, Nigel W., and Tompkins, Emma L. (2005). "Successful Adaptation to Climate Change across Scales." *Global Environmental Change* 15(2) (July): 77–86. doi:10.1016/j.gloenvcha.2004.12.005.

Patterson, Matthew. (2007). *Automobile Politics: Ecology and Cultural Political Economy* (New York: Cambridge University Press).

Philippopoulos-Mihalopoulos, A. (2011). "Law's Spatial Turn: Geography, Justice and a Certain Fear of Space." *Law, Culture and the Humanities* 7(2) (June 1): 187–202. doi:10.1177/1743872109355578.

Pirie, G. H. (1983). "On Spatial Justice." *Environment and Planning A* 15(4): 465–73.

Pratt, Geraldine. (1999). "Geographies of Identity and Difference: Marking Boundaries." In *Human Geography Today*, edited by Doreen Massey, John Allen, and Phil Sarre (Cambridge: Polity Press), 151–67.

Qian, Junxi, Qian, Liyun, and Zhu, Hong. (2012). "Representing the Imagined City: Place and the Politics of Difference during Guangzhou's 2010 Language Conflict." *Geoforum* 43(5) (September): 905–15. doi:10.1016/j.geoforum.2012.04.004.

Quastel, Noah. (2009). "Political Ecologies of Gentrification." *Urban Geography* 30(7) (October 1):694–725. doi:10.2747/0272-3638.30.7.694.

Robbins, Paul. (2007). *Lawn People: How Grasses, Weeds, and Chemicals Make Us Who We Are* (Philadelphia: Temple University Press).

Robbins, P., Polderman, A., and Birkenholtz, T. (2001). "Lawns and Toxins—An Ecology of the City." *CITIES* 18(6): 369.

Schlosberg, David. (2013). "Theorising Environmental Justice: The Expanding Sphere of a Discourse." *Environmental Politics* 22(1): 37–55. doi:10.1080/09644016.2013.755387.

Smith, Neil. (1984). *Uneven Development* (Athens, GA: University of Georgia Press).

Smith, Neil. (1996). *The New Urban Frontier: Gentrification and the Revanchist City* (New York: Routledge).

Smith, Richard G. (2003). "World City Actor-Networks." *Progress in Human Geography* 27(1) (February 1): 25–44. doi:10.1191/0309132503ph411oa.

Soja, E. (1999). "Thirdspace: Expanding the Scope of the Geographical Imagination." In *Human Geography Today*, edited by Doreen B. Massey, John Allen, and Phil Sarre (Cambridge: Polity Press), 260–78.

Soja, Edward W. (2010). *Seeking Spatial Justice* (Minneapolis: University of Minnesota Press).

Sze, Julie and London, Jonathan K. (2008). "Environmental Justice at the Crossroads." *Sociology Compass* 2(4) (July): 1331–54. doi:10.1111/j.1751-9020.2008.00131.x.

Sze, Julie, London, Jonathan, Shilling, Fraser, Gambirazzio, Gerardo, Filan, Trina, and Cadenasso, Mary. (2009). "Defining and Contesting Environmental Justice: Socio-Natures and the Politics of Scale in the Delta." *Antipode* 41(4) (September 1): 807–43. doi:10.1111/j.1467-8330.2009.00698.x.

Taylor, Bob Pepperman. (1994). "Henry Thoreau, Nature, and American Democracy." *Journal of Social Philosophy* 25(1) (March): 46–64. doi:10.1111/j.1467-9833.1994.tb00304.x.

Taylor, Dorceta E. (2000). "The Rise of the Environmental Justice Paradigm." *American Behavioral Scientist* 43(4) (January 1): 508–80.

Taylor, P. J. (1994). "The State as Container: Territoriality in the Modern World-System." *Progress in Human Geography* 18(2) (June 1): 151–62. doi:10.1177/030913259401800202.

Thoreau, Henry David. (2009). "Walking." http://thoreau.eserver.org/

Tuan, Yi-Fu and Hoelscher, Steven. (2001). *Space and Place: The Perspective of Experience* (Minneapolis: University of Minnesota Press).

Vigdor, Jacob L. (2002). "Does Gentrification Harm the Poor?" *Brookings-Wharton Papers on Urban Affairs* 2002(1): 133–82.

Walker, Gordon. (2009). "Beyond Distribution and Proximity: Exploring the Multiple Spatialities of Environmental Justice." *Antipode* 41(4): 614–36. doi:10.1111/j.1467-8330.2009.00691.x.

Whatmore, Sarah and Thorne, Lorraine. (2000). "Elephants on the Move: Spatial Formations of Wildlife Exchange." *Environment and Planning D: Society and Space* 18(2): 185–203. doi:10.1068/d210t.

CHAPTER 12

CHALLENGING THE HUMAN X ENVIRONMENT FRAMEWORK

SAMANTHA FROST

Introduction

For decades now, scholars in political theory and other cognate fields have challenged, reconfigured, and rearticulated assumptions about who is a political subject—about which kinds of people are to be accounted as bona fide political actors or as citizens and what the attendant panoply of rights and responsibilities might or should be. As scholars have identified, made explicit, and called into question presumptions about the superior nature, character, or value of particular groups, ideas about gender, racial ancestry, ethnicity, national origin, class, able-bodiedness, sexuality, age, and religious creed have been teased out of and insinuated into theories of political subjectivity. Attendant to this specification and internal differentiation of concepts of political subjectivity has been an expansive reconsideration of the issues, domains, and objects that fall within the purview of politics. What "counts" as politics is not just the activities found in formal political and legal institutions but rather local communities, education, health, sexuality, family, economic and labor relations, culture . . . and the very production of identity. In short, as the "who" of politics has expanded, the "what" has too.

More recently, scholars have added to this critical project an effort not just to decenter particular groups of people from theories of politics but to dislodge the presumptions about the exceptional nature, character, and value of humans as a species. As Cary Wolfe notes, having repudiated assumptions that inclusion within the category of political subject should be restricted to select groups, "it was but one short step . . . to insist that species too should be set aside" (2003: xii). The idea behind this setting-aside of species as a qualification for political subjectivity is not just to expand received categories so as to include a broader cohort of creatures under the rubric of "rights-bearing subject." Rather, it is to elucidate how "the 'human,' . . . is not now, and never was, itself" (Wolfe 2003: xiii). The very notion of the human—a notion that has long underwritten the definition of citizen or political subject—has itself become suspect.

As the suspicion about the human has been elaborated through analysis and critique, a corollary reconsideration of the relationship between humans and their environment has also been undertaken. The general spirit of the critique has been to deny that there is any coherence or integrity to the oft-made distinction between humans and their habitats. The critical efforts to challenge and transform the norms and categories through which we understand the relationship between humans and their environments generally demand that humans reform how they relate to them—how they perceive them, orient themselves to them, or value them. But exactly how these ethically or aesthetically transformed relations might vivify or energize environmental politics is unclear. The reason is that in elaborating the interconnectedness of humans, non-human creatures, and their habitats, and in elucidating the forms of agency or effectiveness that non-human creatures and habitats have irrespective of human intervention and intention, these approaches diminish the human as an agent—just as (human) collective political action is urgently needed.

But the critiques that diminish or chasten the human do not of necessity lead to political paralysis vis à vis looming environmental and climatic catastrophe. Two of the major posthumanist approaches to rethinking the human in relation to the environment—actor network theory and object-oriented ontology—each offer a gestalt that enables us to perceive how our myriad everyday actions have wide-ranging destructive effects upon the world. And although they often portray their arguments as incompatible with one another (Latour, Harman, and Erdelyi 2010), together they give us conceptual tools to move past feelings of futility and fatalism and to discern how our remediating political efforts might be effective.

Questioning the Human

The diminution of the distinctive specialness of humans entails not just a critique of anthropocentrism or the idea that humans and their spirited genius are the key movers and shakers in any account of the social and political world—although it does concern this to some extent. More fully, it constitutes a critical engagement with the ideas, assumptions, concepts, and norms that make of the human a moral and political exception.

The idea here is not simply to rebut the concept of the human as a natural or self-evident category. Nor is it simply to question the presumptive superiority of the human, a superiority that makes humans the loci of recognition and respect and thereby the bearers of social, moral, and political rights and prerogatives (Habermas 2003). More specifically, the idea is to suggest that the criteria for inclusion in the category of the "human," and the special moral and political status attributed to humanity, are manufactured through fairly strenuous philosophical, scientific, and cultural practices—and thus have been, and in many important respects remain, merely aspirational.

To claim that the human is aspirational—that it "is not now, and never was, itself"—is not only to deny that the human is a clearly defined and stable category but also to propose that it is precisely an unstable category and consequently that its definition and outline are a product of an unceasing process of differentiation. To put the point slightly differently, the human is a project through which the human is differentiated from its backgrounds and others. Elizabeth Grosz, for instance, observes that Western philosophy "has attributed to man a power that animals lack"—the power of reason, of speech, of intelligent response, or the moral capacity to experience shame (Grosz 2011: 12). Cary Wolfe goes further to claim that " 'the human' is achieved by escaping or repressing not just its animal origins in nature, the biological, and the evolutionary, but more generally by transcending the bonds of materiality and embodiment altogether" (2010: xv). Such escape and transcendence is often conceived in terms of a distinctively human capacity for self-creation and self-mastery, or as Rosi Braidotti notes, "the almost boundless capacity for humans to pursue their individual and collective perfectibility," a perfectibility defined "in terms of autonomy and self-determination" (2013: 13, 23). So, whereas animals are trapped within the givenness of their bodies, caught by the pressing immediacy of their instincts, blind to the tricks of reason, stupid to the distillations and metaphors of language, and unable to produce and pass on the social forms and memories that create a culture separate from nature, humans are not. In this view, humans' exception to what is the case or the rule for all other creatures is what grants them singular value and moral and political prerogative.

But within the terms of the posthumanist critique, this quixotic vision of a self-sovereign human subject is more a politically potent fantasy than a set of actual features of human existence. In denying language, consciousness, reasoning, and culture to any creature other than the human, this vision not only makes the human "the mark and measure of creativity" but also "obscures the animal conditions for the emergence of so-called human qualities" (Grosz 2011: 21). No sooner are bees, crows, orcas, or chimpanzees found capable of such "human" arts as dance, creative thinking, cultural formation, or war than these criteria for defining the human are replaced by other characteristics or activities deemed exceptionally human. As a project of self-differentiation, as an aspiration, the human turns out to be not much more than an illusory product of its own processes of self-recognition (Agamben 2004: 26). Indeed, Agamben names those seemingly irrepressible practices of human differentiation and self-recognition "the anthropological machine" (2003). Considering the efforts required to hold open the gap between the human and its philosophical and historical others, William Connolly proposes that we conceive of the specifically human subject as "a formation" of politics rather than "a ground" for politics (2013: 400).

The Environment is Not Without

Just as the challenges to the exclusionary definitions of the citizen have impelled a reconceptualization of the spaces and domains of politics, so challenges to human exceptionalism have entailed a reconsideration of the fields or domains within which humans act. As the notion of the human as separate from nature, distinct from animals, possessed of a bounded self, and thoroughly cultural and political has been called into question, so too has the figuration of the background, the nature, or the environment against which or through separation from which the human has been defined. In fact, through focusing on the corporeity or embodiedness of human beings, scholars have been able to show that the distinctness, boundedness, and cultural integrity of the human are illusory: the environment enters within.

An important means of criticizing the notion that the environment is merely the context, background, or scene within which humans act has been to challenge the assumption that the crude surface of the gross physical human body traces a boundary that differentiates and distances a human from his or her environs. In this view, the embodied human does not simply move in a field of action but rather absorbs manifold substances from and sheds elements of itself into its habitat. Julie Guthman and Becky Mansfield (2013) point out that, conceived as molecular substances ingested through nutrition, breathing, and other forms of passive and active absorption, the environment quite literally composes and decomposes us. The environment transits the permeable skin and mucous membranes of the body, it "actually comes into the body," shaping what and how the body develops, lives, and grows (Guthman and Mansfield 2013: 495). Similarly alert to the myriad toxins that pervade the environment and (thus) our porous bodies, Stacy Alaimo suggests that we think of "human corporeality as trans-corporeality, in which the human is always intermeshed with the more-than-human world" (2010: 2). This trans-corporeality entails that we conceive of the environment not as the background against which the human is made distinct (Alaimo 2010: 142), not as "an external, blank, or inert space," but rather as "the active emergent substance of ourselves" (Alaimo 2012: 563–4).

When the environment is no longer conceived as a field of action external to the human but rather as a constitutive element composing the embodied human, then the distinction between nature and culture, the given and the made, also falters. Anne Fausto-Sterling observes that "living bodies are dynamic systems that develop and change in response to the social and historical contexts" (2012: xiii). There is no point in an individual lifetime or in evolutionary history at which we can identify and specify the separate and distinct entities: body and environment/society. It is not that one set of substances and forces "contributes to the organism's 'nature' and another ... influences its 'nurture'" (Oyama et al. 2001: 4). Rather, through our responsive engagement with the world and other creatures, our bodies incorporate not only the material–chemical but also the social and symbolic dimensions of our lived habitats (Fausto-Sterling 2012;

Slavich and Cole 2013). If we attend to the ways that both the forces and effects of the material and organismic world and the forces and effects of culture shape how humans develop, grow, and evolve within individual lifetimes as well as across generations, then "the distinctions between the physical and social body start to erode" (Fausto-Sterling 2012: 79).

The embedded, compositional relation between humans and their environments also requires that we take a different accounting of the animals and creatures that fall within the orbit of the human. This calling into question of the distinctness between the human and the animal is not a matter of whether humans actually speciated all those many years ago (although exactly how this speciation took place is in question following discoveries that humans are genetically intermixed with or related to Neanderthals, Denisovans, and other *homo* variants (Aiello 2010; Lordkipanidze et al. 2013; Callaway 2014)). Rather, it is a matter of taking stock of the significance of the relationships between humans and other creatures. This move bids that we acknowledge the ways that animals—as pets, livestock, and co-habitants of particular locales—have intermixed their spit, meat, DNA, and various effluvia with the humans with whom they have shared their lives. Donna Haraway uses the term "naturecultures" to designate this kind of imbrication and mutual shaping of human and creaturely existence (2008: 2). Humans have co-evolved with their companion species—not just the canine, equine, bovine, porcine, or feline creatures but all the rodents, fleas, and microbes too that have inhabited our bodies and spaces and either enhanced or diminished our physical survival. But this taking stock also extends beyond the relations established through companionship, use, and various forms of cohabitation. As Myra Hird (2009) points out, human life is crucially dependent upon the microbiome; there are bacteria, fungi, viruses, and microbes who inhabit our bodies and whose symbiotic co-existence with/in us is the enabling condition of our physical growth, health, and well-being. From this perspective, it is not simply that humans should not be considered as separate from nature or from animals but more that they should be considered as composite with them: we grow together and persist in living symbiotically.

Displacing the Human

The environment has for a long time been thought of as the background, the domain, or the space within which humans live their busy lives. Alternatively, figured as Nature, it is the backdrop and the basis for the formation of the political, the imaginatively prior condition from which humans carve and distinguish the realm of culture and politics. Significantly, then, the re-figuration or refusal of a clear distinction between humans and their various material and non-human others displaces the anthropos as the relevant point of reference in social and political thought, especially in thinking about environmental politics (Hird 2009; Marder 2013). There are two general approaches through which this reconsideration of the relationship between humans and the material, creaturely world has been elaborated. On the one hand, there are scholars following actor network theory for whom relations among humans, creatures, and objects actually compose them as humans, creatures, and objects. On the other hand, there are scholars who identify as object-oriented ontologists for whom humans, creatures, and objects are ontologically autonomous or distinct from the relations in which they are tangled. While these two sets of scholars differ on the extent to which the *relations between* or the *autonomy of* elements of the world is their most salient feature, both offer important perspective on the ways that human activities shape the world—and the ways that the world, in its plural forms, acts as an agent in its own right. The recognition that non-human creatures and other features of the material world are agents transforms how we might conceive of or imagine the problems of environmental degradation and global climate change.

Environment as Networks of Agents

For those thinkers who foreground the connections, relations, and interdependencies of all creatures and objects, a primary task is to reject the notion that objects are the philosophical complement of the "subjects" in the subject–object binary. What this means is that objects are not considered as passive, inert lumps of matter whose effects on the world derive from external (human) forces acting upon them. Instead, objects are considered as agents themselves, either because of a vibrancy that is inherent in matter's modes of self-organization or because of their imbrication in the various material and social relations through which they are rendered intelligible, observed, and used (De Landa 1997).

Such a recognition of the ways in which objects act in and through their interconnection with other objects and with human institutions and practices demands a revised account of agency. As Jane Bennett (2010) contends, we must relinquish the idea of individual agents and think instead in terms of "a heterogeneous assemblage" that produces effects through its various and changing interrelations (23). In this view, the networks of interactions in which objects, creatures, institutions, and practices are embedded do not necessarily or always have humans and their actions at their center, as the origin or principle of action. Rather, agency is a kind of "efficacy or effectivity" that is "distributed across an ontologically heterogeneous field" (Bennett 2010: 23). Bernard Stiegler (1998) illustrates this insight by explaining that technical objects are not merely passive machines designed and operated by human agents. Through their mechanical, technological, or digital actions, through their very working existence, technical objects transform their milieux and set the conditions for their further development and elaboration (Stiegler 1998: 81). For Stiegler, the notion that technical objects contribute to their own evolution calls into question the idea of the human as the primary and anterior animating force behind technical development. To foreground the agentic capacities made possible and put into motion through networks of human, creaturely, and material object relations is to draw out "the irreducible imbrication of human/nonhuman or natural/

social processes" (Coole 2013: 454). In fact, if we trace the ways in which effectivity is "distributed," we are compelled to "posit a certain nonhuman agency as the condition of possibility of human agency" (Bennett 2010: 98).

When agency is conceived as distributed through networks of relations, the environment is figured as "us" rather than other, which is to say that it is no longer positioned as a kind of alterity (Alaimo 2010: 2). With the human displaced as a central figure, the environment is conceived as intricate and extensively interconnected ecologies in which individual and collective social, economic, and political activities provoke creaturely and habitat adaptations that in turn require transformations in activity and habit from social and political actors. The environment and human activity constantly transform one another; their mutual responses to their mutual responses make it impossible to distinguish an "environmental" process or event from a "social" or "political" one (Singer 1996).

When scholars analyze environmental degradation and global climate change through the framework of these networks of relations, they claim that we must reorient ourselves towards the environment both ethically and politically. Our recognition of the way that the effects of our actions depend upon, multiply, and amplify other agentic effects within those relations compels us to "re-think the basic tenets of our interaction with both human and non-human agents on a planetary scale" (Braidotti 2013: 5–6). Jane Bennett proposes that we cultivate an openness and sensitivity to the interdependencies that constitute the human–non-human world, "a greater sense of the extent to which all bodies are kin in the sense of inextricably enmeshed in a dense network of relations" (2010: 13). This reorientation entails that we work actively to dispel "a prejudice against a (nonhuman) multitude misrecognized as context, constraint, or tool" and instead bring these agentic objects, creatures, and patterns of action and interaction within the ambit of ethical and political consideration, or at least bring their perspectives to bear in democratic political processes (Bennett 2010: 108). And while this alternative orientation to the ecological worlds that humans, non-humans, and objects together create and inhabit "gives some priority to the human estate, but it does so by emphasizing our manifold *entanglements* with nonhuman processes, both within the body and outside humanity" (Connolly 2013: 401, emphasis in the original).

Ironically, though, as the human is displaced as an exceptional agent in order to account for "entanglements with nonhuman processes" with distributed effects, the extent to which cascading transformations in climate and environment alike are the result of specifically human activity becomes increasingly obvious. In other words, as Rosi Braidotti observes, the collective self-awareness produced by the tracking of human enmeshment in dense networks of relations prompts us to acknowledge that even as we might topple the human agent from the pillar of exceptionalist hubris, that agent must also be called to task and held responsible for the destruction it has wrought (2013: 23). Indeed, drawing on the claim by Paul Crutzen and Eugene Stoermer that the current geological era should be known as the "Anthropocene," Dipesh Chakrabarty urges us to recognize that "humans are a force of nature in the geological sense" (2009: 207).

Chakrabarty contends that imminent climate disaster and environmental catastrophe are products not just of capitalism but of human activity more generally. Evidence suggests that even though there are indeed networks of ecologies through which humans, non-humans, and local and regional objects and processes interact, human activity in particular is "a main determinant of the environment of the planet" (Chakrabarty 2009: 209). So although our analyses of manifold networks of human and non-human agents may incline us to deny that humans are "a geological agent, . . . we appear to have become one at the level of species" (2009: 221). In view of this, it may be insufficient to cleave to the notion that agents are a labyrinthine tangle of heterogeneous human and non-human actors. The "calling to task" enjoined by Braidotti demands an addressee—and that addressee must, in the end, be humans.

The displacement of the human that enables us to appreciate the extent to which humans have reshaped the climate and the environment in turn "poses for us a question of a human collectivity, an us" (Chakrabarty 2009: 222). The inescapable question about the nature of the "we" implied in the question "what should or can we do?" entails that we learn to think in terms of the human species, to engage in "species thinking," even as we cannot yet imagine how to conceive of the human species qua global collective as a subject (Chakrabarty 2009: 213). If environmental degradation and global climate change push us to re-imagine humans as specifically political actors with the largest share of responsibility for the current predicament, then rather than sidelining or diminishing the category of the human as agent, we must, as Cary Wolfe proposes, rethink and animate differently its founding elisions and conditions (2010: xvi).

Furthermore, Diana Coole points out that in order to make a "more ecologically and aesthetically sensitive ethos" effective in bringing about transformation, scholars will have to engage in "critical analysis of the social structures that ethical beings inhabit and of the resistances or constraints they entail" (2013: 463). Which is to say that without "an empirical, scientific and political investigation . . . it is difficult to appreciate the damage and challenges current forms of production and consumption involve or to think realistically about ways materially to transform them" (Coole 2013: 463). Aside from the fact that the forms of reason, science, and knowledge that are demanded by such an investigation are precisely those that have been seen as a problematic and defining mark of the human qua exception (Chakrabarty 2009: 210), the prospective findings of such investigations also bring to light a further political difficulty. To broach and to investigate the problem of environmental degradation and global climate change is to confront a myriad interconnecting relations and actants. As each action is traced through expansive networks and interconnectivities to ascertain its impact on the environment and climate, its unending reverberation could result in our being "paralyzed" by the insight that "everything is interconnected" and consequently by "the obligation to 'take everything into account'" (Latour 2004: 198). How could we account for the impossibly unwieldy "interconnected everything" of the global climate or the environment? Once we recognize the multitudinous interconnections between expansive networks of objects, processes, practices, and creatures, we can see both that every thoughtless action has a contributing effect and that the efficacy of every remediating effort is quickly dissipated. Our actions are at once too effective and not effective enough.

Environment as Hyperobject

In contrast with the (albeit reluctant) recognition by actor network theorists that we must somehow recuperate or re-imagine the human as agent if we are to redress climate and environmental disaster, object-oriented ontologists advocate a chastening of the human so thorough-going as to effect a complete diminution of the human as an effective agent. For these latter thinkers, who foreground the existence of objects independently of their capture in perceptual and utilitarian relations with humans, the task is to undo the subject–object binary by demoting human subjects from any position of superiority vis à vis objects. The idea here is not bring objects within the ambit of the notion of agents—as if to extend a humanly referenced "you too" to objects—but rather to construe humans as themselves "objects *among* objects" (Bryant 2011: 22, emphasis in the original). What motivates these thinkers is the question of how our understanding of humans' place in the world is transfigured when the world is not just "a correlate of our existence" (Meillassoux 2012: 7) or when the "human-world relation has no privilege at all" (Harman 2011: 119).

Central to this approach is the idea that all objects exist in "astonishing autonomy" (Morton 2013b: 45). This autonomy means that what objects are and the ways they persist are not exhausted by what appears to our perceptual apparatus (Harman 2011: 72–3). Objects are partially concealed from human perceptual apprehension—and from other objects' and creatures' apprehension as well (Bryant 2011: 26). Through this concealment, objects are said to "withdraw from access," which is to say that what we can and do see or know of an object "can't fully express the object" (Morton 2013b: 44). Every object always exceeds our efforts to circumscribe or define it. And importantly, this excess is not a humbling mark of human insufficiency but rather an index of the robust fullness and complexity of the world.

Objects' autonomy or withdrawal means that they have a reality that is not reducible to their "impact on other things" (Harman 2011: 73). But this reality-beyond-relation does not imply an atomistic world of solitary objects. Within this theory, objects are not "in-relation" so much as they "contain other objects, and are contained 'in' other objects" (Morton 2013b: 45). Objects co-exist through composing each other. Co-existence as "containing" and "being contained" conveys the density of the material world and is in part what makes objects inaccessible: if objects co-exist, what an object is cannot be finally, properly, and definitively delineated. Because objects co-exist, "everything is an object, including the seemingly special one we call *subject*" (Morton 2013b: 63).

For these thinkers, the notion that objects withdraw from our perception helps to explain the almost insuperable difficulty activists and experts have experienced in trying to generate an effective collective political response to environmental and climate disaster. Timothy Morton (2013a) describes the environment and the climate as "hyperobjects" in order to mark the specific manner in which they recede from our perception and apprehension. It is not just that, like all other objects, hyperobjects withdraw from our access. Rather, they are so gigantic and so multi-dimensionally dense that they exceed our capacity even to imagine or hold in our thoughts. If an object is not reducible either to "its parts" or to "its 'whole' " (Morton 2013b: 44), then the environment and the climate—as hyperobjects—also cannot be reduced to their parts, to the relations between their parts, or to a whole formed by the sum of those parts. And yet, our tendency is to talk of the environment, the climate, or even ecologies as if their dimensions can be delineated or defined. When analysts or activists present the problems of environmental degradation and global climate change as problems with "the environment" or "the climate" conceived as totalities, they invoke phenomena so vast both spatially and temporally that the information they garner cannot evoke the feelings of urgency in individuals or political collectivities that might translate into action. Which is to say that this lack of adequate representational tools can "hinder our efforts to mobilize and act decisively" (Nixon 2011: 2). Morton points out that efforts to represent the problems of environmental degradation and global climate change via computer-generated images, predictive data, and statistics do not adequately capture what those hyperobjects are and cannot convince the public that the problems are real. He contends, "[h]yperobjects are not just the stuff of charts and simulations, but rather are . . . huge objects consisting of other objects: global warming comprises the sun, the biosphere, fossil fuels, cars, and so on" (2013a: 199). To represent the hyperobjects of environmental degradation or global climate change as problems of "the environment" or "the climate," as if they are units, is to reduce and circumscribe them, to create a picture or a frame that distances us from and blinds us to the wretched intimacy with which we live with growing disaster.

For Morton, then, it is not just the violence wrought by patterns of human activity that needs to be countered but also "the distance that reifies the pattern into a world picture" (2013a: 127). Challenging this imagination of the environment as a coherent, identifiable thing, Levi Bryant points out that "the world does not exist. . . . [t]here is no 'super-object,' Whole, or totality that would gather all objects together in a harmonious unity" (2011: 32). This is not to say that the world we live in and perceive is an illusion. Rather, as Morton explains, it is to claim that "[t]here is no space or environment as such, only objects. . . . 'Space' and 'environment' are ways in which objects sensually relate to the other objects in their vicinity" (Morton 2013b: 43).

On the face of it, then, for object-oriented ontologists, the problems of environmental and climate disaster are primarily aesthetic both in the sense that they concern the puzzles of representation and the attendant difficulties of affect or motivation—of effecting the being-moved that will inspire or compel people to engage the problems. And indeed, exactly how to represent these hyperobjects ethically and politically is hard to imagine. We do not yet have a mode of representation that can capture the in-it, of-it, with-it, not-it existence of the objects that co-exist as hyperobjects. Morton suggests that if we could develop such a mode of representation, it would enable us better to locate and mark environmental degradation and global climate change politically. For instance, rather than seeing climate change as out there and beyond, we could see it as constituted by and manifest in "these raindrops falling on my head" or "that early flowering of shrubs in my yard" (Morton 2013a: 48–9).

However, to think about hyperobjects in terms of the objects that co-exist to compose them is not quite the same as seeing a global problem in a local form; a kind of metonymic or synecdochal scaling. For the spatial vastness and internal multiplicity of hyperobjects is textured by strange forms of temporality that link the everyday to conditions hundreds and sometimes thousands of years from now. Morton illustrates this strange orientation toward time by pointing out the forms of futural anticipation demanded by the management of radioactive plutonium waste—which has an extraordinarily long half-life. Morton observes that "[t]wenty-four thousand years into the future, no one will be meaningfully related to me. Yet everything will be influenced by the tiniest decisions I make right now" (2013a: 122). In a bizarre twisting of the forms of identification upon which ideas of responsibility are often predicated, "[t]he future self is thus unimaginably distant in one sense, and yet hyperobjects" make our relation to that self strangely "intimate" (2013a: 123).

This additional temporal dimension of the hyperobjects we call environmental degradation and global climate change produces an exasperating relationship to everyday life: will a different kind of light bulb, a hybrid car, a recycled bottle make a difference to this gigantic, multifaceted phenomenon whose existence and unfolding stretch from this moment through humanly unimaginable time? The need to feel that each little effort does matter, even as it is not clear how it does or at what spatial or temporal scale, can provoke "paralyzing despair about the impossibility of making a difference in the big scheme of things" and thereby "contribute to the wider abdication of political agency" (Foote and Mazzolini 2012: 6). One reusable cup can seem to be a mere drop in a vast expanding ocean of garbage.

Significantly, and perhaps more dispiritingly, what is at issue here for object-oriented ontologists is not merely the question of how to represent hyperobjects in a way that will educate and inspire. An additional dimension of the problems of climate change and environmental degradation is that, in their very autonomy, the hyperobjects that are the climate and the environment move and act independently of our intention and in manner beyond our ken. As Bryant notes, once we come to recognize this "finally subjectless object," what we have before us, within us, around us, is "a variety of nonhuman actors unleashed in the world as autonomous actors in their own right, irreducible to representations and freed from any constant reference to the human" (2011: 23). The idea that, as humans, we could mitigate or redress the momentum of the unfolding disasters that confront us is not precisely another mismeasure of how important humans are. Rather, it is a mis-estimation of objects' autonomy, of the kinds of actions objects and hyperobjects undertake without the slightest regard for what humans might will, intend, or attempt. Indeed, in a hauntingly pessimistic coda to his analysis of hyperobjects, Morton asserts that specifically "[n]onhuman beings are responsible for the next moment of human history and thinking" (2013a: 201). In his view, if we cannot come to terms with and engage this fact, it is because our thinking is "nowhere near posthuman enough" (2013a: 201). In fact, contemplating the "ecological emergency inside of which we have now woken up," Morton suggests that what is left to us is to rediscover how to think and live under the rule of an intemperate, inscrutable, and unpredictable agent. He notes, "Heidegger said that only a god can save us now. As we find ourselves waking up within a series of gigantic objects, we realize that he forgot to add: *We just don't know what sort of god*" (2013a: 201, emphasis in the original).

Beyond Paralysis and Fatalistic Despair

Clearly, posthumanist thinking provides resources with which we can come to understand how seemingly innocuous activities in our daily lives ramify into environmental degradation and global climate change. These analyses also enable us to understand how the extensive enormity of these problems resist integration into daily affairs in ways that might make collective action to redress them seem feasible. In fact, the very strength of these analyses can make the likelihood of broad-based changes effected through environmental politics seem gravely underwhelming. Under one framework, every remedy undertaken appears to have its potential effect so diffused through a million sets of interconnections that it seems futile from the outset. Under the other framework, any ameliorative action appears to target objects and processes that proceed with a momentum and logic so distant and indifferent to understanding, prediction, or control that the only real option is a benumbed fatalism. What both approaches need—and, in part, offer—are means to circumscribe fields of intervention so that care and concern for the climate and the environment might be translated into effective political action.

Karen Barad notes that, when we examine anything, we perform "agential cuts" that section objects-emerging-in-relation into discrete empirical data (2003: 815). Although there is no natural or philosophically given scale of values according to which we might make such cuts, we may have to do so experimentally, respectfully, and with an openness to reconsidering the resultant strategies if they turn out to be dangerous or offensive in ways we have not initially anticipated (Latour 2004: 197–9; Connolly 2013: 401).

Working within the approach that foregrounds networks of relations and interdependencies, Diana Coole suggests that such experimental cuts could be made vertically. In this case, whatever meager efforts we can muster will trace like a ribbon through partial sets of relations, weaving up through what Coole terms "the micro, meso, and macro" levels of the ecologies that constitute our world (2013: 464). But even if the ribbons of effects are provisionally limited or curtailed so that they do not spider out into lacy webs, to have to reach from "embodied quotidian" life through "governance structures" to "the planetary" in its various dimensions (Coole 2013: 464) is still to risk having the initiative to do better dissipate into a futile almost-nothing. But perhaps the manner in which object-oriented ontologists conceive of co-existence could enable us to perform "agential cuts" that put a break on the compulsive/compulsory pursuit of the next effect-in-relation.

Morton's dramatic pessimism seems to emerge because, in spite of his insight that a hyperobject is composed of and contains many objects, he slips into thinking of the environment or the climate as primarily a coherent and unified gigantic entity. If we leaven his conclusion with his own argument that hyperobjects contain and comprise other objects through co-existence, we may engineer some promising possibilities for thinking about environmental politics. The notion of co-existence grants—or indeed, insists—that objects contain and are contained in one another. Because objects have autonomy even as they are contained and containing, they have discrete edges or some density or integrity. This density or autonomy enables us to say that this action, habit, or object *here* is (non-exhaustively) global warming or environmental degradation; not all of it, not reducible to just a part of it, but it nonetheless. Morton proposes something to this effect when, in dismantling the distancing picture of the "environment," the "climate," or the "world," he remarks that climate change is a hyperobject comprising "the sun, the biosphere, fossil fuels, cars, and so on" (Morton 2013a: 199).

In resolving hyperobjects into the objects they contain, in understanding the climate or the environment as hyperobjects composed of innumerable objects, large and small, near and far, we can experience "a weird effect of withdrawal and disturbing intimacy all at once" (Morton 2013a: 189). This intimacy comes not from focusing on human connections with other interconnected agents, as if we "belong . . . to something bigger," but rather from "a sense of being close, even too close, to other lifeforms, of having them under one's skin" (Morton 2013a: 139). The sense of intimacy provoked through perceiving the co-existence of objects provides a way to conceive of climate and environmental catastrophe not as akin to an impetuous god but rather as discrete objects in our lives. In the terms of such an analysis, to change those lesser objects is to change both what the hyperobject contains and how it is composed; to transform cars, to use alternative fuels, to develop efficient intercity public transit, or to implement the greening of cities is to transform the objects that together compose and are contained in that worrisome and threatening hyperobject known as the environment or the climate. If it is through the intimate press of co-existence that the environment and climate become claustrophobically and motivatingly close (Morton 2013a: 132), then perhaps widespread, possibly coordinated small projects aimed at discrete objects and problems are the best hope for environmental politics.

References

Agamben, Giorgio. (2004). *The Open: Man and Animal*. Translated by Kevin Attell (Stanford, CA: Stanford University Press).

Aiello, Leslie C. (2010). "Five Years of *Homo floresiensis*." *American Journal of Physical Anthropology* 142(2): 167–9.

Alaimo, Stacy. (2010). *Bodily Natures: Science, Environment, and the Material Self* (Bloomington, IN: Indiana University Press).
Alaimo, Stacy. (2012). "Sustainable This, Sustainable That: New Materialisms, Posthumanism, and Unknown Futures." *PMLA* 127(3): 558–64.
Barad, Karen. (2003). "Posthumanist Performativity: Toward an Understanding of how Matter Comes to Matter" *SIGNS: Journal of Women in Culture and Society* 28(3): 801–31.
Bennett, Jane. (2010). *Vibrant Matter: A Political Ecology of Things* (Durham, NC: Duke University Press).
Braidotti, Rosi. (2013). *The Posthuman* (Malden, MA: Polity Press).
Bryant, Levi R. (2011). *The Democracy of Objects* (Ann Arbor, MI: Open Humanities Press).
Callaway, Ewen. (2014). "Modern Human Genomes Reveal Our Inner Neanderthal." *Nature* doi:10.1038/nature.2014.14615.
Chakrabarty, Dipesh. (2009). "Climate of History: Four Theses" *Critical Inquiry* 35 (Winter): 197–222.
Connolly, William. (2013). "The 'New Materialism' and the Fragility of Things." *Millennium—Journal of International Studies* 41(3): 399–412.
Coole, Diana. (2013). "Agentic Capacities and Capacious Historical Materialism: Thinking with New Materialisms in the Political Sciences." *Millennium—Journal of International Studies* 41(3): 451–69.
De Landa, Manuel. (1997). *A Thousand Years of Nonlinear History* (Brooklyn, NY: Zone Books).
Fausto-Sterling, Anne. (2012). *Sex/Gender: Biology in a Social World* (New York, NY: Routledge).
Foote, Stephanie and Mazzolini, Elizabeth, eds. (2012). *Histories of the Dustheap: Waste, Material Cultures, Social Justice* (Cambridge, MA: MIT Press).
Grosz, Elizabeth. (2011). *Becoming Undone: Darwinian Reflections on Life, Politics, and Art* (Durham, NC: Duke University Press).
Guthman, Julie and Mansfield, Becky. (2013). "The Implications of Environmental Epigenetics: A New Direction for Geographic Inquiry on Health, Space, and Nature-Society Relations." *Progress in Human Geography* 37(4): 486–504.
Habermas, Jurgen. (2003). *The Future of Human Nature* (Malden, MA: Polity Press).
Haraway, Donna. (2008). *When Species Meet* (Minneapolis, MN: University of Minnesota Press).
Harman, Graham. (2011). *The Quadruple Object* (Arlesford, UK: Zero Books).
Hird, Myra. (2009). *The Origins of Sociable Life: Evolution After Science Studies* (New York, NY: Palgrave Macmillan).
Latour, Bruno. (2004). *Politics of Nature: How to Bring the Sciences into Democracy* (Cambridge, MA: Harvard University Press).
Latour, Bruno, Harman, Graham, and Erdélyi, Peter. (2010). *The Prince and the Wolf: Latour and Harman at the LSE* (Arlesford, UK: Zero Books).
Lordkipanidze, David et al. (2013). "A Complete Skull from Dmanisi, Georgia, and the Evolutionary Biology of Early *Homo*." *Science* 342(October 18): 326–31.
Marder, Michael. (2013). *Plant-Thinking: A Philosophy of Vegetal Life* (New York, NY: Columbia University Press).
Meillassoux, Quentin. (2012). *After Finitude: An Essay on the Necessity of Contingency* (New York, NY: Bloomsbury Academic).
Morton, Timothy. (2013a). *Hyperobjects: Philosophy and Ecology after the End of the World* (Minneapolis, MN: University of Minnesota Press).

Morton, Timothy. (2013b). *Realist Magic: Objects, Ontology, Causality* (Ann Arbor, MI: Open Humanities Press).

Nixon, Rob. (2011). *Slow Violence and the Environmentalism of the Poor* (Cambridge, MA: Harvard University Press).

Oyama, Susan, Griffiths, Paul E., and Gray, Russell D., eds. (2001) *Cycles of Contingency: Developmental Systems and Evolution* (Cambridge MA: MIT Press).

Slavich, George M. and Cole, Steven W. (2013). "The Emerging Field of Human Social Genomics." *Clinical Psychological Science* 1(3): 331–48.

Singer, Merrill. (1996). "Farewell to Adaptationism: Unnatural Selection and the Politics of Biology." *Medical Anthropology Quarterly* 10(4): 496–515.

Stiegler, Bernard. (1998). *Technics and Time, 1: The Fault of Epimetheus*. Translated by Richard Beardsworth and George Collins Stanford (CA: Stanford University Press).

Wolfe, Cary, ed. (2003). *Zoontologies: The Question of the Animal* (Minneapolis, MN: University of Minnesota Press).

Wolfe, Cary. (2010). *What is Posthumanism?* (Minneapolis, MN: University of Minnesota Press).

CHAPTER 13

ENVIRONMENTAL MANAGEMENT IN THE ANTHROPOCENE

DAVID SCHLOSBERG

IN the film *Beasts of the Southern Wild*, a Katrina-like storm is headed for the Louisiana bayou, where the main characters, six-year-old Hushpuppy and her father, live. As the storm approaches, the father doesn't flee like many others, but instead hunkers down in their small shack. Inside, he puts Hushpuppy in a "boat" (actually, more like a trunk), and puts water wings on her arms, explaining that if the waters come up, they'll just float away. After the storm passes, they venture out on their boat, looking at the decimation, including animals that have drowned. And Hushpuppy laments, "For the animals that didn't have a dad to put them in the boat, the end of the world already happened. They're all down below, trying to breathe through water."

The dad can be seen as a metaphor for environmental management—how we protect what we see as most important in the world from various storms, increasingly of our own making. This is the dilemma of environmental management in the Anthropocene—we've created the storm, so now can we also build the boats and protect the animals, human and non-human? The argument of this chapter is that this new era of human-induced environmental change challenges all of the old justifications and approaches to environmental management. The point is to take a closer look at how we might rethink the normative and ethical underpinning of our attempts to manage and protect environments, in an age when human beings impact the very way the planet works. Ultimately, the issue is not simply recognizing the reality of the Anthropocene, but coming to understand how we can become more receptive to, and manage human immersion in, radically changed environmental systems.

After laying out the definition of this new era we are coming to realize and address, I will take a brief look at four possible responses, with a specific focus on how the idea of a human-shaped Anthropocene impacts the normative underpinning for various types of human management of a climate-changing environment. Four different normative approaches to environmental management will be examined. I will note key limitations of two key approaches—classic preservation and conservation ethics, and the limits and boundaries discourse. And I will explore two very different paths that are potentially supercharged by the Anthropocene—the hubris of a new generation of prometheans, and the potential of an ecological receptivity embodied in a politics of sight. The goal is to explore and critique a number of potential ways to ground ecologically sound and politically pragmatic environmental policies in response to, and within, the Anthropocene.

The Anthropo-scenery

There has been much written lately on the Anthropocene,[1] though the idea has been around for at least 150 years; Steffan et al.'s history (2011) lays out how authors since George Perkins Marsh have been examining this relationship between *Man and Nature* (1864).[2] More recently, McKibben (1989), in his first foray into writing on climate change, argued that while human beings were once "a species tossed about by larger forces, now we *are* those larger forces" (xviii, emphasis in the original); *The End of Nature* meant the beginning of the Anthropocene. Crutzen and Stoermer (2000) put forth the original scientific argument for a new human-influenced geological age. But from its origins in empricial studies in the natural sciences, the Anthropocene is now a growing conceptual issue in the humanities and social sciences. As Chakrabarty (2009) observes, human beings now act with the power of a geophysical force, like tectonic plates or volcanoes. We are the *Earthmasters*, as Hamilton argues (2013)—we've already geoengineered our way into this problem. The question, of course, is what the empirical reality of human-impacted global systems means in normative terms.

Here, there are a number of challenging arguments surrounding the meaning of the Anthropocene. Some critics insist we focus too much on the universal nature of the idea—that the age is really not just about "human" impacts, but the impacts of *certain* humans or social practices. Maybe a better term is the Capitalcene, or the Manthropocene. Similarly, we might explore the vulnerability created by the concept—for example, the relationship between the big acceleration of environmental impacts and the great divergence in terms of inequality. Here, the issue is less "human" impacts, and more the effects on different communities (see Di Chiro, this volume, for more on these issues).

One key controversy arose out of Revkin's (2014) suggestion of the possibility of what he called a "good" Anthropocene. Revkin accepts the empirical reality of the new era, but insists that there is a way to more positively engage with (and in) this new reality. It's not that the reality of the Anthropocene is "good,"[3] but that we can approach our response either by continuing to focus on the catastrophe or on the development of more positive human traits that can engage our current condition. This approach (which I will address more fully in the final section) has been thoroughly attacked by Hamilton

(2014), who argues that a simplistic "positive" outlook ignores the worst impacts on the most vulnerable—that for most living beings there is and will be no good at all in the Anthropocene. Worse, Hamilton sees this focus on a positive attitude as maladaptive, as it "impedes appropriate action"—though Revkin responds that all of the efforts of "shouting catastrophe" have not brought satisfactory action either. The question is one of focusing on the specific powers and processes behind the reality of the Anthropocene and its obvious realization in climatic change, or on the ethical and normative design of what Revkin calls "soft landings" for the vulnerable.

Of course, one need not choose one side in that false dichotomy. Both agree that the Anthropocene is a real and significant shift, and that any future will consist of a constant exposure to new environmental realities, an ongoing fight against the worst offenders, and an attempt to rethink human–non-human relations in this new era. The difference is in the political and ethical response.

Crist (2013) goes further than Hamilton, however, insisting that even the acceptance of the term "Anthropocene" is simply a surrender—that the current discourse around the idea refuses to challenge human domination, champions human centeredness, and proposes technological and managerial approaches to a human imposed era of the subjugation of the rest of nature. For Crist, the Anthropocene simply *submits and affirms* human centrality and domination. Worse, it shrinks the discursive space for challenging this domination of the biosphere, and blocks discussion of alternative forms of human life on earth. Similarly, Hettinger insists that the Anthropocene is "an arrogant overvaluation of humans' role and authority," that it undermines "the importance of nature preservation, restoration, and rewilding," and it will have us simply become managers of the earth we have created, promoting ecosystem invention and geoengineering (2014: 4)—a point I will return to later.

Significantly, none of these critics disagrees on the empirical nature of our problem—the reality of the Anthropocene; none disagree that the era is also an illustration of human hubris, self-centeredness, and interference in ecological systems (or, the hubris of those with the power to implement...). All also agree on the necessity of a constructive ethical way forward as well—a more engaged understanding of the human relationship with the environment in which we are immersed. But whereas some critics see the term itself as symptomatic of the problem, I see immense normative potential in the very *idea* of the Anthropocene. As I argue in this chapter, the fact that visibility is key to the Anthropocene—the realization that future geologists will see a distinct impact on the planet that begins in the industrial age—holds promise.

Simply put, the Anthropocene will not recede until human beings do. Given this, can we figure out what it means to be the parent that puts the animals on the boat—or will we remain the source of the storm that ends their worlds and decimates ours? So for this exercise, the focus is on how particular existing normative frames for environmental management are impacted by the empirical reality of the Anthropocene. The central question is about how we can develop ways to think about and manage ecosystems, animal habitats, and human needs as we impact the very nature of those systems.

Response One: Environmental Management and the Past

The first approach to environmental management I want to address goes right to the essence of the dilemma. In the Anthropocene, one of the major groundings of our approach is simply taken away from us.

Much environmental management is based on a classic enlightenment framework: we break down problems into parts, and apply expertise to them via bureaucracies and administration. Dryzek (2013) calls this kind of old school approach administrative rationalism. But what kind of expertise is normally applied? Management of environmental systems has traditionally depended on knowledge of the past: the historical rate of snowmelt and flow of rivers, the range and migrations of various flora and fauna, the history of take, size, and species in fisheries. Environmental management has long taken the past as a standard around which to design conservation and restoration. This connection to history and reference to past, stable conditions is deeply embedded in standard terms like "preservation," "conservation" biology, and "restoration" ecology.

We often manage environments based in a range of preservationist or conservationist environmental ethics or values—setting aside "wilderness areas," nature reserves, or iconic places in order to keep them ever thus. But the combined impact of both climate change and the Anthropocene make our knowledge of, and valuing of, the historical status of environments irrelevant. To put it bluntly, this preservation norm is passé—past environments can no longer function in newly climate-changed space. Our move into the Anthropocene, out of the relative stability of the Holocene, undermines this traditional knowledge base of environmental management.

An example comes with the field of ecological restoration. The field originally defined itself as focused on moving ecological systems back to "indigenous, historic ecosystem" conditions (Higgs 2012). In this incarnation, ecological restoration aimed to repair human damage to the natural world and ecosystems by taking those systems back to a time before such damage began. One example is the proposed restoration of ponderosa pine forests in Northern Arizona. Crudely put, the prescription is simple: look for very old tree stumps from before European settlement, plant new trees there, cut down all the remaining overgrowth, and bring back a fire regime to allow grasslands to come back along with the pine forests (Mast et al. 1999). The problem is that, under the Anthropocene and climate change in particular, the high altitude region of northern Arizona will no longer be able to support ponderosa pines. The days of this particular species in that particular place are truly numbered; it is estimated that the ponderosa pine forests will not last.

It's getting hotter, fish are moving down (or up) the coast, spring is coming early, fires are more frequent and intense. Ecosystems are stressed—which only makes them even more vulnerable. Nothing is like it was, and it will only be more so in the future. Even insurance companies are dropping the past as a basis of expertise and management. On things like flood insurance, they are switching from actuary tables based on past experience to those based on future predictions.

The use of the past as a baseline natural world to be restored or mimicked is no longer possible, and, to put it bluntly, the era of preservation as the basis of environmental management is over. And this is certainly recognized in the field; it is quite amazing to see major figures in the Nature Conservatory arguing that "Conservation's continuing focus upon preserving islands of Holocene ecosystems in the age of the Anthropocene is both anachronistic and counterproductive" (Kareiva, Lalasz, and Marvier 2012).

But old-school conservation biologists continue to fear the spread of the acceptance of the idea of the Anthropocene, as it "will undermine both conservation and restoration objectives" (Caro et al. 2011). Such critics (aligned with those of Crist and Nettinger noted earlier) suggest conservationists simply stop talking about the Anthropocene, and focus on pristine ecosystems unaffected by human activity. Unfortunately, of course, there is no such thing; the world these critics imagine no longer exists (and we would be surprised, no doubt, if such ecologists wanted people to stop talking about climate change—another empirical reality). Overall, a historical approach focused on preserving the now, or putting things back to the way they were, is a normative basis for environmental management that is untenable and indefensible in the physical reality of the Anthropocene.

This does not mean that we cannot restore or protect ecosystems in some way. Such a classic approach may still be possible in small pockets of localized ecosystem management in regions where the impacts of climate change will not undermine the conditions of the Holocene right away.

But there is another way of thinking about, and grounding, restoration. The Society for Ecological Restoration did something extraordinary a few years back; it officially redefined restoration away from its traditional focus on the past, to "the process of assisting in the recovery of an ecosystem that has been damaged, degraded, or destroyed." So the focus is on functioning ecosystems, on resilience, on relationships and sustainability in new conditions—and, crucially, on learning about these new ecosystems that we are creating. History may still be important—it may serve to provide examples, both natural and cultural, of collaborative human–non-human functioning. But we can no longer simply model future restoration on past empirical knowledge of a particular place.

Still, the nostalgic historic restoration idea remains. The newly popular notion of rewilding focuses on bringing megafauna (or closely related surviving relatives) back into environments where they have been eliminated (Monbiot 2013). Rewilding means reintroducing missing plants and animals and then stepping back and letting nature get on with it. The problem, of course, is that sometimes rewilding is seen as a return to the past—a way to let nature get back to the way it was. Monbiot, for example, seems to use both the idea of the past and the value of a functioning system in his argument. A climate-changed environment, however, simply cannot support the old systems rewilders want to restore, and reliance on a notion of the past is just another variation on the conservation ideal that has become moot in the Anthropocene. Should we really let old megafauna loose in an environment that has changed to the point that it can no longer sustain them?

To be fair, unlike some others, Monbiot does discuss focusing on functioning ecosystems rather than the past alone. He discusses the ecological value of species reintroduction and the value of trophic cascades; for example, bringing wolves back into Yellowstone not only cut deer population and changed their behavior, but this allowed trees and grasses to grow back, which attracted birds and small critters, protected riverbanks, and brought a range of additional benefits. So my point is not that we can't do restoration or rewilding, but that the normative underpinning of those efforts has to be clear—not based on some now unattainable historical ideal, and certainly not on a traditional conception of the 'wild' as a past, or apart from human influence. The normative grounding has to pay attention to the physical impacts of the Anthropocene on place.

Response Two: Limits and Boundaries

The second approach to environmental management I want to address has a different sort of problem—it's not realistic, but more for political than ecological reasons.

One of the currently favored discourses of the Anthropocene is actually a very old approach, long in the environmental literature—that of boundaries and limits. For example, Rockström and colleagues, in an influential piece for *Nature*, argued that there are a number of "planetary boundaries that must not be transgressed" (Rockström et al. 2009: 472). These limits denote a "safe operating space for humanity with respect to the Earth system;" and a keen attention to them is the only way to keep us from pushing "the Earth outside the stable environmental state of the Holocene, with consequences that are detrimental or even catastrophic for large parts of the world" (472). Rockström and his colleagues identify nine key ecological processes, and set such boundaries or limits for each. The very fact that we have exceeded the boundaries on at least three of these indicators illustrates that we are, indeed, in the Anthropocene, where human activity changes global ecological systems.

The point to be made here is not about the particular boundaries, but the boundary approach itself. This clearly follows the earlier discourse of limits, specifically the limits to growth (Meadows et al. 1972), which has been part of the environmentalist and conservationist discourse for decades. We have had many years (now past) to prevent overshoot, or capacity reached, or limits transgressed. The political problem is that four decades of an environmental discourse of limits to growth has really come to nothing.

Actually, it's worse than that, and the problem is a political–structural one. Limits discourse immediately faces opposition. However justifiable it may be in both economic and ecological terms, dominant actors in political and economic systems cannot buy into such talk of boundaries. Any environmental advocate can attest to the standard response to any limits proposal: you greenies are out to kill jobs and the economy. Those committed to this status quo often paint environmentalists as anti-growth in order to dismiss them.[4]

As Dryzek et al. (2003) have written previously, states have an imperative *for* growth, and while we have seen innumerable examples of environmental discourse couched against that imperative in the last few decades, these campaigns tend to fail. It may seem obvious to use 350.org's success as a counter example—and there is no more clear environmental organization based on the concept of boundaries as one that takes a limit as its very name. But it is important to note that while the group appeals to environmentalists tied to the limits discourse and the particular boundary of carbon emissions, the brilliance of the group's divestment campaign is that, for business, investment in carbon-based fuels—especially coal—is a growth risk, while renewables are the far more tenable long-term growth investment. In other words, 350.org appeals to the growth language of the business community and the state, not limits alone.

While the argument is sensible, and while the boundaries approach is a representation of mainstream ecological discourse, these metaphors simply do not often work in the political arena. So it should not be surprising that at the 2012 United Nations Conference on Sustainable Development in Rio de Janeiro, planetary boundaries were mentioned in the draft conference declaration—but deleted from the final version as too controversial.

Ecological boundaries are quite a reasonable concept for and from environmental science, but highly problematic as a political discourse. And so a strict and politically unsophisticated focus on limits leaves us without a pragmatic language to address environmental management in the Anthropocene. We may argue that we should get politics to listen to the real world and adopt a limits or boundaries or de-growth discourse, and use that as a normative grounding for environmental management based in science. Maybe so, but 30 years of sustainable development negotiations, and over 20 on CO_2, clearly illustrate the problem with that kind of normative grounding of the problem.

As with the traditional conservationist response, the limits response is evolving, however, and may re-emerge as a potential grounding to action in the Anthropocene. We continue to see arguments against growth—slow growth, anti-growth, de-growth—and many are increasingly coming not only from left environmentalists and the scientific community, but some progressive and mainstream economists as well. One key argument here is that a major shift to address a boundary concern such as carbon will not actually be a limit to growth—in fact, there may be economic benefits. That could certainly change things, but note the shift—the language moves clearly away from limits and boundaries, to benefits. So my critique remains: a strict and politically unsophisticated focus on limits, or limits to growth, leaves us without a pragmatic language to address environmental management in the Anthropocene.

Response Three: Double Down on Hubris

The managerial approaches above take a defensive posture of some kind—they look to the damage caused by Anthropocene and hope to reverse or protect ecological systems from the worst of its impacts. But there is another way to look at the Anthropocene, and at human ability to affect global systems and the workings of the natural and ecological systems and individuals. Maybe the current result of our hubris is simply an opportunity to apply more hubris—in the form of new technologies.

Geoengineering, of course, is a key idea getting a lot of play as a potential response to the Anthropocene—one that embraces the basis of the age by expanding human power to engineer the planet. But while we hear a lot about geoengineering to slow the impacts of climate change, this more purposeful approach need not stop there. Another response to the Anthropocene could include the engineering and redesign of various qualities of the human species itself, and or those of other animals, to enable us all to adapt to new environments.

Keith (2000) was one of the first to advocate the prospects of geoengineering the climate system to avoid the worst impacts of climate change. The idea covers a range of potential techniques, from seeding the oceans with iron to capturing carbon dioxide. But the most often discussed tactic is that suggested by Crutzen (2006), of injecting sulfate aerosols into the atmosphere to block solar radiation and, so, the heating of oceans, ice caps, and land. One reason this tactic is most discussed is because we actually have examples of it working in the way we would want—the very real and measured cooling effect of volcanic eruptions. The *Economist* (2011) proposes to use geoengineering in order to maintain or artificially recreate the best of Holocene conditions. "Embrace" the Anthropocene, they argue, and shape the desired environmental conditions, rather than "retreat onto a low-impact path" of boundaries. This is old fashioned, technological-fix, prometheanism. And yet it is an oft-discussed model of environmental management for the Anthropocene—more management and techo-optimism to fix past mismanagement and misplaced techno-optimism.

Geoengineering has been critically discussed at length, and it is not really possible to add more to the caution laid out by skeptics such as Gardiner (2010) or Hamilton (2013). Gardiner has attacked the idea that we can "arm the future" with preparation for geoengineering; he is particularly concerned with the potential moral corruption of current generations as we appear to diminish our own responsibility for creating a climate-changed world. Hamilton argues quite directly that it is a faith in human hubris that seems to be the litmus test for support or dismay with the idea of geoengineering.

But given our lack of moral responsibility combined with this kind of hubris—key components of the Anthropocene—why stop with *geo*engineering? Liao and colleagues (2012) argue that human engineering, or "the biomedical modification of humans to make them better at mitigating climate change" (207), could include things like taking pills to develop an aversion to meat, or to enhance altruism and empathy. We could manipulate human DNA so we develop cat-like eyes (so we'll need less energy), or, more directly, shrink the size of human beings to decrease both their physical and ecological footprint. Maybe we use genetic engineering to develop resistance to the world we've made; Di Chiro (2004: 142) has written critically of a potential "future of genetically resistant 'Roundup Ready® communities' living, working, and playing happily alongside the toxic effluent of American industry."

Rather than manage the entire global ecological system to provide an environment fit for human beings in their current form, human beings could potentially manipulate our own evolutionary path in order to better fit with the environment we have produced. Thinking about Hushpuppy again, maybe we can engineer biological water wings for people who live along a rising coastline—genetic implants of pufferfish cells right into human biceps. If one response to the Anthropocene is to take a stronger grip on the steering wheel and geoengineer the climate, why should we not apply the same treatment to ourselves as well?[5]

This combination of hubristic human knowledge and (belated) ethical responsibility could be applied not only to planetary climate systems and our own bodies, but to the bioengineering of non-human animals as well. The Anthropocene is already forcing some species to adapt in unique ways; species are moving and changing in response to human impacts on the planet. If human activity is impacting the direction of the evolution of the non-human, why not push them in certain directions—for their own preservation and survival? One recent art project by photographer Vincent Fournier (2012)—aptly entitled *Post-Natural History* and undertaken with the assistance of a geneticist—imagines the use of synthetic biology and genetic engineering to assist animals to survive climate change. Ideas include the basic—like making a rabbit much more intelligent. But it also includes the more fanciful: fungi that grow in arid environments, or armored mammals with metallic scales that help maintain body temperature in a warming climate. After the storm, Hushpuppy says that the animals down below are trying to breathe through the water. Maybe we can make that possible for them—reintroduce gills, and engineer a sort of devolution to an earlier state.

These are not just art projects or fanciful thinking; human beings already do such things. American researchers are developing "new breeds of animals that can stand up to the hazards of global warming"—one idea is to insert the genes of heat-hearty African chickens into current stocks. Of course, this engineering is not new; the Center for PostNatural History, in Pittsburgh, maintains a full catalog of living, preserved, and documented specimens of postnatural origin—from Dolly the sheep to transgenic mosquitoes. Engineering nature is already an environmental management strategy, and in an Anthropocene we might justify these practices for both the good of other species, as well as for human desires or needs.

In addition to a focus on individual animals, we might combine the ideas of geo- and bio-engineering to enable entire ecosystems to remain viable—for example, adjust a number of species in a reef ecosystem to withstand increasing temperatures, higher acidity levels, and rising ocean levels. Again, this isn't just fanciful—it's a profession. There is already an American Ecological Engineering Society, complete with its own *Journal of Ecological Engineering*. It started more focused on sustainability, but seems to be moving in the direction of biotech and synthetic ecologies.

Another quite active research project—an interesting collaboration between theorists, designers, and the sci-fi author Bruce Sterling—is *Next Nature*. The premise is that we have always designed human culture out of nature; human life has always been artificial—we just have good and bad examples to work from. Holland, artificial but aware of the natural world, is the ideal (not coincidentally, most of the theorists are Dutch). But at least the next nature idea is fully aware of our destructive capabilities.

Similarly, in his essay entitled "Love Your Monsters"—a reference to the lesson of Mary Shelley's *Frankenstein*—Latour makes the argument that the "environment is exactly what should be even more managed, taken up, cared for, stewarded, in brief, integrated and internalized in the very fabric of the polity" (Latour 2011: 20). With modernization and technology comes the responsibility, as he says, to care for the monsters we have created—and not fear the continued refinement of technologies. So is assisting animals to survive by changing their very genetic makeup an added unethical act, or is speeding up and influencing the evolutionary process the most ethical thing we can do for all of the species we are currently forcing into extinction?

The point here is that some *embrace* the technological hubris that brought us to this point, and encourage the expansion of the Anthropocene in order to address its impacts. "For nature to survive, it may have to become artificial," says one commentary on Fournier's project (Walsh 2012). While Liao's intention was to point out the absurdity of geoengineering by contrasting it with other forms of bioengineering to which many of us have more of an inbuilt resistance, there is no doubt that what seems a step too far now will become a much more regular topic of conversation and actual management proposals. This is environmental governance with a reflexive hubris.

Response Four: A Politics of Sight

To recap, the idea of historical grounding is moot, limits has political limits, and hubris hasn't exactly worked for us or the environment. So how might we rethink a normative grounding for our relationship with, and management of, the non-human realm we now impact on a global scale? The argument here is that another way to think about environmental management seeks a basis in more receptive, reflexive, and co-evolutionary relationship encompassing humans and ecosystems—a combined ecological and political efficacy. Such an approach is not only theoretical, but also a growing practice, what I am calling a politics of sight for the Anthropocene. The point is to bring attention to the previously hidden, and visualize the ongoing human relationship with the non-human. Helpfully, the idea of the Anthropocene gives us an opportunity to both see and reflect on the human impact on the environment.

A politics of sight is closely aligned to much work that has been done on the politics of receptivity, both in political theory generally, and in environmental theory in particular. Receptivity, however, has been almost entirely focused on *listening* rather than sight. As Kompridis argues, reflexivity is about moving beyond our current passiveness or learned invisibility—the process of receiving information, but then disposing of it, and learning not to see (2011: 263). But Kompridis falls back to a focus on listening: "Becoming receptive to such a call means facilitating its voicing, letting it become a voice that we did not allow ourselves to hear before, and responding to it in a way that demands something of us that we could not have recognized before."

Dobson (2010) notes that receptivity in the form of listening has been present in environmental political theory for some time—the call to listen to the non-human realm. Dryzek (1990) argued that we should extend a conception of communicative rationality to include "signals" from the non-human world in political decision-making. Similarly, Plumwood (1998) insisted that environmental politics demands we listen to "the remote," in terms of both vulnerable human and non-human populations left out of political conversations. And Latour's (2004) extension of the idea of "actants" to the non-human exemplifies such a call to listen to a broader array of utterances and inputs to political processes.[6] As Dobson notes, these types of approaches "implicitly or explicitly suggest that 'giving voice to nature' is less a matter of finding ways of literally making nature speak, and more a question of listening harder to what it already has to say" (Dobson 2010: 764).

But Dobson also understands receptivity in a broader sense; it "is something akin to 'listening'—but also more than listening. It involves the development of *all* the receptive capacities—a category that includes listening, but is not exhausted by it" (760). It is that opening that I want to explore—receptivity beyond listening alone. Let me illustrate the idea with a few examples and illustrations.

David Foster Wallace's famous graduation speech to Kenyon College, published as *This Is Water* (2009), actually discusses a type of receptivity—what he calls "simple awareness." He begins with an apt parable:

> There are these two young fish swimming along, and they happen to meet an older fish swimming the other way, who nods at them and says, "Morning, boys, how's the water?" And the two young fish swim on for a bit, and then eventually one of them looks over at the other and goes, "What the hell is water?"

While the essay covers much ground, the focus is on mindfulness—to pay attention and always see the water. It is an argument for a multi-sensory critical receptivity.

Wallace, however, did not get to the core of *how* it is we come to forget about the water, to be in it without seeing it—the creation of what I call an "immersive ignorance." Miéville's *The City and The City* (2009) illustrates exactly that. The setting of the book is two cities that actually share the same physical, geographical space; they can only exist as distinct from one another if the citizens of each learn to make the other city and its citizens invisible, even as they pass them on the street. Learning in these two cities is aimed at making what we are immersed in our everyday lives—the very people, buildings, and streets we pass every day—invisible. That invisibility is taught, expected, and enforced. While Miéville's work is often used to illustrate the way we make the poor, homeless, or "others" in our own cities invisible, the learned disappearance of things right in front of our faces is also applicable to our relationship with the non-human world. The acceleration of the industrial age, key to the Anthropocene, has been, in part, about obscuring the reality of the environment in which our everyday lives are immersed. The development of the Anthropocene has depended on a taught blindness to that other city, the natural systems we walk through, and that provide the context for our basic needs.

And yet visibility itself is key to the concept of the Anthropocene; it is based on the idea that future geologists will see a distinct impact on the planet that begins in the industrial age. The effort to recognize this new geologic era of human influence is one of *making visible* what we have previously refused to recognize. The Anthropocene *enables* sight, and, so, reflection. Such a vision requires heightened critical reflexivity about our ecological selves, a life with constant awareness of the environmental systems in which human life is immersed. It opens us to a *receptivity* to our impacts on the planet and, so, a potential reconstruction of the relationship between human and non-human.

There are two different aspects to a kind of politics of sight in the environmental arena. First is the classic uncovering or exposure of the treatment of individual animals that we've seen since Greenpeace starting videotaping the slaughter of whales. These images had not been part of the public conception of whaling, and yet now they are quite common. This politics of sight is the essence of a reality TV show, *Whale Wars*, and movies like *The Cove*. The strategy continues with the various attempts to expose the practices and treatment of animals in abattoirs, or their abuse in live transport.[7]

But beyond these illustrations, there is another side to a politics of sight, in particular about exposing not just practice and treatment, but the very construction of learned invisibility or immersive ignorance. Pachirot's *Every Twelve Seconds* (2011), for example, is about the intentional production of invisibility among the workers in industrialized slaughterhouses. The point is not simply to show the abuse of cows in abattoirs, but about exposing a whole uncomfortable and destructive system that we have learned to make invisible, even when its products are in plain sight every day in the supermarket. As Pachirot notes, the hope of his book is "that its detailed account of industrialized killing will invite readers to seek a more thoughtful relationship with the nonhuman creatures with whom we share the planet and a more critical stance toward the mechanisms of distance and concealment that currently operate . . ." (ix). This kind of politics of sight—which is what Pachirot calls his task—is about using such sight to encourage a receptivity to the understanding of the human role in living in and affecting environments. For me, this is about *seeing* the Anthropocene in the everyday.

This is not necessarily about stopping meat-eating, but understanding our relationship with non-human animals, even as they feed us. In Sydney, a local café has a pet pig, aptly named Kevin Bacon, which customers pass on the way in to eat their bacon sandwiches and pork pies. Some have attacked the café for its hypocrisy in caring for animals as pets when they serve their kind; this was actually the justification used for the kidnapping of poor Kevin. Defenders of the café argued that this is exactly the point, and having him right there enforces that visibility. Just seeing Kevin Bacon makes us see the water, it pushes us beyond an immersive ignorance of the basic use of other animals for food.

One of the most famous cases of what I would categorize as this kind of politics of sight has come from the Copenhagen Zoo. In February 2014, the zoo euthanized a young giraffe, Marius, it said could not viably participate in a captive breeding program to preserve and strengthen the species. While zoos frequently put down animals for this reason, the difference in this case is that the Copenhagen Zoo chose to make the process very public and visible. Zookeepers killed and dissected the giraffe in front of a crowd of visitors, including children. Large chunks of Marius were then fed to the lions in the zoo—again, in front of a crowd of spectators, seen in photos released by the zoo itself. There is an obvious argument to be made about whether or not the zoo could have found a safe home for Marius to live out his (non-breeding) life—but that's a separate argument. Once they decided to kill him, the very public visualization of the killing, the dissection, and, especially, the consumption was an active politics of sight on the part of the Copenhagen Zoo. And they were wildly successful; the event was shown globally and stirred debate specifically on the environmental management of endangered species in captive breeding programs.

In another example, and obviously on a larger scale, we are starting to see an insistence on the visibility of the impacts of climate change, and a politics of sight by either activists or governments. In adaptation planning, we are increasingly seeing downscaled impact studies that often visually illustrate drought range, sea level rise, urban heat islands, etc. Scientists and local governments are using these visualizations to prompt reflection and action on climate vulnerability, and to develop governance strategies for adaptation. From the Louisiana coastline to post-Sandy planning in New York, and to floods in Great Britain and adaptation planning in Sydney, the visibility of impacts are being used to bring about reflexivity—an understanding of the impacts of climate change and the vulnerability of local populations.

The point here is that this kind of visualization pushes us to look upon and reflect on the source of our food, on captive breeding to preserve species, on climate change, and on the broad relationship between human and non-human. This practice of a politics of sight can bring us face to face with the Anthropocene, and out of the immersive ignorance of our inattention. This is not to claim that making visible the violence and vulnerability of our current impacts on the non-human will lead directly to a more ethical and sustainable relationship, but it is difficult to imagine how we can create an opening for such a relationship without a politics of sight making the consequences of our current actions that much more perceptible. The first step in environmental management of this age is exactly this kind of recognition, receptivity, and vision.

Concluding Thoughts

The ultimate argument here is that there is a value to, and an immense opportunity in, a recognition and visualization of the Anthropocene. This kind of sight and receptivity is key to any shift to a more sustainable environmental management of the ecological systems of the planet. Such an ecologically receptive and reflexive perspective requires us to live with a constant awareness of the environmental systems in which human life is immersed in an ever changing, and ever challenging, Anthropocene. This receptivity and reflexivity can be prompted and fed by a deliberate politics of sight—exposing the abattoirs, the hidden cities, the internal ecosystems, the impacts of climate change. It is possible to use a very visible Anthropocene to move from an immersive ignorance to an ecological receptivity.

Certainly, such a grounding for environmental management seems more ecologically viable than a grasping for the past, more politically viable than a limits approach, and ethically less problematic than continued technological hubris—a politics of sight insists upon an ecological efficacy as a response. One way or another we will find out if human beings are capable of putting an ecological reflexivity into practice—whether we can put ourselves and the rest of the planet in the boats and visualize, evolve, and manage a more functioning Anthropocene.

Acknowledgments

Many people constructively commented on earlier versions of this chapter, and presentations of the ideas. Thanks in particuar to John Meyer, Teena Gabrielson, Robyn Eckersley, Rom Coles, Nikolas Kompridis, and Lauren Rickards. Thanks also to John Dryzek and Dick Norgaard, who co-authored an earlier shot at the topic for our *Climate-Challenged Society* (2013).

Notes

1. Thanks to Tim Luke for the concept of anthropo-scenery from which this section takes its title.
2. Tellingly, Marsh's book was reprinted a decade later as *The Earth as Modified by Human Action*.
3. Though the "good Anthropocene" was the title of the talk in question, and the impetus for the negative response.
4. This political efficacy critique is different from other common flaws in the use of the limits discourse—e.g. those that use the reality of *global* limits as a normative justification for *local* policies such as limiting immigration or population growth. Such mistaken, political uses of the empirical reality of ecological boundaries is a different issue than the efficacy problem discussed here.

5. The combination of geoengineering and human engineering is at the center of the plot of Stanley Kim Robinson's climate fiction opus *2312*.
6. There are key exceptions; Bennett (2004), e.g., notes the impact that the *sight* has on us as a crucial part of "thing power."
7. There has been a huge crackdown on these practices—but I think it's unfortunate that they're being called 'ag-gag' laws by the opposition. There are some limits on reporting and speech, but the main focus of these anti-whistleblower laws are on film and video—they are a direct attempt to keep sight from the public.

References

Bennett, Jane. (2004). "The Force of Things: Steps Toward and Ecology of Matter." *Political Theory* 32(3): 347–72.

Caro, Tim, Darwin, Jack, Forrester, Tavis, Ledoux-Bloom, Cynthia, and Wells, Caitlin. (2011). "Conservation in the Anthropocene." *Conservation Biology* 26(1): 185–8.

Chakrabarty, Dipesh. (2009). "The Climate of History." *Critical Inquiry* 35(2): 197–222.

Crist, Eileen. (2013). "On the Poverty of Our Nomenclature." *Environmental Humanities* 3: 129–47.

Crutzen, Paul. (2006). "Albedo Enhancement by Stratospheric Sulphur Injections: A Contribution to Resolve a Policy Dilemma?" *Climatic Change* 77: 211–19.

Crutzen, Paul, and Stoermer, E. F. (2000). "The Anthropocene." *Global Change Newsletter* 41: 17–18.

Di Chiro, Giovanna. (2004). "Producing 'Roundup Ready®' Communities? Human Genome Research and Environmental Justice Policy." In *New Perspectives on Environmental Justice: Gender, Sexuality, and Activism*, edited by Rachel Stein (New Brunswick, NJ: Rutgers University Press), 139–60.

Dobson, Andrew. (2010). "Democracy and Nature: Speaking and Listening." *Political Studies* 58: 752–68.

Dryzek, John. (1990). "Green Reason: Communicative Ethics for the Biosphere." *Environmental Ethics* 12(2): 195–210.

Dryzek, John. (2013). *Politics of the Earth: Environmental Discourses*, 3rd edn. (Oxford: Oxford University Press).

Dryzek, John S., Downes, David, Hunold, Christian, Schlosberg, David, with Hans-Kristian Hernes. (2003). *Green States and Social Movements: Environmentalism in the United States, United Kingdom, Germany, and Norway* (Oxford: Oxford University Press).

Dryzek, John, Norgaard, Richard, and Schlosberg, David. (2013). *Climate-Challenged Society* (Oxford: Oxford University Press).

Economist. 2011. "A Man-made World: Science is Recognizing Humans as a Geological Force to be Reckoned With." May 26.

Fournier, Vincent. (2012). "Post Natural History." Available at http://www.vincentfournier.co.uk/site/index.php?r=slideshow/view&id=8

Gardiner, Stephen M. (2010). "Is 'Arming the Future' with Geoengineering Really the Lesser Evil? Some Doubts About the Ethics of Intentionally Manipulating the Climate System." In *Climate Ethics: Essential Readings*, edited by Stephen M. Gardiner, Simon Caney, Dale Jamieson, and Henry Shue (Oxford: Oxford University Press), 284–309.

Hamilton, Clive. (2013). *Earthmasters: The Dawn of the Age of Climate Engineering* (New Haven: Yale University Press).

Hamilton, Clive. (2014). "The Delusion of the 'Good Anthropocene:' Reply to Andrew Revkin." June 17. Available at http://clivehamilton.com/the-delusion-of-the-good-anthropocene-reply-to-andrew-revkin/

Hettinger, Ned. (2014). "Valuing Naturalness in the 'Anthropocene': Now More than Ever." In *Keeping the Wild: Against the Domestication of Earth*, edited by G. Wuerthner, E. Crist, and T. Butler (Washington, DC: Island Press), 174–9.

Higgs, Eric. 2012. "History, Novelty, and Virtue in Ecological Restoration." In *Ethical Adaptation to Climate Change: Human Virtues of the Future*, edited by Allen Thompson and Jeremy Bendik-Keymer (Cambridge, MA: MIT Press), 81–102.

Kareiva, Peter, Lalasz, Robert, and Marvier, Michelle. (2012). "Conservation in the Anthropocene: Beyond Solitude and Fragility." *Breakthrough Journal*. Available at http://thebreakthrough.org/index.php/journal/past-issues/issue-2/conservation-in-the-Anthropocene/

Keith, David. (2000). "Geoengineering: History and Prospect." *Annual Review of Energy and the Environment* 25: 245–84.

Kompridis, Nikolas. (2011). "Receptivity, Possibility, and Democratic Politics." *Ethics and Global Politics* 4(4): 255–72.

Latour, Bruno. (2004). *The Politics of Nature: How to Bring the Sciences into Democracy* (Cambridge, MA: Harvard University Press).

Latour, Bruno. (2011). "Love Your Monsters." In *Love Your Monsters: Postenvironmentalism and the Anthropocene*, edited by Michael Shellenberger and Ted Nordhaus (Oakland, CA: Breakthrough Institute), 16–23.

Liao, S. Matthew, Sandberg, Anders, and Roache, Rebecca. (2012). "Human Engineering and Climate Change." *Ethics, Policy, and the Environment* 15(2): 206–21.

McKibben, Bill. (2006 [1989]). *The End of Nature* (New York: Random House).

Mast, Joy Nystrom, Fule, Peter Z., Moore, Margaret M., Covington, W. Wallace, and Waltz, Amy E. M. (1999). "Restoration of Presettlement Age Structure of an Arizona Ponderosa Pine Forest." *Ecological Applications* 9: 228–39.

Meadows, Donella, Meadows, Dennis, Randers, Jorgen, and Behrens, William III. (1972). *The Limits to Growth* (New York: Signet).

Miéville, China. (2009). *The City and the City* (London: Macmillan).

Monbiot, George. (2013). *Feral* (London: Penguin).

Pachirat, Timothy. (2011). *Every Twelve Seconds: Industrialized Slaughter and the Politics of Sight* (New Haven, CT: Yale University Press).

Plumwood, Val. (1998). "Inequality, Ecojustice and Ecological Rationality." *Social Philosophy Today* 13: 75–114.

Revkin, Andrew. (2014). "Exploring Academia's Role in Charting Paths to a 'Good' Anthropocene." Available at http://dotearth.blogs.nytimes.com/2014/06/16/exploring-academias-role-in-charting-paths-to-a-good-anthropocene/

Rockström, Johan et al. (2009). "A Safe Operating Space for Humanity." *Nature* 461 (September 24): 472–5.

Steffen, Will et al. (2011). "The Anthropocene: From Global Change to Planetary Stewardship." *AMBIO: A Journal of the Human Environment* 40(7): 738–61.

Wallace, David Foster. (2009). *This Is Water* (New York: Little, Brown and Company).

Walsh, Bryan. (2012). "Imagining the Future Animal." *Time Lightbox*. Available at http://lightbox.time.com/2012/07/18/imagining-the-future-animal/#1

ENVIRONMENT, COMMUNITY, AND BOUNDARIES

CHAPTER 14

INTERSPECIES

RAFI YOUATT

Introduction

There has been a resurgence of scholarly interest in the conceptual and practical relations between humans and other species. Responding to the ever deeper enmeshment of human life into ecological processes, the intensification of animal production and biological management, and a troubling set of intra-human political developments that rely on the species concept, interspecies analyses tend to share an interest in decentering human agency, both as an analytic matter and as a normative and theoretical project. This new work presents environmental political theory (EPT) with an unusual but engaging challenge. An interest in other species has in some ways always guided what many environmental political theorists study, and as such they have taken on interspecies issues more closely than many. Concepts like flourishing (Nussbaum 2006), intrinsic value (McShane 2007), and ecological holism (Nelson 2009), for example, have brought interspecies questions to the fore from moral perspectives and often sought to consider their translation into the political and policy sphere (Van De Veer and Pierce 2002). EPT and animal studies have also had a significant history of engagement, which connects directly to interspecies questions. In an empirical sense as well, EPT has been oriented towards interspecies questions in terms of its subject matter, to the extent that environmentalism has often been folded in with issues such as wilderness politics, habitat conservation, biodiversity, and the maintenance of functioning, complex ecosystems involving both human and non-human life.

In this context, the chapter seeks to illuminate what the new interspecies work adds to existing scholarship in EPT, in what ways it is different and distinctive, and the ways in which EPT can add to the interspecies turn. While this turn is located by some at the intersection of posthumanism and animal studies, I suggest in the first part of the chapter that an interspecies rubric has been profitably, if somewhat differently, explored at the intersection of politics and ecology in the work of EPT scholars for a number of decades. By bringing this work into conversation with interspecies work outside of EPT, the chapter hopes to contribute to a more politically robust approach to thinking about interspecies questions in ecological contexts. Such a focus can take many forms, and the chapter goes on to explore three possibilities in turn—the boundaries of political community in relation to non-human others; the ways that sovereignty works through interspecies relations; and the workings of political power.

Environmental Thought and Interspecies

The issues of green politics are frequently understood in terms of environment, rather than ecology. That is, they refer to that which surrounds us, where the presumed "us" is an individual or collection of human beings (see Vogel, this volume). However, environment is not just a neutral or passive term describing the environs of humans, but rather is an active practice involving a politics of encircling a particular area and naming it as an environmental site (Luke 1995). This leads to a thinking of environmental politics as an activity referencing the surroundings of humans, somewhere "out there," rather than any kind of relational practice involving multiple living species in a particular space. When politics encounters environmental issues on these terms, then, it is not surprising that we either do not think about the environment as itself a political practice, or that when we do, we think about the valuation and meaning of nature as standing firmly with a human community, where political debate, discussion, and decisions are made.

Ecological politics, by contrast, can put a stronger emphasis on the generative power of interspecies relations. As a scientific practice, ecology involves the study of natural systems that are made up of the relations among species as they exist in abiotic landscapes (Worster 1977). Unlike environmental problems, ecological problems are breakdowns in a particular meshwork of interspecies relations. Thinking ecologically, then, recasts some environmental problems by seeing humans more squarely in the nets of interspecies life, though precisely what this enmeshment entails is a matter of wide debate. One position, following Aldo Leopold (1968), suggests that humans, as members of the biotic community, are essentially equal to any other member of the biotic community, not just in material terms, but in terms of moral considerability. From another perspective, human enmeshment in ecological systems might mean nothing more than a practical starting point from which we might find better solutions to ecological problems. In this vein, many environmental governance reports note that humans are part of nature, but that such entangling is limited to material potency that threatens the long-term sustainability of human life and economy, rather than implying any moral or political obligations to non-humans.

Likewise, ecological science may understand humans, scientifically, as one species among many, with a particularly heavy footprint. But there is by no means any direct pathway from ecological science to political community, and in fact ecology has sometimes been spun back toward human communities in ways that arguably circumvent politics. At best, ecological science can make suggestive inputs for policy-making, or enhance its deliberative decision-making. But because such inputs must go through science, it assumes that the political action still takes place in a human political community. In short, at the heart of the green politics problematique is the assumption that political community is exclusively human, even as its knowledge-making and material practices are themselves interspecific (that is, occurring across species lines).

Older valences of this distinction sometimes used the terminology of shallow environmentalism and deep ecology. The former term was employed as a pejorative by those espousing the latter, implying a reformist bent rather than a radical one (Naess 1985; Bookchin 1988; Fox 1990). Deep ecology, meanwhile, was criticized as mystical and apolitical or overly authoritarian (Ferry 1995). Put into the terms of environmental ethics, the debate played out in somewhat overdrawn terms as anthropocentrism against eco-centrism (Rolston 1988; Callicott 1989). While it is not necessary to rehearse these debates in full here, there are two significant points relevant to interspecies issues. The first is that shallow ecology is perfectly possible, as is deep environmentalism. What is required to thicken or thin these approaches to interspecies issues was generally framed as a perspective on the relationship to existing structures of politics, economy, and culture, understood as radical or reformist. But it may also lie equally in the quality and depth of the relationship between human species and non-human species—a view of all species as having intrinsic value, for example, is wide-ranging and thus might appear radical; but if the quality of relation does not exceed this claim and encompass some of the contextual and complicated ways that particular species engage and interact with one another, then it may be seen as not particularly thick.

The second point is that "centrism" itself may not be the most useful way to approach ecological issues, in that there is no need to be anything-centric in order to engage interspecies relations. As Kerry Whiteside (2003: 191–2) has suggested, the values we hold about the environment, whether anthropocentric, eco-centric, or otherwise centric, are the results of an encounter or confrontation between human and non-human nature. As such, no values reside in the "core" of things, or in natural objects, and it therefore makes more sense to think about the ways that value is generated through processes such as labor, conservation, wilderness-making, or agriculture.

Although there has been significant debate about the reach of moral considerability beyond humans, the argument that political community itself might go beyond the human has been more difficult to sustain, coming up against assumptions about human language, identity, and consciousness. But against the charges of anthropocentrism that presuppose a fundamentally *moral* problem at the heart of human political community, it is more useful from an EPT perspective to locate the anthropocentrism of political community as a problem and artifact of *political* practice, including political thought, rather than a purely moral issue.

Animal Turns

One place such work has been undertaken is in animal studies (including animal rights theory). Animals are only one part of the living world of species, but they are nonetheless particularly important in ecological terms, as central parts of ecosystems, and within (ostensibly) human societies where varieties of human–animal relations (pets, livestock, rodent control) are pervasive. Because animality, as a shared set of characteristics that is presumed to be mute, reactive, and non-political, spans both human and non-human animals, it also provides an important place from which to think about the three aspects of interspecies relations mentioned at the outset. Finally, animality and nature are linked by the way that species barriers are an important constitutive element of their politics.

Early work in this area focused on individual animals, advancing either utilitarian arguments about individual animal pain and pleasure (Singer 1990), or extending a Kantian approach to advocate for the moral rights of animals (Regan 1983). Often provocatively framed via arguments from the margins, which asked people whether anything other than species-hood differentiated a non-speaking child or severely disabled adult from an animal, this work helped to push a somewhat fringe political movement into more mainstream political consciousness (Sunstein and Nussbaum 2004).

When Gary Varner (1998) asked whether animal rights activists could be environmentalists, his question was relevant not just to moral philosophy on questions of value, but also to the possibility of political critique and action that linked these two domains. The early encounters of animal rights theory with environmental political theory were marked by disagreements about the relevant units or levels of political and moral consideration. The former focused on individual creatures, while the latter focused on species or ecosystems. They also focused on different contexts, with environmental theory focusing more on wilderness and wild animals, rather than industrial farming, animals in captivity, or domesticated animals. But even when they looked at the same context and shared significant points of critique, their optics and politics remained somewhat incommensurable, one seeing hog farming as an ecosystem including pigs, farmers, hog lagoons, and rivers, while the other saw a collection of individual animals.

Whereas this early work emphasized animals as sentient creatures, it did not always seek to locate "animal" itself as a cross-species term with political implications for human and non-human life, nor did it always call into question the supposed impossibility of animal "response" (Wolfe 2003; Calarco 2008; Derrida 2008). Moreover, while animal ethics and philosophy, like its environmental counterpart, has been important in motivating political action, it has sometimes made its arguments in non-political terms, seeing questions of whether species, individuals, or ecosystems have *rights* to be primarily a question about whether they have *intrinsic value* (Callicott 1989: 154). But this brushes aside the political quality of rights, which do not fall cleanly from a moral space, but are political constructions, forged by social movements, individuals, and communities within existing social, political, and legal contexts.

Yet the extension of rights past animal rights and environmental rights for humans is significantly strained, especially because of the individualistic basis of rights (Eckersley 1995). In practice, such circumventions have been made through controversial fictions of personhood, which establishes the singularity of a collective subject as a rights-holder, such as great apes, livestock, or most broadly, animals. But rights and personhood bump up against and even evades some of the important questions surrounding interspecies relations. The most important aspect of recognizing that animals or ecosystems have a right to be legal persons is that a human being can represent their interests in a court of law. Such a model may well lead to concrete improvements in interspecies relations. But it is interesting that it draws on existing understandings of non-human life as unable to represent themselves, and requiring acts of ventriloquism that, inevitably, constitute them in new and potentially hierarchical ways within human discourses (Haraway 1992). While the ideas that animals have interests or that we can talk "as if" ecosystems have discernible interests are in some ways a significant departure, they also run the risk of incorporating non-human life further into systems that are designed for their domination and management.

It is particularly interesting that contemporary forms of personhood for animals and nature have come almost entirely not as "natural persons" but as "legal persons" where, like corporate personhood, their fictive basis is more apparent. While recognizing animals or nature as natural persons would involve deep difficulties, the fact that natural personhood refers only to humans draws on a two-tiered imaginary of real persons who are humans, and fictive legal inventions for non-real persons. In the case of animals, the generalized quality of personhood undermines some of the very uniqueness that it is supposed to enhance—it is arguably not as persons that we ought to consider dolphins, and perhaps not only as species, but as individuals involved in social and communal relations. In short, interspecies engagement with 'natural persons' of multiple species is arguably needed in order to generate not just ecological ethics, but also a working politics.

Along these lines, Val Plumwood's (2002) turn toward a "dialogical interspecies ethics" suggests that interspecies encounters are an indispensable way to ground what is an otherwise abstract sensibility about the value of nature. Because "abstract affirmations ... do little to put flesh on the bones of an environmental ethic" (186), Plumwood argues that contact with other species is an important part of realizing ecological projects that are based on something other than instrumental value. For Donna Haraway (2003, 2008), direct forms of interaction between species, and especially the training she undertakes with her dog, motivates her reflections on companion species. She suggests that touch modifies accountability, and that we cannot entirely grasp interspecies ethics or the political questions that relate to them, through textual reflection. While not all species should involve such points of direct encounter, Haraway uses this as a springboard to reflect on the politics of eating, tracking wildlife with cameras, and laboratory animals.

More recent work on animals has moved more directly to take contextual factors into account, and thereby has shifted more clearly into what we think of as ecological politics. One strand of work has emphasized the ways that rights for non-human animals are bound by urban, wild, and "liminal" contexts (Palmer 2010; Donaldson and Kymlicka 2011), suggesting that political rights ought to be, in effect, a joint product of human practices and animal activities. Another strand of work emphasizes the ways that the liberal state in the United States already treats animals in deeply political ways, and as such, they may be considered to be covered under the liberal social contract (Smith 2012). The crucial point, for both, is that focusing on animals can point to the ways that political life not only addresses other species or impacts them, but rather is already constituted in interspecific ways. The relevant questions, then, are about how such an interspecies politics works in practice.

Interspecies and Politics

Emerging perspectives on interspecies relations are diverse and pluralistic, spanning a number of fields. As such, "interspecies" as a domain of social theoretic knowledge does not represent a strong theoretical claim, but rather, areas of scholarship that sometimes overlap.[1] First, it considers the way that actual, material relations between different living species, human and non-human are related to ecological and political outcomes. That is, while "intraspecies" might describe the social sciences and social theories of human life, interspecies references engagements among particular human communities and particular animals, plants, insects, or bacteria. In this guise, its ontology comes directly from the Linnaean classification system, taking species for granted, and seeks to explore how relations across species lines are either affected by human politics or generative of it. Work in political ecology on the Brazilian Amazon, for example, addresses the ways that large-scale state-led development projects of the mid-twentieth century adversely affected existing networks of rubber tappers and rubber trees, and many other species in the forest; at the same time, it shows the generative political importance for counter-movements of rubber tappers to be involved in relations of extraction, production, and restoration with other species, involving enmeshment in processes such as tropical forest nutrient cycling and ecological symbiosis (Hecht and Cockburn 2010).

Second, it thinks about the ways that conceptual logics operate across species to structure environmental and political contexts. Such logics include human political institutions such as sovereignty or community, the logics of war, development, humanitarianism; and the taxonomic project of biological classification itself. In this valence, interspecies calls the politics of species into question, whether endangered species acts or human rights, and seeks to show how such "cuts" in the fabric of life include and exclude (Barad 2003).

Third, and perhaps most ambitiously, interspecies involves an effort to rethink the nature of social relations across species lines, including the boundaries of political life itself. While not going as far as some of the new materialisms that understand politics as potentially involving any and all kinds of things, some of the fruit of interspecies analysis and critique is a newer and richer understanding of political life as a multispecies endeavor in which humans take part. Some new materialist approaches to politics arguably understand the line between the living and the non-living to be less important than moments of association among things (Latour 2004; Bennett 2010). Interspecies perspectives by contrast suggest that we might think about politics as taking place more squarely in the domain of the living, where feeling pain, interpreting the world in a non-deterministic way, reproducing, making habitat choices, and sentience are more central. Such issues lie at the heart of environmental political thought, including its intersection with animal theory.

While interspecies questions have been focused largely on questions of ethics and rights in moral frameworks, then, such questions sometimes sidestep the important intervening variables of politics. A focus on politics opens up new categories and practices for analysis and avenues for change: community, sovereignty, and power are three exemplary instances considered here, though by no means the only ones.

Political Community

One crucial question is whether the political community is something that can or ought to be expanded to include non-human life. Recent developments in a number of countries such as Ecuador, Bolivia, and New Zealand involve innovations such as constitutional rights for nature and legal personhood for ecosystems (Arsel 2012). The current body of animal rights and welfare laws likewise relies on changing sensibilities about which species have previously unrecognized capacities that make them seem more like humans, such as dolphins and chimpanzees, while also granting some protections to animal species who are understood as being quite different from humans. One account of these developments sees it as an expansion of political community to include previously unrecognized political subjects, particularly within liberal polities.[2]

Yet seeing community in these terms poses at least two dangers. By seeing political community as having a core that is then applied or extended outwards, the stability of that center is itself taken for granted, and is left untroubled. Additionally, the capacities that are required for membership in political community are left intact, such as human language or a highly developed sentience. It is only by resemblance to the human that other species make it into the club. While community is made somewhat interspecific, its core remains human.

The second danger is that it misses the ways that political community is, in many ways, already interspecific, and draws lines that include and exclude without taking species as its first point of reference. To see this perspective, political community has to be thought of in less formalistic terms (voting, citizenship), and more in terms of the collective practices that promote and recognize the well-being of some subjects rather than others. For example, consider the mixed species communities, as Mary Midgley (1983) has formulated them, which refer to an on-the-ground situation where different species share daily life, including resources, and interact on a regular basis. Far from a species-wide allegiance trumping all allegiances to animals, many people will fight for the rights of specific animals over those of geographically or socially distant humans. Likewise, animals who have become domesticated will give allegiance to their existing forms of community when challenged from outside—think of dogs who encounter coyotes. Unlike the more abstract Leopoldian conception of biotic community, Midgley takes care to think of this on-the-ground community in terms of direct relationships between humans and other species (sympathies, bonds, compassion). At the same time, it is not an entirely ecological community, in the sense used in ecological sciences of mutuality, etc., because it is rooted not just in behavior and material benefits, but in experiential terms, difficult though that may sometimes be to judge in the animal case.

To take a small example, there are pets in New York City who can inherit property and wealth after their owner's death, have legal teams representing their interests, such as defense against premature euthanization, and enjoy high-quality health care and standards of living. The same species of dog, by contrast, might be picked up on the streets of Arizona and euthanized in a pound, as happened to a recent dog veteran of the Afghan war. Species is not the deciding factor in these two trajectories. What matters here are the categories that law uses to see life, the structural and material power of social class, and the trajectories of patriotism, war, and life after returning home (Johnston 2012). It involves public spaces where sovereign law and quasi-law is given free rein to manage and commit violence against life (animalized) in the name of life (human) without necessary regard to the species of life involved. It involves the power of wealthy private spaces where life can be protected and where particular kinds of life are bred. Most broadly, one can draw the lines around the kinds of lives that count and those that do not without regard to species at all. At work, instead, is an interspecies form of politics, one organizing and excluding and sorting within a community that is made of many species and whose operations cannot be reduced entirely to human agents.

It is not an expansion of political community that is generally at stake for environmental politics, in the sense of extending membership within a polity. Rather, it is a recognition of the interspecific quality of existing political communities, both in political thought and as a matter for practical analysis. By insisting that, in effect, the line dividing *bios* and *zoe* has always operated across the species divide, it becomes possible to see that environmental issues that insist on casting all green politics in terms of human use are reproducing a particular interspecies set of relationships. Rather than extend rights or incorporate the previously excluded, we need to reconfigure and redistribute, in ways that ally human and non-human who bear disproportionate burdens.

It is this context, then, that Donna Haraway's (2008) point rings true: "There is no rational or natural dividing line that will settle the life-and-death relations between human and non-human animals; such lines are alibis if they are imagined to settle the matter 'technically'" (297). Instead, as Haraway urges us, the very question for political life is "collective engagement on the ways of life and death" (299), across and within species lines. This stance, she insists, is "not relativism," but rather a way of gesturing to the instability of political questions that need to be worked out, "where neither human exceptionalism nor the oneness of all things could come to the rescue" (298). We cannot settle the questions of who lives and dies, who suffers and who flourishes, by resorting to a cosmopolitan humanism, since such a humanism is plainly at odds with the way that actually-existing humanisms work. Nor can we answer the question by insisting on the value of all life, always and at all times, since such an ecology is at odds with what ecological existence actually means. The beginning of answering these questions lies instead in the insufficient but necessary act of affirming a political community that is already interspecific, conceptually and practically.

Sovereignty

Sovereignty and environmentalism have an uncertain and uneasy relationship. Some have argued that sovereignty is the best hope environmentalists have for enacting green policy in a strong but democratic fashion (Eckersley 2004). Others have suggested that sovereignty is inherently anti-environmental in its conceptual logic, because it necessarily reduces nature to a form of standing reserve and readies it for exploitation (Smith 2009). Approaching sovereignty from an interspecies perspective amplifies these questions in many ways, but also adds slightly different questions. It suggests that sovereignty is itself an interspecific construct, founded not just on a logical relationship with nature, but also on specific and traceable figures of non-human species. The figure of the wolf, for example, with its capacities for stealth and predation, has been read as a particularly generative touchstone for sovereign power (Derrida 2009), and related in interesting ways to actual human–wolf relations (Emel 1998). However, it is one species among many in a "bestiary" of human–animal relations, each of which contribute to structuring sovereignty in unique ways. A further set of issues pertains to whether other species can, in some ways, be understood as sovereign communities, in a way that is both theoretically cogent (given the way that sovereignty itself relies on an political mobilization of an apolitical understanding of the animal) and politically feasible (Goodin, Pateman, and Pateman 1997; Donaldson and Kymlicka 2011). Considering sovereignty in this tri-partite manner means thinking about it as: an interspecific construct and practice that affects human and non-human, a logic that reaches from human to other species, and a concept that might apply to other species (and as such, stand as a critique of practices surrounding the first two).

Consider the example of the grey wolves on Isle Royale National Park in Lake Superior, near the US–Canadian border (Peterson 2007; Youatt forthcoming). As first claimed by the United States, Isle Royale involved more traditional constructions of sovereign power, in the wars and treaties negotiated, signed, and enforced with the British, Native American tribes, and Canada. Bound up with the politics of westward expansion and with symbolic dimensions of sovereign American power, wolves were hunted and eradicated throughout many parts of the West for the next century. Appearing on Isle Royale in the mid-twentieth century after crossing over on an ice-bridge, wolves on Isle Royale have been the subjects of longest running study of wolves in the mainland United States. As part of a turn toward ecological management, the data on wolf–moose relations is part of a new era of ecological management, one where sovereign power does not seek to kill outright, but rather co-exists with new forms of power aimed at maximizing life through new forms of knowledge and management. In recent years, as wolves on Isle Royale have veered toward extinction, imperatives to intervene have been increasingly called upon to provide sufficient genetic diversity in order for the wolf population to survive.

Yet wolves also raise questions about whether they might enact a kind of sovereignty, as particularly social creatures with complex forms of hierarchy and communication. Some have argued they have a sense of justice (Bekoff and Pierce 2009), while political theorists have suggested that some animals such as wolves ought to be recognized as sovereign communities. In short, wolves not only have individual life projects, or capabilities, but are enmeshed in communities that exhibit sovereign qualities. The claim for animal sovereignty is far from legal or political reality. More importantly, the sovereignty of wolves and other highly social species cannot be a matter of extending existing modes of human sovereignty, given sovereignty's own problematic relationship with animality and given the different temporal, spatial, and semiotic ways that the sovereignty of wolf communities is articulated. However, its articulation can stand as a critique of aspects of Westphalian sovereignty: its relationship to nature as a form of "standing reserve" (Smith 2009); its claim to full and exclusive control over internal territory including dominion over the living creatures who live there; its conceptual relationship with animality; and its ecological myopia. Turning sovereignty into an ecological institution that advances environmental politics, then, might become possible only if we can start to see and think about human sovereignty interspecifically.

Power

Such thinking about community and sovereignty suggests a different view of social power as well. While power across species lines is usually thought in the coercive terms of force, an interspecies approach suggests the importance of seeing it in the more diverse, fluid, and multi-faceted terms of social theory. Without attempting to provide anything like a full review of political theoretic approaches to power, it is nonetheless fair to say that power has been central to environmental politics. To take one example, a focus on power informs significant strands of political ecology, which have asked probing questions about how geopolitics, capitalism, and expert knowledge intersect particular environmental political cases (Peet and Watts 1996; Peet, Robbins, and Watts 2011). How have power relations structured international conservation efforts like peace parks in Southern Africa (Buscher 2013)? In what ways does power produce environmental subjects and identities (Luke 1999; Agrawal 2005)? How has neo-liberalism pervaded environmental efforts from above, and how have local communities found ways of undertaking resource management that have been over-ridden? Most broadly, how are actual ecologies—structured wholes of interspecies relations, relating to the non-living landscape both natural and technological—produced through power relations? These empirically grounded studies draw on a rich critical tradition of theorizing power that moves beyond power as domination, to interpreting and critiquing structural and discursive modes of power in environmental politics.

However, to generalize, most of this work has been concerned with power as something that operates and might reside among humans, rather than seeking to understand the ways that power itself resides in an interspecies matrix.[3] When power has been thought of across species lines, it has tended to emphasize a relationship of domination or instrumental use of nature. How does an interspecies perspective change the way we think about and approach political power?

To take one case, engaging with knowledge that is created about honeybees is, in an environmental context, often understood to be addressing the widespread collapse of the bee population in the United States, known as colony collapse disorder. This problem threatens human agricultural activities, as well as portending other ecological changes. As a problem of power, there is no easy way to describe the human relationship with bees as anything other than power-over, or a form of domination and instrumental use with unintended consequences. Yet bees highlight the intricacies that come with more associational forms of power between humans and bees, such as seductive power and forms of "power-with" (Allen 2003). Moments of associational power allow the production of food through pollination, through associations that range from wild bee colonies approaching agricultural lands, to highly commercialized mobile bee-keeping operations. In neither extreme is the bee dispensable for food production, at least not without very high cost. Hobby beekeeping, as a multispecies expression of power-with in urban contexts, affiliates with different aspects of class, cultural, and ethnic difference—while beekeeping might motivate a particular community interest in locally produced honey, such products are often only available at higher prices at farmer's markets and are promoted within the context of modes of green gentrification. At other times, they stretch across those same axes of difference, allowing new alliances to form around the keeping of animals in cities, or crystallizing groups of non-beekeepers who think bees have no place in cities.

These networks of associational interspecies power affect the ways that politics works, in ways that are not reducible to human power alone. Bees, too, respond to multiple cues in the environment in interesting ways—getting lost on their way back to the hive, interacting with other species of bees, gauging a threat, stinging—in ways that still leave humans uncertain about causes of colony collapse disorder: Climate change? Cell phone signals? Pesticides? Such associational power, however, is not unilaterally positive, and thus partly belies the idea that this is a "politics of nonhuman friendship" (Bingham 2006). Honeybees are also deeply enmeshed with the development of US military force, which has made use of its "power with" bees to research and develop new forms of swarm-based technology (Kosek 2011).

Such a politics does not only exist at a micro-level. To take another example, consider efforts to conduct a global species census, as a paradigmatic case of environmental knowledge production that marshals many of the significant players in global environmental politics in an effort to improve global conservation of biodiversity (Youatt 2008, 2015). Approaches focused on power relations between humans might understand this project as part of an emerging form of environmental governance, leading either toward new forms of sustainable practices and ecological modernization, or, for more critically oriented scholars, towards an increasingly interventionist eco-managerialism or green governmentality. An interspecies perspective on power would not depart entirely from these interpretations nor resolve their disagreements; rather, it would ask how power circulates through interspecies interactions, and in what ways such interactions tell us something about political life or prod us to ask new questions about our practices of political ecology. For example, in insisting that the biodiversity census is mostly about intra-human biopolitics, the abilities of non-human life to avoid becoming governed by biopolitical processes go missing—its resistances, its escapes, its different temporal horizons of reproduction, its migrations.

An interspecies approach to power has as its upshot a deeply contextualized account of how power works across species lines. It works against claims about human–nature relations that involve largely an exercise of human power over nature (in its newest guise, appearing as the Anthropocene), and against claims that human power is best understood as checked by the power of nature (limits discourse; calls for sacrifice). Power, in interspecies frame, is relational, practice-centered, and rarely held as a capacity by any given entity. As such, it points toward a certain kind of environmental politics that is less inclined to see global environmental crisis as a matter of metastasized human power over nature, and more towards a kind of pragmatism that involves shifting modes of interspecies alliance, enmity, and inquiry.

Conclusion

This chapter suggests the importance of thinking about environmental politics by starting with concrete forms of interspecies relations, both materially and conceptually. It has explored some of the ways that environmental political theory has already contributed to interspecies analyses, and examined some of the ways that political community, sovereignty, and power can be located and understood as practices occurring across species lines. To close, it is important to note that interspecies approaches suggest a direction for environmental politics that is, paradoxically, not based on species. In particular, it suggests the possible importance of exploring and developing politics based on subspecies levels of human–non-human life, such as particular wolf packs engaging particular human communities of different scales; particular bee colonies in urban spaces rather than wild spaces; particular individual relationships of life and death involving pets, livestock, and humans.

At the same time, the multi-decade discourse in environmental politics that emphasizes the global political and ecological agency of human beings as a species is equally in need of deeper questioning, as it represents neither an accurate diagnosis nor a viable direction for forward political progress. The Anthropocene, to take the most recent manifestation of species thinking, is not the result of a generalized "anthropos" at all, but of particular groups of humans interacting with particular groups of non-humans. A politics of species, then, is a significant part of what interspecies politics aims to end, for both human and non-human.

Notes

1. The idea of "interspecies" as a "scholarly rubric" is articulated explicitly in Livingston and Puar (2011). To their two dimensions of the interspecies approach, I add a third here.
2. For the classic account of the rights of nature as a progressive and ever-widening enfranchisement in liberal societies, see Nash (1989). The legal argument for the rights of nature in the American context was first made by Stone (1972), which influenced the drafting of the rights of nature articles in the 2008 Ecuadorian Constitution.
3. Exceptions include Robbins (2007). See also Youatt (2008) and Kirksey and Helmreich (2010).

References

Agrawal, Arun. (2005). "Environmentality: Community, Intimate Government, and the Making of Environmental Subjects in Kumaon, India." *Current Anthropology* 46(2): 161–90.

Allen, John. (2003). *Lost Geographies of Power* (Oxford: Blackwell).

Arsel, Murat. (2012). "Between 'Marx and Markets':? The State, the 'Left Turn' and Nature in Ecuador." *Journal of Economic and Social Geography* 103(2): 150–63.

Barad, Karen. (2003). "Posthumanist Performativity: Toward an Understanding of How Matter Comes to Matter." *Signs: Journal of Women in Culture and Society* 28(3): 801–30.

Bekoff, Marc and Pierce, Jessica. (2009). *Wild Justice: The Moral Lives of Animals* (Chicago: University of Chicago Press).

Bennett, Jane. (2010). *Vibrant Matter: A Political Ecology of Things* (Raleigh: Duke University Press).

Bingham, Nick. (2006). "Bees, Butterflies, and Bacteria: Biotechnology and the Politics of Nonhuman Friendship." *Environment and Planning A* 38(3): 483–98.

Bookchin, Murray. (1988). "Social Ecology vs. Deep Ecology." *Socialist Review* 88(3): 11–28.

Buscher, Bram. (2013). *Transforming the Frontier: Peace Parks and the Politics of Neoliberal Conservation in Southern Africa* (Durham: Duke University Press).

Calarco, Matthew. (2008). *Zoographies: The Question of the Animal from Heidegger to Derrida* (New York: Columbia University Press).

Callicott, J. Baird. (1989). *In Defense of the Land Ethic* (Albany: SUNY Press).

Derrida, Jacques. (2008). *The Animal That Therefore I Am*. Translated by David Wills. Edited by Marie Louise Mallett (New York: Fordham University Press).

Derrida, Jacques. (2009). *The Beast and the Sovereign*. Translated by Geoffery Bennington (Chicago: University of Chicago Press).

Donaldson, Sue and Kymlicka. Will. (2011). *Zoopolis* (New York: Oxford University Press).

Eckersley, Robyn. (1995). "Liberal Democracy and the Rights of Nature." *Environmental Politics* 4(4): 169–98.

Eckersley, Robyn. (2004). *The Green State: Rethinking Democracy and Sovereignty* (Cambridge, MA: MIT Press).

Emel, Jody. (1998). "Are You Man Enough, Big Enough, and Bad Enough? Wolf Eradication in the US." In *Animal Geographies: Place, Politics, and Identity and the Nature-Culture Borderlands*, edited by Jennifer Wolch and Jody Emel (New York: Verso), 91–118.

Ferry, Luc. (1995). *The New Ecological Order*. Translated by Carol Volk (Chicago: University of Chicago Press).

Fox, Warwick. (1990). *Towards a Transpersonal Ecology: Developing New Foundations for Environmentalism* (Boston: Shambhala Publications).

Goodin, Robert E., Pateman, Carol, and Pateman, Roy. (1997). "Simian Sovereignty." *Political Theory* 25(6): 821–49.

Haraway, Donna. (1992). "The Promises of Monsters: A Regenerative Politics for Innappropriate/d Others." In *Cultural Studies*, edited by Lawrence Grossberg, Cary Nelson and Paula A. Treichler (New York: Routledge), 295–337.

Haraway, Donna. (2003). *The Companion Species Manifesto: Dogs, People, and Significant Otherness* (Chicago: Prickly Paradigm Press).

Haraway, Donna. (2008). *When Species Meet* (Minneapolis: University of Minnesota Press).

Hecht, Susanna and Cockburn, Alexander. (2010). *The Fate of the Forest: Developers, Destroyers, and Defenders of the Amazon* (Chicago: University of Chicago Press).

Johnston, Steven. (2012). "Animals in War: Commemoration, Patriotism, Death." *Political Research Quarterly* 65: 359–71.

Kirksey, S. Eben and Helmreich, Stefan. (2010). "The Emergence of Multispecies Ethnography." *Cultural Anthropology* 25(4): 545–76.

Kosek, Jake. (2011). "The Natures of the Beast: On the New Uses of the Honeybee." In *Gloal Political Ecology*, edited by Richard Peet, Paul Robbins, and Michael Watts (New York: Routledge), 227–51.

Latour, Bruno. (2004). *Politics of Nature: How to Bring the Sciences into Democracy* (Cambridge, MA: Harvard University Press).

Leopold, Aldo. (1968). *A Sand County Almanac* (Oxford: Oxford University Press).

Livingston, Julie and Puar, Jasbir. (2011). "Interspecies." *Social Text* 29(1): 1–14.

Luke, Timothy. (1995). "On Environmentality: Geo-Power and Eco-Knowledge in the Discourses of Contemporary Environmentalism." *Cultural Critique* 31: 57–81.

Luke, Timothy. (1999). "Environmentality as Green Governmentality." In *Discourses of the Environment*, edited by E. Darier (Malden, MA: Blackwell), 121–51.

McShane, Katie. (2007). "Why Environmental Ethics Shouldn't Give Up on Intrinsic Value." *Environmental Ethics* 29(1): 43–61.

Midgley, Mary. (1983). *Animals and Why They Matter* (Athens: University of Georgia Press).

Naess, Arne. (1985). "Identification as a Source of Deep Ecological Attitudes." In *Deep Ecology*, edited by Michael Tobias (Santa Monica: IMT Productions), 256–70.

Nash, R. (1989). *The Rights of Nature: A History of Environmental Ethics* (Madison: Unviersity of Wisconsin Press).
Nelson, Michael P. (2009). "Holism." In *Encyclopedia of Environmental Ethics and Philosophy*, edited by J. Baird Callicott and Robert Frodeman (Farmington Hills, MA: MacMillan), 490–93.
Nussbaum, Martha. (2006). *Frontiers of Justice: Disability, Nationality, Species Membership* (Cambridge, MA: Harvard University Press).
Palmer, Clare. (2010). *Animal Ethics in Context* (New York: Columbia University Press).
Peet, Richard and Watts, Michael, eds. (1996). *Liberation Ecologies: Environment, Development, Social Movements* (New York: Routledge).
Peet, Richard, Robbins, Paul, and Watts, Michael. (2011). *Global Political Ecology* (New York: Routledge).
Peterson, Rolf. (2007). *Wolves of Isle Royale: A Broken Balance* (Ann Arbor: University of Michigan Press).
Plumwood, Val. (2002). "Towards a Dialogical Interspecies Ethics." In *Environmental Culture: The Ecological Crisis of Reason* (New York: Routledge), 167–95.
Regan, Tom. (1983). *The Case for Animal Rights* (Berkeley: University of California Press).
Robbins, Paul. (2007). *Lawn People: How Grasses, Weeds, and Chemicals Make Us Who We Are* (Philadelphia: Temple University Press).
Rolston, Holmes. (1988). *Environmental Ethics: Duties to and Values in the Natural World* (Philadelphia: Temple University Press).
Singer, Peter. (1990). *Animal Liberation* (New York: Avon Books).
Smith, Kimberly K. (2012). *Governing Animals: Animal Welfare and the Liberal State* (New York: Oxford University Press).
Smith, Mick. (2009). "Against Ecological Sovereignty: Agamben, Politics, and Globalization." *Environmental Politics* 18(1): 99–116.
Stone, Christopher. (1972). "Should Trees Have Standing?: Toward Legal Rights for Natural Objects." *Southern California Law Review* 45: 450–501.
Sunstein, Cass and Nussbaum, Martha, eds. (2004). *Animal Rights: Current Debates and New Directions* (New York: Oxford University Press).
Van De Veer, Donald and Pierce, Christine, eds. (2002). *The Environmental Ethics and Policy Book* (Belmont, CA: Thomson).
Varner, Gary. (1998). *In Nature's Interests?* (Oxford: Oxford University Press).
Whiteside, Kerry. (2003). *Divided Natures* (Cambridge, MA: MIT Press).
Wolfe, Cary, ed. (2003). *Zoontologies: The Question of the Animal* (Minneapolis: University of Minnesota Press).
Worster, Donald. (1977). *Nature's Economy: A History of Ecological Ideas* (New York: Cambridge University Press).
Youatt, Rafi. (2008). "Counting Species: Biopower and the Global Biodiversity Census." *Environmental Values* 17(3): 393–417.
Youatt, Rafi. (2015). *Counting Species: Biodiversity in Global Environmental Politics* (Minneapolis: University of Minnesota Press).
Youatt, Rafi. forthcoming. "Sovereignty and the Wolves of Isle Royale." In *Political Theory and the Animal*, edited by Judith Grant and Vincent Jungkunz (Albany: SUNY Press).

CHAPTER 15

FLORAL SENSATIONS

Plant Biopolitics

CATRIONA A. H. SANDILANDS

From Sensations to Politics

In her fascinating book *The Flower of Empire*, Tatania Holway traces the ways in which the giant "floral sensation" of the South American water lily *Victoria regia* played a key role tying together colonial botany, bourgeois horticulture, and institutions of Victorian imperial spectacle. The lily, which first came to the attention of the Royal Geographical Society in 1837 (the inaugural year of Queen Victoria's reign), soon became a British obsession. Not only did "the very mention of *Victoria regia*... call forth visions of Britain's imperial grandeur... [but also] the effort to retrieve this peerless exotic from the equatorial wilds where it grew and to cultivate it in England became an epic quest that captured the world" (2013: 1–2). This plant was a participant in the massive project of colonial botany that saw thousands of exotic species transported to Europe for purposes of taxonomic classification and, often, profitable utilization (Schiebinger 2004); moreover, it was also a player in the transformation of English gardening from a mostly subsistence practice (except for the elite) to a nationwide preoccupation with horticultural display that gave rise to institutions as diverse as public botanical exhibitions and massed arrangements of bedding plants (Boddy 2013).[1] Although this chapter is not about the complex role of plants in British imperialism and horticulture, it could be: as Theresa Kelley (2013) demonstrates, for example, exotic species' sensational *differences* from more familiar European plants both cemented their role as a form of colonial currency and facilitated their entry into public debate in the eighteenth and nineteenth centuries because of their overwhelming disruptions of existing systems of botanical understanding.

To continue instead with the larger idea of "sensation" on which this chapter turns, there was recently a line of larger-than-usual bedding plants available at some North American garden centers sold under the brand "Giant Floral Sensations™." The striped purple and white petunias were particularly showy: indeed, like *Victoria regia*, *Petunia axillaris* and *P. integrifolia* came to European attention from South America, and also became important players in the unfolding of Western garden aesthetics. Unlike giant water lilies, however, petunias are no longer quite so sensational: they are, in some circles, considered horticultural clichés, a status only intensified by their routine appearance in front of suburban corporate headquarters and in mass produced plastic hanging baskets. Indeed, petunias are no longer really individual specimens; they are design elements, and their value inheres precisely in their *lack* of uniqueness, their regularity and conformity to industrial aesthetic and maintenance demands: season-long bright flowers, uniform height, drought tolerance. Here, the truer sensation of these plants concerns the "™" on the label in each pot: the trademark is followed by the phrase "propagation prohibited by law." Given Monsanto's 2005 purchase of the seed and plant company Seminis—giving it an estimated 85 to 90 percent share of the US nursery market—it is highly likely that those petunias were Monsanto's at some point along the line. What that lineage means is, first, that the plants were likely radically hybridized so as not to be capable of open pollination (as many petunias are) and, second, that a gardener could technically be prosecuted for successfully rooting a cutting.

This consideration of lilies and petunias as botanical sensations indicates the ways in which plants are caught up, in diverse ways, in specific relations of knowledge, power, colonialism, commodification, technology, accumulation, and desire. In other words, plants are subjects of *biopolitics* which, following Foucault, Agamben, and others, refers to the ways *life* is inserted into *power*, perhaps most intensively and invasively at the current neo-liberal/biotechnological conjuncture. For Foucault, power is not simply a question of the sovereign's ability to kill or "make die," but instead involves a diffuse web of institutions and relations—*dispositifs* or *apparatuses*—in which certain bodies and organisms are *made to live* in particular ways through complex relations and practices of power, knowledge, and corporeality. Organized around understandings of population and species, and also identity and desire, biopolitics concerns the simultaneously massive and intimate management of living: everything from environmental policy to personal pleasure. As Foucault puts it, biopolitics consists of "a closely meshed grid of material coercions rather than the physical existence of a sovereign" (2003: 36): whereas "for millennia, man remained what he was for Aristotle: a living animal with the additional capacity for a political existence; modern man is an animal whose politics places his existence as a living being in question" (1984: 143).

Acknowledging the problem of anthropocentrism that Nicole Shukin identifies as endemic to most biopolitical thought—namely, that it has "been constrained by [its] reluctance to pursue power's effects beyond the production of human social and/or species life" (2009: 11)—this chapter argues that understanding plants as part of the complex enmeshments of biopolitics allows us to consider not only the ways in which plants are treated as objects of various forms of extraction, production, consumption, and manipulation, but also the ways in which different plants' specific *capacities* are a crucial part of their diverse involvements in the multispecies relations of, say, imperial display and neo-liberal exchange (giant water lilies and petunias *do* particular things in particular contexts; so do corn, kudzu, and clover). This argument suggests a second gloss on the term botanical sensation, one in which plants are not simply infinitely manipulable bundles of vegetal resources, but rather complexly embodied and actively *sensate* creatures whose individual and evolutionary lives are deeply intertwined with our own and whose biological abilities have an active influence on the ongoing development of biosocial communities in both evolutionary and everyday relations.

In his book *What a Plant Knows*, biologist Daniel Chamovitz explores the extensive experimental research that currently exists demonstrating that plants see, smell, feel the sensation of touch, know where they are in space (proprioception), and remember, as in storing information for a relatively long period of time.[2] He avoids the contested notion of vegetal intelligence in favor of a strong argument for plant *awareness*: he notes, for example, that "they differentiate between red, blue, far-red and UV lights and respond accordingly [;] they . . . respond to minute quantities of volatile compounds [VOCs] wafting in the air . . . [; they] know when they are being touched and can distinguish different touches [;] . . . they can change their shapes and ensure that shoots grow up and roots grow down [; and they] are aware of their past: they remember past infections and the conditions they've weathered and modify their current physiology based on these memories" (2012: 137–8). Although he is careful to distinguish plant from human awareness, he nonetheless emphasizes that plants respond to their environments in ways that involve constellations of sensation and behavior, not just mechanical unfoldings of genetic potential (there is, of course, considerable debate about this issue). In addition, while plants also have many additional sensory capacities that are not analogous to ours (Pollan 2013), it is quite interesting to note that in some cases, the precise chemical or physical process that appears to enable a sensory response in a plant is remarkably similar to the one enabling human or other animal response, for example, the fact that the laying down of a short-term memory is a matter of potassium imbalance and the passage of electrical signals in both animal neurons and Venus flytrap leaf cells (Chamovitz 2012: 119).

But it is the issue of plant *communication*—which occurs primarily through the emission and reception of VOCs (i.e., scent)—that is, perhaps, most significant to a biopolitical emphasis on the importance of plant capacities to biosocial organization: plants are not only sensate, but they are also able to broadcast their responses to sensation to insects, to other plants, and even to people, prompting actions by these other organisms even in everyday time, and thereby demonstrating active intervention in the world at the level of the individual plant as well as the species. Of course, exuding scent is an evolutionary adaptation, one of many ways in which particular plant species broadcast their attractiveness to pollinators, either generally or specifically. Pollan (2001) might argue that the fact that humans also like some flower scents over others confers on lavender a potential reproductive advantage over skunk cabbage: note which one of these species has achieved nearly global garden distribution. Likewise, in some cases a plant's *response* to scent also seems to be about reproductive adaptation: as Chamovitz shows us, for example, the ethylene emitted by rotting apples that causes other nearby apples to ripen rapidly "ensures not only that the entire fruit ripens uniformly but that neighboring apples will also ripen, which give off even more ethylene, leading to [a . . .] ripening cascade of McIntoshes. . . . A full display of soft fruits brought on by the ethylene-induced wave guarantees an easily identifiable market for animals, which then disperse the seeds" (2012: 31).

But then there is the question of plant *signaling*: since about 1983, there has been a proliferation of research indicating that specific plants respond, *in the moment*, to predation, sending out deterrent chemical signals to predators, sending out warnings to nearby plants (including plants of different species) to do the same, and even sending out signals to insects to come and prey on the predators. To give one example among the hundreds available: wild tobacco plants (*Nicotiana attenuate*) respond to predation in several ways. Their first line of defense is, of course, their general toxicity: nicotine is poisonous. But for some reason, hawkmoth caterpillars are immune to the effects of the nicotine. So the plants have developed several more contextually communicative responses. First, when threatened with an overabundance of caterpillars—which they register chemically through the caterpillars' saliva—the plants send VOCs into the air to attract another insect, the Big-eyed bug (*Geocoris pallens or punctipes*) that feeds voraciously on both hawkmoth eggs and larvae; in one experiment, the bugs arrived within a matter of hours. In addition, when chemically triggered by caterpillar predation, the plants also develop epidermal outgrowths (trichomes) that are specifically *attractive* to the caterpillars but that, when eaten, cause the caterpillars themselves to exude an odor that is attractive to the bugs. And finally, significant predation also causes the plants to dramatically alter their pollinator relations, switching within a matter of days from attracting the nocturnal hawkmoths (which are the main pollinator as well as predator) to attracting diurnal hummingbirds (whose offspring do not eat the plants); in order to do so, the plants come to flower at a different time of day, the shape of the flower changes, and so does the chemical composition of the nectar (Buffie 2012).

There are several points to be made, here. First and most obviously, it seems clear from this research that plants share many registers of sensate and communicative biosocial involvement with human beings. As Elaine Miller (2002), Michael Marder (2013), and Kelley (2013) all point out, in different ways, this observation is not new, and it has troubled Western philosophy at least since Aristotle: plants are clearly alive, sensitive, and responsive (one need only watch a sunflower) and yet they are generally figured as lacking those precise qualities of living that are seen to constitute a fully formed *life*. To put it simply, plants complicate the bifurcation of animacy from inanimacy in obvious ways, which has historically given rise to an array of categorical attempts to devalue, for example, the principle of vegetality as against animality and humanity. As Marder notes, for Aristotle, the fact that plants do not engage in locomotion—their movement inheres in subtle changes of state such as growth and decay—renders them not just differently alive, but less fully so: plants share with humans only "the mere act of living," the proper life of humanity being concerned with something other than nutrition and growth. For Hegel, "plant growth is seen as purposeless because the vegetal soul does not attain to any higher capacities other than those of endless nourishment and propagation [;] . . . it may reach completion only from the external standpoint of those who will impose *their* ends onto these essentially goalless living things" (Marder 2013: 25); as Kelley adds, "for Hegel... plants [also] looked categorically unreliable: some seemed to move; most seemed to procreate...; and still others looked like animals..." (2013: 221). In the context of a philosophy determined that the movement of spirit should prevail over originary nature, suspect botanical life had to be stripped of its unsettling power and placed in the cosmic hierarchy at a level safely below more intelligible modes of being alive. And in different ways for Heidegger and Levinas, for example, because the plant is not fully separate from its environment, it is denied a relation to alterity, reflexivity, and worldliness: what humans may have in common with plants becomes subordinate to some other element that exalts our difference and superiority (Marder 2013).

There are, of course, important nuances to this history. Miller, for example, traces the figure of "the vegetative soul" through nineteenth-century German philosophy, highlighting the ways in which ideas about plants were key to understandings of organicism in thinking: "the vegetative soul, in contrast to the animated soul, emphasizes rootedness, vulnerability, interdependence, and transformative possibility rather than a separation of soul from body, actualization, and a stance of aggressiveness and self-preservation" (2002: 18). Marder discusses Nietzsche and his concept of nutritive desire, which is a faculty that is shared between humans and plants and is also the basic "expression of the overflowing will to power" (2013: 39) so central to his work. And as noted earlier, Kelley brilliantly depicts the ways in which the extraordinary burst of "monstrous" plants into European consciousness brought about by colonial botany had a profound effect on both the developing science of taxonomy (which plants continue to confound) and on philosophy, leading Goethe in particular to challenge Hegelian teleology in favor of a view of plant growth "as a series of remarkable, even inventive adaptations and new directions"(2013: 229) rather than as an imperfect, incomplete modality of living.

But even with these important botanical fascinations and resistances, plants, like animals, are caught up in the workings of Giorgio Agamben's "anthropological machine," in which one crucial operation of biopolitics consists in the iterative struggle over the distinction between *zoe* and *bios*, "bare life" and "political life," the natural life of nutrition, growth, and decay and what is considered meaningfully human. The struggle with the relation between *zoe* and *bios* lies, in fact, at the center of the always-fraught negotiation of what it means to be human, but the logic of that negotiation is always *ex post facto*: the idea of the human as an meaningful entity is presupposed on some basis or another, and something else, understood as not-human, is then excluded. Famously, in *The Open*, Agamben shows that the constant redrawing of this line is a key biopolitical moment in which life is brought to the service of power; in Western culture, life is never defined, but rather "ceaselessly articulated and divided" (2004: 13). For Agamben, of course, the slippery distinction concerns the one made between humans and "mere" animals; here, the distinctions between vegetality and animality, and vegetality and humanity, are at least equally important. For plants are so clearly identified with *bare life* that the possibility that they might possess something other than what Aristotle referred to as mere "psychic potentiality," that substratum of generalized nutritive liveliness out of which a *life* might eventually emerge, is almost impossible to imagine. Animal lives, for us, generally require something more than mere habitual succession; they require an intelligibly responsive relationship to an external environment, and so it is no accident that end-of-human-life discourses engage the "non-responsive" human body in relation to the vegetative, and not the animal. Animal lives, for us, generally require some kind of rudimentary recognition of self in relation to environment, so it is no accident that Cary Wolfe, in the midst of a nuanced argument about Judith Butler's work on the shared corporeal precarity of humans, animals, and environments, writes that: " 'not everything included under the rubric of precarious life'—*plants, for example*—'warrants protection from harm' " (2013: 19; my emphasis). This fundamental biopolitical distinction is why the research presented above is so important: to say that plants are *aware* of and *responsive* to their environments brings at least one cog in the anthropological machine to a halt. In other words: plants inhabit a biopolitical space in which their lives are not recognized as fully lived because of anthropocentric assumptions about the nature of a "proper" life; contemporary research into plant sensation and behavior underscores both the arbitrariness and the politics of this distinction, and asks us to think differently about plants as parts of our political communities.

Despite his categorical dismissal of the plant kingdom as a whole, Wolfe rightly emphasizes that biopolitics are not only or even primarily a matter of inclusion and exclusion—of the line between human and animal, animal and plant, human and plant—but more a question of the specific *dispositifs* organizing particular bodies in and through particular relations of power. When Foucault writes that humans are now "animals whose politics place our existence as living beings in question," he is moving well beyond the distinction between *zoe* and *bios* and into an examination of the ways in which it is, in fact, our biopolitical relations, our beings as members of species entangled with other species, that are the stuff of the ever-increasingly intimate and pervasive political specifications of modernity. Wolfe's view, of course—like Shukin's—is that animals are not only *one* thing to humans. Contrasting the multi-billion dollar pet insurance industry with factory farming, for example, he demonstrates that some nonhuman animals are incorporated into biopolitical relations as at least quasi-subjects (most famously, those Great Apes to whom formal rights have been granted in New Zealand and several European countries), and others such as broiler chickens and laboratory rats are forced to live under conditions of what Derrida calls "virtually interminable survival, in conditions that previous generations would have judged monstrous, outside of every presumed norm of a life proper to animals" (quoted in Wolfe 2013: 45). Likewise, Shukin's version of this process of specification turns on the idea of "rendering" as a central dynamic of what she calls animal capital: at the same time as animals are rendered *representationally* as part of a spectacular naturalization of capital (cute animals selling cellular technologies), they are also rendered *physically*, en masse, into meat, glue, fertilizer, and most pointedly, pet food. The second large point is, then, that plants are also very much bound up in and organized by these relations: although plants generally share certain qualities as organisms (chlorophyll, photosynthesis, multiple cellulose cell walls, indeterminate growth patterns, etc.), their specific places in biopolitics are not simply a matter of their general, excluded "vegetality," but instead a product of a more complex system of material power relations in which some plants are, in fact, *not* just bare life. This is not to say that plants should be considered biopolitical subjects in the same manner as animals (indeed, we should be as skeptical of the idea of "the plant" as Derrida is of "the animal"); plants simply do different things, both for themselves and for us. The insight does suggest, however, alongside the work of geographers Leslie Head, Jennifer Atchison, and Catherine Phillips, that an understanding of the *agency* of plants is not only important to the formulation of a more ethical relationship with them, but also to a more accurate understanding of what is going on in the biopolitical specification of diverse plant/human relationships (Head, Atchison, and Phillips 2014). In other words, understanding plants as having certain capacities that are at once prior to, organized by, and responsive to biopolitics requires that we think beyond our generally habitual, knee-jerk mechanization and instrumentalization of plants toward an understanding of the ways in which we are collectively implicated biopolitical subjects.

From Biopolitics to Ethics

The instant we begin to think about plant–human relations as a plurality rather than a singularity—and people such as foresters, foragers, farmers, gardeners, botanists, and harvesters do so on a daily basis often without the benefit of having read Derrida—we begin to be able to discern something like a constellation that is every bit as complex and contradictory as the one Wolfe describes for animals. Some plants are highly respected and prized as living presences or, at least, as valuable commodities: there is a white oak tree in Athens, Georgia that, because of a deed signed in the 1820s or 1830s, legally "owns itself" and is a valued town citizen with more property rights than many people (Atlas Obscura); in a similar vein, California tree-sitting activist Julia Butterfly Hill publicized her intimate relationship with "Luna," a giant redwood, as part of her campaign to prevent logging in the old growth forest in the 1990s (Hill 2000); and Paul Cloke and Owain Jones describe the ways in which individual trees were key "actants" in conservation politics in a Bristol cemetery (Cloke and Jones 2004: 322). There is such a thing as "orchid tourism," and there are strict national and international regulations prohibiting orchid poaching and smuggling. On the other hand, many plants are treated as raw material for human manipulation: *Phalaenopsis* orchids are artificially propagated on a mass scale and sold in IKEAs and supermarkets worldwide (Sandilands 2010), and industrial agriculture manipulates plants chemically, physically, and genetically with the sole purpose of producing the highest and most reliable yield in the most profitable manner possible. Potatoes, for example, increasingly grown as sources of high quality industrial starch rather than directly for food, are subject to intense genetic modification to optimize amylopectin content, and genetic use restriction or "terminator" technologies even propose to remove from certain plants, including but not only potatoes, their capacity to reproduce independently (GMO Compass).

One highly visible node of plant biopolitics circulates around the opposition of indigenous to "exotic-invasive" species in many current gardening and ecological discourses: certain plants are carefully nurtured and others are carefully exterminated (sometimes very violently, as in Head, Atchison, and Phillips 2014). In eastern North America, one such invasive plant is dog-strangling vine, or the less menacing "DSV" for short (*Cynanchum rossicum*); citing the concern that DSV aggressively out-competes desirable, indigenous flora and interferes with the management of timber plantations, the Ontario Invasive Plant Council (OIPC) published a "Best Management Practices" guide that is primarily oriented to evaluating the relative merits of different ways of going about killing the plant: digging, mowing, clipping, tarping, poisoning. While the biopolitics of invasive species are complex, what is particularly striking about DSV is that, in these bio-managerial terms, it is always already killable, a form of life that—unlike indigenous plants—should have no protection *as* a life; for the OIPC, at least, it is necessary to put this being *to death* for the life of the greater ecology or economy (of course, DSV has no apparent value to humans or it might not be so expendable). And yet, DSV—like most weeds—is "invasive" precisely because its outstanding capacities for proliferating in disturbed soils and traveling along roads and railways allow it to take up residence just about anywhere that humans go (Sandilands 2013). As Richard Mabey documents in his thoughtful book *Weeds*, the tenacity and opportunism of invasive plant species are qualities that one might conceivably find admirable, especially in the human beings among whom DSV so clearly thrives, and especially in the neo-liberal context in which the plant has found such particular purchase. He himself admits to admiring the "insinuation of alien species" as "exquisitely intimate and precise" (2010: 256). And yet the infinite killability of invasive species has not only spawned an entire international surveillance and eradication industry, but also demonstrated what happens when plants are rendered purely as examples of bare life: whereas the lively capacities of some plants are admired and encouraged, in the case of invasives, they are always already excessive and detestable.[3]

Of course, thinking about plants' active appearances in these diverse biopolitical relations shows us that the essential nature of their lives is *not* that of bare life or base vegetality. We are so accustomed to thinking about plants as occupying a hierarchical space somewhere between inanimate things and animals that we have few opportunities to consider that plants are actually creatures whose articulations of being alive are simply just stupefyingly *different* from our own. Where both philosophy and biology indicate some important similarities between humans and plants—including common origins, similar electrochemical processes of sensation, and even modalities of movement—the fact is that plants and animals have adapted to their environments in such radically different ways that it is, in some ways, nonsensical to speak about the one as "higher" than the other, even though doing so is of course, biopolitically, probably inevitable. Chamovitz emphasizes the ways in which plants' rooted pursuit of solar energy—as opposed to mobile pursuit of other beings to eat—has given rise to modes of sensitivity and communication that are, in many respects, much more sophisticated than our own. Karen Houle (2011) emphasizes that terrestrial plants are "in" their environments, earth *and* air, in ways that are both quantitatively and qualitatively different from mammalian inhabitations because of their unique sensitivities; even from our perspective, plants are both landscape and *in* the landscape. Marder emphasizes that plants exist with and in a radically different temporality from our own; in addition, a plant is not a unified self in the same manner as a human. As he writes, "the plant is . . . not contemporaneous with itself, in that it is a loose alliance of multiple temporalities of growth—some of its parts sprouting faster, others slower, still others decaying and rotting—and in that it does not relate to itself, does not establish a self-identity" (2013: 104).

Depending on the context, biopolitical apparatuses may either accentuate or flatten these differences. To give three mundane, microscopic examples: Germinating tomato seedlings in a sunny late-winter window brings their temporality into closer alignment with specific human desires. Pruning the dead twigs from climbing roses in the spring and deadheading their spent blooms in the summer concentrates their complex being into a more singular identity, one centered on the moment of blooming (and not seeding). Nurturing a bonsai tree (which Pollan thinks cruelly manipulative, 2013) takes advantage of the plant's specifically vegetal sensitivities to its conditions of place in order to create a tree that is as perfectly proportioned in a shallow pot as are its larger, genetically identical kin outdoors. The point is not that we should somehow stop using plants for human ends, especially, for eating; it is, instead, to recognize not only that plants are actively involved in biopolitics because of their unique capacities, but also that our social interactions with these capacities involve multiple encounters with their *difference* that we cannot even begin to fathom as such, even as we routinely harness these differences to our desires. As a result, any more mindful, ethical relation to plants cannot simply involve an anthropomorphic extension of our needs to respond to theirs; plants demand that we pay attention to the fact that life is not a singular force differently arranged in specific bodies to which we can respond as "life," and that the nature of specific bodies transforms the experience and unfolding of living itself, and therefore our responses to plants as living and responsive beings. Plants, then, also seriously challenge forms of ethical and political thinking that are premised on the extension of anthropogenic experiences to those of non-human beings: their lives make very different kinds of demands.

In 2008, the Swiss Federal Ethics Committee on Nonhuman Biotechnology issued a report titled *The Dignity of Living Beings with Regard to Plants: Moral Consideration of Plants for Their Own Sake* (Willemsen 2008). This report is quite extraordinary, not least because it involved a legislatively mandated commission, including biologists and philosophers, taking seriously the idea that plants might be morally considerable for reasons other than those concerning basic human utility. The document (which demonstrates more dissensus than anything else) considers the merits of a range of positions on the treatment of plants, ranging from whether or not they merit ethical considerability on the basis of something like sentience, to whether genetic modification is an offense to plant dignity, to whether the proper object of consideration for plants is the individual, the community, or the species. In one example, the report notes that: "two positions represented on the Committee require—with varying justifications—restraint in handling plants. There are also different meanings to 'handling with restraint.' We could understand it to mean that plants may not be arbitrarily impaired or destroyed. Restraint can however also mean a requirement to handle plants carefully and considerately, and to limit their use and exploitation. Handling plants includes the social practice of instrumentalising them in a disproportionate and therefore impermissible way" (10). The majority of the committee supported some version of this argument.

Amazing though it is that the conversation was even had, the Report completely fails to imagine what plants might actually require in the complex of biosocial and political relations in which they are, with us, enmeshed. The only thing that the Committee members agreed upon unanimously was that "an arbitrary harm caused to plants [is] morally impermissible. This kind of treatment would include, [for example], decapitation of wild flowers at the roadside without rational reason" (20). Although it certainly wouldn't hurt for people to think more carefully about what they do to and with individual plants, the facts are that decapitating those flowers—depending on the flower—might help distribute their seeds (in fact, distribution is one of the most important things that humans do for plants); that according to Chamovitz plants don't have the capacity to feel pain as such (stress is a different thing); that they should be not singular beings whose integrity is compromised with the loss of a part; and that whether or not a given human action is arbitrary does not especially matter to the plant, whose being is as affected by being grazed for food as picked for disposal. Simply put, we cannot consider ethical relations to plants without a willingness to engage with their profoundly different articulations of life, in specific contexts, and involving close attention to the ways in which they act in specific biosocial communities.

Thinking about animals, Wolfe is critical of Robert Esposito's ethical insistence on *life* as the basis of a complete normative model, "the principle of unlimited equivalence for every single form of life" (quoted in Wolfe 2013: 56), which we might also roughly ally with both biocentrism in general and the more radical recommendations of the Swiss Committee in particular. The problem with this view, for Wolfe, is that "if all forms of life are taken to be equal, then it can only be because they, as 'the living,' all equally embody and express a positive, substantive principle of 'Life' not contained in any one of them" (56). Ironically, then, the basis of ethics in this position is that individual beings are considered not on the basis of their particular being, but on their abstract affirmation of a larger principle that has little to do with them. As this chapter has argued, plants demand that we understand living not as a singular experience, but as contingent, multiple, changing, and inextricably relational. We cannot understand biopolitics without attending to the ways in which plants are actively involved in their unfolding; likewise, we cannot understand plants without attending to the ways in which their differences are biopolitically articulated in and with their environments, including us. To raise a notion of "plant rights," for example, however politically provocative it might be, is ultimately to bark up the wrong metaphysical tree. In Marder's terms:

> To skirt the pitfalls of efforts aimed at bringing the entire vegetal world into the fold of moral philosophy... [we need] to cultivate a way of thinking not only *about* plants, understood as epistemic or moral objects, but also *with* them.... What is required

> therefore is the cultivation of a certain intimacy with plants, which does not border on empathy or on the attribution of the same fundamental substratum to their life and to ours; rather, like all intimacy, it will take place (largely) in the dark, respectful of the obscurity of vegetal life. (2013: 181)

As this chapter has argued, such a dark plant intimacy requires a new kind of biopolitical attention to the specific relations in and through which we find ourselves entangled with plants. Although, as biologist Stefano Mancuso suggests, "because plants are sensitive and intelligent beings, we are obliged to treat them with some degree of respect" (quoted in Pollan 2013: 102), it is clearly inadequate to anthropomorphize their capacities and interests in the service of an abstract conception of life or justice. To take plants seriously requires us to attend to the sensational mutuality of our biopolitical co-constitution; to understand biopolitics, in turn, requires that we take plants seriously, sensations and all.

Notes

1. The lily is also part of a different biopolitical configuration in the Amazon Basin. It plays a role in the origin stories of many indigenous peoples (Galeano 2009); it appears on the Guyanese coat of arms; its seeds are edible.
2. He acknowledges that, popular wisdom about "talking to plants" notwithstanding, they do not have an experimentally demonstrated capacity to respond to sound per se; Michael Pollan, in his 2013 overview of research on plant intelligence, disagrees.
3. "Invasiveness" is, of course, a discourse that involves plants, animals, and even some humans.

References

Agamben, Giorgio. (2004). *The Open: Man and Animal*. Translated by Kevin Attrell (Stanford, CA: Stanford University Press).

Atlas Obscura. (2014). "The Tree that Owns Itself." http://www.atlasobscura.com/places/tree-owns-itself

Boddy, Kasia. (2013). *Geranium* (London: Reaktion Books).

Buffie, Erna, dir. (2012). *Smarty Plants: Uncovering the Secret World of Plants*. Canadian Broadcasting Corporation, *The Nature of Things*/Merit Entertainment Inc.

Chamovitz, Daniel. (2012). *What a Plant Knows: A Field Guide to the Senses* (New York: Farrar, Strauss and Giroux).

Cloke, Paul and Jones, Owain. (2004). "Turning in the Graveyard: Trees and the Hybrid Geographies of Dwelling, Monitoring and Resistance in a Bristol Cemetery." *Cultural Geographies* 11: 313–41.

Foucault, Michel. (2003). *"Society Must Be Defended": Lectures at the College de France, 1975–1976*. Edited by Mauro Bertani and Alessandro Fontana. Translated by David Macey (New York: Picador).

Foucault, Michel. (1984). *The History of Sexuality: Volume I, An Introduction.* Translated by Robert Hurley (Harmondsworth: Vintage Books).

Galeano, Juan Carlos. (2009). *Folktales of the Amazon.* Translated by Rebecca Morgan and Kenneth Watson (Westport, CT: Libraries Unlimited).

GMO Compass. (2008). "Potatoes." http://www.gmo-compass.org/eng/grocery_shopping/crops/23.genetically_modified_potato.html

Head, Leslie., Jennifer Atchison and Catherine Phillips. (2014). "The Distinctive Capacities of Plants: Re-thinking Difference via Invasive Species." *Transactions of the Institute of British Geographers.* doi:10.1111/tran.12077

Hill, Julia Butterfly. (2000). *The Legacy of Luna: The Story of a Tree, a Woman, and the Struggle to Save the Redwoods* (New York: Harper Collins).

Holway, Tatania. (2013). *The Flower of Empire: An Amazonian Water Lily, the Quest to Make it Bloom, and the World it Created* (New York: Oxford University Press).

Houle, Karen. (2011). "Animal, Vegetable, Mineral: Ethics as Extension or Becoming? The Case of Becoming-Plant." *Journal for Critical Animal Studies* IX(1/2): 89–116.

Kelley, Theresa. (2013). *Clandestine Marriage: Botany and Romantic Culture* (Baltimore: Johns Hopkins University Press).

Marder, Michael. (2012). "Resist Like a Plant! On the Vegetal Life of Political Movements." *Peace Studies Journal* 5(1): 24–32.

Marder, Michael. (2013). *Plant-Thinking: A Philosophy of Vegetal Life* (New York: Columbia University Press).

Miller, Elaine. (2002). *The Vegetative Soul: From Philosophy of Nature to Subjectivity in the Feminine* (Albany: SUNY Press).

Pollan, Michael. (2001). *The Botany of Desire: A Plant's Eye View of the World* (New York: Random House).

Pollan, Michael. (2013). "The Intelligent Plant." *New Yorker*, December 23 & 30: 92–105.

Sandilands, Catriona. (2010). "Calypso Trails: Botanizing Expeditions on the Bruce Peninsula." *Dalhousie Review* 90(1): 5–22.

Sandilands, Catriona. (2013). "Dog Stranglers in the Park? National and Vegetal Politics in Ontario's Rouge Valley." *Journal of Canadian Studies* 47(3): 93–122.

Schiebinger, Londa. (2004). *Plants and Empire: Colonial Bioprospecting in the Atlantic World* (Cambridge, MA: Harvard University Press).

Shukin, Nicole. (2009). *Animal Capital: Rendering Life in Biopolitical Times* (Minneapolis: University of Minnesota Press).

Willemsen, Ariane, ed. (2008). *The Dignity of Living Beings with Regard to Plants: Moral Consideration of Plants for Their Own Sake* (Berne: Federal Ethics Committee on Non-Human Biotechnology).

Wolfe, Cary. (2013). *Before the Law: Humans and Other Animals in a Biopolitical Frame* (Chicago: University of Chicago Press).

CHAPTER 16

COSMOPOLITANISM AND THE ENVIRONMENT

SIMON CANEY

In the last 35 years there has been a renewed interest in, and discussion of, "cosmopolitanism." Many theories are described as "cosmopolitan," both by their defenders and their critics. However, the term is used in many different ways. This chapter analyzes the concept of "cosmopolitanism" and explores the relationship between it and the environment.

Before beginning the analysis I should make two preliminary comments about the relationship between cosmopolitanism and the environment. The first is that many cosmopolitan theories have not dealt explicitly with the environment. Rather, the environment features implicitly, as a background assumption, in their theories, but its role and significance are often not made explicit. In such cases my aim is to bring out the tacit assumptions made, and make them visible. Second, and in addition to this, in some cases connections *can* be made between cosmopolitan ideals and the environment that have not been drawn by cosmopolitan thinkers themselves. In such cases, I highlight these latent connections for they are implications of cosmopolitan principles, even if cosmopolitans themselves have not observed or drawn attention to those implications.

The Nature of Cosmopolitanism

First, it is necessary to define cosmopolitanism.[1] To do so, it is useful to bear in mind Rawls's distinction between a "concept" and a "conception" (1999a: 5, 8–9). As Rawls employs these terms, a "concept" is the core basic idea. Concepts are often vague and can be interpreted in different ways: Rawls refers to these different interpretations of the concept as "conceptions". With this in mind we can say that the core concept of "cosmopolitanism" is the idea that persons are "citizens of the world." They are not, or not just, citizens of separate countries, but are—and should see themselves—as members of the world as a whole. One can identify (at least) three key "conceptions" of contemporary cosmopolitanism—what I shall call *cosmopolitanism about justice, political cosmopolitanism*, and *cosmopolitanism about the good life*. I shall now introduce each in turn.

Cosmopolitanism about Justice

To introduce cosmopolitanism about justice it is helpful to begin by outlining the core elements of a theory of justice and then, using that, to specify what distinguishes a cosmopolitan account of these elements from other different normative approaches. Theories of justice generally include principles of civil justice and principles of distributive justice. In what follows I focus solely on principles of distributive justice because they are most relevant for our focus here on the environment. Theories of distributive justice include the following kinds of features:

(a) the *units* to which principles of justice apply (do principles of justice apply to non-human animals, individuals, firms, nations, states, or something else?);
(b) the *scope* of distributive justice (which particular units are governed by a principle of distributive justice?);
(c) the *distributive* principle (what distributive principle (or principles) should apply?)
(d) the *metric* of justice (what is it that persons should have fair shares of?).

With this framework in mind we can now introduce cosmopolitanism about justice for this fourfold framework helps to bring out what is key to a cosmopolitan approach. More specifically, cosmopolitanism can be defined in terms of its positions on (a) and (b). Furthermore, it makes no specific claims about (c) and (d); and there is indeed considerable disagreement amongst cosmopolitans about (c) and (d). Let us start with (a): a cosmopolitan approach holds that the units to which principles of justice apply are "individuals". Collective units—like nations or states—do not have any value in and of themselves.[2] Whatever value they have can be explained in terms of whether they promote the interests of individual human beings or are authorized by individual human beings. If we turn now to (b): on a cosmopolitan approach, some principles of distributive justice have a *global* scope. They include all persons within their remit. To combine (a) and (b): cosmopolitans claim that some principles of justice include *all individuals* within their scope (Pogge 2008: 175).

This kind of cosmopolitanism can be contrasted with a nationalist view that holds that principles of distributive justice apply only within the nation (Miller 1995), and with statist views that hold that principles of distributive justice apply only within states.

Political Cosmopolitanism

Having introduced one variety of contemporary cosmopolitanism we may turn now to a second variety—what is sometimes referred to as "political cosmopolitanism".[3] This kind of cosmopolitanism interprets the ideal of being a citizen of the world to mean that there should be global political institutions and thus that everyone is a citizen of the world in the sense that they are members in a global political system. In an extreme version it calls for a world state. Very many cosmopolitans, however, call for a post-sovereign order—one in which powers are distributed at different levels (Caney 2005a: ch. 5; Pogge 2008: ch. 7). Those who take this route call for a system of multi-level governance, with political institutions at the global, regional, state-level, and substate-level. Proponents of this view might hold that *no* body should be sovereign, and that authority can be distributed at different levels. Notwithstanding these differences of emphasis, what these kinds of cosmopolitanism have in common is a commitment to global political institutions that have some authority over other political units.

Cosmopolitanism about the Good Life

I turn now to a third kind of cosmopolitanism—what I shall term "cosmopolitanism about the good life."[4] This kind of cosmopolitanism is a claim about what constitutes a good life. It holds that persons are citizens of the world in the sense that for a person to lead a good life does not require him or her to conform to his or her national or regional traditions or ways of life. Rather, according to cosmopolitanism about the good life, persons can flourish (in some versions, they can *only* flourish) by drawing on the ideas and ideals of different countries.

Having identified three different strands in cosmopolitanism it is worth making clear how I understand the concept of the "environment." Here I use it to refer to the natural world including the earth's lithosphere (the earth's crust) and pedosphere (its soil) and the natural resources contained therein, the atmosphere, the hydrosphere and the biosphere.[5] Our focus will include the treatment of both natural resources and also the creation of harms to the environment (such as climate change, ozone layer depletion, the nitrogen and phosphorus cycles, biodiversity loss, ocean acidification, air pollution) and thus what have been termed "planetary boundaries" (Rockström et al. 2009).

With these definitions in mind we can turn now to the substantive analysis. Since so much has been written about cosmopolitanism about justice, and, since moreover, there are many links between it and the environment, the bulk of the remainder of this chapter will be on the relationship between cosmopolitanism about justice and the environment.

Contractarian Cosmopolitanism and the Environment

An important starting point for our inquiry is Charles Beitz's *Political Theory and International Relations* (1979/1999). Beitz develops two quite separate arguments. Both of them operate as internal critiques of Rawls's *A Theory of Justice* (1971/1999). Furthermore, both of them have implications for the environment but they do so in different ways.

Beitz's "Natural Resources" Argument

To start with his first argument: Beitz operates with Rawls's argument that we can derive principles of justice for a society from considering what agents who are unaware of their talents, conception of the good, and identity would agree to in a hypothetical contract (Rawls 1971/1999a). Furthermore Beitz accepts, for argument's sake, Rawls's suggestion that there should be a separate international contract to determine the principles that should govern international relations.

Beitz argues, however, that the parties to that international contract would not confine themselves to Rawls's modest principles of international law, which are restricted to principles of just war, self-determination, and the freedom and equality of sovereign states (1999a: 332–3). Rather, he argues, they would accept a global natural resource principle (1999: 136–43). Beitz argues that "the distribution of resources" is, and here he quotes Rawls's famous words, "arbitrary from a moral point of view" (1999: 140; the Rawls's quotation comes from Rawls 1999a: 63). Countries like Saudi Arabia are just lucky to have plenty of oil and others are lucky to have rich mineral resources. Given this, no one can claim to have a special moral right to them and they should be treated as owned by everyone. The parties would thus choose the following principle:

> [E]ach person has an equal prima facie claim to a share of the total available resources, but departures from this initial standard could be justified (analogously to the operation of the difference principle) if the resulting inequalities were to the greatest benefit of those least advantaged by the inequality. (1999: 141)

This clearly has major impacts for the enjoyment of the world's resources and would call for redistribution from some countries to others to compensate for lack of natural resources.

Two further points about Beitz's conclusion should be made here. The first is that some, building on Beitz, have employed this framework to discuss specific environmental problems like climate change. For example, Steve Vanderheiden applies

Beitz's principle to the emission of greenhouse gases and argues on this basis for a version of the view that permits to emit greenhouse gases should be distributed on an equal per capita basis (2008: 101–9, 223–30). Note though that in doing so he is focusing on just one good (the use of the absorptive capacity of the atmosphere and oceans), whereas Beitz's principle applies to all natural resources, and so it is not clear why greenhouse gases per se should be equalized as opposed to the total bundle of resources (Caney 2012: 264–82). In other words, one might ask why we should treat greenhouse gases in isolation.

Second, it bears noting that others have proposed slightly different variants on Beitz's natural resource principle. For example, Thomas Pogge has defended what he terms a Global Resource Dividend. Put at its simplest, this involves charging states for their use of natural resources and using the resources levied to assist the world's least advantaged (2008: ch. 8). As such, it treats the world's natural resources as subject to cosmopolitan principles of justice. In addition to this Brian Barry also once argued that the world's natural resources belong to humanity as a whole and thus may be taxed and the revenues disbursed to countries lacking in natural resources (1980: 36, 38). More generally, a number of political philosophers, commonly referred to as "left-libertarians," argue that everyone should have an equal share of the world's natural resources (this is the "left" part) but they own their body and talents and are entitled to whatever they produce or trade with their fair share of resources and their talents (the "libertarian" part) (Steiner 1994; Vallentyne and Steiner 2001).

The conclusion of Beitz's first argument—that there should be a global natural resource principle—is, thus, one that enjoys support from a number of different perspectives, and, as we have seen, it has considerable environmental implications.

Beitz's "Global Interdependence" Argument

Beitz, however, does not simply rest on this argument. He also advances a second critique of Rawls, which calls for a different distributive principle. This argument still works within Rawls's framework, but instead of holding two contracts (one domestic and one international) it argues that there should be just one—global—original position (including persons from throughout the world, none of whom know who they are). Beitz's reason for this starts with Rawls's concept of the "basic structure." This refers to the system of institutions and rules that have a major impact on people's lives (Rawls 1999a: 6–10). Rawls assumes in *A Theory of Justice* that the basic structure corresponds to the system of institutions that exist within states. Beitz's second argument challenges this and argues that there are global relations of interdependence. Therefore there should be a global original position (Beitz 1999: 143–53).

Now in making his case, Beitz draws extensively on the empirical literature about economic integration. His focus is on international trade and investment (see, for example, 1999: 144–5). He makes no reference to what we might term ecological interdependence. However, given the findings of the environmental sciences, we can see that global environmental phenomena might be invoked to support his claims about the scope of principles of distributive justice. Global climate change is one case in point, but others such as biodiversity loss, the use of biofuels in one part of the world affecting food prices elsewhere, the effect of CFCs on the ozone layer and so on, provide support for the view that we are living in an ecologically interdependent world. These kinds of relations have the features that Rawls attributes to the basic structure (Rawls 1999a: 6–7): they have deep and unavoidable effects on people's basic interests (in this case their interests in food, water, land, and health). Given their global character, an argument could be made that they constitute a global scheme of interdependence.

Of course, to make a compelling case, an advocate would have to perform two key tasks. First, they would need to provide an account of just how much integration and of what kind was necessary to generate principles of distributive justice; and then, second, they would need to provide the relevant empirical evidence (Caney 2005b: 396–7). So, much more argument is needed to vindicate this line of reasoning. Nonetheless the key point is that the existence of global environmental interdependence might—if Beitz's argument is right—provide the basis for adopting principles of distributive justice with a global scope.

To sum up: Beitz offers two arguments that differ in a number of ways. They rest on different presuppositions (one resting on global interdependence and the other not); they differ in the principles they recommend (one calling for prima facie *equality* of *natural resources* and one for the difference principle for all primary goods). Furthermore, they differ in the way that they treat the environment. For the first argument is about the *content* and *metric* of justice (cosmopolitan justice requires equal natural resources), whereas the second argument can be used (though Beitz does not himself use it) to guide our thinking about the *scope* of distributive justice.

Human Rights and the Environment

Having discussed Beitz's contractarian approach to cosmopolitanism, we turn now to consider cosmopolitan approaches that appeal to human rights and explore their environmental implications.

Shue on Basic Rights

One very influential statement of cosmopolitanism that emphasizes a commitment to human rights is Henry Shue's book *Basic Rights* (1996; first published in 1980). Shue's main aims in *Basic Rights* are to argue that there are basic rights to "subsistence" as well as to "liberty" and "security," to identify the correlative obligations, and to address objections to these basic rights. The environment does not loom large in his analysis of basic rights, and he does not draw attention to, or emphasize, any strong links between his basic rights and the environment. However, as we shall see, his commitment to subsistence rights does have implications for the treatment of the environment. To see this we need to unpack Shue's core claims.

Shue makes several key arguments. The first is that the right to subsistence is a "basic right." Shue uses the term "basic right" in a technical sense. For him rights are basic rights "only if enjoyment of them is essential to the enjoyment of all other rights" (Shue 1996: 19–20). Shue's claim then is that subsistence rights are basic rights because without the capacity to meet one's socio-economic needs one is unable to exercise other rights such as freedom of association or movement or participation. One cannot enjoy other rights if one does not have enough to live and to perform basic bodily functions (Shue 1996: 22–34).

Having argued for this, Shue then examines what correlative obligations are entailed by basic rights. Many argue that rights entail simply negative duties to abstain from certain kinds of action (like murder or torture). Shue argues, however, that rights—including familiar rights like the right to physical integrity—entail not simply negative duties on others to abstain from certain kinds of action, but also positive duties to assist others. Shue identifies three correlative duties: the (negative) duty "to avoid depriving" people, the (positive) duty "to protect from deprivation," and the (positive) duty "to aid the deprived" (1996: 68). Shue's central point is that the enjoyment of any right requires not simply negative duties not to harm people but also positive duties too; and, this is true of the right to physical security or to certain freedoms as well as the right to subsistence (1996: ch. 3).

Now, apart from some comments in passing (1996: 25), Shue does not apply this directly to the environment. However, his account of the right to subsistence contains within it some environmental commitments. To see this we need to consider the content of the right to subsistence more fully. Shue describes it as follows:

> By minimal economic security, or subsistence, I mean unpolluted air, unpolluted water, adequate food, adequate clothing, adequate shelter, and minimal preventive public health care. (1996: 23)

Thus defined, it is clear that realizing the right to subsistence has a number of environmental preconditions. For example, ensuring "unpolluted air" puts limits on the emission of exhaust fumes, the burning of biomass for cooking, the location of waste, and the creation of other kinds of environmental pollution. In addition to this, "unpolluted water" has implications for the use of fertilizers (overuse of which can affect water quality), and puts limits on the dumping of waste in rivers and oceans. The third element Shue mentions—"adequate food"—requires preventing dangerous climate change because this results in desertification and the loss of land to rising sea levels and salination. Adequate food also requires preventing the release of toxic waste into rivers and oceans. So Shue's "subsistence rights" do have some important and unequivocal environmental preconditions.

Now Shue himself did not explore these links between rights and the environment (though see 2014: ch. 8), but he did write a series of important papers about one environmental problem in particular—namely climate change. Interestingly, these writings tended to eschew the language of rights. Instead Shue presented arguments on less contentious grounds (such as a duty not to harm (2014: 168)), or by arguing that they enjoy support from a number of different principles. For example, Shue argued that affluent countries should bear the main responsibility for tackling climate change, and did so by arguing that it flowed from three separate principles. In particular, it can be grounded by appealing to the principle that those who create an environmental problem should pay, that those with the ability to pay should pay, and the principle that persons should not be pushed beneath a decent standard of living (2014: ch. 9). In his most recent work, however, Shue has employed the notions of rights to characterize the harmful effects of climate change (2014: ch. 16: see also Caney 2009b).

Pogge on Negative Duties, Harm, and Human Rights

Having considered Shue's cosmopolitan account of basic rights, it is instructive to contrast it with Thomas Pogge's account of global justice, for Pogge distances himself from one core component of Shue's approach, namely Shue's affirmation of positive duties of justice. Like Shue, Pogge does not himself emphasize the environment in his thought. However, as with Shue, Pogge's cosmopolitan account of justice also has clear implications for the treatment of the natural world and can be fruitfully applied to ecological issues.

We can characterize Pogge's account of global justice in terms of two key components—a normative claim and an empirical one. To start with the normative claim: Pogge holds that principles of justice should be applied to institutions. He maintains that when institutions foreseeably result in a state of affairs in which persons are prevented from enjoying core interests, and when they could reasonably be designed in ways that do not do this (so the harms are avoidable), then they are unjust. As he puts it, "any institutional design is unjust when it foreseeably produces an avoidable human rights deficit" (2008: 25). Furthermore, if agents uphold and maintain institutions that impose this avoidable human rights deficit on others then they are violating a negative duty of justice not to impose unjust orders on others. In Pogge's view they are *harming* others because they are choosing to uphold and maintain a system that forseeably and avoidably deprives others of access to core goods, where harm is defined in terms of how they fare in comparison to a moralized baseline (that is, a baseline reflecting what they are entitled to) and not what their situation was before.

Turning now to his empirical claims: Pogge argues that the governments of affluent countries have failed to comply with this negative duty not to harm others. Furthermore, this has resulted in extensive global poverty. The large proportion of the world living on less than 1 or 2 dollars a day, for Pogge, arises because powerful Western governments impose unjust trade and other laws on developing countries. To substantiate this empirical claim Pogge draws attention to several ways in which affluent governments produce poverty in other countries. First, they uphold what he terms the "international resource privilege": by this he means that they treat existing governments (no matter how democratic or just they are) as the rightful owners of the resources in a country (2008: 119–20). Second, they uphold what he terms the "international borrowing privilege": by this he means that they treat existing governments (again irrespective of how democratic or just they are) as if they can take out loans which their subjects or subsequent governments are required to pay back (2008: 120). Both privileges, Pogge argues, helps sustain unjust governments: for example, they enable dictators to sustain themselves in power, incentivize coups, and the international borrowing privilege means that incoming democratic societies are burdened with paying off the debts of their authoritarian predecessors (2008: 120–1). All of these perpetuate poverty. So, by honoring them, Western governments bear some responsibility for the ensuing poverty.

His conclusion then is that those governments—and their citizens—have duties to eradicate poverty, but this is not a (positive) duty to aid the poor so much as a (negative) duty not to bring about their poverty.

Now Pogge has not applied this to the environment. His argument about the ways in which affluent governments harm members in developing countries does not appeal to environmental degradation, and focuses instead very much on their trade policies (such as the two privileges just mentioned) and their design of the system of international trade (2008: 18–19). However, one could adopt Pogge's framework for environmental problems like global climate change. The argument would be that affluent members of the world are also culpable of violating the negative duty not to act in ways that foreseeably and avoidably deprive others of the capacity to enjoy core human rights. Individuals do this, as consumers, for many affluent individuals emit high amounts of greenhouse gases—more than they need to emit. Their governments also do this by subsidizing the fossil fuel industry, by supporting and facilitating high emissions lifestyles (for example, by building new airports, by designing urban infrastructure in ways that do not reduce transportation emissions) and by not investing in, and transferring clean technology. Individuals thus also bear a responsibility, as citizens, not to support governments which act in these ways.

These policies—though they do not constitute imposing a set of *institutions* on members of other countries—do, however, fit Pogge's framework for they are (a) avoidable (governments of high emitting countries could do otherwise); and the harmful impacts are also (b) foreseeable (the malign effects of high emissions of greenhouse gases is recognized by the overwhelming majority of climate scientists and has been known for several decades at least). So, one can see the creation of global climate change (to take one example) as an instance of a failure by advantaged persons to honor the negative duty not to impose unjust burdens on others. Furthermore, one could extend this to other kinds of environmental degradation such as destroying the ozone layer, destroying biodiversity, causing ocean acidification, depleting scarce non-renewable natural resources, and overusing renewable natural resources. Pogge's theory provides a powerful framework for thinking about environmental degradation and can highlight the ways in which some can use the environment in ways that undermine the core rights and interests of others.

A More General Account

The preceding two sections have considered two specific cosmopolitan approaches. In this section we shift from assessing how *particular* cosmopolitan theories of justice relate to the environment to examining the ways in which cosmopolitan theories of justice *in general* make assumptions about, or have implications for, the environment. As we shall see, the environment bears on accounts of the content of cosmopolitan principles of justice in two kinds of ways.[6] Or to put the same point in a different way: the ensuing analysis brings out two ways in which the environment needs to be taken into account for a cosmopolitan account of the content of justice. To see this consider what I term the *environmental impacts claim* and the *environmental preconditions claim* (Caney 2012: 293–4).

The *environmental impacts claim* makes the simple but important point that human activities (including the kinds of activities protected and enabled by principles of justice) have an important impact on the natural world. This is true for all theories of justice. Consider, for example, right-libertarian theories. These ascribe private property rights to individuals over land and natural resources: they thereby permit people to act in ways that change the natural world. They may cut down trees or mine the earth; they might plant crops or use up scarce resources. They might release some greenhouse gases or create other environmental hazards and unless checked these are potentially very harmful. Libertarian rights will have an environmental impact.

The same is true of egalitarian liberal theories. These theories call for the fulfillment of persons' core needs at the very least and, in some cases, they call for socio-economic equality. We can get a sense of the ways in which the realization of such theories has environmental impacts by examining one core need, namely access to food. Meeting this need requires fertilizer on crops. However, this results in the emission of nitrous oxide (a greenhouse gas). Fertilizer often results in high levels of nitrogen that can cause eutrophication and result in algal blooms which, in turn, have harmful effects on marine life. In addition to this, access to food also requires energy for cultivation (for example, tractors and combine harvesters), storage, and transportation, and the production of energy of course frequently involves the use of fossil fuels (which contributes to both poor air quality and to climate change). Alternatively, energy can be created by using hydroelectric plants (which involve building dams and often flooding land, thereby destroying flora and fauna or involving loss of forests) or burning biomass (which can result in poor air quality and indirect land use change). An alternative is, of course, the use of nuclear energy but this too clearly has environmental impacts. So enabling persons to enjoy access to food has profound environmental impacts. The same is true of other needs such as providing shelter (construction is a major source of greenhouse gases). Furthermore, since energy is critical to almost all vital interests, the energy impacts of realizing egalitarian liberal ideals of justice are enormous. Indeed, since *all* theories of justice either permit, or call for, the use of energy then all will have environmental impacts.

We thus have good reason to endorse the *environmental impacts claim*: the kinds of interests and activities protected by many orthodox theories of justice have environmental impacts.

One might, however, ask: But why does this matter? Answering this takes us to the second claim, what I termed the *environmental preconditions claim*. This holds that the enjoyment of the kinds of activities and interests affirmed by cosmopolitan principles of justice presuppose certain environmental preconditions. Take health. The enjoyment of good health has a number of environmental preconditions. For example, it requires clean air (which requires a limit on emissions from vehicles and burning of biomass) and drinkable water (which requires a limit on the release of waste into rivers). It also requires the protection of the ozone layer for the depletion of the ozone layer would result in eye cataracts and skin cancer. Good health also requires limits on the emission of greenhouse gases since dangerous climate change has harmful impacts on human health. The protection of health thus requires that humans not degrade the natural world in many ways.

Similar points could be made about protecting access to food. This too requires a stable climate system, and climate change poses serious threats to agriculture. Or consider another interest—persons' interests in life—this is threatened by storm surges, extreme precipitation, and extreme temperatures, and these, in turn are associated with climate change.

Health, food, and life, thus, all have environmental preconditions. These interests are fairly uncontroversial and different cosmopolitan accounts of justice will agree on their centrality. There are, however, likely to be other cases where different cosmopolitan theories—because they are committed to different accounts of the metric of justice—may well identify different kinds of environmental preconditions. Where this is the case, we need to arbitrate between different accounts of the metrics of justice and select one over others.

Consider the "capabilities" approach pioneered by Nussbaum (2011) and Sen (2009: Part III). Some adopt this approach and explore its implications for valuing and protecting environment. David Schlosberg, for example, conceives of justice in terms of protecting and promoting capabilities, and hence emphasizes the importance of protecting "the environmental underpinning of existing lists of human capabilities" (2012: 453). A similar view is taken by Breena Holland who also draws on the capabilities approach to argue that "protecting human capabilities requires protection of an 'ecological meta-capability'" (Holland 2014: 24, see ch. 4). Some, though, reject a "capabilities" approach: some argue that justice is concerned with the satisfaction of people's preferences and others that its focus should be on a person's enjoyment of Rawlsian primary goods. And it is worth noting that protecting either Rawlsian primary goods or persons' preference satisfaction might have different implications for environmental protection to accounts of justice that are concerned with realizing persons' capabilities. In addition to this, welfarist metrics may very well endorse the substitution of human capital for natural capital (Dobson 1998), whereas others may think that justice requires protecting natural capital. So, different metrics of justice might issue in different accounts of the preconditions of realizing justice.[7]

If we now combine the *environmental impacts claim* and the *environmental preconditions claim* then we can see that these have important implications for a cosmopolitan theory of distributive justice. What is crucial is that for a cosmopolitan theory of justice to honor its own commitments the realization of its own principles of justice must not result in environmental impacts (via the *environmental impacts claim*) that undermine the realization of its own principles of justice (the *environmental preconditions claim*).[8] Put more bluntly, it must put limits on people's use of natural resources and their creation of environmental burdens—limits imposed by a concern for ensuring that people have the kind of environment necessary to enjoy their entitlements in the future. If this is not done, and the environmental impacts exceed the boundaries required by the commitment to securing the environmental preconditions then we are producing an unsustainable outcome and living beyond our means.

Political Cosmopolitanism and the Environment

This then raises the question of what might be done to realize these cosmopolitan ideals of environmental justice. One answer to this takes us from *cosmopolitanism about justice* to *political cosmopolitanism*, where the latter, recall, is defined in terms of a commitment to supra-state political institutions since some argue that supra-state authorities are needed to realize important environmental objectives.

Stated more fully, someone might make the following three-step argument. First, it starts from the claim that there are cosmopolitan principles of justice that require protecting the integrity of the global environment. It then argues, second, that we should choose whichever political structures best realize cosmopolitan ideals of justice. The third step in the argument contends that a system of states is unable to provide the necessary protection and that a system including supra-state authorities is more effective. The sheer number of states in the world will result in insuperable collective action problems, and, in addition to this, there are unjustly motivated states who will seek their own self-interest. Given this, it is argued, a layer of supra-state authorities is required to realize cosmopolitan environmental justice (Pogge 2008: 189–90). This might involve global legislative institutions with the authority to pass laws protecting environmental sustainability or a strengthened international legal system.

These kinds of proposals are hotly contested. One can identify three kinds of points that political cosmopolitans need to address. First, some will dispute the third step, and argue that global political authorities are not required because a statist order is as good as, or better than, the mooted cosmopolitan reforms. The charge here is that such institutional reforms are unnecessary or ineffective.

Second, some might argue that the argument above ignores other moral considerations and that the reforms violate these other moral considerations. Some (including Rawls 1999b) are fearful that supra-state institutions pose a serious threat to individual liberty. Others might argue that the good of collective self-determination is not given sufficient significance in a cosmopolitan order (Miller 1995). So, in addition to questions about its efficacy in addressing global environmental problems, political cosmopolitans also need to address concerns about whether their proposals clash with other more important ideals.

Third, even if the political cosmopolitan reforms are better than alternatives at realizing environmental objectives, and even if they do not compromise other more weighty moral ideals, another objection might be made. Some might argue that such reforms are utopian in the sense that they will never come about. Either those with an interest in perpetuating global environmental injustice will prevent global political authorities from being created; or whilst global political authorities with an environmental remit might be created, they will be captured by powerful actors who seek to thwart their initiatives.

The argument that political cosmopolitan institutions are needed to realize cosmopolitan ideals of environmental justice, thus, needs to be able to address these three challenges.

At this point it bears noting that there are other arguments for supra-state institutions that do not rest on the essentially consequentialist line of reasoning just presented. For example, some like Held, ground political cosmopolitanism on an appeal to democratic principles. This argument has two steps. First Held argues that "those whose life expectancy and life chances are significantly affected by social forces and processes ought to have a stake in the determination of the conditions and regulation of these, either directly or indirectly through political representatives" (Held 2004: 100: see also Pogge 2008: 190ff). Second, he argues, that the social forces and processes that significantly affect persons' lives are global in nature. Held's main emphasis is on economic interdependence. However, one might also draw on facts about the kinds of global ecological interdependence that currently exist to argue that there need to be global political institutions to regulate the global environment and thereby enable persons to have "a stake" in the "social forces and processes" that affect the environment within which they live and which determines their "life expectancy and life chances" (Held 2004: 100). Thus, in the same way that someone might appeal to facts about global ecological interdependence and combine it with Beitz's (second) argument about the scope of distributive justice to derive cosmopolitan principles of distributive justice, so someone might appeal to facts about global ecological interdependence and combine it with Held's argument about the scope of the democratic decision-making to derive democratic institutions with a cosmopolitan scope.

Quite what supra-state institutions would be required remains the subject of some dispute. Some start from a recognizably similar starting point to Held but do not endorse his institutional prescriptions. For example, in their book *Democratizing Global Climate Governance*, Hayley Stevenson and John Dryzek emphasize the importance of democratic deliberation. However, they call instead for democratizing the discourses that shape the political decision-making processes—what they term "discursive representation" (Stevenson and Dryzek 2014: 130–42)—and a " 'Chamber of Discourses' that brought together representatives of all the various discourses present in global civil society" (2014: 197–8).

Related to this, some might argue that realizing Held's democratic ideals does not require abandoning a system of states and erecting supra-state institutions with authority over states. They might instead call for an order in which states retain their sovereignty but have genuine democratic oversight over the multilateral negotiations. This leads to a more general point. Rather than operate with a dichotomous contrast between, on the one hand, a statist order in which states face no limits on their autonomy, and, on the other hand, a world state which has complete authority, it is probably more helpful to think of a continuum between these two extremes. The task for those who call *either* for a political framework that best realizes the cosmopolitan ideals of environmental justice *or* for a world in which persons can shape the forces that determine their lives is to chart where on that continuum represents the best combination of supra-state governance and local autonomy.

Concluding Remarks

It is time to conclude. Thus far, the standard arguments both for cosmopolitan theories of justice and for cosmopolitan political institutions have, with some exceptions, largely been developed without reference to the environment. However, as we have seen in this chapter, this does not entail *either* that cosmopolitan theories of justice or proposals for supra-state institutions have no implications for the treatment of the natural world *or* that facts about the environment have no implications for arguments for cosmopolitan theories of justice or supra-state institutions. As the analysis of cosmopolitan arguments has illustrated, cosmopolitan theorists have good reason to take on board the significance of environmental change for the application and realization of their principles (Caney 2005c, 2009b, 2012). Furthermore, as those same arguments also attest, in a world marked by profound and increasingly global ecological interdependence those concerned with protecting the environment have good reason to explore further the resources offered by cosmopolitan thought.

Notes

1. Cosmopolitan ideas flourished among the Cynics and Stoics and later among Enlightenment thinkers. My focus in this chapter, however, is on contemporary cosmopolitanism. For discussion of both earlier and contemporary cosmopolitan ideas, see Caney (2009a).

2. It should be noted that it is not committed to the assumption that only human beings have moral status or that only human beings should be included in the scope of justice.
3. Others have used different terms for the same idea. Beitz terms it "institutional cosmopolitanism" (Beitz 1994: 120) and Pogge uses the term "legal cosmopolitanism" (Pogge 2008: 175).
4. This kind of cosmopolitanism has been termed life "cosmopolitanism about culture" (Scheffler 2001: 111ff; see also Waldron 1995).
5. My categorization corresponds to, and is indebted to, that used by John McNeill in his illuminating account (McNeill 2000).
6. Note I focus in what follows on the relationship between the content of justice and the environment, and I set aside the relationship between the scope of justice and the environment.
7. For a discussion of the ways in which different metrics of justice might result in different evaluations of the impacts of climate change, see Page (2006: ch. 3).
8. See Holland's discussion of "capability thresholds" and "capability ceilings": Holland (2014: 25).

References

Barry, Brian. (1980). "Do Countries Have Moral Obligations? The Case of World Poverty." *The Tanner Lectures on Human Values*, delivered at Harvard University October 27, 1980. This is available at: http://tannerlectures.utah.edu/_documents/a-to-z/b/barry81.pdf

Beitz, Charles R. (1994). "Cosmopolitan Liberalism and the States System." In *Political Restructuring in Europe: Ethical Perspectives*, edited by Chris Brown (London and New York: Routledge) 119–32.

Beitz, Charles. (1999). *Political Theory and International Relations* (Princeton: Princeton University Press) with a new afterword by the author.

Caney, Simon. (2005a). *Justice Beyond Borders: A Global Political Theory* (Oxford: Oxford University Press).

Caney, Simon. (2005b). "Global Interdependence and Distributive Justice." *Review of International Studies* 31(2): 389–99.

Caney, Simon. (2005c). "Cosmopolitan Justice, Responsibility, and Global Climate Change." *Leiden Journal of International Law* 18(4): 747–75.

Caney, Simon. (2009a). "Cosmopolitanism and Justice." In *Contemporary Debates in Political Philosophy*, edited by Thomas Christiano and John Christman (Oxford: Blackwell), 387–407.

Caney, Simon. (2009b). "Human Rights, Responsibilities, and Climate Change." In *Global Basic Rights*, edited by Charles Beitz and Robert Goodin (Oxford: Oxford University Press): 227–47.

Caney, Simon. (2012). "Just Emissions." *Philosophy & Public Affairs* 40(4): 255–300.

Dobson, Andrew. (1998). *Justice and the Environment: Conceptions of Environmental Sustainability and Theories of Social Justice* (Oxford: Oxford University Press).

Held, David. (1995). *Democracy and the Global Order: From the Modern State to Cosmopolitan Governance* (Cambridge: Polity).

Held, David. (2004). *Global Covenant: The Social Democratic Alternative to the Washington Consensus* (Cambridge: Polity).

Holland, Breena. (2014). *Allocating the Earth: A Distributional Framework for Protecting Capabilities in Environmental Law and Policy* (Oxford: Oxford University Press).
McNeill, John. (2000). *Something New Under the Sun: An Environmental History of the Twentieth Century* (London: Penguin).
Miller, David. (1995). *On Nationality* (Oxford: Clarendon Press).
Nussbaum, Martha C. (2011) *Creating Capabilities: The Human Development Approach* (Cambridge, MA and London, England: Harvard University Press).
Page, Edward A. (2006). *Climate Change, Justice and Future Generations* (Cheltenham: Edward Elgar).
Pogge, Thomas. (2008). *World Poverty and Human Rights: Cosmopolitan Responsibilities and Reforms*, 2nd edn. (Cambridge: Polity).
Rawls, John. (1999a). *A Theory of Justice*, rev edn. (Oxford: Oxford University Press).
Rawls, John. (1999b). *The Law of Peoples with "The Idea of Public Reason Revisited"* (Cambridge, MA: Harvard University Press).
Rockström, Johan et al. (2009). "Planetary Boundaries: Exploring the Safe Operating Space for Humanity," *Ecology and Society* 14(2): article 32. This is available at: http://www.ecologyandsociety.org/vol14/iss2/art32/
Scheffler, Samuel. (2001). *Boundaries and Allegiances: Problems of Justice and Responsibility in Liberal Thought* (Oxford: Oxford University Press).
Schlosberg, David. (2012). "Climate Justice and Capabilities: a Framework for Adaptation Policy." *Ethics & International Affairs* 26(4): 445–61.
Sen, Amartya. (2009). *The Idea of Justice* (London: Allen Lane).
Shue, Henry. (1996). *Basic Rights: Subsistence, Affluence, and U. S. Foreign Policy*, 2nd edn. with a new afterword (Princeton: Princeton University Press).
Shue, Henry. (2014) *Climate Justice: Vulnerability and Protection* (Oxford: Oxford University Press).
Steiner, Hillel. (1994). *An Essay on Rights* (Oxford: Blackwell).
Stevenson, Hayley and Dryzek, John S. (2014). *Democratizing Global Climate Governance* (Cambridge: Cambridge University Press).
Vallentyne, Peter and Steiner, Hillel. (2001). *Left-Libertarianism and Its Critics: The Contemporary Debate* (Basingstoke: Palgrave Macmillan).
Vanderheiden, Steve. (2008). *Atmospheric Justice: A Political Theory of Climate Change* (New York: Oxford University Press).
Waldron, Jeremy. (1995). "Minority Cultures and The Cosmopolitan Alternative." In *The Rights of Minority Cultures*, edited by Will Kymlicka. (Oxford: Oxford University Press), 93–119.

PART IV

ENDS, GOALS, IDEALS

SUSTAINABILITY

CHAPTER 17

SUSTAINABILITY—POST-SUSTAINABILITY—UNSUSTAINABILITY

INGOLFUR BLÜHDORN

A Paradigm Exhausted?

To many observers, *sustainability*, for more than two decades the beacon of global environmental politics, today seems an exhausted paradigm. In the second half of the 1980s, the United Nations World Commission on Environment and Development (WCED) had raised the concepts *sustainability* and *sustainable development* to prominence, famously defining the latter as "development that meets the needs of the present without compromising the ability of future generations to meet their own needs" (WCED 1987: 43). Its report *Our Common Future* framed the environmental issue in a way that enabled a diverse range of societal actors to embrace it; and the 1992 Conference on Environment and Development (UNCED) in Rio then fully mainstreamed the sustainability paradigm. Indeed, in the wake of the Rio Earth Summit sustainable development became an essentially hegemonic eco-political frame that pushed all other perspectives on nature, society, and their mutual relationship far into the margins of public and policy discourse. Two decades later, however, there is considerable concern that "the sustainable development agenda no longer exerts the pulling power it once had" and that the concept is "under growing pressure amid a perceived failure to deliver change" (Bulkeley et al. 2013: 958f). Despite the threats of climate change and a tightening ecological, economic, and social crisis, global leaders at the Rio+20 Summit (again held in Rio, 2012) displayed "little political appetite" for any fast and sweeping transformative action (Bulkeley et al. 2013; Linnér and Selin 2013).

Still, the concept of sustainability and the policy strategy of *ecological modernization* that is widely associated with sustainable development retain the status of hegemonic eco-political frames (Brand 2010), though sustainability is, more than ever, a fuzzy term that does not imply any commitment to the kind of structural change that radical ecologists and many scientists regard as essential if "serious harm and societal collapse" are to be prevented (Meadowcroft 2013: 991). In fact, in practical policy-making the ever present terms sustainability and sustainable development seem to have adopted a meaning exactly opposite to what, for many, the concepts originally meant: Rather than using the global financial and economic crisis since 2009 as a unique opportunity to initiate a radical transformation of the modern growth economy and consumer culture, national governments and international bodies are bending over backwards to restabilize and sustain the established socio-economic order—however self-destructive it is now widely acknowledged to be, ecologically, economically, socially, and also for democracy (Wilson and Swyngedouw 2014).

From the perspective of eco-activists and ecologically committed policymakers, this sustained *politics of unsustainability* (Blühdorn 2011, 2013) in ecological, economic, social, and democratic terms may, indeed, be perceived as a comprehensive failure of the sustainability paradigm. At least from a sociological point of view, however, there is also an impressive story of success to tell: After all, there is, undoubtedly, more knowledge and public awareness of the multiple sustainability crises than at any earlier stage. As a concept, sustainability is more present in public discourse than ever before. Virtually all societal actors and institutions portray themselves as fully committed to the goal of sustainability. This goal has been adopted as a key objective in constitutional documents, pieces of legislation, policy programs, and international agreements. All this signals considerable success! It not only raises the question why so much knowledge, awareness, and commitment yield so little structural change, but also why an unwieldy—and in many respects counter-intuitive—notion such as sustainability could become so powerful in the first place. Why is a paradigm that has provided so extensive evidence of its failure to deliver radical structural change nevertheless not abandoned in favor a more effective approach? How has the agenda of sustainability metamorphosed into the prevailing politics of sustained unsustainability?

In what follows, the objective is not to criticize those who profess commitment to sustainability without supplementing their rhetoric with commensurate action, nor to expose the power of self-interested elites (such as Republican deniers of climate change in the United States) who systematically blockade any move toward a transformation of the existing order of unsustainability. These are very important tasks! Yet, at least equally important as investigating its *failure*, is the task to explore the curious *success* of the sustainability paradigm. In fact, this contribution proceeds from the assumptions that (a) the sustainability paradigm, despite its inability to deliver to eco-activist expectations, is by no means exhausted but, actually, very responsive to the particular requirements of modern liberal consumer societies; and that (b) if a transformation of these societies in line with the demands of many ecologists, climate scientists, and sustainability researchers is possible at all, a much more profound understanding of the prevailing politics of unsustainability is required than is provided by the wide literature on power relations (for example, Luke 1995; Klein 2008; Swyngedouw 2010) and different forms of denial (Dunlap and McCright 2011; Norgaard 2011; Foster 2014). The next section first of all explores why the paradigm of sustainability is widely perceived to have failed focusing, in particular, on the misguided attempt to decouple eco-politics from the category of the *subject* and the *emancipatory project*. The third section is about the shift towards *post-sustainability*. It investigates prevalent norms of subjectivity and identity which underpin the ways in which advanced modern societies perceive environmental issues, frame environmental problems and negotiate related policy responses. The fourth section then elaborates on the conceptualization of contemporary eco-politics as the *politics of unsustainability*. It investigates how the paradigm of sustainability—in its contemporary appearance—rather than having failed and being exhausted, very effectively addresses the complex needs of liberal consumer societies.

Genealogy of the Perceived Failure

When trying to assess why and in what respects the paradigm of sustainability may be seen to have failed, calling to mind against what kind of background this thinking gained prominence and what kind of promise it had actually entailed is a useful starting point. Since the 1960s, in particular, rapid economic development in the industrialized countries and the spread of the consumer culture had triggered fast and profound environmental change, whilst the expansion of education systems and the increasing availability of information had increased public environmental awareness, raised expectations in terms of quality of life beyond material accumulation, and nurtured emancipatory claims for political self-determination (Commoner 1971; Inglehardt 1977). At the same time, the re-emergence of mass unemployment in the industrialized North, the persistence of deep poverty in the global South, and the threat of new mega-technologies such as nuclear technology (civil and military) raised profound doubts about the underlying logic of industrial capitalism (Marcuse 1972; Kelly 1984). All this added up to a diagnosis that Ulrich Beck later captured with his concept of the *risk society* (Beck 1992) and gave rise to a novel blend of concerns to which neither traditional-style conservationism nor the new environmental protection programs which some progressive national governments were launching at the time could offer an adequate response. Thus, radical *ecologism* (Dobson 2007) emerged as a new brand of eco-political thinking that took a much more holistic approach than any of its predecessors. It diagnosed a profound crisis not only in the natural environment but in the social, economic, and cultural dimensions of modern society, too (Habermas 1984, 1987). Radically challenging the established socio-economic and political order of the industrialized countries as well as the latter's relationship to the developing world, radical ecologists demanded a comprehensive transformation of economic structures, the political system, and personal lifestyles, as well as cultural values and notions of identity. Yet, whilst it offered a much more profound problem analysis, and although its demands for comprehensive socio-cultural change seemed thoroughly plausible in theory, radical ecologism was also widely perceived as unrealistic in political practice, as overly ideological and as anti-modernist.

In particular, it appeared as a distinct threat to established notions of *progress* and the convenience and pleasures of modern lifestyles. Its critique of consumer capitalism triggered deep ideological divisions leading into a confrontational, often deadlocked, style of eco-political discourse.

It was against this particular background that the WCED's notions of sustainability and sustainable development developed their coercive attractiveness. They promised to take the environmental crisis seriously, acknowledged the existence of non-negotiable bio-physical limits, and demanded respect for "the bounds of the ecologically possible" (WCED 1987: 55). They recognized the problem of Third World poverty and the unsuitability of the industrial countries' model of development as a blueprint for the global South. They conceded the necessity of comprehensive structural change, yet they held out an alternative to the demands of radical ecologism that seemed much more palatable and feasible than a wholesale departure from capitalist industrial capitalism and the consumer culture. Their promise that the environmental crisis, in industrialized as well as developing countries, could be addressed from within the existing socio-economic system and would not require radical system change was compelling not only for environmentally aware economic actors, reformist policymakers, and the politically moderate public, but it also appealed to many radical ecologists who believed that a suitably *strong* interpretation of the sustainable development concept might indeed be conducive to the achievement of radical ecologists' objectives (Dobson 1996; Jacobs 1999).

But although the sustainability paradigm seemed to acknowledge many concerns which were central to the thinking of radical ecologists, it distinguished itself sharply through its belief and promise that a combination of improved scientific understanding, technological innovation, managerial perfection, and the internalization into the market of hitherto unaccounted or externalized costs could rectify the destructive tendencies of consumer capitalism. Essentially, it conceptualized environmental problems as a matter of inefficient resource use and, accordingly, the sustainability paradigm remained firmly committed to established notions of progress and development. Indeed, it regarded the logic of modernity and modernization, which many radical ecologists had portrayed as the core problem, as the very solution. It suggested that even the principle of growth was thoroughly compatible with the conditions of finiteness. The WCED report of 1987 stated unambiguously that sustainable development is "far from requiring the cessation of economic growth" (1987: 40). Quite the contrary, it presented economic growth as an "essential" tool to "avert economic, social and environmental catastrophes," particularly in the developing world (1987: 89). Hence the WCED demanded that the international "economy must speed up world growth" (1987: 89). In contrast to radical ecologists, it thus reconfirmed the most basic principle of the established economic order, placing its primary emphasis not only on *development* rather than the restrictive qualifier *sustainable*, but more specifically on *economic* development in the traditional sense of economic *growth*.

Insofar as it had never intended to suspend the principles of capitalism, the consumer market, or the modernist logic of progress and efficiency, the critique that the sustainability paradigm has failed to deliver radical structural change may, thus, be based on inappropriate norms of assessment. Yet, the proponents of sustainable development also raised unjustified expectations. Particularly significant was the promise that the sustainability paradigm would emancipate eco-political thinking from its earlier dependence on soft and subjective criteria (aesthetics, religion, ethics) and thus render environmental policy much more effective than it had ever been before. Indeed, earlier forms of environmental thought had tried to support their demands and motivate environmental action by invoking aesthetic norms (preserve beauty of nature), religious imperatives (protect divine creation), or the ethical principle to respect the integrity and dignity (intrinsic value) of nature—all of which had proved too weak a foundation for a kind of environmental policy that would change established socio-environmental relations and attitudes toward nature. The sustainability paradigm, in contrast, promised to base environmental policy on a foundation of hard science and objective truths. It sought to specify the Brundtland Report's two norms of reference—the "bounds of the ecologically possible" and to the "needs" of present and future generations—in bio-physical rather than aesthetic, moral, or cultural terms. The scientific diagnosis of bio-physical limits was expected to facilitate much more focused and effective policy responses. Technological innovations and increased reliance on market-based policy instruments would, furthermore, improve the political acceptability of environmental policy.

Accordingly, sustainability researchers set out to quantify the availability of particular *resources*, calculate the stock of *natural capital*, determine the *carrying capacity* of regional ecosystems and the Earth at large, measure the *ecological footprint* of specific lifestyles or forms of social behavior, explore which *ecosystem services* are indispensable for modern society, understand the *material-flows* that make up the *nature/society metabolism*, and so forth. Similar effort was invested into defining key functions of human existence and yardsticks of individual and social well-being so as to identify the "needs" of present and future generations. These efforts were supplemented by the push for new efficiency technologies which radically reduce both the consumption of natural resources and modern society's waste and emissions output. Yet, in their endeavor to measure, map, quantify, and innovate, sustainability research and technology developers tended to neglect that the accumulation of scientific knowledge and technological know-how, however detailed and sophisticated, can never be a substitute for normative judgment. Science and technology on their own can neither define environmental limits—because "normative judgments are essential to give social and political meaning" to the notion of limits—nor specify "the positive social goods that are to be secured through the recognition of such limits" (Meadowcroft 2013: 988). Science can gather empirical information, measure and explain processes of environmental change, and try to calculate how particular patterns of human behavior and societal development may impact on natural ecosystems or the global climate. But the empirical data it delivers do, as such, never qualify as problems and nor do they necessitate or by themselves trigger any form of social action—unless they are put into relation to, and are perceived to conflict with, established social values, expectations, and aspirations. Ultimately, so-called *environmental* problems are perceived violations of *social* norms—and as such they are beyond the realm of the natural sciences and technological solutions (Redclift

1993). Thus, with its focus on bio-physical conditions, its fixation on objective truth, and its belief in technological fixes, the sustainability paradigm did not simply neglect the irreducibly normative character of environmental policy and politics, but it systematically failed to grasp the actual core of eco-political discourse.

In fact, the sustainability paradigm left the whole range of subject-related concerns, which had figured so prominently in radical ecologism, essentially unaddressed. On the one hand, the Brundtland report and the sustainability paradigm had, from the outset, adopted an anthropocentric perspective. Human welfare and well-being were, just like social justice and the eradication of poverty, key concerns and the primary reason for considering ecological limits and protecting the environment. On the other hand, however, the emancipatory and subject-related concerns which had so central a position in the thinking of radical ecologists, were never part of the WCED's sustainability agenda. The liberation of human beings from the widely perceived reification, instrumentalization, exploitation, and domination of human beings through the logic of rationalizing modernity and the spirit of capitalism were not relevant concerns. Yet, exactly these so-called *post-material needs*, that is, the new demands of increasingly educated, articulate, and self-confident citizens in post-industrial societies, for cultural and political self-determination, self-realization, and self-expression were a core element of the *new social movements* and a feature that distinguished eco-political discourses of the 1980s from both, older social movements such as the labor movement and earlier environment-related discourses such as conservationism (Inglehart 1977, 1997; Touraine 1981). The WCED's notion of sustainability, however, explicitly aiming to render environmental policy independent from categories like culture, subjectivity, and identity, remained insensitive to the emancipatory struggle. Similarly, the ecological modernization promise that new efficiency technologies and market-based resource management policies can resolve the environmental crisis not only disregarded the fact that normative judgments are required to establish what qualifies as a *resource* and what forms of resource-use may be considered as *efficient*, but it, too, failed to recognize that environmental crises, problems, and concerns are inextricably linked to matters of subjectivity and identity.

Toward Post-sustainability

Such norms of subjectivity and identity are crucial when it comes to defining *what* ought to be sustained, for *whom*, for *how long*, and for *what reason* (Redclift 1993; Luke 1995). They underpin the perception of environmental problems, determine what kind of policy responses are regarded as suitable and efficient, and power the implementation of such policies. And just as much as their neglect is a key parameter explaining why the sustainability paradigm is widely perceived to have failed, it is also crucial when it comes to explaining why contemporary liberal consumer democracies, nevertheless, do not abandon the sustainability paradigm in favor of a different approach. Indeed, the ongoing transformation of prevalent norms of subjectivity and identity is a much-neglected factor in explaining the success of this paradigm and understanding how the politics of sustainability—if it ever really had a genuinely transformative agenda—has silently metamorphosed into the prevailing politics of sustained unsustainability.

The central category here is, arguably, the modernist notion of the *autonomous subject* which has its origins in the Protestant–Kantian tradition of thought and has been installed as a quasi-transcendental—yet always unfulfilled—norm through a long sequence of emancipatory struggles. For the new social movements, exactly this unfulfilled promise was the foundation not only for the social demands they articulated, but also for the way in which their more radical currents, in particular, framed environmental issues. Indeed, radical political ecologists demanded that nature has to be accredited the same intrinsic value and status of subjectivity, that is, the same autonomy, dignity, and integrity that modern citizens claim for themselves and consider as their inalienable right. Explicitly, or often just implicitly, this idea of the autonomous subject is the normative point of reference for environmental concerns, and the normative yardstick by which ecological limits would have to be defined and legitimate human needs identified. Underneath all narratives of threats to the survival of the human species and other life on earth, it became the normative foundation for ecological imperatives and eco-political policy prescriptions—even where ecological thought aimed to adopt an eco- rather than anthropocentric point of view. But in the course of its long journey to hegemony and beyond, this specifically modernist, quasi-transcendental norm did not remain static. For norms of subjectivity and their interpretation are in fact always in flux, changing in line with the ongoing evolution of modernity.

Two interrelated changes which, in eco-political terms, are particularly relevant are, first, the transformation of the ways in which individuals in contemporary post-industrial societies realize, articulate, and experience their subjectivity and identity and, secondly, the incremental differentiation, fragmentation, and flexibilization of prevalent notions of identity. The former had for a long time been debated by the critical left as the permeation of the supposedly autonomous subject by the market, its colonization by the culture and consumer industries, and its manipulation by the advertising machine. More recently, however, it has been acknowledged in less normative terms that for purposes of their identity construction and self-expression individuals in advanced post-industrial societies very strongly rely on acts of consumption and the choices provided by the market (Featherstone 2007). Social theory has acknowledged this in that it has begun to conceptualize modern individuals primarily as consumers rather than—as the Marxist tradition had done—as producers (Bauman 2005: 23–4, 2007: 54); market actors have shifted from selling products to selling brands as carriers of lifestyles and identities; and governments and policymakers are increasingly addressing citizens as customers making well-informed consumer choices in the free market. Thus emancipation, empowerment, and autonomy are ever less a matter located *beyond* the market but an agenda pursued *within* its boundaries. The emancipatory struggle for self-realization and consumer capitalism have become mutually compatible rendering the abolition of the latter not only unnecessary but, indeed, undesirable.

The latter, that is, the pluralization and flexibilization of identity, had for a long time been discussed under the headings of popular culture and postmodernization (for example, Kellner 1995). More recently, Zygmunt Bauman has sought to capture this socio-cultural shift with his paradigm of *liquid modernity* (Bauman 2000). He suggests that individual identity, which had once been conceived of as unitary, consistent, and solid, is becoming increasingly fragmented, volatile, and liquid. Indeed, the bourgeois–modernist tradition had understood identity formation as a steady and life-long process of maturation culminating in a rounded and stable personality defined by firm moral principles, consistent tastes and interests, and reliable features of character. Yet, as contemporary societies are becoming ever more differentiated and subject to accelerated change; as the life-worlds of modern individuals are becoming ever more extended, complex, information-rich, and virtualized, this traditional notion of identity is giving way to multiple, fragmented, and flexible forms of identity. The qualities in demand today are versatility, mobility, and openness to change. Life-long learning and strategic image management are imperatives of the modern labor market and professional success. Also, more flexible notions of identity, which are more open to inherent contradictions, appear to facilitate a much richer experience of life and more personal fulfillment, whereas the earlier ideals of subjectivity and identity—with their implicit demands for consistency, commitment, loyalty, and rational-cum-moral self-discipline—are becoming impracticable and burdensome. Accordingly, the more progressive parts of contemporary societies, in particular, are adapting their understanding of their Self and their norms of identity. Such value change may be seen as an "evolutionary process in which those values that are best suited to cope with life under given existential conditions have a selective advantage" (Inglehardt and Welzel 2005: 23).

Critics of hegemonic neo-liberalism continue to describe these developments, quite legitimately, in terms of *alienation*, the incremental *decline* of the individual and the expansion of the apparatus of *domination* and control. Yet, taking into account its emancipatory drivers and potentials, this cultural shift can also be framed in terms of liberation from norms which no longer reflect the aspirations and life-world realities of contemporary citizens. As regards its eco-political implications, this modernization-induced value- and culture-shift may be conceptualized as a *post-ecologist turn* (for example, Blühdorn 2004). Whilst radical ecologists and the emancipatory new social movements had been driven by the longing for, and the belief in, the *authentic Self* and identity beyond the individualized and predominantly materialist consumer lifestyle, *real fulfillment* beyond the alienating treadmill of competitiveness and efficiency, *pacified social and natural relations* beyond social and ecological instrumentalization, exploitation, and destruction, and *genuinely empowering forms of political and economic organization* beyond the only formally democratic order of liberal consumer capitalism (for example, Goldsmith 1972; Die Grünen 1980), contemporary consumer-citizens are much less likely to experience this profound unease with the *alienating* order of scientific-technological-industrial modernity. The belief in a better alternative has largely evaporated, and scientific-technological-industrial modernity with its consumerist lifestyles has been firmly embraced.

Ever expanding needs in terms of, for example, mobility, technology, communication, or shopping opportunities have become essentially non-negotiable. Prevalent notions of well-being and quality of life imply that ways *must* be found to meet them. Accordingly, the supposedly categorical imperatives (ecological and social) which ecologists believed in *must* be reviewed; environmental policy and eco-political action *must* be amended to conform to, rather than challenge, the consumer market. Of course, contemporary eco-political communication is also shaped by an unprecedented awareness of the multi-dimensional unsustainability of post-industrial consumer societies. Yet, prevalent norms of subjectivity and identity imply that sustaining the established socio-economic order has itself become a categorical imperative. Indeed, in a number of respects, *unsustainability* is itself a constitutive feature of contemporary self-realization: notions of identity are inherently flexible, fluid, and non-identical, that is, they are not intended to be sustained but to be remolded as and when required. And as the ever more strongly consumption-based lifestyles and patterns of self-realization cannot be generalized, they inherently rely on ever increasing social inequality and exclusion.

So, in the wake of the post-ecologist turn, eco-political approaches which are based on the (reinterpreted) norm of the autonomous subject as their ultimate point of reference invariably lose their transformative capacity. They can no longer generate, legitimate, and implement criteria for remolding the established order of unsustainability. Quite the contrary, prevalent norms of subjectivity, identity, and self-realization demand that the established order of unsustainability and the logic that supports it are sustained. They turn *sustaining the unsustainable* into an imperative, destroy the normative foundation of the criticism that the paradigm of sustainability has failed, and necessitate a much more positive reassessment of policy approaches—voluntary agreements, corporate social responsibility, ethical consumerism, green growth—which neither aim for, nor deliver, profound structural change. In fact, from a post-ecologist perspective, the paradigm of sustainability now actually appears as a major success! Rather than having failed, it has paved the way toward environmental policy approaches which accommodate and deliver to the changing aspirations and identity needs of modern individuals. Supplementing approaches which focus on power structures, this focus on the change of social values and norms makes a significant contribution to explaining why the paradigm of sustainability could ever become so hegemonic and why it is being defended with so much resolve. Rather than being exhausted, the paradigm seems set to retain its significance and have a promising future as the politics of unsustainability.

The Politics of Unsustainability

This politics of unsustainability distinguishes itself from earlier phases of eco-politics in that an unprecedented level of scientific understanding and public awareness of the social and bio-physical implications of modern lifestyles, patterns of self-realization, and socio-economic structures coincides with an equally unprecedented determination to maintain these emancipatory achievements regardless of their ecological and social impact. Whilst it fully acknowledges the social, ecological, and economic unsustainability of the established socio-economic order, this politics of unsustainability is ever less about trying to change social values, prevalent lifestyles, and socio-economic structures to comply with any categorical eco- or social imperatives. Instead, its focus is on managing the inevitable consequences, social and ecological, of the resolve to sustain the established value preferences and the related socio-economic order. Rather than attempting to suspend or even reverse the prevailing logic of unsustainability, its main objective is to promote societal *adaptation* and *resilience* to sustained unsustainability. Inter alia, this implies trying to push minor changes in consumer behavior and the development of new technologies, which may help to reduce, on the production side, the empirical impact (social and ecological) of liberal consumer capitalism. But having taken on board that eco-political discourse is not primarily about empirically measurable conditions but about the social concerns which the latter may or may not trigger, an at least equally (and probably even more) important dimension of the *governance of unsustainability* (Blühdorn 2013, 2014) is to manage the *social perception* and *communicative processing* of changing societal and bio-physical realities, and thereby to reduce their capacity to raise socio-political conflict.

A key strategy for this is, first, the continued *depoliticization* of eco-political issues. This entails, inter alia, that eco-political issues are framed as matters of scientific knowledge, technological innovation, and managerial perfection—an effort that has always been central to the paradigm of sustainability and the policy approaches of ecological modernization. But beyond that, depoliticization also entails the relocation of definitional power, issue competence, and decision-making capacity away from the realm of the political—and the societal grassroots, in particular—to specialist bodies or authorities which are equipped with relevant expertise and shielded from political contestation. These depoliticized institutions—also including the market—are ascribed the ability to deal with matters of (un)sustainability more competently, effectively, and efficiently than political bodies ever could. In fact, political institutions themselves, in an effort to manage public expectations and the conflicting pressures to address and at the same time sustain the condition of unsustainability, now explicitly emphasize the limitations of their own abilities and the extent to which their actions are circumscribed by imperatives which are beyond their control. This is reflected in the dual shift of emphasis in policy-making, first, from producers to consumers and, secondly, from traditional-style regulation to voluntary agreements. On the one hand, this depoliticization of environmental issues may appear as disempowering and disowning the grassroots movements which once put the environment on the political agenda. On the other hand, however, the outsourcing of commitments and responsibilities to assumedly more effective service providers is fully in tune with the emancipation of modern individuals—as discussed earlier—from the previous social and ecological commitments which are seen to conflict with (non-negotiable) modern lifestyle preferences and personal aspirations.

In fact, the non-negotiability of these values, lifestyles, and aspirations is itself one of the imperatives which circumscribes government action and, therefore, such practices of depoliticization may actually claim much more democratic legitimacy than contemporary critics of *post-democracy* and *post-politics* (for example, Crouch 2004; Dean 2009; Wilson and Swyngedouw 2014) may want to concede. In addition, they are embedded in, and mediated by, a policy discourse of co-optation and re-empowerment.

Indeed, practices of *engagement* and *activation* are a second core ingredient of the governance of unsustainability. Recognizing their own limitations and acknowledging that modern demands for self-determination necessitate a shift from traditional-style, centralized government to decentralized, participatory forms of governance, governments and public administrators are not only soliciting the services of depoliticized expert bodies, but are also trying to engage a variety of non-state actors including private businesses, charities, civic interest groups, and individual citizens. Participatory, often informal and apparently non-hierarchical *stakeholder networks* are proliferating as a policy tool employed to reduce the potential for political conflict, facilitate consensus-based policy-making, share responsibility, and improve policy implementation. This new discourse of engagement and activation also entails that individual citizens and their households are addressed as the level where real societal change can and should be effected. Citizens are portrayed as commanding a wealth of readily available information and a broad variety of market choices which enables them, as socially and ecologically *responsible consumers*, to shape and propel society's transformation towards sustainability. This discourse presents consumer-citizens—rather than economic or political elites—as the real center of power, demands that every individual *contribute their bit*, and suggests that the sum of individualized consumer choices and small-scale behavior changes (for example, recycling household waste, not printing every email, using public transport more regularly, changing light bulbs) will deliver what neither the globalized economy nor the decapacitated state are able to achieve. Thus the task to define sustainability criteria, that is, to decide what exactly it may mean to *shop ethically, travel lightly*, and *live responsibly* is shifted to the individual, and the inconvenience and disadvantages which may accompany socially and ecologically informed consumer behavior are privatized.

Such strategies of decentralizing responsibilities which have traditionally been ascribed to (and claimed by) the state and such practices of individualization and responsibilization are firmly in line with neo-liberal thinking and may, accordingly, be portrayed as the project of self-interested elites. Yet, they also resonate with the social movements' and radical ecologism's great confidence in the ability of emancipated individuals and their civil society associations to effect change. Therefore, just like the practices of depoliticization, these strategies, too, have much more solid societal foundations than their critics may want to acknowledge: the accentuation of the emancipated and empowered individual speaks to contemporary citizens' desire to experience themselves as autonomous subjects, and the principles of voluntarism, state restriction, and personal responsibility maximize the space modern individuals retain to accommodate their own manifold commitments. Citizens may take action or make particular lifestyle choices where this supports their self-perception and identity-construction. But they can delegate responsibilities to service providers where this seems more convenient; and they may also pursue ecologically or socially detrimental avenues where external pressures or non-negotiable priorities seem to leave no acceptable alternative. Thus these practices of co-optation and activation maximize social inclusion into the politics of exclusion.

Thirdly, the governance of unsustainability strongly relies on the *neo-democratic, neo-social, and neo-ecological discourse* that orchestrates the ongoing depoliticization of modern liberal democracies, the steady rise of social inequality, and the continued exploitation of the natural environment. As the conditions of the post-growth economy, that is, the factual absence and apparent unachievability of any significant economic growth, powerfully reinforce the long-established awareness of natural finiteness, the non-negotiable continuation of prevalent value priorities, lifestyles, and patterns of self-realization is, more evidently than ever, possible only for certain parts of society; and it invariably implies that equivalent reductions must be achieved elsewhere. Accordingly, securing societal support and generating political legitimacy is an ever more difficult task—which is further complicated by the fact that, seemingly in contradiction to the above-mentioned preferences for delegation and outsourcing, expectations concerning democratic participation, representation, and legitimation continue to rise. In this particular constellation, new forms of social discourse have evolved in which a wide range of societal actors not only emphasize their firm commitment to environmental sustainability, but also to democracy and social justice. Indeed, in contemporary consumer democracies, the new social movements' values of *new politics* seem to have been more firmly embraced and mainstreamed than the emancipatory movements themselves would ever have thought possible (Dean 2009). The terms engagement, responsibility, self-determination, inclusion, fairness, or empowerment resound through public political debate; yet in the wake of the post-ecologist turn they have all been reinterpreted in line with the logic of the market and the changing identity needs of contemporary individuals. On the one hand, invoking these emancipatory values is a tool for securing societal support and generating legitimacy, on the other hand, their reinterpretation makes sure that they do not obstruct the post-ecologist priorities of contemporary individuals. As a matter of fact, these refashioned norms are an important tool for identifying social groups which may legitimately be excluded: they provide criteria to distinguish between those who *engage, do their bit, behave responsibly*, etc—as defined in the depoliticized manner and reflecting the post-ecologist needs of advanced modern society—and those who don't and may, therefore, be regarded as socially irresponsible and not deserving societal support, for example in terms of public welfare provision.

Together, these practices of depoliticization, co-optation, individualization, and responsibilization, and the neo-emancipatory discourse into which they are embedded, ensure that there is rich societal engagement and a high level of sustainability-related activity, without the established, and non-negotiable, socio-economic structures being challenged in any serious manner. In fact, remaining firmly within its boundaries, these activities reliably reproduce and further consolidate the established order; but at the same time they provide societal actors with ample opportunity to articulate their firm commitment to the goal of sustainability. This is exactly what renders them so effective as tools for the governance of unsustainability. They allow the wide range of political, economic, and civil society actors to demonstrate that they fully understand the seriousness of the multiple sustainability crises and make genuine efforts to take appropriate action. They enable individual citizens to present and experience themselves as socially and ecologically committed, but at the same time hold on to their values, lifestyles, and identities of unsustainability. Elsewhere I have conceptualized such social practices as the *politics of simulation* which is specifically geared to the inherently contradictory value preferences emerging in the wake of the post-ecologist turn (Blühdorn 2011, 2014). But from a social–theoretical point of view, in particular, it is essential not to misread this politics of simulation as a tool devised by a small power elite to oppress and rule the masses! Instead, it is the project of a new, and in its aspirations inclusive, alliance of societal actors, which entirely redraws established socio-political division lines. Undoubtedly, the politics of unsustainability is about managing—and facilitating—ever increasing levels of social inequality and exclusion. But it is essential to recognize that the governance of sustainability is a decentralized, participatory, and collective effort engaging a wide range of societal actors. And at least as much as it is about minimizing the social conflict that sustained unsustainability invariably breeds, the governance of unsustainability must be regarded as an individual as well as societal coping strategy for the paradoxes and the irresolvable dilemmas of an eco-politics that has no extra-social normative point of reference (Blühdorn 2015).

Conclusion

So, the analysis has revealed in what respects, or from which perspective, the paradigm of sustainability may be regarded as having failed to deliver and as being exhausted. Yet, it has also revealed why the sustainability concept has become so powerful and indeed hegemonic, and in what respects it may be regarded as very successful and expected to retain considerable future importance. This is neither simply because its reliance on modern science rather than cultural, religious, or ideological norms rendered the paradigm acceptable to a wide range of societal actors who had previously been divided by deep ideological rifts. Nor is it just because it did not demand a wholesale departure from the capitalist growth economy and consumer culture. Going well beyond these undoubtedly important points, its most significant strength is, arguably, its openness to diverse interpretations of exactly what sustainability may imply politically and, accordingly, its ability to accommodate the change of social values and identity needs in the post-ecologist constellation. It is for this reason, in particular, that the sustainability paradigm is set to retain its hegemonic status.

Talking of the sustainability paradigm—as well as radical ecologism—in generalizing terms as if they were monolithic bodies of thought, this analysis has paid little attention to the differences between the diverse interpretations of the sustainability concept. Also, it has not dealt with issues of power and with political actors who have consistently endeavored to block sustainability policies. Instead it has highlighted that science will invariably remain unable to generate objectively valid eco-political imperatives and uncontested policy agendas, and that sustainability research will have to fully acknowledge that ecological communication is, at its root, always about the perceived violation of socially negotiated norms. Accordingly, any sustainability research that wants to reach beyond the sheer reproduction of neo-emancipatory discourses, and beyond contributing to the governance of unsustainability, needs to break out of the mainstream of technocratic thinking, economistic analysis and its assigned role as policy advisor to the governors of unsustainability. It needs to take account of the radical re-subjectivation of eco-politics, the particular conditions under which it occurs, and the new eco-political constellations and social practices which it entails. As the politics of unsustainability continues to unfold, any eco-political theory that wants to retain a critical ambition will need to focus on unpacking the prevailing societal self-descriptions and investigating the communicative strategies that facilitate the governance of unsustainability.

References

Bauman, Z. (2000). *Liquid Modernity* (Cambridge: Polity).

Bauman, Z. (2005). *Liquid Life* (Cambridge: Polity)

Bauman, Z. (2007). *Consuming Life* (Cambridge: Polity).

Beck, U. (1992), *The Risk Society* (Cambridge: Polity).

Blühdorn, I. (2004). "Post-ecologism and the Politics of Simulation." In *Liberal Democracy and Environmentalism: The End of Environmentalism?*, edited by M. Wissenburg and Y. Levy (London: Routledge), 35–47.

Blühdorn, I. (2011). "The Politics of Unsustainability: COP15, Post-ecologism and the Ecological Paradox." *Organization & Environment* 24(1): 34–53.

Blühdorn, I. (2013). "The Governance of Unsustainability. Ecology and Democracy after the Post-democratic Turn," *Environmental Politics* 22(1): 16–36.

Blühdorn, I. (2014) "Post-ecologist Governmentality: Post-Democracy, Post-Politics and the Politics of Unsustainability." In *The Post-Political and its Discontents. Spaces of Depoliticisation and Spectres of Radical Politics*, edited by J. Wilson and J. Swyngedouw (Edinburgh: Edinburgh University Press), 146–66.

Blühdorn, I. (2015). "A Much-needed Renewal of Environmentalism? Eco-politics in the Anthropocene." In *The Anthropocene and the Global Environmental Crisis: Rethinking Modernity in a New Epoch*, edited by C. Hamilton, F. Gemenne, and C. Bonneuil (London: Routledge), 156–167.

Brand, U. (2010). "Sustainable Development and Ecological Modernization—The Limits to a Hegemonic Policy Knowledge." *Innovation—The European Journal of Social Science Research* 23(2): 135–52.

Bulkeley, H., Jordan, A., Perkins, R., and Selin, H. (2013). "Governing Sustainability: Rio+20 and the Road Beyond." *Environment and Planning C* 31: 958–70.

Commoner, B. (1971). *The Closing Circle* (New York: Knopf).
Crouch, C. (2004). *Post-democracy* (Cambridge: Polity).
Dean, J. (2009). *Democracy and other Neoliberal Fantasies. Communicative Capitalism and Left Politics* (Durham NC: Duke University Press).
Die Grünen. (1980). *Das Bundesprogramm* (Bonn: Die Grünen).
Dobson, A. (1996). "Environment Sustainabilities: An Analysis and a Typology." *Environmental Politics* 5(3): 401–28.
Dobson, A. (2007). *Green Political Thought* (London: Routledge).
Dunlap, R. and McCright, A. (2011). "Organized Climate Change Denial." In *The Oxford Handbook of Climate Change and Society*, edited by J. Dryzek, R. Norgaard, and D. Schlosberg (Oxford: Oxford University Press), 144–160.
Featherstone, M. (2007). *Consumer Culture and Postmodernism* (London: Sage).
Foster, J. (2014). *After Sustainability: Denial, Hope, Retrieval* (London: Earthscan).
Goldsmith, E. (1972). *A Blueprint for Survival* (London: Penguin).
Habermas, J. (1984). *The Theory of Communicative Action Vol. 1* (Boston: Beacon Press).
Habermas, J. (1987). *The Theory of Communicative Action Vol. 2* (Boston: Beacon Press).
Inglehart, R. (1977). *The Silent Revolution: Changing Values and Political Styles Among Western Publics* (Princeton, NJ: Princeton University Press).
Inglehart, R. (1997). *Modernization and Postmodernization: Cultural, Economic, and Political Change in 43 Societies* (Princeton, NJ: Princeton University Press).
Inglehart, R. and Welzel, C. (2005). *Modernization, Cultural Change and Democracy: The Human Development Sequence* (Cambridge: Cambridge University Press).
Jacobs, M. (1999). "Sustainable Development as a Contested Concept." In *Fairness and Futurity. Essays on Environmental Sustainability and Social Justice*, edited by A. Dobson (Oxford: Oxford University Press), 21–45.
Kellner, D. (1995). *Media Culture: Cultural Studies, Identity and Politics. Between the Modern and the Postmodern* (London: Routledge).
Kelly, P. (1984). *Fighting for Hope* (London: South End Press).
Klein, N. (2008). *The Shock Doctrine: The Rise of Disaster Capitalism* (London: Allen Lane).
Luke, T. (1995). "Sustainable Development as a Power/Knowledge System." In *Greening Environmental Policy: The Politics of a Sustainable Future*, edited by F. Fischer and M. Black (London: Paul Chapman), 21–32.
Marcuse, H. (1972). *Counter-revolution and Revolt* (Boston: Beacon Press).
Meadowcroft, J. (2013). "Reaching the Limits? Developed Country Engagement With Sustainable Development in a Challenging Conjuncture." *Environment and Planning C: Government and Policy* 31: 988–1002.
Norgaard, K. (2011). *Living in Denial. Climate Change, Emotions and Everyday Life* (Cambridge, MA: MIT Press).
Redclift, M. (1993). "Sustainable Development: Needs, Values and Rights." *Environmental Values* 2: 3–20.
Swyngedouw, E. (2010). "Apocalypse Forever? Post-political Populism and the Spectre of Climate Change." *Theory, Culture & Society* 27: 213–32.
Touraine, A. (1981). *The Voice and the Eye* (Cambridge: Cambridge University Press).
Wilson, J. and Swyngedouw, E., eds. (2014). *The Post-Political and its Discontents. Spaces of Depoliticisation and Spectres of Radical Politics* (Edinburgh: Edinburgh University Press).
World Commission on Environment and Development, WCED (1987), *Our Common Future* (New York: Oxford University Press).

CHAPTER 18

POPULATION, ENVIRONMENTAL DISCOURSE, AND SUSTAINABILITY

DIANA COOLE

THIS chapter begins with a conundrum. It would seem a logical inference that global ecologies would be more sustainable with a stable population and that population growth, especially when combined with rising living standards, is a significant factor in deteriorating environmental indicators. Equally, there are many countries where having fewer bodies to support and less human capital to nurture might be expected to make a significant contribution to preserving biodiversity and enhancing personal well-being. Such claims are not of course unchallenged but arguably they are compelling enough to warrant the kind of serious consideration they attracted during the 1960s and '70s. The conundrum is that suggestions for stabilizing or reducing world population have since then become so controversial that there is little appetite for putting them on environmental policy agendas or for considering them within environmental political theory, even though numbers are now far higher and environmental conditions look considerably worse.

While conservatives and the political right have their own reasons for disavowing population politics, progressive thinkers—including Greens (Beck and Kolankiewicz 2000)—have been among the most vehement critics of Malthusian doctrines over recent decades. Their reluctance to consider the topic of overpopulation is nonetheless unsurprising. The principal variables at stake are fertility, mortality, and migration, each of which is a treacherous ethical field for political actors. On a broader level, merely to ask whether there are too many human beings on the planet is to challenge deep-seated ontological beliefs about the sanctity of life and the exceptionalism of a human species with the right and capacity to dominate nature. This is a field, too, where distrust of political elites seems especially strong. Policies whose intention is to reduce fertility are regularly linked to coercive means of population control, while there is a pervasive suspicion that those who recommend fewer people actually aspire to reducing certain categories of person, with some lives being judged less valuable than others (Hardt and Negri 2004: 166). Indeed, constructivist critics often contend that there is no real, material issue here at all but rather, a discursive problematization designed to shore up racial privilege against "the other". In sum, there are many reasons why political theorists are reluctant to consider policies for reducing our burgeoning numbers or to acknowledge the material benefits of stabilization.

Yet the numbers are disturbingly large and the current generation of retiring baby-boomers will witness a trebling of world population in their lifetime. UN (medium variant) projections are for our current seven billion plus to reach 9.6 billion by mid-century and, on the basis of optimistic assumptions that worldwide fertility is converging to a sub-replacement level, to 10.9 billion by 2100 (UN 2013). This growth is of course uneven and now occurs mainly in developing countries where ecological footprints are smaller. Yet, as living standards rise and with poverty eradication a core demand of social justice movements, challenges for vulnerable ecosystems are becoming more intractable (IPCC 2014). Populous emergent economies like China and India now cast doubt on any simple distinction between developing and developed countries as a new global middle class oriented to high consumption emerges. With mounting evidence of the costs of unsustainable pollution levels, increasing exhaustion of non-renewable resources, biodiversity loss through the destruction of natural habitats, the surrendering of iconic landscapes and open spaces to human settlement, the increasing density of cities whose ecological footprints radiate ever wider in pursuit of water, energy, and food security, and general environmental degradation that is likely to worsen with climate change, stabilizing or reducing human numbers would seem prima facie to be a sensible ingredient of mitigation or adaptation strategies. As Sir David Attenborough argues, a common feature of these social and environmental problems is that they all become "more difficult—and ultimately impossible—to solve with ever more people" (Attenborough 2011: 6). Consumption is an important factor here, as is the prevailing economic model of global capitalism. Yet, population serves as a multiplier of profligate consumer behavior, while economic growth has itself become one of the principal rationales for promoting population growth, especially in those low-fertility countries where stabilization is currently feasible yet resisted.

Two key questions arise here: does the planet have the biophysical capacity to support 11 billion human bodies at a decent material level; and even if it does, will the environmental and existential costs be worth paying? The first is a more objective, empirical question that is disputed through competing modeling exercises. The second is a more normative question that considers the quality of life in a crowded, urbanized world of depleted green spaces and intensified competition for resources. The former depends a great deal on which negative externalities are included when calculating the impact of further demographic and economic growth on natural capital. The latter involves value judgments about lifestyle choices and the good life that are mediated by cultural diversity and material opportunities. It is here that environmental political theorists could in principle make a valuable contribution.

The aims of this chapter are to present some of the arguments that have been made in favor of stable or declining numbers, to explain some of the reasons the issue has become so toxic, and to suggest some of the areas where it does seem pertinent to revisit this matter in the context of twenty-first century conditions despite the significant obstacles to doing so.

Zero Population Growth as a Progressive Environmental Cause

This section reconstructs some earlier environmental arguments in favor of stabilizing growth rates. Systematic concern about overpopulation emerged in eighteenth-century Europe in response to demographic changes integral to the modernization process. It took some 10,000 years for humans to reach a billion (around 1804) but after 1750 European growth rates began to accelerate and numbers would double to two billion by 1927 (Livi-Bacci 1997: 65). Mainly, this accelerated growth was welcomed, especially by classical economists like Adam Smith who equated prosperity with plentiful cheap labor and were sanguine that numbers would remain congruent with demand for workers. But in 1789 T. R. Malthus warned in his *Essay on the Principle of Population* that overpopulation threatens starvation and endangers economic growth itself.

Malthus proposed as a universal law that unchecked, population will increase much faster (exponentially) than advances in food production (Malthus 2004; Mayhew 2014). This was not an environmental argument as such, but it was a warning that demographics and resources can become dangerously unbalanced. Although he underestimated the increased food production industrialization would permit, thus allowing more people to be supported, what Malthus recognized more generally was that at any level of technology, numbers and resources must achieve equilibrium. Preferably this occurs through voluntary reductions in fertility (preventive checks) but otherwise, famine and epidemics will restore a balance through higher mortality (positive checks). Like other leading classical economists, Malthus saw some more definitive limits, notably of arable land in "old" countries like Britain where most productive farmland was already under cultivation.

Much of Malthus's unpopularity stems from his later suggestion that withholding Poor Law relief would be demographically prudent. Britain was better able to resolve its problems by importing food (and exporting people to the new world), but recurrent Indian famines during the nineteenth and twentieth centuries were widely regarded as proof of Malthus's warning. The Green Revolution of the 1970s mainly allayed these fears of food shortages as new biotechnologies increased crop yields. Subsequently, however, environmental degradation caused by the intensive irrigation and chemical fertilization required, in conjunction with predictions of detrimental climate change effects on agriculture (itself a significant source of greenhouse gas emissions), ongoing population increases, and renewed concern about global limits to productive land and fresh water, has provoked renewed Malthusian concern (Shiva 2000; Alexandratos 2005). Most commentators remain cautiously optimistic that through efficiency, free trade, technology, and good governance, ecological constraints can be managed sufficiently to feed the world; but only if radical changes in farming practices, dietary habits, and food distribution occur (Foresight 2011; McMahon 2013).

If demographic remedies are rarely included among contemporary responses to scarcity ("insecurity"), another perspective that is noticeable for its absence from most policy reports is one that John Stuart Mill, another classical economist, introduced in the mid-nineteenth century. Mill blamed overpopulation for depressing working class wages but drawing on romantic poets like Wordsworth, he also articulated more explicitly ecological concerns about the detrimental existential, aesthetic, and affective effects of growth on everyday experience. In his *Principles of Political Economy* (1848) he acknowledged that there may be no fixed threshold beyond which numbers become unsupportable, but he also questioned the benefits of continued population and economic growth for their own sake. Mill invited his readers to ask why persistent growth is valuable once a certain threshold of need satisfaction has been met, if the price is loss of tranquility or access to natural beauty. He envisaged a bleak future in which all fertile land is cultivated, with "every flowery waste or natural pasture ploughed up, all quadrupeds or birds which are not domesticated for man's use exterminated as his rivals for food, every hedgerow or superfluous tree rooted out, and scarcely a place left where a wild shrub or flower could grow without being eradicated as a weed in the name of improved agriculture" (Mill 1970: 116). It is not difficult to transcribe his unease into contemporary images of countryside covered in glass and plastic, solar panels and wind turbines. This may provide viable, even green, life support systems for large future generations, but the provocative question Mill posed was whether this should be considered a desirable option.

Such concerns became prominent during the 1960s as a postwar babyboom accompanied economic reconstruction and engendered new anxieties about the high costs of population and economic growth, both of which were advancing exponentially. World population had recently exceeded three billion and doubling times were quickening as growth rates reached 2.2 percent per annum. When Rachel Carson's *Silent Spring* was published in 1962 it produced shocking evidence of the effects of pollution on natural species. As Paul Ehrlich would note in *The Population Bomb* (1968), when "a population becomes more wealthy, it tends to consume more resources per person per year" (Ehrlich 1972: 107). It was affluent, "over-developed" populations that were the main problem for these neo-Malthusians. Some of the environmental movement's most influential texts emerged during this period, with many recommending a steady-state economy and urgent intervention to halt population increases. In addition to Ehrlich's work they included Barbara Ward and René Dubos's *Only One Earth* (1972), The Club of Rome's *The Limits to Growth* (1972), *The Ecologist*'s "Blueprint for Survival" (1972),

Arne Naess, "The Shallow and the Deep, Long-Range Ecology Movement. A Summary" (1973), E. F. Schumacher's *Small is Beautiful* (1973), and James Lovelock's *Gaia. A New Look at Life on Earth* (1979). Their demographic message was echoed in seminal writings from the New Left and the Women's Liberation Movement, such as Herbert Marcuse's *An Essay on Liberation* (1969) and Shulamith Firestone's *The Dialectic of Sex* (1970). Ending the population explosion was adopted as a radical cause grounded in critical theory.

The limits to growth paradigm that framed these works represented a powerful conjunction of forces in which ecological sensitivity combined with critical analysis of late capitalism, a beguiling vision of a post-industrial future predicated on values compatible with biophysical limits, grassroots movements inspired by a radical counter-culture, and innovations in computer modeling that allowed large data sets to be used for projecting future scenarios. Collectively they supported a view that without a transformation of humans' instrumental relationship to nature and of the prevailing socio-economic structure, the world is heading for catastrophe.

Of particular significance was the emergence of a normative approach epitomized by Arne Naess's deep ecology (Naess 1973). Rejecting anthropocentric assumptions, its exponents argued that supporting more people at the cost of extinguishing other species is morally indefensible, with a diminished human population being a requirement of biotic integrity (Cafaro and Crist, eds. 2012). In 1964 the US government passed a Wilderness Act that spoke of preserving the "primeval character" of parts of "the earth and its community of life" in a natural condition, thus ensuring "that an increasing population, accompanied by expanding settlement and growing mechanization" does not "occupy and modify" everything wild (US government 1964: section 2). Even President Nixon warned that "one of the most serious challenges to human destiny in the last third of this century will be the growth of the population," with privacy, living space, and "attractive countryside" under particular threat (Nixon 2006: 777, 782). Official reports in the United States (1972) and the United Kingdom (1973) recommended population stabilization.

Among critical theorists, this demographic advice was accompanied by a thorough critique of consumer capitalism. New Left thinkers condemned long hours of alienated toil performed in order to satisfy "false" and ultimately unsatisfying needs engendered by advertising and the culture industry. "The need for possessing, consuming, handling, and constantly renewing, gadgets, devices, instruments, engines," Marcuse argued, only increases voluntary servitude to "a market ever more densely filled with merchandise" (Marcuse 1972: 21). Inversely, future happiness was equated with less but more creative work, a relationship to objects that appreciates their aesthetic qualities without reducing them to utilitarian or status possessions, and a harmonious relationship with nature achieved through a "new sensibility." Marcuse insisted that a "new standard of living, adapted to the pacification of existence, also presupposes reduction in the future population" (Marcuse 1964: 243). Firestone agreed. Like other early second-wave feminists she identified women's liberation with their escape from the tyranny of reproduction and the nuclear family (Firestone 1970: 158). This would help defuse the menace of overpopulation, she argued, by dismantling the stubborn patriarchy that sustains it. The assumption was that once they achieved reproductive autonomy, women would choose small families or childlessness.

These normative and critical positions were underwritten by empirical data showing the world apparently heading for disaster. The concept of limits to growth was popularized by the title of the book published by scientists at MIT and commissioned by the Club of Rome. Feeding data of current trends into their World3 computer model and interpreting their findings from the perspective of systems theory, the authors warned of positive feedback loops and system overload on a finite planet. The only sustainable scenario to emerge was a steady-state economy and stable population; even with optimistic technological possibilities factored in, continued growth overwhelmed the planet's homeostatic mechanisms. The political problem was that modern Western culture "has evolved around the principle of fighting against limits rather than learning to live with them" (Meadows and Meadows 1972: 150). This last observation was borne out by the derision with which limits to growth discourses were treated. Clearly their principal thesis offended pro-growth economic ideologies, but the question remains why an argument that briefly prevailed in the mid-twentieth century when world population was half its current total has been so comprehensively reviled since.

Anti-Malthusianism since 1974

Reconstructing the complicated factors that have silenced the population issue since the mid-1970s is an immense task that incorporates numerous geopolitical and ideological contingencies. Some of the more salient anti-Malthusian positions, in particular as they affect environmental thinking, are summarized in this section with the most important period of paradigm change being 1974–94.

The key to ending population growth is controlling fertility. A significant shift in progressive Western opinion occurred, however, as disenchantment with family planning programs emerged. Feminists still regarded access to new reproductive technologies and legal abortion as essential for women's liberation. But thinkers like Angela Davis pointed out their ambiguous significance for working class women and women of color who had experienced abortions and sterilizations in response to poverty or eugenics policies (Davis 1982: ch. 12). This was judged part of a wider tendency to treat women's fertility instrumentally in pursuit of broader social goals or even to blame women for overpopulation. In addition, as feminist attention shifted during the 1980s from gender equality to sexual difference, women's nurturing capacities were revalorized: a position that was not exactly pro-natalist but that did reject the former anti-natalism. The Old Left remained suspicious of arguments that attributed poverty to population rather than over-consumption or maldistribution and, as attention shifted to developing countries, postcolonialists judged neo-Malthusianism indelibly racist (Hardt and Negri 2004: 165–9). This equation, which renders it shameful to ascribe blame for social or environmental ills to overpopulation, has arguably been the most potent reason for deterring critical thinkers and publics from engaging with population matters (Coole 2013). Critics invariably ask who is being judged excessive and thus blamed; usually, they answer, it is the poor, especially those from the global South. The New Left, meanwhile, suffered a common fate with other radical ecological and limits to growth exponents as their positions were dismissed by an ascendant New Right. Exemplified by the Reagan Administration, this brought together two anti-Malthusian forces. Neo-liberalism reverted to a pre-Malthusian position in welcoming population growth as a driver of sustained economic growth (demographic revisionism) while social conservatism invigorated pro-life positions and strengthened older religious aversions toward small family norms, abortion, and birth control.

Declining fertility anyway defused the issue of rapid population growth in developed countries during the later 1970s. The issue was now relocated to developing regions just embarking on transition. This completely changed the geopolitical and ideological landscape in which demographic matters were rehearsed, with several landmark world conferences convened by the United Nations witnessing deep antagonisms between the global North and South but also facilitating the emergence of new transnational discourses. Here the relationship between population, development, and environment became the main focus and economics, its principal framework.

During the 1970s the US government was strongly promoting family planning programs in countries like India, where it worried that destabilization caused by rapid population growth might turn them toward a communist development model (Szreter 1993). These cold war motivations antagonized developing countries, which argued on the one hand that population control was a racist agenda driven by neo-colonial ambitions and on the other, that it was the unequal economic conditions reproduced by the world economic order, not high fertility among the world's poor, that was responsible for poverty and underdevelopment in the global South (Finkle and Crane 1975). Meanwhile, despite their hostility to population control in international meetings, populous states like India and China were imposing stringent fertility controls at home. As the Reagan Administration turned against population policies in the mid-1980s, such programs were designated coercive abuses of couples' right voluntarily to choose their family size.

In particular, though, it was the emergence of anti-Malthusian demographic and economic arguments, for which population and economic growth are mutually and positively reinforcing and the promise of equilibrium is embedded in a teleological modernization narrative, that had the greatest transformative effect in disavowing a population issue. Several interlocking strands of this still hegemonic discourse may be identified. First, rational choice theorists maintained that contrary to the Malthusian belief that rising living standards encourage larger families, the high cost of childrearing in developed urban economies reduces demand for them (Becker 1960). Under free market conditions fertility will therefore automatically fall (White House 1984). This was complemented by a second theory, demographic revisionism, whose principal exponent, Julian Simon, argued that population growth is anyway economically beneficial in the longer term. This is because higher densities stimulate technological innovations, while larger numbers constitute a bigger labor force that increases productivity and enhances the ingenuity needed, for example, to overcome natural constraints that might otherwise render resources inelastic (Simon 1977; Bauer 1981; Hodgson 1988). This argument is reinforced by a third, the environmental Kuznets Curve, which hypothesizes that although environmental damage and inequality may surge during the development process, beyond a certain income threshold better-educated, wealthier publics will be motivated to protect their natural capital and stabilize their consumption, with the fruits of development yielding revenue that can be used to ameliorate the ecological damage inflicted by larger numbers of prosperous consumers. Lack of evidence to support the downturn, for example in carbon dioxide emissions, has induced considerable skepticism toward such claims (Stern 2006: 191–2). But this theory is part of a wider assemblage that encourages complacency about population growth because economic growth is attributed capacities to restore equilibrium.

Expectation that a renewed, albeit higher-level, equilibrium will mark the end of demographic modernization is enshrined in a fourth approach to which most demographers currently subscribe: demographic transition theory (DTT) (Kirk 1996; Lee and Reher 2011). This describes a series of demographic stages that are integral to the modernization process. Following a low, pre-modern equilibrium maintained by high mortality and fertility rates, transition refers to a period of rapid population growth in which development first causes mortality decline and subsequently—but only after a delay whose duration is crucial in determining eventual numbers—fertility decline. In theory, this process culminates in a stable equilibrium between low mortality and fertility regimes of the kind currently materializing in developed regions. Although DTT does not argue in favor of demographic or economic growth, it does therefore deny any long-term problem of overpopulation since Malthusian worries become merely transient responses to a temporary transition phase. The crucial question, however, is whether transition will be completed as universally and automatically as experts often assume, or requires robust intervention from policymakers.

Meanwhile, the prospect of stabilization is being actively challenged from the perspective of a fifth argument that is more explicitly pro-growth and unhappy with the idea of completing transition. Transitional stages affect age structure and toward the end, fertility decline plus longer life expectancy result in population ageing. Because this means a shrinking labor force and higher dependency ratio it presents an acute, albeit temporary, fiscal challenge for developed economies. Nations that compete to increase GDP growth in a competitive global economy, while also striving to balance their budgets, are responding by trying to rejuvenate their populations (Coole 2012). Their motivation is encapsulated in the concept of a "demographic dividend": a temporary feature of low-dependency cultures as they pass through a stage where fertility has declined but the population has not yet aged, thus yielding a disproportionately large working-age population. Countries whose dividend is passing are understandably reluctant to abandon this productive advantage and therefore strive to avoid the stable or even reduced numbers that transition entails. Pro-natalism and net migration are their main strategies (Grant and Hoorens 2006).

The first is usually promoted in the form of family-friendly policies but the second has quickly become immersed in the circuits of racist politics that are a legacy of earlier hostilities. Suffice it to say that policies designed to expand the populations of post-transitional, affluent regions run contrary to suggestions that this is where falling numbers could be most environmentally beneficial (Coleman and Rowthorn 2011). Were the United States, for example, to return to its 1950 level rather than growing to the 460 million plus projected for 2050, it would shrink from its current 320 million to 158 million. For the United Kingdom—a country that, according to its 2011 census, is expanding at a historically unprecedented rate—a corresponding trajectory would mean returning to the 50.6 million of 1950 rather than growing to the 73 million projected for 2050 (UN 2013a). A similar story can be told for Australia, France, and many other developed nations (although not for Japan). In these cases, however, recommending population stabilization immediately becomes entrameled in an insidious immigration politics. As the "dividend" window closes in populous emergent economies like China, they too are being urged to raise their fertility rate (Yi 2007), regardless of its environmental impact.

A final body of argument, and one of particular importance for environmentalists, concerns sustainable development. The concept was pioneered by the Brundtland Report, *Our Common Future* (1987), at the behest of the UN World Commission on the Environment and Development (WCED). The report itself was quite demographically bold. With numbers nudging five billion it asserted that "present rates of population growth cannot continue" because of a widening gap between numbers and resources, with children born in affluent countries placing especial burdens on resources (World Commission 1987: paras 4.4, 4.8). But it also admitted that this had "proved to be one of the more difficult concerns with which we had to struggle" due to seemingly "unbridgeable" differences between diverse cultural, religious, and regional perspectives (Chairman's Foreword: 8). In fact, this would be almost the last major UN report to express this level of concern. The Commission took an agnostic view regarding population's causal role in underdevelopment but advised urgent action to lower fertility rates, especially in Africa. Strategies such as banning child labor, building social security for the elderly, and educational campaigns that supplement family planning services by explaining the merits of small families, were recommended. Since higher densities nevertheless looked inevitable, additional support was given for building what would today be called resilience: helping people adjust to "problems of overcrowding and excessive population densities" by teaching the "tolerance and empathy required for living in a crowded world" (1987: para 4.61).

The reason for including sustainable development as a plank in the anti-limits to growth edifice, however, is the concept's subsequent itinerary. Sustainable development helped paper over deep disagreements between the global North and South. It was in the North that ecological concerns were paramount and these were mainly now allocated as developed nations' responsibility. The global South was understandably adamant that its development prospects should not be impeded by the resource profligacy and ecological or demographic sensibilities of affluent countries. By the 1980s their focus on economic development in any case resonated with neo-liberal regimes for which sustained, market-led global economic growth was a panacea. Unwittingly, sustainable development became a formula that allowed both sides to endorse an approach for which biophysical limits, radical ecologism, and neo-Malthusian positions are anathema.

Population Matters in the Twenty-First Century

The preceding overview explains some of the reasons for the conundrum with which this chapter began. The chapter ends, however, by mentioning signs of a cautious return of the population question and some of the challenges involved in reframing it. One factor remains incontrovertible: world population increased massively during the twentieth century and although the growth rate has slowed considerably, barring some unforeseen catastrophe the number of human bodies that planet Earth must sustain on a daily basis by 2100 will be immense, at three to four billion more than currently according to the latest estimates. Worldwide, this will require huge changes in political and economic capacity. It will also place enormous demands on the biophysical world, whose contribution we have become used to rendering as "natural capital" or "ecosystem services" and whose deficits are increasingly framed in terms of securitization or business opportunities. The environmental areas most vulnerable to this spread of humanity are probably biodiversity, especially inasmuch as it defies or fails to contribute to economic reckoning, and, related to its loss, a gradual aesthetic–existential impoverishment of everyday experience as the presence of non-human otherness is attenuated. Inhabiting more crowded, congested spaces and coping with infrastructural deficits may yield some economies of scale and metropolitan exhilaration, but beyond a certain threshold it simply makes ordinary life more difficult, unpleasant, and competitive for most humans, especially poor ones, as well as for other species.

It is in light of these demographic horizons that the population question is being hesitantly reprised in popular books and policy reports. These tend to divide between pessimistic prognoses of systems collapse and optimism that in combination with new technologies, market incentives plus effective governance can reorient consumer behavior in sufficiently sustainable directions to accommodate the additional billions. Within the more popular genre, Stephen Emmot's *10 Billion* (Emmott 2013) and Alan Weisman's *Countdown* (Weisman 2013) are good examples of Malthusian pessimism that stress an urgent need to reduce fertility, while Danny Dorling's *Population 10 Billion* (Dorling 2013) endorses a more optimistic "possibilism" grounded in faith that fertility decline is fast enough for projected numbers to be manageable. Official reports are also increasingly likely to include population growth among major imminent challenges, especially in the case of statistical studies that can readily incorporate demographic data and which mainly reveal growth to be an aggravating factor across environmental externalities such as global warming, food production, or resource insecurity (for example, Stern 2006; RCEP 2011; Foresight 2011; World Bank 2012; IPCC 2014).

Reinforcing such arguments are computer simulations that show the effect of bigger populations on specific sustainability indicators such as greenhouse gas emissions. A study by O'Neill et al., for example, shows gains in carbon efficiency being negated by more consumers, inviting the conclusion that "reduced population growth could make a significant contribution to global emissions" such that "family planning policies would have a substantial environmental cobenefit" (O'Neill et al. 2010: 17525). By modeling the cumulative impact of individuals' descendents as a carbon legacy of current fertility choices, Murtaugh and Schlax similarly find that "the potential savings from reduced reproduction are huge compared to the savings that can be achieved by changes in lifestyle" (Murtaugh and Schlax 2009: 18). For the most part these kinds of report refrain from advocating demographic remedies but a notable exception is the Royal Society's *People and the Planet* (2012). This concludes that "a gradual and equitable decline in numbers will serve humanity best," especially if complemented by reductions in material consumption by the more affluent and by "changes to the current economic model" of persistent economic growth (Royal Society 2012: 83). As this makes clear, population reduction would on its own be no panacea: the population question cannot be asked in isolation from consumption. Yet neither issue is being addressed with much verve or efficacy: for the most part solutions to environmental overload rely on strategies that are internal to the dominant pro-growth model (green entrepreneurialism, market mechanisms, even population growth itself) and on faith in its intrinsic capacity to restore equilibrium. From this perspective a far more radical, critical, and integrated approach is needed.

In any case, population projections give little succor to complacency. The last two UN world revisions (in 2010 and 2012) both revised totals upward. The difference between low and high variant projections is 2.5 billion people in 2050 and ten billion by 2100: disparities that rest on an average of merely one child more or fewer per woman (UN 2013a). The implication is that while transition to a stable population cannot be guaranteed, there is scope to hasten it and thereby also to reduce the level at which it occurs. In its 2012 Revision the UN is explicit that an 11 billion peak (its medium projection) is contingent on taking urgent action: "without further reductions of fertility, the world population by 2100 could increase by nearly six times as much as currently expected." Were 2005–10 fertility rates to be sustained then closer to 28 billion could be the tally (UN 2013a, summary of findings: 3).

But even if stabilizing or reducing numbers were endorsed, could this feasibly be achieved without coercive methods or the framework of population control associated with them? During the mid-1990s, macro-level demographic concern was reframed as primarily an issue of women's reproductive health rather than in terms of resource shortages and environmental harm, thus helping to foreclose what was now defined as a "numbers game" antithetical to couples' right to choose their family size (Campbell

2007). An indication of how this issue might be renegotiated appears in *Return of the Population Growth Factor. Its Impact upon the Millennium Development Goals*, a report issued by Britain's All-Party Parliamentary Group on Population, Development and Reproductive Health. In hoping that "we will find a way to speak, from a human rights perspective, about both the importance of population stabilisation and the importance of supporting the rights of individuals to reproductive freedom" (APPGP 2007: 1) the Group's Chairwoman suggests a new synthesis of macro- and micro-level approaches. The concept of "unmet need" plays an important role here in legitimizing renewed international support for family planning programs. Surveys reveal that some 200 million women worldwide would voluntarily use modern contraception were it available. This would enhance their reproductive autonomy (Stephenson, Newman, and Mayhew 2010). This supply-side approach could help also to reduce the estimated 40 percent of conceptions that are unplanned even in developed countries, where information and services are often far less comprehensive than is assumed. But demand-side educational strategies are also surely needed in order to explain, including to those affluent couples who can afford more offspring, why small families are an environmentally responsible choice. Liberal governmentality provides numerous examples of equivalent attempts at behavior modification, such as regarding personal health regimes, which are regarded as perfectly acceptable. Indeed, despite a widespread reluctance to formulate a broader theoretical position on an optimum population level, the majority of countries do in fact have policies directed at reducing or, increasingly, raising their population growth and fertility rates (UN 2013b).

Whether high population growth causes underdevelopment or vice versa; whether, even if low fertility does follow from economic development, population will stabilize fast and low enough to avoid a chronic ecological crisis and how its effects will be distributed; whether the onset of climate change effects leaves us time or opportunity to await the establishment of a new equilibrium between numbers, consumer demands, technological innovations, and already stretched biophysical systems; whether the pursuit of poverty reduction, and of the Western lifestyles desired by a globally emergent middle class, are feasible in a world of 11 billion without either gross inequality or profound ecological destruction; whether, even if all can be sustained, and even sustained equitably, this will be worth the price of species extinction and loss of wilderness or green countryside; whether consumers can be persuaded to limit their demands and change their habits in order to support more people: these are some of the most pressing questions for the coming century. A major challenge for environmental theorists will be to find a politically and ethically acceptable way to frame these questions, given the profound misgivings and rationalities, the poisonous legacies and hegemonic interests, summarized in this chapter.

Ultimately, whether a world with fewer people is more sustainable and more conducive to equality, social justice, and quality of life is not a question that can be settled solely by statistics, computer models, and objective calculations of capacity. It requires a sustained critical analysis of interests invested in population/economic growth and a holistic appraisal of its existential costs at the level of everyday lives and ecosystems.

It invites normative reflection on the good life: a task for which political theorists are especially well-equipped. If they can construct a compelling, congenial vision of desirable lifestyles existing within realistic constraints under twenty-first century conditions, then today's theorists might rescue overpopulation concerns from assumptions that they are solely the currency of pessimists, racists, and misogynists. Or it may be the case that the conundrum mentioned at the start is simply irresolvable at present, especially as energetic migration flows vie with fertility as the main driver of population growth in developed regions and race combines with gender in new ways to render the topic unspeakable. In which case, Malthus might belatedly prove to have been right all along.

References

Alexandratos, N. (2005). "Countries with Rapid Population Growth and Resource Constraints: Issues of Food, Agriculture, and Development." *Population and Development Review* 31(2): 237–58.

All-Party Parliamentary Group on Population, Development and Reproductive Health. (APPGP). (2007), *Return of the Population Growth Factor. Its Impact upon the Millennium Development Goals* (London: Print Management Systems). Available at http://www.appg-popdevrh.org.uk

Attenborough, Sir D. (2011). "RSA President's Lecture 2011: People and the Planet."

Bauer, P. T. (1981). *Equality, The Third World and Economic Delusion* (Cambridge MA: Harvard University Press).

Beck, R. and Kolankiewicz, L. (2000). "The Environmental Movement's Retreat from Advocating U.S. Population Stabilization (1970–1998): A First draft of History." *Journal of Policy History* 12(1): 123–56.

Becker, G. S. (1960). "An Economic Analysis of Fertility." In *Demographic and Economic Change in Developed Countries*, by Universities-National Bureau (New York: Columbia University Press).

Campbell, M. (2007). "Why the Silence on Population?" *Population and Environment* 28: 237–46.

Cafaro, P. and Crist, E., eds. (2012). *Life on the Brink. Environmentalists Confront Overpopulation* (Athens GA: University of Georgia Press).

"Chinese Statements on Population at Bucharest, 1974, and Mexico City, 1984." *Population and Development Review* 20(2): 449–59.

Coleman, D. and Rowthorn, R. (2011). "Who's Afraid of Population Decline? A Critical Examination of its Consequences." *Population and Development Review* 37 (supplement): 217–48.

Coole, D. (2012). "Reconstructing the Elderly: A Critical Analysis of Pensions and Population Policies in an Era of Demographic Ageing." *Contemporary Political Theory* 11(1): 41–67.

Coole, D. (2013). "Too Many Bodies? The Return and Disavowal of the Population Question." *Environmental Politics* 22(2): 195–215.

Davis, A. (1982). *Women Race and Class* (London: The Women's Press).

Dorling, D. (2013). *Population 10 Billion. The Coming Demographic Crisis and How to Survive It* (London: Constable).

Ehrlich, P. (1972, orig. 1968). *The Population Bomb* (London: Pan/Ballantine).

Emmot, S. (2013). *10 Billion* (London: Penguin).
Finkle, J. L. and Crane, B. B. (1975). "The Politics of Bucharest: Population, Development, and the New International Economic Order." *Population and Development Review* 1(1): 87–114.
Firestone, S. (1970). *The Dialectic of Sex* (London: The Women's Press).
Foresight. (2011). *The Future of Food and Farming* (London: The Government Office for Science).
Grant, J. and Hoorens, S. (2006). "The New Pronatalism? The Policy Consequences of Population Ageing." *Public Policy Research* 13(1): 13–25.
Hardt, M. and Negri, A. (2004). *Multitude. War and Democracy in the Age of Empire* (New York: The Penguin Press).
Hodgson, D. (1988). "Orthodoxy and Revisionism in American Demography." *Population and Development Review* 14(4): 541–69.
Intergovernmental Panel on Climate Change (IPCC) (2014). *Fifth Assessment Report*.
Kirk, D. (1996). "Demographic Transition Theory." *Population Studies* 50(3): 361–87.
Lee, R. and Reher, D. (2011). "Introduction: The Landscape of Demographic Transition and Its Aftermath." *Population and Development Review* 37 (supplement): 1–7.
Livi-Bacci, M. (1997). *A Concise History of World Population*, 4th edn. (Oxford: Blackwell).
Malthus, T. R. (2004, orig. 1798). *An Essay on the Principle of Population* (Oxford: Oxford University Press).
Marcuse, H. (1964). *One-Dimensional Man* (London and New York: Routledge).
Marcuse, H. (1972 orig. 1969). *An Essay on Liberation* (Harmondsworth: Penguin).
Mayhew, R. (2014). *Malthus. The Life and Legacies of an Untimely Prophet* (Cambridge MA: Harvard University Press).
McMahon, P. (2013). *Feeding Frenzy. The New Politics of Food* (Suffolk: Profile Books).
Meadows, D. and Meadows, D. et al. (1972). *The Limits to Growth. A Report for the Club of Rome's Project on the Predicament of Mankind* (New York: Universe Books).
Mill, J. S. (1970, orig. 1848). *Principles of Political Economy*. Edited by D. Winch (Harmondsworth: Penguin).
Murtaugh, P. A. and Schlax, M. G. (2009). "Reproduction and the Carbon Legacies of Individuals." *Global Environmental Change* 19: 14–20.
Naess, A. (1973). "The Shallow and the Deep, Long-range Ecology Movement. A Summary." *Inquiry* 16(1): 95–100.
Nixon, R. (2006). "President Nixon on Problems of Population Growth." *Population and Development Review* 32(4): 771–82.
O'Neill, B. et al. "Global Demographic Trends and Future Carbon Emissions." *PNAS* 107(41): 17521–6.
Royal Commission on Environmental Pollution (RCEP). (2011). *The Environmental Impacts of Demographic Change in the UK* (London: The Stationary Office Ltd.) Available from http://www.official-documents.gov.uk
Royal Society. (2012). *People and the Planet* (London: Royal Society).
Simon, Julian. (1977). *The Economics of Population Growth* (Princeton NJ: Princeton University Press).
Stern, N. (2006). *The Stern Review. The Economics of Climate Change*. Available at http://webarchive.nationalarchives.gov.uk
Shiva, V. (2000). "Poverty and Globalisation". BBC Reith Lectures 2000, *Respect for the Earth*: lecture 5. Transcript available at http://www.bbc.co.uk/radio4/features/the-reith-lectures/transcripts/2000

Stephenson, J., Newman, K., and Mayhew, S. (2010). "Population Dynamics and Climate Change: What are the Links?" *Journal of Public Health* 32(2): 150–6.

Szreter, S. (1993). "The Idea of Demographic Transition and the Study of Fertility Change: A Critical Intellectual History." *Population and Development Review* 19(4): 659–701.

UN, DESA. (2013a). *World Population Prospects: The 2012 Revision*. http://esa.un.org/wpp/Documentation/publications.htm

UN, DESA. (2013b). *World Population Policies Report 2011* (UN, New York). Available at http://www.un.org/en/development/desa/population/publications/policy/world-population-policies-2013.shtml

US government. (1964). *Wilderness Act*. The Act can be downloaded from http://www.wilderness.net/nwps/legisact

Weisman, A. (2013). *Countdown. Our Last, Best Hope for a Future Earth?* (New York: Little, Brown and Co).

White House Office of Policy Development. (1984). "Policy Statement of the United States of America at the United Nations International Conference on Population." Reprinted in *Population and Development Review* 10(3): 574–9.

World Bank. (2012). *Turn Down the Heat. Why a 4° Centigrade Warmer World Must be Avoided*. http://climatechange.worldbank.org/sites/default/files/Turn_Down_the_heat_Why_a_4_degree_centrigrade_warmer_world_must_be_avoided.pdf

World Commission on Environment and Development (WCED). (1987). (The Brundtland Report), *Our Common Future*. United Nations, Annex to document A/42/427.

Yi, Z. (2007). "Options for Fertility Transition in China." *Population and Development Review* 33(2): 215–46.

CHAPTER 19

ARE THERE LIMITS TO LIMITS?

ANDREW DOBSON

INTRODUCTION

THE question that forms the title of this chapter is prompted by what has come to be known as the "limits to growth" thesis, and its centrality to the theory and practice of green—or environmental—politics. Ever since Christmas 1968 when the crew of the Apollo 8 spacecraft took the iconic "Earthrise" photograph, which emphasized the finitude of the planet, and the publication of *The Limits to Growth* report in 1972, which outlined the implications of this finitude for political, social, and economic systems aspiring to ever-increasing economic growth, the idea of "limits" has been a key—and contested—feature of environmental politics. However, the importance of limits to this politics has waxed and waned over the years. It was perhaps inevitable that it would be questioned by those who had a stake in business as usual, and also by those who in entirely good faith were unpersuaded by the claims made in the 1972 report. It has also come in for criticism from those within the green movement, working in the mainstream of politics, who have found the limits message to be an electoral liability, and by some in the global South who see in limits to growth a form of Malthusianism that inevitably leads to a focus on "overpopulation" and an analysis centered on blaming "the poor" for the world's ecological problems.

In this chapter I will briefly outline the limits to growth thesis, describe and assess some of the critical reactions to it, and comment upon its relevance today. I have argued elsewhere (Dobson 2006) that limits to growth is (or was) one of the three main building blocks of an ideology I called "ecologism," so the career of the concept is important for an understanding of the development of the ideology, and of its nature today. My argument will be that from its initial highpoint in the early 1970s, the thesis declined in importance during the 1980s and 1990s under sustained and effective attack, from those who felt that it was just plain wrong, from those who argued that, while there might be some truth in it, its challenge could be met by more reformist and less radical policies than those suggested in, or implied by, the 1972 report, and by those in the global South who see it as a thinly disguised way of diverting blame for ecological problems from the rich and powerful to the poor and dispossessed. (It is worth pointing out that while the limits thesis was being called into question during this period, the team that put the original report together published two updates (in Meadows et al. 1992 and Meadows et al. 2005 respectively) which amounted to a reiteration of the original message: that infinite growth in a finite system is an impossible aspiration). The limits argument has in any case seen something of a renaissance in recent years in the wake of the "peak oil" debate and a generalized renewed concern about the effects of continued economic growth. Climate change has also had a role to play, though in a slightly more nuanced way. From a limits point of view, climate change is caused by the inability of the global "sinks" for greenhouse gases to cope with the level of emissions that human activity has generated since the beginning of the Industrial Revolution. I say "nuanced" because from another point of view, climate change is more obviously related to excess (of production, emissions, etc.) than it is to limits. All of this has led to debates about "degrowth" and "post-growth" which look quite similar to those that took place in the 1970s. Perhaps the biggest difference is that those who advocate degrowth now are doing so in the belief that resource scarcity and its implications are not a putative condition of the future but an actual condition of the present.

The Limits to Growth Thesis

The authors of the 1972 report identified "5 trends of global concern": "accelerating industrialization, rapid population growth, widespread malnutrition, depletion of non-renewable resources, and a deteriorating environment" (Meadows et al. 1974: 21). They then created a computer model containing the variables relating to these trends with a view to mapping their future development given different kinds of scenario. In the first computer run the team assumed "business as usual," extrapolating current trends into the future up to the year 2100. In this run, the determining feature in eventual system collapse was the depletion of non-renewable resources. The standard response of the skeptic at this point is to say that it is a mistake to take what we currently believe to be the stock of non-renewable resources as a guide to those that will be available to us in the future. The skeptic will draw a distinction between, for example, "conventional" and "non-conventional" gas, where the former refers to a deposit that has accumulated in one relatively easily accessible space, while the latter refers to gas that is trapped in impermeable rock and which needs to be released by unconventional means such as "hydraulic fracturing" (or "fracking"). The conclusion the skeptic will draw from this is that the limits team has underestimated the amount of non-renewable resources available to us, and that therefore the timetable for collapse is unduly pessimistic.

At this point, the heuristic power of this approach to illustrating the limits to growth becomes clear. Instead of confronting the skeptic head on and making a counterclaim regarding the scarcity of non-renewable resources, the limits team programmed a computer run which allowed for a doubling in the availability of such resources. This move both disarms the skeptic (to some extent at least) and shows that, far from solving the growth problem, doubling the amount of non-renewable resources available to us simply results in a different kind of collapse—due this time to the uncontrolled pollution resulting from increased industrial growth. The rest of *The Limits to Growth* report is taken up with following this serial problem-solving approach through to its conclusion. Even with solutions in place to each of the five problematic global trends, the computer model suggests eventual collapse:

> The result is still an end to growth before the year 2100. In this case growth is stopped by three simultaneous crises. Overuse of the land leads to erosion, and food production drops. Resources are severely depleted by a prosperous world population (but not as prosperous as the present US population). Pollution rises, drops then rises again dramatically, causing a further decrease in food production and a sudden rise in the death rate. (Meadows et al. 1974: 141)

Once the modeling was complete, Meadows and her colleagues drew two overall conclusions: first, that technology cannot solve the limits to growth problem, and second, that the five global trends on which they focus are interrelated. The limits argument is not that technology will play no role in the sustainable society, but that technologies must be deployed in the knowledge that solving one problem may exacerbate another. This notion echoes the "holism" that one often finds in green social thought. It is also to say that achieving sustainability is as much a political, social, and economic challenge as it is a techno-scientific one.

Responses to the Limits to Growth Thesis

Technological Optimism

The limits to growth thesis has prompted three types of critical response. First, there are those who argue that the report underestimates the capacity of human ingenuity to overcome these limits. While this could refer to ingenuity of all types, including ingenuity in regard to social, political, and economic arrangements, it generally refers to technological ingenuity—including the technology of policy-making. This is an especially important fault line between limits to growth and its critics since those who argue in favor of limits argue for the necessity of radical social change,[1] as this—they say—is a necessary condition for living with limits. Those who argue against the limits to growth idea, though, focus on technological ingenuity in the belief that resource-based and other environmental problems can be dealt with through the deployment of clever (social) science and its practical applications. This position is often referred to as one of "ecological modernization." According to ecological modernizers, environmental problems related to economic growth can be dealt with by new policy-making principles, such as integrating the possibility of environmental damage into cost benefit analysis. More particularly, they argue that limits to growth can be significantly if not wholly pushed back by efficiency gains created by smarter techniques of production and distribution. This has been popularized as the "dematerialization" thesis, or the Factor 4 or Factor 10 movement, according to which, with suitable efficiencies one can get either four or 10 times the product from the same amount of input, thus reducing the environmental impact of production by approximately four or 10 times. Critics of this approach point out that, even assuming fourfold efficiencies, resource consumption would be eight times higher after 100 years and 243 times higher after 200 years, assuming growth rates of 3.5 percent per year (Xue 2010: 9). Neither side has gained the upper hand in this process of claim and counterclaim. Supporters of the limits idea constantly refer back to the finite planet depicted through the window of Apollo 8 and argue that, at some point, either non-renewable resources will run out, or the planet's capacity to absorb waste at a rate and level consistent with a comfortable life of humans will be exhausted. Ecological modernizers and dematerialists rest their case on historical experience and on the seemingly endless capacity of human beings to solve problems that they have created.

Substitutability

Some of the sting can be drawn from the limits to growth thesis by arguing for the substitutability of resources, and this is at the heart of the second response to the limits to growth thesis. After all, the decline in the availability of any given resource is less pressing if that resource can be replaced by another, perhaps even more plentiful, one. It is important to note, though, that the word "replaced" can be understood in a number of ways, and the success of the substitutability argument depends to some extent on understanding it in a quite particular way. Take energy for example. We are interested in energy for what it can do for us, and all other things being equal we are not interested in any particular form of energy as long as it does the job. In this sense, different sources of energy are substitutable for each other. So while it might be pointed out that coal will run out in, say, 300 years, this cannot be regarded as a limit to growth as long as some other form of energy is available.

But not all resources are like this—trees, for example. Of course in some senses one tree, or even species of tree, is much like another. So while it might be true that some species of tree provide better wood for building than others, we can build a wooden shelter using pretty much any kind of tree. But not all trees are substitutable in this way—they may be invested with cultural and historical meaning, for example, such that they are seen as irreplaceable to those for whom they have such meaning. Imagine a classic English village green with a yew tree on it. Imagine that the village magazine is called *The Yew Tree*. Imagine that a crucial piece of development (say flood drainage works) requires that the yew tree be removed, but that the developers undertake to replace the yew tree with another tree—even another yew tree. Would this substitution be acceptable to the village residents? Some might not be especially bothered, but others might regard the yew tree as embodying irreplaceable—"uncopiable"—historical and cultural value. For these others, even moving the original yew tree to some other part of the village might well be an indefensible move, since part of its historical and cultural value resides in its specific location in the village's topography.

The power of this example, such as it is, rests on an argument from the unique cultural value of objects. This taps into the debate about "weak" and "strong" sustainability. Those who argue from the point of view of weak sustainability say that human capital can substitute for natural capital. This means that natural capital does not need protecting or conserving in its own right, since any loss of natural capital can be compensated for by human capital. In contrast, the strong sustainability position holds that human and natural capital are complementary rather than interchangeable. This implies that (some) natural capital requires protection in its own right because it cannot be substituted for by human capital (Beckerman 1995; Daly 1995; Holland 1997). Those who argue, in the example above, that the village's yew tree cannot be substituted for by another one, are arguing for a particular form of strong sustainability. In this case, what cannot be substituted for adequately is the original yew tree, because of its unique cultural/historical value.

But those who argue against the limits to growth thesis from a substitutability point of view will say that cultural value is generally not at issue: few would oppose the substitution of gas by nuclear energy, for example, on the grounds that the former has a unique and irreplaceable historical and cultural value. What *is* at issue, it will be said, is the degree to which *natural* objects can be substituted for. This substitution can itself take two forms: first, one natural object for another, and second, natural objects for human made objects (or, as it is often put, natural capital for human capital). The idea and practice of substituting natural objects for one another lies behind the increasingly popular "offsetting" approach to land use planning. The problem with which policymakers are confronted is that development can cause damage to habitats and other environmental assets. The challenge is to square the circle in such a way as to allow for development while preserving these assets. In this context, "Biodiversity offsets are conservation activities designed to deliver biodiversity benefits in compensation for losses in a measurable way. Good developments incorporate biodiversity considerations in their design but are still likely to result in some biodiversity loss. One way to compensate for this loss is by offsetting: the developer secures compensatory habitat expansion or restoration elsewhere" (DEFRA 2011: 22). For offsetting to work, habitats need to be turned into "a symbolic numerical measure, in order to make two different places commensurable with each other, and also able to assume the monetary value (price) required for a marketized exchange" (Hannis and Sullivan 2012: 10). Critics of this approach say that this drive to commensurability eradicates what is of value in the natural objects, or collections of objects, in question: their very uniqueness. Substitutability helps us to overcome a limit, but arguably at the cost of reducing richness and diversity.

The discussion above refers to the substitution of one natural object, or collection of objects, for another, or others. There is also the possibility of substituting human made objects for natural ones—the substitution of human capital for natural capital. This idea is captured by the Nobel prize-winning economist Robert Solow, who writes that, "the duty imposed by sustainability is to bequeath to posterity not any particular thing . . . but rather to endow them with whatever it takes to achieve a standard of living at least as good as our own . . . We are not to consume humanity's capital, in the broadest sense" (1992: 15). The inhabitants of our imaginary village, above, would radically disagree with Solow on the grounds that their duty to the future is, precisely, to "bequeath to posterity . . . [a] particular thing"—in their case, the yew tree. Solow, in contrast, believes in the perfect substitutability of human made from natural capital. Thus every loss of natural capital can be compensated for by increases in capital of human origin. Put crudely, plastic trees can be designed to perform the same ecological functions as real ones, and the loss of real ones represents no decline in the "overall capital base" (Bartelmus 1994: 65).

Even from a functional point of view, Solow's substitutability view might be regarded as having its shortcomings. Ecological economists such as Herman Daly and John Cobb talk of the complementarity, rather than the substitutability, of resources. Thus: "Capital cannot ultimately substitute for resources because capital itself is composed of resources . . . labor and capital complement the material resources that are transformed into a product" (Daly and Cobb 1989: 409). More pithily: "what good is the capital represented by a refinery if there is no petroleum?" (Daly and Cobb 1989: 198).

This is the point at which the sustainability debate meets the limits to growth debate, since:

> If natural and man-made capital were substitutes (weak sustainability) then neither could be a limiting factor. If, however, they are complements (strong sustainability), then the one in short supply is limiting. Historically, in the "empty world" economy, man-made capital was limiting and natural capital superabundant. We have now, due to demographic and economic growth, entered the year of the "full world" economy, in which the roles are reversed. More and more it is the remaining natural capital that now plays the role of limiting factor. The fish catch is not limited by fishing boats, but by remaining populations of fish in the sea. (Daly 1995: 50)

So the success of the substitutability response to the limits to growth thesis depends to some extent on the practical viability of substituting human for natural capital. It also depends on dealing with any objections there might be to talking of nature in terms of "capital" at all. The example of the village yew tree, above, should make it clear that these objections might also be of some moment. Recognition of this will help us to avoid the tendency to think that arguments over limits to growth can be solved by the deployment of empirical argument: there is an ineluctably ethical component to the debate as well.

Economic Growth as a Precondition for Environmental Protection

The third response to the limits to growth thesis comes from those who argue that economic growth is a necessary condition for environmental sustainability—or that environmental problems produced by growth can be solved by smarter growth. One of the most sophisticated and best known versions of this response is based upon the so-called "environmental Kuznets curve." The Kuznets curve was originally developed by Simon Kuznets (1955; see also Stern 2004), and it describes the supposed relationship between inequality and economic development. According to Kuznets, as an economy develops, inequality increases, then after a certain point of development—when a certain average income is achieved—inequality decreases. The environmental version of the Kuznets curve suggests that environmental quality decreases as an economy develops, but then once a certain average income is achieved, environmental quality increases. On this account, economic growth—in the long run at least—is beneficial for environmental sustainability.

There is certainly an on-the-face-of-it plausibility to the environmental Kuznets curve hypothesis: one does not have to follow the news for very long to be aware of mounting air pollution problems in rapidly developing countries such as China, whereas already industrialized—or post-industrialized—countries such as the UK have relatively smoke-free cities. Moreover, we hear Chinese environmental officials placing their faith in the historical experience of countries such as the UK, averring that China only has to follow the development path of so-called advanced industrial countries in order to experience the same environmental improvements. These are Kuznets remarks in all but name. But the hypothesis is open to objection. So while, for example, the evidence suggests that local pollutants follow Kuznets predictions, global ones do not (York, Rosa and Dietz 2003; Dinda 2004). Our putative Chinese environmental official, then, might be right about the smog, but development would almost certainly be accompanied by an increase in global pollutants such as those associated, for example, with climate change. It is also possible that environmental quality in relatively developed countries improves because environmentally damaging activities are relocated to developing countries. In this sense, environmental degradation is effectively outsourced/exported from richer countries to poorer ones. There are signs, indeed, that this is what is happening (Cole, Elliott, Okubo 2012), as industrial production is relocated from Europe and North America to Southeast Asia, and as China follows a similar pattern by buying up tracts of the continent of Africa. At some point, this "race to the bottom" will reach the bottom, and countries at the end of the chain will be forced to mitigate and/or adapt to environmental degradation, rather than export it elsewhere.

An Attack on the Poor and Vulnerable?

In his *An Essay on the Principles of Population* (1798), Thomas Malthus argued that the tendency for population to grow at a faster rate than food supply would lead to starvation. This led him to argue for population restraint, through moral stricture, restricting the circumstances in which the poor and/or those with psychological defects could get married. While Malthus talked exclusively about the relationship between population growth and food supply, the idea that population might outstrip a range of resource supplies has given rise to the term "Malthusianism." This is usually a pejorative term, either because Malthus is taken simply to have been wrong about population outstripping food supply (and, by extension, other resources too), or because of his focus on the poor as the root of the problem of resource supply. The first of these two critiques takes the form—in the context of the reaction to *The Limits to Growth*—of ecological modernization, discussed earlier. I will discuss the second now.

One response to the limits to growth thesis was Garrett Hardin's "lifeboat ethics" (1974). Hardin argued that in resource terms the world is like a lifeboat, with room for 60 people in it, surrounded by 100 swimmers. The lifeboat represents the rich countries and the swimmers represent poor countries. This metaphor trades on the limits to growth argument by stressing the apparently fixed availability of resources available on the lifeboat. Hardin argued that taking all 100 swimmers on board the lifeboat would result in disaster, as there are only sufficient resources for 60. This, for Hardin, leaves one option: leave the 100 swimmers in the water.

The combination of Malthus and Hardin has led to wholesale suspicion in the global South of the limits to growth argument. To the extent that it draws on Malthus it appears to blame the poor for resource scarcity, and to the extent that it draws on Hardin it appears to deny the poor a fair share of the resources there are. Neither of these conclusions necessarily follows from the limits to growth argument, however. First it can be argued that resource scarcity is much more obviously the fault of the rich than of the poor because their lives are more resource intensive. It is well known and widely accepted that the per capita carbon emissions of rich countries are greater than those of poor countries, for example. It is also true that the distribution of carbon emissions within countries is uneven—there are poor people in rich countries and rich people in poor ones. All this suggests that the limits to growth thesis does not lead inexorably to blaming the poor for resource scarcity, because in actual fact it is the rich who "overuse" resources.

Nor do we need necessarily to conclude, as Hardin does, that the only course of action in the context of resource scarcity is to distribute resources unequally. At least as far as the satisfaction of basic needs is concerned, it can be persuasively argued from a human rights point of view that resources should be equally distributed. This suggests that limits to growth is indeterminate as far as normative conclusions are concerned: it does not lead, necessarily, to any particular conclusion regarding social and political arrangements.

The Return of Limits to Growth

Peak Oil

It is fair to say that three of these responses to the limits to growth idea—ecological modernization, substitutability, and versions of the environmental Kuznets curve—were convincing enough to push the idea from center stage for much of the 1990s. Lurking in the background, though, was M. King Hubbert, and a theory to which his work gave rise has breathed new life into the limits to growth argument. This renaissance of the limits to growth position has spawned a set of new terms around which the debate now revolves: "peak everything" (Heinberg 2007), degrowth, transition, and resilience. In the 1950s, Hubbert—a geoscientist—argued that the rate of oil production in any given location (from the local to the global) would follow a Bell curve. This curve has a peak, which represents the maximum rate of production, after which the rate will go into decline. Given the degree to which modern societies are reliant on oil for production, food, housing, transport, and recreation, and the increase in oil production and consumption as developing countries power up their societies, the peak oil thesis sets up collapse scenarios very similar to those envisaged in the original limits to growth report. Arguments have raged over the timing of the peak oil moment: has it passed, are we in the middle of it, or is it yet to come? Whatever the exact answer to this question, one striking difference between the limits to growth report of the early 1970s and the contemporary peak oil debate, is that, while the former suggested that depletion would occur sometime in the future, the latter is located in the here and now. This is one reason why the idea of peak oil has made such an impact: the relative immediacy of its potential effects.

Economic Growth and Environmental Degradation: Relative and Absolute Decoupling

Peak oil is evidently a challenge to the business as usual prospectus of ecological modernization, and it seems fair to regard it as a reassertion of the limits to growth thesis in a more particular form. But it is not the only route to this reassertion. It will be remembered that at the heart of ecological modernization lies the idea that economic growth and environmental degradation can be decoupled, such that we can simultaneously have more of the former and less of the latter. Tim Jackson, among others, has drawn our attention to the need to distinguish between relative and absolute decoupling. As he puts it, "Relative decoupling refers to a decline in the ecological intensity per unit of economic output. In this situation, resource impacts decline relative to the GDP. But they don't necessarily decline in absolute terms. Impacts may still increase, but at a slower pace than growth in the GDP" (Jackson 2009: 48). Relative decoupling amounts to an endorsement of the ecological modernization idea: that more efficient use of tools and technology can decrease the environmental impact associated with the production of each unit of economic output—or, simply, doing more with less. But if one subscribes to the idea of ecological limits, relative decoupling is clearly not good enough because impacts are still increasing. In contrast to this, writes Jackson, "The situation in which resource impacts decline in absolute terms is called 'absolute decoupling.' Needless to say, this latter situation is essential if economic activity is to remain within ecological limits" (2009: 48). Jackson says that absolute decoupling is essential for long-term sustainability, but suggests that the distinction between relative and absolute decoupling is rarely drawn in sustainability debates. In his view, the chances of absolute decoupling based on technological advances alone are slim, and there is little if any evidence for it ever having been achieved in any sector. There is more than an echo here of the conclusion reached by the limits to growth team in the original report after they ran their final world model computer simulation with "unlimited" resources, pollution controls, increased agricultural productivity, and "perfect" birth control: "The result is still an end to growth before the year 2100 . . . The application of technological solutions alone has prolonged the period of population and industrial growth, but it has not removed the ultimate limits to that growth" (Meadows et al. 1974: 141).

Planetary Boundaries

Peak oil and the debate over the possibility for the absolute decoupling of economic growth and environmental degradation are two of the responses to the business as usual economic modernization idea. A third contemporary reassertion of the limits to growth idea comes in the form of the notion of "planetary boundaries." This concept, which is best known through the work of Johan Rockström and his colleagues (Rockström et al. 2009), relies heavily on the limits to growth idea and the systems analysis methodology that underlay it. Rockström distinguishes between thresholds and boundaries. The former are "non-linear transitions in the functioning of coupled human–environmental systems" (2009: 2) which are intrinsic to those systems. One example of a non-linear transition is what is commonly referred to as "runaway climate change." The idea is that, at a certain tipping point, linear and rather predictable changes flip into a different dimension in which feedback loops generate rapid and unexpected change. Some argue that the recent decline in Arctic sea ice is an example of such a non-linear transition in its early stages. Boundaries, on the other hand, are human-determined variables which involve normative decisions regarding safety, risk, and uncertainty. Taking into account what we know about these variables in the context of "a state conducive to human development" (2009: 23) Rockström and his colleagues suggest that three of the nine boundaries they identify have already been transgressed—climate change, the rate of biodiversity loss, and the rate of interference with the nitrogen cycle (2009: 23).[2] The conclusion reached by the planetary boundaries team is very similar indeed to that found in the original limits to growth thesis: "[the dynamics of the system] lull us into a false sense of security because incremental change can lead to the unexpected crossing of thresholds that drive the Earth System, or significant subsystems, abruptly into states deleterious or even catastrophic to human well-being. The concept of planetary boundaries provides a framework for humanity to operate within this paradox" (2009: 23).

Degrowth and Re-localization

Now, as when the limits to growth thesis was first presented, one outcome of the perceived imminence of the large scale changes presaged by peak oil is the amount of time spent thinking about the transition to a society in which absolute decoupling is the norm. Those who work in the field of degrowth do not doubt that we are heading for such a society: "The reality is that we are approaching a time of economic contraction" (Heinberg 2007: 18). The question is whether we will get there "intelligently or in an uncontrolled, chaotic fashion" (Heinberg 2007: 8). The global economic crisis which began in 2008 is a warning in regard to what can happen if contraction is uncontrolled and chaotic: "We know that simply contracting the economy plunges our societies into disarray, increases the rate of unemployment and hastens the demise of the health, social, educational, cultural, and environmental projects that provide us with an indispensable minimal quality of life" (Latouche 2009: 8). A considerable amount of thought is now being given to the conditions and preconditions for a controlled energy and resource descent, consistent with equity and fairness (see, for example, Dobson 2014). This has breathed new life into another element of the early ideology of ecologism which seemed to have withered in the face of the ecological modernization response to the original limits to growth thesis. Once ecological modernization took hold in the environmentalist imaginary the idea of the "green state" prospered. It seemed obvious that, while the market would be a necessary feature of the mechanisms for ecological modernization, regulation would be the catalyst for initiating the "race to the top" that such modernization involves. The source of this regulation is the state and its agents—hence the idea of a green state. This is a far cry from Alan Carter's view that the state is at the heart of an "ecologically hazardous dynamic" (Carter 1999). Both the globalization of environmental degradation and ecological modernization seemed to sound the death knell of the anti- or post-state politics represented by Carter; the old green adage "think globally, act locally" appeared hopelessly naive and unrealistic. During this period, far-reaching attempts were made to describe what a "green" or "eco" state would look like (De Geus 1996; Eckersley 2004).

In contrast, analysts of the degrowth or post-growth society argue for re-localization in much the same way and for much the same reasons as those who argued for the ideology of ecologism in the 1970s and 1980s. So as Serge Latouche—a central figure in degrowth thinking—writes, "Re-localization . . . has a central role to play in our concrete utopia, and almost immediately suggests a political programmed. Degrowth appears to give a new life to the ecologist's old slogan of 'Think globally, act locally' " (2009: 44). In a sonorous echo of ecological decentralist thinking from 30 or 40 years ago, Latouche offers a series of ecological and political (democratic) reasons for re-localization: "less transport, transparent production lines, incentivizing sustainable production and consumption, reducing dependency upon capital flow and multinationals ... [it] ... facilitates a more democratic approach to the economy, reduces unemployment, increases participation ... encourages solidarity ... improves the health of citizens in the rich countries by encouraging sobriety and reducing stress" (2009: 50). On this reading, limits to growth is not a penance to be borne but an opportunity to be grasped: an opportunity for healthier, happier, and fairer lives for all. In this sense, peak oil has sparked anew the old debates around the possibilities of green utopianism.

The Transition Movement

Nowhere is this more obvious than in the real world phenomenon to which peak oil has given rise: the Transition movement. Founded in the UK town of Totnes in 2005, the Transition movement now numbers communities in the United States, Canada, Italy, Japan, Germany, Ireland, New Zealand, Chile, the Netherlands, Brazil, and beyond (Smith 2011: 99). The key assumption behind the Transition movement is that peak oil will inevitably bring in its train low energy forms of living. Transitioners share the analysis, outlined above, that this change could be either catastrophic or benign, and they believe that it is more likely to be benign if preparations are made now for living in low energy societies. A key term for transitioners is "resilience": they believe that complex, energy-rich societies lack the resilience that will enable them to confront the massive changes that peak oil will bring in its train. For transitioners, preparedness comes in the form of Transition towns/communities, founded and operated in the here and now. Once again, the language of the Transition project is reminiscent of the decentralist ecological utopianism which followed the limits to growth report of 40 years ago. As the founder of the Transition movement, Rob Hopkins, puts it: "Rebuilding local agriculture and food production, localizing energy production, rethinking health care, rediscovering local building materials in the context of zero energy building, rethinking how we manage waste, all build resilience and offer the potential for an *extraordinary* renaissance—economic, cultural and spiritual" (quoted in Smith 2011: 100; emphasis in the original).

Conclusion

So, to return to the title of the chapter, are there limits to limits? About 10 years ago it seemed as though there were—at least as far as the idea, and its impact upon green/environmental/ecological thinking and practice, were concerned. The notion seemed to have run aground, beached by a combination of techno-optimism from without and skepticism about its apolitical naturalized determinism from within (Bettini and Karaliotas 2013). However, the rise of the discourse of peak oil, a renaissance of the debate around the possibility and necessity of a path to prosperity without growth, and a revamped version of the limits to growth thesis in the guise of the idea of planetary boundaries, all amount to a recognizable second wave of limits to growth thinking. Accompanied as this is by a raft of thinking around what a re-localized post-growth society might look like, the current situation is very much back to the future. Or should that be Groundhog Day?

Notes

1. I have in mind here the distinction between "environmentalism" and "ecologism", defined as follows: "environmentalism argues for a managerial approach to environmental problems, secure in the belief that they can be solved without fundamental changes in present values or patterns of production and consumption"; "ecologism holds that a sustainable and fulfilling existence presupposes radical changes in our relationship with the non-human natural world, and in our mode of social and political life" (Dobson 2006: 2–3). The "radical social change" referred to here relates to ecologism.
2. The other boundaries are ocean acidification, land use, freshwater, ozone depletion, atmospheric aerosols, and chemical pollution. The distinction between "thresholds" and "boundaries", based on the idea that the latter are human-determined variables while the former are not, is open to question. The example given by Rockström of a threshold—climate change—is surely human-determined, especially when coupled with the adjective "runaway". A question we would have to answer is "runaway for whom or what?", and the answer to this question will involve normative debate regarding the objects of concern (Humans? Non-humans? Which non-humans?).

References

Bartelmus, Peter. (1994). *Environment, Growth and Development: The Concepts and Strategies of Sustainable Development* (London: Routledge).

Beckerman, Wilfred (2005). "How Would You Like Your 'Sustainability,' Sir? Weak Or Strong?" *Environmental Values* 3(3): 191–209.

Bettini, Giovanni and Karaliotas, Lazaros. (2013). "Exploring the Limits of Peak Loyal: Naturalising the Political, De-politicising Energy." *The Geographical Journal* 179(4): 331–41.

Carter, Alan. (1999). *A Radical Green Political Theory* (New York and London: Routledge).

Cole, Matthew, Elliott, Robert, and Okubo, Toshihiro. (2012). "International Environmental Outsourcing," paper presented at the 10th Annual Conference of the Euro-Latin Study Network on Integration and Trade, Milan, Italy (http://www10.iadb.org/intal/intalcdi/PE/2012/10379a03.pdf accessed July 21, 2014).

Daly, Herman. (1995). "On Wilfred Beckerman's Critique of Sustainable Development." *Environmental Values* 4(1): 49–55.

Daly, Herman and Cobb, John. (1989). *For the Common Good: Restructuring the Economy toward Community, the Environment and a Sustainable Future* (Boston: Beacon Press).
DEFRA. (2011). "The Natural Choice; Securing the Value of Nature." *Natural Environment White Paper* (NEWP) (http://www.defra.gov.uk/environment/natural/whitepaper/ accessed January 14, 2014).
De Geus, Marius. (1996). "The Ecological Restructuring of the State." In *Democracy and Green Political Thought*, edited by Brian Doherty and Marius De Geus (London and New York: Routledge), 185–206.
Dinda, Soumyananda. (2004). "Environmental Kuznets Curve Hypothesis: A Survey." *Ecological Economics* 49: 431–55.
Dobson, Andrew. (2006). *Green Political Thought*, 4th edn. (London and New York: Routledge).
Dobson, Andrew. (2014). "The Politics of Post-Growth." Green House Think Tank (http://www.greenhousethinktank.org accessed June 22, 2015).
Eckersley, Robyn. (2004). *The Green State: Rethinking Democracy and Sovereignty* (Cambridge, MA, and London: MIT Press).
Hannis, Mike and Sullivan, Sian. (2012). *Offsetting Nature? Habitat Banking and Biodiversity Offsets in the English Land Use Planning System* (Weymouth, Green House) (http://www.greenhousethinktank.org/files/greenhouse/home/Offsetting_nature_inner_final.pdf accessed January 14, 2014).
Hardin, Garrett. (1974). "Living in a Lifeboat." *Bioscience* 24(10): 561–8.
Heinberg, Richard. (2007). *Peak Everything: Waking Up to the Century of Decline in Earth's Resources* (Forest Row: Clairview Books).
Holland, Alan. (1997). "Substitutability: or, Why Strong Sustainability is Weak and Absurdly Strong Sustainability Is Not Absurd." In *Valuing Nature? Economics, Ethics and the Environment*, edited by John Foster and Alan Holland (London: Routledge), 119–34.
Jackson, Tim. (2009). *Prosperity Without Growth?—Steps Towards a Sustainable Society* (London: Sustainable Development Commission).
Kuznets, Simon. (1955). "Economic Growth and Income Inequality." *American Economic Review* 45 (March): 1–28.
Latouche, Serge. (2009). *Farewell to Growth* (Cambridge: Polity Press).
Meadows, Donella, Meadows, Dennis, Randers, Jørgen, and Beerens III, William. (1974). *The Limits to Growth* (London: Pan).
Meadows, Donella, Meadows, Dennis, Randers, Jørgen, Beerens III, William. (1992). *Beyond The Limits: Global Collapse or a Sustainable Future* (London: Earthscan).
Meadows, Donella, Meadows, Dennis, Randers, Jørgen, Beerens III, William. (2005). *The limits to Growth: The 30-year Update* (London: Earthscan).
Johan Rockström et al. (2009). "Planetary Boundaries: Exploring the Safe Operating Space for Humanity." *Ecology and Society* 10(2): 1–33 (available at http://www.ecologyandsociety.org/vol14/iss2/art32/ PDF version; accessed February 28, 2014).
Smith, Amanda (2011), "The Transition Town Network: A Review of Current Evolutions and Renaissance," *Social Movement Studies*, Volume 10 Number 1: 99–105
Solow, Robert (1993), "An Almost Practical Step toward Sustainability," *Resources Policy* (September): 162–172 (available at http://www.stanford.edu/class/econ155/coursework/CourseMaterials/Readings/Solow-Sustainability.pdf accessed January 15, 2014).

Stern, David. (2004). "The Rise and Fall of the Environmental Kuznets Curve." *World Development* 32(8): 1419–39.
Xue, Jin. (2010). "Arguments For and Against Economic Growth" (http://www.barcelona.degrowth.org/fileadmin/content/documents/Proceedings/Xue_Jin.pdf accessed January 13, 2014).
York, R., Rosa, E. A. and Dietz, T. (2003). "Footprints on the Earth: The Environmental Consequences of Modernity." *American Sociological Review* 68(2), 279–300.

CHAPTER 20

GREEN POLITICAL ECONOMY

Beyond Orthodox Undifferentiated Economic Growth as a Permanent Feature of the Economy

JOHN BARRY

Introduction: Origins and Overview of Green Political Economy

A potted historical evolution of green economic thinking would include Aristotle's distinction between "*oikonomia*" or management of the household and "*chremastistics*" or money-making; the French Physiocrats in the eighteenth century in relation to their analysis of the importance of the land and agriculture to the economy; Thomas Malthus as an early proponent of "limits to growth"; Karl Marx in relation to his foundational critique of capitalism and class exploitation and for his analysis of the inner workings of capital accumulation; John Stuart Mill's defense of the "stationary state" economy in the mid-nineteenth century (a forerunner of Herman Daly's later work in the 1970s on "steady-state economics"); twentieth-century thinkers such as E. F. Schumacher, for his "small is beautiful" concept, "Buddhist economics" and the injunction for "an economics as if people mattered" (Schumacher, 1973); Ivan Illich for his trenchant critique of dehumanizing institutions and defense of the convivial economy (Illich 1973); Herman Daly, the founder of modern "ecological economics" (Daly 1973); and Dennis and Donella Meadows and the Club of Rome for their ground-breaking "Limits to Growth" reports from the 1970s, and on (Meadows et al. 1972; Meadows et al. 2004).

And yet despite this lineage, green political economy, as a "heterodox" school of economic thinking, is marginal and lacks influence and status in comparison to dominant neo-classical economics. By neo-classical economics I mean a form of asserted value-neutral, objective knowledge of the human economy, which assumes a view of the human being as "homo economicus" (rational, selfish, and possessive), and a view of the human economy as ecologically disembedded, that is, ecologically ignorant. It is marked by an ideological preference for the free market and capitalism (Barry 2012: 121–2), even though it rarely uses the term "capitalism," nor countenances alternative non-capitalist forms of economics or ways of organizing the human economy. For Stanford:

> Neoclassical economics is dedicated to the study of capitalism; in fact, other kinds of economies (that existed in the past, or that may exist in the future) are not even contemplated. Yet the term "capitalism" does not appear in neoclassical economics textbooks. *Instead, economists refer simply to "the economy"—as if there is only one kind of economy, and hence no need to name or define it.* This is wrong . . . "the economy" is simply where people work to produce the things we need and want. There are different ways to organize that work. Capitalism is just one of them. (Stanford 2008: 33; emphasis added)

As Molly Cato notes "Green economics is not, as yet, an academic discipline with a major place in the universities" (Cato 2008: 5), and there are very few self-declared "green economists" or "green political economists" within the academy or elsewhere. By "green economics" I mean something distinct from both "environmental economics" and "ecological economics." While environmental economics does discuss ecological "externalities" and resource problems, it does so from within the dominant neo-classical, capitalist/market model, and neither questions economic growth nor offers a deeper or integrated view of the economy as both ecologically embedded (and therefore limited) as well as politically, culturally, and socially embedded (and therefore a political creation not "naturally given"). Ecological economics does move us further toward a scientific/metabolic and energy/resource understanding of the human economy. However, while it does not rule out explicitly normative ethical and political concerns, these prescriptive elements are not a systematic feature of its approach. Green political economy on the other hand is explicitly political, critical, and prescriptive and takes the economy and how we think about it is a site of contestation and an exercise in power. This power is on the one hand the power and struggle of ideas and, related to that, how those ideas that win or are dominant create the economy they prescribe. In other words, dominant framings or conceptualizations of the economy, such as neo-classical/capitalist economics, do not "objectively" or "neutrally" simply *describe* an economy that "just is," but rather actively *prescribe* and bring into being an economic system aligned with normative and ideological assumptions.

It is as pioneers of an "old/new" approach to understanding the economy and its relationship to the non-human world, politics, ethics, and human well-being, and its challenge to a dominant neo-classical economic theory and capitalist economic practice, that we can explain the striking lack of visibility of this green economic approach. Add to that the fact that those holding this perspective are also by default "dissidents" in relation to the ruling economic orthodoxy, who also seek to reveal the political, philosophical, and cultural roots and assumptions underpinning dominant views of "economics" and the "economy," and one can easily understand why these dissident pioneers are invisible.

An extremely important feature of green political economy and its spelling out of an economics of sustainability is its scientific basis: its integration of the insights of the natural sciences, especially ecology, thermodynamics, and systems thinking. This concern has been there from the origins of modern green political economy in the work of Nicholas Georgescu-Roegen and Herman Daly, to contemporary scholars such as Molly Cato and Tim Jackson (Barry 2012). For example, green political economists suggest we should analyze and appraise our energy options not just from a financial/profit/monetary perspective, but also in terms of energy returned on energy invested (EROEI) (Murphy 2014), that is, how much energy we expend on extracting an energy resource. In this case, fracking (or extracting shale gas), from a green political economic perspective, should be assessed not simply from a cost or "energy security" perspective but from an energy/thermodynamic perspective. Does it make sense to expend more energy (which could be used for other purposes) to extract shale gas? Yet, despite this accumulating evidence, the neo-classical economic paradigm and its commitment to unsustainable economic growth still reigns dominant both in terms of how we understand the economy and "economics" in public policy.

The Battle of Ideas over the Economy

The intellectual debate between green political economy and neo-classical economics is one that lies partly within the framework of the academic production of knowledge, but is also a debate that goes far beyond the academy. This is also an ideological battle, only part of which occurs within the academy. Neo-classical economics supports a particular view of the economy and society, one which, with a few exceptions, is supportive of a capitalist organization of the economy, private ownership of the means of production, and production for profit; justifies an unequal distribution of income and wealth; promotes free trade, deregulation, and economic globalization; and above all is committed to promoting orthodox economic growth. By orthodox "economic growth" is meant "undifferentiated, monetary/GDP measurements of economic growth as a permanent feature of the economy" (Barry 2012). *In short, neo-classical economics supports the prevailing capitalist status quo, yet does not make this explicit, and therefore underpins actually existing unsustainability: neo-classical economics sustains the unsustainable.*

This is of course an old Marxist insight—namely that conceptions about and debates regarding the economy and economics are, in part, about power relations within society, seeking ideological and intellectual hegemony. This ideological hegemony translates not simply into political power in determining state policies for example, but is equally a form of cultural hegemony informing how we "commonsensically" think about, assess, and evaluate the economy and economic issues. Perhaps the most vivid expression of an ideological position that has achieved this preeminent position is that it neither presents itself as an ideological position nor is perceived as such by others. Rather it is viewed as "commonsense" or "normal." Once a particular way of conceptualizing and thinking about the economy is widely shared and commonsensical, alternative modes of thinking about the economy are by default deemed "nonsensical," and indeed this has and continues to be the most common reaction to non-neo-classical economic perspectives—green or others.

In other words, a sign of the ideological success of neo-classical economics is that it has, by and large, managed to perform the sleight of hand of replacing "capitalism" with "the economy," such that whenever we "commonsensically" talk about "the economy" we are in fact, usually, talking about a particular mode of economic organization, namely capitalism. A category mistake has been made: the confusion and conflation of "capitalism" with the "economy." Think of when an "economist" is called to comment in the media: it is without exception a neo-classical economist who will (generally speaking) talk about (and defend) capitalism. Rarely do we hear non-neo-classical economists in our media, or if we do these are not accorded the label of "economists" but "political commentators," nicely eliding the fact that those called "economic experts" are also political commentators.

Part of the ideological project of green political economy, I would suggest, lies in its aim, at one and the same time, *to repoliticize and democratize thinking about economics* and democratize the economy through, for example, strategies of localization or the promotion of social enterprises. This is the real meaning of Cato's view of green political economy growing "from the bottom up and from those building a sustainable economy in practice" (2008: 5). This democratic impulse does not mean that a green political economy perspective does not recognize that complex aspects of the economy require expertise and forms of knowledge only a few will possess. But this is compatible with requiring democratic oversight and transparency in respect of these complex aspects of managing the economy. On the other hand, if we look at the ways in which the very complexity of certain types of economic activity, primarily but not limited to the financial sector, is partly to blame for creating the current economic crisis, then simplifying the economy and making it more transparent does make a lot of sense. So apart from the standard response of calling for more regulation in response to the current economic crisis, a green economic perspective makes the case for also de-complexifying the economy (and in the process making it less unsustainable and more resilient). This imperative to de-complexify is a democratic impulse in which, *inter alia*, re-localization, enhancing community self-reliance, reducing the distance between production and consumption, and reducing the material throughput of the economy are needed to create a "human-scale" economy capable of being democratically controlled and regulated, embedded in, rather than disembedded from community. Here democratization necessarily leads to less unsustainability.

The Critique of Economic Growth

Another aspect of the ideological battle of ideas about the economy from a green perspective is the claim that economic growth is an ideological belief that has to be imposed upon a society and is not something that people "naturally" gravitate toward. It is only by understanding economic growth as the ideology of the ruling classes that we can explain the paradox at the heart of the green critique of growth. Namely, why and how could economic growth be supported by the majority of people (not just the elites), given the abundant ethical, political, and psychological arguments against it, and the wealth of empirical evidence demonstrating that (after a threshold) orthodox, undifferentiated economic growth does not improve peoples' lives and goes against their interests in flourishing? How in short, can such a belief system continue past the point where it no longer contributes to real freedom, genuine prosperity or human well-being and flourishing? How can such "cancerous growth" continue to be not only supported but actively desired? How, reminding ourselves of the insights of the early Frankfurt school and Marcuse, in the midst of material abundance and plenty (in so-called "developed" capitalist societies) can people be induced to believe that their lives are governed by its opposite, namely generalized scarcity, and thus be disciplined into wage labor and into producing and consuming more and more?

Another founder of green economics, James Robertson, notes why the "new economics" is so threatening: it challenges "powerful established interests, and call[s] into question existing institutional structures, existing organizational values, and existing expansionist tendencies in government, business and the careerist professions, and conventional economic orthodoxy" (Robertson 1997: 13). Yet Robertson's analysis is somewhat abstract. So to fill this gap as I see it in the generally well-developed (if not generally accepted) green critique of orthodox economic growth, I wish here to touch upon four sources of evidence for the ideological and class character of economic growth—drawn from historical analysis, development studies, deliberative democracy, and orthodox economics.

First, some historical evidence. It is clear that Marx's view of capitalism emerging "dripping from head to toe, from every pore, with blood and dirt" (Marx 1967: 760) is, despite the overdramatic expression, basically true. There was massive popular and sustained resistance by peasants, craft guilds, and others, resulting in uprisings, revolutions, sabotage, and other acts of resistance and opposition to the imposition from above of the discipline of wage labor, enforced movement from the land to the city, the use of machine technology, enclosure of the commons, the factory system, etc. As Polanyi details, the emergence of capitalism resulted in the spontaneous "double movement" of social forces rising to resist and protect society and social relations from the unfettered free market (Polanyi 1947). A large part of this was forcibly compelling people to produce more goods and more wealth, despite norms of pre-industrial, peasant culture being oriented toward producing enough rather than accumulating a large surplus. The habit of accumulation or producing more and more, rather than enough, had to be imposed from above by those who benefitted most from it, the emerging capitalist class. A good example of this class bias of economic growth is the way in which technological improvements have been since the emergence of capitalism (and continue to be today) used not to result in *more people working less, but less people working more*. Simply put, it is in the interests of the owners of capital to institute and maintain an economic system geared toward generating a *surplus*, whereas it had been in the interest of peasants to produce a *sufficient* amount.

Secondly, we have the evidence from development studies about the ways in which economic growth had to be forced upon, and how it was and is resisted by, people in non-Western, so-called "underdeveloped" societies. It is interesting and telling that early green critiques such as Illich (1973), Shiva (1988), Latouche (1993), and Escobar (1995), drew much of their insights about the problems of global capitalism from their studies and experiences of the "developing world." On the one hand, there is the arrogance of using Western experiences of development to categorize all other societies as "developing," "underdeveloped," or "undeveloped," that is, using Western metrics to judge and rank all societies. On the other, there is the documented resistance of non-Western societies and people (mostly non-elites and peasants) to capitalism, the imperative of economic growth, factory-time and its work discipline, and production for accumulation and consumerism for leisure. And there are clearly similarities between the forms of resistance to economic growth in the "majority world," and the resistance historically to capitalism in Europe.

Thirdly, there is some evidence of the disjuncture between elites and citizens when it comes to certain risky technological policies in relation to promoting economic growth. That is, results from deliberative citizens' experiments seem to indicate that the public is more risk adverse and more inclined to support precautionary approaches than political and economic elites (Dryzek et al. 2009). As they note, "If precautionary worldviews are as pervasive in reflective publics as we suggest, then the generally Promethean positions of governing elites cannot be legitimated by deliberative means—at least when it comes to issues of technological risk" (Dryzek et al. 2009: 34). This is suggestive of the view that the more open and deliberative the political process the less likely we are to see policies for technologically risky economic growth policies. This suggests that alternatives to economic growth such as "economic security" (discussed in the next section) may enjoy more democratic support. Finally, from conventional economic theory we have what is known as the "backward bending labor supply curve." This is the rather simple hypothesis that beyond a threshold, further increases in wages will not lead people to work more. In other words, once workers have attained enough or sufficient wages, they prefer other things than working for a wage and consuming (Barry 2012).

What is an Economy for? From Economic Growth to Economic Security

A long-standing green commitment is to re-orientate the economy toward enhancing and being judged by its capacity to promote "quality of life," "well-being," and "happiness" rather than orthodox economic growth. As the new economics foundation puts it,

> the purpose of economy should be to enhance the well-being of the citizens of the country, in a way that is socially just, and environmentally sustainable. That is, the level of economic growth achieved in an economy is not a sufficient measure of that economy's success or failure to deliver prosperity to society. This is because economic growth does not, in itself, tell us anything about our quality of life." (new economics foundation 2008: 1–2)

The economy and economic growth are, after all, means not ends in themselves. We live in societies with economies, not economies with societies, a view which profoundly challenges neo-classical economics and the neo-liberal worldview. I outline here how "economic security" could be a replacement for economic growth, and present a green economic case for a new type of economy, in which redistribution and reducing socio-economic inequality are central (Wilkinson and Pickett 2009). A model of green political economy cast in terms of "economic security" has the advantage of presenting a positive and attractive discourse for addressing the problems of "actually existing unsustainability" (Barry 2012). Using the language and analysis of economic security introduces ways of arguing and presenting the case for a less growth-orientated economy and high consumption society, which at the same time aims to raise quality of life while lowering inequality. At the same time it is important (not least strategically) that a green critique of "growth" should be viewed as a critique of orthodox and *undifferentiated growth* as measured by conventional economics. That is, lest a critique of economic growth be viewed as critique of any and all types of growth, it is important to stress that greens reserve their critique for what Daly calls "uneconomic growth"—the expansion of forms of activities which (after a threshold) undermine or compromise human flourishing. Thus it is perfectly consistent for greens to support growth in, for example, education, public health, public transport, or subsidized organic farming, but criticize the growth of consumerism, the quantity of arms and weapons an economy produces and trades, and the size of domestic/household credit card debt.

Many potential contenders for what should replace economic growth have been canvassed over the last 150 years—from John Stuart Mill's "stationary state" (Mill 1848/1900), to more recent work on "quality of life," "well-being," and "prosperity" (Jackson 2009) for example. All share a number of components and have a large degree of overlap—the one I wish to explore here is the notion of "economic security" (Barry 2009). I take this term from a 2004 report by the International Labor Organization (ILO) entitled *Economic Security for a Better World*, which found that "economic security" coupled with democratic representation and equality were the main determinants of well-being, tolerance, and social stability (International Labor Organization 2004c). The report defines economic security as "composed of *basic social security*, defined by access to basic needs, infrastructure pertaining to health, education, dwelling, information, and social protection, as well as *work-related security*. (International Labor Organization 2004a: 1, emphasis in the original). The report found that:

> People in countries that provide citizens with a high level of economic security have a higher level of happiness on average, as measured by surveys of national levels of life-satisfaction and happiness... *The most important determinant of national happiness is not income level—there is a positive association, but rising income seems to have little effect as wealthy countries grow more wealthier. Rather the key factor is the extent of income security, measured in terms of income protection and a low degree of income inequality.*" (International Labor Organization 2004b: 1; emphasis added)

Such findings, also echoed in the work of others such as Wilkinson and Pickett (2009) and Standing (2002), give some empirical support to long-standing arguments stressing the need for policies to lower socio-economic inequality as necessary to enhance individual and collective socio-economic security and increase well-being.

It is also relevant to note other observed links between in/security, economic growth, and well-being. One of the principal psychological determinants of excessive consumption has been found to be feelings of personal insecurity, status competition, and vulnerability—whether about one's body shape, sensitivity to peer judgments, or externally generated and reinforced views of self–other relations that undermine personal or other forms of security and self-esteem (De Graff et al. 2005; Chaplin and John 2007). For example, psychologist Tim Kasser points out that individuals in America, when faced with short-term insecurity or pain (psychological or physical), increasingly turn to money and possessions as a way of coping with distress, rather than seeking comfort and support in social interaction and community or family relationships, since these have been eroded, in part, due to the pressures of economic globalization and the imperative of orthodox economic growth (Kasser 2008). Yet it is precisely those non-monetary, non-possessive relationships that have a greater positive impact on our overall levels of happiness and well-being.

However, this does not necessarily mean (as critics are wont to point out) that a focus on economic security as a main objective of macro-economic policy means an end to entrepreneurialism or innovation. A fair question to ask, and one any alternative to our current economic growth focused model needs to take seriously, is how to ensure that stagnation and regress will not be the outcome of a post-growth economy. However, we have reasons for thinking that development "comes from innovation, from consuming different things, rather than more of the same things" (Wilkinson and Pickett 2009: 221). And once one begins to free up key economic goals—such as "innovation" from its technological–economic straightjacket, "growth" from its reduction to material wealth or capital accumulation, "work" from being identified solely with formally paid "employment," and so on—there is reason to suppose that *more, not less, innovation and creativity* and innovation beyond technological or institutional spheres will be the result of living in such a society, rather than stagnation or regress. In fact, such forms of innovation and creativity are *necessary features and therefore "required"* for low carbon, high well-being lives and communities, and not some "added extra" (Cato and Hillier 2010).

This problem of economic insecurity (experienced at an individual or collective level) can also be applied at the level of the existing economic system itself. An economic system that has only two options—continual growth or collapse—cannot be stable or secure. On the one hand, this economic system is unsustainable, that is, it is simply *biophysically impossible* to achieve continual economic growth. Much hope is (mis)placed on the idea of "decoupling" orthodox economic growth from energy, resource, and pollution impacts, often associated with "ecological modernization" and the "environmental Kuznets curve" hypothesis. Both suggest that orthodox economic growth is compatible with reducing environmental impact. Rather like the ancient myth of Achilles lance, which could heal the wounds it inflicted, the argument (based in neo-classical economics) is that growth which causes environmental degradation can, after a point, reverse this and deliver environmental improvements. Yet as a recent study has concluded, "the statistical analysis on which the environmental Kuznets curve is based is not robust. There is little evidence for a common inverted U-shaped pathway that countries follow as their income rises" (Stern 2014: 14).

Thus, we have little empirical evidence that this is either possible on the scale required, or that such "decoupling" within advanced industrial economies is possible (Barry 2003). For Jackson this decoupling is a "myth" and "assumptions that capitalism's propensity for efficiency will allow us to stabilize the climate and protect against resource scarcity are nothing short of delusional" (Jackson 2009: 7). This is the case even if growth is associated with more egalitarian and redistributive policies, that is, within alternative views that less inequality does not undermine orthodox economic growth (Kirby and Murphy 2010; Putterman, Roemer, and Silivestre 1998). So while clearly better from the point of view of equality and providing economic security, "egalitarian growth" is, qua continuous economic growth, also biophysically impossible and therefore unsustainable.

On the other hand, capitalist stagnation brings with it its own dangers, that is, no-growth is *not socially desirable* or politically acceptable (Jackson 2009). Economic stagnation—as with the global economic crisis experienced since 2008—is associated with high levels of unemployment, social dislocation, disinvestment, and a lowering of well-being. This macro-level or system level critique of the capitalist economy represents an updated version of Marx's analysis of the endemic "crisis-ridden" character of capitalism. Hence, more radical conceptions of green political economy often accept significant elements of the Marxist analysis of capitalism, though without necessarily going along with its proposed solutions for or alternatives to capitalism, since most (though not all) streams of Marxism are committed to economic growth. It is the "myth" of exponential and permanent economic growth itself that is the problem and needs to be abandoned. *Rather than focusing our energies on increasing the ecological and energy efficiency of capitalist production and orthodox economic growth, what we need to be doing is exploring ways of increasing the ecological and energy efficiency of human flourishing.*

Economic Security, Equality, and Well-Being

One of the most significant impacts of a shift away from economic growth as a central goal would be the undermining of the justification of socio-economic inequalities. The latter are usually justified or tolerated on the grounds that inequalities are necessary "incentives" to motivate people (via the promise of differential, unequal rewards) toward entrepreneurial activity, "hard work," etc., and thus stimulate economic growth. As early proponents of the "steady-state economy" pointed out, the shift from a society geared toward economic growth to a society where material growth is not a priority may lead to more extensive redistributive measures. This is a point made many years ago by forerunners of green economic thinking such as Herman Daly (1973). That is, there are significant redistributive implications of moving beyond a growth paradigm. According to the orthodox growth view, growth is needed to eliminate poverty (by making the "economic pie" bigger, not slicing it differently), through the process of "trickle down." If, however, the option of baking a bigger pie is neither (ecologically) possible nor (socially) desirable, then poverty elimination can be solved only by more direct redistributive measures. And in so doing the link between poverty and inequality is explicitly revealed. That is, inequality causes poverty, not vice versa. As the authors of the ILO report note, "Inequality is part of insecurity, particularly when that inequality is substantial. And the unequal distribution of insecurities is part of socio-economic inequality" (International Labor Organization 2004b: 3). So if one argues for a post-growth economy, then it does mean that the traditional political strategy for simply managing inequalities is no longer an option.

There are other problems with inequality in relation to human well-being that I wish to highlight here. The *first* is that the more unequal a society the greater the status competition and the lesser the overall well-being. As Wilkinson and Pickett note "The problems in rich countries are not caused by society not being rich enough (or even by being too rich) *but by the scale of material differences between people within each society being too big.* What matters is where we stand in relation to others in our own society" (2009: 25; emphasis added). As Jackson contends, this "unproductive status competition increases material throughput and creates distress" (Jackson 2009: 154) as a result of competition between individuals for social status. And in modern consumer-capitalist societies the main way in which social comparison is performed is through material goods and the "mandatory" practices of consumerism and consumption.

The *second* is that, as Wilkinson and Pickett's research demonstrates, highly unequal societies almost always come out worse on a range of policy issues including obesity, childhood mortality, drug use, literacy, social mobility, trust, teenage pregnancy, and incidence of mental illness. As they put it, "Economic growth, for so long the great engine of progress, has, in the rich countries, largely finished its work. Not only have measures of wellbeing and happiness ceased to rise with economic growth but, as affluent societies have grown richer, there have been long-term rises in rates of anxiety, depression, and numerous other social problems. *The populations of rich countries have got to the end of a long historical journey*" (Wilkinson and Pickett 2009: 5–6; emphasis added). Thus, this suggests that economic growth is not to be somehow rejected "in principle" as being "intrinsically" bad or wrong, but is to be seen in terms of a society's evolution over time, and as a policy that needs to be periodically reviewed, rather than a "locked-in" or permanent feature of a society. And one threshold (apart from obvious ecological ones) that can be identified to signal the point beyond which economic growth needs to be reconsidered, is when greater and greater levels of inequality are required for economic growth, which reduces the range of components central for human flourishing. Other thresholds could be more directly related to human flourishing, such as mental health, social trust, or measurements of community and solidarity.

The *third* striking implication of inequality is its negative effect on social trust, social solidarity, and sense of community (Lane 2000). This has significant implications for democracy, based on the principles of both equality between citizens and fellow feeling as members of the same community. It is of particular concern for a green republican notion of politics. In short, large degrees of inequality undermine a sense of a community of equals. This can lead to the danger of hierarchical and paternalistic relations between supposedly equal citizens. This carries with it the possibility of relations of domination, including those based on internalized senses of inequality and inferiority. As Wilkinson and Pickett note, "The problem is that second-class goods make us look like second-class people" (Wilkinson and Pickett 2009: 222). Such forms of social stratification (around race, class, ethnicity, sexuality, or gender) are not compatible with the equality required for democratic politics, and living in a democratic society of equals.

A *fourth* and related problem with inequality is one particular to democratic politics, namely how inequality undermines and compromises democracy. Simply put, a substantial degree of equality is a precondition for democracy. As Stout observes, "Wherever economic power is both concentrated in the hands of a few and easily convertible into unconstrained political power, it makes no sense to speak of political life as democratic. The power of the rich is unconstrained because too few people are bothering to constrain it. *Power is always accumulating in novel ways, posing new threats to liberty and justice*" (Stout 2007: 6; emphasis added). In that context, as work stretching from Goodin and Dryzek in the early 1980s (Goodin and Dryzek 1980), to more recent work of Solt (Solt 2008), we find that less well-off citizens, those most disadvantaged and marginalized in society due to inequality, give up on discussing political matters and effectively withdraw from politics. This of course leaves politics and the shaping of what politics means (like neo-classical economics in relation to economics) in fewer and fewer hands.

Conclusion

Green political economy can be thought of as motivated by creating an economy as if we mean to stay around to enjoy it, not as a process of liquidating the planet, exploiting people, unequally distributing the fruits of that economic growth, and calling it "progress." In terms of the critique of economic growth, green political economy questions *undifferentiated, orthodox GDP measurements of growth, where growth is viewed as a permanent feature of an economy or a permanent economic objective*. Economic growth beyond a threshold becomes an ideology which serves the interests of elites, and its ideological promotion (by neo-classical economics) is intrinsically connected to the contemporary practices of global capitalism. And "threshold" can be roughly understood in terms of the need for an explicitly political and democratic process whereby the point beyond which economic growth increases rather than decreases inequalities, continues rather than reverses our unsustainable development pattern, and leads to a decline rather than an increase in human flourishing: this is the threshold beyond which economic growth has become "uneconomic growth." Green political economy thus indicates the need for a paradigm shift in how we understand the economy and the organization of the economy away from orthodox, undifferentiated economic growth as a permanent feature of the economy toward seeing it as a contingent and historically specific feature, a step toward a green, sustainable economy organized around the objective of increasing the ecological efficiency of human flourishing (Boyle and Simms 2009).

References

Barry, J. (2012). *The Politics of Actually Existing Unsustainability: Human Flourishing in a Climate Changed, Carbon-Constrained World* (Oxford: Oxford University Press).

Barry, J. (2009). " 'Choose Life' not Economic Growth: Critical Social Theory for People, Planet and Flourishing in an 'Age of Nature'." *Current Perspectives in Social Theory* 26: 93–113.

Barry, J. (2003). "Ecological Modernisation." In *Environmental Thought*, edited by J. Proops and E. Page (Cheltenham: Edward Elgar), 191–214.

Boyle, D. and Simms, A. (2009). *The New Economics: A Bigger Picture* (Cheltenham: Edward Elgar).

Cato, M. S. (2008). *Green Economics: An Introduction to Theory, Policy and Practice* (London: Earthscan).

Cato, M. S. and Hillier, J. (2010). "How Could We Study Climate-related Social Innovation?: Applying Deleuzean Philosophy to Transition Towns." *Environmental Politics* 19(6): 869–87.

Chaplin, L. N. and John, D. R. (2007). "Growing Up in a Material World: Age Differences in Materialism in Children and Adolescents." *Journal of Consumer Research* 34: 480–93.

Daly, H., ed. (1973), *Toward a Steady State Economy* (San Francisco: W.H. Freeman & Co.).

De Graaf, J., Wann, D., and Naylor, T. (2002). *Affluenza: The All-consuming Epidemic* (Vermont: Berett-Koehler).

Dryzek, J., Goodin, R., Tucker, A., and Reber, B. (2009). "Promethean Elites Encounter Precautionary Publics: The Case of GM Foods." *Science, Technology, and Human Values* 34: 263–88.

Escobar, A. (1995). *Encountering Development: The Making and Unmaking of the Third World* (Princeton: Princeton University Press).

Goodin, R. and Dryzek, J. (1980). "Rational Participation: The Politics of Relative Power." *British Journal of Political Science* 10(3):273–92.

Illich, I. (1973). *Tools for Conviviality* (London: Marion Boyers).

International Labor Organization (2004a). "Definitions: What We Mean When We Say 'Economic Security'", available at: http://www.ilo.org/public/english/protection/ses/download/docs/definition.pdf (accessed February 1, 2010).

International Labor Organization (2004b). "Economic Insecurity Is a Global Crisis: ILO Report Shows How and Where Economic Security Index Linked to Happiness," available at: http://www.ilo.org/public/english/protection/ses/download/docs/happiness.pdf (accessed February 1, 2010).

International Labor Organization (2004c). *Economic Security for a Better World* (Geneva: International Labor Office), available at: http://www.ilo.org/public/english/protection/ses/index.htm (accessed November 10, 2004).

Jackson, T. (2009). *Prosperity without Growth: Economics for a Finite Planet* (London: Earthscan).

Kasser, T. (2008). "Pain and Insecurity, Love and Money." *Psychological Inquiry* 19: 174–8.

Kirby, P. and Murphy, M. (2010). "Globalisation and Models of State: Debates and Evidence from Ireland." *New Political Economy* 16(1): 19–39.

Lane, R. (2000), *The Loss of Happiness in Market Democracies* (New Haven: Tale University Press).

Latouche, S. (1993). *In the Wake of the Affluent Society: An Exploration of Post-Development* (London: Zed Books).

Marx, K. (1967). *Capital: A Critique of Political Economy, Vol. I* (New York: International Publishers).

Meadows, D., Meadows, D., and Randers, J. (1972). *The Limits to Growth: A Report for the Club of Rome's Project on the Predicament of Mankind* (New York: Universe).

Meadows, D., Randers, J., and Meadows, D. (2004). *Limits to Growth: The 30-Year Update* (White River Junction, Vermont: Chelsea Green Publishing).

Mill, J. S. (1878/1900). "Of the Stationary State." In his *Principles of Political Economy, Vol. IV* (London: Longmans, Green and Co.).

Murphy, D. (2014). "The Implications of the Declining Energy Return on Investment of Oil Production." *Philosophical Transactions of the Royal Society, A*, 372: 20130126–20130126.

new economics foundation. (2008). *Think Piece for the Commission for Rural Communities: Economic Well-being* (London: new economics foundation), available at: http://www.rural-communities.gov.uk/files/NEF%20Final%20think-piece.pdf (accessed February 18, 2011).

Polanyi, K. (1947). *The Great Transformation: The Political and Economic Origins of Our Time* (Boston: Beacon Press).

Putterman, L., Roemer, J., and Silivestre, J. (1998). "Does Egalitarianism Have a Future?" *Journal of Economic Literature* 36(2): 861–902.

Robertson, J. (1997). *The New Economics of Sustainable Development: A Briefing for Policy Makers, A Report for the European Commission*, available at: http://www.jamesrobertson.com/book/neweconomicsofsustainabledevelopment.pdf (accessed February 21, 2011).

Schumacher, E.F. (1973), Small is Beautiful: Economics as if People Mattered (London: Blond and Briggs).

Shiva, V. (1988). *Staying Alive: Women, Ecology and Development* (London: Zed Books).

Solt, F. (2008). "Economic Inequality and Democratic Political Engagement." *American Journal of Political Science* 52(1): 48–60.

Standing, G. (2002). *Beyond the New Paternalism: Basic Security as Equality* (London: Verso).
Stanford, J. (2008). *Economics for Everyone: A Short Guide to the Economics of Capitalism* (Toronto: Pluto Press).
Stern, D. (2014). *The Environmental Kuznets Curve: A Primer*, Centre for Climate Economic and Policy Working Paper, 1404 (Australian National University, Canberra).
Stout, J. (2007). "The Spirit of Democracy and the Rhetoric of Excess." *Journal of Religious Ethics* 35(1): 3–21.
Wilkinson, R. and Pickett, K. (2009). *The Spirit Level: Why More Equal Societies Almost Always Do Better* (London: Allen Lane).

JUSTICE, RIGHTS, AND RESPONSIBILITY

CHAPTER 21

ENVIRONMENTAL AND CLIMATE JUSTICE

STEVE VANDERHEIDEN

THE call by activists and scholars for "climate justice" as a core objective of international efforts to minimize the harm associated with climate change builds upon an older discourse of "environmental justice" (EJ), adapting its analyses for its own purposes and extending the concept in several important ways. Both view anthropogenic environmental harm in terms of its implications for social justice, and focus especially upon the effects of such harm on the disadvantaged. But climate justice imperatives involve analyses and demands not found in early EJ discourse, which grew out of more localized pollution issues and a more parochial politics than are found in current debates over international climate policy. Viewing EJ discourse as having evolved over three generations of movements and normative theorizing, however, more closely links the two, and illustrates the scope and application of an applied justice analysis now capable of illuminating the nature of a wide range of environmental threats to human welfare and framing demands for reform. Such an analysis also identifies key objectives and constraints for cooperative efforts to address anthropogenic environmental threats which, when cast in terms of justice, demand responses that take equity as seriously as sustainability and are as concerned with human dignity and welfare as with the integrity of biophysical systems.

The policy basis for climate justice imperatives can be found in the 1992 United Nations Framework Convention on Climate Change (UNFCCC), which calls upon signatory parties to protect the climate system for the benefit of current and future generations of humankind and to do so in accordance with several justice principles to be discussed in this chapter. Since climate change is expected to produce harmful impacts across the globe, but to concentrate much of the worst damage upon the world's most vulnerable persons and peoples, this reference to the interests of current generations invokes an ideal of global justice (Harris 2009), where the demands of justice cross national borders and protect all regardless of nationality. Since many of its most serious impacts are expected to be felt in the future, as accumulated atmospheric greenhouse gases remain in the atmosphere for over a century beyond their initial emission, the UNFCCC casts the justice imperative in intergenerational terms, as well. But perhaps the more urgent call for justice can be found in terms by which those parties are tasked with cooperating in protection of the planet's climate system. Parties to the treaty are, in short, urged to design a cooperative international response to the injustice of climate change that is itself bound by ideals of justice, shifting focus from problems to remedies while taking in a wider set of principles than can be found in early EJ movements and discourse.

This chapter surveys the origin and development of EJ discourse from its early use as a civil rights strategy to resist the siting of hazardous waste facilities in the neighborhoods of poor people of color in the United States to its more contemporary variant as a directive for equitable global cooperation in pursuit of environmental sustainability. Here, the primary focus will be upon the ideas rather than the movements that gave rise to them, and with the capsule history of changes in EJ discourse intended to show how different justice conceptions and principles have come to be used to advocate for social and environmental change rather than to reveal the full landscape of contemporary EJ politics. Next, it examines debates among climate justice scholars and activists over the demands of justice as applied to problems of global climate policy efforts, as an illustration of the diagnostic and prescriptive force of justice analyses in this context. Given controversies over which justice principles to apply to such problems, as well as how one or more might be translated into concrete directives for action or policy, this examination reveals both the potential and the limits of wielding abstract normative ideals in the service of social mobilization or policy development. The chapter concludes by considering other contemporary environmental problems that third generation EJ discourse might constructively engage along with several new issues that might drive further evolution of the EJ analytical framework.

Environmental Justice

How does this discourse of climate justice build upon and extend the older EJ tradition? What features of EJ analysis needed to develop in order to accommodate the kinds of justice issues now recognized as inherent to international climate change mitigation efforts? In order to appreciate the evolution of environmental justice as a conceptual frame used by social movements as well as a set of principles grounded in normative theory, it is instructive to view EJ discourse as having developed over several generations, with successive generations marking significant transformations of the discourse from previous ones.

In their first generation, EJ discourses were primarily developed and used in reference to socially unequal vulnerability to pollution exposure, as a function of toxic waste sites in the United States being disproportionately located near poor people of color. Robert Bullard's pioneering work demonstrating race to be a significant factor in exposure to hazardous waste in the United States (1990) grew out of his earlier effort to marshal evidence about correlations between race and pollution exposure in Houston, which he undertook as an activist effort rather than a scholarly research project. Given announced plans to locate a waste facility in his middle class African-American neighborhood, Bullard hoped to demonstrate patterns of unequal vulnerability within the city as part of a Fourteenth Amendment "equal protection" antidiscrimination case to enjoin those plans. Although his challenge was unsuccessful in the courts, since it demonstrated racially unequal vulnerability but not the intentional racism that the court required, the linkages that his work established gave rise both to a civil rights strategy for resisting the imposition of toxic waste disposal within poor neighborhoods of color and a scholarly research area built around exploring causal linkages between race, class, and environmental quality (Chavis and Lee 1987).

Three conceptual features characterized this first generation of EJ appeals, based around US anti-toxics campaigns. First, their primary focus was upon the socio-spatial distribution of environmental hazards, especially those having to do with exposure to toxic waste. Access to environmental amenities such as parks or open space was not yet viewed as an issue of justice, given the reliance upon the negative framing of claims to equal protection from harm rather than a more positive claim to equal access to some range of goods. Second, the focus was upon local hazards, not those with remote sources or those that were regional or global in nature, which could not be traced to some set of responsible parties. As a quasi-legal challenge, the EJ frame was developed in order to be applied against particular decisions by identifiable authorities whose actions could be enjoined, where the resulting inequitable vulnerability could at least be foreseen even if not expressly intended, relying upon what Iris Young terms a liability model of responsibility (2006). Environmental threats such as climate change were not yet viewed as amenable to that frame, since the causal agency leading to such problems is far too diffuse to readily invite analyses under antidiscrimination law and the unequal vulnerability of poor people of color not yet appreciated and not the clear result of any decisions in question. Finally, first generation EJ discourse primarily focused upon race as a determining factor in unequal vulnerability within a single national community, seeking to distinguish its effects from those of socio-economic class. Given the EJ strategy of invoking antidiscrimination law in the service of better protections of the vulnerable from environmental harm, and since such laws recognize racial minorities but not poor people as a protected class, the EJ lens in its first generation was not developed for application to poverty-related threats.

A second generation of EJ discourse can be seen in what Bullard describes as the move from a demand for "not in my backyard" to "not in anyone's backyard" (that is, a shift in focus to the reduction in production of hazardous wastes, not merely in more equitable siting of storage facilities). This shift can be seen in the 1991 First National People of Color Environmental Leadership Summit's "Principles of Environmental Justice" (PEJ), which calls for "universal protection from nuclear testing, extraction, production and disposal of toxic/hazardous wastes and poisons" and demands "the cessation of the production of all toxins, hazardous wastes, and radioactive materials" (Principles 4 and 6).

As Schlosberg (2009) notes, EJ discourse evolved from a primary focus upon substantive policy outcomes understood primarily in terms of the distribution of hazards or vulnerability among peoples into a call for more equitable participation by and recognition of those most affected by environmental injustice. These new foci can also be seen in the PEJ, which demand the "right to participate as equal partners at every level of decision-making" (Principle 7) and call for public policy to "be based on mutual respect and justice for all peoples" (Principle 2). Finally, whereas first generation EJ campaigns sought injunctive remedies that would halt or prevent actions deemed as unjust, relying upon civil rights tactics and antidiscrimination law to halt objectionable actions, the second generation of EJ remedies included demands for compensation, appropriating tort and liability law in the service of righting past wrongs, which supplements demands for injunctive relief with restorative justice.

While still primarily domestic in its focus and directed at local sources of environmental hazards rather than transboundary pollution or anthropogenic hazards that lack an identifiable set of responsible parties, this second generation of EJ analyses casts a wider conceptual net than did the first generation, including a more sophisticated set of objectives along with additional demands and remedies. Evolutionary changes that facilitated adaptation of EJ discourses to the demands of climate change politics included the shift from the initial demand that exposure to pollution-related hazards be more equitably distributed to the second generation claim that justice requires the production of fewer pollutants in general, as vulnerability to greenhouse gas pollution is not affected by the location of greenhouse gas emission sources and so cannot be reduced by their mere spatial redistribution. While developing country representatives to climate policy conventions, along with their advocates in both the scholarly and activist communities, have called for a global redistribution of emissions rights in order to accommodate development interests (Vanderheiden 2008), they recognize that any such redistribution would need to be accompanied by significant reductions in overall emissions if the injustice of climate change were to be avoided. The demand to compensate those harmed by ongoing pollution as a matter of justice, supplementing injunctive relief, would pave the way for a key demand of contemporary climate justice activism, which calls for transfers from high emitting nations to those expected to experience the most serious climate-related impacts.

The third generation of EJ discourse, and that most closely associated with demands for climate justice, adds two additional elements to the framing of anthropogenic environmental harm as injustice. First is the wider scope of concern associated with global environmental harm, where pollutants transcend national borders and affect the vulnerable regardless of their source but without a set of responsible parties causally connected with the harm in a sufficiently direct manner to establish liability. National governments cannot remedy global environmental injustice caused by phenomena such as climate change, insofar as they can regulate pollution only within their borders, so third generation EJ discourse necessarily appeals to international civil society and mobilizes international cooperation, as quintessentially seen in climate justice movements. As a result, third generation EJ discourse is less parochial than were earlier generations, as the agents to which it appeals and the legal bases of proposed remedies are transnational or global, based in treaties calling for domestic regulatory efforts to curb pollution that originates in the widely dispersed causal agency of individual action. Second, the equity issue or distributive concern is not merely with inequitable vulnerability to pollution, as in prior generations, although this concern remains important to defining EJ issues. Third generation EJ discourses also apply equity principles to the remedial costs associated with minimizing the pollution-related harm in question. With climate change, then, not only is the higher vulnerability of the world's poor viewed as unjust, maintaining the earlier EJ focus upon unequal vulnerability, but newer analyses also prescribe principles to inform the just allocation of mitigation and adaptation costs, or what are commonly termed the burden-sharing principles of climate justice (Harris 2009; Vanderheiden 2011).

Building upon this third generation of EJ discourse, demands for climate justice include the framing of anthropogenic climate change as a justice issue, involving the imposition of negative externalities that result from activities disproportionately enjoyed by the affluent upon the global poor, along with the demand that responses to climate change conform to ideals or principles of justice. The UNFCCC prescription of "common but differentiated responsibilities" (CBDR) as the basis of the allocation of national climate change mitigation burdens is typically understood as expressing an ideal of distributive justice for guiding climate policy efforts. To the extent that responsibility for climate change is *common* to all in that all humans emit some greenhouse gases as an unavoidable part of daily life, the CBDR principle holds that all should in some way accept some burdens in reducing those emissions or controlling their effects. But to the extent that individual or national emissions are *differentiated*, according to this principle, so also should remedial burdens be unequally assigned. Bigger polluters should accept a greater remedial burden, whether in terms of costly domestic emissions cuts for higher emitting nations or in contribution of resources used to fund mitigation and adaptation projects elsewhere.

Far from first generation EJ discourse, which was primarily concerned with equitable exposure to environmental hazards, climate justice discourse emanating from third generation EJ discourse rejects the notion that exposure to pollution-related hazards might be permissible if only equitably distributed, applying its distributive criteria more forcefully to the allocation of remedial costs than to the way unmitigated hazards differentially affect persons and people. In the process of its evolution, however, EJ discourse has been adapted to capture a wider range of environmental threats and grounded in a plurality of normative and legal principles, increasing its flexibility but at some cost to its clarity and coherence. Scholarly debates about climate justice not only illustrate the range of EJ discourses, they also reveal the extent to which the multiplicity of justice principles contained within the current ideal of environmental justice can lead to disagreement about which justice principles are required of EJ objectives, and how these principles can be translated into practice or into the development of environmental policy.

Three Justice Principles

In terms of which justice principles to apply to the allocation of national climate change mitigation burdens as a matter of climate justice, scholars and activists debate the role played by each of three distributive principles mentioned by the UNFCCC. In a single sentence, that treaty directs state parties to "protect the climate system for the benefit of present and future generations of humankind, on the basis of equity and in accordance with their common but differentiated responsibilities and respective capabilities" (Article 3.1), invoking "equity" as one principle by which national parties might be asked to contribute toward international climate policy efforts, along with CBDR as a second distinct principle and "respective capabilities" (widely viewed as reflective of the relative affluence of parties) as a third such principle. Without further clarification in the treaty for how to combine these three principles into a single metric for national burden allocation, proposals for interpreting this language and constructing policy solutions that combine some mix of equity, responsibility, and capacity have flourished within the climate justice literature and activist community without any one emerging as dominant.

Taking equity as a guiding principle, climate justice scholars typically view climate policy as a resource-sharing issue, proposing terms by which the capacity to absorb emissions without changing climate might be equitably assigned amongst various parties. Perhaps the most common equity-based proposal would require all nation-state parties to converge around equal per capita emissions at some point, which might for developed countries require significant reduction from current emission rates but could for some developing countries entail modest per capita emissions gains. For this reason, this interpretation of climate justice imperatives has been termed "contraction and convergence," since it allocates national burdens in terms of how much each must do to move from the status quo to per capita equality (Meyer 2000). Another equity-based proposal seeks to allocate costs equitably by asking each party to reduce their emissions from some baseline level by an equal percentage, as with the 1997 Kyoto Protocol's proposal to require all Annex I developed countries to reduce emissions by an average of 5 percent from 1990 baseline levels. In neither case does any country's past emissions play any direct role in its assigned share of total burdens, in contrast to responsibility-based approaches discussed below.

According to the second principle, remedial burdens would vary according to each nation's "responsibilities" for climate change, which is typically understood in terms of its past emissions. As a "polluter-pays" principle, CBDR assigns higher burdens to those parties that are more responsible for the present accumulations of greenhouse gases in the atmosphere, in proportion to that greater responsibility, and lesser burdens to those countries that have in the past been less responsible for climate change. In contrast with an equal per capita approach like the one associated with equity, which looks forward to some future per capita target and asks each party to undertake whatever efforts are necessary to achieve it, this responsibility-based principle looks backward at what various parties have done in the past and assigns present and future burdens accordingly. Whereas both would assign relatively higher burdens to countries with relatively high current emissions and relatively lower burdens to those with relatively lower current emissions, they rely upon distinct normative analyses and treat the status quo differently. For those embracing a responsibility-based interpretation of climate justice, a nation's responsibility has to do with what has been done in the past, up to now, while what is being done in the present is not immediately relevant. In contrast, an equity-based principle has to do with what must be done in the future, while what was done in the past is not directly relevant to the assignment of burdens.

Within the category of polluter-pays or responsibility-based interpretations of climate justice, considerable variation exists among those endorsing strict liability formulations of CBDR and those instead defining responsibility in terms of fault. Viewing responsibility for climate change strictly, national parties would be responsible for climate change in proportion to their full historical emissions, or at least for those going back to early industrialization, at which point significant variations in national per capita emissions began to appear and from which time data concerning national emissions has been estimated. Since greenhouse gases emitted two centuries ago continue to affect global climate, this "historical responsibility" view of the demands of CBDR counts the full quantum of past emissions in calculating remedial burdens.

By contrast, applying a fault-based liability standard to CBDR leads to two important modifications of the historical responsibility approach, both of which exempt significant shares of national emissions from the calculation of national burdens by claiming that these represent causal but not moral responsibility for climate-related harm (Vanderheiden 2008). The first exempts as faultless each nation's emissions prior to some baseline year, on grounds that human knowledge of the causes and effects of climate change prior to the dissemination of such knowledge was such that each party's causal responsibility for climate change was not accompanied by moral responsibility. Prior to 1990, advocates of this approach argue, national governments could not reasonably have known that their policies affecting national emissions could lead to harm, so they cannot now be faulted or held responsible for this harm. However, their responsibilities can validly be differentiated on the basis of their post-1990 national emissions, as that year marked not only the publication of the Intergovernmental Panel on Climate Change's first assessment report confirming the link between certain human activities and climate change but was also the year at which those parties pledged to freeze their emissions in the 1992 UNFCCC.

Relying upon a similar analysis of fault, in which parties are held to be morally and thus remedially responsible only for that share of their past emissions for which they could reasonably have been expected to exercise some control, a second exception to strict liability calculations has been proposed. Since some baseline level greenhouse emissions appear to be an unavoidable necessity of human survival, and therefore cannot be further reduced without reducing human population or inflicting upon peoples such draconian limitations that they are forced to undergo significant suffering, some propose that "subsistence emissions" be a second category of national emissions that are not counted in the calculation of each party's remedial burdens (Shue 1993). According to this analysis, some countries with very low per capita emissions may now be at or below the threshold of survival emissions, and might therefore not be responsible for climate change at all (in a fault-based moral sense, as they would be still be responsible in a causal sense). In allocating remedial burdens, only the "luxury emissions" that exceed each nation's subsistence threshold, perhaps going back to 1990 if both fault-based exemptions are employed simultaneously, would count in the calculation of remedial burdens, which would be assigned in proportion to post-1990 luxury emissions.

Further exemptions to each nation's emissions records could also be proposed under this fault-based interpretation of the UNFCCC's CBDR principle. National emissions resulting from natural events such as volcanic eruptions could be exempted as outside the control of state parties and thus not their fault in calculating their national liability. Certain kinds of natural advantages or disadvantages that affect each nation's past and current emissions, such as the availability of non-fossil fuel-based energy or extreme temperatures that require more energy for the heating and cooling of buildings, might likewise be viewed as faultless sources of variations in national emissions, and have been proposed as reasons to further modify each nation's remedial burdens from what otherwise would be prescribed under an accounting of its relevant past emissions. The common feature of all such analyses, however, lies in their common use of responsibility as the key justice principle around which remedial burdens are to be assigned, even if they diverge in how national responsibilities are to be differentiated.

A third principle can be seen in the "respective capabilities" phrase that immediately follows the CBDR language in the UNFCCC text. Apart from their variable past responsibility, nations differ significantly in their ability to further reduce their emissions, and such differences may be obscured by approaches that look only at past emissions records. Invoking an "ability to pay" principle, some scholars and activists have argued that one nation's greater national wealth or higher per capita income ought also to be taken into account in determining its remedial burdens, since variations in mitigation "ability" determine the extent to which each party would be asked to sacrifice for the cooperative effort (Baer et al. 2009; CSE 2010). While rarely invoked on its own, capacity-based accounts are often politically popular options for allocating remedial burdens amongst parties experiencing divergent circumstances, since they ask those able to do more to take on a greater role in solving common problems while allowing those less able, and therefore more reluctant to help, to participate in cooperative actions at a lower commitment level. While this might be viewed as merely a pragmatic concession, one can interpret capacity-based considerations as a demand of justice, as for example from the consideration that justice requires the equal sacrifice of welfare in pursuit of common endeavors, in combination with the observation that equal monetary contributions or percentage cuts to some baseline of national emissions might not have equal effects upon national welfare. Those advocating capacity-based principles therefore often combine them with one or more other principles, as with Simon Caney's

(2005) proposal for basing national mitigation burdens upon a combination of past emissions and national affluence.

Levels of Analysis

Taking its cues from the UNFCCC identification of nation-states as the relevant parties to the convention and agents responsible for mitigating climate-related harm, the dominant approach to theorizing climate justice likewise takes nations or states to be relevant units of analysis. By this account, climate change represents an injustice committed by relatively affluent states through their disproportionately high rates of greenhouse gas emissions, against relatively poor states with their comparatively low per capita emissions and (often) higher vulnerability to climatic change. Applying a CBDR principle would assign remedial burdens to nation-states on the basis of their per capita emissions, but would remain silent on the question of how these burdens are to be internally allocated within such states. Insofar as some nations were more vulnerable than others to climate-related harm, they would as nations have claims upon a larger share of resources made available for adaptation projects (or, alternatively, to compensate them for their imposed suffering if adaptation fails or is impossible) which, through financing mechanisms like the Green Climate Fund, would require differential contributions from states on the basis of their differentiated responsibility, viewed in terms of some quantum of their greenhouse gas emissions.

Critics of the nation-state model point out the wide disparity in individual emissions in both industrialized and developing countries, often noting that big individual polluters in poorer countries compare with those in more affluent states and that poor residents of developed countries often bear a closer resemblance in both their responsibility for and vulnerability to climate change to residents of developing countries than to their more affluent compatriots. Rather than applying CBDR principles at a national level of analysis exclusively, some argue, they should also or instead be applied at an individual level (Harris 2009). In combination with a macro-level view that focuses upon states, one version would employ a two-stage burden allocation process, first allocating national burdens in proportion to national responsibility and then translating those national targets into individual burdens in a second stage, relying upon the same CBDR principle in assigning persons with higher emissions greater remedial burdens. In another version, differences in national per capita emissions would play no role, with remedial burdens being assigned according to individual criteria only. A version of this latter approach can be seen in proposals for personal carbon allowances (Hyams 2009), which grants those holding title to them permission to emit up to some determinate threshold but prohibits further emissions, taxing them above that individual quota in order to mimic the effects of a trading system for such allowances or else involving actual trading of personal credits.

In addition to nation-states and individuals, other entities have been proposed as having decarbonization obligations as a matter of climate justice. Firms and municipalities commonly take on non-binding pledges to reduce their emissions, citing climate justice concerns and hoping to influence other actors to do the same, as do households, neighborhoods, organizations such as universities and professional associations, and multinational organizations such as the European Union (Fisher 2014). In some instances where emissions from some activity are not clearly attributable either to particular persons or states, as when a commercial airline departs from one country and lands in another while carrying passengers and cargo bound for still other destinations, analyses of how much each might be allowed to emit before contributing to climate injustice employ analyses at levels in between states and persons as a pragmatic device, given complications inherent in assigning emissions upward to states or downward to individuals. On other occasions, such intermediate actors are targeted with climate change mitigation imperatives because they have more control over their carbon footprints than do either nations or persons, as with "green" or "sustainable" ratings of manufacturers or service providers on the basis of their carbon footprints relative to others (Newell and Paterson 2010).

Further Evolution of Environmental Justice Analysis

Global climate change offers one of several applications of this third generation of EJ discourse, given the fragmented agency and dispersed causality from which the accumulation of greenhouse gases originates. By extending its account of responsibility to include inequitable contributions to aggregative problems by large numbers of uncoordinated parties, and by replacing the limited focus of first generation EJ discourses on injunctive relief and redistribution rather than cessation of pollution-related harm with sustainability imperatives and mechanisms for redressing past injustice, third generation EJ analysis could be applied to environmental issues that have not previously been regarded as raising issues of justice. With some minor revision of existing EJ discourse to account for their distinctive features, other forms of resource depletion and ecological degradation that result not from a small number of identifiable actions undertaken by a few culpable parties could be challenged as unjust, with remedies bound by the constraints of one or more justice principles. Chronic water scarcity in many of the world's poorest and most vulnerable regions could be linked to excessive use by the affluent elsewhere, although unsustainable use differs from the pollution theme that links the first three generations of EJ analysis. Likewise, the unsustainable use of the world's fisheries and agricultural capacity, both of which exacerbate existing disadvantages through environmental drivers, could be cast as an issue of environmental rather than economic or social justice insofar as it depended upon claims about egalitarian entitlement to the planet's ecological capacity, as some have articulated.

Similarly, climate change policy responses invite further justice analyses than have thus far emerged within third generation EJ discourses, including demands for more inclusive, responsive, and accountable institutions for directing mitigation and adaptation efforts. Calls for climate justice have likewise sought to invoke a form of resource egalitarianism similar to that discussed above (Hayward 2007), through which the injustice of climate change has less to do with the effects of greenhouse pollution than with the inequitable allocation of or access to natural resources, whether in terms of the carbon sinks that allow for benign greenhouse emissions or the water and mineral resources that facilitate a relatively cost-effective transition to a low-carbon energy economy. Regardless of how EJ discourse continues to evolve, the concept has up to now gained considerable currency in popular and scholarly circles as the result of the considerable purchase that its principles contain, whether in legal, political, or philosophical applications. For this reason, EJ theories and analyses are likely to remain central to the ongoing development of environmental political theory into the foreseeable future.

References

Baer, P., Athanasiou, T., Kartha, S., and Kemp-Benedict, E. (2009). "Greenhouse Development Rights: A Proposal for a Fair Global Climate Treaty." *Ethics, Place & Environment* 12(3): 267–81.

Bullard, R. (1990). *Dumping in Dixie: Race, Class, and Environmental Quality* (Boulder, CO: Westview).

Caney, S. (2005). "Cosmopolitan Justice, Responsibility and Global Climate Change." *Leiden Journal of International Law* 18(4): 747–75.

Centre for Science and Environment (CSE). (2010). "Who is Responsible?" (New Delhi: CSE), available at http://www.cseindia.org/userfiles/Who%20is%20responsible(1).pdf Last accessed June 18, 2015.

Chavis, Jr., B. F. and Lee, C. (1987). *Toxic Wastes and Race in the United States* (New York: United Church of Christ Commission for Racial Justice).

Fisher, S. (2014). "The Emerging Geographies of Climate Justice." *The Geographical Journal* (doi: 10.1111/geoj. 12078).

Harris, P. G. (2009). *World Ethics and Climate Change: From International to Global Justice* (Edinburgh: Edinburgh University Press).

Hayward, T. (2007). "Human Rights Versus Emissions Rights: Climate Justice and the Equitable Distribution of Ecological Space." *Ethics & International Affairs* 21(4): 431–50.

Hyams, K. (2009). "A Just Response to Climate Change: Personal Carbon Allowances and the Normal-Functioning Approach." *Journal of Social Philosophy* 40(2): 237–56.

Meyer, A. (2000). *Contraction and Convergence: The Global Solution to Climate Change* (Bristol, UK: Green Books).

Newell, P. and Paterson, M. (2010). *Climate Capitalism: Global Warming and the Transformation of the Global Economy* (New York: Cambridge University Press).

Schlosberg, D. (2009). *Defining Environmental Justice: Theories, Movements, and Nature* (New York: Oxford University Press).

Shue, H. (1993). "Subsistence Emissions and Luxury Emissions." *Law & Policy* 15(1): 39–59.

Vanderheiden, S. (2008). *Atmospheric Justice: A Political Theory of Climate Change* (New York: Oxford University Press).

Vanderheiden, S. (2011). "Globalizing Responsibility for Climate Change." *Ethics & International Affairs* 25(1): 65–84.

Young, I. M. (2006). "Responsibility and Global Justice: A Social Connection Model." *Social Philosophy and Policy* 23(1): 102–30.

CHAPTER 22

ENVIRONMENTAL HUMAN RIGHTS

KERRI WOODS

In the words of the Dalai Lama, "a clean environment is a human right." Many, many people around the world struggle to secure this right for themselves, their families, and communities. Indeed, some have died in the attempt. Given (i) the urgency of environmental problems—global problems such as anthropogenic climate change and biodiversity loss, and local ones such as industrial pollution, deforestation, toxification of waterways—and (ii) the very serious social and political risks faced by many environmental activists, particularly in developing countries, it is not surprising that there has been growing interest in the idea of environmental human rights.

We find this in the burgeoning academic literature in the field, but also in legal and political practice. At the grassroots level, activists have long framed their claims addressing particular environmental struggles in terms of human rights, and international NGOs like Amnesty International now also recognize environmental human rights amongst their campaigns. In 2012, the United Nations High Commissioner for Human Rights mandated an Independent Expert on the Environment to report to the Human Rights Commission. Yet, environmental concerns were largely absent from human rights declarations and covenants in the early stages of the development of human rights after the landmark 1948 Universal Declaration of Human Rights. Similarly, political theorists interested in human rights had almost nothing to say about the environment until the beginning of the twenty-first century.

There are different ways of thinking about the idea of environmental human rights. We might understand environmental human rights to be rights *of* the environment—that is, rights embedded in constitutional law or similarly authoritative law and attributed to the biosphere, or an ecosystem, or some other entity that constitutes a human environment—rights that can be exercised against human beings. These would be strictly speaking environmental rights, but might be called human rights because of the canonical status of human rights law.

More often, though, we find environmental human rights understood to be rights held by human beings, and stipulating the entitlement of human beings to some sort of environmental good. Here the possibilities include rights claimed by environmental activists, such as free speech and free association rights, as well as rights to be informed of proposed developments and their likely environmental impacts. There is nothing terribly new in this conception of environmental human rights—essentially these are long-recognized civil and political rights applied to the case of environmental issues. Specifically *environmental* human rights, which represent a departure from traditionally accepted human rights, would be either rights to particular environmental resources, or to a specified standard of environmental quality, well-being, or sustainability. Both of these latter types of rights have been explored in some detail by environmental political theorists, and it is on these types of rights that I will focus my discussion.

My aim here is to unpack the idea of environmental human rights, beginning with the question: why adopt a human rights approach to theorizing claims to environmental goods of one sort or another? Suppose we are concerned with questions like, what do we owe future generations? Or, should people in one country have a say about the ways another country approaches its environmental resources? My question in the first section is, why would we approach these questions in terms of human rights at all? In the second section, I move on from this problem to look at the various ways in which environmental human rights might be conceptualized, and in the third section I look at what an account of human rights entails in terms of rights holders and duty bearers. The importance of this last topic lies in the ways in which environmental political theorists might use the human rights framework and the extent to which environmental human rights represent an innovation in the concept of human rights itself.

Why Adopt a Human Rights Approach?

Human rights emerged in legal and political practice in the aftermath of the Second World War. They have developed into an authoritative language in which to advance moral and political claims. Thus, human rights exist at (at least) two levels: (i) they are a legal tool, both at a global level and in the constitutions of most countries; and (ii) they are a powerful discourse. To say "this practice violates my human right" is to say that an important wrong is taking place, and it ought to be stopped. Human rights are remarkably widely accepted, in word if not always in deed—hardly anyone wants to be "against" human rights, even if many governments fail to fully respect human rights in their actions and policies.

Given this remarkable standing of human rights, it is unsurprising to find that environmental scholars and activists have appropriated the language of human rights when analyzing and articulating demands of entitlements to environmental goods. Theorizing moral claims via the medium of an established and apparently accepted normative framework is quite obviously a promising approach. If environmental claims can be shown to be consonant with this accepted normative architecture, then environmental activists will have a powerful justificatory tool at their disposal. Moreover, the global scope of human rights seems prima facie well-suited to the global nature of the environment itself and the most pressing environmental challenges, such as climate change and biodiversity loss.

Human rights, being as they are the embodiment of claims for equality and justice, seem ideologically compatible with the broad arc of environmental aims. Environmentalists often (not quite always) hold that environmental problems arise from a broader set of moral and political problems that are reflected in the persistence of social and political inequalities and injustices evident around the world. Insofar as it is true that the very idea of human rights presupposes the moral equality of all human beings, it seems obvious that human rights represent a significant challenge to the status quo. Many environmentalists would be sympathetic to this challenge. There seems, then, to be a neat conceptual and normative fit between the concept of human rights and the general aims and moral commitments of environmentalism that would lead an advocate of the latter to embrace the idea of environmental human rights.

There are, however, two sets of concerns that may give pause for thought. One is practical, the other conceptual. In practical terms, what the global human rights regime suggests is that the protection of human rights is first and foremost the responsibility of nation-states, and specifically of the nation-state of the citizen(s) whose rights are under discussion (see, *inter alia*, Beitz 2009). This is partly because, in effect, states are the only plausible agents able to command the necessary resources (O'Neill 2001, 2005). But states are also the primary agents of justice in a human rights framework because embedded within the global human rights regime is a normative commitment to the values of sovereignty and self-determination.

Here we encounter a potential worry for environmentalists keen to embrace the idea of environmental human rights. Pollution of air and waterways does not respect state borders. In some instances, the sovereignty-based global order has a good record of achieving cooperation to address urgent environmental issues. The 1987 Montreal Protocol is an example of a global agreement that successfully addresses an environmental problem generated by multiple diffuse actors but with localized displaced effects, specifically a dangerously depleted ozone layer in the Southern hemisphere.

But sovereign rights have often been asserted by those seeking to defend environmentally unsustainable practices. The principle of sovereign rights over natural resources within a territory is at odds with the idea that the earth is a commons that belongs to all. Within the realist tradition of International Relations theory we are told that it is "rational" for state actors to accord priority to the interests of their own state, even at the expense of international collaboration that could lead to a "win–win" scenario, such as in the case of the Montreal Protocol. There is a significant body of literature calling into question this realist approach, but it remains the case that electoral practices of liberal democracies, which foster short-termism, and the political–economic nexus that is crucial to the stability of the economy in most countries, create significant disincentives for political leaders to do anything other than prioritize the positions of their own states over the short term. These features of the sovereignty-based order compounded the challenge of reaching global agreement to undertake coordinated action on climate change, as on other global environmental problems.

As for human rights in general, the norm of sovereignty presents an interesting paradox for environmental human rights. On the one hand, human rights represent a universal standard, a standard against which all states agree to be judged and in doing so accept some limit to their sovereignty. On the other hand, enshrined in the International Bill of Rights[1] is the right to self-determination, which gives moral authority to the claim that a state has a sovereign right to determine for itself its own affairs and to reject the interference of outsiders (O'Neill 2005).

The other concern about a human rights approach relates to the concept of human rights itself. Any normative framework grounded in the rights of humans *qua* humans is self-evidently anthropocentric. There is a long tradition of moral and political theorizing on environmental issues that takes as its point of departure a rejection of the anthropocentrism of Western legal, moral, and political thought and practice (see, *inter alia*, Marshall 1995; Attfield 1999). For many, the environmental problems we now face are not just the product of an economic system that fails to count the costs of environmental externalities, but rather they are the product of a way of thinking about social and political life that emerged predominantly in the West and that paradigmatically took the relationship between human and non-human to be one of mastery and domination. As such, it would be at best misguided to look for a framework for addressing the current environmental crisis in the very tradition that produced these problems. This business-as-usual approach to environmental political theory seems unlikely to generate the radical conceptual (sometimes spiritual) shift that is held to be crucial to realigning the human–non-human dynamic (see, for example, Naess 1973).

Environmentalists who take it to be axiomatic of being "green" that one accepts the precept that non-human nature has intrinsic value would be very surprised, and perhaps somewhat alarmed, by the turn toward something like political orthodoxy that seems evident in the move to embrace environmental human rights. Human rights, it is true, have historical roots in calls for revolution and emancipation (Ishay 2008). But it is also true that to accept human rights as a framework for theorizing a given set of claims is to accept an institutional order that many would want to reject, and that discloses a set of moral presuppositions that are in fact controversial. These include not only the normative principle of sovereignty, but also the presupposition that the individual human being has a special moral value, that the individual exists in an antagonistic relationship to her community, and particularly to political authority within her community. One need not be an eco-centrist to see that to take on the mantle of human rights is to take an approach to environmental political theorizing that is at home in the liberal tradition of political theory in a way that more radical approaches to environmentalism would not be.

For some, this will be an advantage. If environmental political theory is to be persuasive, it needs to be intelligible to a wide audience. Liberal democracies, for all their deficiencies, remain a remarkably popular and resilient method for organizing a political community. Moreover, human rights, as the institutional benchmark of liberal democracies, have acquired a remarkable status as a global "standard of civilization" in Jack Donnelly's (1998) phrase. Some, of course, will note that, throughout history, standards of civilization have tended to be exclusionary devices. But I would not want to underplay the extent to which human rights as both an institution and an idea are intimately connected to the norms of freedom and equality. That being the case, the attraction of the human rights framework as a platform for advancing environmental claims is self-evident.

However, we should remember that human rights do not represent an institutional framework for delivering the good life, let alone the green good life. Human rights are moral minimums that protect human beings' entitlement to the necessary conditions for a life consistent with human dignity. That being the case, the standard of environmental sustainability that a human rights approach promises need not be as high as might be delivered by some other approach. For example, if we were to begin with a theory about the value of the non-human environment, rather than its value *for* humans, we might find ourselves committed to preserve a great many more species, and their habitats, than if we begin with a theory about the minimum that is necessary in order for humans to lead a decent life. Human rights protect moral minimums, but many environmentalists will argue that we have a moral duty to go beyond the minimum. Against this, the advocate of human rights may rightly point out that human rights do not constitute a total ethical theory—they are minimum standards because they are the most basic and fundamental, and thus, most morally urgent demands. One need not stop there. It is perfectly consistent to defend a human rights approach to securing some particular environmental goods at the same time as advocating a stewardship approach (say) which takes us beyond the minimum.

It is noteworthy that in the drafting of canonical human rights texts in the latter half of the twentieth century environmental issues did not feature at all. Human rights protect against standard threats to human dignity (Shue 1980). For some environmentalists it is cause for concern that the human rights framework is traditionally silent on environmental issues. Indeed, the absence of environmental claims in canonical human rights texts suggests that humans do not see themselves as ecologically embedded beings (Woods 2010). Human rights are not Platonic forms, they are made—articulated and institutionalized—by human beings. They are thus a reflection of how human beings see themselves in moral and political terms; morally because they highlight those goods and capacities that we hold to be crucial to a minimally decent life, and politically in the sense that the functionality of human rights tells us much about the ways in which responsibility for ensuring the protection of human rights is to be ordered. For skeptics of human rights, the values embedded in the human rights framework are a product of the biases of those who created it—they are too liberal, too statist, too anthropocentrist. But for proponents of environmental human rights there is an opportunity to be found in the fact that human rights are human-made. Just as socialist and feminist thinkers have done, environmentalists might undertake an immanent critique of the traditionally liberal concept of human rights, and thereby develop an account of human rights that is fully fit for environmental purposes (Eckersley 1996; Hayward 2005; Hiskes 2009). Thus, when considering whether or not to embrace the idea of environmental human rights, it matters how human rights are conceived.

How Have Environmental Human Rights Been Conceived?

In the introduction I mentioned two ways of thinking about environmental human rights: (i) rights to particular environmental resources, or (ii) rights to a specified standard of environmental quality, well-being, or sustainability. Rights to particular environmental resources—most obviously land—are particularly important in the case of marginalized communities whose livelihoods or even residence is threatened by development projects. These sorts of rights are to some extent recognized in international treaties protecting the rights of indigenous peoples, but are also invoked in the context of any struggle where development threatens the short- or long-term well-being of an affected community (Hancock 2003). There is an interesting mix of characteristics evident in these sorts of human rights. On the one hand, rights to land look like traditional liberal property rights, and thus sit very easily within the liberal tradition of rights theorizing that can be traced to John Locke's (1985 [1690]) account of natural rights. On the other hand, the 2007 United Nations Declaration on the Rights of Indigenous Peoples recognizes rights to land and environmental resources justified by the rich cultural, spiritual, and social significance these entities have for indigenous peoples. What this suggests is that the human rights paradigm is capable of recognizing and legally protecting a relationship between the human and the non-human that is very different from the Western tradition of dominance and mastery that environmentalists reject.

Other examples of claims to particular environmental goods include a proposed human right to water, which is held to be implicitly endorsed in the United Nations' Millennium Development Goals (Alvarez 2003). Understood in these terms, environmental human rights seem to fit within what Juan Martinez-Alier (2001; see also this volume) calls "the environmentalism of the poor," that is, the struggle for rights and justice enacted by people who may not think of themselves as environmentalists, but simply as activists whose lives and livelihoods are threatened by apparently rapacious capitalism. This environmentalism of the poor is described by Martinez-Alier in contrast to the rather more privileged environmentalism of Western liberals who may be deeply concerned by species extinction, biodiversity loss, and the pollution of the global commons, but whose lives and communities are often insulated from the immediacy of these threats. As with other human rights, there are widely differing experiences of the threats to human dignity which may inflect the conceptualizations of human rights espoused in different social and political contexts.

A somewhat different way of thinking about rights to environmental goods would be to speak in terms of a right to emit greenhouse gases (effectively, a right to make use of carbon sinks). This is different from the example of rights to land or water insofar as carbon (or other waste) sinks are a less tangible resource, and are generally more diffusely located in physical space. In essence, this approach to environmental human rights tries to tackle directly one of the most pernicious effects of market externalities. In debates about climate justice we encounter human rights arguments that suggest that the right to a minimally decent standard of living necessarily entails a right to emit a certain level of greenhouse gases (Shue 2007), which would be contingent on the specific needs of the individual (for example, children might need more heat than adults) and the accessibility of cleaner energy alternatives (for example, green tariffs on a national grid in an industrialized economy, or ease of access to a national grid in an industrializing economy). Henry Shue's aim here is to draw a distinction between subsistence emissions (which are legitimate) and luxury emissions (which are not), but it seems to me that Tim Hayward (2007) is right to resist the idea that there can ever be, even implicitly, "a human right to pollute."

Hayward's own idea is that we may find great normative purchase in considering the implications of rights to ecological space. What he means by ecological space is an attempt to capture the totality of material throughput in any human endeavor. Each person, and each action, occupies a certain amount of ecological space which may or may not be physically proximate to them. The ecological footprint of our lives could then be measured against the ecological space that exists in a particular community (or globally). Again, the idea is not that a right to use up resources is ever countenanced. Rather, by exposing the enormous imbalance in the use of ecological space we starkly illustrate the extent to which those living in the rich countries are in massive ecological debt to those in the poorer countries and to future generations. The concept of rights has less work to do here; environmental justice becomes a question of distribution.

A third interpretation of environmental human rights, and the one that is most often advanced within environmental political theory, posits a right to a certain standard of environmental quality (for an overview, see Woods 2010; Toft 2013). There have been several formulations of this interpretation, both speaking generally in terms of a "safe environment" (Nickel 1993), and more specifically in terms of a right to a stable climate (Vanderheiden 2008, see also Vanderheiden's chapter on climate justice in this volume) or rights against "dangerous" climate change (Bell 2011). These approaches suggest that what is needed is a new human right—an environmental one. Influential here is James Nickel's early essay in which he defends a human right to a safe environment, on a threshold model. Simon Caney also tells us that human rights "represent moral 'thresholds' below which people should not fall" (2010: 164). The threshold idea presents some challenges for thinking clearly about human rights obligations. The argument crucially depends upon there being a critical threshold in environmental (un)safety, which, if passed, constitutes a threat to human rights. Before that threshold, it may be bad that (say) there is an oil spill, or an unstable climate, but it is not a bad of the magnitude of human rights issues. If human rights "trump" lesser moral and political claims

(Dworkin 1984), then we will want to know when a given environmental problem is a human rights concern, and when it is not.

James Nickel deals with this problem directly: "How safe must the environment be? The total elimination of all risks is impossible... A better approach is to specify that the environment, or the level of safety from environmental risks, should be satisfactory or adequate for health.... The fact that terms such as 'satisfactory' and 'adequate' are vague is not a significant problem in this context.... International human rights typically set broad normative standards that can be interpreted and applied by appropriate legislative, judicial, or administrative bodies at the national level" (Nickel 1993: 285). To claim a human right to a safe environment and rely on the global, local, and national institutions to interpret critical thresholds (or to infer from existing human rights that we have a right to be protected from climate change) is not qualitatively different from claiming a human right to education, say, or even freedom of expression. The basic structure of Nickel's proposed right to a safe environment is endorsed in other formulations of environmental human rights. Hayward (2005) argues that the right to an environment adequate for health and well-being should be enshrined in the constitution of every liberal democracy, on the grounds that this is consistent with the implementation of existing accepted human rights. As Hayward (2005: 31) notes, the "declaratory formulation" that he, Nickel, and others adopt is entirely constituent with other iterations of human rights. There is scope for flexibility within this formulation for different nation-states to interpret the necessary and sufficient conditions for this standard of adequacy, and again the concept of a critical threshold below which no environment should be allowed to fall seems to be implied.

Although I am broadly sympathetic to this approach, for me, there remains an unresolved tension here. The question of where the threshold lies remains a political one, to be decided by each community and each generation. It will be contingent upon levels of technological development, on population size, and on the lifestyle preferences of the population. We may collectively decide we are prepared to put up with rather less biodiversity than currently exists, without it necessarily threatening human rights. Do we really *need* white rhinos? On the other hand, environmental human rights understood in threshold terms might well be best achieved by halving the human population of the planet. Clearly, any plausible method of doing so would violate other human rights. But the point here is that the threshold is contingent on several factors, one significant factor being simply the number of humans any given environmental context is used to support. It is not clear what the human rights framework tells us about population ethics, but it is startling that this is a question that is largely neglected in the literature (see Diane Coole's contribution to this volume).

Caney's early work similarly proposed a human right against climate change (thus a new human right) but he has since modified his position to say that anthropogenic climate change violates already accepted human rights, and as such we have duties to mitigate, or, where this fails, to facilitate adaptation (Caney 2005; cf. 2010). He concentrates on three human rights that he finds endorsed in multiple canonical human rights treaties, including the International Bill of Rights: (1) the right to life, (2) the right to health, and (3) the right to subsistence (Caney 2010). Anyone with a passing familiarity with debates about climate change will know that each of these is threatened if the predictions of the International Panel on Climate Change (IPCC) are correct. Insofar as this is true, then it follows, Caney argues, that persons have a duty not to contribute to anthropogenic climate change, and where they fail in this duty (as most of us unavoidably do) we have duties to mitigate or compensate appropriately. Note that we have moved here from human rights as presupposing a statist framework to human rights as a mechanism by which we may identify individual duties. I will say more about this in the next section.

Clearly, the human rights approach provides a powerful argument. Insofar as the same argument might credibly be made with respect to biodiversity loss, one can infer that Caney's strategy applies to other environmental problems beyond climate change. Thus, accepting the threshold idea (and its potential problems), we might proceed by arguing for a new human right—an environmental one—or we might proceed by pointing out the extent to which already accepted human rights deeply depend upon a "safe" or "adequate" or "clean" environment if they are to be realized.

Whose Rights, Whose Duties?

In understanding the concept of environmental human rights, it is also important to analyze the normative contours that delineate rights holders and duty bearers. Who, then, can be said to have environmental human rights? Human rights are typically understood to be held by all human beings, simply in virtue of their humanity. This much need not be controversial for a theory of environmental human rights, but environmentalists may well want to challenge the practice of restricting fundamental rights only to human beings.

If we take the term human rights to mean not just rights held by humans, but the most fundamental or basic rights there are, which are morally or lexically prior to other moral and political claims, then we might reasonably wonder why non-human animals, or perhaps ecosystems, or the biosphere itself, might not legitimately hold such rights. There is much more to say about this, but the basic thought is that human rights *qua* fundamental rights protect entities that are held to be of great moral value, yet it is not obvious that only humans have such value. Moreover, if we try to explain precisely why humans and only humans have that special value, what qualities it rests on that are unique to humans but possessed by all humans, we often run into serious difficulties (Singer 2009; see also the chapters by Frost and Youatt in this volume for more on this).

Leaving aside the question of whether non-humans can be bearers of human rights, there is another constituency of potential human rights claimants that needs to be considered. Particularly in debates about climate change, we often encounter claims that the human rights of future generations will be violated by the action (or inaction) of people alive today (Hiskes 2009; Caney 2010; Bell 2011). Indeed, the long-term impact of climate change is such that future generations will in all likelihood feel the most severe effects of it. That being the case, the question of whether or not future persons can be said to have human rights that impose duties on those living now has great significance.

For some, it is intuitively obvious that future persons can be, and indeed are, bearers of human rights that are normatively operative now. Future people will have fundamental interests that we can be reasonably sure we can predict with some accuracy—they will need food, shelter, water, and a reasonably stable climate, a reasonable degree of biodiversity and other ecosystem support services. Insofar as this is true, and insofar as we accept that present persons have rights to a given standard of environmental resources, it seems intuitively defensible to say that future persons have a moral claim to a like degree of protection.

However, there does seem to be an important difference between the moral standing of actually existing persons and future persons who we may reasonably predict will exist but who do not exist now (Feinberg 1974; Partridge 1990). Derek Parfit's (1984) much discussed "non-identity problem" presents us with a difficulty. A simple gloss of Parfit's rather complex idea might go as follows: Environmental policy *ECO*, adopted now, would influence the patterns of living of current people, so it would influence which people met and mated and became parents. (In some discussions this is even taken to the level of influencing the precise gametes that are combined in the case of the same parents, influenced, say, by whether the parents drive home from work or take public transport, thus arriving later.) Environmental policy *POLLUTE* would have a different influence, so the offspring that parents produce in the context of policy *ECO* would be different from the offspring that are produced in the context of policy *POLLUTE*. This being the case, Parfit's thesis suggests that we cannot say that the children who grow up after policy *POLLUTE* have been harmed by the environmentally damaging impacts of this policy, relative to what their lives would otherwise have been, because the fact is that their lives *would not otherwise have been*. Their lives would not have been better under policy *ECO*; they would not have been born at all under policy *ECO*, because different offspring altogether would have come into being instead.

In short, the non-identity problem suggests that a person cannot be harmed by an event that also caused them to be brought into existence, because the non-factual baseline against which harm is being compared would be non-existence. If this is true then it follows that a given course of action or policy cannot coherently be said to violate the human rights of future generations, because the people who comprise the future generations affected would not otherwise have existed.

Many have disregarded this philosophical puzzle, holding that the significance of the non-identity problem for environmental political theory has been overstated. (Parfit himself takes the view that it makes no difference to the content of our moral obligations to future generations, though for him it does make a difference to the terms in which these can be expressed and the justificatory arguments that can be offered in support of them.) Derek Bell argues, "Current persons have a duty not to undertake actions that will violate the rights of the actual future people who will exist—even if those particular future people would not have existed but for those very actions" (Bell 2011: 110). Moreover, the average expected lifespan of most reasonably affluent people in

Western democracies is such that many of those people alive today will overlap, at least briefly, with future generations whose lives are likely to be impacted by anthropogenic climate change. That being the case, we might follow Bell and others in holding that the non-identity problem does not completely disable a human rights-based argument in support of duties associated with climate change.

It is significant that Bell shifts attention from the status of rights bearers to the responsibilities of duty bearers. Whether or not the non-identity problem is fully resolved, what matters, from Bell's point of view, is that we can use an account of human rights held by future persons to give us clarity on the moral obligations held by persons alive today. This represents a significant shift in the purpose of human rights. Human rights are no longer the urgent claims of persons whose dignity and well-being is gravely threatened; rather, human rights are a mechanism for understanding what we in the here and now ought morally to do for persons who will be in years to come.

This change in the function and orientation of human rights speaks to the point raised earlier about there being an opportunity in the fact that human rights are human made. While it is true that human rights as they exist in law are undeniably statist institutions, human rights as they exist in moral and political discourse can be invoked as means of claiming moral authority for one's position. In saying "this is a human right" we do not simply make an observation about the human rights that exist in positive law, we are also, implicitly, saying something like, "this is a basic, fundamental entitlement that ought to be recognized in positive law and acted on by governments." By focusing on the duties of individuals, theorists of climate justice who invoke human rights take this further, by linking the moral authority of human rights to duties of individuals to effect political change. The function of human rights here is to justify burdens that are to fall on the capable, rather than to defend entitlements of the threatened.

Within political theory, much discussion of environmental human rights, and in particular of human rights against climate change, follows this shift in focus. If environmental human rights are to be effective in delivering the ends for which environmentalists invoke them, then it is crucial that duty bearers can be identified, and that the extent and content of their duties can be determined and justified. It is also important that the universalism inherent in the idea of human rights, and its long tradition of association with a revolutionary and emancipatory spirit, need not overshadow the legacy of the statist conceptualization of human rights as institutionalized in the post-Second World War international regime. What advocates of environmental human rights suggest is that the concept of human rights is a powerful tool for advancing the claim that all human beings are entitled to a standard of environmental well-being, wherever and whenever they happen to be.

Conclusion

In this chapter I have addressed three key questions in order to unpack the concept of environmental human rights: (1) Why adopt a human rights approach? (2) How have environmental human rights been conceived? and (3) What does an account of environmental human rights entail for rights holders and duty bearers? This last question is perhaps the most controversial, raising as it does the question of the moral status of future generations (as well as non-humans) and ultimately the nature of human rights themselves.

Human rights have been employed as a means of justifying duties which environmental political theorists have long defended via other ethical languages. From a human rights point of view we might find the direction of the justificatory argument a little unorthodox. In a sense, rights have a secondary role here; it is the duties that persons have with respect to the environment that are key. One might wonder what work the concept of human rights is really doing here. Invoking human rights affords the theorist access to a powerful normative architecture, but one which puts human value at the center of the moral story—it is for the sake of current and future humans (not non-humans nor its own sake) that the environment must be protected and maintained. One could defend an account of duties to respect the environment more directly via a moral argument about the intrinsic rather than instrumental value of the environment. But such arguments have failed to persuade in sufficient numbers to motivate the widespread action that is evidently needed. What invoking human rights brings, then, is the authority, accessibility, and intelligibility of a widely endorsed moral, political, and legal framework.

Note

1. Three human rights agreements are together referred to as the International Bill of Rights: The Universal Declaration of Human Rights (1948), The International Covenant on Civil and Political Rights (1966) and the International Covenant on Economic, Cultural and Social Rights (1966).

References

Alvarez, Ignacio J. (2003). "The Right to Water as a Human Right." In *Linking Human Rights and the Environment*, edited by R. Picolotti and J. D. Taillant (Tuscon: University of Arizona Press), 71–81.

Attfield, Robin. (1999) *The Ethics of the Global Environment* (Edinburgh: Edinburgh University Press).

Beitz, Charles R. (2009). *The Idea of Human Rights* (Oxford: Oxford University Press).

Bell, Derek. (2011). "Does Anthropogenic Climate Change Violate Human Rights?" *Critical Review of International Social and Political Philosophy* 14(2): 99–124.

Caney, Simon. (2005). "Cosmopolitan Justice, Responsibility, and Global Climate Change." *Leiden Journal of International Law* 18(4): 747–75.

Caney, Simon. (2010). "Climate Change, Human Rights, and Moral Thresholds." In *Human Rights and Climate Change*, edited by S. Humphreys (Cambridge: Cambridge University Press), 163–77.

Eckersley, Robyn. (1996) 'Greening Liberal Democracy: the Rights Discourse Revisited'. In *Democracy and Green Political Thought: Sustainability, Rights and Citizenship*, edited by B. Doherty and M. de Geus (London: Routledge) 212-236.

Feinberg, Joel. (1974). "The Rights of Animals and Future Generations." In *Philosophy and Environmental Crisis*, edited by W. Blackstone (Athens, GA: University of Georgia Press).

Hancock, Jan. (2003). *Environmental Human Rights: Power, Ethics and Law* (London: Ashgate).

Hayward, Tim. (2005). *Constitutional Environmental Rights* (Oxford: Oxford University Press).

Hayward, Tim. (2007). "Human Rights versus Emissions Rights: Climate Justice and the Equitable Distribution of Ecological Space." *Ethics and International Affairs* 21: 431–50.

Hiskes, Richard P. (2009). *The Human Right to a Green Future* (Cambridge: Cambridge University Press).

Ishay, Micheline R. (2008) *The History of Human Rights* (Oakland, CA: University of California Press).

Marshall, Peter. (1995). *Nature's Web: Rethinking Our Place on Earth* (London: M. E. Sharpe).

Naess, Arne. (1973). "The Shallow and the Deep, Long-Range Ecology Movement. A Summary." *Inquiry* 16: 95–100.

Nickel, James. (1993). "The Human Right to a Safe Environment: Philosophical Perspectives on its Scope and Justification." *Yale Journal of International Law* 18: 281–96.

O'Neill, Onora. (2001). "Agents of Justice." *Metaphilosophy* 32(2): 180–95.

O'Neill, Onora. (2005). "The Dark Side of Human Rights." *International Affairs* 81(2): 427–39.

Parfit, Derek. (1984). *Reasons and Persons* (Oxford: Oxford University Press).

Partridge, Ernest. (1990). "On the Rights of Future Generations." In *Upstream/Downstream: Issues in Environmental Ethics*, edited by D. Scherer (Philadelphia, PA: Temple University Press), 40–66.

Shue, Henry. (1990). *Basic Rights: Subsistence, Affluence and US Foreign Policy* (Princeton, NJ: Princeton).

Singer, Peter. (2009). "Speciesism and Moral Status." *Metaphilosophy* 40(3–4): 567–81.

Toft, Kristian Høyer. (2013). "The Human Rights Approach to Climate Change: An Overview." *Environmental Ethics* 35: 209–25.

Vanderheiden, Steve. (2008). *Atmospheric Justice: A Political Theory of Climate Change* (Oxford: Oxford University Press).

Woods, Kerri. (2010). *Human Rights and Environmental Sustainability* (Cheltenham: Edward Elgar).

Woods, Kerri. (2014). *Human Rights* (Basingstoke: Palgrave Macmillan).

CHAPTER 23

RESPONSIBILITY FOR CLIMATE CHANGE AS A STRUCTURAL INJUSTICE

ROBYN ECKERSLEY

INTRODUCTION

ENVIRONMENTAL protection is generally accepted as a public good, and the task of preventing environmental degradation is widely understood as a collective responsibility. But there is much disagreement about how this responsibility is to be shared among states, corporations, and citizens in a globalizing world. Indeed, the increasing integration of the global economy through the processes of liberalization has, paradoxically, challenged the conventional liberal grammar of responsibility, which is rooted in notions of individual agency, direct causation, and culpability.

How we frame problems, and how we think about the relationship between agents and structures, shapes how we think about responsibility. The dominant frame for thinking about environmental problems comes from economics: such problems are "negative externalities," which are the unintended and unwanted side-effects of normal practices of production and consumption. This framing serves to naturalize the practice of privatizing gains and socializing losses and thereby absolves economic agents of responsibility until such time as regulators step in or "third party" victims turn to litigation.

The purpose of this chapter is explore what is gained, and what might be lost, if the harmful impacts of climate change are understood as the product of structural injustices, and whether this necessarily requires a forward looking rather than backward looking understanding of responsibility. In posing the problem this way I critically engage with Iris Marion Young's reflections on responsibility in her posthumously published book *Responsibility for Justice* (2011).[1] Unlike individual injustices, where undeserved harms can be traced to the wilful or negligent acts of identifiable "culprits," structural injustices are undeserved harms that are collectively produced through recurrent social practices that are considered "normal" and therefore non-blameworthy. To address this particular type of injustice, Young argued that it is necessary to avoid a backward looking, "liability model" of responsibility that focuses on blaming particular culprits. Instead, she defended a more critical, forward looking account of shared responsibility based on accountability, grounded in her "social connection" model, according to which all those who participate in the social structures that systematically produce undeserved harm bear responsibility for challenging, debating, and transforming those structures to reduce such harm.

Although Young's primary focus was poverty, and the particular problem of sweatshop labor in developing countries, her arguments can be readily applied to climate change. Here the primary injustice is that many of the world's poorest and least developed communities will suffer the worst impacts of climate change despite making the least contribution to the problem. At the same time, their marginal social structural position in the economy and the state system not only exposes them to most of the risks, and few of the benefits, generated by these social structures but also places them in a particularly weak position to orchestrate their transformation in ways that will reduce their vulnerability.

Of course, Young is not the only political theorist to reflect on responsibility or structural injustices. Both have been major themes in environmental political theory (EPT) and there is a rich literature within EPT and cognate fields that specifically focuses on assigning responsibility for mitigation and adaptation to states, individuals, and other actors (for example, Caney 2005, 2010; Vanderheiden 2008, 2011; Gardiner 2011; Page 2012). There is also a mounting environmental critique of the limitations of existing practices of corporate responsibility, and more general accountability practices in governance, alongside growing interest in new norms of responsibility in public and private governance and environmental citizenship (Dobson 2003), all of which seek to cater for the distinctive nature of transboundary environmental harm (for example, Mason 2008). And environmental justice scholars have shown that the skewed distribution of environmental risks and harms reflects not simply a structural problem of distributive justice but also a lack of social recognition of, and political participation by, the affected groups (Schlosberg 1999 and 2007). However, it is probably Ulrich Beck's critique of "organized irresponsibility," which forms a key plank in his theory of the risk society (for example, Beck 1995), that most resonates with Young's structural analysis. Despite these strong overlaps, her arguments are distinctive in at least two interesting respects.

First, whereas most of the climate ethics debates have focused on moral responsibility, Young is primarily interested in clarifying the special character of *political* responsibility for structural injustices. Of course, political responsibility cannot be dissociated from moral responsibility, and this essay will certainly highlight these connections. Yet not all forms of moral responsibility necessarily relate to structural injustices, or have a political character in the sense that they involve a public. Young's contribution is to sharpen our thinking about responsibility so that we are better equipped to reflect, communicate, and act politically in pursuit of the public good of environmental protection, which may therefore be understood as a "structural justice."

Second, Young's critique of the backward looking, liability model of responsibility poses a potential challenge to the arguments mounted by many developing countries and climate justice activists for the historical responsibility of developed countries for their cumulative emissions since the beginning of industrialization. A considered reply to this challenge holds the promise of revisiting with fresh eyes the long-standing stalemate between developed and developing countries over this vexed issue.

The discussion that follows is organized around these two distinctive features of Young's account. I begin by outlining in a little more detail Young's critique of the liability model and her alternative account of the political responsibility of citizens for structural injustices. Next I focus on the daunting character of this responsibility for citizens in relation to climate change, and offer some refinements of Young's analysis of the relationship between power and responsibility. I then move from citizens to states by providing a critical exploration of the implications of her critique of the liability model to arguments for the historical responsibility of states for climate change. In the conclusion, I connect Young's thinking on political responsibility to the sociological literature on risk and responsibility and draw out some of the unavoidable political and moral tensions that emerge from the analysis.

The Liability Model

In the English language, "responsibility" is one of those especially over-burdened words. Being responsible can mean any of the following: simply causing an outcome; being culpable and therefore morally blameworthy for an outcome; being legally liable for an outcome; being accountable or answerable for a problem; having certain duties associated with professional roles or capabilities, or arising from the membership of a particular community; or being obligated, or volunteering, to get a job done. Cutting across these different meanings are various categories of responsibility—moral, legal (strict or fault-based), professional, and political.

Young's critique of the "liability model" of responsibility takes aim at conventional (liberal) moral and legal accounts of responsibility that combine causal responsibility, culpability, and the associated obligation to provide redress. This is a powerful and appealing understanding of responsibility that is reflected in conventional moral intuitions as well as the criminal law, the law of torts, and international public law, including the principle of state responsibility for environmental harm. This liability model evolved to handle cases involving a relatively clear chain of causation between the harm suffered by identifiable victims and the actions or inactions of identifiable wrongdoers (which may include individuals, incorporated organizations, or states) who can be found to have breached a moral principle or duty of care. However, for Young, this model of responsibility is not only unable to address structural injustices generated by the activities of literally billions of individuals and organizations engaged in cooperation and competition; it also works actively to obscure the structural character of injustices in ways that make it hard to achieve collective action.

Young fleshes out this central claim with a set of interrelated arguments. First, she maintains that the liability model is politically unproductive because it is isolating, and focuses only on the immediate or proximate causes of discrete harms. Moreover, the act of singling out culpable individuals has the effect of absolving everyone else (Young 2011: 105–6).[2]

Second, the liability model judges wrongfulness on the basis of existing rules and institutions, yet it is precisely many of these rules and institutions that need to be called into question insofar as they legitimate the systemic production of injustices. The liability model therefore plays an ideological role in naturalizing existing social structures, thereby foreclosing critical reflection on the very practices that reproduce such structures and preventing the kinds of reforms that are required to prevent structural injustices.

Third, the liability model is backward looking in focusing on fact-finding and fault-finding in relation to past events. In contrast, addressing structural injustices requires a forward looking approach that challenges and seeks to transform the social practices that continue to produce harm in the present and future.

Finally, Young argues that the search for blameworthy agents tends to produce a highly defensive response from those who are accused of acting wrongly, which deflects attention away from the hard work that needs to be done by everyone to transform social structures.

Young's critique is part of a growing chorus of attempts in EPT and cognate fields to move beyond the liability model of responsibility toward a more critical understanding of responsibility that is appropriate to a global risk society. These arguments are forcefully made by Ulrich Beck, who laments how systems of organized irresponsibility have locked in a cynical fatalism over an increasingly "self-endangering society" (Beck 1995: 64–5). Likewise, Chad Lavin (2008) calls for a post-liberal account of responsibility while Andrew Linklater defends an understanding of "complex responsibility" that entails critically reflecting on the ways in which personal conduct, existing norms, and social institutions inflict undeserved harm on distant others (Linkater 2011: 101–2). But how is this broader notion of responsibility to be shared and discharged in relation to the structural injustices of climate related harm?

Political Responsibility

Since globalization has made political borders more porous, Young argues that political responsibility for structural injustices arises "not from living under a common constitution, but rather from participating in the diverse institutional processes that produce structural injustice" (Young 2011: 105). This includes participating in transnational economic exchanges. As she explains:

> The social connection model of responsibility says that individuals bear responsibility for structural injustice because they contribute by their actions to the processes that produce unjust outcomes. Our responsibility derives from belonging together with others in a system of interdependent processes of cooperation and competition through which we seek benefits and aim to realize projects . . . All who dwell within the structures must take responsibility for remedying injustices they cause, though none is specifically liable for the harm in a legal sense. (Young 2011: 105)

For Young, political responsibility is not about heroism or charity. Rather, it requires a particular kind of solidarity that must be forged between individuals who may have little in common but for a preparedness to engage in a public debate and collective action for the sake of preventing structural injustices (2011: 120). This account returns to the Latin root of the word responsibility, *respondeo* (to answer), and to the French *répondre* (as in RSVP) (Lucas 1995: 5). Indeed, for Lucas, "the central core of the concept of responsibility is that I can be asked the question 'Why did you do it?' and be obliged to give an answer" (1995: 5).

In the case of climate change, this question can also take the form "Why did you not do anything?" This is a question that older generations must answer younger generations, rich countries must answer poor countries, and everyone must answer those who speak on behalf of non-human others. Clearly, political responsibility is not just about answering questions but also asking them. Indeed, responsibility *qua* answerability does not arise if questions are not asked. Exercising political responsibility for structural injustices such as climate change is necessarily public spirited or other-regarding in the sense that it acknowledges and honors social connection to others through the very practice of asking and answering others in ways that address collective practices, meanings, and collective consequences. Conversely, failing to ask or anticipate questions, ignoring or resisting questions, or answering them untruthfully or disingenuously, is tantamount to failing to recognize others by denying one's social connection to others. This understanding of responsibility is grounded in a relational ontology of the self, which draws inspiration from Derrida and Levinas, among others. From Derrida, Young accepts that answering to the other is more originary than answering to one's self, since relations to others are prior to the self (Young 2011: 121). And from Levinas, Young acknowledges that we experience responsibility most primordially in embodied encounters with others, but that these proximate and singular encounters enable us to realize the singularity and equivalence of all other potential encounters with others, and that both are necessary dimensions of responsibility (2011: 162–3). Although Young seeks to replace "blame" with the less loaded notion of "accountability," this is a rather subtle distinction since it does not signal any shyness about criticism. Political responsibility necessarily presupposes a questioning and judging public so we can expect to see shaming and censure by those who raise questions, and discomfort and embarrassment for those who are called to account.

Young's account of political responsibility is primarily directed toward citizens rather than states. While she acknowledges that states have a crucial role to play in transforming structural injustices, they do not act as neutral arbiters over the struggle between the interests that produce structural injustices and those who are most disadvantaged by them. Rather, whether such claims will be accepted by key decision-makers will largely turn on the outcome of struggles in the public sphere (Young 2011: 151). Whether, and how, citizens exercise political responsibility for the structural injustice of climate related harm is therefore crucial in shaping the responsibilities of states. I shall therefore address the challenges facing citizens before turning to the vexed question of state responsibility.

Citizens: The Vertigo of Political Responsibility

Young's particular account of political responsibility, which goes well beyond being a law abiding citizen and exercising one's right to vote, might strike many as overwhelming. Indeed, many might find it paralyzing, given the enormity of the task of weaning the global economy off fossil fuel consumption and other emissions-generating activities, and the fact that climate related harm is only one of many structural injustices in a globalized world. How should we negotiate this "vertigo of political responsibility" (Young 2011: 124), given our multiple social connections and multiple and competing responsibilities?

In a sympathetic critique of Young, Jacob Schiff has reflected on the difficulties of exercising political responsibility for structural injustices that are woven into the fabric of our everyday lives (Schiff 2008: 106). He notes that such responsibility may be experienced as so "agonizing and infinite" as to demand a degree of bad faith and the concealment of inconvenient truths from oneself as a form of insulation from the overwhelming burdens of existence (Schiff 2008: 108). If so, then the exercise of political responsibility for climate change is also likely to be exceptional, and most people will outsource political responsibility for climate change to their political representatives, disengage and retreat from the problem or simply deny it. However, as Schiff points out, lying to oneself presupposes that we know the truth of the problem and allow ourselves to forget or conceal it so that we can act against what we know to be right (108). Yet there are also many people who do not recognize the problem, or rather misrecognize it, because they are ensnared in the dominant practices and associated categories of thought and perception embodied in language, which reinforce the legitimacy of prevailing social structures.

Given these challenges, what should we expect of citizens and how are they to be judged? Young acknowledges the unavoidable tensions we all face between the responsibilities that arise from interactions with others in close proximity (such as family and friends) and the responsibilities that arise from participation in social structures. Indeed, she argues that to acknowledge this tension is to acknowledge that "it is impossible to say that we ever discharge our responsibilities" (163). This probably explains her interest in developing "rhetorics of responsibility that are specifically political and that have fewer echoes of moralistic or juridical language" than the liability model (2011: 118). Nonetheless, she argues that the more that privileged groups attend to their immediate responsibilities, the more they will reinforce structural injustices by virtue of their structural position (2011: 164). Young's defense of the virtues of public-spirited political questioning and engagement shares and builds upon Hannah Arendt's critique of the passive politics of privatized, bourgeois life that avoids civic engagement and elevates personal and/or family security and prosperity above all else, whatever the cost to others.

Turning specifically to political responsibility, Young insists that this responsibility must be shared while also accepting that not everyone can be expected to exercise the same kind or degree of political responsibility (Young 2011: 143–4). To develop this claim, Young sketches some broad "parameters of reasoning" for guiding reflection on how differently situated actors might exercise political responsibility to address structural injustices based on how much power or privilege they may have, what their interests are, and whether they have "collective ability" (Young 2011: 142–51). For Young, power in this context is understood to mean the ability to influence the social structural interactions that produce unjust outcomes. That is, each actor's abilities or capabilities are largely (though not exclusively) derived from their social structural position. Social structures position people in particular relationships, which shape their capabilities and the range and kinds of options available to them, generating positions of relative privilege and under-privilege. For example, owners of capital are in a better position to make decisions to invest in renewable energy research, development, and production, or divest from the fossil fuel industry, than wage laborers or the unemployed. In contrast, the degree of "collective ability" refers to whether actors are part of organizations with a large membership (such as unions, nongovernment civic, or religious organizations), which have much greater potential for collective action than individuals who act alone or in smaller groups (2011: 146–51). In short, we should exercise our political responsibility by using our membership of organizations, our roles in the workforce and society, and whatever other capabilities we have as citizens and consumers, to drive the necessary structural transformation to a low carbon, sustainable society.

However, as Young acknowledges (building on the heritage of Karl Marx), one of the key challenges is that there is typically an inverse relationship between power and privilege, on the one hand, and the interest to transform social structures, on the other. Those who are the major beneficiaries of such processes have the greatest power to transform them but typically have little interest in doing so, and vice versa. This is starkly illustrated in the case of climate change, where the executives, workers, and states that are highly dependent on fossil fuel extraction and consumption remain mostly in denial of their complicity in hastening the possibility of catastrophic climate change, and remain largely deaf to the pleas of the most climate vulnerable, such as communities in low-lying nations and coastal areas. In response, Young suggests that the most vulnerable and marginalized can seek the support and assistance of others with greater power and privilege, but with less of an interest in perpetuating structural injustices, to mobilize on their behalf. Young also notes that many organizations and corporations may come to see their longer-term interests as aligned with transformation. In the case of climate change, this might include insurance companies, banks, pension funds, and other investors concerned about the possibility of holding stranded assets, along with a wide range of businesses that stand to gain from decarbonization or suffer from a failure to decarbonize.

Power and Responsibility

Young's parameters of reasoning provide a useful first cut in thinking about how citizens might discharge their political responsibility. However, they contain some tensions and also raise further questions regarding the applicability of her arguments to states and other actors.

First, the tensions. Young's social connection model assumes that citizens are rational and autonomous agents, capable of recognizing universal moral principles, making and executing moral political choices, asking questions in the public sphere, and exerting influence on social structures. However, her constructivist sociology acknowledges that citizens often bear little resemblance to the unencumbered, freely choosing individual of liberal moral theory (Hoover 2012: 237), since they are unavoidably ensnared in social structures (most notably, the relations of exchange in a neo-liberal, global capitalist economy) and therefore constrained in what they can think, desire, and do by their particular social position. Her "parameters of reasoning" seek to negotiate this tension by acknowledging the constraining effects of social structures on individual capability, but this negotiation rests on a rather thin and instrumental account of power as influence (Schiff 2013). Admittedly, Young's focus was confined to the intentional, agential power of citizens to exert influence on social structures. Nonetheless, had she developed a broader understanding of power for this particular purpose, she would have highlighted a greater range of challenges, and opportunities, for social transformation. Young would be the first to concede that power is much more than the relative capacity possessed by differently situated social agents to transform social structures. Power is not only intentional, active, and agential; it can also be diffuse, unintended, structural, and productive (via discourses), and its effects can arise from doing nothing (for example, Lukes 2005; Barnett and Duvall 2005).

Although Young does not provide any systematic account of the role of discursive power in legitimizing structural injustices, she has sharp antennae for the various strategies employed by privileged agents to evade, avoid, and deny responsibility for structural injustices (which typically include "hiding behind" the liability model). These include: 1) Reification—the pretence that the processes that produced undeserved harm are natural, a matter of bad luck, or otherwise inevitable and therefore unavoidable and unchangeable; 2) Denial—the failure to acknowledge any connection between social practices, and the injustices that are suffered by others; and 3) Immediacy—the idea that we *only* have responsibility to our immediate neighbors or compatriots, not distant others (2011: ch. 6). These are precisely the strategies of evasion and avoidance of responsibility for preventing dangerous climate change employed by many states, political parties, corporations, and citizens in developed countries. And they are arguably far more politically potent in stalling effective action on climate change than the more blatant, and often desperate, propaganda strategies of the organized climate denial movement, which has a particularly strong base in English speaking jurisdictions. So how might the forward looking climate responsibilities of the wealthy and the privileged be framed in ways that might serve to galvanize positive action rather a defensive reaction? Replacing liability/guilt with accountability/shame moves the debate from the legal and moral sphere to the political sphere but it depends for its success on those who are publicly criticized sharing a sense of social connection to, and moral concern for, others in order to be swayed to accept responsibility. This can be a tall order.

Second, Young confines her focus to the political responsibilities of citizens on the grounds that states lack the motivation to take responsibility for climate change, and the policies they enact will largely turn on the outcome of struggles in the public sphere. However, public spheres are not confined to the domestic level and the politics of assigning, accepting, claiming, defending, or shirking responsibility are also basic to international politics (Bukovansky et al. 2012). What, then, are the implications of her critique for framing state responsibilities for climate change?

States: Historical Versus Political Responsibility?

Young's critique of the liability model of responsibility appears to provide a fundamental challenge to all those wishing to pin historical responsibility on the early industrializers, as well as to those seeking compensation for "loss and damage" from the present and future harmful impacts of climate change that are already locked in since industrialization. An uncritical application of Young's argument would run as follows: we should avoid the fraught process of trying to pin blame and liability on the biggest historical emitters for their past actions because it does not spread responsibility wide enough. It is isolating, backward looking, deflects attention from shared responsibility, does not challenge existing economic institutions, produces a defensive reaction by those singled out, and is politically unproductive. The United States, in particular, has been strongly resistant to the liability model and/or the idea of historical responsibility as a basis for burden sharing, and has argued that we must look forward and not backward by focussing on the regions of the world where the biggest future growth in emissions is expected. For their part, major emitters in the developing world, such as China and India, have avoided stringent international commitments until such time as major developed countries such as the United States accept historical responsibility. According to Young's line of argument, a new regime of responsibility for climate change would need to acknowledge shared responsibility of all states in order to prevent exactly this kind of stand-off. Yet it would also need to recognize that responsibility needs to be calibrated in accordance with each state's different capabilities derived largely (but not exclusively) from their social structural position in the society of states and the global capitalist system. In other words, political responsibility for mitigation should be aligned with the relevant capabilities of states to prevent future emissions growth, which means that the primary focus for mitigation should be on all major emitters in order "to get the job done."

Translated into the language of climatic ethicists, Young's arguments align with the forward looking Ability to Pay Principle (APP) rather than the backward looking Polluter Pays Principle (PPP). The latter has attracted a range of objections, the most significant of which are the defense of excusable ignorance by the polluter, the challenge of measurement, the fact that most past individual polluters are now dead (although many states and corporations endure), and that the PPP leaves unaddressed climate related harms that cannot be attributed to the polluter (for example, Vanderheiden 2008, 2011; Caney 2010; Meyer and Roser 2010; Gardiner 2011; Page 2012).

Yet these objections have been met with a range of considered replies, including modified versions of the PPP, the defense of the Beneficiary Pays Principle (BPP) and/or the development of hybrid models that include elements of the PPP, APP, and BPP (discussed further later in the chapter). It is beyond the scope of this chapter to rehearse these arguments in detail but the key point for present purposes is that most of these climate justice debates have been confined to the morality rather than politics of assigning responsibility. One of the few exceptions is Pickering and Barry (2012), who assess both the moral and political value of framing the climate responsibilities of developed states in terms of a climate or carbon debt based on their historical contribution. While they concede that it is possible to develop a coherent moral account of historical responsibility, they nonetheless conclude that it provides a politically unhelpful frame in the climate negotiations for reasons that are consistent with Young's: it poses the risk of overemphasizing retrospective liability at the expense of future distributive concerns, its adversarial nature, and the problems associated with measurement. Indeed, they suggest that "many developing countries (including highly vulnerable small island states) have themselves eschewed the rhetoric of climate debt in favour of other strategies for boosting collective responsibilities to address climate change" (679). Drawing on John Dryzek's distinction between bonding rhetoric (which preaches to, and seeks to mobilize, the already converted) and bridging rhetoric (which seeks to reach across polarized divisions and find common ground), they argue that historical responsibility constitutes a form of bonding rhetoric that is inflammatory to many developed countries (especially the United States) and unlikely to advance the negotiations (679). Bridging rhetoric (such as collective responsibility) is therefore to be preferred since it is more likely to facilitate deliberation and compromise.

Given the diminishing window of opportunity to reach a fair and effective agreement, these arguments certainly have practical political merit. But it also needs to be asked: what are the political consequences of rejecting historical responsibility based on the PPP? A complete rejection of the liability model or the PPP seems unduly lopsided and ahistorical in the case of climate related harms: it wrongly assumes that responsibility *qua* liability and responsibility *qua* accountability are mutually exclusive and fails to acknowledge how present capabilities are historically derived and connected to present structural injustices. An outright rejection of the liability model could also be seen as justifying a politics of appeasement that serves to uphold the status quo advantages of the major cumulative emitters, thereby providing little comfort to late developers but especially those who are the most vulnerable to climate change and also the least responsible for generating emissions. This is no less politically unproductive from the standpoint of many late developers as an uncritical application of the liability model of responsibility since it plays into the hands of the most advantaged at the expense of the most disadvantaged.

However, Young's analysis of historical responsibility for slavery suggests that she too would probably reject such an uncritical application of her arguments. First, she accepts that liability and political responsibility can co-exist.[3] Second, although she rejects the case for reparations for the historical injustice of slavery when the perpetrators and victims are long dead, she nonetheless argues that unrepaired past injustices create a present political responsibility to deal with unfinished business (2011: 176–9). That is, ensuring public recognition of the continuities between present structural injustices and the past practices that produced them provides added weight to the political case for the transformation of present racialized structures. She also argues that those who are the beneficiaries of racialized structures "can properly be called to a special moral and political responsibility" to recognize their privilege and its connection with past wrongful practices and to work toward changing present structures, even if it entails reducing their own privileges and opportunities (2011: 187).

Likewise, it matters how state capabilities are derived. Those states that have economically benefited from a longer history of emissions should have a greater responsibility to mitigate and to provide finance for mitigation and adaptation for less developed countries, and this can be achieved under the BPP without attaching the "blame" associated with the PPP, *qua* liability model. As Edward Page has explained, the BPP is distinguishable from the PPP insofar as it entails "giving up" rather than "paying back" a benefit unwittingly but unjustly acquired (Page 2012: 314). Indeed, a refusal by developed countries to "disgorge their fair share of climatic benefits for the sake of the global climate response would put states in the position of condoning the setbacks of interest to which their affluence can be historically linked" (2012: 315).

Those critical theorists who have placed structural injustice to the front and center of their analysis of climate change have highlighted the structural links between the past and present skewed distribution of benefits and burdens in the international economy. A notable example is Parks and Roberts (2010), who locate the structural injustice of climate change in the context of the more general unequal flows of energy, resources, and materials between the North and the South arising from the colonial legacy and the shifting division of labor in an increasingly integrated global economy. It is this unequal load displacement or "unequal ecological exchange" that underpins the claim that the North owes an ecological debt to the South on the grounds that it has used an excessive proportion of "ecological space" at the expense of the South. The carbon debt is merely one component of this larger ecological debt and it arises not just from the colonial legacy but from the constantly shifting international division of labor. That is, participation in international trade tends to decrease emissions in many wealthy countries, which have increasingly specialized in the service sector, while increasing them in developing countries where heavy industry has become increasingly concentrated. This enables citizens in developed countries to enjoy the benefits of carbon intensive good imported from, say China, without having to accept responsibility for the emissions associated with their production. Yet this unequal ecological exchange can flow in different directions, depending on how different local and national economies are "inserted" into the global economy, but either way it escapes the territorial and production-based accounting system of the climate regime.

While the BPP provides a useful principle to "catch" early industrializers and carbon free riders through emissions offshoring, the virtues of Young's social connection model would appear to provide strong grounds for the responsibility of the wealthy to transform international economic structures to address the skewed distribution of benefits and burdens produced by international exchanges irrespective of any direct link between their enjoyment of the climate related benefits and the burdens suffered by others, simply by virtue of participation in international economic exchange. As Simon Caney (2010: 212) has shown, no single principle can frame responsibility in ways that provide comprehensive justice for the most vulnerable. And this is becoming increasingly apparent in the global risk society (see also Bukovansky et al. 2012: ch. 4). The PPP leaves unaddressed climate related harms that cannot be attributed to particular polluters; the BPP is limited by the degree to which the beneficiary actually benefited from unwittingly causing a harm (which may not be sufficient to cover the loss suffered, or assistance required, by the victim); and the APP cannot discriminate between the innocent and the culpable among the wealthy, or the "clean" and "dirty" rich. That said, the BPP provides a helpful ethical and political bridge between the forward looking responsibility to mitigate (a matter of distributive justice), and the backward looking responsibility to assist and compensate (a matter of compensatory or remedial justice) (Vanderheiden 2011; Meyer and Roser 2010). Indeed, as Miller points out, this kind of remedial responsibility can be both backward and forward looking (Miller 2007: 99–104).

None of the above arguments should rule out the application of the liability model in cases where states (or indeed corporations) continue to produce significant emissions in full knowledge of the consequences for the most vulnerable states and communities. While a strict version of the PPP from the beginning of industrialization is too punitive, given that the earlier industrializers did not know that their emissions generating activity would cause harm, a culpability/liability based responsibility can be invoked from the time when the science of climate change became widely known and a matter of international concern, such as from the beginning of the negotiations for a climate change treaty in the late 1980s.

Conclusion

Young's reflections on political responsibility for structural injustices are a response to profound shifts in the social relations of risk and responsibility. Her reflections highlight the different ways in which the liability model is unable to deal with growing interdependence and the increasingly complex, incalculable, and uninsurable character of risks generated by the social structures of the (neo-liberal) risk society (Voigt 2008). Her social connection model pushes in the direction of a new understanding and practice of "extended responsibility" that moves beyond the interests of contractual parties and principal–agent models of responsibility, and the language of "negative externalities," to embrace a broader and a more risk-averse guardianship or trusteeship model of responsibility for all social agents that acknowledges pervasive and complex social and ecological interconnectedness (Christoff and Eckersley 2013: 190–3).

Two broader insights emerge from the foregoing discussion. The first is that while we need a post-liberal understanding of environmental responsibility to adapt to a more complex, interdependent world, this does not mean that the traditional liberal understanding of responsibility should be obliterated. The liability model still has an important role to play in providing corrective justice to the vulnerable for so long as structural injustices persist and the necessary connections between culpability and harm can be drawn and there is no motivation on the part of the powerful to transform social practices. Indeed, as Anthony Langlois has shown, in the anti-sweatshop campaigns examined by Young it is, ironically, the application of the liability model rather than the exercise of political responsibility by corporations that largely explains the positive changes in corporate practices (Langlois 2014: 56–9). More generally, a hybrid model that includes elements of the PPP, BPP, and APP is most likely to produce an agreement that will serve the needs and interests of differently situated states and other social actors, including the most vulnerable.

Second, bringing structural injustices into the foreground of responsibility, especially when based on the PPP or even the BPP, is politically confronting. Conversely, allowing these principles to recede into the background of political negotiations is likely to remove obstacles to agreement about the allocation of responsibility from the standpoint of those social actors that have derived their privilege from past and/or present existing social structures. But this produces a major predicament or Catch-22: this backgrounding leaves intact social structures that can be expected to generate a further widening of the gulf between those who enjoy the benefits and those who suffer the burdens produced in the global risk society, and this will further strip the capability of the already vulnerable to shape their destiny while also making it harder to reach any common ground with the most privileged. As Parks and Roberts (2010) have argued, deep disagreement about the allocation of responsibilities in the international climate negotiations is a predictable outcome of a starkly unequal world, which has produced different understandings of fairness, causation, and responsibility between (and increasingly within) the North and South. Indeed, the same can be said for the negotiation of national climate policy. In short, unchecked inequality undermines trust and cooperation. It follows that if trust is to be built and cooperation over climate change enhanced, then inequality must be addressed. In the international sphere, Parks and Roberts suggest broadening the negotiation agenda to include issues such as trade, investment, debt, and intellectual property rights (136). However, this brings us back to our dilemma: if some kind of new international economic deal were to serve as a precondition for a new climate deal by developing countries, then we can expect the stalemate to deepen, to the detriment of the most marginal and disempowered given the diminishing window of opportunity to produce a fair and effective agreement. Indeed, even without this expanded agenda, the negotiations leading to the scheduled 2015 climate agreement have all but given up on reaching agreement on the equitable allocation of responsibilities by leaving it to individual states to put forward their own "nationally determined contributions" on the basis of their own understanding of equity.

Against this background, it is fitting to return to the political responsibility of non-state actors, especially citizens, to provide the necessary motivation and political mobilization for states to negotiate a fair and ambitious agreement. In bringing social connections to the foreground of public engagement Young's reflections direct attention to the tight links between the ideals and practices of political responsibility, public accountability, and deliberative democracy. Political responsibility means asking critical questions, and being answerable to others in the sense of revealing, explaining, and justifying what one has done (and not done), what one wishes to get done by way of collective action, and doing so publicly. Herein lies the surest path away from "organized irresponsibility" and the awful prospect of catastrophic climate change.

Notes

1. Iris Marion Young died in August 2006, before completing the final revisions to her book. The final editing was completed by her husband, David Alexander.
2. An earlier and more condensed version of these arguments appears in Young (2006).
3. For example, Young accepts that corporations can be held liable for damages for profiting from slavery in the past, since corporations are fictitious persons under the law and can "live" well beyond the life of an ordinary person (2011: 175–6).

References

Barnett, Michael and Duvall, Raymond. (2005). "Power in International Politics." *International Organization* 59: 39–75.

Beck, Ulrich. (1995). *Ecological Politics in an Age of Risk*. Translated by Amoz Weisz (Cambridge: Polity Press).

Bukovansky, Mlada, Clark, Ian, Eckersley, Robyn, Price, Richard, Reus-Smit, Christian, and Wheeler, Nicholas J. (2012). *Special Responsibilities: Global Problems and American Power* (Cambridge: Cambridge University Press).

Caney, Simon. (2005). "Cosmopolitan Justice, Responsibility, and Global Climate Change." *Leiden Journal of International Law* 18: 747–75.

Caney, Simon. (2010). "Climate Change and the Duties of the Advantaged." *Critical Review of International Social and Political Philosophy* 13(1): 203–28.

Christoff, Peter and Eckersley, Robyn. (2013). *Globalization and the Environment* (Lanham: Rowman and Littlefield).

Dobson, Andrew. (2003). *Citizenship and the Environment* (Oxford: Oxford University Press).

Gardiner, Stephen. (2011). *A Perfect Moral Storm: The Ethical Tragedy of Climate Change* (Oxford: Oxford University Press).

Hoover, Joseph. (2012). "Reconstructing Responsibility and Moral Agency in World Politics." *International Theory* 4(2): 233–68.

Langlois, Anthony. (2014). "Social Connection and Political Responsibility: An Engagement with Iris Marion Young." *St Antony's International Review* 10(1): 43–63.

Lavin, Chad. (2008). *The Politics of Responsibility* (Urbana and Chicago: University of Illinois Press).

Linklater, Andrew. (2011). *The Problem of Harm in World Politics: Theoretical Investigations* (Cambridge: Cambridge University Press).

Lucas, J. R. (1995). *Responsibility* (Oxford: Clarendon Press).

Lukes, Steven. (2005). "Power and the Battle for Hearts and Minds." *Millennium* 33(3): 477–93.

Mason, Michael. (2008). "The Governance of Transnational Environmental Harm: Addressing New Modes of Accountability." *Global Environmental Politics* 8(3): 8–24.

Meyer, Lukas H. and Roser, Dominic. (2010). "Climate Justice and Historical Emissions." *Critical Review of International Social and Political Philosophy* 13(1): 229–53.

Miller, David. (2007). *National Responsibility and Global Justice* (Oxford: Oxford University Press).

Page, Edward. (2012). "Give it up for Climate Change: A Defence of the Beneficiary Pays Principle." *International Theory* 4(2): 300–30.

Parks, Bradley C. and Roberts, J. Timmons. (2010). "Climate Change, Social Theory and Justice." *Theory, Culture & Society* 27(2–3): 134–66.

Pickering, Jonathan and Barry, Christian. (2012). "On the Concept of Climate Debt: Its Moral and Political Value." *Critical Review of International Social and Political Philosophy* 15(5): 667–85.

Schiff, Jacob. (2008). "Confronting Political Responsibility: The Problem of Acknowledgment." *Hypatia* 23(3): 99–117.

Schiff, Jacob. (2009). "Power and Responsibility: A Reconsideration." Paper prepared for the Annual Meeting of the Canadian Political Science Association, University of Ottawa, Ottawa.

Schiff, J. L. (2013). "Power and Responsibility." In *Political Responsibility Refocused: Thinking Justice after Iris Marion Young*, edited by Genevieve Fuji Johnson and Loralea Michaelis (Toronto: University of Toronto Press), 42–62.

Schlosberg, David. (1999). *Environmental Justice and the New Pluralism* (Oxford: Oxford University Press).

Schlosberg, David. (2007). *Defining Environmental Justice* (Oxford: Oxford University Press).

Vanderheiden, Steven. (2008). *Atmospheric Justice: A Political Theory of Climate Change* (New York: Oxford University Press).
Vanderheiden, Steven. (2011). "Globalising Responsibility for Climate Change." *Ethics and International Affairs* 25(1): 65–84.
Voigt, Christine. (2008). "State Responsibility for Climate Change Damages." *Nordic Journal of International Law* 77: 1–22.
Young, Iris Marion. (2006). "Responsibility and Global Justice: A Social Connection Model." *Social Philosophy and Policy* 23(1): 102–30.
Young, Iris Marion. (2011). *Responsibility for Justice* (Oxford: Oxford University Press).

CHAPTER 24

ENVIRONMENTAL JUSTICE AND THE ANTHROPOCENE MEME

GIOVANNA DI CHIRO

> It matters what thoughts think thoughts.
> It matters what stories tell stories.
> It matters what worlds world worlds.
>
> —Donna Haraway, 2014

At the end of the twentieth century, environmentalists from all corners of the world woefully acknowledged that the battle to *prevent* climate change before it started had been lost. From the high expectations at the 1992 United Nations (UN) Earth Summit in Rio for international unity on the global environmental crisis, to the crushing disappointment of the UN's Copenhagen Accord in 2009, the late twentieth-century aspirations that the world community would act decisively to prevent global warming before it irreversibly altered all earth systems was now relegated to the dustbin of history (Bond 2012; Costanza et al. 2014; Jamieson 2014). The culprit, identified in the late 1980s and later spelled out in the text of the UN Framework Convention on Climate Change (UNFCCC), was "dangerous *anthropogenic* interference with the climate system" caused by "high levels of *anthropogenic* emissions of carbon dioxide and other greenhouse gases."[1] Fossil fuel-powered human activities had generated the crisis of global warming and despite the high hopes for global accord envisioned in earlier pronouncements of "Our Common Future" (WCED 1987), humans had not been able to prevent themselves from polluting their own nest. While having recognized from the outset that specific human populations (the rich in global North countries and elites in the global South) were primarily responsible for producing and profiting from dangerous levels of greenhouse gas emissions, and that other specific human populations (poor communities from the North and South) would suffer the worst effects, by the turn of the twenty-first century, climate scientists had proclaimed that *we* had seen the enemy and it is *us* (the human species). Humans have become such a dominant force of nature through our high levels of anthropogenic emissions, extractions, and exterminations that *we* have created a new geological epoch dominated by *ourselves*. This planetary-scale story, based on considerable scientific evidence chronicling the transformation of earth by one voracious species, *Homo sapiens*, has instigated the invention of a new word: the *Anthropocene* (the age of humans).

This proposal by environmental scientists to quantify, name, and formalize a new species-centric geological epoch paints an overwhelmingly disastrous picture of human behavior and human presence on earth. While the general idea of "common but differentiated responsibilities" by the rich and the poor still appears as a talking point in international environmental policy, and while a movement advancing "climate justice" for the world's least responsible and most vulnerable human populations, and moreover, for the rights of Mother Earth, has been growing worldwide, in the early decades of the twenty-first century the Anthropocene discourse of *pan-human* culpability has garnered much interest. The rapid adoption of Anthropocene discourse in environmental circles (primarily in the Anglophone world) presumes that, by virtue of being human, we are *all* to blame and we are *all* responsible for global warming and ecological decline. This recent geo-historical and explanatory "turn" raises the question not only whether the Anthropocene is the right framework for understanding the global environmental crisis (are *all* humans the problem?), but whether it is the best story for mobilizing action on climate change and making possible a more livable and just world.

The use of the term "Anthropocene" has skyrocketed since it was first popularized by scientists Paul Crutzen and Eugene Stoermer in 2000. Initially a concept limited to in-house debate amongst biogeochemists and other environmental scientists from professional organizations including the Geological Society of America and the International Union of Geosciences (Zalasiewicz et al. 2010), the Anthropocene has strayed beyond these specialized, scientific disciplines into broader academic, environmentalist, and popular cultural realms. The scientific rationality and technical merits of an Anthropocene epoch, however, are not settled and remain controversial among many experts (Autin and Holbrook 2012; Schneiderman 2014). Nevertheless, some analysts have suggested Anthropocene has assumed the character of a gene-like "meme"[2] transmitted across disciplinary spheres (Nixon 2014). In the early twenty-first century, Anthropocene has become a *keyword*, capturing the imagination of diverse academic fields and diverse publics concerned about the deteriorating state of the planet.

While the term Anthropocene originated from within the biological and physical sciences, its etymological core (Human/Anthropos) signals an important role for the social sciences and the humanities, especially for their methodological emphases on critical analyses of discourse, culture, and politics (Rose et al. 2012; Sörlin 2012). As Donna Haraway (2014) has argued, it matters what thoughts, knowledges, or stories are marshaled to theorize and transform a profoundly damaged world. *Keywords* matter in producing particular kinds of eco-politics. I am interested in what kinds of environmental politics are mobilized, and by whom, with the use of the term Anthropocene. Is it a useful keyword—and a good story—to think and act with?

The keyword and storytelling device of the Anthropocene emerges historically at the same time as the awareness of the crisis of climate change is on the increase and when the dominant environmental policy discourse for human agency is framed as "global environmental governance," a passive idiomatic construction that has become rhetorically bundled with an equally technocratic policy prescription lexicon: "mitigation," "adaptation," "resilience," "sustainability." Critics have noted that the Anthropocene story has surfaced at the height and expansion of neo-liberal capitalism, when the political will for "mitigation" has lost steam and climate action has been relegated to "adaptation" (Dryzek et al. 2011; Jamieson 2010). Despite the pledge in UN climate agreements and institutions to protect "Our Common Future," the paucity of funding earmarked for adaptation suggests that human-centric individualism and privatization, the hallmarks of deregulated, neo-liberal corporate capitalism, not "human commonality," are the controlling narratives of the day (Klein 2014). Now responsible for their own adaptation and resilience, individual cities, towns, neighborhoods, and people are left to pull themselves up by their bootstraps as climate change proceeds apace (Reid 2012; Ribot 2013).

Could the neologism Anthropocene, with its emphasis on a *pan*-species narrative, help build a collective project uniting humanity in a commitment to stop global warming and climate catastrophe? In this essay, I examine how Anthropocene is deployed as a keyword in environmental studies and environmental politics discourse and is replicated as an "idea worth spreading" through the popular storytelling apparatus of the *keynote speech*. I focus on the use of Anthropocene in keynote speeches in the early decades of the twenty-first century, when the life and death effects of global warming are being felt around the world and when the international scientific community predicts future disasters of even larger scope. I argue that this meme-like diffusion of the Anthropocene keyword has occurred primarily within particular social, cultural, and political contexts (Euro-Australo-American academic environmental studies and environmental politics) and does *not* surface, nor has it gained any epistemic or political traction, in other contexts that are *equally* concerned with the social and ecological impacts of runaway climate change (environmental justice/climate justice organizations and social movements). My goal is to think about the consequences of the Anthropocene keyword as a concept for understanding, theorizing, and acting on climate change at this particular historical moment.

"Welcome to the Anthropocene": Environmental Politics of Keywords and Keynotes

Anthropocene's status as a keyword is evident in its adoption as the thematic subject of an array of international conferences, academic panels, popular scientific lectures, and keynote addresses on the topic of environmental crisis and climate change. One of the first public appearances of Anthropocene as an environmental keyword was in 2010 in an Internet-based TED Talk by Will Steffen, an Australian earth system scientist who introduced the term to a popular audience. Committed to Anthropocene as an "idea worth spreading" from the arcana of the geosciences to a wider public, Steffen's TED Talk, titled "The Anthropocene," clearly explained the evidence documenting the negative impact of anthropogenic activities on the earth's systems including ocean acidification, glacier and ice sheet melting, massive species extinction, and severe climate instability.[3] Steffen's popular science lecture aimed to lay the scientific groundwork supporting a global environmental policy agenda for establishing a "safe operating space for humanity with respect to the earth system" (Rockström et al. 2009: 475).

Following Steffen's and other scientists' advice that humanity must determine its "safe operating space" on the planet, in 2012 a video titled "Welcome to the Anthropocene" opened (or keynoted) the Rio+20 United Nations Conference on Sustainable Development.[4] The three-minute, fast-paced video consists of a screen-size image of the globe superimposed with an uninterrupted succession of the hockey stick-shaped graphs illustrating the "great acceleration" of human activities in the past 250 years including steadily rising CO_2 emissions, tropical forest loss, and population growth. The British-accented, female voiceover in the video invites the audience to reflect on the "relentless pressure" humanity has inflicted on the planet now that "we have entered the Anthropocene," yet we should have confidence that "our creativity, energy, and industry offer hope" to shape our future. "As the population grows to 9 billion," she continues, "we must find a safe operating space for humanity and for the sake of future generations."[5]

The Rio+20 keynote video, a sort of "welcome to the party" approach, is upbeat and even celebratory about the human zeal, ingenuity, and progress symbolized by the Anthropocene. The Anthropocene story told in this UN video climaxes with the eco-modernist (Pearce 2013) "green economy" policy framework promoting both market-based approaches to climate mitigation represented by the Clean Development Mechanism (CDM) and REDD+, and the advancement of the new technologies of geoegineering (carbon dioxide removal or solar radiation management) and nuclear and renewable energy. To date, there are still no binding emissions reductions policies, adaptation strategies, or action plans agreed upon by all UN member states. For some environmental critics, the UN's Anthropocene "party" has been a big flop (Hamilton 2013; Conca and Dabelko 2014; Jamieson 2014).

Echoing the UN's attempt at hospitality to mobilize action on climate change, the "Welcome to the Anthropocene" motif resurfaced in the titles of two Environmental Studies conferences held in the United States in June 2014.[6] Both conference titles and the subject matter of each conference's keynote speeches exemplify two common, and polarized, responses to the Anthropocene as an ethically or politically mobilizing story for the era of climate crisis.

Environmental Studies Conference I: "Welcome to the Anthropocene: From Global Challenge to Planetary Stewardship"

The annual conference of the Association for Environmental Science and Studies (AESS), the largest interdisciplinary professional association for environmental studies in the United States, was held at PACE University in New York City in June 2014. The title sets the tone for the conference's overall agreement with the epochal status of Anthropocene. In "Paths to a 'Good' Anthropocene," the AESS keynote speaker, Andrew Revkin (Dot Earth blogger at the *New York Times*), affirms his readiness to take on the Anthropocene challenge and opens his talk by giddily exclaiming "Wow! What a wonderful time to be alive!"[7] Putting a positive spin on the idea of "The Great Acceleration" of the advance of human civilization, he describes the familiar scientific graphs depicting exponentially rising human population, resource use, and waste as the "the astonishing pulse of *us*!." Always emphasizing the sunny side, Revkin claims that buoyant humor and boy-like enthusiasm (in contrast to the gloominess and self-righteousness of the greens) projects excitement and optimism, attitudes more likely to foster civic action on the climate problem.

Revkin's response to the Anthropocene—"it's the best word we have"—represents an eco-modernist perspective. Eco-modernism, or ecological modernity (Mol et al. 2000), maintains that the acceleration of technological innovations and energy transitions that fueled the Industrial Revolution and created modern capitalist economies allowed us to bring many millions of people out of abject poverty into increasingly prosperous lives, and with relatively less impact on the environment (for example, Nordhaus and Shellenberger 2007). Embracing the Anthropocene, for Revkin, is simply naming and "taking full ownership" of this truth. Suggesting that humans need a strong dose of "anthropophilia" to get through these tough times, Revkin muses: "We have to accept ourselves, flaws and all, in order to move beyond what has been something of an unconscious, species-scale pubescent growth spurt, *enabled by fossil fuels in place of testosterone*" (emphasis added).[8]

The "unconscious" sexism in equating the naturalness of human and masculine exceptionalism in the repeated telling of the Story of Man is nothing new, and demonstrates Revkin's obliviousness or unwillingness to engage with decades of feminist-environmentalist and eco-feminist analyses on the topic of the rise of Western modernity and its social and ecological consequences (Shiva and Mies 1993; Plumwood 1994; Merchant 2005). Thus, the rise of the keyword Anthropocene begs the question, does the Anthropos (Human/Man: Greek) in the Anthropocene have a sex, gender, class, or race?[9] Apparently it does, if the examples of human ingenuity and awesomeness in Revkin's keynote address are any indication. Those possessing what he calls the "human traits" of innovation, resourcefulness, and enthusiasm, which are in need of "acceleration" to respond positively to the inertia of our modern (suburban and urban) lifestyles and to innovate exciting environmental sustainability projects, are, almost exclusively, white, male, academic, and Euro-American. The universal "we" and "us" embodied in the species idiom of Anthropocene in this keynote talk thus obscure the extensive scholarship on diverse human histories and resilient naturecultures (Haraway 2014) that are imagining and producing innovative approaches to climate mitigation, adaptation, and sustainability.

Revkin's objective is to spur environmental activism with get-up-and-go optimism and he argues that "it's time to grasp the uncomfortable, but ultimately hopeful, idea" that "We Are Perfect" (the words appearing on his final slide with his email and twitter addresses listed underneath). Evidently irritated by Revkin's assertion of humanity's perfectness in this keynote speech, ethicist Clive Hamilton, author of *Requiem for a Species: Why We Resist the Truth About Climate Change* (2013), responded vociferously in the blogosphere.[10] Hamilton criticizes the technological utopianism championed by environmental optimists like Revkin for what he considers the minimizing of the urgency of the problem, and for the inadequacy of the individualistic, personal lifestyle, and techno-utopian consumer-based solutions. This attempt to de-escalate political urgency by "going green," he argues, is a time worn tactic used by those parties financially invested in the status quo to "exercise political power to stop governments from imposing policies that will facilitate the transition to the low-carbon future."[11] In response to Hamilton's doomer prognosis that "there is no such thing as a 'good' Anthropocene," Revkin countered with the assertion that our human creativity and industry does not just enhance sustainability, it enhances the planet: "The natural world should be better for our efforts and our ingenuity."[12]

Environmental Studies Conference II: "Welcome (?) to the Anthropocene"

The eco-modernist idea that "the natural world should be better off" in the Anthropocene with the benefits of human ingenuity and enhanced technology sends many of the environmental thinkers who participated in the annual conference of the International Society of Environmental Ethics (ISEE) into paroxysms of rage. Held contemporaneously with AESS in June 2014, ISEE's conference was convened at the more "natural" setting of a scenic conference center in Colorado bordering on the majestic snow-capped peaks of Rocky Mountain National Park.[13] In the conference's keynote presentation titled "Age of Man Environmentalism and Respect for an Independent Nature," philosopher Ned Hettinger argued that the discourse of the Anthropocene, together with its unapologetic anthropocentrism, "manifests a culpable failure to appreciate the profound role non-human nature continues to play on Earth and an arrogant overvaluation of human's role and authority." Worse, it has "helped spawn 'Age of Man Environmentalism' (AME)" by "downplaying the importance of nature preservation, restoration, and re-wilding and it will have us simply become managers of the earth we have created, promoting ecosystem invention and geo-engineering" (2014: 4).

Hettinger criticizes academics and conservationists who have been seduced by the Anthropocene concept. AME's construction of the Anthropocene, Hettinger argues, on the one hand, *overexaggerates* human influence on nature (the earth will ultimately out-survive the age of humans, and be better off without us) and, on the other hand, *undervalues* the importance of still-existing natural areas (conservation zones, wilderness areas). It does this, he claims, with the fallacious argument put forward by some misguided conservationists, or "neo-greens" (for example, Kareiva et al. 2012) that we already live on a domesticated planet since there is no such thing as pre-human, pristine, untouched wilderness, and the desire for such represents a misanthropic ideal denying growth, prosperity, and economic development for the world's "marginalized and demonized groups" (2014: 4).

Hettinger reads the ascendance of the Anthropocene as a triumphalist celebration of human power and control over non-human nature. Yet, in his critique, he seems not to notice his gendered framing of "Age of Man Environmentalism" in his nostalgia for what he considers the oldie-but-goodie versions of environmentalism, that is, those versions that *used to* value preservation and conservation of real wilderness and real nature, but instead capitulated to the vices of anthropocentrism. Putting the quotation marks in a different place, feminist scholars would argue that the Age of "Man Environmentalism" well describes the gendered, racialized, and dichotomous constructions of nature and society underlying dominant Euro-American environmental thinking from early on (Merchant 1992/2005; Seager 1993; Boag 2003). The human–environment dualism characteristic of many Western philosophical standpoints (and reproduced in the mainstream environmentalism Hettinger memorializes), as eco-feminists, environmental justice scholars, and other critics have shown, lies at the root of the exploitative and unsustainable modern, industrial economies that have brought us to the edge of climate catastrophe in the first place. In his rage against the Anthropocene and his longing for the old environmentalism that valued an "independent Nature," Hettinger forgets these potent analyses of the dangers and oppressiveness of splitting humans from nature.

Just Say No to the Mis-Anthropocene: Where is the Social Justice in the Anthropocene Meme?

Both the proponents *and* critics of the keyword Anthropocene deploy the totalizing, species-wide discourse of Universal Man: "We" are the tyrants or "We" are the saviors. However, environmental justice research has well documented that it is poor communities and communities of color around the world who have borne the brunt of modernity's "Great Acceleration" while reaping few of the rewards (Faber 2008). Telling the story of environmental decline and catastrophe very differently, environmental justice (and more recently, climate justice) scholars and activists foreground the deep history of environmental racism when analyzing the *disproportionate* impact of the history of fossil-fuel driven, modern industrial development (Guha 1997; Martinez-Alier 2004; Carmin and Agyeman 2011; Di Chiro 2013; Schlosberg and Collins 2014).

In contrast to the storytelling trope of the Anthropocene as having started with the Euro-American Industrial Revolution of the mid- to late eighteenth century, when global capitalism through extracting and exploiting both humans and nature began its steady ascendance, many environmental and social historians identify fifteenth-century European expansionism and colonialism as origin points of the takeover of nature and human nature alike (Guha 1997; Grove 1998). The species/racial project of European colonialism in denying "species-being" to colonized peoples while alienating them from and stealing their land, knowledge, resources, and labor was early theorized by Frantz Fanon as he argued "when you examine at close quarters the colonial context, it is evident that what parcels out the world is to begin with the fact of belonging to or not belonging to a given race, a given species"; the "world cut in two" at the root of colonialism "is inhabited by two different species" (1963: 93). By truncating history and disregarding the critical environmental justice frame, the Anthropocene's aggregate Anthropos does not account for "unequal human agency, unequal human impacts, and unequal human vulnerabilities" (Nixon 2014) when narrating the story of anthropogenic blight.

The critiques of the human hubris and anthropocentrism embedded in Anthropocene discourse point to the imperative to recognize the anthropogenic devastation wrought on the non-human and other-than-human worlds, but by not recognizing the deeper history of colonialism often fail to address the persistent dehumanization, racism, eugenics, and other social injustices experienced by human groups who are still not "welcomed" as fully human (Escobar 1994/2011; Harvey 1998; Ray 2013).[14] Recognizing these shortcomings of Anthropocene as a keyword for asserting humanity's "species-being" and thereby its limited capacity to generate the collective "we" necessary to mobilize the political force to address anthropogenic climate change, some authors choose either not to use Anthropocene or to make it do different kinds of ideological and political work (Gibson-Graham 2011; Dibley 2012; Chakrabarty 2013; Haraway 2014).

Environmental writer Derrick Jensen, for example, vehemently opposes the Anthropocene proposition because its species centrism is "grossly misleading" by including all of humanity in its "sociopathic" behaviors of genocide and ecocide (driving indigenous cultures from their land and driving the extinction of millions of other species). He writes that "humans aren't the ones 'transforming'—read, killing—the planet. Civilized humans are. . . . The word 'Anthropocene' attempts to naturalize the murder of the planet by pretending the problem is 'man,' and not a specific type of man connected to this particular culture" (2013).

Likewise, historian Dipesh Chakrabarty, in a keynote talk titled "The Anthropocene's Invitation" at the Haus der Kulturen der Welt in Berlin in 2013, "declines the invitation of Anthropocene" but *accepts* the challenge to talk about anthropogenic global warming and to address the pressing issues of global climate change. Chakrabarty calls attention to the too easy slippage into "repressive universalism" echoing the critiques of climate justice scholars and activists by noting natureculture histories are not homogeneous and the story of the rise of modernity and climate change is rooted in social injustice as much as in the exploitation of non-human nature.[15] Chakrabarty lays the groundwork for an "enlightened anthropocentrism" that critiques the eco-modernist discourses of human exceptionalism, and proposes instead an eco-centric anthropocentrism as a political framework with the power to generate effective environmental alliances and policies.

Offering another socially critical perspective at the 2014 annual conference of the Modern Languages Association (MLA) in a plenary presentation titled, "The Great Acceleration and the Great Divergence: Vulnerability in the Anthropocene,"[16] environmental humanities scholar Rob Nixon explains that the Anthropocene story arises in the early twenty-first century expansion of neo-liberal capitalism, a time in which most societies around the world have experienced a deep and widening chasm between the super rich and the ultra poor. Nixon argues that the Anthropocene's narrativization of the great *acceleration* of the human species impact on the earth downplays the parallel story of a great *divergence* in human inequality and disparities. This omission, or underemphasizing, of the social inequalities and injustices at the heart of global, neo-colonial, corporate capitalism—and, thus, of environmental degradation and climate change—is a serious flaw in the Anthropocene storyline that starts with: "Once upon a time, humans took over the earth and destroyed it." As Raj Patel has argued, this story relies heavily upon apocalyptic narratives of impending catastrophe, familiar tropes in Western politics both on the left and right that have provided "alibis for misanthropic, racist, and cold-blooded policy."[17] As a planetary, apocalyptic, species-wide story about Humanity having brought the "End Times" on itself, the Anthropocene, he continues, "can very easily become the *Misanthropocene*."[18] The misanthropy lurking in the plot of Anthropocene's epic, species-totalizing story hinders the potential for human imagination and coalition and limits possibilities of gaining critical insights from examples of resistance (to eco-colonialism) and resilience (through sustainable lifeways) accomplished by those who have been left behind, colonized, or bulldozed over in the service of global domination of the earth.

Drawing on feminist political ecology and cultural studies of science and technology, in a keynote talk titled "Anthropocene, Capitalocene, Chthulucene: Staying with the Trouble," at UC Santa Cruz in 2014, Donna Haraway maintains that the Anthropocene story, which favors either "game over" climate politics (McKibben 2012; Sassen 2014) or "We Are Perfect"/geoengineers to the rescue (Revkin 2014), tends toward normalizing the story of human exceptionalism and planetary decline, leading not to better stories imagining "more livable presents and more livable futures," but often instead to the temptation to despair and denial.[19] Arguing in support of a "regenerative," joyful, and clear-eyed eco-politics Haraway states: "We need stories that are non-despairing, non-cynical, non-defeatist, and not in denial about the possibilities of flourishing on a damaged planet."[20] If we need a "big story" to demarcate the earth's current predicament, Haraway considers the more historically accurate "Capitalocene"—the era in which an assemblage of political, cultural, economic, scientific, and technological apparatuses fueled by fossil energy becomes consumed with "making more fossils as fast as possible." For Haraway, however, the Anthropos-centrism in the stories of Anthropocene and Capitalocene makes both insufficient, too readily lending themselves to "cynicism, defeatism, and self certain and self-fulfilling predictions, like 'game over, too late' discourse." She ultimately rejects the invitation to embrace the "big stories" of the Anthropocene, calling instead for the flourishing of smaller stories of *sympoiesis* (together-making) peopled by diverse human and non-human players generating practices of "thought, love, rage, and care" (31) and cultivating "multispecies muddles" taking response-ability for ongoingness on a damaged planet.

Environmental Justice and the Regenerative Politics of Flourishing

Although the Anthropocene meme burst out of the confines of the sciences and has assumed the status as keyword, it has not broken into the world of environmental justice politics. For peoples around the globe living in contaminated neighborhoods, impoverished villages, or colonized territories, whose claims to full humanity and human rights are still not guaranteed, a proposal to tone down human-centeredness or to relinquish the fight for human rights may reek of indifference to the ongoing brutality of racism, colonialism, and environmental injustice. Environmental justice and global climate justice proponents "affirm the sacredness of Mother Earth, ecological unity, and interdependence of all species,"[21] while at the same time advocate for an *environmental human rights* perspective as the most effective responses to a damaged planet and runaway climate change, a position that resonates with Chakrabarty's concept of "enlightened anthropocentrism." For these communities, Anthropocene just doesn't make historical or political sense (Di Chiro 2008).

Sustainability for All

At a 2014 Environmental Protection Agency (EPA) conference in Washington, DC commemorating the twentieth anniversary of the Executive Order on Environmental Justice, keynote speaker Jalonne White-Newsome never uttered the word Anthropocene, but issued a strong critique of the paradigm of domination and environmental injustice underlying the US history of progress and manifest destiny, which has left a legacy of toxic environments and poor health in communities of color and low-income communities and has contributed to the current global warming crisis.[22] A climate justice policy analyst at West Harlem Environmental Action (WEACT) in New York City, White-Newsome called on the audience of environmental scientists, government representatives, civil rights leaders, and community activists to honor the histories of abolitionism, anti-colonial struggle, and civil rights activism by building solidarity and collaborations to create a sustainable future for all communities.

Challenging the usual demographics of audiences attending conferences focusing on climate science or environmental studies, White-Newsome commented that "when you're in a room with environmentalists or the EPA talking about climate or energy policy and you don't see any faces of color, then you should know that that conversation is incomplete." She reminded the audience that environmental justice communities from around the world still suffer from the "slow violence" (Nixon 2011) of the cumulative effects of unabated "legacy pollutants" in their water, air, soil, and bodies, and "when you add climate change, that makes it even worse." To address these ongoing issues of environmental injustice, White-Newsome and WEACT simultaneously work on strategies for climate mitigation, adaptation, and community resilience.

Using the storytelling device of imagining the "weather forecast" of a possible future, White-Newsome envisioned a set of proactive "climate conditions" and actions in the United States that would embody environmental justice values and priorities:

> While conditions might be dry now, I see extreme climate legislation that passes the House and Senate unanimously, and includes special consideration, and resources for populations more at risk for climate consequences, and that provides for planning, infrastructure improvements, and health education.
>
> I see a cold mass of arctic air transitioning us from fossil fuel dependency to more renewable energy sources, which are decentralized and give communities and neighborhoods the power to make, create, and sustain their own energy.
>
> And while temperatures might be above normal, I predict that the meaningful and purposeful participation and engagement of EJ [environmental justice] communities across the country will help shape strategies for mitigation and adaptation to address climate change across the country.[23]

In the conclusion of her keynote, White-Newsome contends that the "extremes" of climate chaos require "extreme resilience, extreme clean energy, and extreme involvement of environmental justice communities." Quite the opposite of the anti-humanist slant of the Anthropocene story, White-Newsome's environmental justice perspective maintains that "working together to achieve climate justice for *those most marginalized will provide climate benefits for all*."[24] Responses to climate chaos must "mind the EJ gap" as she puts it, and in collaboration with EJ communities most directly harmed, must develop participatory and scientifically sound solutions to sustainability. The EJ gap in the United States, however, is gapingly wide and consistently hits a "green ceiling" with people of color representing a scant 12–16 percent of environmental organizations and environmental studies institutions nationwide (Taylor 2014). The vast majority of participants being "welcomed" to the Anthropocene at AESS (the aforementioned conference in New York City) were white, and few panels at the conference highlighted environmental or climate justice. WEACT has been organizing in New York City for 30 years, but did not have a seat at the table at the nation's largest environmental studies conference addressing how to move from "global challenges to planetary stewardship" in the Anthropocene.

People Powered Regeneration and a Just Transition Toward Living Economies

Refusing the apocalyptic and human species-bashing rhetoric inclined toward cynicism and angst, climate justice advocates like White-Newsome are taking action to push for policies to reduce the fossil fuel-based pollution that both creates global warming and endangers human health, and to build partnerships for "integral development"[25] (collective human rights to livelihood integrated with the rights of Mother Earth) to create a "just transition" toward climate-friendly economies and thriving, resilient communities around the world. For example, the New York City Environmental Justice Alliance (NYC-EJA), a network of city-based EJ organizations, and UPROSE, a multi-racial, intergenerational EJ organization in Brooklyn are leading the community-based "mitigation, adaptation, and resilience" efforts in this mega-city. In the aftermath of the flooding of New York City's lower boroughs in 2012 from Superstorm Sandy, NYC-EJA and UPROSE established the Climate Justice Community Resiliency Center, the city's first community-led planning project dedicated to "just adaptation" and community resiliency, and they organize an annual Youth Climate Justice conference teaching young people how to take action on climate change.[26] These environmental/climate justice initiatives illustrate regenerative people power, not human hubris.

The early twenty-first-century Anthropocene meme has likewise *not* found its way into the climate activism of many indigenous organizations, yet diverse coalitions of indigenous peoples actively challenge the "false solutions to destroy the Earth's balance, assassinate the seasons, unleash severe weather havoc, privatize life and threaten the very survival of humanity" (Kari-Oca Declaration 2012)[27] and engage in ecologically sustainable practices of "embodied resilience" (Adger et al. 2012; lewallen 2014). For example, regenerative political alliances among young environmental justice activists and Native American and First Nations tribes across the Americas have emerged to fight the extraction of shale gas and oil on indigenous lands and to demand that institutions of higher education divest their financial endowments from fossil fuel stocks and re-invest in a renewable economy.[28] At a student-led event titled "Power Up! Divest From Fossil Fuels" held at Swarthmore College in 2013, leaders of frontline communities delivered stirring keynote addresses describing their environmental justice struggles to protect their communities from the dangers of tar sands development, mountaintop removal coal mining, oil and chemical refineries, and hydrofracking operations.

The keynote speeches by First Nations activists Crystal Lameman (Beaver Lake Cree) and Leanne Betasamosake Simpson (Mississauga Nishnaabeg) forcefully critiqued the climate-destroying, exploitative, and extractivist mindset of modern, industrial society, central tenets in Anthropocene discourse, yet neither activist deployed the term.[29] Distinct from Anthropocene's narrative of humans vs. nature, Lameman and Simpson's stories express the interconnectedness of naturecultures and conceptualize an eco-politics grounded in multi-species relationality, what some refer to as cosmo-vision (Desmarais 2007; Walsh 2011) or cosmo-politics (Stengers 2010; Di Chiro 2013). In her speech, Simpson refers to the idea of "collapse," so central to Anthropocene discourse, yet her account of collapse is a story of multi-species environmental injustice perpetrated by the destructiveness of settler colonialism:

> Indigenous peoples have lived through environmental collapse on local and regional levels since the beginning of colonialism—the construction of the St. Lawrence Seaway, the extermination of the buffalo in Cree and Blackfoot territories and the extinction of salmon in Lake Ontario. Our elders have been warning us about this for generations now—they saw the un-sustainability of settler society immediately. (Klein 2013)

In contrast to many environmentalists who decry the onset of the Anthropocene in modes of sadness and angst, Simpson and other First Nations and indigenous activists do not respond with requiem or defeat. Arguing that the interconnected traumas of colonialism and ecological decline must be faced and healed, Simpson asserts, lamenting the end of the world or "counting down to oblivion" do not inspire active hope: "The impetus to act and to change and to transform, exists whether or not this is the end of the world." Simpson continues, "If a river is threatened, it's the end of the world for those fish. It's been the end of the world for somebody all along. The *sadness and the trauma* of that is reason enough for me to act" (Klein 2013).

At an international conference focused on "Encountering the Anthropocene" held in Sydney, Australia, in February 2014, in his keynote talk titled "Sustainability, Country, and Social Reconstruction in the Fitzroy Valley," Steve Kinnane (Marda Marda, Mirrowoong Country) argued that "there are lessons to be drawn about creating sustainable livelihoods" in the face of the Anthropocene from the positive stories of survival and resistance to the traumas of settler colonial violence told by many Australian Aboriginal communities.[30] Subjected to generations of cultural repression and economic depredation, Aboriginal peoples have developed strategies for coping with the everyday needs of social reproduction including dealing with lack of electricity, unreliable telecommunications, insecure shelter, and inadequate food,[31] all problems that will be exacerbated across Australia and around the world as the climate crisis worsens. In an action research study on Karajarri people's adaptations to climate change funded by the National Climate Change Adaptation Research Facility, Kinnane and his colleague Anna Dwyer (Karajarri, Kimberly Region), found that people were "worrying for their country"[32] having observed and experienced many changes in the local ecology. Yet, as Dwyer noted, when researchers used the term Anthropocene to label the crisis and to engage members of the community, people often responded with alarm fearing Anthropocene was a coming plague or a force that would terrorize their land and families.[33]

Proposing instead the more aspirational word, *Sustainocene*, Kinnane recounted stories of resilience where communities thrive by developing their own relevant understandings of sustainability founded on "caring for country" through cultural governance, natural resource management, cultural revival, and strategies to enhance community well-being. For Kinnane, the "small stories" of resilience growing from Karajarri programs inspire innovations in local natural resource management and provide climate solutions. These stories also generate knowledge about how to address "social" traumas such as food insecurity, domestic violence, substance abuse, and youth disempowerment: problems that affect community sustainability, but are not typically recognized as "environmental." As the "impacts of the Anthropocene increase," Kinnane argues, "these are problems the likes of which will be experienced by populations everywhere."[34]

The responses by Aboriginal communities to social and ecological trauma place human experience and the "sympoeisis" of multi-species relationality inside the stories of resistance, survival, and regeneration. As Judy Atkinson (Jiman, West Queensland) argues in *Trauma Trails: Recreating Song Lines* (2002), the ceremonies and "song lines" produced by Aboriginal societies teach the people how to deal with the cultural violence and trauma resulting from colonial dispossession and disconnection to culture, history, and country. In honoring the connections and responsibilities to country and community, which includes relationships with non-human entities like dingo, emu, water, and rock, "our ceremonies teach us how to be human" (2002: 23). The anti-humanism and apocalypsism of Anthropocene cannot conceive of these millennia-long approaches to interspecies understanding, resiliency, and sustainability.

In August 2014, a national convening of the "Our Power Campaign," an international network of environmental and climate justice organizations, gathered hundreds of activists together to build a just transition to "more resilient, equitable, and living economies." Held in Richmond, California, near the site of an explosion at the Chevron Oil Refinery in 2012 that sent 15,000 people to the hospital (Cagle 2013), the conference offered community-based, action research-oriented workshops focused on developing equitable and sustainable approaches to regional food systems, public transportation, community-generated renewable energy, zero waste, affordable and durable housing, and ecosystem restoration and stewardship. The conference's keynote speakers pledged to "build the bigger *we*" by creating multi-racial, multi-class, and transnational coalitions for climate justice and respect for the rights of Mother Earth/Pachamama.[35] The diverse stories, ceremonies, "multispecies muddles," and rich coalitions of the movement for climate justice are hopeful signs that responses to the present and future realities of global climate change will be more than cynicism, defeatism, or the re-domination of nature by human Earthmasters.[36]

The generativity of these diverse political assemblages cannot be captured in the universal "we" of the Anthropocene story. It matters which stories, knowledges, and worlds/words make our environmental politics. As Haraway has noted, "the doings of situated, actual human beings matter. It matters which ways of living and dying we cast our lot with rather than others. It matters not just to human beings, but also to those many critters across taxa which and whom we have subjected to exterminations, extinctions, genocides, and prospects of futurelessness" (2014: 30). Despite the recent ascendency of the species-centric story of Anthropocene, communities and social movements around the world are co-producing new narrative–political tools for mobilizing, organizing, and "dancing a new world into being" (Klein 2013); they are not giving up hope, wallowing in angst and disgust, or relinquishing the future to more of the same Anthropos. Creating generative, receptive environmental politics and coalitions means casting our lot and our lives with some and not others. As the planet heats up, as the great acceleration of depletions and extinctions pile up, and as intra-human and inter-species divergences speed up, which keywords will inspire new stories for environmental justice in the twenty-first century? Some stories make better eco-politics than others.

Notes

1. Emphasis added. Full version of the UNFCCC text is available at http://unfccc.int/essential_background/convention/background/items/1353.php
2. A meme is defined as a new idea, image, phrase, or behavior that is rapidly transmitted and diffused within and between cultural contexts through various communication, educational, and information technologies and practices.
3. Will Steffen, "The Anthropocene," TEDx Canberra, November 14, 2010. http://tedxtalks.ted.com/video/TEDxCanberra-Will-Steffen-The-A
4. The video was produced by the International Geosphere-Biosphere Programme (IGBP). Available at http://www.anthropocene.info/en/home
5. "Welcome to the Anthropocene" (http://www.anthropocene.info/en/home).
6. Also in 2014, Elizabeth Kolbert's Pulitzer Prize-winning book, *The Sixth Extinction: An Unnatural History*, draws on the hospitality motif. Her fifth chapter, titled "Welcome to the Anthropocene" recounts the story of the scientific debates surrounding the naming of this new geological epoch (New York: Henry Holt and Company, 2014).
7. Available at https://www.youtube.com/watch?v=VOtj3mskx5k
8. Andrew Revkin, "Embracing the Anthropocene," DOT Earth, May 20, 2011. Available at http://dotearth.blogs.nytimes.com/2011/05/20/embracing-the-anthropocene/?_php=true&_type=blogs&_r=0
9. The Conference on Anthropocene Feminism, Center for 21st Century Studies, at University of Wisconsin-Milwaukee, April 10–12, 2014, was one of the first dedicated explicitly to feminist critical analyses of Anthropocene.
10. Clive Hamilton. (2014). "The Delusion of the 'Good" Anthropocene," http://clivehamilton.com/the-delusion-of-the-good-anthropocene-reply-to-andrew-revkin/
11. Nathaneal Johnson. (2014). "Is the Anthropocene a World of Hope or a World of Hurt?" *Grist Magazine*, http://grist.org/climate-energy/is-the-anthropocene-a-world-of-hope-or-a-world-of-hurt/
12. Andrew Revkin. (2014). "The Good, the Bad, and the Anthropocene," http://dotearth.blogs.nytimes.com/2014/07/07/the-good-the-bad-and-the-anthropocene/
13. Highlands Retreat Center, Allenspark, Colorado, June 9–12, 2014.

14. In July 2014, people protesting the shooting of an unarmed, black teenager in Ferguson, Missouri, by a white police officer, carried posters stating "I Am A Man" and "I Am a Woman," invoking the centrality of the issue of *human* rights for blacks during the 1960s US civil rights movement and, continuing today in the early twenty-first century. See Dyson (2014).
15. Dipesh Chakrabarty. (2012). "Climate Change, Climate Justice, and the Anthropos of the Anthropocene," Humanities Research Institute at Australian National University, June 15, 2012. http://rsha.anu.edu.au/events/climate-change-climate-justice-and-anthropos-anthropocene See also Dipesh Chakrabarty. (2013). Keynote address, "History on an Expanded Canvas: The Anthropocene's Invitation," https://www.youtube.com/watch?v=svgqLPFpaOg Berlin, Germany. Available at http://www.hkw.de/en/programm/projekte/2014/anthropozaen/anthropozaen_2013_2014.php
16. Prepared for the Presidential Forum on "Vulnerable Times," at the annual meeting of the Modern Language Association, Chicago, IL, January 9–12, 2014.
17. Raj Patel. (2013). "Misanthropocene?" *Earth Island Journal* (Spring), http://www.earthisland.org/journal/index.php/eij/article/misanthropocene/
18. Patel. (2013). "Misanthropocene?"
19. Donna Haraway. (2014). "Anthropocene, Capitalocene, Chthulucene: Staying with the Trouble," Anthropocene: Arts of Living on a Damaged Planet Conference, UC Santa Cruz, May 8, 2014. http://vimeo.com/97663518
20. Donna Haraway. 2014. "SF: String Figures, Multispecies Muddles, Staying with the Trouble". Keynote Presentation, Research Creation Working Group, Department of Art and Design, University of Alberta, March 24, 2014. Uploaded onto youtube on June 12, 2014. Available at https://www.youtube.com/watch?v=Ii3vuI-o614
21. Principles of Environmental Justice, The First National People of Color Environmental Leadership Summit, Washington, DC, October 24–27, 1991.
22. "Climate Justice and Environmental Justice: Honoring the Past, Looking Toward the Future," Washington, DC, February 26, 2014. http://www.epa.gov/environmentaljustice/events/20th-anniversary.html
23. "Climate Justice and Environmental Justice: Honoring the Past, Looking Toward the Future."
24. "Climate Justice and Environmental Justice: Honoring the Past, Looking Toward the Future."
25. In Bolivia and Ecuador "integral development" is embodied in the concept "*buen vivir*" ("living well" or "collective well-being"). See Walsh (2011).
26. Climate Justice Community Resiliency Center, http://uprose.org/?page_id=1547
27. "Kari-Oca 2 Declaration." Indigenous Environmental Network, June 21, 2012. http://www.ienearth.org/kari-oca-2-declaration
28. Fossil Fuel Divestment Student Network, http://studentsdivest.org/
29. Power Up! Convergence trailer of video in production by Zein Nakoda, https://www.youtube.com/watch?v=ZUo5fAfKq-I
30. Steve Kinnane, "Sustainability, Country, and Social Reconstruction in the Fitzroy Valley." Keynote, Conference on "Encountering the Anthropocene," Sydney Environmental Institute, University of Sydney, February 26–28, 2014. https://www.youtube.com/watch?v=3_xq3r9doUU
31. Kinnane, "Sustainability, Country, and Social Reconstruction in the Fitzroy Valley."

32. The use of the term "country" translates to the Aboriginal concept of human and nature interconnectedness and interdependence (see Rose (2004)). Some changes that Karajarri communities have observed and worry about include extreme high tides, falling populations of bush turkey and kangaroo, trees and bushes fruiting out of season, salmon running out of season, and traditional water holes drying up.
33. Anna Dwyer, "People Worrying for their Country: Karajarri Country and Climate Change." Conference on "Encountering the Anthropocene," Sydney Environmental Institute, University of Sydney, February 26–28, 2014.
34. Kinnane, "Sustainability, Country, and Social Reconstruction in the Fitzroy Valley."
35. Our Power Convening, August 6–9, 2014, https://storify.com/OurPower/richmond2014
36. Examples of dynamic, climate justice political assemblages include: Our Power Campaign (http://www.ourpowercampaign.org/), *buen vivir* (Gudynas 2011), just sustainability (Agyeman 2013), integral development (Orr 2014), transition towns (Edwards 2010), living economies/community economies (J. K. Gibson-Graham et al. 2013; Shiva 2014).

References

Adger, W. Neil, Barnett, Jon, Brown, Katrina, Marshall, Nadine, and O'Brien, Karen. (2012). "Cultural Dimensions of Climate Change Impacts and Adaptation." *Nature Climate Change* 3: 112–17.

Atkinson, Judy. (2002). *Trauma Trails: Recreating Song Lines* (Melbourne, Vic: Spinifex Press).

Autin, Whitney and Holbrook, John. (2012). "Is the Anthropocene an Issue of Stratigraphy or Pop Culture?" *GSA Today* 22(7): 60–1.

Boag, Peter. (2003). "Thinking Like Mount Rushmore: Sexuality and Gender in the Republican Landscape." In *Seeing Nature Through Gender*, edited by Virginia Scharff (Lawrence, KS: University Press of Kansas), 40–59.

Bond, Patrick. (2012). *Politics of Climate Justice: Paralysis Above, Movement Below* (Scottsville: University of Kwazulu-Natal Press).

Cagle, Susie. (2013). "A Year After a Refinery Explosion, Richmond, Calif., is Fighting Back." *Grist Magazine*, August 6, 2013. Available at http://grist.org/climate-energy/a-year-after-a-refinery-explosion-richmond-cali-is-fighting-back/

Carmin, JoAnn and Agyeman, Julian, eds. (2011). *Environmental Inequalities Beyond Borders: Local Perspectives and Global Injustices* (Cambridge, MA: MIT Press).

Chakrabarty, Dipesh. (2009). "The Climate of History: Four Theses." *Critical Inquiry* 35 (Winter): 197–222.

Conca, Ken and Dabelko, Geoffrey. (2014). *Green Planet Blues: Critical Perspectives on Global Environmental Politics* (Boulder, CO: Westview Press).

Costanza, R., Alperovitz, G., Daly, H., Farley, J., Franco, C., Jackson, T., Kubiszewski, I., Schor, J., and Victor, P. (2014). "What Would a Sustainable and Desirable Economy-in-Society-in-Nature Look Like?" In *Creating a Sustainable and Desirable Future: Insights from 45 Global Thought Leaders*, edited by R. Costanza and I. Kubiszewski (Singapore: World Scientific), 33–49.

Crutzen, Paul and Stoermer, Eugene. (2000). "The Anthropocene." *Global Change Newsletter* 41: 17–18.

Desmarais, Annette Aurelie. (2007). *La Via Campesina: Globalization and the Power of Peasants* (Halifax, NS: Fernwood Publishing).

Dibley, Ben. (2012). "'Nature is Us': The Anthropocene and Species-being." *Transformations* 21. Available at http://www.transformationsjournal.org/journal/issue_21/article_07.shtml

Di Chiro, Giovanna. (2008). "Living Environmentalisms: Coalition Politics, Social Reproduction, and Environmental Justice." *Environmental Politics* 17(1): 276–98.

Di Chiro, Giovanna. (2013). "Climate Justice Now!" Imagining Grassroots EcoCosmopolitanism." In *American Studies, Ecocriticism, and Citizenship*, edited by Joni Adamson and Kimberly Ruffin (NY: Routledge), 204–19.

Dryzek, John, Norgaard, Richard, and Schlosberg, David, eds. (2011). *The Oxford Handbook of Climate Change and Society* (New York: Oxford University Press).

Dyson, Michael Eric. (2014). "Where Do We Go After Ferguson?" Sunday Review, Opinion, *New York Times*. November 29.

Edwards, Andres. (2010). *Thriving Beyond Sustainability: Pathways to a Resilient Society* (Gabriola Island, BC: New Society Publishers).

Escobar, Arturo. (1994/2011). *Encountering Development: The Making and Unmaking of the Third World* (Princeton: Princeton University Press).

Faber, Daniel. (2008). *Capitalizing on Environmental Injustice: The Polluter-Industrial Complex in the Age of Globalization* (Lanham, MD: Rowman & Littlefield Publishers).

Fanon, Frantz. (1963). *The Wretched of the Earth* (New York: Grove Press).

Gibson-Graham, J. K. (2011). "A Feminist Project of Belonging for the Anthropocene." *Gender, Place & Culture* 18(1): 1–21.

Gibson-Graham, J. K. (2013). *Take Back the Economy* (Minneapolis: University of Minnesota Press).

Grove, Richard. (1998). *Ecology, Climate and Empire: Colonialism and Global Environmental History, 1400–1940* (Isle of Harris, UK: Whitehorse Press).

Gudynas, Eduardo. (2011). "Buen Vivir: Today's Tomorrow." *Development* 54(4): 441–7.

Guha, Ramachandra. (1997). *Varieties of Environmentalism: Essays North and South* (New York: Routledge).

Hamilton, Clive. (2010). *Requiem for a Species: Why We Resist the Truth about Climate Change* (Washington, DC: Earthscan).

Hamilton, Clive. (2013). *Earthmasters: The Dawn of the Age of Climate Engineering* (New Haven: Yale University Press).

Haraway, Donna. (2014). "Anthropocene, Capitalocene, Chthulucene: Staying with the Trouble." Paper delivered at the Anthropocene: Arts of Living on a Damaged Planet Conference, UC Santa Cruz, May 8, 2014. http://vimeo.com/97663518

Haraway, Donna. (2014). "Staying with the Trouble: Sympoiesis, String Figures, Multispecies Muddles." Paper delivered at the Conference on Gestes Spéculatifs, Centre Culturel International de Cerisy, France, June 28–July 5, 2013.

Harvey, David. (1997). *Justice, Nature and the Geography of Difference* (Hoboken, NJ: Wiley-Blackwell).

Hettinger, Ned. (2014). "Valuing Naturalness in the "Anthropocene": Now More than Ever." In *Keeping the Wild: Against the Domestication of Earth*, edited by G. Wuerthner, E. Crist, and T. Butler (Washington, D.C.: Island Press), 174–9.

Jamieson, Dale. (2010). "Adaptation, Mitigation, and Justice." In *Climate Ethics: Essential Readings*, edited by Stephen M. Gardiner et al. (New York: Oxford University Press), 263–83.

Jamieson, Dale. (2014). *Reason in a Dark Time* (Oxford: Oxford University Press).

Jensen, Derrick. (2013). "Age of the Sociopath." *Earth Island Journal* (Spring). Available at http://www.earthisland.org/journal/index.php/eij/article/age_of_the_sociopath/

Johnson, Nathaneal. (2014). "Is the Anthropocene a World of Hope or a World of Hurt?" *Grist Magazine*. Available at http://grist.org/climate-energy/is-the-anthropocene-a-world-of-hope-or-a-world-of-hurt/

Kareiva, Peter, Marvier, Michelle, and Lalasz, Robert. (2012). "Conservation in the Anthropocene: Beyond Solitude and Fragility." The Breakthrough Institute. Available at http://www.thebreakthrough.org/index.php/journal/past-issues/issue-2/conservation-in-the-anthropocene

Klein, Naomi. (2013). "Dancing the World Into Being: An interview with Idle No More's Leanne Betasamosake Simpson." *Yes! Magazine*. Available at http://www.yesmagazine.org/peace-justice/dancing-the-world-into-being-a-conversation-with-idle-no-more-leanne-simpson

Klein, Naomi. (2014). "The Change Within: The Obstacles We Face Are Not Just External." *The Nation*. Available at http://www.thenation.com/article/179460/change-within-obstacles-we-face-are-not-just-external?page=0,1

lewallen, ann-elise. (2014). "Resilience Embodied." *Resilience: A Journal of the Environmental Humanities* 1(1) (January): 11

Martinez-Alier, Juan. (2004). *The Environmentalism of the Poor* (London: Edward Elgar).

McKibben, Bill. (2012). "Global Warming's Terrifying New Math." *Rolling Stone Magazine*. Available at http://www.rollingstone.com/politics/news/global-warmings-terrifying-new-math-20120719?page=5

Merchant, Carolyn. (1992/2005). *Radical Ecology: The Search for a Livable World* (New York: Routledge).

Mol, Arthur and Sonnenfeld, David A., eds. (2000). *Ecological Modernization Around the World: Perspectives and Critical Debates* (Ilford, UK & Portland, OR.: Frank Cass & Co.)

Nixon, Rob. (2011). *Slow Violence and the Environmentalism of the Poor* (Cambridge, MA: Harvard University Press).

Nixon, Rob. (2014). "The Great Acceleration and the Great Divergence: Vulnerability in the Anthropocene." Presidential Forum, *Profession*, 2014 Modern Language Association of America. http://profession.commons.mla.org/2014/03/19/the-great-acceleration-and-the-great-divergence-vulnerability-in-the-anthropocene/

Nordhaus, Ted and Shellenberger, Michael. (2007). *Break Through: Why We Can't Leave Saving the Planet to Environmentalism* (New York: Mariner Books).

Orr, David. (2014). "Reflections on Resilience in a 'Black Swan' World." *Resilience: A Journal of the Environmental Humanities* 1(1) (January).

Patel, Raj. (2013). "Misanthropocene?" *Earth Island Journal* (Spring). http://www.earthisland.org/journal/index.php/eij/article/misanthropocene/

Pearce, Fred. (2013). "New Green Vision: Technology As Our Planet's Last Best Hope." *Yale Environment 360* (July 15). http://e360.yale.edu/feature/new_green_vision_technology_as_our_planets_last_best_hope_/2671/

Plumwood, Val. (1993). *Feminism and Mastery of Nature* (New York: Routledge).

Ray, Sarah Jaquette. (2013). *The Ecological Other: Exclusion in American Culture* (Tucson, AZ: University of Arizona Press).

Reid, Julian. (2012). "The Disastrous and Politically Debased Subject of Resilience." *Development Dialogue* 58: 67–80.

Ribot, Jesse. (2013). "Risk and Blame in the Anthropocene: Multi-scale Climate Change Analysis." Conference Paper #7, Conference on Food Sovereignty: A Critical Dialogue, Yale University, September 14–15, 2013.

Rockström, J. et al. (2009). "A Safe Operating Space for Humanity." *Nature* 461(7263): 472–5.

Rose, Deborah Bird. (2004). *Reports From a Wild Country: Ethics of Decolonisation* (Sydney: University of New South Wales Press).

Rose, Deborah Bird et al. (2012). "Thinking Through the Environment, Unsettling the Humanities." *Environmental Humanities* 1: 1–5.

Sassen, Saskia. (2014). "Countdown to Oblivion: The Real Reason We Can't Stop Global Warming." *Salon*. http://www.salon.com/2014/05/18/countdown_to_oblivion_the_real_reason_we_cant_stop_global_warming/

Schlosberg, David and Collins, Lisette. (2014). "From Environmental to Climate Justice: Climate Change and the Discourse of Environmental Justice." *WIREs Clim Change*. doi: 1002/wcc.275.

Schneiderman, Jill. (2014). "Critical Thinking in/for the Anthropocene: A Feminist Perspective on Geological Nomenclature." Paper presented at AESS Conference, PACE University, New York, NY, June 12, 2014.

Seager, Joni. (1993). *Earth Follies: Coming to Feminist Terms with the Global Environmental Crisis* (New York: Routledge).

Shiva, Vandana. (2014). "Economy Revisited. Will Green be the Colour of Money or Life?" Global Research, July 26. Available at http://www.globalresearch.ca/economy-revisited-will-green-be-the-colour-of-money-or-life/5393406

Shiva, Vandana and Mies, Maria. (1993). *Ecofeminism* (Halifax, NS: Fernwood Publications).

Sörlin, Sverker. (2012). "Environmental Humanities: Why Should Biologists Interested in the Environment Take the Humanities Seriously?" *BioScience* 62(9): 788–9.

Stengers, Isabelle. (2010). *Cosmopolitics* (Minneapolis: University of Minnesota Press).

Taylor, Dorceta. (2014). "The State of Diversity in Environmental Organizations: Mainstream NGOs, Foundations & Government Agencies." *Green 2.0*. http://diversegreen.org/report/

Walsh, Catherine. (2011). "Afro and Indigenous Life—Visions in/and Politics: (De)colonial Perspectives in Bolivia and Ecuador." *Bolivian Studies Journal* 18: 47–67.

WCED (World Commission on Environment and Development). (1987). *Our Common Future: The Brundtland Report* (Oxford: Oxford University Press).

Zalasiewicz, Jan., Williams, M., Steffen, W., and Crutzen, P. (2010). "The New World of the Anthropocene." *Environmental Science and Technology* 44: 2228–31.

FREEDOM, AGENCY, AND FLOURISHING

CHAPTER 25

THE LIMITS OF FREEDOM AND THE FREEDOM OF LIMITS

JASON LAMBACHER

INTRODUCTION

THE aspiration toward freedom is a vital element of the human condition, especially in contemporary societies. Life is diminished without the feeling that freedom, and enjoying freedoms, is an attainable possibility. But "freedom" is a loaded term—conceptually, ideologically, and politically. Distinguishing the various ways this concept resonates in political discourses and connecting freedom to related ideas such as "agency," "responsibility," and "flourishing" is a difficult task in political theory. *Environmental* political theory is faced with the additional challenge that freedom is typically imagined irrespective of *ecological* contexts. This detachment from context—indeed the idea that freedom is about the absence of contextual limitations—leads to considerable tension between green thought and conventional ways of thinking about freedom. Green concepts—such as *carrying capacity* and *limits to growth*, as well as an array of regulatory policies and behavioral prohibitions that have emerged in the past 40 years—have allowed critics of environmentalism to frame it as restrictive, and potentially even authoritarian. On the surface, green politics does appear to interfere with freedom of choice and the maximization of preferences in private life. Looking deeper, however, it becomes clear that this is only one way to view freedom. Freedom, in fact, is not a unitary, or universal, concept. Clusters of freedoms—like property, civil rights, vocation, sexuality, or leisure—have internal tensions and are often in conflict with other freedoms. Green notions of freedom exhibit a similar diversity. Rather than a liability, this diversity can be an important foundation for environmental political legitimacy and social creativity.

If freedom and environmental values do *not* have inherent oppositional tension, how should environmental political theory assess its potential? While restricting freedoms is rightly connected to policy regulation, rule by experts, and stern imperatives of responsibility, living in an age of ecological limits is much more than a politics of the forbidden. Any notion of green freedom begins with an understanding of ecological limits—and what respecting those limits necessitates—but what this means for us by way of authentic response is open to interpretation and autonomous experimentation. Indeed, environmental political theory should take the opportunity to explore green notions of freedom as one of the most powerful ways to conceive of human endeavors in an ecological context. As I will argue, responses to ecological challenges can illuminate visionary and imaginative pathways to human and ecological emancipation. Freedom in green politics raises penetrating questions of meaning and purpose, which inform identities, practices, and policies that reflect desires for *both* freedom *and* ecological integrity. Moreover, certain freedoms are *enabled* by *freedom from* rampant materialism and isolated, over-worked, and stressed lifestyles. When examined with a tone that minimizes guilt, fear, or punishment, green freedom emerges as a set of motivational ideals and innovative practical opportunities. Heeding ecological limits may lead to pragmatic strategies of avoidance, but freedom inspires us to *live* green ways of life. In this way, efforts to realize green forms of freedom can be authentic, ecologically responsible, and consciously human.

This chapter engages a green politics of freedom in two sections. The first sketches a selective historical portrait of how freedom has been conceived as both in tension and in harmony with "nature." The second explores a few lines of inquiry that invite environmental political theorists to investigate how freedom resonates in green politics.

Limits and Freedom: Divergent Perspectives

It is a propitious time to reconsider the critical status of freedom in environmental political theory. The "doom and gloom" rhetoric that has long been a feature of green political discourse has made freedom antagonistic to ideas about sustainable living. On the one hand, if the requirements of staving off ecological collapse are imminent, then freedoms become subsumed under a politics of authoritarianism, whether by despots, technocrats, or environmentalists. On the other hand, if ecological catastrophes are inevitable, many may conclude that ignoring complex problems is the best strategy, in part to maintain vestiges of their "free" life. At first glance, therefore, the eruptive emergence of ecological challenges and subsequent awareness of living in an "age of limits" would seem to confront freedom with skepticism. The historical perspective, however, is much broader and worth closer scrutiny.

There have been two fundamentally different ways to conceive of the relationship between freedom and ecology—one where ecological risks pose a *threat* to freedom and one where living ecologically is an *expression* of freedom. Western theory, in particular, has long maintained a distinction between "freedom" and "necessity," where freedom is mainly about liberation from necessity, limitation, and coercion, manifesting itself prominently as an ability to make authenic choices. From Aristotle, whose vision of freedom is a political accomplishment that triumphs over brute animality, to Vaughan, who exemplifies the Medieval view that freedom is attained through the spirit struggling to separate itself from matter (Merchant 1980: 107), to Kant's modern idealism which views freedom as a metaphysical achievement that transcends nature, the struggle against nature is a defining feature of being both human and free. It should be noted that this dualism is more a feature of Western thought than, say, East and South Asian, animist, and indigenous ethical traditions that tend not to be as rigid when it comes to categorical divisions between "freedom" and "nature."

The project of opposing nature in Western theory eventually shifted to more material and scientific ways of not just struggling against nature but *dominating* it, often with remarkable technological success. For Bacon, dominating nature is explicitly linked to freedom through the augmentation of human power (Bacon 2000). Hobbes rejects the *vita contemplativa* as a path to freedom, for freedom is experienced not by a "mind reposed" but by an absence of impediments to the restless pursuit of "power after power that ceaseth only in death" (Hobbes 2008: 149, 188). The "labor theory of value" theorists, a category that links classical liberalism with Marxism, also saw the expansion of freedom through the exploitation of nature, whether through private property regimes or socialized modes of production. As Hans Jonas remarks, the chorus in *Antigone* could once sarcastically mock the pretentiousness of human power as "clever beyond all dreams," but we now know that human power can no longer be dismissed so easily, for the "Anthropocene" created by modern achievements *is* clever beyond Greek dreams (Jonas 1984: 2). Dominating nature may yield freedom to enjoy certain powers of control and manipulation, but this kind of freedom is deeply problematic to green theory.

The emergence of the "limits to growth" discourse in the 1970s amplified the discursive tension between ecologism and freedom in interesting ways (Meadows et al. 2002). With advancing ecological crises becoming impossible to ignore, debates shifted from questions about what humans are doing to nature to what nature will do to us as a consequence of our actions, what William Leiss calls the "revenge of nature" (Leiss 1994). Testing ecological limits could lead to any number of ecological transitions that could materially alter, and perhaps thwart, the human freedom to act by overshooting the earth's carrying capacity for food, fuel, and resources (though this would certainly be felt differently along class, race, and geographic lines, at least initially). Garrett Hardin, William Ophuls, and William Catton captured, in different ways, a dystopian mood that portrayed the political consequences of a murky future of constrained choices and radically un-free ways of life (Catton 1980; Ophuls 1997; Hardin 2005). As Andrew Dobson characterizes the apparent inexorability of an authoritarian future, "Dystopia, then, for political ecology, is written into the dynamics of present social, political, and economic practices" (Dobson 2003: 69). As with Dosteovsky's Grand Inquisitor or Hobbes' Leviathan, who are there to save us from the "curse" of freedom or the chaos of anarchy, environmentalism could be seen as curbing freedoms and civil liberties in the name of ecology, prudence, and survival. The popular environmental equation I=PAT (Impact = Population x Affluence x Technology) could be interpreted, for instance, as constraining the freedom to have children, become prosperous, or innovate technologically. The apparent political unpopularity of such prospects created a fierce backlash, especially in the United States, where "freedom" is a confusing but potent political ideology (often supporting comical memes for just about anything).

It is interesting to note here a profound shift in how freedom as such is evaluated as anti-ecological. The philosophical view that transcending nature is a distinguishing feature of freedom changes into empirically and scientifically driven predictions of gloomy ecological trends that some believe will lead to restrictions on freedom as a matter of political necessity. This transformation is worthy of more historical and critical scrutiny.

However, this is only one side of the story. The "ecological turn" also provoked a reconsideration of what human freedom in an ecological context means. Rousseau's thesis that humanity is born free but is everywhere in chains influences a late modern current that links society with dependence and repression, and freedom with self-sufficiency that is found in natural, unalienated ways of life (Rousseau 1993). The "dark side" of modernism was exposed with ferocity by Horkheimer and Adorno, who pointed out links between scientism, instrumental rationality, ecological degradation, and social control (Horkheimer and Adorno 1991). Freud explained how the outward denial of limits could negate subjective experiences of freedom (Freud 1989). And as Piers H. G. Stephens points out, some dystopian literature is helpful in showing how "nature" represents a realm of freedom from economic and social systems that deign to control life (Stephens 2004: 76).

The ecological turn has also inspired a looking back to older traditions that have positively associated freedom and nature in order to constitute new ecological ethics and politics. Romantics (including transcendentalists like Thoreau), Buddhists, and a myriad mystical and wilderness traditions have long sought to experience the freedom thought to be found in nature's example of authenticity, autopoeisis, and symbiosis. The Japanese philosopher Dogen sees freedom as the universe experiencing itself through the self, not as the illusion of a self imposing itself on external objects, an insight important to contemporary Japanese ideas of liberation and aesthetics (Dogen 1992). The Norwegian cultural concept of *friluftsliv*, or "free air life," refers to qualities of exaltation, exploration, and freedom only experienced outdoors. Heidegger's concept of *Gelasseinheit* entails an ethic of forbearance, of "letting be," that is taken to be a mature form of freedom (Heidegger 2010). Aldo Leopold argues that, "An ethic, ecologically, is a limitation on freedom of action in the struggle for existence," but the "land ethic" he endorses "changes the role of Homo sapiens from conqueror of the land-community to plain member and citizen of it" (Leopold 1966: 238, 240). Many arguments that use the precautionary principle, as with climate change or the extinction crisis, speak about preserving freedoms for future generations, on both prudential and ethical grounds. Freedom and nature in all of these accounts—and doubtless there are more—are intimately related and tend to reinforce each other.

Another strain of political thinking sought freedom in environmental social movements, especially through their potential to overcome the ecological destructiveness of capitalist and socialist forms of production (Marcuse 1994). The 1980s' liberation ecology movements, particularly in Latin America, explicitly linked social with ecological emancipation (Peet and Watts 1996). Murray Bookchin's social ecology perspective sees, as Robyn Eckersley puts it, "nature as the *ground* of freedom" that helps to overcome hierarchical relations of domination (Eckersley 1992: 149). Douglass Torgerson shows how the theater of environmental protest and activism can engender transformative social experiences of shared solidarity and point the way to new horizons of political possibility (Torgerson 1999). Finally, eco-villages and eco-village networks represent an attempt by intentional communities to model and prefigure forms of meaningful freedom through the practices of small-scale communal life (Litfin 2013).

This relatively tidy contrast of conceptualizing freedom as either against or with nature is, it should be conceded, slightly misleading. In fact, freedom in the landscape of *environmental* political theory can be further examined through different standpoints and their attitudes toward freedom, as in green forms of liberalism, Marxism, feminism, civic republicanism, postcolonialism, Prometheanism, primitivism, and anarchism. There isn't space here to explore these perspectives in depth, but in brief, green liberalism focuses on the compatibility of rights with the land ethic and avoiding harm to non-human nature while maintaining a plurality of goods (Dagger 2006). Green Marxists tackle the centrality of property regimes in capitalism and the empty formalism of abstract rights in the context of materially unequal societies, finding freedom in forms of un-alienated labor aligned with ecological settings. Eco-feminists criticize how freedom is constructed to assume masculine conceptions of the self as exercising choice outside of social or ecological contexts, while also advocating a more relational and embodied account of the self that acknowledges both material and social constraints on individual action (Plumwood 1993; King 2005; Teena Gabrielson *personal communication*). Green civic republicans find freedom in a political realm that balances rights and duties, regulates the market in the service of sustainability, and offers an expansive vision of inter-generational justice based on obligation and virtue (Barry 2008). Ecological postcolonialism emphasizes the freedom to be found in liberation from colonial regimes and, more recently, economic globalization and transnational conservation regimes, by advancing political and ecological self-determination (Castro 2010). Promethean greens wish to harness the freedom of technological innovation and creative ingenuity, which increasingly is modeled on biomimicry and principles found in nature (Beattie and Erlich 2004). Primitivists, in contrast, think that freedom emerges through liberation from technology and the conventions of "civilization" (Zerzan 2012). A variety of green anarchisms, though disparate, unite in the belief that freedom is the highest political value and that a closer connection to nature organically emerges with the absence of hierarchical authority—that is, without institutions of the state, property, or religion (Parson 2008; Goldman 2011).

Fissures between freedom and environmental politics are also associated with numerous *practical* tensions in what is called "lifestyle politics." A few examples are germane to illustrating these problems: a politics of consumption, property rights, and mobility. In daily life, the freedom to consume is one of the more pedestrian freedoms. Consumer "sovereignty" is often appealed to, especially by commercial and political pressures that compel imperatives of economic growth (Princen et al. 2002). Consumers are sensitive to overt attempts to constrain what they buy, how much, and for what purpose, and tenaciously guard their "freedom to consume" almost as a matter of right. Even if one is otherwise conscious of the impact of consumption on environmental degradation, it can be challenging to connect the dots between individual consumption and the cumulative impact of consumption in general. There is frequent dissonance between being free as a consumer and free as an ecologically mindful citizen. One can be sympathetic to environmental regulations as a citizen by recognizing their collective import, but still be reluctant to curb the freedom to consume as a private individual (Sagoff 2007). Similarly, polities can democratically agree that some environmental regulations are desirable, but often not when they constrain economic growth. An environmental politics of consumption, then, is mainly about what version of freedom—the consumer's or the citizen's—is in control of discursive and policy issues.

A related argument is the challenge that green freedom poses to property rights, especially for Lockean conceptions of property (Ryan 1977). In liberal societies (in particular) property rights are central, and many individuals cling to a vision of themselves as rights bearing individuals whose property is viewed almost with a sense of sacredness, even in the midst of sprawl, pollution, species loss, and other problems. Green freedom challenges private property as a pre-political right sealed from politics and ethical scrutiny. At the same time, there is increasing recognition that environmentalism shouldn't be limited to the regulation of public lands or entities. Through a variety of means—conservation easements, land swaps, and habitat corridors—environmentalists work collaboratively with private property owners in the service of ecological goals, something which a green scholarship of freedom should explore with more rigor.

Another example of practical tension in lifestyle politics is about mobility. How we transport ourselves to home, work, or play is often taken to be a matter of personal freedom. Though the construction of roads, railways, and bike lanes are primarily a matter of public domain, transportation is for many a matter of personal choice. Dictating this choice, through taxes, fees, or other incentives and disincentives to mobility, can be seen as interfering with this freedom to choose how to move from place to place. In reality, a politics of mobility is highly influenced by the path dependence of previous infrastructure histories. One can only get around most parts of ex-urban California effectively by car, while in Japan a car is less efficient than taking trains or subways. An environmental politics of mobility influences where people live, what transportation systems are available, and where jobs are located. The extent to which these issues are matters of freedom and choice is tenuous, yet people still see how they get around as something they decide, even when a full range of transportation options is not available.

There are many other examples that typify the problems between personal choices and collective ecological responsibility. It should not be surprising that a politics of freedom and issues of class and group divisiveness lies at the center of many of these disputes. These different perspectives on freedom and ecology, therefore, cannot reduce to a single substrate. The relationship between independence and interdependence is layered and complex. And so the question of freedom in environmental politics has a much different texture depending on individual and collective frames, lines between public and private, and disagreements about what "freedom" means in practical detail. All this being said, the dominant way of conceiving freedom as the absence of limitations opens up positions of critique and points to alternative ways of energizing the concept of freedom in green politics.

The Freedom of Limits

How can freedom be positioned as a strong and productive concept in environmental political theory? As a source of imaginative, aesthetic, and practical reflection about the world and the human place in it, green freedom leads us to ask fundamental questions about action, agency, and responsibility. Theorizing freedom tends to prioritize the new, but there is certainly ancient wisdom to draw on in regards to living a good life in an ecological context. The challenge for green theorists is to be open to the old and the new, and provide future generations with similar opportunities to experience green modes of freedom. Moreover, it sounds paradoxical, but restraining certain freedoms can actually give rise to *other* freedoms—freedoms that have been degraded or that we don't even know we lack. As Goethe reminds us, "No one is more enslaved than the man who believes himself to be free and is not" (Goethe 2008: 151). And as Zizek remarks, "We 'feel free' because we lack the language to articulate our unfreedom" (Zizek 2002: 2). Theories of green freedom can help us think through these problems.

Green forms of freedom first invite an immanent critique of the dominant ideological forms of freedom in contemporary politics. The critique emphasizes that ecologically destructive kinds of freedom have three main characteristics: promoting rights irrespective of ecological contexts, demanding that productivism and consumerism expand indefinitely, and the disavowal of any special obligation to care for non-human nature. Why are these characteristics troubling to a green conception of freedom? On a basic level, the exercise of freedom and rights is not possible without functioning ecological systems. Therefore, appealing to "freedom" as an abstract right in a decontextualized way does not justify one's choices a priori, for the context in which one makes, or is able to make choices, is key. As Nancy Hirschmann writes, "Freedom is precisely a combination of self-creation and what happens to you, the internal as well as the external, the combination of and the dynamic between the two. If freedom is concerned with the capacity to choose, then social construction requires us to think about the broader conditions in which choices are made" (Hirschmann 2003: 39). Ecological limits can be construed as a context in which our choices are not only *constrained* but also *constructed*. Berlin's famous distinction between negative and positive liberty is a relevant association here (Berlin 1969), though green theory has trouble accepting its neat analytical division, which is similar to the vexing problem of clearly distinguishing between "private" and "public." Environmental political theory insists that the context in which choices are made and the outcomes they bring about are part of a critical discourse about the responsible exercise of freedom. Especially problematic, again, is when freedom is assumed to imply the absence of limitations, a position often associated with liberalism. Yet liberalism need not be the "evil genius" behind the ecological crisis, as Marcel Wissenburg argues. He rightly points out that there is a compelling case to be made that, *inter alia*, if liberals cherish choices, a plurality of healthy environments are important to the exercise of choice where there is a "maximum protection of ecological diversity combined with maximum freedom for individuals to pursue a green life" (Wissenburg 2006: 29). Nevertheless, if freedom is to have valence in green theory, the atomizing effects and abstract tendencies of negative liberty need to be confronted. Theorizing freedom within particular social and ecological contexts calls to attention a danger pointed out by Berlin, notably that "freedom for the pike is death to the minnows" (Berlin 1969: 124). That is, freedom for some can inhibit freedom for others. A green theory of freedom should therefore always be viewed critically in the context of *relationship* with others.

Beyond critique, freedom is a potent motivational source in green politics. Imagining green forms of positive liberty can be energizing, both for individuals and collectives. Recognizing how this can be accomplished requires cognitive and material shifts in our aspirations toward freedom. Green freedom is about contributing to a *quality* of life that people help to create, for themselves and others. This requires time for reflection about purposeful living and political opportunities to engage with others directly. It may not be easy to get out of the "iron cage," as Weber persuasively characterizes the modern world (Weber 1958), but freedom in environmental politics needs to be strongly distinguished from possessive materialism. Many are becoming convinced that less materialistic lifestyles and more social equity *increases* happiness and an expanded sense of freedom. To build on this growing sentiment, especially in societies marked by the primacy of economic productivity, green theorists should forcefully advocate more space for thinking, contemplation, and unhurried phenomenological experiences as important modes of freedom.

Many theorists would resist an attempt to see freedom as anything other than the individual pursuit of the good life. Individual frames are important, but a more promising stream for theorizing green freedom is to understand it as relational. This way of viewing freedom is less about independence and more about integral interconnections with others—people, species, ecosystems, bioregions, and even all sentient beings. As Vandana Shiva writes, "Earth democracy ... is the freedom for all species to evolve within the web of life, and the freedom and responsibility of humans ... to respect the rights of other species" (Shiva 2013). A relational construction of freedom cannot accept the exercise of freedom that comes at the expense of other people or through egregious exploitation of the environment—direct or indirect. In this sense, freedom can effectively be linked to environmental justice perspectives about the social and ecological impacts of harm and ideas of responsibility and flourishing. Phillip Pettit's civic republican perspective on freedom as non-domination is also relevant in this sense to casting freedom in relational contexts (Pettit 1997), particularly for theorizing conditions under which an ethos of non-domination extends to other species and ecosystems. And following E. O. Wilson, thinking about freedom as relational might help to prevent what he calls the emerging "Eremocene," an age of loneliness characterized by a world of shrinking biodiversity and increasing ecological homogeneity (Wilson 2014).

Freedom in an ecological frame is guided by the opportunity to live "freely" whilst other lifeforms and systems are also permitted to evolve in their own ways. Environmental political theory is generally suspicious of fixed answers to what this means, as there is no "original harmony" prescribed by either human nature or natural principles. As John Barry writes, there is no "reading off" hypothesis that predetermines particular social or political arrangements from examples found in nature (Barry 2007: 27–8). Following William Connolly, theorists of freedom and creativity should "break both unified narratives and closed explanatory theories" (Connolly 2014: 444). Doing so can help us see that there cannot be just one model of an ecologically sustainable society and that there is considerable room for imagining and thinking through alternatives. For instance, attitudes toward freedom are different in arguments for, say, a green state vs. green anarchism, though both can offer valid pathways to sustainable societies. Green theory encourages a plurality of ways to live respectfully, consciously, and deliberately in nature *as modes of freedom* by challenging the growth paradigms and engaging others in robust deliberation about what green freedom can mean.

Thinking about ecological limits and freedom can thus provide an important context for reflexivity. The presence of environmental risks gives us occasion to reflect on what the activities of freedom are doing to our ecological relationships, and to other human beings. At the same time, limits encourage us to think differently about what autonomy means given certain ecological constraints. Green freedom in this sense is about the creation of values, technologies, and strategies for political aspiration. It can therefore be a broad motivational force rather than a defensive ideology centered around private preferences. As such, it is about inspiring *possibilities* and inviting creative reflection on the political conditions necessary for the flourishing of humans and non-humans alike. In this respect, green appeals to freedom, following Piers H. G. Stephens, can harness the "childlike faculties of wonder, delight, and fascination with the independent processes of the world" in order to deepen an experience of genuine human liberty (Stephens 2004: 86). At the very least, this leads to an appreciation that "nature," whatever it may mean, is not merely the playground for human agency and control. It also invites us to explore what freedom grounded in experiences of nature may mean for individuals and communities alike. We may also consider that freedom is something more than human, with the recognition that, as Connolly characterizes it, "we [humans] are distinctive, but not unique" (Connolly 2014: 442).

Furthermore, green freedom benefits considerably from an Arendtian approach to political action that sees freedom not as a matter of being but of *becoming*—which is about natality and new beginnings, not the uncovering of some sort of essence. Green forms of freedom should be seen less in terms of ideas that we are "born free." Rather, they can be achievements experienced when acting with others, as seen in many green social movements. Arendt rightly suggests that freedom is a form of virtuosity—the performance of lives that express meaningful values (Arendt 2006). As Frances More Lappé writes, "We can then experience real freedom: not freedom from rules but freedom with power—freedom to participate in creating rules that promote life" (Lappé 2011: 132). This kind of active freedom can't be scripted in advance, though, again, the freedom to articulate and practice environmental values certainly draws inspiration from older lifeways that model ecologically balanced relationships. An exhilarating sense of discovery—or rediscovery—of what is possible, what is new and creative, should be kept alive for those who help to shape green politics. There is a powerful creative element in freedom, and green freedom is no exception.

Cynics might see these perspectives as naive utopianism. But arguing that we can, to a degree, freely create, interpret, and re-envision green values does not mean that *any* world can be conceived. Green politics shouldn't promise "prophecies of bliss" (Jonas 1984: 17–19). And as Andrew Dobson reminds us, neither ecological conditions nor the human condition is infinitely malleable (Dobson 2003). Freedom as "infinite malleability" paints fantastical varieties of green utopianisms, which explains why Dobson rightly thinks that environmentalism can inspire many different causes yet leave "confusing" political benefits and burdens (Dobson 2003: 67). At the same time, we should recognize that freedom in detached utopianism ignores ecological contexts and is significantly liable for current environmental crises.

Engagement with ecologically utopian thought can be helpful, however, because it offers diverse and vivid accounts of what green freedom can look like. As Marius De Geus argues, utopian works, be they utopias of sufficiency or abundance, are important for raising critical awareness of issues in the present, many of which are "quiet" problems whose cumulative effects unfold over long periods of time (De Geus 1999: 31). Green utopian works also stoke political curiosity by encouraging people to envision how freedom and sustainable living can coalesce. Of course, we should be mindful that the terms "utopian" and "dystopian" carry much dramatic cargo and there may be nothing especially utopian *or* dystopian about a sustainable society that values ecological limits and does so in a way that nurtures appeals to freedom. Freedom may be a high aspiration, but freedoms are mostly experienced in the mundane—as matters of habit, routine, practical detail, and everyday choices.

Freedom is not the same as agency, though they are certainly connected. The former comes from imagination and striving, the latter is about the capacity to act. The critical point is less about the abstract question of whether humans are "free" to respond to ecological challenges that we are mostly responsible for making, and more about the contextual ways in which the "choice architecture," as Thaler and Sunstein put it, can be "nudged" in a more ecological direction, for both individuals and polities (Thayler and Sunstein 2009). Thus, another promising line of inquiry is to show that while living sustainably may restrict some choices, it need not diminish freedom of action. Richard Dagger (drawing on Pettit) distinguishes "option freedom" from "agency freedom." Option freedom refers to the number of choices that a person may have. Pettit writes that a choice between "20 barely discernible beers" means little to someone who would rather drink something else (or a different style of beer) (Dagger 2006: 211). Agency freedom is the capacity to exercise autonomy, and thus is concerned with the *value* of options available and the context in which they are experienced (Dagger 2006: 211). Maximizing option freedom may increase the number of choices immediately but endanger both option and agency freedom in the long run by destroying ecological contexts in which one can capably exercise choices, as well as causing, as Barry Schwartz argues, considerable anxiety about the dizzying array of options (Schwartz 2004). Green freedom is less about the number of choices one has than about the contexts that expand agency freedom within an ecological ethic. In other words, pursuing agency freedom may involve "sacrificing" some options, but sacrifice is not necessarily limiting and may, in fact, be "a form of self-expression and self-fulfillment" (Hall 2010: 63). We may restrict some options so that, say, other species may live, but doing so can deepen a sense of our own freedom, for we are living deliberately and with a sense of purpose. Focusing on the value of agency freedom might then open us up to other freedoms we might not know we lack, such as an abundance of time, meaningful work, connections to others, resilient communities, and refreshing experiences of wildness and the diversity of life.

Finally, green politics also invites us to evaluate the *value* of freedom as a political ideal, aside from its conceptualization. On the surface, it seems that freedom is a good that can't be exhausted—we always want more of it. But we are complex creatures and it is fair to say that freedom doesn't always hold a trump card. Sometimes we want guidance, teaching, ritual, or grace. Despite the ubiquitous rhetoric of freedom in contemporary life, most of us don't think that our actions always represent the profound exercise of authentic choices and existential autonomy. Rather than evading discourses of freedom in environmental political theory, we would do best to consider the value of it in a way that puts it in conversation with other important environmental ideas, such as agency, responsibility, care, equality, and flourishing.

Conclusion

Freedom is indeed a vital concept in environmental political theory. Green freedom challenges ideologically comfortable assumptions in contemporary societies and the power of those who benefit from the status quo. As environmentalists have confronted the material excesses and ecological hazards of liberal, social, and corporatist states, anti-environmentalists have skillfully framed environmentalism as anti-freedom. And to the extent that ideologies of negative liberty dominate conceptions of freedom, it can be difficult to see how freedom can be a robust concept for green theory. As Elizabeth Anker points out, we live in "a culture steeped in images of sovereign power, heroic action, and neoliberal valuations of choice and self-reliance" (Anker 2014: 456). While these images can be "greened" to an extent, there is more potential for freedom in environmental political theory than these particular constructions of liberty suggest.

Much environmentalism does admirable work in preparing us to reckon with a future where ecological limits will play a larger role in politics. But environmentalism has too often recklessly deployed a politics of doom and gloom rhetoric that emphasizes logics of catastrophe accompanied by fear, guilt, and punishment. This wakes people up but often shuts people down, and ultimately taps meager sources of motivation. A politics of fear is often behind appeals to self-interest or ethical duty. Aside from making people defensive and combative, motivation through self-interest is too narrow in effect, and ethical commands miss an opportunity to generate affective enthusiasm by a critical mass of people.

Avoiding the dangers that limits imply is a necessary but insufficient approach to our ecological challenges. Emphasizing the *freedom to* create ecologically sustainable societies is therefore critically important. I argue that this is a creative endeavor, at once joyful, comic, and serious, and need not be cast only in a gloomy and tragic vein. Joseph Meeker's position that "saving the environment" need not be played out as a tragedy is worth remembering, especially his endorsement of "play ethic" tactics of reconciliation—like novelty, spontaneity, wit, and imagination (Meeker 1987: 10). Ecological limits exist and we need to be clear that they constrain action, but green theorists should explore how they liberate other kinds of freedom. Environmental political theory can help by articulating a language of *green* freedom that has vibrant and constructive impact. The appeal of freedom nourishes imagination, gives energy to action, and inspires political movements. As Emma Goldman supposedly remarked, "If I can't dance, I don't want to be part of your revolution." This is another way of saying that the transition to sustainable societies should be accompanied by celebration and the varied expressions of human freedom. The challenge is to enable a politics of freedom that is generative and leads to the flourishing not only of people, but other species, landscapes, and systems. Freedom as a concept has tremendous political resonance. Environmental political theorists should waste no time in exploring more deeply what the limits of freedom and the freedom of limits can mean for green politics and our collective future.

References

Anker, Elizabeth. (2014). "Freedom and the Human in 'Evolutionary' Political Theory." *Political Research Quarterly* 67(2): 456.

Arendt, Hannah. (2006). *Between Past and Future* (London: Penguin Books).

Bacon, Francis. (2000). *The New Organon* (Cambridge: Cambridge University Press).

Barry, John. (2007). *Environment and Social Theory*, 2nd edn.(London: Routledge).

Barry, John. (2008). "Toward a Green Republicanism: Constitutionalism, Political Economy, and the Green State." *The Good Society* 17(2): 3–11.

Beattie, Andrew and Erlich, Paul. (2004). *Wild Solutions: How Biodiversity is Money in the Bank* (New Haven: Yale University Press).

Berlin, Isaiah. (1969). *Four Essays on Liberty* (Oxford: Oxford University Press).

Castro, Joao Augosto de Araujo. (2010). "Environment and Development: The Case of Developing Countries." In *Green Planet Blues*, 4th edn., edited by Ken Conca and Geoffrey Dabelko (Philadelphia: Westview Press), 30–7.

Catton, William. (1980). *Overshoot: The Ecological Basis of Revolutionary Change* (Urbana: University of Illinois Press).
Connolly, William. (2014). "Species Evolution and Cultural Freedom." *Political Research Quarterly* 67(2): 442.
Dagger, Richard. (2006). "Freedom and Rights." In *Political Theory and the Ecological Challenge*, edited by Andrew Dobson and Robyn Eckersley (Cambridge: Cambridge University Press), 211.
De Geus, Marius. (1999). *Ecological Utopias: Envisioning the Sustainable Society* (Utrecht: International Books).
Dobson, Andrew. (2003). "Janus-Faced Utopianism: The Politics of Ecology." In *Explorations in Environmental Political Theory: Thinking About What We Value*, edited by Joel Jay Kassiola (Armonk, NY: M. E. Sharpe), 67.
Dogen, Eihei. (1992). *Shogogenzo: Zen Essays*. Translated by Thomas Cleary (Honolulu: University of Hawaii Press).
Eckersley, Robyn. (1992). *Environmentalism and Political Theory: Toward an Ecocentric Approach* (Albany: SUNY Press).
Freud, Sigmund. (1989). *Civilization and its Discontents* (New York: W. W. Norton).
Goethe, Johan Wolfgang. (2008). *Elective Affinities: A Novel*. Translated by David Constantine (Oxford: Oxford University Press).
Hall, Cheryl. (2010). "Freedom, Values, and Sacrifice." In *The Environmental Politics of Sacrifice*, edited by Michael Maniates and John M. Meyer (Cambridge: MIT Press), 63.
Hardin, Garrett. (2005). "The Tragedy of the Commons." In *Debating the Earth: The Environmental Politics Reader*, edited by John Dryzek and David Schlosberg (Oxford: Oxford University Press), 25–36.
Heidegger, Martin. (2010). *Country Path Conversations* (Bloomington: Indiana University Press).
Hirschmann, Nancy. (2003). *The Subject of Liberty: Toward a Feminist Theory of Freedom* (Princeton: Princeton University Press).
Hobbes, Thomas. (2008). *Leviathan*. In *Modern Political Thought*, 2nd edn., edited by David Wooton (Indianapolis: Hackett), 122–302.
Horkheimer, Max and Adorno, Theodore. (1991). *Dialectic of Enlightenment* (New York: Continuum Press).
Jonas, Hans. (1984). *The Imperative of Responsibility: In Search of an Ethics in the Technological Age* (Chicago: University of Chicago Press).
King, Ynestra. (2005). "Toward an Ecological Feminism." In *Debating the Earth: The Environmental Politics Reader*, 2nd edn., edited by John Dryzek and David Schlosberg (Oxford: Oxford University Press), 399–407.
Lappe, Frances Moore. (2011). *EcoMind: Changing the Way We Think, to Create The World We Want* (New York: Nation Books).
Leiss, William. (1994). *The Domination of Nature* (Montreal: McGill-Queens Press).
Litfin, Karen. (2013). *Ecovillages: Lessons in Sustainable Community* (Oxford: Polity Press).
Leopold, Aldo. (1966). *A Sand County Almanac* (New York: Ballantine Books).
Marcuse, Herbert. (1994). "Ecology and Revolution." In *Ecology: Key Concepts in Critical Theory*, edited by Carolyn Merchant (Atlantic Highlands: Humanities Press International), 67–70.
Meadows, Donella et al. (2002). *The Limits to Growth: The 30 Year Update* (White River Junction: Chelsea Green Publishing).

Meeker, Joseph. (1987). *The Comedy of Survival: Literary Ecology and a Play Ethic* (Tucson: University of Arizona Press).
Merchant, Carolyn. (1980). *The Death of Nature: Women, Ecology, and the Scientific Revolution* (San Francisco: HarperCollins).
Ophuls, William. (1997). *Ecology and the Politics of Scarcity* (New York: W.H. Freeman).
Parson, Sean. (2008). "Understanding the Ideology of the Earth Liberation Front." *Green Theory and Praxis: The Journal of Ecopedagogy* 4(2): 50–66.
Pettit, Philip. (1997). *Republicanism: A Theory of Freedom and Government* (Oxford: Oxford University Press).
Plumwood, Val. (1993). *Feminism and the Mastery of Nature* (London: Routledge).
Princen, Thomas et al. (2002). *Confronting Consumption* (Cambridge: MIT Press).
Peet, Richard and Watts, Michael, eds. (2006). *Liberation Ecologies: Environment, Development, and Social Movements* (London: Routledge).
Rousseau, Jean Jacques. (1993). *The Social Contract and Discourses* (London: Everyman).
Ryan, Cheyney C. (1977). "Yours, Mine, and Ours: Property Rights and Individual Liberty." *Ethics* 87(2): 126–41.
Sagoff, Mark. (2007). *The Economy of the Earth* (Cambridge: Cambridge University Press).
Schwartz, Barry. (2004). *The Paradox of Choice: How More is Less* (New York: HarperCollins).
Shiva, Vandana. (2013). "What I Learned in the Forest." *Yes! Magazine* 64 (Winter):.46–51.
Stephens, Piers H. G. (2004). "Nature and Human Liberty: The Golden Country in George Orwell's 1984 and an Alternative Conception of Human Freedom." *Organization & Environment* 17(1): 76, 86.
Thaler, Richard and Sunstein, Cass. (2009). *Nudge: Improving Decisions about Health, Wealth, and Happiness* (London: Penguin Books).
Torgerson, Douglass. (1999). *The Promise of Green Politics: Environmentalism and the Public Sphere* (Durham and London: Duke University Press).
Weber, Max. (1958). *The Protestant Ethic and the Spirit of Capitalism.* Translated by Talcott Parsons (New York: Scribner).
Wilson, Edward O. *A Window on Eternity.* (New York: Simon and Schuster, 2014).
Wissenburg, Marcel. (2006). "Liberalism." In *Political Theory and the Ecological Challenge,* edited by Andrew Dobson and Robyn Eckersley (Cambridge: Cambridge University Press), 29.
Zerzan, John. (2012). *Future Primitive Revisited* (Port Townsend: Feral House Press).
Zizek, Slavoj. (2002). *Welcome to the Desert of the Real* (New York: Verso).

CHAPTER 26

BODIES, ENVIRONMENTS, AND AGENCY

TEENA GABRIELSON

Among the many catch phrases identified with modern Western environmentalism, "Think Globally, Act Locally" might easily be considered its signature statement. On the rise is the slogan "Doing Your Bit," adopted in the UK to urge citizens to act environmentally in their every-day lives. Environmentalists urge us to preserve, conserve, save a whale!, plant a tree, reduce, reuse, recycle, buy green, buy local, turn it off, turn it down . . . and the list of imperatives goes on. Yet, demands on the individual, like these, are made as enormous and complex collective challenges, such as climate change, the global distribution and circulation of toxic substances, invasive species, and pernicious viruses, and the worldwide loss of biodiversity, seem to practically eviscerate individual efficacy. Humans, as a species, have made a powerful impact on the world, but we have yet to gain much traction in collectively, and justly, adapting to the demands this new world is likely to make. This disjuncture, between our collective, and largely unintentional, power and our well-intentioned, but largely ineffectual individual action suggests the value of rethinking the conceptions of agency embedded in much liberal-democratic political thought.

While the concept of agency has long been central to understandings of freedom and autonomy, political projects of self-determination and political expression, and notions of democratic citizenship, it is only recently that scholars have begun to disentangle it from a larger web of, predominantly liberal, concepts including intention, responsibility, freedom, autonomy and empowerment.[1] Since roughly the early 2000s, a broad swath of researchers across the humanities and social sciences has taken interest in theorizing agency. This essay reviews much of that literature to flesh out the implications that stem from adopting various conceptions of agency for forging an inclusive and progressive ecological politics. It begins with a brief description of the traditional liberal conception of "sovereign agency" and its liabilities for contemporary politics. In the second section, I draw on the work of feminists and disability theorists to suggest the value of conceptualizing agency as relational, socially distributed, and embodied. Touching on the intimacy between questions of agency and ontology, the third section sketches the recent "turn to the ontological" before describing three quite different environmentally-minded motivations for extending agency to non-humans. I conclude the essay with a brief discussion of wildfire to suggest how accounting for the agency of non-humans may produce more effective environmental thinking and action.

Agency as Sovereignty

In his recent book, *Melancholic Freedom: Agency and the Spirit of Politics*, David Kyuman Kim offers a fairly traditional definition of agency, writing: "in its most basic sense, [agency] is the capacity for self-initiated, intentional action, that is, the ability of an agent (self, consciousness, ego, or even representative body, people, or community) to determine for itself acts and consequences in the world" (2007: 8). In this definition, as in many, agency is conceived as a moral attribute of the individual tied to the twin faculties of physically acting in the world and articulating a justification for those actions. Acting with intention, or by choice, the agent draws upon his or her reasoning ability to express one's subjectivity and thereby can be held responsible for his or her actions. The deliberative faculty provides a robust source for questioning and opposing traditional forms of authority, legitimating alternative political structures, and transcending the demands of the body and nature itself. It also forms the basis for cultivating respect for norms, fulfilling obligations, holding individuals accountable for their actions, and choosing one's life plan.

Historically, this conception of agency has marked the Western ideal citizen as a reasoning, independent, autonomous agent. Within the context of the nineteenth-century rise and consolidation of the liberal state in the United States, liberal agency took its shape in the development of, among other things, theories of crime and punishment, narratives of educational promise and self-made men, policies of Native American removal, and the concomitant delineation of the effective boundaries of the polity (Forbes 2016). Those excluded—the criminal, the cognitively disabled, the enslaved, Native Americans, and women, among others—occupied a liminal space somewhere between the citizen and the beast and, as such, were thought to participate in the inhuman. For many political theorists today, the capacity for justification continues to define political agency, leaving children, the cognitively disabled, future generations, animals, non-human nature, and things in the category of "nonagents" in need of guardianship or representation (LaVaque-Manty 2002: 137–54).

Much research in the social sciences and humanities has been dedicated to recovering the agency of the dispossessed and to conceptualizing the ways that social structures evolve and differentially enable and constrain individuals. These efforts work to more fully humanize the excluded. But, the persistent emphasis on the prize of liberal agency continues to marginalize those who either do not seek to or cannot achieve this aspirational conception of personhood. In casting all forms of action against the standard of liberal agency which, historically, has been available to very few, if any, citizens, "sovereign agency" severely limits the field of politically meaningful actors and obscures the varieties of agency at work in the world. This oversimplified conception of agency extracts the individual from the larger contexts that shape all action and overstates the power and efficacy of the individual, particularly, in relation to what is often characterized as a passive environment.

Contemporary articulations of the "agent as sovereign" can often be traced to Lockean liberalism and the conception of the self upon which it is built. As Piers H. G. Stephens argues, the Lockean self is individualistic, fundamentally acquisitive, and socially disconnected; it is "at root, 'a wanting thing', . . . [that] naturally lends itself to instrumental modes of perception" (2010: 9). For Stephens, it is not so much liberalism, generally, as the inherently narrow, impermeable, and isolated conception of the Lockean self that reduces human experience to acquisition, reason to instrumentalism, and freedom to economic liberty. For greens, this conception is particularly problematic because it reduces agency to the training of the appetites and the natural world to a mere resource for economic production (Stephens 2010: 11). As Charles Taylor explains it, the modern subject is *sovereign* over both his actions and his body; one is "free and rational to the extent that he has fully distinguished himself from the natural and social worlds" so much so that "the subject withdraws from his own body, which he is able to look on as an object" (1995: 7). In this way, both the body and the natural world come to serve as mere backdrops to human agency.

As surprising as it may seem, traces of this conception appear in the literature on green citizenship, where individuals are urged to take rational control over the body and the private sphere through green "lifestyle" practices such as restraining consumption and managing household waste, attesting to the power of the Lockean conception of the self in structuring Western understandings of citizenship (Dobson 2003).[2] While such practices, if adopted widely, contribute to a more sustainable future, this "individualization of responsibility," as Michael Maniates refers to it, abstracts the individual from the complex and collective processes of production and consumption, thereby inflating individuals' expectations of their own efficacy while depoliticizing environmental action and reinforcing a paradigm of green consumerism (2001).

Nonsovereign Agency

In response to the anemic and atomistic Lockean self, Stephens recommends a Millian and pragmatic liberalism that values freedom and social diversity for their contribution to the experiential process of a full and capacious development of the self (2010). Here, the self is conceived as constitutively *relational* and forged, fostered, and cultivated through encounters with others and the larger world. The environment becomes more than a mere resource, offering aesthetic value and an opportunity to enrich human connections both with non-human nature and one another by advancing a model through which we work *with* nature's dynamics "rather than imposing preset patterns upon it" (Stephens 2010: 18). Stephens' pragmatist view shares much with contemporary feminist accounts, many of which seek to show that while the conception of agency as sovereignty successfully incorporates the centrality of will and desire to human action, it does not consider the ways that social contexts shape those very desires (Hirschmann 2003). As Hirschmann explains, a mainstream conception of freedom "focused as it is on intentionality, identifiable agency, and purposiveness" can never see the ways that large-scale social structures such as capitalism and patriarchy systematically constrain the parameters of freedom for some while empowering others (2003: 23–4). Recent works in green-governmentality build on these insights to examine how particular state policies, deliberative tools, and discursive constructions are deployed in an effort to shape and cultivate environmental identities with differential effects on empowerment (Hobson 2013). More critical than prescriptive, works like these engage the notion of agency obliquely, illuminating the contexts that shape its articulation as well as the extent to which it is enabled or constrained.

Seeking to address inequalities in agency due to structural dynamics, Sharon Krause defines agency as the "affirmation of one's subjective existence through concrete action in the world" (2013: 196). Krause retains the notion of a self that precedes action, but rather than conceive of agency as an attribute of the individual, she argues that it is better understood as a product of inter-subjective exchange or as *distributed* through social assemblages, which she defines as the "social (and material) interactions through which individuals come to have meaningful effects on the world" (2013: 202). In contrast to Philip Pettit's theory of non-domination (2001) or Charles Taylor's work on recognition (1994), Krause shifts focus from the individual to the larger social arena highlighting the role that social interactions play in the exercise of agency. Drawing on Arendt (2006), Krause points to two significant limitations on individual action that recommend her nonsovereign conception of agency: first, the effect of one's actions is dependent upon how others receive that action; and second, an individual's actions may outstrip his or her intentions. Later in the chapter, I will address the second of these constraints further, but the first demands that we consider agency, as Catriona Mackenzie explains, as always a matter of "degrees and domains" (2008: 527). From this perspective, our efficacy is always contingent, and may also be dynamic, precisely because it is dependent upon the attitudes, power, and disposition of those receiving it. Applying these insights to environmental attitudes and action, Emily Huddart Kennedy's work shows that neighborhood networks have the potential to reinforce ecologically sustainable behaviors (2011). In contrast to individualistic conceptions of environmental obligation, Kennedy positions consumption choices within collectives to show the political potential of these actions, and argues that "ecological citizens are more potent agents of cultural change as a collective than as individuals" (2011: 843).

Adopting a relational and socially distributed conception of agency goes some distance to resolve what Val Plumwood describes as the results of "contemporary hegemonic constructions of agency" which posit a "hyper-separated autonomous self" (2002: 27). However, for both feminists and greens, agency must also be conceptualized as *embodied* in order to account for humans' dependencies both on one another and the natural world. While feminist relational approaches have underscored the extent to which agency is constrained by the social, political, economic, and cultural institutions within which the individual finds herself, Christine M. Koggel urges greater attention be given to the embodied realities to which these conditions give rise. Koggel writes, "Taking agency seriously involves taking embodiment seriously, and this is because empowerment is enabled through bodies—bodies that are fed, sheltered, safe, healthy, and engaged in meaningful participation and communal activities" (2009: 251). This is not to say, merely, that agency is dependent upon material well-being, but to show that, like desires, bodily needs *are shaped* by relationships and social structures that extend from the household and community to global institutions.

Yet, as much as the body is a site upon which power relations are inscribed, many argue it is also the source of a distinctive kind of agency. Taking a phenomenological approach, Diana Coole asserts that agency is necessarily embodied, but envisions it as a capacity immanent to an intersubjective social field (2005). Where Krause and Koggel focus on the subject, Coole proposes an "agentic spectrum" (entailing no developmental progression) that includes the corporeal agency of the body, the agential capacities of the singular individual, and those of "transpersonal" collectives. Because humans react to a whole range of sensory information and corporeal signals that bodies convey prior to reflection—including comportment, facial expressions, stress sweat, unintentional gestures, and heart rate to name a few—bodies exercise agential capacities that carry significant social and political meaning (Coole 2007). Whether explicitly recognized or not, these agential capacities of the body can be powerful means of enhancing one's status or of excluding and silencing others, and thus are significant to democratic theory.

Responding to Coole's work, Krause acknowledges corporeal agency, but only to the extent that it reveals an inner subjectivity. Krause's principal concern is to enlarge the orbit of individual responsibility in light of the body's ability to reveal our identity at the very moment that it outstrips our intentions.[3] Too often, she claims, we participate in and "unwittingly perpetuate patterns of domination (our own as well as that of others)" (2011: 306). Here, I want to raise two points for consideration. First, Krause's work not only considers the agency of the body, but also the embodiment of normativity. In this case, the body becomes a sort of delayed reflection or echo of the normative commitments of the subject. The white female who tightens her body and clutches her bag at the approach of an African-American man or the same woman who, in the office, excessively defers to male authority reveals through her body's actions normative commitments.[4] Yet, these commitments may be the product of social structures "outside" of the self and even detrimental to self-actualization, making agency neither directly intentional nor liberatory. Krause's objective is to bring our awareness to the body's agency and the normative commitments it reveals such that we might take responsibility and bring it in line with our intentions.

But, Krause is quick to differentiate normative from "natural" forms of corporeal agency, the second issue I want to raise. She claims, "To be nauseated at the tone or content of a political speech and to convey this displeasure through unintentional gestures and expressions is an exercise of agency in a way that flu-induced nausea is not" (2011: 307). While this may seem intuitively plausible, it is a distinction that has increasingly come into question by feminists, posthumanists, and greens for its tendency to uphold traditional binaries between reflective subjectivity and bodily materiality, interiority and exteriority, culture and nature, humans and animals. Krause, I think, makes this distinction precisely because she wants to retain the connection between identity and intention, even as she loosens it. Yet, in doing so, she places the "self" squarely within the realm of reason and reflection and in opposition to the material body, thereby denying the ways that our bodies "are the agents of our lived experience and subjectivity" (Garland-Thomson 2011: 600). The body in its sociality becomes politically meaningful, while the biological body is depoliticized.

This distinction becomes problematic particularly because traditional accounts of agency have tended to presuppose physical ability, conceive of barriers to freedom as external to the self, and disregard the variability in bodies and the "fit" of individuals with their environment (Garland-Thomson 2011; Hirschmann 2012: 217). Theorized from the position of the normalized, "healthy" body, where "health is life lived in the silence of the organs," freedom becomes an achievement of the will alone and meaningful agency is reserved to the ambit of the reflexive self (Canguilhem 1991: 91). Using disability theory, Nancy Hirschmann contests this account by demonstrating that the "able" body is actually socially constructed or *made* able by the social, cultural, ecological, and built environment. Greater attention to the ways that particular environments—wheelchair accessibility, peanut-free lunch rooms, unisex bathrooms—enable specific bodies is likely to produce a more inclusive polity by normalizing difference and socializing the costs of enhancing agency. For corporeal feminists and disability theorists, the *noisiness* of the body, whether initiated internally or in its fit with the built and natural environments, demands that we understand it as an integral aspect of the self, as recalcitrant to the will as it may be (Grosz 1994; Gatens 1996; Garland-Thomson 1997). Viewed in this way, social inequalities and the attitudes that support them become manifest not only in the unintentional actions (whether normative or biological) of the corporeal body, but also in the thoughtless construction of the built environment and the reckless degradation of the natural one.

One of the chief problems with traditional environmentalism has been a similar tendency to adopt a particularly Western conception of nature, as wild or pristine, and as Charles Mills refers to it, a "somatic norm" or a conception of a particular body—white, wealthy, and able—as ideals that then reinforce traditional patterns of privilege (Guha 1989; Mills 1997; Ray 2013). Elsewhere, Katelyn Parady and I have argued that greens have much to gain by adopting a corporeal and porous understanding of the self that begins with the fact of humans' inescapable embeddedness in both social and natural contexts that shape subjectivity and condition our collective agency (2010). By envisioning agency as embodied, and the body as positioned both socially and physically in natural and built environments, including the degraded urban, manicured suburban, and industrial extraction zone, we give greater recognition to the diverse attachments individuals have to their environments. Yet, attention to the physical environment and the institutional shaping of bodily needs is insufficient. While such a view shifts our attention from human ability to human vulnerability, dependency, and precarity (Butler 2004), as Garland-Thomson's work suggests, we must also attend to the *systematic* differences in how particular bodies "fit" with their environment to fully grasp the uneven terrain of material vulnerability.

Agential Capacities

Thus far, the relational, socially distributed, and embodied conception of agency that I have been describing has still been, primarily, an attribute of the subject, and, certainly, a capacity of humans. However, a wide range of scholars spanning the humanities and social sciences have sought to decenter the human subject by adopting an ontological reorientation that looks for *agential capacities* beyond the human and conceives of agency as collectively produced by a variety of participants, including non-human animals, plants, and things. A range of motivations spur the crafting of a more capacious conception of agency including commitments such as better capturing the interdependencies among science, technology, and politics in the lived experience of late modernity (Braun and Whatmore 2010), compensating for an excessive focus on linguistic and discursive constructions of identity in social analyses (Alaimo and Hekman 2008), eroding the nature/culture dualism and the disciplinary divides between the natural and social sciences to which it has contributed (Latour 2005), imagining more sustainable ways to live (Alaimo 2010; Bennett 2010), and, finally, developing tools to better understand the workings of power from the household to the global scale (Barad 2007; Coole 2013).

Tying these varied motivations together is an effort to identify the *processes of materialization* and the qualities of agency as they emerge in "the irreducible intermeshing of human and non-human systems" that compose our common world (Coole 2013: 457). For thinkers such as Bruno Latour, Jane Bennett, Andrew Pickering, and Karen Barad, the non-human natural world is not a passive resource or object, but a key participant or "actant," as Latour defines it, in a "dance of agency" that includes the human, non-human nature, and artifice (Pickering 1995; Latour 2005). Drawing from a range of theoretical sources including Spinoza, Bergson, Heidegger, Merleau-Ponty, Agamben, and Deleuze and Guattari (to name the most prominent), "new materialists" emphasize the generative and emergent processes of becoming (over being), the dynamic and contingent fluxes of the material world, and the "lively immanence of matter" (Coole and Frost 2010: 9). There are significant differences regarding the conceptualization of materiality: as inherently indeterminate (Barad 2007); constitutively relational (Latour 2005); autonomous, but largely inaccessible (Harman 2009); or, as the differentiated flows of substances, media, and the surfaces between them (Ingold 2011). Yet, despite these differences, most new materialists view agency not as an attribute of the subject, but as *widely distributed, temporally emergent, and collectively expressed.*

In what follows, I highlight the work of a few new materialists explicitly engaged with questions of environment and sustainability: political theorist, Jane Bennett; anthropologist, Tim Ingold; and sociologist, Noortje Marres. In doing so, I focus on two primary and related questions: First, how ought we to conceptualize non-human agency? And, second, in what ways does non-human agency matter for contemporary ecological politics? Both questions are addressed in Jane Bennett's explicitly eco-political project as she explores how our understanding of public problems might change if we took seriously the "capacity of things—edibles, commodities, storms, metals—not only to impede or block the will and designs of humans but also to act as quasi agents or forces with trajectories, propensities, or tendencies of their own" (2010: viii). At the least, Bennett argues, if humans can only exercise their agential capacities in collectives that include non-human agencies then democratic theory ought to focus, not on the individual, but on an "(ontologically heterogeneous) 'public' coalescing around a problem" (Bennett 2010: 108). In this sense, non-human agency matters for its contributions to human agency and for its reshaping of traditional political concepts.

While Bennett, and other new materialists, distinguish the aleatory agency of things from the—sometimes—intentional agency of humans, some theorists still worry over the loss of reflexivity and responsibility entailed in the emphasis on efficacy (Krause 2010; Coole 2013). Bennett's response to such concerns is to argue that attending to "thing power" will actually enlarge the scope of individual responsibility. In this regard, her approach is similar to that of Krause. Bennett's hope is that in changing the way we *think* about the material world, we will cultivate an ethical disposition that restrains an arrogant anthropocentrism while also providing a sort of opening for revaluing *things*, and thereby considering more ecologically sustainable ways of living (2004, 2010). But, as John Meyer argues, in doing so, Bennett essentializes materiality and thereby returns to a moralizing idealism, reminiscent of earlier eco-centric approaches, that disregards the inevitable plurality of humans' material experience and the environmental commitments that stem from it (Meyer 2015).

Bennett's work (and that of other new materialists) has also been criticized for emphasizing the constant flux of the material world in a way that fails to sufficiently account for the enduring character of deep structural inequalities (Sutherland 2013) and for urging a shift in our ethical sensibility when it ought, *first*, to be put to the ends of critique and explanation. As Diana Coole writes, "without a better understanding and critique of the circuits through which matter flows—that is, an empirical, scientific and political investigation—it is difficult to appreciate the damage and challenges current forms of production and consumption involve or to think realistically about ways materially to transform them" (2013: 463).

Finally, both Krause and Bennett problematically draw the readers' attention to the distributed character of agency, principally, to heighten *individual* obligations. I find this counterproductive at a time when we not only face enormous and complex collective challenges, such as climate change, the global distribution and circulation of toxic substances, invasive species, and the worldwide loss of biodiversity, but also have very few mechanisms for holding collectives responsible for their actions. The scale of environmental problems today dwarfs the capacity for individual action; which is not to say that we should be unconcerned with empowering individuals. However, overloading average individuals with further responsibility in a context in which individual action appears all but fruitless seems unlikely to reap positive change and may even provoke resentment. An inclusive, ecological politics must attend to those instances in which individuals feel unable to extract themselves from particular assemblages, to the socio-material processes that contribute to the differential positioning of persons within assemblages, and to theorizing forms of responsibility that address both the intentional and unintentional consequences of our collective agency (Eckersley, this volume; Young 2011).

Where Bennett looks to material agency to reform our ethical commitments, Tim Ingold adopts a phenomenological approach that aims to take materials seriously as conditions for a more inclusive agency conceived as a capacity not of reflection, but of perception and movement. Ingold rejects the position that non-humans inhabit meaningless worlds and seeks to return humans to "the continuum of organic life" where creatures act in response to their sensory engagement with the world (2011: 31). From this perspective, to ask whether or not agency should be extended to animals or winds or rocks is to pose the question poorly. Ingold writes, "Bringing things to life, then, is a matter not of adding to them a sprinkling of agency but of restoring them to the generative fluxes of the world of materials in which they came into being and continue to subsist" (29). By focusing not on matter as such, but on *materials*, Ingold turns our attention to the highly specific relationships between creatures and their environments as they come to inhabit and act within them. Like Garland-Thomson's work on disability and the built environment, Ingold asks us to attend to the capacities, relations, and materials that offer the conditions for an actor's fit with its environment and thereby its agency.

Extending the realm of meaningful action to much of the non-human natural world, Ingold refuses agency to non-living entities like stones, air, and water (arguing they are instead the dynamic media within which life is immersed) so as to retain and acknowledge the complexity of living organisms in contrast to inert matter. However, he also opens organisms to the flows and frictions of the wider material world by envisioning them as *porous*, rather than as bounded by impermeable barriers. For greens, adopting a conception of the human body (and other living bodies) as open to constant connection and interaction with the material world, or a notion of trans-corporeality as Stacy Alaimo (2010) describes it, allows us greater traction in tracing systematic inequalities in material well-being and vulnerability while acknowledging the deep rootedness of humans (and other living creatures) in particular environments. Ingold's approach is attractive for its repositioning of humans within the larger field of living creatures, its ability to capture long-held, but evolving, intuitions regarding the diverse qualities and capacities of humans, animals, plants, and the inorganic, and its attention to the qualities of materials that swirl about, sustain, and infuse living bodies. My chief concern, however, is that this approach fails to account for the extent to which all materiality is also *discursively constituted* (for humans) and thereby open to political contestation.

As Gay Hawkins' work on the many meanings of everyday plastic bags demonstrates (from unacceptable trash to obvious convenience), all varieties of the non-human can become loaded with normative values, including conflicting ones (2010). Noortje Marres' work is informative on this score in that she asserts that the key question may not be whether or not non-humans have normative capacities, but "how they become *invested* with specific normative *powers* through the deployment of particular settings and devices" (2013: 419; emphasis added). Both Hawkins and Marres focus on the processes through which things become enrolled in political contest, thereby highlighting the plasticity of the material world to discursive construction and specifying one path (surely there are many others) by which non-humans come to participate in contemporary political life. Taking an empirical approach attentive to the diversity of human/non-human assemblages, Marres further specifies this process by asking us to consider how "objects, and by extension ontologies, have political and moral capacities 'by design'" (2013: 423). Using the example of the eco-show home, Marres demonstrates how a number of objects and settings, such as large visual thermostats, are invested (by humans) with moral and political capacities that, then, further shape human behavior. Marres adopts what she calls an experimental approach that demands careful empirical attention to the diversity of assemblages, practices, and discursive constructions that constitute the agency of any particular thing and thereby assist in specifying how particular non-humans become participants in contemporary political life.

Wildfire

To conclude, I take up, very briefly, the example of wildfire to illustrate the value of conceptualizing agency as emerging from the intra-action of a variety of actants, both human and non-human. Our language suggests that, historically, we have granted fire a greater degree of "liveliness" than we have many other ecological processes. Fires breathe, consume, roar, and die. From a phenomenological perspective, fires respond to terrain, fuel quality and loading, variations in vegetation, climatic conditions, air currents, and suppression efforts. But wildfires in the early 2000s in the US Mountain West (and elsewhere) burn differently than did those in the mid-twentieth century and before. In many respects, the story of fire in this region depends upon evolving conceptions of agency. Initially considered an act of God, by the end of the nineteenth century forest managers conceived of fire as a natural occurrence that could be controlled through human action. Seeking to eviscerate the agency of fire and asserting that of humans over the natural world, early US conservationists initiated a policy of fire suppression where fires were fought and conservation victories were won.

Decades of such victories issued in increasing numbers of uncontrollable fires. Advances in ecology took the role and effect of fires more seriously as research revealed the ecological functions of limited and more frequent burns for forest health and the preservation of both non-human and human habitats. But, to conceive of fires strictly as ecological or physical processes depoliticizes them. Simply conferring agency upon fires recognizes their powerful effect, but does little to explain the extent to which they have come to "matter" as portents of the new world climate change is producing and embodiments of the diverse cultural and economic commitments that contributed to decades of fire suppression, current fire policy, and the now unprecedented conditions of Western US forests. Ideally, I think, we would like fire to act a bit more responsibly. This wish, with its fantastic and cheeky expectation of normative capacity, points to the limits of mere extensions of agency while revealing the inseparability of questions of agency and ontology. On the other hand, one might demand that we (humans) take more responsibility for our fires. But, isn't that what decades of fire suppression policy intended to do, while failing to adequately account for the ecological function and material force of fire?

With this discussion, I aim only to gesture toward the advantages of viewing fire as a discursive-material phenomenon constituted by a particular assemblage of actors, both human and non-human, and agency as a collective, embodied, distributed, and emergent capacity of the world in which we all participate, differently. This approach, taken in somewhat different forms, by Mol (2003), Latour (2005), and Barad (2007), demands we conceive not of the force of fire and the agency of firefighters or fire ecologists, but of the collectives, historical and contemporary, that intra-act to produce powerful, but unevenly distributed, effects. Such a view is more likely to show, for instance, how discursive constructions of wildfire contribute to media coverage which in turn creates political incentives for suppression. It is also more likely to turn our attention to the way failure to regulate housing or recreational development near forested lands is increasing the costs and risks related to fires. Such analyses suggest that an effective fire policy must consider how agency is produced amongst a variety of actors that include county commissioners, the wind, members of convict crews, insurance premiums, fire modelers, golf course managers, Congress, the grade of a slope, land-owners, firefighters, the rain, developers, reporters, fire itself—and a host of others. Such accounting is exhausting, but promises a greater appreciation of the collectives that produce action in the world and its unequal effects on the inhabitants of that world. If we are to adapt to the new world already in the making, rethinking bodies, environments, and agency in relation to one another may give us greater purchase in the much needed areas of both tracing discursive-material circuits of power and beginning to theorize collective forms of responsibility.

Notes

1. For instance, few, if any, overview or introductory volumes to political theory dedicate a chapter to it or even a listing in the index; see Dryzek, Honig, and Phillips (2006); Goodin and Pettit (2006).
2. While theorists of green citizenship are also concerned with democratic participation and collective action, it is green lifestyle practices that receive the bulk of attention both popularly and in the scholarly literature.

3. This being only one type of the broader category of instances in which our actions produce effects well beyond those we intend. See Arendt (2006).
4. This example is taken from President Obama's description of a common experience for African-American men in his speech on the court ruling in the shooting of Trayvon Martin. See http://www.whitehouse.gov/the-press-office/2013/07/19/remarks-president-trayvon-martin

References

Alaimo, S. (2010). *Bodily Natures: Science, Environment, and the Material Self* (Bloomington: Indiana University Press).

Alaimo, S. and Hekman S., eds. (2008). *Material Feminisms* (Bloomington: Indiana University Press).

Arendt, H. (2006 [1954]). *Hannah Arendt: Between Past and Future* (New York: Penguin Books).

Barad, K. (2007). *Meeting the Universe Halfway* (Durham: Duke University Press).

Bennett, J. (2010). *Vibrant Matter: A Political Ecology of Things* (Durham: Duke University Press).

Braun, B. and Whatmore, S. J., eds. (2010). *Political Matter: Technoscience, Democracy and Public Life* (Minneapolis: University of Minnesota Press).

Butler, J. (2004). *Precarious Life: The Powers of Mourning and Violence* (London: Verso).

Canguilhem, G. (1991). *The Normal and the Pathological* (New York: Zone Books).

Coole, D. (2005). "Rethinking Agency: A Phenomenological Approach to Embodiment and Agentic Capacities." *Political Studies* 53(1): 124–42.

Coole, D. (2007). "Experiencing Discourse: Corporeal Communicators and the Embodiment of Power." *British Journal of Politics and International Relations* 9(3): 413–33. doi: 10.1111/j.1467-856x.2006.00258.x

Coole, D. (2013). "Agentic Capacities and Capacious Historical Materialism: Thinking with Materialisms in the Political Sciences." *Millennium- Journal of International Studies* 41(3):451–68. doi: 10.1177/0305829813481006

Coole, D. and Frost, S., eds. (2010). *New Materialisms: Ontology, Agency, and Politics* (Durham: Duke University Press).

Dobson, A. (2003). *Citizenship and the Environment* (Oxford: Oxford University Press).

Dryzek, J. S., Honig, B., and Phillips, A., eds. (2006). *The Oxford Handbook of Political Theory* (Oxford: Oxford University Press).

Forbes, E. (2016, forthcoming). "'Between the Human and Brutal Creation': Posthuman Agency and the Samuel Frost Corpus." *The Eighteenth Century: Theory and Interpretation* 57(1).

Gabrielson, T. and Parady, K. (2010). "Corporeal Citizenship: Rethinking Green Citizenship through the Body." *Environmental Politics* 19(3): 374–91. doi:10.1080/09644011003690799

Garland-Thomson, R. (1997). *Extraordinary Bodies: Figuring Physical Disability in American Culture and Literature* (Columbia: Columbia University Press).

Garland-Thomson, R. (2011). "Misfits: A Feminist Materialist Disability Concept." *Hypatia: A Journal of Feminist Philosophy* 26(3): 591–609.

Gatens, M. (1996). *Imaginary Bodies: Ethics, Power and Corporeality* (London: Routledge).

Grosz, E. (1994). *Volatile Bodies: Toward a Corporeal Feminism* (Bloomington: Indiana University Press).

Goodin, R. E. and Pettit, P., eds. (2006). *Contemporary Political Philosophy: An Anthology*, 2nd edn. (Malden, MA: Blackwell Publishing).
Guha, R. (1989). "Radical American Environmentalism and Wilderness Preservation: A Third World Critique." *Environmental Ethics* 11(1):71–83.
Harman, G. (2009). *Prince of Networks: Bruno Latour and Metaphysics* (Melbourne, VIC, Australia: Re.press).
Hawkins, G. (2010). "Plastic Materialities." In *Political Matter: Technoscience, Democracy, and Public Life*, edited by B. Braun and S. J. Whatmore (Minneapolis: University of Minnesota Press), 119–38.
Hirschmann, N. J. (2003). *The Subject of Liberty: Toward a Feminist Theory of Freedom* (Princeton: Princeton University Press).
Hirschmann, N. J. (2012). "Feminist Thoughts on Freedom and Rights." *Politics & Gender* 8(2): 216–22. doi:10.1017/S1743923X12000189.
Hobson, K. (2013). "On the Making of the Environmental Citizen." *Environmental Politics* 22(1): 56–72.
Kennedy, E. H. (2011). "Rethinking Ecological Citizenship: The Role of Neighbourhood Networks in Cultural Change." *Environmental Politics* 20(6): 843–60. doi:10.1080/09644016.2011.617169.
Kim, D. K. (2007). *Melancholic Freedom: Agency and the Spirit of Politics* (Oxford: Oxford University Press).
Koggel, C. M. (2009). "Agency and Empowerment: Embodied Realities in a Globalized World." In *Embodiment and Agency*, edited by S. Campbell, L. Meynell, and S. Sherwin (University Park: Pennsylvania State University Press), 250–68.
Krause, S. (2011). "Bodies in Action: Corporeal Agency and Democratic Politics." *Political Theory* 39(3): 299–324. doi: 10.1177/0090591711400025.
Krause, S. (2013). "Beyond Non-Domination: Agency, Inequality and the Meaning of Freedom." *Philosophy & Social Criticism* 39(2): 187–208. doi: 10.1177/0191453712470360.
Latour, Bruno. (2005). *Reassembling the Social: An Introduction to Actor-Network-Theory* (Oxford: Oxford University Press).
LaVaque-Manty, M. (2002). *Arguments and Fists: Political Agency and Justification in Liberal Theory* (New York: Routledge).
Mackenzie, C. (2008). "Relational Autonomy, Normative Authority and Perfectionism." *Journal of Social Philosophy* 39(4): 512–33.
Maniates, M. (2001). "Individualization: Plant a Tree, Buy a Bike, Save the World?" *Global Environmental Politics* 1(1): 31–52.
Meyer, J. (2015). *Engaging the Everyday: Environmental Social Criticism and the Resonance Dilemma* (Cambridge: MIT Press).
Mills, C. (1997). *The Racial Contract* (Ithaca, NY: Cornell University Press).
Mol, A. (2003). *The Body Multiple: Ontology in Medical Practice* (Durham: Duke University Press).
Pettit, P. (2001). *A Theory of Freedom* (Oxford: Oxford University Press).
Pickering, A. (1995). *The Mangle of Practice: Time, Agency, and Science* (Chicago: University of Chicago Press).
Plumwood, V. (2002). *Environmental Culture: The Ecological Crisis of Reason* (London: Routledge).
Ray, S. J. (2013). *The Ecological Other: Environmental Exclusion in American Culture* (Tucson: University of Arizona Press).

Stephens, P. H.G. (2010). "Green Liberalisms: Nature, Agency and the Good." *Environmental Politics* 10(1): 1–22. doi: 10.1080/714000559.
Sutherland, T. (2013). "Liquid Networks and the Metaphysics of Flux: Ontologies of Flow in an Age of Speed and Mobility." *Theory, Culture, & Society* 30(5): 3–23. doi: 10.1177/0263276412469670.
Taylor, C. (1994). "The Politics of Recognition." In *Multiculturalism: Examining the Politics of Recognition*, edited by A. Gutmann (Princeton, NJ: Princeton University Press), 25–73.
Taylor, C. (1995). *Philosophical Arguments* (Cambridge: Harvard University Press).
Young, I. M. (2011). *Responsibility for Justice* (Oxford: Oxford University Press).

CHAPTER 27

CULTIVATING HUMAN AND NON-HUMAN CAPABILITIES FOR MUTUAL FLOURISHING

BREENA HOLLAND AND AMY LINCH

THE commitment to flourishing in various traditions of political thought has been an important bridge between anthropocentrically conceived political theory and the more encompassing concerns of environmental political theory (EPT). The idea that mutual flourishing is the purpose of political association, and therefore the proper standard for evaluating the organization of relationships and resources within a society, is one compelling basis for theorizing human obligations within a broader ecological context. Ecological systems and the other beings that inhabit them play a crucial role in sustaining human well-being. Yet the potential of these systems and beings to flourish also provides a basis for regarding them on their own terms, as entitled to ecological resources, and as the subject of evaluation in settling conflicting claims to such resources. Toward this end, the theory of human capabilities has been an especially fruitful point of engagement for EPT in theorizing what political associations owe to humans, non-humans, and ecological systems. This theory offers a robust conception of human flourishing and of the capabilities that make such flourishing possible. As an account of justice within political communities, the theory provides a basis for securing the environmental preconditions of human flourishing as a fundamental entitlement, and for extending this support to include the specific excellence or dignity of non-human life. In this chapter we explore how the ideas and concepts from capabilities theory are being engaged, expanded, and redefined to characterize and realize an environmentally and ecologically just politics.

Capabilities Theory and its Relevance to EPT

The theory of human capabilities originally advanced by Amartya Sen and Martha Nussbaum offers a multi-dimensional conception of individual well-being, conceiving of humans as developmental beings, capable of flourishing in many different ways and through many different life activities. While Sen has used this conception of well-being to improve quality of life comparisons in the context of international development, Nussbaum has done so for the purpose of developing a theory of social justice.[1] Efforts to extend Sen and Nussbaum's original work so that it includes a fuller account of environmental value and addresses the capabilities of the non-human natural world comprise a budding area of contemporary environmental scholarship. As Thompson and Bendik-Keymer note, central among the advantages of capabilities theory for conceptualizing and reasoning about environmental values and relationships is that "it is conceived in a protoecological way already" (Thompson and Bendik-Keymer 2012: 17). While the theory's specification of justice as mutual access to the conditions that support lives worthy of the dignity—or inherent potential—of individual beings is anthropocentric in its origins, some have argued that its logic entails a commitment to the flourishing of non-human animals and non-sentient beings. In this chapter we will first introduce capabilities theory as rooted in an Aristotelian ideal of human flourishing, and then discuss its development and application in the area of EPT. We close by pointing to some particularly fruitful areas for further inquiry, theorizing, and analysis.

Human "capabilities" refer to the conditions or states of enablement that make it possible for people to do various things that make up a good or flourishing human life. These things may be complex, such as having self-respect or participating in the life of a community, or more simple, such as maintaining a healthy intake of nutritious food on a daily basis (Sen 1999: 75). In either case, capabilities theory holds that people should experience the conditions that make it possible for them to flourish as human beings. For this they need more than a given income or set of resources; they must have both the internal traits and the external circumstances and provisions that put the possibility of a good life within their reach (Nussbaum 2000: 83–5).[2] For example, both physical health and social norms that allow women to leave the home without the threat of harm are necessary for women to be able to participate in political debate as a chosen component of their flourishing. A capabilities based conception of well-being is meant to capture this connection between one's personal abilities and broader social, economic, and political conditions that determine whether one can effectively put those abilities at the service of one's values. In this sense, capabilities define a person's effective opportunities (Robeyns 2005).

Nussbaum has developed the concept of capabilities as the basis for political justice in liberal democratic societies (Nussbaum 2000, 2006). Drawing on Aristotle, she argues that the purpose and responsibility of political power is to avail people of lives worthy of their particularly human excellences.[3] Optimal human living involves the exercise of choice and rationality, which in turn requires certain material and social conditions. A just society promotes human excellence by nurturing individuals' capacity for choice and providing the external conditions necessary for individuals to have choices in the range of activities that constitute a full human life. Nussbaum identifies ten central human capabilities that specify dimensions of human functioning that collectively are indispensable to a full human life: Life; Bodily Health; Bodily Integrity; Senses, Imagination, and Thought; Emotions; Practical Reason; Affiliation; Other Species; Play; Political and Material Control over One's Environment.[4] A capabilities based justice secures these conditions of flourishing for humans *qua* humans. The specific excellence or dignity of human life guides both specification of the substantive commitments of a just society and standards of distribution. The dignity of human life, in the sense that humans bear particular capacities, warrants provision of the conditions through which those capacities can be realized (Nussbaum 1988, 2006).

Capabilities, in Nussbaum's formulation, are akin to Aristotle's understanding of *virtue* in that they involve both a disposition, or habit of mind, and the material and institutional conditions that enable their existence and expression. Political institutions, for Nussbaum and Aristotle alike, should provide and protect the conditions for the expression of human potentialities that individuals cannot provide on their own. Among these potentials is the ability to be valued and to value others as an end in one's self. A capabilities based conception of justice thus articulates the quality of life to which one is entitled and the obligations one has to others as beings of equal dignity or moral worth. Like Aristotle, Nussbaum identifies the virtues of a just society as arising from and sustained by institutional and material conditions rather than in terms of abstract principles. They are the qualities that we need to live optimally as human beings, but they become discernible through the commitment to human potentialities or the worthiness of human beings to live certain kinds of lives. A capabilities based justice is always open to expansion of its understanding of human flourishing rather than tethered to a finite assertion of well-being.

Sen's "capability approach" to international development is less explicitly indebted to Aristotle, and more explicit in its commitment to political participation and deliberation as a means to a flourishing human life. Sen argues that expanding people's freedoms, or capabilities, should be an explicit goal of development policies. Capabilities should provide the basis for assessing poverty, inequality, and the success of international development strategies (Sen 1999). However, Sen distinguishes himself from Nussbaum in his emphasis on the role of public participation and discussion in specifying and prioritizing a list of capabilities that can serve these purposes (Sen 2004). Sen advances an agency-oriented view of individuals, and frequently expresses the importance of decisional engagement through reciprocity based deliberation (see Crocker 2006: 173) and autonomy, which is conducive to socially reflective judgments that can lead people to prioritize not just their own well-being, but also that of others.[5] He sees a crucial and constructive role for democracy in shaping values and defining political goals. Thus, in Sen's view, valuations of the natural environment should be placed directly in the hands of public reasoning (Scholtes 2010: 297). Public discussion is preferable to incentive based approaches to fostering good environmental values and changing damaging environmental behaviors (Scholtes 2010: 296–7).

Although these ideas are relevant to a variety of questions about the environment, including the distribution of capabilities in the context of scarce resources, Sen has said relatively little about the relationship between the natural environment and human capabilities. Nussbaum, by contrast, has distinguished herself from many liberal political theorists by recognizing relationships to non-human life as a core component of human flourishing, and especially by recognizing the dignity and potential excellences of non-human life as relevant to political justice. However, she has left it to others to specify the theory's implications for understanding the role of environmental relationships in human and non-human flourishing and for establishing how to balance, prioritize, and make tradeoffs between the capabilities of different species.[6] Application of the capabilities approach to these questions forms an emerging field of scholarship. As we discuss in this chapter, scholars have drawn on capabilities theory to argue for protection of the natural environment from an anthropocentric standpoint as a component of human flourishing and as a condition of human flourishing. Others have applied the theory's logic to non-human life in ways that extend and challenge Nussbaum's project, arguing that the non-human world is worthy of recognition as an end in itself.

Cultivating Capabilities in Anthropocentric EPT

When considered alongside many of the most well-known liberal theories of justice, Nussbaum's "capabilities approach" stands out because it conceptualizes people's relationships to nature as a core component of human flourishing. Specifically, in her "capabilities approach" to justice the capability for having relationships with "plants, animals, and the world of nature" is one of the ten central human capabilities that citizens have a right to demand from their government. For Nussbaum, each of these ten capabilities has independent importance as a component of a life worthy of human dignity; therefore a just society will secure and protect the list of capabilities for each individual person. Relationships to plants, animals, and the world of nature are thus taken as a central good of human life because they provide the opportunity for citizens to develop a disposition of character that regards the non-human world with a sense of wonder and recognition of our interdependence.

While this acknowledgement that meaningful relationships to the environment are a central component of human flourishing represents a significant advance in liberal conceptions of justice, it admittedly stops short of theorizing how broader ecological relationships are necessary conditions of these relationships and other capabilities that define the human good. In addressing this limitation, Breena Holland develops the ecological implications of capabilities theory from the standpoint of human flourishing. She argues that protecting the natural environment should be understood as a basic condition of a socially just political community, because damage to it can undermine the full range of entitlements that Nussbaum's capabilities approach treats as central to a life worthy of human dignity. For instance, air pollution is a significant problem in contemporary society that can exacerbate inequalities present from the start of life and seriously undermine the physical, emotional, and professional components of a good life. Holland argues that the list of protections that make it possible for people to flourish should include "sustainable ecological capacity" as a capability of humans. This capability requires "*being able to live one's life in the context of ecological conditions that can provide environmental resources and services that enable the current generation's range of capabilities; [and] to have these conditions now and in the future*" (Holland 2008a: 324, italics in the original). The opportunity for each person to live a good life therefore requires that society do more than protect functioning ecosystems in which people can develop meaningful relationships with plants, animals, and the world of nature on an ongoing basis. It also requires that such ecosystems are able to sustain the ecological conditions contributing to all the other capabilities that make it possible for people to choose to live and flourish as the kinds of beings that they are.

Holland demonstrates that a high degree of ecological protection will result from an approach to environmental valuation and distribution that takes seriously the central role of the environment in the ten human capabilities that Nussbaum posits as vital to a flourishing human life (Holland 2015). For instance, the natural environment is crucial to Nussbaum's architectonic capabilities—*Affiliation* and *Practical Reason*—which are capabilities that suffuse and support all the other central human capabilities. Protecting the associational capability of members of groups whose way of life relies on particular features of the natural environment means protecting the ecological systems that sustain them. As David Schlosberg has similarly argued, when people's cultural identities and ways of life are intimately bound up with particular natural environments, their capability to participate effectively in political decisions—as equals in a political community—is dependent on protecting those relationships (Schlosberg 2007: 16–20). Considering the importance of these relationships, Holland's "capabilities approach to social and environmental justice" advances a functioning natural environment that can provide and sustain these relationships as a "meta-capability" of humans, since it underlies all other capabilities (Holland 2008a, 2015).

Importantly, the anthropocentric environmental ethic Holland advances establishes criteria for distributive justice. A society that protects each person's capabilities at a threshold level will inevitably need to balance the distribution of environmental goods and services that create possibilities for actualizing capabilities through various functionings. Such balancing will entail limiting the capabilities that enable people to engage in activities that damage the environment if the damage has harmful effects on others. For Holland, limiting capabilities—or establishing "capability ceilings" that constrain people's range of choices for how to experience or express their own flourishing—is justified when it is necessary to secure a threshold level of each of the central human capabilities for all people (Holland 2008b). By foregrounding the connection between environmental relationships and the human capabilities they sustain, Holland shows how capabilities theory can expose and resolve conflicting claims to environmental resources that are implicit in people's exercise of their capabilities.

Fabian Scholtes also uses capabilities theory to address harms to others carried out via the natural environment (Scholtes 2010). Scholtes is concerned that the inescapable and irreversible loss of environmental resources will impose the present generation's values on people living in the future by foreclosing the options for future people to use those resources in ways they may value. He argues that this kind of "environmental domination" conflicts with Sen's central goal of leaving people free to lead the kinds of lives they have reason to value (Scholtes 2010: 296). Sen's capability approach to international development cannot achieve its goal of communal self-determination if it continues to assume that environmental resources are substitutable and, consequently, that the present generation is only obligated to leave future generations with a generalized capacity for well-being, rather than with particular environmental resources. For Scholtes, this "simple assumption of a 'fact of substitutability' [of environmental resources] encourages us to ignore how cultures differ regarding how nature matters" (Scholtes 2010: 302).[7] Therefore, it also undermines Sen's commitment to pluralism, and the intended openness of his approach to respecting culturally particular values. According to Scholtes, genuinely preserving the freedoms of future generations will entail restricting the use of nature in the current generation so that future generations at least have the same freedom to value nature as the present generation.

The anthropocentric and instrumental approach to conceiving of the environment's value in relation to human capabilities evident in Holland and Scholtes is particularly compelling for addressing how to assess and adapt to the impacts of climate change. For instance, Holland has argued that climate change will undermine the "ecological conditions for justice," which are met when each person has a threshold level of all of the capabilities necessary for living a good human life, *and* when ecological systems are functioning at a capacity that enables them to provide the resources and services instrumental to these capabilities (Holland 2008a). A flourishing human life therefore requires a stable climate system (Holland 2012; Heyward 2011). Similarly, David Schlosberg has proposed defining the emissions allocations codified in global climate policies in terms of what is needed for social and economic development to make people capable of living flourishing lives amidst changing climate conditions (Schlosberg 2012b: 457–8). Applying his own procedural account of capabilities justice, Schlosberg advocates a decision context for developing climate adaptation policies that brings attention to the environment's instrumental importance to people's basic capabilities as individuals and as members of distinct cultural communities that are especially vulnerable to the impacts of climate change (Schlosberg 2012b: 455).[8]

Beyond Anthropocentrism: Justice as the Flourishing of All Beings

Capabilities theory has been extended to the non-human world by a number of scholars who see its core intuition that moral worth arises from the specific excellences of beings as a basis for recognizing the entitlements of other life forms. Thus understood, various entities—individual organisms, animals, species, and ecosystems—have capabilities that are worthy of political protection, independent of their instrumental importance to humans. Nussbaum has elaborated her original account of capabilities justice to include the flourishing of non-human animals among the list of political goals in a just society.[9] Specifically, Nussbaum argues it is reasonable to imagine that citizens who hold different conceptions of the good could come to an "overlapping consensus" that animals have intrinsic ends that society should promote (Nussbaum 2006: 388).[10] She then considers what it would mean to treat animals as subjects of justice and proposes protecting a list of capabilities for animals analogous to the list of capabilities she wants to protect for humans. Nussbaum argues, "there are a wide range of types of animal dignity, and of corresponding needs for flourishing" (Nussbaum 2006: 327). A capabilities approach that treats animals justly "is attentive to the variety of activities and goals that creatures of many types pursue... [and] is capable of yielding norms of interspecies justice that are subtle and yet demanding, involving fundamental entitlements for creatures of different types." Like the capabilities approach to human justice, a capabilities approach to animal justice sees animals as ends in themselves with an inherent good or dignity. It therefore establishes the moral entitlement of animals to the conditions that enable that good (Nussbaum 2006: 337).

Implicit in Nussbaum's reasoning is an understanding that securing the conditions of flourishing for any being, humans and non-humans alike, requires prior commitment that the being is worthy of a certain kind of regard and of receiving certain resources. Since a society's commitment to the possibility of specific ways of flourishing influences the distribution of resources that make such flourishing possible, the status quo condition of any being may not be a reliable indicator of its particular excellence. Just as habits of valuation among groups of people might deny resources to some of their members, which in turn influences the apparent potential of those members that would warrant their worthiness of those goods, human habits of valuation of animals affect their capacity to perceive the inherent excellence of animals and what development of this excellence requires. Nussbaum's articulation of ten specific capabilities that are essential to the expression of other potentialities is an attempt to circumvent this problem in the human sphere. However, since non-human beings cannot make claims on humans regarding their own capabilities directly, they are reliant upon people's capacity to observe and recognize their inherent excellences and the environmental conditions they require. Consequently, virtues of humans that support just relationships with non-humans may only become possible to imagine if societies commit to the value of such relationships as political goals.

Furthermore, a capabilities justice rooted in the dignity or moral worth of particular beings requires considering them in relation to the possibilities of flourishing as that kind of being, and how that flourishing might be expressed given their individual circumstances. Nussbaum is adamant that for animals, as for humans, it is the individual being that is the bearer of capabilities. Damage to species should be understood in terms of damage to the species' individual members. She states clearly, "this individual damage should be the focus of ethical concern within the capabilities" (Nussbaum 2006: 357). Likewise, justice for animals requires protecting ecological systems only to the extent that they further the good of the individuals that depend on them.

David Schlosberg contests this view on the grounds that both humans and non-humans flourish as systems, and that systems should be regarded as more than the sum of their parts. Rejecting the inherent individualism of Nussbaum's capabilities approach, Schlosberg suggests that we should think about life forms in their dynamic and vital relation to others. He argues that we more accurately portray the interdependence of life forms at a systems level and can thus achieve more far-reaching protections by thinking about ecosystems in terms of their *integrity*. For Schlosberg, Nussbaum's way of "atomizing nature into isolated animals devalues a form of life, and the way that this form of life flourishes." Positing a more eco-centric approach to capabilities justice, Schlosberg treats systems as "living entities with their own integrity" (Schlosberg 2007: 148). Like individuals, habitats and ecosystems also have a kind of unfolding or realization of potential (Schlosberg 2007: 148; Kamsler 2006: 206). Capabilities justice should entail "a recognition of the potential of a landscape or an ecological community to maintain its integrity, and to flourish" (Schlosberg 2007: 148). Grounding an approach to capabilities justice in notions of integrity rather than dignity will make it possible to develop "a broader notion of ecological justice" that applies to individual humans and non-humans as well as to systems (Schlosberg 2007: 144). Schlosberg does not resolve the tension between nurturing the flourishing of individual animals and nurturing the flourishing of species and ecological systems (Bendik-Keymer 2014: 176). Nonetheless, by positing recognition of the integrity of ecological life as a political goal of a just society, he advances the discussion of how this might be achieved both in the concrete terms of resource distribution and as a condition of particular civic virtues.

Rather than proposing an alternative philosophical concept to extend capabilities justice to non-humans, other scholars see the potential for valuing the non-human world as an end in itself in Nussbaum's theory as currently formulated (Bendik-Keymer 2014: 176). Jeremy Bendik-Keymer argues that Nussbaum's grounding of capabilities theory in the Aristotelian logic that a being's particular excellence warrants a life worthy of its highest expression entails a biocentric outlook that apprehends dignity in all living beings. Nussbaum (like Aristotle) contends that all life has "something wonderful and worthy of awe" (Nussbaum 2006: 93–4). We recognize dignity, and thus the worthiness of respect, through the experience of wonder beings inspire in us (Nussbaum 2006: 349, 2011: 29; Bendik-Keymer 2014: 179). Yet, as Bendik-Keymer demonstrates in reconstructing Nussbaum's argument, recognizing all life as having dignity does not mean that all beings are subjects of justice (Bendik-Keymer 2014: 181). Nussbaum limits justice to beings that pursue their own functioning and experience harm subjectively because these attributes indicate a being's stake in its own existence, which for her is necessary to imagine a being as the subject of political claims. Katy Fulfer also recognizes the biocentric commitment in Nussbaum's theory, but she argues that predicating inclusion in the realm of justice on sentience is a failure of imagination and an artifact of the anthropocentric origins of Nussbaum's capabilities approach. From Fulfer's point of view, the capacity to flourish is sufficient for inclusion in the realm of justice under the logic of the capabilities approach, thus it can be readily extended to include non-sentient life.

Both Bendik-Keymer and Fulfer emphasize the moral and perceptual habits of humans that support a commitment to the dignity of all life. In line with Schlosberg's concern with ecosystem integrity, Fulfer sees in capabilities theory the prospect for perceiving dignity in interdependence and need. She proposes something akin to gratitude as the basis for human recognition of the dignity in non-sentient life and in ecosystems as organic wholes. Dignity arises from the interaction between people, or between people and sentient beings, and acknowledgement of interdependence and asymmetrical dependency in those relations (Nussbaum 2006: 356; Fulfer 2013: 33–5). Thus, for Fulfer the dignity of ecosystems is inherent in humans' dependence upon them. The dignity that makes something worthy of justice is a relational moral property that comes into being through recognition of mutual dependence. It can therefore inhere in relationships between humans and ecosystems, as well as between humans and between humans and non-sentient beings.

Bendik-Keymer makes two observations about Nussbaum's restriction of justice to sentient beings despite her commitment to the dignity in all life: First, it severs the longstanding relationship between dignity and justice within the human rights tradition, which holds that beings with dignity are worthy of justice. Nussbaum maintains a distinction between our duties *to* others, which arise from others' capacity to make claims on us as subjects of justice, and our duties *regarding* others, which do not hinge on the criteria of movement and sentience. The latter duties arise from obligations independent of justice, but they are no less binding. Second, it posits wonder as the crucial virtue or capacity through which people recognize their duties regarding beings who are different from them in ways that make empathy an implausible basis for apprehension of their moral worth. As Bendik-Keymer highlights, wonder leads us to see the order of another being, as "beautiful, even awe-inspiring," and thus as worthy of treatment as its own end (Bendik-Keymer 2014: 187). While empathy is the principal virtue of a political order that holds human beings as ends in themselves, it is insufficient for actualizing a biocentric ecological order in which human beings regard all life as an end in itself (Bendik-Keymer 2014: 187).

Bendik-Keymer's treatment of Nussbaum's argument suggests an emergent radical potential in capabilities theory to formulate human obligation to the non-human world and illuminate the moral virtues necessary to sustain a biocentric global justice.

By expanding recognition of dignity to all life while continuing to relegate justice to beings who are able to have a stake in their own existence, Nussbaum provides a theoretical basis for distinguishing the kinds of beings who warrant certain protections and the types of protections they require (an application taken up by Keulartz and Swart, which we discuss later). Furthermore, in emphasizing wonder as the means through which humans recognize the dignity of all life, however remote from human experience, Bendik-Keymer sees Nussbaum as pointing to a previously undeveloped aspect of human excellence. If empathy has been, as he contends, a central virtue of a human rights tradition that associates dignity with human life and thus with worthiness of justice, wonder opens the possibilities for recognizing value in difference. Presumably a biocentric capabilities regime requires nurturing the capacity for wonder among its citizens. This move simultaneously decenters human subjectivity as the basis of value and posits the capacity to recognize the inherent dignity of life as a crucial dimension of fully realized human subjectivity. In this way, Bendik-Keymer's reading of Nussbaum's biocentrism returns us to treating our respect for the dignity of life in the non-human world as a condition or component of our own flourishing.

Pelenc et al. develop concrete implications of the capability to value the other as a component of a flourishing human life by expanding Sen's account of human agency to include "ex ante responsibility." In doing so they make Sen's capability approach more effective in addressing the environmental dimension of sustainable (human) development (Pelenc et al. 2013: 78). Ex ante responsibility is "a responsibility before acting—or even before having the responsibility to act" (Pelenc et al. 2013: 82). It includes a responsibility to consider whether an action should be taken, and what the action's impact on nature will be, before taking that action. In this context it defines a capability to impute responsibility on oneself, potentially limiting one's own freedom, voluntarily (Pelenc et al. 2013: 85). Pelenc et al. treat this distinctly human responsibility as correlative to the power of initiative humans have to create uncertain but potentially catastrophic outcomes for life on earth. Thus, ex ante responsibility is commensurate with our potential to destroy the natural habitat on which present and future generations depend. As an expression of human agency and freedom of choice, it is exercised when one acts based on comprehensive consideration of the effects of the action (Pelenc et al. 2013: 86).

However, because one's environmental impacts are often a product of circumstance rather than choice, Pelenc et al. argue that responsibility for the environment cannot be understood to apply only at the level of individual action. It can and must also be a responsibility that is shared with others, as it is a condition of people's capability to forge the collective capacity for responsible action (Pelenc et al. 2013: 87). In this context, an individual realizes her capability to act with ex ante responsibility when she commits herself to acting in concert with others to protect the environment for collective rather than merely individual concerns (Pelenc et al. 2013: 88). Such exercises of responsibility are expressions of collective agency that compensate participating individuals for the implied and voluntary losses of their individual well-being (Pelenc et al. 2013: 90). David Schlosberg's research on collective action in response to environmental injustice supports this understanding of the interconnection between individual agency and the capacity to commit to a collective. His observations regarding the communal formulation of environmental claims, and the capacity for collective agency as a crucial component of central human capabilities that is dependent upon environmental resources, inform his proposal that capabilities theory should treat whole communities of people—not just individuals or ecosystems—as having capabilities requiring protection as a matter of justice (Schlosberg and Carruthers 2010). This would reflect how communities have themselves actually characterized environmental degradation (that is, as a threat to their community's thriving). Furthermore, as we mentioned earlier, it would protect the conditions of individual and community capabilities for effective political participation.

Keulartz and Swart's work specifying the human obligation to other species points to the kind of questions people must answer in taking responsibility for non-human life. They apply Nussbaum's approach to animal justice as an ethical framework to find the optimal balance between "specific care" (directed at individual animals and their individual needs) and "non-specific care" care (directed at the level of populations and ecosystems that sustain animals in the wild). This latter type of care, as Keulartz and Swart explain, "does not prevent suffering caused by natural conditions, since such conditions are a fact of life in the wild" (Keulartz and Swart 2012: 130). They argue instead that we should understand our obligations of care for animals as variable, depending on the kind of environment (natural vs. non-natural) an animal is in, and how those conditions are changing.

Keulartz and Swart advance this type of balancing between specific and non-specific care as precisely what Nussbaum begins to theorize in her proposal to base justice for animals on the extent to which their essential capabilities can be realized (Keulartz and Swart 2012: 132). Applying this capabilities based criterion of animal flourishing, Keulartz and Swart argue that we have duties of non-specific care in wild areas such as wildlife parks, which entail taking measures that preserve or restore animals' wild habitats, but not securing animals' individual welfare (Keulartz and Swart 2012: 130). In more confined environments, such as zoos, the flourishing of captive animals depends on the options and opportunities animals have to perform species-specific activities, while also trying to protect some of their original habitat so the species can be reintroduced into the wild (Keulartz and Swart 2012: 134–5). This may entail substituting one form of an animal's natural ability for another, by providing spaces and experiences in which animals can engage in behavior expressive of their natural practices. Finally, when it comes to circus animals, individual care is crucial to animal flourishing, which requires consideration of both the norm of flourishing for the species and the particular capacities of the individual animal. In this last context, capabilities justice for animals requires assessing, on a case-by-case basis, the two-way interaction between animal and trainer, as well as the possibilities for the animal's resistance, in order to determine "whether the happiness that results from the labor of training can compensate for the lack of non-specific care and the deficit of species specific care" (Keulartz and Swart 2012: 139).

Keulartz and Swart's application of Nussbaum's capabilities approach to animal justice demonstrates how a virtuous person can navigate a strategy for recognizing, protecting, and promoting the capabilities of animals and their natural habitats (Keulartz and Swart 2012: 131). However, while Keulartz and Swart do flesh out what a capabilities based animal justice would require in the context of existing relationships with domesticated and wild animals, and their habitats, they do not treat the capabilities and flourishing of ecosystems as valuable independent of their value as habitat to particular animals or species. Thus, what it means to promote the capabilities of ecosystems, and how this can be exercised as a human virtue in contemporary society are questions that are crucial to further theorizing and application of capabilities theory. Let us conclude then, by considering potential future directions for cultivating capabilities in EPT.

Conclusion: Cultivating Capabilities for a Flourishing Future

Capabilities theory has engendered a growing literature in EPT, exploring questions of environmental value and resource distribution within approaches to justice and international development, and conceptualizing the environment as a condition of human flourishing, as a component of human flourishing, and as an end in itself. This literature has shown that capabilities—as an account of well-being and justice—provide an effective means for defining the kinds of obligations humans have to others within political communities as well as across national boundaries, generations, and species. It further allows us to formulate the role of environmental stewardship and care for non-human species as an aspect of a full human life and to envision the material and institutional circumstances that would nurture this nascent capacity of human judgment and sentience. Finally, it posits the dignity of all life in a way that enables us to imagine decentering human subjectivity as the basis of moral worth while simultaneously envisioning the transformation of human experience this would entail. Capabilities theory has informed these discussions both at a high level of abstraction and at the level of policy regarding the kind of practices that optimize capabilities and the processes through which competing claims for recognition and resources might be settled.

Part of the theory's distinct potential lies in its recognition of the co-constitution of the material, institutional, and ethical dimensions of human experience at the outset. It takes human beings as materially constituted and sustained without reducing human potentiality to the circumstances that shape them at any given time or place. Rather, it emphasizes the emergence and becoming of humans as creative and ethical beings as its central values. Its developmental conception of human life and commitment to the dignity of each being on its own terms synthesizes the classical understanding of humans as relational beings and liberal individualism by looking through the lens of what it would mean for each being to flourish. Concern for the individual necessarily entails concern for the community that supports individual flourishing and the ecological conditions that underlie people's physical and social well-being. The theory's commitment to individual agency always points back to the distribution of power and resources necessary for people to recognize and act on their responsibility to the conditions of their own flourishing and forward to new possibilities for relationships with other humans and non-humans that arise from this recognition.

For the purpose of challenging existing paradigms and creating space for new relationships between humans and other species in the context of a rapidly changing climate, this reflexive aspect of capabilities theory seems particularly relevant. The inability of the natural world to hold humans to account puts the natural world under a human charge. The qualities through which humans recognize and value the natural world are crucial to focus on because they are vital both to perceiving these obligations and to securing the conditions through which they might be realized. A capabilities based approach to theorizing these qualities would ask: What institutional and material conditions support the human capability to value the natural environment as an end in itself? Similarly, what material and institutional conditions are necessary to support the capability to regard others as equally worthy of fully human lives and thus to accept the limits on one's own capabilities that Holland demonstrates are necessary to securing fundamental capabilities for all people? We might also ask (as, for example, Scholtes does in considering the impact of development on future generations) how existing institutions mediate human relationships with the environment in ways that support or inhibit the capability of people to value the environment and act on the basis of that value.

where to go next

The political conditions that render people capable of valuing others in relation to the natural environment and the natural environment as an end in itself also require further elaboration. Pelenc et al. convincingly derive the responsibility for environmental stewardship from the commitment to human agency in Sen's capability approach. What would securing this aspect of the capability for agency mean in practice? Specifically, what kind of information and voice do people need as a matter of political entitlement to be able to exercise their agency with respect to the natural world? Schlosberg's work on this issue highlights the capability for *Affiliation* as a condition of the capability for political agency and *Control over One's Environment*, pointing out the loss of the agency that results when environmental degradation undermines community integrity, and thus the ability for community members to make public claims to particular resources. Schlosberg's procedural account of capabilities justice could be used to evaluate and design the political processes necessary for protecting the kind of political agency that is central to Amartya Sen's account of justice and for elaborating the content of Nussbaum's capability for political *Control over One's Environment*, which entails "effective political participation."

While Bendik-Keymer provocatively points us to a politics of wonder opened up by Nussbaum's biocentric individualism, theorizing such a politics will require a more specific articulation of what it means to value non-human beings as ends in themselves. Keulartz and Swart have derived what it would mean to support the capabilities of a subset of captive animals and their habitats, but there is further work to be done in identifying how to support the capabilities of other kinds of animals and other forms of life under different conditions and in different contexts. Of particular importance is exploration of how we can treat animals as ends in cases where they are also instrumental to human well-being. Particular proposals for resolving conflicts between the capabilities and flourishing of individual animals and the capabilities and flourishing of whole species and ecological systems, also calls for deeper exploration. This would include, as Elizabeth Cripps (2010) has proposed, an elaboration of the central capabilities of ecosystems, which Schlosberg intends to treat as worthy of political protection in a socially just political community.

The urgency of this project is highlighted as certain environments are disappearing, and with them the choice over how one can relate to the physical world and to others whose identities and ways of life are bound up with their environmental relationships. Amidst an uncertain and changing global ecology, cultivating capabilities is both a condition and an expression of the political power necessary to forestall irreversible environmental loss.

Notes

1. See Robeyns (2005: 103–5) and Crocker (2008: 104–89) for an overview of Sen and Nussbaum's work. Also see Nussbaum (2000: 11–15) distinguishing her own "capabilities approach" from Sen's "capability approach."
2. In contrast to Nussbaum, Sen (1999: 190–2) might describe the relevant conditions as including both "well-being" freedom or achievement, and "agency" freedom.
3. See Nussbaum (1988) for her early linking of capabilities to Aristotelian thought.
4. See Nussbaum (2000: 78–80) for the full definition of each of these capabilities.
5. e.g. this is why Sen (2013) advocates education and empowerment of women as a means to limiting the impact of population growth on the natural environment.
6. See Kamsler (2006: 198), who originally noted in responding to Nussbaum's development of capabilities theory, that there is nothing inherent in capabilities theory to prevent expanding and applying it in these ways.
7. See Heyward (2011: 10) for an example of this problem related to climate change.
8. See Schlosberg (2007) for what we have characterized as his procedural account of capabilities justice.
9. Even in her early work on capabilities Nussbaum (1988: esp. 173, fn. 29) recognized the advantages of the framework for developing an account of what humans owe to others species and living things in general, based on an understanding of their particular telos or optimal functioning.
10. See Cripps (2010) for an argument that such an overlapping consensus is unrealistic.

References

Bendik-Keymer, Jeremy. (2014). "From Humans to All of Life: Nussbaum's Transformation of Dignity." In *Capabilities, Gender, Equality: Towards Fundamental Entitlements*, edited by Flavio Comim and Martha Nussbaum (Cambridge, UK: Cambridge University Press), 175–91.

Cripps, Elizabeth. (2010). "Saving the Polar Bear, Saving the World: Can the Capabilities Approach do Justice to Humans, Animals *and* Ecosystems." *Res Publica* 16: 1–22.

Crocker, David. (2006). "Sen and Deliberative Democracy." In *Capabilities Equality: Basic Issues and Problems*, edited by A. Kaufman (New York: Routledge), 155–97.

Crocker, David. (2008). *Ethics of Global Development: Agency, Capability, and Deliberative Democracy* (Cambridge, UK: Cambridge University Press).

Fulfer, Katy. (2013). "The Capabilities Approach to Justice and the Flourishing of Nonsentient Life." *Ethics and the Environment* 18(1): 19–38.

Heyward, Clare. (2011). "Climate Justice and the Capabilities Approach." *Maitreyee: The E-Bulletin of the Human Development and Capability Association* March 11: 9–11.

Holland, Breena. (2008a). "Justice and the Environment in Nussbaum's Capabilities Approach: Why Sustainable Ecological Capacity Is a Meta-Capability." *Political Research Quarterly* 61(2): 319–32.

Holland, Breena. (2008b). "Ecology and the Limits of Justice: Establishing 'Capability Ceilings' in Nussbaum's Capabilities Approach." *Journal of Human Development and Capabilities (Special Edition on Ideas Changing History)* 9(3): 399–423.

Holland, Breena. (2012)."Environment as Meta-Capability: Why a Dignified Life Requires a Stable Climate System." In *Ethical Adaptation to Climate Change: Human Virtues of the Future*, edited by Allen Thompson and Jeremy Bendik-Keymer (Cambridge, MA: MIT Press), 145–64.

Holland, Breena. (2015). *Allocating the Earth: A Distributional Framework for Protecting Capabilities in Environmental Law and Policy* (Oxford, UK: Oxford University Press).

Kamsler, Victoria. (2006). "Attending to Nature: Capabilities and the Environment." In *Capabilities Equality: Basic Issues and Problems*, edited by A. Kaufman (New York: Routledge), 198–213.

Keulartz, Jozef and Swart, Jac. A. A. (2012). "Animal Flourishing and Capabilities in an Era of Global Change." In *Ethical Adaptation to Climate Change: Human Virtues of the Future*, edited by Allen Thompson and Jeremy Bendik-Keymer (Cambridge, MA: MIT Press), 123–44.

Nussbaum, Martha. (1988). "Nature, Function, and Capability; Aristotle on Political Distribution." In *Oxford Studies in Ancient Philosophy.* 6 Supplementary Volume. (Oxford, UK: Clarendon Press), 145–84.

Nussbaum, Martha. (2000). *Women and Human Development: The Capabilities Approach* (New York: Cambridge University Press).

Nussbaum, Martha. (2006). *Frontiers of Justice: Disability, Nationality, Species Membership* (Cambridge, MA: Harvard (Belknap) University Press).

Nussbaum, Martha. (2011). *Creating Capabilities: The Human Development Approach* (Cambridge, MA: Harvard (Belknap) University Press).

Pelenc, Jerome, Lompo, Minkieba Kevin, Ballet, Jérôme, and Dubois, Jean- Luc. (2013). "Sustainable Human Development and the Capability Approach: Integrating Environment, Responsibility and Collective Agency." *Journal of Human Development and Capabilities* 14(1): 77–9.

Robeyns, Ingrid. (2005). "The Capability Approach: A Theoretical Survey." *Journal of Human Development* 6(1): 93–114.

Schlosberg, David. (2007). *Defining Environmental Justice: Theories, Movements, and Nature* (Oxford, UK: Oxford University Press).

Schlosberg, David. (2009). "Capacity and Capabilities: A Response to the Greenhouse Development Rights Framework." *Ethics, Place and Environment* 12(3): 287–90.
Schlosberg, David. (2012a). "Justice, Ecological Integrity, and Climate Change." In *Ethical Adaptation to Climate Change: Human Virtues of the Future*, edited by Allen Thompson and Jeremy Bendik-Keymer (Cambridge, MA: MIT Press), 165–83.
Schlosberg, David. (2012b). "Climate Justice and Capabilities: A Framework for Adaptation Policy." *Ethics and International Affairs* 26(4): 445–61.
Schlosberg, David and Carruthers, David. (2010). "Indigenous Struggles, Environmental Justice, and Community Capabilities." *Global Environmental Politics* 10(4): 12–35.
Scholtes, Fabian. (2010). "Whose Sustainability? Environmental Domination and Sen's Capability Approach." *Oxford Development Studies* 38(3): 289–307.
Sen, Amartya. (1999). *Development as Freedom* (New York: Alfred A. Knopf).
Sen, Amartya. (2004). "Capabilities, Lists, and Public Reason: Continuing the Conversation." *Feminist Economics* 10(3): 77–80.
Sen, Amartya. (2013). "The Ends and Means of Sustainability." *Journal of Human Development and Capabilities* 14(1): 6–20.
Thompson, Allen and Bendik-Keymer, Jeremy. (2012). "Introduction: Adapting Humanity." In *Ethical Adaptation to Climate Change: Human Virtues of the Future*, edited by Allen Thompson and Jeremy Bendik-Keymer (Cambridge, MA: MIT Press), 1–24.

CHAPTER 28

CONSUMPTION AND WELL-BEING

PAUL KNIGHTS AND JOHN O'NEILL

Well-being and Limits

Recent debates on sustainability, consumption, and happiness have seen the renewal of an ancient controversy: Are there bounds to the goods required for a happy or flourishing life? The classical answer to that question, shared for example in Aristotelian and Epicurean traditions, was that bounds do exist to the goods required for a happy life. That answer survives into some central texts of modern economics, most notably Ramsey's influential paper on saving which still informs basic economic discussion of intergenerational saving. Ramsey assumes that there is a "maximum obtainable rate of enjoyment or utility" which he terms "Bliss" (Ramsey 1928: 545). The point of saving is for a community to achieve that level of goods at which members reach or approximate to Bliss.

While Ramsey's paper remains influential, the specific assumption that there is a maximum state of utility, a point of Bliss, is one that has disappeared from the standard assumptions in economics. The standard economic textbook denies that there are bounds to the goods required for a happy life. Gauthier states the assumption thus: "Appropriation has no natural upper bound. Economic man seeks more" (Gauthier 1986: 318). The question of whether there do or do not exist upper bounds to the goods required for a good life is one that has been brought into new relief by environmental problems and sustainability.

The Concept of Consumption

The term "consumption" itself is used in a variety of different senses (Williams 1988: 78–9). In its basic sense the concept of consumption is used to refer to the process of using up material and energy in human life processes (Williams 1988: 78–9). To consume is to act such that the availability of an object or resource is reduced (Knights 2012: ch. 1). In that sense, there are strong reasons to assume that if sustainability requires a reduction of throughput of energy and materials, then sustainability requires a reduction in consumption. However, the term "consumption" has been extended beyond this in recent uses under the influence of marketing, economics, and other social sciences to include the activities that a person engages in as a "consumer" understood as a purchaser of goods and services in a market. As such reference is made for example to the consumption of images and cultural goods. As Williams notes, the predominance of this market model has meant a further extension of the term into domains such as politics, education, and health. His comment on this extension is still an apposite one: "In any of these fields, but also in the ordinary fields of goods and services, to say *user* rather than *consumer* is still to express a relevant distinction" (Williams 1988: 79; emphases in original).

Maintaining this distinction matters for a number of reasons. First, the generalization of a market model of consumption reflects and reproduces a form of marketization. Important social distinctions and relations, for example between citizens in politics, student and teacher in education, patient and doctor in health, and artist and audience in the cultural sphere, each with their associated practices and internal goods, are reduced to the relation of purchaser and provider concerned with the exchange and acquisition of commodities (Keat 1991). A second claim that appeals to the distinction between use and consumption is to be found in the work of Arendt. For Arendt in consumer society the rate of use of objects is accelerated to the point that "the objective difference between use and consumption, between the relative durability of use objects and the swift coming and going of consumer goods dwindles to insignificance" (Arendt 1958: 125). The durable common world of fabricated use objects that are the products of work gives way to a world of consumer goods which are treated as parts of the cycle of labor: "we must consume, devour, as it were, our houses and furniture and cars as though they were the 'good things' of nature which spoil uselessly if they are not drawn swiftly into the never-ending cycle of man's metabolism with nature" (Arendt 1958: 126). The reduction of many use objects to objects of consumption undermines our understanding of a common world of fabricated but relevantly stable objects that are shared across generations. Finally, understanding the differences between consumption and other uses of goods is important to conceptualizing the relationships between the good life and the reductions in the use of materials and energy required for sustainability.

In referring to the using up of material and energy, a distinction between two kinds of consumption can be drawn. First, materials and energy are "used up" in the productive process itself—in what is sometimes called "productive consumption" (Marx 1973: 90). Second, there is the consumption of the final objects of the productive processes by consumers. The classical question remains important for sustainability: can a reduction in consumption be achieved without a loss in well-being?

One influential answer to this question is that it can without the need for any reduction in the consumption of final goods by consumers. Shifts in productive activity through technological change and resource substitutability will allow for continuing increases in the consumption of final goods to be pursued with lower energy and resource use. Consumption of raw materials in the productive process itself will be reduced without requiring the reduction in final consumption goods. One recent expression of this view is to be found in the work of Mark Sagoff. While accepting the claim that ever increasing consumption of such goods might not be good for us, he rejects the claim that there exist physical and ecological limits to increasing individual consumption or to increased consumption through population growth (Sagoff 2008: 132ff). Since resource and energy limits are a function of technological development, as technology advances so can the frontier of any such limits. As technological development renders final consumption goods less energy and resource intensive, the apparent limits will recede. If state regulation and subsidy did not distort market signals, an innovative market economy could deliver increasing final consumption (Sagoff 2008: 125). The view that markets, technology, and resource substitutability can deliver sustainability with increasing growth in final consumption is widespread in economic literature in both the neo-classical and Austrian traditions.

There are a number of reasons to be skeptical about this view. The first reason has to do with rebound effects that go back to Jevons' paradox (Jevons 1866; Jackson 2009). Falls in the resource and carbon intensity of goods in a market economy will, other things being equal, result in a relative cheapening of the goods. This will either increase consumption or displace it elsewhere, potentially undoing any resource and energy savings. A decline in carbon and material intensity may be a necessary condition for an absolute decline in material and energy use. However, it is not sufficient. The second reason concerns justice in consumption. Development in basic consumption of the least well off is a condition of global justice. However, that increase itself will place large additional burdens on ecological limits. A reduction in luxury consumption is a condition for subsistence consumption to improve as justice requires (Shue 1993). The third reason concerns the time scale for the reduction of greenhouse gases. The avoidance of dangerous climate change requires rapid and deep cuts in the emissions of greenhouse gases that cannot be achieved through technological change alone in the requisite time-span (Anderson and Bows 2011). There are strong reasons for skepticism that technology alone could deliver sustainable outcomes.

If consumption is to decline without a loss of well-being one cannot rely on technological change. The older classical arguments have renewed importance. Are there bounds to the goods required for a good life? The answer depends on the assumptions made about well-being and the good life. Recent neo-classical economics assumes a preference satisfaction account of well-being: well-being consists in the satisfaction of preferences, the stronger the preferences, the greater the improvement in well-being. If one assumes that a rational agent will always prefer more to less, it follows that one can always improve well-being through offering more. There are no limits to the goods required for a good life. The two main rivals to this account of well-being do recognize the existence of limits: subjective state theories that assume well-being is a matter of being in the right mental states, for example in classical hedonist theories, pleasure and the absence of pain; and objective state theories that assume that well-being consists in the realization of some objective states, such as close personal relations, autonomy, achievement, and knowledge. The Epicurean and Aristotelian answers to the question of limits—that there are bounds to the goods that are required for a good life—are premised for the Epicurean upon a subjective state and the Aristotelian on an objective state account of well-being or happiness. Both have seen revivals as a response to problems of sustainability.

Two Theories of Well-being

The revival of hedonic accounts of well-being (Kahneman et al. 1997, 1999; Layard 2005; Frey 2010) has seen a renewed interest in an Epicurean answer to the question of whether there are limits required for the good life. Hedonic accounts of well-being are subjective state accounts of well-being. Well-being is a matter of being in the right mental states. The promise of recent hedonic psychology is that, through both global evaluation and experience sampling methods, states of subjective welfare can be measured and their determinants empirically investigated: "Hedonic psychology... is the study of what makes experiences and life pleasant and unpleasant. It is concerned with feelings of pleasure and pain, of interest and boredom, of joy and sorrow and of satisfaction and dissatisfaction" (Kahneman et al. 1999: ix). While this research is often presented as a return to Bentham (Kahneman et al. 1997; Layard 2005), the central environmental claims involve a return to Epicurean themes about the limits of the goods required for a good life. A classical Epicurean theme is that the view that there are no limits to the goods required for a good life is founded on errors about the nature and determinants of happiness. Once the good life is properly understood in hedonic terms, it is evident that there are limits to the goods required for its realization: "Natural wealth is both limited and easy to acquire. But wealth [as defined by] groundless opinions extends without limits" (Epicurus *Principal Doctrines* 15, in Inwood and Gerson 1988). The claim made by the hedonic environmentalist (for example, Porritt 2003) is that the findings in recent hedonic research confirm this view. Hence a decoupling of consumption and the improvement of well-being is possible. There is evidence that beyond a certain point, growth in GDP is not correlated with a change in reported life satisfaction (Easterlin 1974). While the relative income of different groups within a society is correlated with different levels of life satisfaction, beyond a minimal threshold absolute increases are not. Increasing opportunities for consumption are no longer indicative of increasing well-being.

There are two standard explanations of these findings. The first concerns the fact of hedonic adaptation—the tendency of the intensity of at least some good or bad experiences to lessen as individuals adjust to a new state of affairs in which they find themselves. Individuals adapt both to gains in goods—for example to lottery wins—and to losses—for example those who find themselves in wheelchairs after accidents will adjust and after a period their subjective well-being tends to return to previous levels (Frederick and Loewenstein 1999). While changes in circumstances can produce an immediate shift in subjective well-being, over a period individuals adapt and shift to a prior reference point.

The second is an older argument about positional goods that is independent of any hedonic perspective but is still invoked in this context. Positional goods are those goods whose worth depends on their consumption by others. In a market economy where individuals pursue their personal improvement through positional goods each agent makes an individual choice for a good that is affected by the same choice by others and hence there is no increase in life satisfaction (Hirsch 1977). In particular, the race for status and relative income as positional goods is self-defeating. Increased income and consumption is not matched with any increase in life satisfaction.

The consequence of both hedonic adaptation and the pursuit of positional goods is that individuals find themselves on a hedonic treadmill in which as they consume more they want more and subjective well-being remains static. The hedonic environmentalist argues that the solution is to pursue those goods that are not subject to these treadmill effects and are shown to be closely correlated to subjective well-being: the quality of familial relationships, the security and intrinsic worth of work, health, personal and political freedoms, and the quality of wider social relationships in a community including in particular the degree of mutual trust within a community. The conclusion that is drawn by the hedonic environmentalist is that we can move to a low consumption economy which sustains happiness.

The promise of hedonism as the basis for the claim that lower consumption can be combined with the maintenance and even possible improvement of well-being has rendered it popular in environmental discourse (Porritt 2003). However, there are major problems with the approach. The first and most basic are the well-known objections to subjective state theories of well-being. Other things matter to well-being in addition to psychological states of feeling good. As Kahneman himself notes in a paper with Sugden: "human well-being may be thought to depend, not only on the sum of moment-by-moment affective experiences... but also on other aspects of life, such as autonomy, freedom, achievement, and the development of deep interpersonal relationships, which cannot be decomposed into momentary affective experiences" (Kahneman and Sugden 2005: 176). The point underpins the standard experience machine objections to hedonism (Nozick 1974: 42–3). We would not agree to enter an experience machine, no matter how reliable it was at giving us all the experiences of a good life of friendship, achievement, and autonomy, since what matters is having friends, realizing certain achievements, etc., not just the experience of having friends, realizing certain achievements, etc. Similarly in the environmental case, we want to actually live in an unspoiled natural environment, not just have the experience of doing so. Given the choice, most of us would desire to live in a natural world, not to live in a simulation of it, even if the experiences were identical.

In addition to these general problems there are more specific difficulties with hedonist accounts of well-being in discussions of intergenerational justice and concern. Consider first intergenerational justice. Hedonic adaptation renders hedonic metrics poor metrics for the purposes of determining injustice generally. The less well-off will adapt to their situation and may not experience it as hard: "A thoroughly deprived person, leading a very reduced life, might not appear to be badly off in terms of the mental metric of desire and its fulfilment, if the hardship is accepted with non-grumbling resignation" (Sen 1992: 55). The point has implications for intergenerational justice since one might expect those in the future who suffer the negative consequences of current decisions to similarly adapt. A world geo-engineered in response to climate change may lack blue skies, a biologically impoverished world may lack many species of flora and fauna we experience today, but the absence of blue skies and biological species may no longer be experienced as a loss but simply a background condition of life. Given adaptation, a subjective well-being metric will fail to capture potential harms that matter for intergenerational justice.

Second, hedonic theories of well-being fail to offer an adequate account of why the future matters to us. A central claim in the Epicurean tradition is that what happens after a person's death is a matter of indifference for that person's life: "See likewise of how little concern to us were the ages of eternal time that passed before we were born. Nature holds this up to us as a mirror of the time that will be after our death" (Lucretius 1965: Book 3, 972–5). Consequently concern for future generations can only be an impersonal ethical matter that is not tied to how well a person's own life is going. This account fails to acknowledge the ways in which the central projects and relations that constitute our lives have a future beyond our deaths and that the way things turn out matters for how well our lives can be said to go. From intergenerational familial relations, through work activities and political engagements, the way our projects turn out is not a matter of indifference to us (O'Neill 1993: ch. 3).

Can the central claims of recent hedonic research about the possible decoupling of consumption and well-being be retained without being subject to the particular problems associated with hedonism? Objective state theories of well-being promise that they can; the claim that there are limits to the goods required for a good life was articulated by Aristotle: "[T]he amount of household property which suffices for a good life is not unlimited, nor of the nature described by Solon in the verse 'There is no bound to wealth stands fixed for men'. There is a bound fixed . . ." (Aristotle 1948: Book 1, ch. 8). According to objective state theories that descend from Aristotle, well-being consists in the realization of certain objective states such as close personal relations, autonomy, achievement, and knowledge. The two central versions of objective state theories of well-being appeal to the concepts of needs (Wiggins 1998, 2006; Gough 2014; O'Neill 2010) and of capabilities and functionings (Sen 1995; Nussbaum 2000).

(a) Needs: While some needs claims are purely instrumental to meeting some optional ends—if I am to have a luxury cruise in the Caribbean, then I need £4000—others are absolute or categorical in the sense that the ends themselves are not optional. Rather the ends are "unforsakeable," a condition of living a minimal level of human flourishing at all, and as such a person can be said to be harmed if they are not met (Wiggins 1998).
(b) Capabilities: The capabilities approach takes individuals' quality of life to be a matter of their freedom to achieve valuable functionings. Functionings are "what people are actually able to do and be" (Nussbaum 2000: 5), and capabilities are the freedoms or opportunities individuals have to achieve those functionings, even if they do not choose to.

The contrast between needs and capabilities approaches to well-being is itself open to some debate. The contrast is undone somewhat if sentences describing needs take a verb phrase as their object, for example, "Joe needs to be able to eat adequately" rather than a noun phrase, for example, "Joe needs food" (Wiggins 2006: 31–2). Thus specified many needs claims will effectively be equivalent to claims about functionings and capabilities. However, some differences may remain. For example, needs claims tend to be about conditions required to achieve functionings rather than capabilities.

Objective state theories of well-being can articulate and defend the claim that there are bounds to the goods required for the good life in two ways. First, in common with hedonic environmentalists, proponents of objective state theories can claim that current consumption levels in richer regions of the world are excessive and are compromising their inhabitants' well-being, such that a reduction in consumption is compatible with maintaining or even improving well-being (Jackson and Marks 1999; Stiglitz et al. 2009: ch. 2). Secondly, unlike hedonic environmentalism, objective state theorists can claim that current consumption levels compromise the well-being of present generations insofar as they decrease the likelihood that future generations will be in a position to continue, appreciate, preserve, and value the projects that were of importance to us.

With regard to the first argument, appeal can be made to empirical data which shows that rising GDP, above a certain level, is not correlated with improvements in capabilities to achieve valuable functionings (Stiglitz et al. 2009: ch. 2). However, appeal may also be made to data which is commonly assumed as emerging from firmly within the hedonic tradition. Much is made within the recent revival of Epicurean hedonism of the empirical data on reported life satisfaction which appears to show that while per capita consumption has risen in the past 60 years within rich countries, aggregate welfare has plateaued over this period. This data is derived from the World Values Survey and the Gallup World Poll, both of which ask the question: "All things considered, how satisfied are you with your life as a whole these days?" Respondents rank their answer on a scale from 1 (dissatisfied) to 10 (satisfied). In order for the data derived from the answers given by respondents to this question to be understood as pertaining to subjective well-being it must be the case that respondents understand the concept of "satisfaction" to be referring only to psychological states, and to be asking them to sum particular episodes of happy feelings. But it is highly plausible that the life satisfaction survey question is understood by respondents to be calling for them to assess not only their subjective states of feeling good and feeling bad, but also what they have been able to do and become in dimensions of their life that are significant to them. This requires an assessment of the more objective conditions of their life, such as the quality of their neighborhood for bringing up their children, housing, opportunities for leisure, the quality of their work life, and so on. The assumption that the data only reveals subjective well-being appears to be at least partly due to a scope fallacy, where "a subjective assessment of well-being" and "an assessment of subjective well-being" are conflated (O'Neill 2006). Life satisfaction surveys can be understood to be surveys of subjective assessments of objective well-being. How far this data itself adequately tracks objective assessments of objective well-being remains an important problem. Since a person's assessment of the achievement of a particular level of objective well-being will itself depend on the person's expectations, subjective assessments of objective well-being can themselves be subject to the problems of adaptation. A person with low functioning might assess an improved condition highly, whereas a person with a high state of functioning might give a low assessment to that condition if it is the outcome of a loss.

The second argument that objective state theorists can make to the effect that current consumption levels compromise the well-being of present generations is that they do so in virtue of the effect that unsustainable consumption is likely to have on the capacity of future generations to be in a position to continue, appreciate, preserve, and value the projects that were of importance to us. Unlike hedonism, objective state theories of well-being can provide an account of how the way the future turns out has a bearing on how well our life can be said to be going now. It can do this by claiming that the welfare value of particular moments, or episodes within larger time frames, cannot be ascertained independently of the larger narrative structure in which they occur. The future determines what appraisal we can give to the present (O'Neill 1993: ch. 3, 2006). This applies not only within lives, but also, crucially, to what happens after our deaths, since the narrative that can truly be told of our lives will often include reference to the way that central projects and relationships that were important to us when we were alive fared after our death. Hedonism fails to provide such an account. If all that matters to the welfare value of some event at any moment of time is the quality of the experience at that moment then this can be ascertained quite independently of what happens at any moment before or after. It is fixed by the quality of the experience at that instant. Whether or not the event was pleasurable or painful and by how much can be ascertained independently of what happened before or after (O'Neill 2006: 163). In failing to allow that what happens after our deaths matters to an appraisal of how well our lives are going now, hedonism cannot explain why consuming sustainably, such that future generations are bequeathed the conditions that make it possible for them to continue our current important projects, matters for how well our lives go. Articulations of arguments for sustainable consumption that are grounded in objective state theories of well-being, however, can allow that the future matters to us.

The shortening of time horizons that is a feature of a market economy and consumer society undermines such cross generational projects. This point was central to classical republican political thought and underpins Arendt's distinction between use and consumption noted earlier. For Arendt, in consumer societies public objects like buildings are built not as ties over generations but as goods that are created and destroyed like objects that are literally consumed. The temporal cycles of markets and the competition for political office undermine commitments to projects with a longer time frame to come to fruition. Such projects give individuals a stake in the future. Neither, in these conditions, can we expect that future generations will preserve and value the scientific, political, and cultural projects of central importance to current generations. In this way, objective state theorists can argue that the narrative of current generations will be ended tragically, and this appraisal affects how well our lives can be said to be going now, providing a kind of reason to consume sustainably relating to our own well-being that hedonism cannot. Thus, in the context of a new environmental situation in which future generations are threatened with degraded conditions of life, a new justification to the claim that there are bounds to the goods required for a good life emerges; we cannot be said to be living a good life if the central projects of importance to us that we believed or hoped would be continued and valued by future generations will be abandoned by them as a result of our unwillingness to create and support institutions that secured the conditions for them to be able do so.

The Sources of Consumption Without Limits

Aristotelian and Epicurean approaches to well-being, while sharing the view that there are bounds to the goods required for the good life, offer different accounts of the nature of well-being. There is, however, a second way in which they differ in their account of the limits, namely their account of the explanation as to why individuals pursue goods without bounds. The explanations are independent of the specific theories of well-being.

Epicurus's account of the source of the limitless pursuit of goods is a purely cognitive one. Individuals pursue goods without limits due to false beliefs. "The stomach is not insatiable as the many say, but rather the opinion that the stomach requires an unlimited amount of filling is false" (Epicurus *Vatican Sayings* 59, in Inwood and Gerson 1988: 31). This view is echoed in more recent work on happiness within the psychological literature which similarly tends to take the source of the pursuit of goods without limits to lie in cognitive errors by individuals. In contrast, Aristotle's answer is institutional. He contrasts the form of acquisition of goods in the classical household, in which acquisition is limited by the needs of householders, with the forms of acquisition that are characteristic of commercial society in which wealth is pursued for its own sake and acquisition appears to lack limits: "There is no limit to the end it seeks; and the end it seeks is wealth of the sort we have mentioned [that is, wealth in the form of currency] and the mere acquisition of money" (Aristotle 1948: Book 1, ch. 8). This distinction between two modes of acquisition has been influential in more recent critical discussion of market societies (O'Neill 1993: ch. 10). Marx explicitly appeals to it in *Capital*. Where he differs from Aristotle is in his claim that acquisition without limits is not simply a vice, *pleonoxia*, that is fostered by market society, but rather, in the form of capital accumulation, is an activity that is required by the capitalist to survive against competitors (Marx 1970: ch. 4). Polanyi also takes Aristotle's distinction as his starting point for understanding the ways in which market societies disembed the economy from social and moral relations (Polanyi 1957: 53–5). The structural and institutional determinants of consumption without limits matter. We live in economies in which increasing consumption is a condition for the stability and reproduction of the economic system itself—where falls in "consumer confidence" are indications of an economy in crisis. This argument is important in considering responses to the gap between increasing consumption and static or even declining well-being. To frame the solution in Epicurean terms of shifting the beliefs and values of consumers fails to address the structural determinants of increasing consumption. Political and economic responses to consumption and sustainability need to address not just false beliefs but the institutional and structural determinants of behavior and hence address again fundamental questions in political economy about the organization of economic life.

References

Anderson, K. and Bows, A. (2011). "Beyond 'Dangerous' Climate Change: Emission Scenarios for a New World." *Philosophical Transactions of the Royal Society A* 369: 20–44.

Arendt, H. (1958). *The Human Condition* (Chicago: University of Chicago Press).

Aristotle. (1948). *Politics*. Translated by E. Barker (Oxford: Clarendon Press).

Easterlin, R. (1974). "Does Economic Growth Improve the Human Lot? Some Empirical Evidence." In *Nations and Households in Economic Growth: Essays in Honor of Moses Abramovitz*, edited by P. A. David and M. W. Reder (London: Academic Press), 89–125.

Frederick, S. and Loewenstein, G. (1999). "Hedonic Adaptation." In *Scientific Perspectives on Enjoyment, Suffering, and Well-Being*, edited by D. Kahneman, E. Diener, and N. Schwartz (New York: Russell Sage Foundation), 302–29.

Frey, B. (2010). *Happiness: A Revolution in Economics* (Cambridge, MA: MIT Press).

Gauthier, D. (1986). *Morals by Agreement* (Oxford: Oxford University Press).

Gough, I. (2014). Climate Change and Sustainable Welfare: The Centrality of Human Needs (London: NEF working paper).

Hirsch, Fred. (1977). *Social Limits to Growth* (London: Routledge, Kegan and Paul).

Inwood, B. and Gerson, L., eds. (1988) *Hellenistic Philosophy* (Indianapolis: Hackett).

Jackson, T. (2009) *Prosperity without Growth* (London: Earthscan).

Jackson, T. and Marks, N. (1999). "Consumption, Sustainable Welfare and Human Needs—With Reference to UK Expenditure Patterns Between 1954 and 1994." *Ecological Economics* 28: 421–41.

Jevons, W. (1866). *The Coal Question*, 2nd edn. (London: Macmillan and Co).

Kahneman, D. and Sugden, R. (2005). "Experienced Utility as a Standard of Policy Evaluation." *Environmental & Resource Economics* 32: 161–81.
Kahneman, D., Wakker, P., and Sarin, R. (1997). "Back to Bentham? Explorations of Experienced Utility." *The Quarterly Journal of Economics* 112: 375–405.
Kahneman, D., Diener E., and Schwarz N., eds. (1999). *Well-Being: Foundations of Hedonic Psychology* (New York: Russell Sage Foundation Press).
Keat, R. (1991). "Consumer Sovereignty and the Integrity of Practices." In *Enterprise Culture*, edited by R. Keat and N. Abercrombie (London: Routledge),216–30.
Knights, P. (2012). *Consumption, Environment and Ethics: An Analysis of Moral and Welfare Arguments for Reducing Personal Consumption* (Ph.D. Thesis, University of Manchester).
Layard, R. (2005). *Happiness: Lessons for a New Science* (London: Allen Lane).
Lucretius. (1965). *On Nature*. Translated by R. Greer (Indianapolis: Bobbs-Merrill).
Marx, K. (1970). *Capital I* (London: Lawrence and Wishart).
Marx, K. (1973). *Grundrisse* (Harmondsworth: Penguin).
Nozick, R. (1974). *Anarchy, State and Utopia* (Oxford: Blackwell).
Nussbaum, M. (2000). *Women and Human Development: The Capabilities Approach* (Cambridge: Cambridge University Press).
O'Neill, J. (1993). *Ecology, Policy and Politics: Human Well-Being and the Natural World* (London: Routledge).
O'Neill, J. (2006). "Citizenship, Well-Being and Sustainability: Epicurus or Aristotle?" *Analyse & Kritik* 28: 158–72.
O'Neill, J. (2010). "The Overshadowing of Need." In *Sustainable Development: Capabilities, Needs, and Well-Being*, edited by F. Rauschmayer, I. Omann, and J. Frühmann (London: Routledge), 25–42.
Polanyi, K. (1957). *The Great Transformation* (Boston: Beacon Press).
Porritt, J. (2003). *Redefining Prosperity: Resource Productivity, Economic Growth and Sustainable Development* (London: Sustainable Development Commission).
Ramsey, F. P. (1928). "A Mathematical Theory of Saving." *Economic Journal* 38: 543–59.
Sagoff. M. (2008). *The Economy of the Earth*, 2nd edn. (Cambridge: Cambridge University Press).
Sen A. (1992). *Inequality Reexamined* (Oxford: Clarendon Press).
Sen, A. (1995). *Development as Freedom* (Oxford: Oxford University Press).
Shue, Henry. (1993). "Subsistence Emissions and Luxury Emissions." *Law and Policy* 15: 39–60.
Stiglitz, J. et al. (2009) Report by the Commission on the Measurement of Economic Performance and Social Progress http://www.stiglitz-sen-fitoussi.fr/documents/rapport_anglais.pdf
Wiggins, D. (1998). "The Claims of Need." In D. Wiggins, *Needs, Values, Truth*, 3rd edn. (Oxford: Clarendon Press), 1–58.
Wiggins, D. (2006). "An Idea We Cannot Do Without." In *The Philosophy of Need*, edited by S. Reader (Cambridge: Cambridge University Press), 25–50.
Williams, R. (1988). *Keywords* (London: Fontana).

PART V

POWER, STRUCTURES, AND CHANGE

IDENTIFYING STRUCTURAL CONSTRAINTS AND POSSIBILITIES

+ biblio
+ how specific really were
Matthew + Joe's proposals?
. diary

CHAPTER 29

CAPITAL, ENVIRONMENTAL DEGRADATION, AND ECONOMIC EXTERNALIZATION

ADRIAN PARR

NEO-LIBERAL principles of individualism, privatization, consumption, and unconstrained choice underpinning advanced capitalism are rapidly becoming the predominant strategy used in response to widespread environmental degradation and climate change. Whether we are speaking of changing our personal choices to buy green or investing in the growing market in carbon offsets there is very little difference between the two. Both assume we can leave pollution, species extinction, the increasing frequency and intensity of extreme weather events, diminishing water quality and quantity, food scarcity, trash, and dirty energy up to the market to solve. Furthermore, this approach to the problem of environmental deterioration leaves unquestioned the unsustainable model of growth that global capitalism relies upon.

This essay describes and analyzes capital's production of negative environmental externalities. Despite a slew of environmental legislation passed by governments the world over—a response to the demands of the environmental movements of the 1960s and 1970s, environmental degradation persists. Indeed, as the continual rise in greenhouse gas (GHG) emissions exemplifies, environmental degradation has worsened. How has this happened? On the one hand, the rise of neo-liberal governance and the forces of patrimonial capitalism have compromised the action of the state; on the other, capital has corrupted the autonomy, discourse, and activist charge of the mainstream of the environmental movement, turning it into an ally of private wealth.

Environmental Fallout: Externalities

Much attention has been given to Thomas Piketty's (2014) groundbreaking analysis, *Capital in the Twenty-First Century*. Growth, he argues, has not been evenly distributed, and since the 1970s public wealth has been steadily transferred into private hands. Simply put, the political climate of neo-liberalism has given private wealth preferential treatment. Piketty explains:

> At the beginning of the 1970s, the total value of private wealth (net of debt) stood between two and three and a half years of national income in all the rich countries on all continents. Forty years later in 2010, private wealth represented between four and seven years of national income in all the countries under study. (Piketty 2014: 173)

Today's global patrimonial capitalism is characterized by a massive transfer of public wealth into private hands and "immense inequities (some individuals are now as wealthy as entire countries)" (Piketty 2014: 471). This situation is unsustainable because as private wealth concentrates in fewer and fewer hands forces of divergence set in, producing severe social inequities that are "potentially incompatible with the meritocratic values and principles of social justice fundamental to modern democratic societies," Piketty explains (2014: 26).

In spite of a very thorough analysis of the social implications of growth and inequality, however, Piketty does not devote a great deal of attention to the environmental impact of these economic developments. Nonetheless, he does describe the connection between patrimonial capitalism, as a phenomenon that has resulted in a massive decline in public wealth, and the relationship this has with natural resource extraction:

> The annual rent derived from the exploitation of natural resources, defined as the difference between receipts from sales and the cost of production, has been about 5 percent of global GDP since the mid-2000s (half of which is petroleum rent and the rest rent on other natural resources, mainly gas, coal, minerals, and wood), compared with about 2 percent in the 1990s and less than 1 percent in the early 1970s. (Piketty 2014: 459)

What Piketty misses is that in addition to the rent-seeking activities associated with the exploitation of natural resources, patrimonial capitalism is producing massive environmental degradation. Environmental degradation refers to changes in the climate, loss of habitat and habitat fragmentation, damage inflicted on ecosystem vitality, decrease in the quality and quantity of natural resources, pollution, toxicity, and biodiversity loss. Factors influencing the degradation of the life-world include rapid urbanization, industrialized agriculture, dirty energy, and a growing global middle class of eager consumers with unsustainable ecological footprints (United Nations 2013).

Eco-marxist critics have long argued that environmental damage is an externalized cost of economic growth (O'Connor 1997). Since the beginning of industrialization the environment has borne the brunt of the economic development burden, providing the raw materials necessary for production while becoming a dumping ground for pollution. Capitalism, as John Bellamy Foster, Brett Clark, and Richard York sum it up, is "incurring an enormous ecological debt" using up "environmental resources and the absorptive capacity of the environment while displacing the costs back on Earth itself" (Foster et al. 2010: 45). All in all, the direct cost of economic growth to the environment and the often indirect costs to communities living in the vicinity of environmental hazards are not factored into the overall cost of a commodity or service (Bullard et al. 1997). In other words, environmental degradation and social injustice are connected negative externalities of capital.

Let's take a moment to sketch out some of the defining features of capital by returning to that eminent and influential thinker, Karl Marx. The linchpin of Marx's understanding of capital is that it is a process, not a thing (Marx 1990 [1867]: 247–57). Marx explains that the process of capital accumulation consists of production, exchange, circulation, and the generation of wealth (money, assets, rent). Commodities are produced for exchange on the market to generate surplus value. Commodities hold both a use and exchange value. A use value is directly consumed and satisfies a human need, whereas the commodity's exchange value is actualized when the commodity is sold. Marx used the formula M-C-M to summarize the process of using money to buy a commodity that is then re-sold for a profit (Marx 1990 [1867]: 248–9). Surplus value isn't realized until the commodity is sold for money. Prior to money entering the equation surplus value exists merely as an unrealized speculative value. In this respect money doesn't just measure value; it is also a medium of circulation. It is the movement arising from exchange that facilitates the accumulation of capital, because through exchange, surplus is generated.

However, price does not accurately represent the real costs of a given commodity. There are a range of social and environmental damages that are part of the production, circulation, and exchange of commodities that are used for free. Neither producers, nor consumers, pay for negative environmental costs such as air and water pollution, aquifer depletion, or deforestation. Some environmental costs, such as the natural resources used in production, do enter the price structure of a commodity as "raw materials," but there are many environmental costs, such as emitting carbon into the atmosphere or water contamination and depletion, that come free. Furthermore, the complex environmental costs arising from each stage of a commodity's global life cycle remain externalized (Patel 2008; Leonard 2010). For example, the real cost of a car does not honestly represent the environmental damage that comes from mining the coal to produce the energy needed in the production of steel, or the chemicals used in plastics or spray paint which contaminate water supplies, nor does it reflect the social and environmental costs of oil spills from the gas used to power the trucks that transport the cars to car dealerships. Then there are future environmental costs such as the amount of GHGs that the car will pump into the atmosphere during its lifetime and which are driving climate change, or the expanding number of landfills dotted around the globe where the car will eventually be dumped.

Capital engenders numerous negative environmental externalities. Carbon emissions from human activities are causing global climate change. In addition, the unsustainable extraction rate of groundwater supplies is placing global water resources under stress (Konikow and Kendy 2005). Then there is the contamination of water supplies and the havoc this wreaks on ecosystems. Environmental accidents such as the BP Deepwater Horizon oil spill in 2010, one of the worst oil spills in US history, spewed approximately 170 million gallons into the Gulf, killing 11 workers and injuring 16 more, with severe effects for flora and fauna and injuring thousands of birds, marine life, and sea turtles. The combination of pollution, climate change, and the destruction of natural habitats has caused the planet's sixth mass extinction of plants and animals, with the present rate of species extinction estimated at between 1,000 and 10,000 times the natural extinction rate (see Tilman et al. 1994; Chivian and Bernstein 2008). This is an alarming indication of biodiversity loss, which threatens to irreparably weaken genetic diversity and trigger extensive ecosystem distress and collapse.

In addition, capital ignores the value added of natural ecosystem processes. Basically producers and consumers are free-riding the benefits of the environment (depleting a public good or service whilst reaping the advantages without paying for it). Indeed, a report issued by Corporate Eco Forum (CEF) in 2013 estimated that nature provided "$72 trillion worth of free goods and services" to the global economy (CEF 2013: 5). Piketty (2014: 62) estimates the price tag of the 2012 global economy to be approximately 70 trillion euros (US$97 trillion), thus nature provided over 72 percent of goods and services to global output for free. The important point is that neither the direct and indirect costs of production and economic growth, nor the benefits of environment, are in the current exchange value. It is the environment and communities that end up absorbing the costs and impacts of this disconnect.

The Regulatory State and Neo-liberal Governance

One way to curb negative environmental externalities is through governmental regulation. The environmental movement of the 1960s and 1970s was an important ingredient in achieving this. It raised the public's environmental consciousness and placed pressure on governments to introduce environmental legislation and legal frameworks to hold polluters accountable. The movement harnessed the social energies invested in other political movements—anti-war, anti-nuclear, labor, civil rights, and feminist—placing these in the service of an environmental agenda. It presented a unified political front traversing the differentiated landscape of identity politics popular at the time.

Celebrated environmental achievements in the United States were the Clean Air Act of 1970 and the Clean Water Act of 1972. In the UK the Clean Air Act was passed in 1968. In Europe Norway introduced a Nature Conservation Act (1970), the European Council declared the first five-year Environment Action Programme (1972), and the Environment Protection Act was approved in Switzerland by popular vote (it didn't come into effect until 1985). In the Southern Hemisphere New Zealand approved its Clean Air Act (1972) and a Marine Reserves Act (1971), whilst Australia introduced the National Parks and Wildlife Conservation Act (1975) and the Australian state of New South Wales passed the Environment and Planning Assessment Act (1979). Numerous political parties with environmental agendas popped up: the Popular Movement for the Environment in Switzerland (1972), the United Kingdom's People Party (1973) that later became the Ecology Party (1975) and then the UK Green Party (1985), and the German Green Party (1980). The rising popularity of environmental politics ushered in numerous non-governmental activist organizations. A few notable examples include Greenpeace (1972), which is committed to promoting peace through environmental protection and conservation, and the fundraising activities of the World Wildlife Fund (1961), aimed at preserving the diversity of life on earth.

Why is it that despite all the successes of the environmental movement toward the latter part of the twentieth century environmental damage continued at a brisk pace? On environmental issues, regulation and legal frameworks only work if governments serve as arbitrators between public and private interests. In the case of climate change and emissions regulations, the rise of neo-liberal governance from the 1970s, followed by an aggressive corporate campaign that cast doubt over climate science, and which morphed into warning the public against the adverse economic effects of emissions regulations, set the environmental movement back.

Developed countries, such as the United States and Australia, dragged their heels over ratifying the Kyoto Protocol (1997) because their governments maintained that it gave developing countries an unfair economic advantage and interfered with domestic economic growth. Understandably, environmentalists argued that the importance of ratifying Kyoto was to avoid catastrophic changes to the earth's climate system, which would impact all. What remained unquestioned however was the neo-liberal premise at the core of Kyoto: property rights.

The policy to institute carbon emissions trading, central to Kyoto and subsequent negotiations, presupposes that the corporate sector owns the atmosphere. You can't sell something if you don't already own it. But such a market gives wealthy countries a right to dump carbon dioxide and buy another's surplus if the emissions cap is exceeded. In their support of Kyoto, leading environmental organizations such as Greenpeace and the David Suzuki Foundation have left unquestioned Kyoto's underlying neo-liberal logic of property ownership and privatizing carbon emissions (Environmental Defense Fund; Greenpeace; Suzuki 2009). This selfsame logic in the context of governance has resulted in the political institution of representative democracy putting its muscle behind private wealth ahead of the public good.

As with the growth of inequality, the neo-liberalization of environmental policy in the United States can be traced back to the Reagan era. Whilst in office, Reagan rolled back many environmental safeguards, opened millions of acres of national land for fossil fuel development, and set about introducing market mechanisms into environmental regulations (Heynan et al. 2007: 11–13). Rolling back on government regulations meant downsizing the public sector; this included cutting the budget of the Environmental Protection Agency (EPA) and slowing down its enforcement program. By 1983 EPA officials resigned en masse. In 1987 Reagan vetoed the reauthorization of the Clean Water Act, only to have this overturned by Congress. Questioning the scientific findings linking pollution to acid rain, Reagan reneged on his promise to Canadian Prime Minister Trudeau to honor his predecessor's agreement to enforce pollution standards in the United States, in order to address American contributions to acid rain in Canada.

Crossing the oceans to the UK another infamous proponent of neo-liberalism, Prime Minister Margaret Thatcher (1979–90), also embarked on a series of cavalier deregulatory initiatives. With the "Big Bang" reforms of 1986 Thatcher reorganized the City of London, deregulating financial markets, turning the City into an international financial center. She instituted a private market in land by repealing the Community Land Act, which had achieved "positive planning through public control over development" (Blowers 1987: 281). And she pioneered the introduction of enterprise zones that exempted developers from paying rates in an effort to liberate "land and property markets from the detailed process of development controls" (Blowers 1987: 282). Greenbelt areas were opened up for development and greater freedoms were accorded industrial and commercial developers. Furthermore, large farming interests were given preference over conservation efforts.

Basically, environmental legislation may be one way to force companies to stop free riding and internalize the costs of negative environmental externalities in capital, but this hinges upon governments introducing environmental legislation and regulation to stop environmental harms from occurring and by bringing the full force of the law to bear on dealing with environmental harms. Neo-liberal governance exacerbates the tension between advancing the public good and a state that facilitates and promotes the free market economy alongside the interests of the private sector, thereby undermining the regulatory mechanism that forces previously externalized costs to be internalized.

On the international stage, neo-liberal governance resulted in financial organizations, such as the International Monetary Fund (IMF) and World Bank, imposing structural adjustment policies on "under-developed" countries. Policies of the IMF and World Bank boosted the power of the corporate sector and free market. Restructuring involved fiscal austerity measures, opening up the local economy to foreign investors, privatizing state-owned industries, introducing export driven economic strategies, and deregulating local currencies. Putting the appalling abuse of human rights to one side for a moment, the environmental consequences of these restructuring efforts were frightful (Cruz and Repetto 1992; George 1992; Owusu 1998). Restructuring measures resulted in environmental protections and regulations being loosened or lifted entirely. For instance, under the IMF program Ghana restructured its forestry sector, replacing the

Ghana Timber Marketing Board with the Timber Export Development Board to facilitate timber exports and the Forest Products Inspection Bureau to oversee production. In addition Ghana lifted forest conservation restrictions (Owusu 1998: 425–9). Natural resource extraction increased to meet the demands of the export market in raw materials. The devaluation of the national currency caused prices on wood products to fall on global markets, spurring on deforestation as demand intensified. Unsurprisingly, during 1983–93 the volume of logs exported from Ghana jumped 806 percent and lumber exports increased 500 percent (Owusu 1998: 428). In addition to natural resources for export, capital began to enforce the privatization of environmental goods and services. For example, between 1990 and 2002 the World Bank made water reform policies a condition of approximately one-third of the loans it granted, forcing lendees to agree to the privatization of the country's water resources (Center for Public Integrity 2003).

On the one hand, the global economy was booming amidst deregulation and the massive restructuring of economies the world over. On the other hand, the environmental situation was worsening and GHG emissions were on the rise. The first Intergovernmental Panel on Climate Change (IPCC) assessment report (1990) confirmed that human activities were connected to GHG emissions and a higher concentration of CO_2 in the atmosphere, which was causing the earth's surface to warm. Admitting there were some uncertainties, the IPCC was confident enough to publicly recommend a reduction in global GHG emissions. Climate change became a public issue and the pressure on industry actors was mounting with grassroots organizations mobilizing their forces around campaigns including the Global Warming Divestiture Campaign. Industry responded by joining forces to combat the legitimacy of climate science, forming industry sponsored think tanks and associations to lobby against environmental regulations that would inevitably hurt their bottom line. The Global Climate Coalition (GCC) (1989–2002) successfully lobbied the US government to avoid mandatory emissions controls in the lead up to the Earth Summit (Rio de Janeiro 1992). With the financial support of the oil, coal, gas, and automobile industries the GCC campaigned hard to persuade the public that GHG emissions would not pose a threat. Indeed, the GCC went so far as to claim there would be substantial benefits to higher levels of CO_2 maintaining this would improve crop production and in turn alleviate poverty. However, as the scientific evidence in support of human activities negatively causing the climate to change mounted, the smear campaign of scientific uncertainty eventually became an untenable position for industry actors to hold.

On 11 December 1997 the Kyoto Protocol was adopted (to be enforced on 16 February 2005). The treaty committed countries to internationally binding emissions reductions of 5 percent below 1990 levels by the years 2008–12. Industry shifted gears, pushing back against environmental regulation and threatening it would lead to job cuts and economic collapse. The GCC announced that slowing emissions by 20 percent "could reduce the US gross domestic product by 4% and cost Americans up to 1.1 million jobs annually" (as cited in Schlichting 2013: 501). The Competitive Enterprise Institute urged the public that the Kyoto agreement would "cripple the economy." The Heartland Institute calculated Kyoto would "cut economic growth by 50% by the year

2050" (Schlichting 2013: 501). Under President George W. Bush the United States withdrew from Kyoto entirely, announcing it would be "harming the economy and hurting American workers" (Reynolds 2001).

The GCC vehemently opposed the United States ratifying the Kyoto Protocol. It spent approximately US$13 million on the anti-Kyoto campaign (Hamilton 1998: 35). Documents have shown that US under-secretary of state (2001–04), Paula Dobriansky, acknowledged the United States "rejected Kyoto in part based on input from you [Global Climate Coalition]" and showed deep appreciation for the active involvement of Exxon executives in formulating US climate change policy (Vidal 2005).

What this brief trot through contemporary environmental history and policy demonstrates is an absence of fair play as the private sector increasingly influenced government to water down its position on environmental protections. The corporate world had reached deep into their pockets to pressure government not to introduce environmental regulations, going as far as to obstruct environmental justice. The environmental movement fought back with the message that GHG emissions would eventually slow economic activity, adding that there were many economic benefits to being at the forefront of clean energy and technological solutions to climate change. Director of Greenpeace US Global Warming Campaign, Kert Davies explained: "President Bush is wrong when he says reducing GHG emissions will hurt the US economy. Bush ignores the economic benefits of US leadership on 21st century energy technology" (as cited in Greenpeace 2001). But with this simple discursive shift to economic justification, the complicity between environmental activism and capital accumulation had begun.

Environmental Opportunism

What we are dealing with is a change in the "dominant form of valuation" as Foster, Clarke, and York write. That is to say, on the one hand, "in our age of global ecological crisis" capitalism profits from the "destruction of the planet" (Foster et al. 71–2); on the other, the "growth of natural scarcity is seen as a golden opportunity in which to further privatize the world's commons" (Foster et al. 70) and accumulate capital. This situation has even given rise to a new model of economic growth, coined "green capitalism" or "green economics." Here, environmental degradation and climate change not only pave the way for the privatization of public assets and common pool resources, but also offer entirely new market opportunities.

With the publication of *Natural Capitalism*, a new model of economic growth was rolled out, promising a competitive advantage and healthy profits for companies that were willing to reduce, reuse, and recycle waste (Hawken et al. 1999). The goal of natural capitalism is to place social, economic, and environmental values "on the balance sheet" so that "nothing is marginalized or externalized" (Hawken et al. 1999: 319). They vouch for an economic system that values all forms of capital.

The thesis of natural capitalism is similar to the one espoused by architect William McDonough and chemist Michael Braungart, who teamed up to write *Cradle to Cradle* (an influential text in the design world). In it they advocate the business sector make better choices that will both improve the bottom line and be environmentally friendly. However, McDonough and Braungart position themselves against the natural capitalism business model of reduce, reuse, and recycle, which they claim relies on an outdated model handed down to us from the Industrial Revolution. Instead of a cradle to grave model they propose business do more with less by closing the loop on waste using the formula "waste equals food." The idea that business is inherently bad for the environment was therefore turned on its head and replaced with a model that views business as providing nourishment for the environment (McDonough and Braungart 2002).

Green economics recognizes that if a value for nature's goods and services can be set, this would provide enough motivation for the private sector to shift to cleaner energy sources, pollute less, and basically start investing in green technologies and business models. In so doing, it identifies a use-value for nature that is both a product of human labor and satisfies a human need, along with an exchange value that comes from selling an environmentally conscious commodity or service. Yet not all aspects of the green economy are involved with producing green commodities or services. The green economy encompasses many activities that accrue capital without necessarily producing anything new. For instance, in the carbon offset market capital is generated by simply owning, or claiming ownership of, a forest. Profits are made from having control over access to water resources. Capital is accumulated through the sale of permits to use a natural resource. These are all examples of rent seeking activities as Piketty has documented—capital is accrued not because anything new is created but because an individual or group has claimed ownership, or monopoly control, over what is otherwise a commons (a resource openly shared by different parties—people, animals, ecosystems). Rents are extracted from the labor of the earth's ecosystems and the reservoir of natural resources provided by the planet. This darker underbelly of power and the undue advantage that arises from this is not sufficiently addressed by green economics.

The optimism surrounding the greening of the economy witnessed the emergence of an entirely new breed of capitalism: the clean green capitalism epitomized by figures such as former Walmart president H. Lee Scott Jr. (2000–09), who led the greening of Walmart initiative. Then there is the re-branding of multinational oil and gas company BP—once referred to as British Petroleum, it adopted an environmentally politically correct image of Beyond Petroleum (see Parr 2009: 16–19, 2013: 130–44). Eventually environmental initiatives entered the corporate responsibility programs of multinational corporations such as Coca Cola, BP, and ExxonMobil; what was once a counterpoint to capitalism—the state of the environment—had become the newest and latest market opportunity.

Examples of the growth in the green economy abound. There is the growing market in carbon trading, carbon offsets, the robust private investment sector in developing and expanding clean and green energy options through the use of solar and wind, and the rise of the green commodity like the fuel efficient Toyota hybrid Prius. In 2008 the voluntary carbon market was worth approximately US$728.1 million (Hamilton et al. 2010). In 2011 Achim Steiner, the UN Under-Secretary General and UNEP Executive Director, reported it was "up 17% to $257 billion—a six-fold increase on the 2004 figure and 93% higher than the total in 2007, the year before the world financial crisis" (UNEP and Frankfurt School 2012: 5).

By the twenty-first century it was becoming publicly offensive for industry actors to continue looking the other way on environmentally unsound business practices, which is a testimony to the political density of environmental degradation. Warnings over not greening the economy laid out in the 2007 Stern Review are just one indication of this shift in attitude. The Stern Review provided an alarming synopsis of the economic costs associated with not lowering GHG emissions: "the overall costs and risks of climate change will be equivalent to losing at least 5% of global GDP each year, now and forever. If a wider range of risks and impacts is taken into account, the estimates of damage could rise to 20% of GDP or more" (Great Britain Treasury 2007: vi).

Big business was vigorously moving from brown to green, verifying just how far society had come in dealing with the magnitude of the environmental problem. However, at the same time the activist corner of environmentalism was falling into obscurity due to its cooptation by the principles of neo-liberalism, which turned the environmental issue into a problem of changing individual consumption patterns. The cultural shift that accompanied public enthusiasm for environmentalism inaugurated the emergence of a new environmentally aware consumer and in the process the deeper systemic issue of the unsustainable nature of endless capital accumulation faded from view (Parr 2009: 15–31; Foster et al. 2010: 377–99). To prevent this shift in focus from negatively impacting the bottom line, environmental externalities were addressed using market mechanisms. This would make green business a win–win as industry actors could re-emerge as both rescuing the environment and bolstering economic activity. Capital had successfully overcome the limit environmental degradation had posed by appropriating it and placing it back in the service of capital accumulation.

However, over the same time period, the benefits of economic gains became even more concentrated within the hands of a few wealthy individuals (the income for the world's wealthiest 1 percent increased 60 percent from 1993–2013 (Oxfam 2013: 2)), while the rest of the world was slipping further and further into a cycle of poverty and environmental degradation. As Naomi Klein bleakly points out, with environmental harms and changes in climate adversely affecting the poor we face a "collective future of disaster apartheid in which survival is determined by who can afford to pay for escape... Perhaps part of the reason why so many of our elites, both political and corporate, are so sanguine about climate change is that they are confident they will be able to buy their way out of the worst of it" (Klein 2007: 530). Actually, they are also confident they can profit from it.

When faced with crisis, such as the looming threat of climate change or the collapse of ecosystems, those who manage the flows of capital seize upon and transform such limits into the new frontiers of capital accumulation. As Klein sums it up, "Not so long ago, disasters were periods of social leveling, rare moments when atomized communities put divisions aside and pulled together. Increasingly, however, disasters are the opposite: they provide windows into a cruel and ruthlessly divided future in which money and race buy survival" (Klein 2007: 522). In *The Shock Doctrine* Klein chronicles how environmental disasters, like other disasters (economic and conflict), are harnessed to push through neo-liberal restructuring measures. This entails displacing entire communities, further disenfranchising the already disenfranchised, and seizing land for redevelopment under the guise of reconstruction.

The corporate opportunism of the reconstruction process that swept through both Sri Lanka after the 2004 Tsunami and New Orleans in the wake of Hurricane Katrina in 2005 resulted in "victimizing the victims, exploiting the exploited" says Klein, quoting her guide Kumari (Klein 2007: 492). The end result in Sri Lanka was that the fishing communities underwent a second "tsunami of corporate globalization," first losing their homes on the beachfront to the tsunami, and second losing out to the tourism industry. In New Orleans privatized reconstruction efforts after the storm neither employed local labor nor invested in developing much needed public infrastructure. Rather, as government resorted to outsourcing its responsibilities, the few scraps of the public that remained in New Orleans were either gutted or privatized.

When we throw trade liberalization into the mix, then the poverty–environmental nexus sharpens. Trade liberalization promotes pollution-intensive industries and environmentally harmful activities to be located in the so-called "developing world" where environmental standards are relatively lenient and regulations that do exist are not effectively implemented because of endemic corruption and bribery.

Conclusions

Environmental degradation is an effect of the unequal relations of power that drive and are driven by capitalist social relations. Put simply, some people exploit the environment and benefit from that exploitation more than others whilst the benefits are not equally distributed. Environmental degradation and crises exacerbate the already skewed global landscape of wealth and poverty. A minority benefits as their wealth and power expands; meanwhile, an exploited majority remains marginalized. Viewed this way, environmental problems are socially structured just as much as they are an expression of hierarchical capitalist social relations. A political trajectory appears as the majority collectivizes around environmental issues to articulate the trenchant systems of exploitation afflicting both people and other than human species. In this regard environmental degradation is both a political object and subject, it is the basis for political struggle and at the same time unequal capitalist social relations are inherent to the problem of environmental degradation. The most important lesson to take away from this is that capital accumulation and environmental degradation are inextricably joined.

It is too easy to explain climate change and environmental degradation as an effect of "human activities." This is a neo-liberal spin, for it places the solution back in the hands of individual people to change their everyday lives. It is the process of capital accumulation that is driving environmental degradation. Making this claim is not to naively dismiss the impact human activities are having on the environment, but more significantly it is to turn the spotlight onto the structure of violence mediating the squeaky clean neo-liberal image of individual freedom and boundless choice whereby the problem of environmental degradation is simply solved by placing a price on nature's resources and services or by just making a greener lifestyle choice.

Human activities do not equally inflict damage on the environment. It is important to resist oversimplifying and thereby depoliticizing what is otherwise a deeply political issue and that means not obscuring how the human activities in question *work*. Human relations are themselves producing and reproducing capitalist social relations and it is important to remember that not everyone in this situation has contributed equally to environmental degradation.

The issue of capitalist crisis summons us to think more closely about the fundamental premises upon which the case for green capitalism rests. Shifting to a green economy and introducing the concept of natural capital into our thinking about the use and consumption of natural resources is not a politically responsible rejoinder to the issue of environmental degradation. Indeed, this displaces the much deeper problem of endless economic growth and the neo-liberal logic driving our response to negative economic externalities.

Negative economic externalities, such as pollution and greenhouse gas emissions, are costs that remain unaccounted for in the price structure of a commodity or service. The question is what to do about them. Will government regulation effectively internalize these costs (Pigou 1920), especially in a political climate that advances private interests ahead of public interests? Or, should we institute new forms of private property so as to create a platform for competition to incentivize the internalization of these costs (Coase 1960)? Both assume markets are transparent rational mechanisms that create neat and tidy relationships between costs and benefits and which translate consumer choices into prices. In this regard both positions can be traced back to liberal thinking. Indeed the very nature of the problem and the dominant solutions to it tell us something important about the situation of the public good: private interests prevail at the expense of the public interest. In other words, the solutions on offer to environmental degradation are reinforcing and legitimating the source of the problem, namely, the transfer of public wealth into private hands.

The green turn in commodity culture at best directs the activist impulse of an otherwise engaged political subject into a narcissist in which environmentalism and the social inequities connected to it become nothing more than the setting for self-realization. At worst it validates capitalist society and the private property relation along with the model of growth underpinning these, both of which landed us in the mess in the first place.

It is fair to say that environmental activism, as a social movement, has been integrated into the process of capital accumulation. The environmental movement needs to urgently revive itself as a social movement and engage in a critique of the deeper structural issues of capital accumulation, economic growth, and the private property relation. How can a price be set on the smells, colors, and textures emanating from a field bursting into bloom as springtime comes around? What price could possibly be put on the enriching sounds of wildlife awaking in the trees and rustling through the leaves? And how might the sensations arising from sunlight and shadow playfully dancing across the forest floor ever have a monetary value? These affective dimensions of life are priceless, and perhaps their affective power comes from the way in which they defy abstraction in the monetary form and the privatization of collective life.

References

Blowers, A. (1987). "Transition or Transformation? Environmental Policy Under Thatcher." *Public Administration* 65(3): 277–94.

BP. (2014). *Alternative energy.* http://www.bp.com/en/global/corporate/sustainability/the-energy-future/alternative-energy.html Accessed February 6, 2014.

Bullard, R. D., Johnson, G. S., and Wright, B. H. (1997). "Confronting Environmental Injustice: It's the Right Thing to Do." *Race, Gender, and Class* 5(1): 63–79.

Chivian, E. and Bernstein, A., eds. (2008). *Sustaining life: How Human Health Depends on Biodiversity* (New York: Center for Health and the Global Environment. Oxford University Press).

Center for Public Integrity and International Consortium of Investigative Journalists. (2003). *Promoting Privatization* (Washington DC: Center for Public Integrity and International Consortium of Investigative Journalists). http://projects.publicintegrity.org/water/report.aspx?aid=45 Accessed May 5, 2014.

Coase, R. H. (1960). "The Problem of Social Cost." *Journal of Law and Economics* 3: 1–44.

Corporate Eco Forum. (2013). *The New Business Imperative: Valuing Natural Capital.* http://www.corporateecoforum.com/valuingnaturalcapital/ Accessed January 4, 2014.

Cruz, W. and Repetto, R. (1992). *The Environmental Effects of Stabilization and Structural Adjustment Programs: The Philippines Case* (Washington, DC: World Resources Institute).

Environmental Defense Fund. "How Cap and Trade Works." http://www.edf.org/climate/how-cap-and-trade-works Accessed April 10, 2014.

Foster. J., Clark, B., and York, R. (2010). *The Ecological Rift: Capitalism's War on the Earth* (New York: Monthly Review Press).

George, S. (1992). *A Fate Worse than Debt* (Hammondsworth: Penguin).

Great Britain Treasury. (2007). *The Economics of Climate Change: The Stern Review* (Cambridge: Cambridge University Press).

Greenpeace. (2001). "U.S withdraws from Kyoto Protocol." *Greenpeace USA.* Feature Story April, 5. http://www.greenpeace.org/usa/en/news-and-blogs/news/u-s-withdraws-from-kyoto-prot/ Accessed January 3, 2014.

Greenpeace. *Kyoto.* http://www.greenpeace.org/international/en/campaigns/climate-change/a/governments/kyoto/ Accessed April 10, 2014.

Hamilton, K. (1998). *The Oil Industry and Climate Change* (Amsterdam: Greenpeace International). http://www.greenpeace.org/international/Global/international/planet-2/report/2006/3/the-oil-industry-and-climate-c.pdf Accessed January 4, 2014.

Hamilton, K., Milo, S., Peters-Stanley, M., and Marcello, T. (2010). *State of the Voluntary Carbon Markets 2010* (New York. Ecosystem Marketplace and Bloomberg New Energy Finance).

Hawken, P., Lovins, A., and Lovins, H. (1999). *Natural Capitalism: Creating the Next Industrial Revolution* (Boston: Little Brown and Company).

Heynan, N., McCarthy, J., Prudham, S., and Robbins, P., eds. (2007). *Neoliberal Environments: False Promises Unnatural Promises* (London: Routledge).

Klein, N. (2007). *The Shock Doctrine: Disaster Capitalism* (New York: Picador).

Konikow, L. F and Kendy, E. (2005). "Groundwater Depletion a Global Problem." *Hydrogeology Journal* 13(1) (March): 317–20.

Leonard, A. (2010). *The Story of Stuff: How Our Obsession with Stuff is Trashing the Planet, Our Communities, and Our Health* (New York: Free Press).

Marx, K. (1990 [1867]). *Capital: Volume 1*. Translated by B. Fowkes (London: Penguin).

McDonough, W. and Braungart, M. (2002). *Cradle to Cradle: Remaking the Way We Make Things* (New York: North Point Press).

O'Connor, J. (1997). *Natural Causes: Essays in Ecological Marxism* (New York: Guilford Press).

Owusu, J. H. (1998). "Current Convenience, Desperate Deforestation: Ghana's Adjustment Program and the Forestry Sector." *Professional Geographer* 50(4) (November): 418–36.

Oxfam. (2013). *Oxfam Media Briefing*. Ref: 02/2013. January 18. http://www.oxfam.org/sites/www.oxfam.org/files/cost-of-inequality-oxfam-mb180113.pdf Accessed January 8, 2014.

Parr, A. (2009). *Hijacking Sustainability* (Cambridge, MA: MIT Press).

Parr, A. (2013). *The Wrath of Capital: Neoliberalism and Climate Change Politics* (New York: Columbia University Press).

Patel, R. (2008). *Stuffed and Starved: Markets, Power, and the Hidden Battle for the World Food System* (New York: Melville House).

Pigou, A. C. (1920). *The Economics of Welfare* (London. Macmillan).

Piketty, T. (2014). *Capital in the Twenty-First Century*. Translated by A. Goldhammer (Cambridge, MA: The Belknap Press of Harvard University Press).

Public Citizen. (2005). *Veolia Environment: A Corporate Profile*, Water for All Campaign. Washington D.C. Public Citizen. http://www.citizen.org/documents/Vivendi-USFilter.pdf Accessed May 5, 2014.

Reynolds, P. (2001). "Kyoto: Why Did the US Pull Out?" *BBC News*. March 30. http://news.bbc.co.uk/2/hi/americas/1248757.stm Accessed January, 3 2014.

Schlichting, I. (2013). "Strategic Framing of Climate Change by Industry Actors: A Meta-analysis." *Environmental Communication* 7(4) (December): 493–511.

Suzuki, D. (2009). "Carbon Offsets as a Tool in the Fight Against Global Warming." *David Suzuki Foundation*. http://www.straight.com/news/david-suzuki-carbon-offsets-tool-fight-against-global-warming Accessed April 10, 2014.

United Nations. (2013). *World Economic and Social Survey 2013: Sustainable Development Challenges* (New York: United Nations Publication, Department of Economic and Social Affairs) http://sustainabledevelopment.un.org/content/documents/2843WESS2013.pdf Accessed February 6, 2014.

Tilman, D., May, R., Lehman, C. L., and Nowak, M. A. (1994). "Habitat Destruction and the Extinction Debt." *Nature* 371: 65–6.

UNEP and the Frankfurt School of Finance and Management. (2012). *Global Trends in Renewable Energy Investment 2012*. http://fs-unep-centre.org/sites/default/files/publications/globaltrendsreport2012.pdf Accessed January 1, 2014.

Vidal, J. (2005). "Revealed: How Oil Giant Influenced Bush." *The Guardian*. Wednesday June 8. http://www.theguardian.com/news/2005/jun/08/usnews.climatechange Accessed December 20, 2013.

World Bank. (2007). *Global Economic Prospects 2007: Managing the Next Wave of Globalization* (Washington, DC: The International Bank for Reconstruction and Development/The World Bank).

CHAPTER 30

ENVIRONMENTAL GOVERNMENTALITY

TIMOTHY W. LUKE

As the introduction and preceding chapters in this collection have illustrated, environmental political theory is becoming much more salient and significant in framing new ethical, political, and social analyses of contemporary life. This comparatively new school of political thought, or style of policy critique, has never ratified a foundational text for itself nor assumed a definitive scholarly profile on the shifting terrains of academe despite its obvious importance. It is not clear at this juncture in its development, however, that a canonical anchor is even feasible. As Goodin (1992: vii) observes about green political theory, "considering the diversity of positions . . . that project would quickly degenerate into taxonomic tedium even if it did not prove altogether impossible." Still, a wide variety of cultural, political, social, technological, and urban thinkers (Ophuls 1977; Merchant 1980; Dryzek 1987; Eckersley 1992; Hay 2002) have contributed many conceptual innovations and moral insights to advance the project of environmental political theorists as they refine their understandings of politics and the environment, particularly as they relate to governmentality.

At a tacit level, critical studies of commercialization, industrialization, rationalization, or urbanization in political theory rarely stray far from deeply embedded conflicts, which rightly should be classified as essentially ecological questions for the economy, society, and state. As individual and collective worries about the viability of human and non-human life on the earth become more urgent with its continuing ecological degradation brought on by global modernization, the political dilemmas that the state and/or society now face in their moral understandings of, and technological dealings with, the environment clearly have become, "the very essence of government—that is, the art of exercising power in the form of economy" (Foucault 1991: 92).

This chapter asserts environmental political theorists must concentrate their intellectual efforts upon both "the ecology" and "the economy" to protect the environment, maintain order, and attain the good life through more effective political interventions. It will first provide an overview of governmentality as this concept was developed by

Michel Foucault. Second, it explores his notion of "milieux" as it relates to environmental governmentality and green political action. Third, it then develops a more specific conceptualization of the operational implementations of governmentality in environmental applications. Finally, it stresses the importance of political reflexivity and resistance in countering the largely managerial impulses behind environmental governmentality to revitalize individual and group engagement in resisting ecological degradation at multiple points of resistance.

Governmentality and the Environment

Governmentality is a useful notion, particularly in its environmental or green articulations, for addressing political questions about the conduct of conduct by individuals and groups in their interactions with the environment, society, and themselves, because "what government has to do with is not territory but rather a sort of complex composed of men and things" (Foucault 1991:93). The operational engagements of governmentality, can help to define, in part, some of environmental political theory's most complex concerns, while they also spotlight a few of the policy solutions put forward to cope with environmental crises. Unlike so much traditional political theory, which endows political agency and moral force mostly to humans (mainly individuals that are older, male, warriors, and propertied within the social order of any given polis), and who perhaps then are empowered as sovereign agents to rule or otherwise serve in different institutional social roles to exert control, environmental governmentality is quite different. This set of practices concerns the exertion of control over the complex interrelations of humans and things, focusing on the conjoined activities of citizens and sovereigns as well as the not-citizen, non-organic, not-resident, or non-human elements of societies.

These social forces typically have been confined to the *oikos* rather than freed in the state due to their lack of positions or privileges to exert control in accordance with custom, law, or philosophy. Green governmentality heeds the presence of traditional political actors, but it also acknowledges how thoroughly the workings of power and knowledge across the whole society produce many other subjects and structures with materially significant differences as agents (Kuehls 1996; Princen 2010; Wapner 2010). Few, if any, of these often occluded players should be ignored by political theory, especially when looking at structural issues tied to environmental governmentality.

From climate change to biodiversity loss, environmental governmentality discourse is engaged in mapping out new domains of truth, in which the knowledge and/or data needed to categorize, judge, and manage the operational mission of economic, political, and social institutions become engaged in managing the "complex composed of men and things" in the built, unbuilt, or yet-to-be-built environment. These codes of knowledge produce powers that, in turn, enable certain specific new modes of subjectivity to emerge from, and then co-evolve with, larger populations, markets, and ecosystems. Environmental governmentality endeavors to provide and police a range of conduct for the conduct of green ways of living, which are sometimes accepted as normal and other times contested as oppressive, irrational, or unjust. Within these eco-managerial maneuvers, this expression of green governmentality requires an ever more complex and sophisticated mobilization of the environmental sciences to be deployed with management-oriented foci.

As Soule and Press (1998: 398) describe developments in the 1960s, "environmental studies programs were pioneers in this rare era of academic experimentation, and ecology—the 'subversive science' was often the centerpiece." However, environmental sciences, when viewed through the lens of governmentality studies, have also become productive power/knowledge nodes "in which are articulated the efforts of a certain type of power and the reference of a certain type of knowledge, the machinery by which the power relations give rise to a possible corpus of knowledge" (Foucault 1980b: 92). Such knowledge extends and reinforces its effects from crisis to crisis, since crisis management has morphed into a major modality of contemporary governance (Baudrillard 2001: 254–63). At the same time, human individuals themselves are being made more responsible, out in the shifting currents of crisis during a time that many now call "the Anthropocene" (Zalasiewicz, Williams, Steffen, and Crutzen 2010: 2228–31), for themselves in managing the conduct of their conduct. Whether it is deemed ecological, green, or sustainable citizenship, these civic subjectivities are positioned in dense networks of expert discourse and technical structure such that power and personhood co-evolve in "the multiplicity of force relations immanent in the sphere in which they operate and which constitute their own organization" (Foucault 1980b: 92).

Governance from without and above as well as within and below soon becomes co-constitutive with environmental governmentality. As "the environment" (Luke 1994: 57–81) circumscribes, surrounds, encircles persons and places, environmental governance authorities and/or managerial experts simultaneously empower human agents with a variety of complex knowledge codes for its strategic disciplinary spatial policing. Environmental advocates, state functionaries, and corporate workers all are asked to keep watch over these sites, guard the systems of sustainability, and manage those populations co-inhabiting such spaces for their survival (Young 1994; Rutherford 2007).

Regardless, politics always remains essential. Reflexive resistance within as well as competitive counter-moves, for example, against managerial imperatives from campaigns for different energy paths to environmental justice campaigns illustrate how individuals can and do organize new opportunities to exert certain freedoms amid these power effects (Schlosberg 2007). Embracing political responsibility and engaging with the policy implementation, deployment, or activation of administrative writs, managerial decisions, and techno-scientific findings can be liberating as new political agendas in many political movements, focusing on policies from saving the rain forests to slowing rapid climate change. Knowledge becomes a basis for freedom-from and freedom-to at the same time as the individuals implement the designs of power in adaptive, collaborative, and inventive environmentalizing practices out in their own organic cultivated fields, wood lots, rooftop solar installations, bicycle commutes, and net-zero LEED buildings (Aggarwal 2005).

Governmentality is an emergent cluster of strategies and tactics for traversing the present with no presumption of determinate origins and goals (Dean 1999). As Lemke (2002: 50) notes, all governmentality analysis must concentrate on how Foucault always was "adumbrating the close link between forms of power and processes of subjectification." Foucault's governmentality studies cash out as "the exposure and contestation of assumptions," but they also at the same time intervene "into the space of the contestation and evaluation of arguments and ideas" (Dean 1994: 119). In tracing the expression of the political assumptions behind ecologically-rooted governmentalization, it is crucial to remember how they not merely "describe the environment" as much they "actively constitute as an object of knowledge and, through various modes of positive intervention, manage and police it" (Rutherford 2007: 56).

Even though Foucault does not turn the full force of his genealogical analytics toward ecological concerns per se, his understandings of biopolitics and governmentality clearly can be seen at work in how "Nature," "the Environment," or "Ecology" are, in part, explicit knowledge formations constructed by scientific experts, government bureaucracies, business concerns, and urban populations (Luke 1995: 57–81). By fabricating such objects of knowledge and targets for action, "the environment" becomes a range of complex spatialities and domain of varied resources in reserve or being made ready for multiple modes of management under various institutions for cultural, economic, political, social, technical, and technical intervention (Luke 2009: 129–59).

Thus, the conditions of environmental governmentality are, either manifestly or latently, core concerns laced through much of environmental political theory's project. Whether the task at hand is protecting the environment, creating sustainable lifestyles, preserving endangered species, conserving scarce resources, or assuring intergenerational equity, the concerns of security, population, territory, and their effective governance are the policy problematic, social forces, and operational spaces designated as decisive for governmentality (Foucault 2007b). Governmentality also entails policing the outcome of many processes pitched at transforming traditional systems of coercive power, feudal justice, and personal authority within modernizing changes, which advance the governmentalization of the administrative state and society (Foucault 2008) as well as the subjectification of individuals whose conduct must meet and match these shifts.

Modernity as Milieux: Power/ Knowledge and Politics

While it is not typically regarded as the most important key to the keep of knowledge, political theory also must not be ignored in careful intellectual deliberations about the environment (Eckersley 1992; Meyer 2001; Hay 2002). The involvement of political thinkers in drawing material connections between the exertion of coercive state power to presumed economic, policy, or technological imperatives, whose solutions are to be found in the sciences of biology, geography, mathematics, or physics, has preoccupied political thinkers from the time of Plato and Aristotle (Orphuls 1977). Moving into the present, generations of thinkers, writing about agriculture, conservation, industrialization, science, technology, and urbanism since the eighteenth century, have laid strong foundations for environmental political theory in the twentieth century (Meyer 2001). It is clear that most of their message has not been heeded (Ophuls 2011). This philosophical stream in the larger currents of political theory perhaps only began to find its own voice during the 1960s and 1970s in the midst of the social, political, and cultural upheavals of that time (Hay 2002); nonetheless, these last five decades were among the worst to ignore the ideas of green political thinkers.

For humans and non-humans to co-exist and survive on the Earth, environmental political theorists, explicitly or implicitly, have begun to recognize that governmentality—or the practices needed to regulate and administer life itself for entire populations in complexes composed of men and things—must be made integral to discourses and policies that guide debates over human survival on the planet. Any effort to govern entails developing theories and practices "to shape the field of possible action of others" (Foucault 1982: 221), and efforts to governmentalize economies, societies, and technologies in environmental registers also now accept that there are many populations of other humans and non-humans in complex coupled systems, like societies/ecologies, humans/non-humans, technologies/markets, that must be governed. While other social forces and institutions also exert governmentalizing guidance, it is plain that states, the state system, and global governance regimes continue to be critical players for environmental policy and political theorists (Young 1994; Kuehls 1996; Luke 1997; Eckersley 2004; Dowie 2009).

Few focused thematics in environmental political theory writing can fuel the environmental governmentalization of state policies as well as the disciplined oversight in many corporate operations, technical activities, and consumer behaviors that conform to evolving new understandings of environmental protection, preservation, and practices (Luke 2009). Today, a wide range of environmental analysts, ethicists, philosophers, and theorists are assessing how the governmentalization of state articulates a "green," "ecological," or "environmental" governmentality (Goodin 1992; Luke 1995; Aggarwal 2005; Rutherford 2007; Brand 2010; McKibben 2010; Gore 2013). Whether one takes more macro-level views of governmentality from above, or peers into micro-level appraisals of governmentality from below, the attention given to this assemblage of power/knowledge apparatuses cannot be diminished.

In most respects, environmental political theory has not run aground on the shoals of minor scholastic quibbles nor has it quailed before today's hard choices to be made by states and societies about environmental governance as it relates to rapid climate change (Vanderheiden 2008), global governance (Speth and Haas 2006), collective sacrifice (Maniates and Meyer 2010), planetary management (Bierman and Pattberg

2012), or resisting unsustainability (Barry 2012). Of course, in confronting the challenge of mitigating climate change, many environmental political theorists morally entreat individuals and societies consciously to choose to be green, more sustainable, intentionally frugal, or even wild (Meyer 2006; Princen 2010; Wapner 2010; Ophuls 2011; Zerzan 2012), not unlike the partisans of moral anarchism resisting the depredations of nineteenth-century industrial society.

Such advice must now be heeded. It can leverage, on the margins of continuous economic changes, many small personal decisions into the political attainment of significant collective adjustments. Political actions did check the degradation of the ozone layer, rain forest destruction is slowing in Brazil, some animal species are being protected, and toxic waste sites are being policed. At the same time, the logic of environmental governmentality maintains its focus on entire populations and wider territories in its quest for security. In steering the conduct of conduct, power, and knowledge both work at these higher, more massive levels of aggregation. This focus is imperative, because environmental destruction is, and has been, materially embedded in immense regional, national, and global infrastructures for transport, industry, agriculture, housing, communication, and marketing. They simultaneously are, in many respects, the *sine qua non* of modern affluence as well as, in several other respects, the common sources of rapid climate change, biodiversity loss, landscape degradation, resource dissipation, and wilderness destruction (Luke 1999).

Choosing to be more green in this context, as a conscious ethico-political act, often can only express itself as green consumerism in sustainable shopping (Szasz 2009), corporate social responsibility campaigns (Dauvergne and Lister 2013), dedicated recycling (MacBride 2011), or alternate transportation systems (Schäfer, Heywood, Jacoby, and Waitz 2009). Making these choices, however, more often appears to reinforce the existing order of ecological degradation (Luke 2006; Parr 2012; Layzer 2012) rather than making truly telling transformations in the world's deepening ecological unsustainability.

When looking more closely at these problematic aspects of environmental governmentality, one must return to Foucault for a larger perspective. He situates the articulation of modernity in multiple milieux when he concludes "sovereignty capitalizes a territory, raising the major problem of the seat of government, whereas discipline structures a space and addresses the essential problem of a hierarchical and functional distribution of elements, and security will try to plan a milieu in terms of events or series or events or possible elements, of series that will have to be regulated within a multivalent and transferrable framework" (Foucault 2007b: 20). Even though he is not entirely clear, and promises further elucidation that never comes, Foucault characterizes the concept of a milieu as "a pragmatic structure," a certain complex number of "overall effects bearing on all who live in it," or multiple circular linkages "produced between effects and causes," which all cascade through economies and societies as "what is needed to account for action at a distance of one body to another ... therefore the medium of an action and the element in which it circulates" (Foucault 2007b: 21, 20–1). More significantly, the milieu cannot be excluded from sovereignty and its effects, since it constitutes another bigger and broader "field of intervention" that, in the final analysis,

> ... instead of affecting individuals as a set of legal subjects capable of voluntary actions—which would be the case of sovereignty—and instead of affecting them as a multiplicity of organisms, of bodies capable of performances, and of required performances—as in discipline—one tries to affect, precisely, a population. I mean a multiplicity of individuals who are and fundamentally and essentially only exist biologically bound to the materiality within which they live. What one tries to reach through milieux, is precisely the conjunction of a series of events produced by these individuals, populations, and groups, and quasi natural events which occur around them. (Foucault 2007b: 21)

For Foucault, milieux seem counter-intuitively only to emerge when the expansive and complex "naturalness" of human species, living and working in definite territories, depend more and more on "artificial" milieux in economies and societies to thrive.

Foucault recognizes milieux as a range of new phenomena; but, he does not extensively dissect them, even though he off-handedly labels the larger of these interactions as "environnmentalite" (Foucault 2004: 266, 2008: 261–2). At most, he senses how the interactivity of techniques of power and codes of knowledge complicate the everyday pragmatics behind human agents, non-human actants, and embedded cultural structures enough to continuously reshape "environmentality." Therefore, he suggests that everyone must focus upon all that "now appears as the intersection between a multiplicity of living individuals working and coexisting with each other in a set of material elements that act on them and on which they act in turn" (Foucault 2007b: 22).

Looking closely into its grand design, the question of freedom is not alien to considerations of governmentality. Assuring that any culture, ideology, or milieu is rooted in the values of freedom clearly is "one of the conditions of development of modern or ... capitalist forms of the economy" (Foucault 2007b: 48). The degrees of freedom accorded to different individual agents and social forces are, of course, matched by deployments of new disciplinary techniques that essentially operate as checks and balances of the expression of these freedoms. Consequently, freedoms are not simply the discretionary privileges granted to this or that person, but rather a coincident empowering and constraining of systems of material mobilization, allowing for "the possibility of movement, change of place, and processes of circulation of both people and things" (Foucault 2007b: 48–9).

Liberal practices of freedom, then, must be understood as "one of the facets, aspects, or dimensions of the deployment of apparatuses of security" (Foucault 2007b: 49). In fact, maintaining stability in these milieux of material mobilization, cultures of disciplinary coordination, and ideologies of collective security is necessary for implementing the governmentalization of states and societies. Part ideology, part technology, this new formulation for "a government of men" is a radical departure from traditional notions of moral authority and political freedom "that would think first of all and fundamentally of the nature of things and no longer of men's evil nature, the idea of the administration of things that would think before all else of men's freedom, of what they want to do, of what they have an interest in doing, and of what they think about doing, are all correlative elements" (Foucault 2007b: 49) in what now mediates environmentality in the actions and apparatuses of green or environmental governmentality.

These alterations in authority evolved haltingly throughout the West in a manner that lent governmentality and its apparatuses a particular primacy over many other types of power by assembling, articulating, and applying a complex array of knowledges. Hence, for Foucault, governmentality is involved inherently in the pragmatic construction and material operation of modern social formations. Indeed, at its core, he placed "the ensemble formed by the institutions, procedures, analyses and reflections, the calculations and tactics that allow the exercise of this very specific albeit complex form of power, which has as its target population, as its principal form of knowledge political economy, and its essential technical means apparatuses of security" that directly mobilize "the tendency, which, over a long period and throughout the West, has steadily moved toward the pre-eminence over all other forms (sovereignty, discipline, etc.) of this type of power which may be termed government resulting, on the one hand, in the formation of a whole series of specific governmental apparatuses, and, on the other hand, in the development of a whole complex of *saviors*" (Foucault 1991: 102–3).

Since environmental political theory does appeal to ethical ideals to effect change, it also can express the exercise of new complex forms of power over human and non-human populations working outside of realms of personal ethical activity and collective ideal thinking. How they are produced and policed typically follow from the machinations of political economy, and their well-being for continued survival is quite often entrusted to essentially complicated technics embedded in apparatuses of security. While the label is serendipitous, the mission of such ensembles ironically can be largely disclosed by recognizing them as ensembles of institutions, procedures, analyses, or reflections that are always already deployed to function as "environmental protection agencies."

Political theory in many of its articulations, as Foucault might suggest, answers to "the question of the *Aufklärung* as its way of gaining access, not to the problem of knowledge, but to that of power" (Foucault 2007: 59). In their liberal and illiberal, conservative and progressive, radical and reactionary writings, political theorists have proven decisive since the Enlightenment for articulating the processes of modernity's "eventualization." That is, the gathering of "groups of elements where, in a totally empirical and temporary way, connections between mechanisms of coercion and contents of knowledge can be identified. Mechanisms of different types of coercion, maybe even legislative elements, rules, material set-ups, authoritative phenomena, etc.," and these layered discursive labors allow the practitioners of political theory to assess "such knowledge in terms of their diversity and heterogeneity, view them in the context of the effects of power they generate inasmuch as they are validated by their belonging to a system of knowledge" (Foucault 2007: 59).

The Machinations of Environmental Governmentality

The implementation of green governmentality design involves more questions than ecological issues tied to green policies and practices. Environments, as Foucault observes, are immense and complex milieux. Mapping and monitoring their ever-changing machinations necessarily engages many cultural, economic, social, technological considerations. This recognition puts much larger domains of freedom on the table, not unlike Haeckel's assessments of ecology, which most ecologists would treat as ongoing investigations into the relation of organisms to their organic as well as inorganic environments. Examining individual organisms, populations of organisms, and all the dimensions of their relations to each other in organic and inorganic environments, therefore, constitutes a challenging operational task due to its complexities, temporal variations, and continuously shifting dynamics when environments span a range of natural and artificial ecologies.

To push deeper into the operative details of green governmentality, the thought and practice of environmentality plausibly requires oversight and guidance of at least five key dimensions—time, motion, matter, metrics, and control—to administer ecologies effectively by causing and directing action "at a distance" (Rose 1999: 125). In capturing control over these fields of force to govern the conduct of conduct of both populations and individuals inhabiting definite territories, green governmentality initiatives become engaged in continuously repositioning the ethics, technics, and economics of individuals in groups co-inhabitating sites with many material elements. Much of their natural engagement is, however, largely artificial. Indeed, the pragmatic structures, individual security, and collective systems of men and things in common habitats all must be made visible, manipulatable, and legible in the productive powers animating their activities.

Among the techniques and technics that are used to "shape the field of possible action of others" (Foucault 1982: 221) via "groups of elements where, in a totally empirical and temporary way, connections between mechanisms of coercion and contents of knowledge can be the politics of knowledge identified" (Foucault 2007: 59), the tools to make visible and legible the interactions of individuals and groups are pivotal. These primary technics force as many as possible to "write things down, and the nature of things people are made to write down, is itself a kind of government of them" (Rose and Miller 2010: 187). To highlight one central, and quite problematic, example here, one can look at the policy-making regime's fixation on decarbonizing the world's energy systems that still depend heavily upon fossil fuels.

Mapping, tracking, or inventorying the fossil fuels behind globalizing industrial democracy, for example, plots out the carbonized "ecological footprints" of individuals and groups in an effort to steer this hydrocarbon-based social order. Wealthy industrial societies rely upon fossil fuels to maintain their prosperity, but today's carbon-centered economy and energy complex is degrading the viability of the planet's atmosphere, waters, soil, and ecosystems. What is monitored becomes normative and normalizing at the same time, so power/knowledge form around such standardized scientific tools. As solutions to "the problematics of governance" (Rose and Miller 2010: 173–205), these technics advance "the general principle of what is called liberalism" (Foucault 2003: 48). The self-fulfilling set of economic and technical principles behind liberalism as a pragmatic system rests upon "freedom," which must be regarded as an "ideology and technique of government . . . understood within the mutations and transformations of technologies of power" (Foucault 2003: 48). For 250 years, individual and collective freedoms have developed in no small part due to the energy-intensive forms of hydrocarbon commerce, petrodollar governance, and carbonized liberalism (Mitchell 2013).

More particularly and precisely, freedom here often is nothing else but the coercive and corrective forces behind the deployment of fossil fueled "apparatuses of security," which are intertwined with "the possibility of movement, change of place, and processes of circulation of both people and things" (Foucault 2003: 48–9). To activate movement, assay changes in place, and assess processes of circulation, ideologies, and techniques of their government develop, for instance, around specific dimensions in their material pragmatics, like "momentality" (time), "movementality" (motion), "mattermentality" (massification), "measurementality" (metrification), and "managementality" (control) to constitute and control "all correlative elements" (Foucault 2003: 49) required to exert the productive powers of governmentality. Not unlike Foucault's assessments of liberal market architecture, these "organizing actions" deal with "the function of intervening . . . on more fundamental, structural, and general conditions" (Foucault 2003: 139) by which individual and collective action can be organized and reordered.

Rendering the organizing actions and all correlative elements of green governmentality visible and legible is, to a certain extent, a quite complex systems operational or logistical exercise. Plainly, all matter can become matter(s) of the state—people, animals, plants, minerals, water, soil, air, etc—that must be identified for service as sites, stocks, or subjects of circulation whose masses of materiality must be inventoried for mobilization or immobilization (Luke 2009). In today's "carbon democracy," it is manifest that "fossil fuels helped create both the possibility of modern democracy and its limits" (Mitchell 2013: 1). These fuels' quantity, qualities, capacity, numbers, fungibility, attributes, supply, etc., require complex metrified registers, making the transparency essential. Once the mattermental extent (Casey 1997: 162–5) of hydrocarbon energy stocks and the measuremental scope (Turnhout, Neves, and de Lijster 2014: 581–97) of these fuel stocks are ascertained, their temporality and motility become readable to momental and movemental knowledges and powers. Whether it is the spread of toxins from a coal-fired power plant ash dumps or a population collapse for an endangered species caused by hydrocarbon pollutants acidifying the seas, the free circulation from place to place in definite motions at certain rates brings elaborate time–motion studies of life-giving and life-taking materialities circulating through ecosystems into view, once again, as "a sort of complex composed of men and things" (Foucault 1991: 93).

Most saliently for environmentality's power/knowledge networks, the finely tuned requisite measurementalities are needed for rendering "men" (car-dependent suburbanites, households consuming oil-intensive agribusiness foods, workers churning out petroleum-based plastic products) and "things" (oil-burning power plants, gasoline-powered vehicles, or coal-illuminated cities) subject to these technologies of power all ready to work in conformity with replicable stable metrics. Finally, the purposive synchronizations of time, motion, and material all cycling through-and-with the embedded milieux of modernity and their pragmatic structures produce traces allowing the fabrication of intricate reliable metrics for measurementality to enable the evolving managementality of the environment and organisms, organisms and their relations to one another, and thus people and things. Once these episodic slices in action can be rendered into discrete, disciplined, and determinate quanta, it also becomes feasible for entities charged with controlling economic and technical actions at a distance to exert their productive powers (Bierman and Pattberg 2010). Thus, the carbon economy and society of modernity fabricate their varied feasible pragmatics in fungible structures to extract and apply fundamental services and stocks in diverse nested systems of governance. Technologies of power, exercised in/as/for organizing structures do simultaneously, "describe the environment" as well as they "actively constitute as an object of knowledge and, through various modes of positive intervention, manage and police it" (Rutherford 2007: 56).

What is more, the advance of authority in a governmental guise—despite the proclivity of political theory to read politics through the traditional terms of *Realpolitik* favored by Machiavelli—cuts loose the coercive juridical power of princes and nobility, kings and court, aristocracy and fealty in favor of a more complex productive power regimen tied into more anonymous technical functionaries working inside the many operational bureaux of "the state." In the security-seeking regulation of human conduct as well as policing the stability-enforcing co-existence of men and things, "governmental reason thus posits the state as the principle for reading reality and as its objective and imperative . . . governing rationally because there is a state and so that there is a state" (Foucault 2007b: 287). Once these pragmatic structures are in place, space will, in turn, usually conform all of these structured actions rising from, but also given to, populations and territories to assure the security of the environmental subjects enabled to conduct their material existence in such spaces.

Politics as Resistance, Reflexivity, and Revitalization

Environmental governance must become a more pressing issue for political activists and theorists. At this point, some activists are intent upon acting on a larger scale devising new deliberative institutions to anchor democratic practices, while others lobby to impose tighter regulations on firms and households to more efficiently use natural resources. Other movements seek to outline reflexive ethical alternatives for Nature's environments by turning to locally sourced food, textiles, and renewable energy.

Still, as the limited success of the past generation's political efforts to do more than create carbon markets, decarbonize economies, and popularize low carbon lifestyles illustrate, their general impact on the economy at large is minimal. The eco-managerial thrust of most environmental governmentality operations make them integral to sustaining the everyday materiality of modernity. Working through international organizations, regional trade pacts, nation-states, third sector organizations, and citizens' groups, many political initiatives, which focus upon the global environment, remain significantly important interventions. Yet, many of their political activities never fully recognize the complex workings of environmental governmentality as they struggle to steer the interrelations of people and things in the milieux of entire populations and territories in new directions.

Whether it is rapid climate change, habitat depletion, biodiversity loss, ocean rise, land degradation, or resource overshoot, the experts trying to govern these threats will call upon the pragmatics of momentality, movementality, mattermentality, and measurementality to marshal the extensive knowledge and mobilize the power they need to attain and actuate the managemental capacities at the heart of environmental governmentality. Different modes of production at different times in history around the world have fought over the natural environment in diverse ways, but the capacities of green governmentality truly bring the administrative reach of artificial authority and deliberate design deeper, faster, and harder into the organizational capabilities of eco-managerialism. As they unfold in their current neo-liberal permutations, these forces often seem irresistible, but political resistance can check their advance (Luke 1999). In the service of conventional economic freedoms, the organizing structures and correlative elements of neoliberalism seem to fuse together in such governance capacities, as they are created by these time/motion/material analyses (Luke 2014).

Plainly, the matrices of eco-managerialism impose varied standardizing metrics to allow local-to-global scales of governance to hold sway over the accumulation, circulation, and utilization of goods and services (Mitchell 2013). Each of these dynamic sub-servos in apparatuses of power rationalize, however, the production and consumption of human and non-human resources under today's emergent planetarian regime of green governmentality. Environmental political theory, in addition to capturing and criticizing the eco-managerial logics of these processes therefore, must provide even more reflexive critiques of green governmentality's growth programs with theory and practice for resistance, ranging from collaborative localism, voluntary frugality, or purposive simplicity to workplace democracy, green municipalism, or communitarian management (Vanderheiden 2008; Schlosberg 2009; Princen 2010). Consequently, environmental political theory can, and should advance an array of political strategies and cultural alternatives to keep power in the hands of local human actors. They must become the social forces that collectively determine on their own, from below and within the milieux of modernity, how capitalism, democracy, and ecology will co-exist in our increasingly processed world.

References

Aggarwal, A. (2005). *Environmentality: Technologies of Government and the Making of Subjects* (Durham: Duke University Press).

Baudrillard, J. (2001). "The Illusion of the End." In *Selected Writings*, 2nd edn, edited by Mark Poster (Stanford: Stanford University Press), 254–63.

Bierman, F. and Pattberg, P. (2010). *Global Environmental Governance Reconsidered* (Cambridge, MA: MIT Press).

Brand, S. (2010). *Whole Earth Discipline: Why Dense Cities, Nuclear Power, Transgenic Crops, Restored Wild lands and Geoengineering are Necessary* (New York: Penguin).

Casey, E. S. (1997). *The Fate of Place: A Philosophical History* (Berkeley: University of California Press).

Dauvergne, P. and Lister, J. (2013). *Eco-Business: A Big-Brand Takeover of Sustainability* (Cambridge, MA: MIT Press).

Dean, M. (1994). *Critical and Effective Histories: Foucault's Methods and Historical Sociology* (London: Routledge).

Dean, M. (1999). *Governmentality: Power and Rule in Modern Society* (London: Sage).

Dowie, M. (2009). *Conservation Refugees: The 100-Year Conflict Between Global Conservation and Native Peoples* (Cambridge, MA: MIT Press).

Dryzek, J. S. (1987). *Rational Ecology: Environment and Political Economy* (Oxford: Blackwell).

Dryzek, J. S., Norgaard, R. B., and Schlosberg, D. (2013). *Climate Challenged Society* (Oxford: Oxford University Press).

Eckersley, R. (1992). *Environmentalism and Political Theory: Toward an Ecocentric Approach* (Albany: State University of New York Press).

Eckersley, R. (2004). *The Green State: Rethinking Democracy and Sovereignty* (Cambridge, MA: MIT Press).

Foucault, M. (1980a). *Power/Knowledge: Selected Interviews & Other Writings, 1972–1977* (New York: Pantheon).

Foucault, M. (1980b). *History of Sexuality, Vol. I: An Introduction* (New York: Vintage).

Foucault, M. (1982). "Afterword: The Subject and Power" In *Michel Foucault: Beyond Structuralism and Hermeneutics*, edited by Hubert Dreyfus and Paul Rabinow (Chicago: University of Chicago Press) 208-26.

Foucault, M. (1988). *Technologies of the Self* (Amherst: University of Massachusetts Press).

Foucault, M. (1991). "Governmentality." In *The Foucault Effect: Studies in Governmentality*, edited by Graham Burchell, Colin Gordon, and Peter Miller (Chicago: University of Chicago Press), 87–104.

Foucault, M. (2003). *"Society Must be Defended": Lectures at the Collège of France, 1975–1976* (New York: Picador).

Foucault, M. (2004). *La Naissance de la Biopolitique Cours au Collège de France 1978–1979* (Paris: Editions du Sevil/Gallimard).

Foucault, M. (2007a). *The Politics of Truth* (Los Angeles, CA: Semiotext(e)).

Foucault, M. (2007b). *Security, Territory, Population: Lectures at the Collège de France, 1977–1978* (New York: Palgrave Macmillan).

Foucault, M. (2008). *The Birth of Biopolitics: Lectures at the Collège de France, 1978–1979* (New York: Palgrave Macmillan).
Foucault, M. (2010). *The Government of the Self and Others: Lectures at the Collège de France, 1982–1983* (Basingstoke: Palgrave Macmillan).
Goodin, R. (1992). *Green Political Theory* (Cambridge: Polity).
Gore, A. Jr. (2013). *The Future: Six Drivers of Global Change* (New York: Random House).
Hay, P. (2002). *Main Currents in Western Environmental Thought* (Bloomington: Indiana University Press).
Kuehls, T. (1996). *Beyond Sovereign Territory: The Space of Ecopolitics* (Minneapolis: University of Minnesota Press).
Layzer, J. A. (2012). *Open for Business: Conservative's Opposition to Environment Regulation* (Cambridge, MA: MIT Press).
Lemke, T. (2002). "Foucault, Governmentality, and Critique." *Rethinking Marxism: A Journal of Economics, Culture & Society* 14(3): 49–64.
Luke, T. W. (1995). "On Environmentality: Geo-Power and Eco-knowledge in the Discourses of Contemporary Environmentalism." *Cultural Critique* 31: 57–81.
Luke, T. W. (1997). *Ecocritique: Contesting the Politics of Nature, Economy and Culture* (Minneapolis: University of Minnesota Press).
Luke, T. W. (1999). *Capitalism, Democracy, and Ecology: Departing from Marx* (Urbana: University of Illinois Press).
Luke, T. W. (2009). "Developing Planetarian Accountancy: Fabricating Nature as Stock, Service and System for Green Governmentality." *Current Perspectives in Social Theory* 26: 129–59.
Luke, T. W. (2014). "Urbanism as Cyborganicity: Tracking the Materialities of the Anthropocene." *New Geographies: Grounding Urban Metabolism* 6: 39–53.
Maniates, M. and Meyer, J. M. (2010). *The Environmental Politics of Sacrifice* (Cambridge, MA: MIT Press).
MacBride, S. (2011). *Recycling Reconsidered: The Present Failure and Future Promise of Environmental Action in the United States* (Cambridge, MA: MIT Press).
McKibben, B. (2010). *Eaarth: Making a Life on a Tough New Planet* (New York: St Martin's Griffin).
Merchant, C. (1980). *The Death of Nature: Women, Ecology and the Scientific Revolution* (San Francisco: Harper and Row).
Meyer, J. (2001). *Political Nature: Environmentalism and the Interpretation of Western Thought* (Cambridge, MA: MIT Press).
Meyer, S. M. (2006). *The End of the Wild* (Cambridge, MA: MIT Press).
Mitchell, T. (2013). *Carbon Democracy: Political Power in the Age of Oil* (London: Verso).
Ophuls, W. (1977). *Ecology and the Politics of Scarcity: A Prologue to a Political Theory of the Steady State* (San Francisco: W. H. Freeman).
Ophuls, W. (2011). *Plato's Revenge: Politics in the Age of Ecology* (Cambridge, MA: MIT Press).
Parr, A. (2012). *Hijacking Sustainability* (Cambridge, MA: MIT Press).
Princen, T. (2010). *Treading Softly: Paths to Ecological Order* (Cambridge, MA: MIT Press).
Rose, N. (1999). *Powers of Freedom, Reframing Political Thought* (Cambridge: Cambridge University Press).
Rose, N. and Miller, C. (2010). "Political Power Beyond the State: Problematics of Government." *British Journal of Sociology* 61: 173–205.
Rutherford, S. (2007). "Green Governmentality: Insights and Opportunities in the Study of Nature's Rule." *Progress in Human Geography* 31(3): 291–307.

Schäfer, A., Heywood, J. B., Jacoby, H. D., and Waitz, I. A. (2009). *Transportation in a Climate-Constrained World* (Cambridge, MA: MIT Press).

Schlosberg, D. (2007). *Defining Environmental Justice: Theories, Movements, and Nature* (Oxford: Oxford University Press).

Soule, M. E. and Press, D. (1998). "What is Environmental Studies." *BioScience* 48(5): 397–405.

Speth, J. G. and Haas, P. (2006). *Global Environmental Governance: Foundations of Contemporary Environmental Studies* (Washington, DC: Island Press).

Szasz, A. (2009). *Shopping Our Way to Safety: How We Changed from Protecting the Environment to Protecting Ourselves* (Minneapolis: University of Minnesota Press).

Turnhout, E., Neves, K., and de Lijster, E. (2014). "'Measurementality' in Biodiversity Governance: Knowledge, Transparency, and the Intergovernmental Science–Policy Platform on Biodiversity and Ecosystem Services (IPBES)." *Environment and Planning A* 46(3): 581–97.

Vanderheiden, S. (2008). *Political Theory and Global Climate Change* (Cambridge, MA: MIT Press).

Wapner, P. (2010). *Living Through the End of Nature: The Future of American Environmentalism* (Cambridge, MA: MIT Press).

Young, O. R. (1994). *International Governance: Protecting the Environment in a Stateless Society* (Cornell: Cornell University Press).

Zalasiewicz, J., Williams, M., Steffen, W., and Crutzen, P. (2010). "The New World of the Anthropocene." *Environmental Science & Technology* 44(7): 2228–31.

Zerzan, J. (2012). *Future Primitive Revisited* (Port Townsend, WA: Feral House).

CHAPTER 31

POLITICAL ECONOMY OF THE GREENING OF THE STATE

MATTHEW PATERSON

Introduction

Are state responses to environmental challenges triggering profound transformations in political structures? This question has become a significant component in debates in environmental political theory, with deep consequences for practical political life and the pursuit of sustainability. Two distinct literatures have emerged around this claim, although they have not largely come in direct contact with each other, except indirectly via debates about the idea of ecological modernization (EM). One deploys the term "green state," and is largely positive in suggesting that we are witnessing some sort of profound shift in political structures and processes. The other interrogates the notion of the "environmental state" developed within environmental sociology from an eco-Marxist perspective, and is rather more skeptical as to claims about any broad transformation, suggesting that the capitalist character of contemporary states fundamentally limits such transformative processes.

My aim in this chapter is to interrogate both of these literatures and to argue that they are both partly correct but partly wrong. Table 31.1 is a schematic account of their arguments and how I respond to them. I interrogate these literatures with two sorts of questions in mind. First, to the extent transformations are underway, what are the forces that drive this process? What sort of analytical perspective might therefore best enable us to understand what drives the process of transformation (or lack of it)? Second, how is the process of state transformation connected to socio-economic processes associated with responses to environmental change? Specifically, does the relationship between capitalism and the state make such transformations impossible? Briefly, I claim that "green state" writers are largely correct that there is a substantial change occurring, but

Table 31.1 Summary of Argument

	Green State	Eco-Marxists	Present argument
Driver	Adding of core functions to the state. Social movement pressure	Imperative of accumulation State role in capitalist development	Imperative of accumulation + legitimation
Explanatory framework	Historical sociology	Political economy	Political economy
Socio-economic process	Ecological modernization	Treadmill of production Neo-liberalization of the environment	(Neo-liberal) ecological modernization

their explanations are weakened by their base in historical sociology, while eco-Marxist "environmental state" writers are correct that the dynamics of capitalism dominate the responses to environmental change but underestimate capitalism's flexibility and adaptability.

Toward a Green State?

In the early 2000s, authors such as Robyn Eckersley, John Dryzek, and James Meadowcroft started to argue that we are witnessing the emergence of a "green state," and a process of the "greening of the State" (in particular Dryzek et al. 2003; Eckersley 2004; Barry and Eckersley 2005). In part a reaction to an anarchist instinct amongst many in the Green movement (for example, Carter 2013), in part an attempt to think through the implications and potential of some of the transformations of state practice being brought about by political responses to various environmental challenges, these authors have suggested in effect that we are witnessing the early stages of a possible process of transformation where the pursuit of ecological sustainability can be regarded as at least potentially a core state function.

At perhaps the most general level, James Meadowcroft (2005) argues that the greening of the state is the latest in the evolution of a series of the functions of the modern state since its emergence in seventeenth-century Europe as a territorial state. Over time, it has become a national, capitalist, liberal, democratic, and welfare state, gaining these aspects as core functions of the state, and the ecological function—securing the conditions of sustainability—is emerging as an additional one.

Dryzek et al. (2003) develop a more detailed empirical analysis of this process in relation to four industrialized states—the United States, the UK, Norway, and Germany. They explore how these states have responded to environmental concerns and what has conditioned the possibilities and constraints on their "greening." Consistent with arguments in historical sociology regarding the emergence and transformation of the state (notably Tilly 1985), their argument is that the driver of the potential ecological transformation of the state resides in the patterns of relations between states and social movements. They explore the four cases via a typology of state–civil society relations to suggest which sorts of conditions are most propitious for the emergence of green states. Their typology has two dimensions—whether relations between the state either includes or excludes civil society (and especially the environmental movement) from its policy-making processes, and whether this inclusion/exclusion is passive or active. They suggest that the four countries they analyze correspond to the four possible types this generates. Thus the United States is passively inclusive, Norway actively inclusive, Germany passively exclusive, and the UK (at least through to the early 1990s) actively exclusive.

They argue on the basis of this typology that the most likely state form for the emergence of green states is the passive-exclusive form exemplified by Germany. This is because the passive-exclusive form enables ideas—both substantive ideas about particular policies, but also broader shifts in culture and values—to filter through to the state through popular pressure, but keeps a distinct public sphere outside the state where such ideas can emerge unconstrained, and also makes an element of an oppositional culture possible, enabling diverse strategies by environmental movements. In particular, what it makes potentially possible is the attachment of the goals of environmental conservation to what they call the economic "core state imperative" via ecological modernization (Dryzek et al. 2003: 2). EM (see, for example, Hajer 1995; Young 2000; or Mol 2001) is a concept that argues that economic growth and sustainability can be rendered consistent with each other—via for example the development of closed-loop production systems, radical increases in resource efficiency, dramatic technological breakthroughs, and the new business models and state–business partnerships that make these possible. EM writers also argue that we are witnessing the early stages of a socio-economic transformation along these lines.

As Dryzek et al. extend this argument to the political sphere, "environmentalist interest in pollution control and conservation of material resources can be attached to the economic imperative via the idea of ecological modernization. Demands to protect the intrinsic value of natural systems cannot make this link" (Dryzek et al. 2003: 161). However, they are clear that it is only by linking green politics to the legitimation (and not just the economic) imperative of the state that more radical and democratic green goals can be articulated and possibly achieved (2003: 193).

Dryzek et al.'s focus for their analysis is on developments internal to each state. By contrast, Eckersley focuses both on shifts in internal state organization and on international dimensions to state greening. Her key points for present purposes are that it is transformations in two central elements in contemporary statehood—sovereignty and democracy—that will enable the greening of the state. On the one hand, shifts in the way that states transform the meaning of sovereignty to expand their responsibilities to those beyond their borders are a condition of possibility of the greening of the state. On the other hand, a radical reworking of democratic institutions and practices will make possible the consideration of ecological concerns beyond the state's territorial limits, but will also enable the development of "strong" ecological modernization strategies. Her overall argument is well expressed in the beginning of her conclusion:

> The anarchic state system, global capitalism, and the administrative state have served in different ways to inhibit the development of greener states and societies. In this book I have shown how three mutually informing counter-developments—environmental multilateralism, ecological modernization, and the emergence of green discursive designs—have emerged to moderate, restrain and in some cases transform the anti-ecological dynamics of these deeply embedded structures. . . . This virtuous relationship, however, cannot be deepened without a move from liberal democracy to ecological democracy. (Eckersley 2004: 241)

The term ecological democracy is intended by Eckersley to refer to a form of democracy that differs from liberal democracy in two key respects. First it rejects liberal democracy's presumption of pre-existing autonomous individuals, whose preferences and interests are therefore unquestionable. Second, it is constituted as a "democracy of the affected" rather than (or more precisely in addition to) a "democracy of membership" (for example, Eckersley 2004: 243). This thus means both that deliberation is a key element in ecological democratic practice (undermining liberal democracy's separation of public and private) and that territoriality (as well as species or temporality, although these are not the focus of her analysis) is unimportant in determining who should get to participate in decisions.

Combined, the analyses of Meadowcroft, Eckersley, and Dryzek et al. provide powerful arguments which suggest that the "green anarchist" position is over-stated: that while there is much which is clearly anti-ecological in contemporary state practice and structures, these should be regarded as historically contingent rather than structurally inherent features of statehood. In sustaining this claim regarding the greening of the state, two elements are key. The first is whether or not states can be treated as having no key features or roles, but simply as evolving complexes of institutions and power that develop specific functions in response to different historical exigencies or pressures. The second is whether different elements in the roles or functions of states are structurally consistent with the function of sustainability and ecological democracy.

For Dryzek et al., for example, to the extent that the state has the securing of economic growth as a structural imperative, this is the result of historical social movements (in this case the eighteenth- and nineteenth-century European bourgeoisie) having successfully attached their interests to already existing state imperatives. Dryzek et al.'s "Brief History of the State" (2003: 1–2) mirrors Meadowcroft's as discussed earlier, and is a narrative of state development familiar in historical sociology (Mann 1986; Dryzek et al. draw explicitly on Skocpol 1979). Dryzek et al. suggest that the transformations currently underway in response to mobilizations by environmental movements can be interpreted in terms of the potential development of an ecological function for states. Eckersley's argument depends on a similar narrative regarding the functions of states. Her "three core challenges"—interstate anarchy, global capitalism, liberal democracy—correspond broadly to the three historically evolved functions of states outlined by Dryzek et al. Eckersley's theoretical move, principally developed in her chapter on interstate anarchy (2004: ch. 2), is in her turn to constructivism (in International Relations) to suggest that the image of international politics as a realm of unremitting competition and hostility between self-regarding sovereign states is only one of a number of possible "cultures of anarchy" (cf. Wendt 1999; Litfin 1998). By contrast, political economy accounts would make a stronger ontological claim for the distinctive historical and structural relationship between capitalism, growth, and the state—in this view capitalism constitutes the state *as such*, and thus detaching a growth imperative from the state is impossible to imagine.

But even if it is the case that the various functions of states are historically constituted and potentially transformable, are these various functions (potentially) consistent with each other and with an emerging function of sustainability? In other words, how plausible is it to suggest that the functions of the state in pursuing territorial security through military power, or economic growth, are consistent with sustainability? Eckersley's response is to suggest that these different functions are not consistent, but that militarism in particular is decline, because of both economic interdependence and democratization, demonstrating the malleability of state imperatives over time. Her response regarding the latter is more evasive. She argues in favor of a "strong" version of EM over a "weak" one (Eckersley 2004: 70–7; see Christoff 1996 on this distinction), but in developing this argument, she has a less than clear answer to the question about the potential compatibility of growth and sustainability:

> On the one hand, the green state would still be dependent on the wealth produced by private capital accumulation, via taxation, its programs and in this sense would still be a capitalist state. On the other, securing private capital accumulation would no longer be the defining feature or primary raison d'être of the state. The state would be more reflective and market activity would be disciplined, and in some cases curtailed, by social and ecological norms. (Eckersley 2004: 83)

The question arises as to whether the two "hands" in this passage can be regarded as compatible with each other; that is, if the green state is dependent on capital for taxes, and capital is dependent on accumulation for profits (out of which taxes would be paid), then how viable is a strategy of limiting overall accumulation? For many state theorists the responsibility of the state for accumulation in capitalist society is more fundamentally structured than this formula by Eckersley suggests (for example, Jessop 1990; Harvey 1990; Hay 1994; Paterson 2000). This thus takes us back to the historical narrative concerning state functions—an alternative reading is the co-evolution of the capitalist social form (wage labor, market competition, the primacy of private property) and the political form of the modern state (territoriality/anarchy, constitutional government, the rule of law), with the former setting certain conditions of operation for the latter.

This political–economic critique of the "green state" literature should not however be taken as a rejection of their general *problématique*. Rather, it suggests a different line of analysis and inquiry as to the conditions of possibility of such a state, and the routes by which it might be pursued. Specifically, the pursuit of a green state entails the pursuit of an "ecological regime of accumulation"—this would be the political–economy equivalent of the notion of "ecological modernization." If a (capitalist) state has, as suggested above, the pursuit of accumulation as one of its main responsibilities, then its role in an ecological context is to attempt to provide a regime of growth which at the same time reduces resource consumption and the production of pollution consistent with a sustainability agenda. It should be noted of course that this argument is not necessarily inconsistent with an argument that such an ecological modernization agenda is essentially incoherent from an ecological point of view; indeed it remains possible that overcoming the accumulation/sustainability tension is impossible. My point would be that from this perspective, if this is the case, then a green state is also impossible, since the state as we know it and capitalism (for which accumulation is the basic premise) are historically and structurally co-existent. A political economy account of the greening process (of both state and economy) thus insists that the pursuit of a green state is necessarily *contradictory*—in the strict sense that it contains both the specific tension of the growth/environment relationship, and the other contradictions already present in capitalist society—and thus cannot be usefully regarded as the addition of a "sustainability function" onto the other functions of the state as suggested most directly by Meadowcroft (2005). Rather, the emergence of the green state will be driven by an ongoing tension between different accumulation and legitimation imperatives that are frequently in contradiction with each other.

From this point of view, therefore the challenge is two-fold. The first is to attempt to articulate what an ecological regime of accumulation might look like, and how it might hold together politically, economically, and ecologically. Thinking through such an ecological regime of accumulation would involve considering its discursive elements (the ideological resources needed to "frame" the problematic such that it persuades sufficient numbers of its viability), technical elements (such as the Environmental Kuznets Curve, the Porter hypothesis on competitiveness and the environment, techniques of environmental accounting), and narrowly political elements (changes in the substantive role of the state, and relations between states, social movements, and firms).

The second challenge however is to legitimize this regime of accumulation. Legitimation would entail articulating which specific interests (economic and social) stand to gain from such a regime of accumulation, working with those interests (sometimes having to work to transform their own sense of their interests), and engaging with resistance. This resistance can come both from those who directly stand to lose from an ecological regime of accumulation (fossil fuel interests, paradigmatically) and those who insist on the impossibility of a green growth regime or object to its particular characteristics (as we see in contemporary resistance to carbon markets for example).

From the Environmental State to Neo-liberal Natures

If the problem with the green state literature might be its treatment of political economy, what then of those literatures which discuss the state and its (potential) transformations from a political–economy point of view? There are a number of ways into this question, but I discuss a particular trajectory of eco-Marxist thought in environmental sociology and geography since the early 1980s, from the notion of the Treadmill of Production (TOP) to the more recent debate about the "neo-liberalization of nature." Both of these debates deal, in rather different ways, with the possibility and character of transformative change within capitalism as states deal with environmental change.

Toward the end of the 1980s, some environmental sociologists (for example, Kloepfer 1989; Jänicke 2006) started to use the term "environmental state" to refer to the set of institutional and regulatory reforms established from the late 1960s onwards by Western states. A significantly less ambitious concept than the "green state" of more recent usage, it nevertheless was intended to signify that Western states had undergone a significant amount of institutional change in directing their regulatory attention to environmental problems. No broad transformation in political structures is however intended by the term; it simply denotes the parts of the state that are now directed to managing and ameliorating (or at least reducing the rate of destruction of) environmental conditions. This conception continues to be used within environmental sociology in particular (for example, Mol and Buttel 2002; Spaargaren et al. 2006), in particular in combination with accounts of ecological modernization and in contrast to those of the TOP writers we move to now.

At around the same time, Allan Schnaiberg (1980) coined the term "the Treadmill of Production" to refer to a dynamic by which the environmental impacts of capitalist societies, in particular the United States, intensified after 1945. Schnaiberg argued that despite official efforts to improve the environmental performance of economies, there is a relentless logic within industrial capitalism that increases environmental degradation and cannot be transformed. The state in this perspective is sometimes seen as a passive permissive condition, sometimes as an active aider and abetter of this treadmill process. Schnaiberg and his colleagues were highly critical of claims about significant transformations, and regarded the features of the "environmental state" as described by other environmental sociologists as inevitably weak in the face of the inexorable processes of degradation generated by capital-intensive economic growth. TOP theorists were unmoved by the shifts in the 1980s, in particular claims about the emergence of ecological modernization as a "new politics of pollution" (Weale 1992). Specifically, they claim that: EM analyses only ever sustain claims about particular firms or sectors (Mol's 1995 study of the chemicals industry is often taken by both sides as a paradigm case) and don't show that these successes are or can be replicated across the economy; that the case selection in EM analyses is biased toward those sectors which have been able to cut environmental impacts; that overall trends still show a continuing increase in environmental degradation produced by the treadmill; and that globalization masks some of these effects by displacing production from the West (for example, Gould, Pellow, and Schnaiberg 2008). The analyses by TOP scholars remains remarkably constant since its original formulation, giving the impression (despite protestations to the contrary, see Gould, Pellow, and Schnaiberg 2008: 29–33) that the TOP is effectively a linear theory concerning the relationship between capitalism and environmental degradation, seeing both an undifferentiated relationship between economic processes and environmental impacts, but also an undifferentiated account of capitalist production itself, and thus a continuous and linear relationship between economic growth and environmental degradation. All of capitalist production is deemed to follow the same treadmill logic, whereby capital intensity determines interests in maximizing production, displacing labor for technology (thereby increasing capital intensity) and externalizing costs. By contrast, might not capital itself be rather differentiated in terms of these processes and thus both dynamics of environmental degradation produced by different parts of capital be different, and relations among different parts of capital regarding the environment be contradictory? I follow up this point empirically in the discussion of climate change later in the chapter.

While TOP theorists in effect argue for a very strong continuity in how both state and economy have dealt with environmental degradation, another eco-Marxist literature emerged in the 2000s that took both the possibility of transformations and the differentiation of capitalist interests more seriously. This is what has become known as the "neo-liberal environments" or "neo-liberal natures" literature, and it is commonplace particularly amongst geographers (Castree 2003, 2008; Heynen et al. 2007; Mansfield 2009). Following the idea of neo-liberal natures, it remains the case that any political transformation is to be understood as driven by processes of capital accumulation and its contestation, but the account of capitalist development itself and thus the possibilities of state transformation are rather more nuanced than in the TOP perspective. In particular, this literature starts with the political–economic rupture of the 1980s, laying emphasis on the shifts that neo-liberalism brought about. In doing so, they draw on a broad range of arguments (more or less ignored by TOP analysis) about what neo-liberalism entails, such as a shift in state economic management from Keynesian to monetarist/"free market," a re-regulation of labor markets, a shift from welfare to workfare, and so on. But neo-liberalism also entails more broadly a resurgence of (global) finance, shifting the balance of forces not only between states and capital, but between financial and productive capital and a "hollowing out" of the state, as various state functions (including some aspects of environmental management) are variously privatized, run down, decentralized to local political units, or re-organized through public–private partnerships under the rhetoric of "governance."

Central to these analyses of environmental politics is the process of commodification. The claim is that neo-liberal approaches to environmental problems are based on opening up space for new forms of commodification. In some instances these approaches involve rolling back existing regulatory systems: rejecting environmental regulation as an unreasonable intrusion into the enjoyment of private property rights to use forests, wetlands, and so on, and sometimes, privatizating of public resources—land, lakes, etc. In other instances it entails the creation of new sorts of private property rights that are legitimized in terms of efficient, market-based responses to environmental problems. Payments for ecosystems services and the establishment of environmental markets (sulphur or carbon trading systems for example) are the key instances of this approach. These are the effect of the combination of a search for new sources of accumulation following the economic crisis from the 1970s onwards (the slowdown in growth and labor productivity produced by the exhaustion of the gains of the classic Fordist era from the 1920s onwards—see Harvey 1990 or Lipietz 1987—as well as the problems encountered within Keynesian macro-economic management), the re-emergence of finance as a dominant force within capitalist economies, and the ideological hegemony of neo-classical economic ideas, which in the environmental context is the application of Robert Coase's (1960) arguments that the best way to internalize externalities (such as pollution) is via the establishment of private property rights in those externalities.

The state is thus in this view undergoing significant transformation in how it deals with environmental change. However, while the "neo-liberal natures" approach is rather more nuanced than the TOP one, it remains the case that for the most part the concrete analyses of the sorts of society–environment relations produced by neo-liberalism are more or less unremittingly negative, as encapsulated in the subtitle of one of the main books in this literature, "false promises and unnatural consequences" (Heynen et al. 2007). As a consequence, the neo-liberal "environmental state," does look rather different to that which existed in the Fordist–Keynesian era, but it is nevertheless limited in environmental terms in similar ways to that identified by TOP scholars. However, this literature similarly underplays the implication of the notion of contradiction for the examination of neo-liberalism's environmental politics. It sees in effect neo-liberalism only as an intensification and particular form of capitalism's more general contradictions in relation to ecological relations—as a new way that capitalism undermines sustainability. Might neo-liberalism, clearly not by its intent but by unintended consequences, have opened up certain possibilities for environmental reform? The rest of this chapter attempts to explore the possibilities here, focusing on responses to climate change. These clearly follow the pattern identified in the neo-liberal natures literature—neo-liberal responses to climate change are indeed dominated by commodification of nature as a strategy, in particular—but what I will try to show is that these neo-liberal responses to climate change do open up space for both a political–economic and a state transformation, as suggested by green state writers.

Climate Change and the Ecological Transformation of the State

If we are to evaluate these competing claims about the extent and causes of state transformation, then climate change is a particularly good case for two principal reasons.

First, because it is rooted principally in the use of fossil energy, it is the most far-reaching environmental issue in socio-economic terms, touching on all aspects of economic activity and daily life. It thus poses substantial challenges to existing political systems and responding adequately can be expected to require transformative politics. Second, it has also become a site of significant governance innovation, both within and beyond states, and thus can provide useful evidence about both the extent and causes of political change.

Establishing the basis for this last claim is important. What is meant by the claim that climate change is a site of significant innovation in governance? There are various such innovations. With regard to governance by states, the principal site of innovation is in the emergence of carbon markets. I focus mostly on these in this section, but it is worth emphasizing that they are accompanied by a huge range of initiatives by multiple actors across different scales. These are increasingly known under the collective rubric of transnational climate change governance (Bulkeley et al. 2014). They include: partnership arrangements among states, businesses, and occasionally NGOs focused on specific technology developments (for example, Renewable Energy and Energy Efficiency Partnership; Global Methane Initiative); initiatives by institutional investors working with NGOs to get companies to disclose greenhouse gas (GHG) emissions and other climate-related risks to affect investor and manager behavior (for example, Carbon Disclosure Project, Investor Network on Climate Risk); cooperation among subnational political units, notably cities, to transform urban GHG performance (for example, C40 cities); and critical engagement by some NGOs seeking to govern corporate, state, and community practice "from below" (for example, Carbon Trade Watch, Transition Towns Network).

Turning to carbon markets in more detail, these emerged in part within the interstate system. Because of the significant obstacles to reaching agreement that they have experienced, international negotiators have experimented with highly novel forms of regulation for international politics. Specifically, they have developed a series of governance strategies oriented around the creation of markets. There are precedents in earlier agreements which restricted certain sorts of markets (the Convention on the International Trade in Endangered Species, for example, or the part of the Montreal Protocol on Substances That Deplete the Ozone Layer which prevent parties from trading in CFCs with non-parties), but none really which focus on the creation of markets as a means to achieving environmental goals.

The substance of these governance mechanisms is by now fairly well-known and will only be introduced briefly here (for fuller introductions see, for example, Newell and Paterson 2010; Stephan and Paterson 2012). The three key elements are in the Kyoto Protocol on Climate Change, and consist of an Emissions Trading System and two carbon offset systems, the Joint Implementation (JI) mechanism and the Clean Development Mechanism (CDM). These governance mechanisms have spawned a rapidly expanding market in carbon emissions. They have also triggered a large range of other such markets, most notably the European Union Emissions Trading Scheme, but also now active markets in the north-eastern United States, California, Québec, New South Wales, New Zealand, Tokyo, several Chinese provinces and cities, soon to emerge markets in South Korea and Kazakhstan, and a voluntary carbon offset market driven by corporate PR demands.

In one sense, these policy innovations are entirely consistent with the arguments of the "neo-liberal environments" literature, which focus a good deal of their attention on the extension of logics of commodification to novel arenas, notably the emergence of environmental markets. But there are three aspects of this process which are worth emphasizing to resist those conclusions. First, they reveal the highly differentiated interests of different types of business. The eco-Marxist perspectives outlined above tend to assume that capital has rather similar interests regarding environmental problems, whereas the emergence of carbon markets, and of transnational climate change governance more broadly, disclose the highly differentiated interests of coal mining companies, insurers and reinsurers, accountants, and financiers, to name just a few. Even among oil companies we see significant differences of strategy arising out of differences of interests among them (Rowlands 2000; Skjaerseth and Skodvin 2001). This differentiation of business interests has been instrumental in enabling these novel initiatives to emerge and have produced new forms of alliance among state, business, and civil society actors.

Second, these commodification processes have created very significant novel forms of political authority. As markets only ever exist with a set of regulatory processes to make them possible, carbon markets have generated a set of governance structures that can be seen as part of the process of the greening of the state. These include the formal structures of the Kyoto Protocol and national regulatory agencies but also the messy public–private hybrids of states, NGOs, and businesses involved in the verification systems, the certification of carbon offsets, the registries, and so on. But they are being driven by a capitalist logic, both of accumulation, as private companies seek new opportunities for commodification and states seek to enable this (the creation of carbon markets in the first place) and of legitimation, as companies and NGOs both seek to generate means of governing such markets (the certification systems) as part of a search for legitimacy of these novel commodifications. In other words it is less useful to see it as an historical process of adding a new function to the state (as in Meadowcroft), or as driven by social movement pressure and the responses by states to that pressure (as in Dryzek et al.), or in evolving notions and practices of sovereignty and democracy (as in Eckersley), but as a contested process centered on the legitimacy of new ways to generate capital accumulation.

The second aspect of this process worth emphasizing is its own contradictions. While these contradictions can be understood in the classic sense of capital being unable to realize its own conditions of reproduction, they can also be understood in the sense that any social project of capital to generate new arenas for accumulation will also have unintended consequences that capital cannot fully control. One aspect of this has been that NGOs have been able to move directly into the space of attempting to govern carbon markets, in particular carbon offsets. But a deeper process is perhaps that the flip side of the commodification of climate is the "carbonification" (Stephan 2012) of finance.

While there is definitely an extension of capitalist logics into the realm of climate change, there is at the same time a reverse process. Carbon is arguably in the process of becoming not only a fetishized commodity but also a money-form (Descheneau 2012). It is becoming increasingly used by a range of actors as a means of judging value in the economic sense. Some actors within carbon markets get paid in carbon credits for their work. Some companies (for example, Tesco, the world's second largest supermarket chain) measure their flow of goods and products in terms of carbon as well as dollars, euros, or pounds, and some store managers claim the carbon measure is a more effective measure of their efficiency as a store than a traditional money measure (Fuller and Bulkeley 2013). There are a number of initiatives from accounting organizations attempting to incorporate carbon into standard financial accounting systems (Thistlethwaite 2011), such as the Carbon Disclosure Standards Board.

Ecological economics has long argued normatively that we should subsume notions of economic value within the ecosystem itself. It could be argued that the processes of developing accounting systems for carbon are doing just that. They do so of course in a narrow manner that reduces ecology to carbon, which is far from unproblematic. But nevertheless it is a significant transformation, at least in terms of its potential. The key point however is that to the extent this is true, it arises precisely out of the engagement of some parts of capital with climate change, as they attempt both to generate new sites of accumulation (carbon markets), legitimize their activities (offsetting, promoting carbon markets as "green finance"), and deal with the risks climate change itself poses to investment.

In addition to suggesting a rather different process driving forward the greening of the state than that in the green state literature, more familiar with processes understood well in eco-Marxist debates, focusing on carbon markets also suggests that the form that such greening takes is different to that either understood by Dryzek and colleagues, Meadowcroft, or Eckersley. It is perhaps closest to Eckersley's in that it does entail significant rearticulation of political authority beyond the currently existing territorial state—more consistent with Dryzek's work on deliberative democracy than on the green state. But the transnational processes involved in these transformations are not so much about the incorporation of transnational elements within state practices—the shift to a democracy of the affected as opposed to of membership, for example—as about the activities of corporations, NGOs, and states extending governance into transnational domains as corporations seek new markets and investment opportunities, states seek to enable and regulate them, and NGOs seek to govern these novel markets directly. The resulting green state (still in emergence) is a messy assemblage with multiple sites of governance operating across different scales—a "global climate governance complex" (Bulkeley et al. 2014). Much of this complex is oriented directly toward creating new sites of capital accumulation, with civil society actors for the most part either excluded, co-opted, or occasionally carving out a space to govern corporate and state actors within the complex.

Conclusions

This chapter has tried to offer an alternative account of the process of the greening of the state. While "green state" writers are right to emphasize at the least the potential for significant transformations in political authority as polities grapple with environmental problems, especially ones with deep systemic implications like climate change, these processes are better understood as being driven by logics of capital accumulation and legitimation than the dynamics of states and social movements as understood by Dryzek and colleagues, or by the emergence of deliberative democratic institutions and shifts in the meaning of sovereignty as emphasized by Eckersley. Conversely, political economy approaches are overly linear in their accounts of how capitalism deals with environmental problems, neglecting the internal contradictions between different fractions of capital and the need for capital to legitimize its accumulation projects as potential triggers for more far-reaching political changes.

My argument is thus that we do indeed see the emergence of various initiatives that signal significant potential transformations of political authority, but that these are been driven by the twin, contradictory, relations between imperatives for accumulation and those for legitimation. Capitalist states are charged with securing the conditions for capital accumulation but at the same time have to deal with legitimation crises caused (a) by capitalism's internal ecological contradictions (producing crises for capital itself such as insurance disasters due to extreme weather events) and the novel conflicts among different parts of business, and (b) by the contestation by social movements both of the ecological degradation produced by capitalism and the state's complicity in that, and of the responses to environmental challenges like climate change that themselves are embedded in highly problematic aspects of capitalism, as evidenced by the controversies over carbon markets. These complicated dynamics help understand the patterns of policy-making by states over environmental problems, both in terms of difficulties in responding to those problems but also in terms of the characteristics of the responses themselves.

At the same time as the dynamics of accumulation and legitimation have started to transform states as they respond to problems like climate change, they have also produced a sprawling set of transnational governance initiatives, both by states and a range of other actors. These initiatives are themselves driven by logics of accumulation and legitimation in large measure, as companies seek to generate new markets, expand control over commodity chains, and respond to NGO pressure, and NGOs seek to regulate and shape emerging patterns of investment and consumption. In some sense, this "global climate governance complex" should be understood as itself an intimate part of the greening of the state—much like in Eckersley's focus on deliberative democratic initiatives beyond state borders but driven instead by capitalist imperatives.

What remains an enormously open question from the point of view of the argument I develop here is whether the state can, in fact, be "greened." Given that we do not know whether capitalism can become sustainable, and there are good reasons to believe it cannot, it follows that states, as co-existent historically and structurally with capitalism, may be transformed to such an extent by for example the emergence of economic systems not dependent on economic growth, or by the ongoing intensification of multiple transnational governance systems, that they no longer become meaningfully understood as states in Weber's (1919) classic sense of the term—they will no longer have "given territories," a "monopoly on the legitimate use of force," and will no longer be an identifiable "human community." What will have emerged is a form of political authority which requires a different sort of vocabulary.

References

Barry, John and Eckersley, Robyn, eds. (2005). *The State and the Global Ecological Crisis* (Cambridge, MA: MIT Press).

Bulkeley, H., Andonova, L., Betsill, M., Compagnon, D., Hale, T., Hoffmann, M., Newell, P., Roger, C., and Van De Veer, S. (2014). *Transnational Climate Change Governance* (Cambridge, Cambridge University Press).

Carter, A. (2013). *A Radical Green Political Theory* (London: Routledge).

Castree, N. (2003). "Commodifying What Nature?" *Progress in Human Geography* 27(3): 273–97.

Castree, N. (2008). "Neoliberalising Nature: The Logics of Deregulation and Reregulation." *Environment and Planning A* 40(1): 131–52.

Christoff, P. (1996). "Ecological Modernisation, Ecological Modernities." *Environmental Politics* 5(3): 476–500.

Coase, R. (1960). "The Problem of Social Cost." *Journal of Law and Economics* 31–44.

Descheneau, P. (2012). "The Currencies of Carbon: Carbon Money and Its Social Meaning." *Environmental Politics* 21(4): 604–20.

Dryzek, J., Downes, D., Hunold, C., and Schlosberg, D. (2003). *Green States and Social Movements* (Oxford, Oxford University Press).

Eckersley, R. (2004). *The Green State: Rethinking Democracy and Sovereignty* (Cambridge MA: MIT Press).

Fuller, S. and Bulkeley, H. (2013). *New Climate Change Initiatives in the UK: Tesco Case Study Report* (Durham: Durham University Geography Department for the Leverhulme Trust).

Gould, K. A., Pellow, D. N., and Schnaiberg, A. (2008) *The Treadmill of Production: Injustice and Unsustainability in the Global Economy* (Boulder: Paradigm Publishers).

Hajer, M. (1995). *The Politics of Environmental Discourse: Ecological Modernisation and the Policy Process* (Oxford: Clarendon Press).

Harvey, D. (1990). *The Condition of Postmodernity* (Oxford: Blackwell).

Hay, C. (1994). "Environmental Security and State Legitimacy." In *Is Capitalism Sustainable? Political Economy and the Politics of Ecology*, edited by M. O'Connor (New York: Guilford Press).

Heynen, N., McCarthy, J., Prudham, S., and Robbins, P. (2007). *Neoliberal Environments: False Promises and Unnatural Consequences* (London; New York: Routledge).

Jänicke, M. (2006). "The Environmental State and Environmental Flows: The Need to Reinvent the Nation-State." In *Governing Environmental Flows: Global Challenges to Social Theory*, edited by Gert Spaargaren, Arthur P. J. Mol, and Frederick H. Buttel (London: Routledge), 83–106.

Jessop, B. (1990). *State Theory: Putting Capitalist States in their Place* (Cambridge: Polity).

Kloepfer, M. (1989). *Umweltstaat* (Trier: Springer-Verlag).

Lipietz, A. (1987). *Mirages and Miracles: Crisis in Global Fordism* (London: Verso Books).

Litfin, K. (1998). *The Greening of Sovereignty in World Politics* (Cambridge, MA: MIT Press).

Mann, M. (1986). *The Sources of Social Power, Volume 1* (Cambridge: Cambridge University Press).

Mansfield, B. (2009). *Privatization: Property and the Remaking of Nature–Society Relations* (Oxford: Blackwell).

Meadowcroft, J. (2005). "From Welfare State to Ecostate." In *The State and the Global Ecological Crisis*, edited by John Barry and Robyn Eckersley (Cambridge, MA: MIT Press), 3–23.

Mol, A. (2001). *Globalization and Environmental Reform: The Ecological Modernisation of the Global Economy* (Cambridge, MA: MIT Press).

Mol, A. P. J. (1995). *The Refinement of Production: Ecological Modernization Theory and the Chemical Industry* (Utrecht: Van Arkel).

Mol, A. P. J. and Buttel, F. H. (2002). *The Environmental State Under Pressure* (Amsterdam: Elsevier JAI).

Mol, A. P. J. and Spaargaren, G. (2002). "Ecological Modernization and the Environmental State." *Research in Social Problems and Public Policy* (10): 33–52.

Newell, P. and Paterson, M. (2010). *Climate Capitalism: Global Warming and the Transformation of the Global Economy* (Cambridge, Cambridge University Press).

Paterson, M. (2001). "Risky Business: Insurance Companies in Global Warming Politics." *Global Environmental Politics* 1(4): 18–42.

Paterson, M. (2000). *Understanding Global Environmental Politics: Domination, Accumulation and Resistance* (London: Macmillan).

Rowlands, I. H. (2000). "Beauty and the Beast?: BP's and Exxon's Positions on Global Climate Change." *Environment and Planning C: Government and Policy* 18: 339–54.

Schnaiberg, A. (1980). *The Environment, from Surplus to Scarcity* (New York: Oxford University Press).

Skjaerseth, J. B. and Skodvin, T. (2001). "Climate Change and the Oil Industry: Common Problems, Different Strategies." *Global Environmental Politics* 1(4): 43–64.

Skocpol, T. (1979). *States and Social Revolutions: A Comparative Analysis of France, Russia and China* (Cambridge: Cambridge University Press).

Spaargaren, G., Mol, A. P. J., and Buttel, F. H. (2006) *Governing Environmental Flows: Global Challenges to Social Theory* (Cambridge, MA: MIT Press).

Stephan, B. (2012). "Bringing Discourse to the Market: The Commodification of Avoided Deforestation." *Environmental Politics* 21(4): 621–39.

Stephan, B. and Paterson, M. (2012). "The Politics of Carbon Markets." Special Issue, *Environmental Politics* 21(4).

Thistlethwaite, J. (2011). "Counting the Environment: The Environmental Implications of International Accounting Standards." *Global Environmental Politics* 11(2): 75–97.

Tilly, C. (1985). "War Making and State Making as Organized Crime." In *Bringing the State Back In*, edited by Peter Evans, Dietrich Rueschemeyer, and Theda Skocpol (Cambridge: Cambridge University Press), 169–91.

Weale, A. (1992). *The New Politics of Pollution* (Manchester: Manchester University Press).
Weber, M. (1919). "Politics as a Vocation," lecture at Munich University.
Wendt, A. (1999). *Social Theory of International Politics* (Cambridge: Cambridge University Press).
Young, S. (2000). *The Emergence of Ecological Modernisation: Integrating the Environment and the Economy?* (London: Routledge).

CHAPTER 32

ENVIRONMENTAL SCIENCE AND POLITICS

MARK B. BROWN

INTRODUCTION

FOR most environmental problems today, science plays a key role in both the perceived causes and proposed solutions. Toxic pollution, species extinction, climate change, and many other environmental risks are widely seen not merely as "side effects" of modern science, but as integral to the social meaning of science itself (Beck 1992). On the one hand, environmentalists have been among the most powerful critics of the technocratic arrogance often associated with modern science. Some environmentalists have even embraced a romantic rejection of scientific knowledge and scientific modes of thought. On the other hand, environmentalists have long relied on science both to understand environmental problems and to legitimate political responses to them. The most common legitimation strategies tend to assume a rationalist image of value-free science as preceding and compelling political decisions. This chapter sketches some of the ways that environmental thinkers have understood the relation between science and politics, arguing for a constructivist–democratic approach that avoids the pitfalls of both rationalist and romantic conceptions of science.

Scientific expertise provides indispensable substantive information for environmental politics and policy, potentially leading to more reasonable and effective decisions. Lay people may be able to observe certain changes in local weather patterns, for example, but we cannot see them as potential aspects of global climate change without the long-term statistical assessments provided by climate science. Similarly, the unaided human senses cannot detect the subtle ecological effects of industrial chemicals, nuclear radiation, and many other environmental risks (Beck 1992: 23–7, 71–6). Additionally, whether or not scientific expertise actually has a substantive impact on environmental policies, it provides a key resource for legitimating such policies. Despite repeated conflicts over the politicization of expertise, science as an institution retains high public trust in wealthy democracies, and political actors of all kinds rely on scientific expertise to promote public support for their claims (National Science Board 2012; Weingart 1999). Parties to environmental disputes may also use scientific expertise strategically to delay decisions by calling for more research or to avoid responsibility by blaming the experts. Finally, at a more general level, science shapes how people conceive environmental issues in the first place. Global scientific advisory bodies like the Intergovernmental Panel on Climate Change (IPCC), for example, have framed climate change primarily as a global physical phenomenon, rather than as a matter of justice and democracy at the regional or local level (Demerit 2001; Miller 2004). And scientific knowledge is a key element in the diffusion of environmental practices like recycling and household energy conservation, arguably infusing daily life with a managerial ethos of collective surveillance and self-discipline (Luke 2011).

The role of science in environmental politics, of course, depends on how people conceive the diverse practices, institutions, and bodies of knowledge associated with the term "science." Throughout much of the twentieth century, efforts to address environmental problems often drew on a "positivist" view of science as a formal, logical, socially insulated method for producing value-free knowledge. From this perspective, which remains widespread in environmental politics, any "politicization" of science—which we might define simply as the deliberate attempt to shape science through politics—threatens to undermine environmental politics and policy-making. For example, when critics rightly objected to the manipulation of science advisory bodies during the administration of US President George W. Bush, they often failed to acknowledge the liberal values that shaped their critiques and instead presented themselves as apolitical defenders of value-free science (Mooney 2005). In this respect, they adopted a conception of science discredited by decades of research in the social studies of science and technology, which has shown how social values and political decisions influence science in all kinds of ways (Jasanoff et al. 1995). Environmental toxicology, for example, relies on value-laden decisions about the burden of proof required to qualify a substance as hazardous to human health and the environment (Douglas 2009). Such analyses generally do not claim that science inevitably reflects dominant interests, as caricatures of "social constructivism" assert. Just because science is constructed in part by society does not mean it cannot produce reliable accounts of non-human realities (Dryzek 2013: 12–13, 78–9). A constructivist conception of science is thus fully compatible with the realist conviction that the world has an independent existence that precedes human efforts to understand and shape it. Nonetheless, constructivism does challenge ongoing efforts to justify environmental policies with reference to an incontestable foundation of scientific truth. In this respect, constructivist views of science dovetail with a broader intellectual shift away from the longstanding conviction that environmentalism requires preserving and protecting pristine non-human nature, unsullied by human intervention (Cronon 1996; Latour 2004; Shellenberger and Nordhaus 2007).

Acknowledging that science and politics, humans and non-humans, inevitably shape each other does not entail an entirely artificial world of human mastery, devoid of the sense of otherness and wonder often associated with non-human nature. "Just because the world has become humanized—with a human signature everywhere—does not mean that there is nothing except humans" (Wapner 2010: 209). The otherness of non-human nature appears in many forms, and if you want to describe the sublime otherness of a fierce winter storm, the sciences may offer limited assistance. Art, poetry, storytelling, and many other non-scientific modes of engagement with non-human nature provide valuable resources for environmental politics. But for purposes of reliable prediction and control—assessing and reducing greenhouse gases, designing habitat restoration projects, building wind turbines, and so on—the sciences offer a key resource for political efforts to shape relations between humans and non-humans.

Seen in this light, environmental politics arguably becomes most democratic when it invokes diverse kinds of knowledge and experience, mediated through different kinds of practices and institutions. Legislatures, courts, and NGOs, for example, offer different representations of citizen interests, just as thermometer records, computer models, and Antarctic ice cores provide different representations of the global climate. Different political institutions represent citizens in different ways, and the various environmental sciences construct representations of nature that serve different but potentially compatible purposes (Brown 2009). In both science and democracy, modern societies have little hope of agreeing on a single authoritative spokesperson, and so we need to find ways of mediating diverse representative claims. A constructivist conception of environmental science thus potentially reinforces a constructivist approach to democratic politics.

Modern Science, Ecology, and Environmental Values

A long tradition of environmental political thought relies on a view of science as value-neutral expertise, supporting a discourse of "administrative rationalism" (Proctor 1991; Dryzek 2013: 75–98). From the late nineteenth century onward, early conservationists in Europe and the United States, and in colonies throughout the world, advocated scientific approaches to the management of natural resources in the public interest. Professional expertise seemed to offer a welcome antidote to political corruption and partisan competition. Natural resource management was defined as a technical problem to be solved by foresters, agronomists, hydraulic engineers, and other experts (Hays 1959). This approach assumed a direct and essential link between professional expertise and publicly interested environmental policy, and it became especially prominent in the United States after the Second World War. According to an idealized "social contract for science," science provided technological innovation and expert advice in exchange for generous public funding and minimal political oversight (Guston 2000). From this perspective, science inevitably produces social benefits, but only if insulated from politics. This conception of science continues to underlie much environmental politics and policy-making.

Another tradition in environmental thought portrays science not as a neutral tool of effective policy, but as an ideological force that rationalizes everything it touches. Romantic thinkers in the tradition of Jean-Jacques Rousseau, Henry David Thoreau, and the Frankfurt School have offered powerful indictments of the rationalism, individualism, and incessant hunger for technological progress prevalent in modern societies. Green theorists working in this tradition often begin by attacking the mechanistic conception of nature associated with Bacon, Galileo, Descartes, Newton, and other founders of modern science (Bocking 2006: 49–51). According to Carolyn Merchant (1980), for example, modern science conceives nature as inert matter to be mastered and exploited for instrumental human purposes. While such arguments are often overblown, it is clear that in both rich and poor countries around the world, science-driven planning has replaced meandering rivers with engineered water management systems, indigenous farming with industrial agriculture, and local control with centralized administration (Scott 1998). Moreover, as shown by feminist critics like Vandana Shiva (1991), techniques for dominating nature often serve to promote elite interests and perpetuate social inequalities. As a result, Peter Hay notes, "for many environmentalists the scientific project has been sullied beyond redemption" (Hay 2002: 122).

Other environmental theorists, in contrast, have sought to develop a new conception of science that avoids the domination of nature. Drawing on thinkers like Herbert Marcuse (1964: 166–7), they have sought a non-mechanistic, non-reductive form of science that would heal the ancient split between mind and body, humanity and nature, art and science. Some point to the indeterminism associated with quantum mechanics or chaos theory, for example, to argue for a conception of science amenable to a green worldview. For commentators like Fritjof Capra, post-Newtonian physics embraces a "non-reductionist paradigm" that echoes the environmental movement's emphasis on uncertainty, holism, and ecological processes (Hay 2002: 131). Others have pinned their hopes for a new science on ecology itself, arguing that "ecology contains the possibility of a different science around which environmentally benign technology and environmentally benign social relations can be constructed" (Hay 2002: 133).

Such arguments often appeal to one of the first and most effective uses of ecological science to promote environmental awareness: Rachel Carson's *Silent Spring* (1962). Written for a broad audience, the book was as striking for its literary as its scientific qualities. Carson intertwined beautiful accounts of plants and animals with startling information on the impact of synthetic pesticides on birds, insects, rodents, humans, and other elements of the "web of life" (64). Carson did not call for banning all pesticides, but she insisted that citizens had a right to not be poisoned without their knowledge or consent. "The public must decide whether it wishes to continue on the present road, and it can do so only when in full possession of the facts" (13). Chemical companies tried for years to discredit the book and its author, accusing Carson of scientific incompetence and communist sympathies, among other things. Indeed, Carson was in many ways an early "counter-expert" who criticized mainstream chemical expertise for its narrow focus, its dismissal of ecological concerns, and its close ties to industrial interests (Beck 1992: 30; Bocking 2006: 26).

Carson is widely credited with sparking the US environmental movement and the boom in environmental legislation of the early 1970s. But environmentalism has a much longer international history, and it emerged as much from economic and political changes as from scientific evidence of pollution (Bocking 2006: 70–1; Nordhaus and Shellenberger 2007). Indeed, the tendency of many American environmentalists to tell an origin story that begins with Carson's *Silent Spring* says less about the historical causes of environmentalism than about the cultural authority of science. Advocates of deep ecology, social ecology, and bioregionalism, for example, often appeal to ecological science as a source of both moral inspiration and intellectual authority. But such arguments are problematic in several ways. They tend to draw on abstract ideas of natural harmony and stability that have little in common with ecology as practiced by ecological scientists. Ecological scientists themselves have tended to resist close links between ecology and environmental values (Bocking 2006: 61). Moreover, attempts to protect nature on the basis of ecological science—in the Amazon, for example, and other parts of the developing world—have often displaced marginalized communities who rely on those natural resources for their livelihood. Most importantly, efforts to base environmental values on ecological science often suggest a technocratic desire to control public opinion and shut down political debate.

To be sure, ecological critiques of modern science have revealed the environmental destruction and human domination associated with modernist ambitions to control nature. But modern science has fostered not only domination but also greater appreciation of nature's moral value and its role in human communities. Charles Darwin's theory of evolution, for example, has been used not only to justify policies based on the "survival of the fittest," but also to foster a sense of kinship between and among humans and other species (Bocking 2006: 53; Desmond and Moore 2009). More generally, by documenting the human dependence on nature, scientific knowledge can be used to challenge anthropocentric hubris and pride (Barry 1999: 30). The social meanings of science are as diverse as the contexts within which science has developed, and we cannot effectively address most environmental problems without the aid of science, including many sciences not usually considered part of ecology. Critiques of modern science have highlighted important limits of administrative rationalism, but they do not eliminate the need for various forms of technical expertise in environmental politics.

Models of Science Advice

Both rationalist conceptions of science and their romantic critics tend to assume a fixed and predetermined relation between science and politics. They merely disagree on whether science will help or hinder environmental goals. In this respect they fail to consider alternative roles for science in politics. While rationalists generally adopt either a technocratic or decisionist view of expertise, a constructivist approach promises more effective and legitimate environmental politics (Habermas 1970: 62–80).

According to a *technocratic* conception, scientists should determine both the ends and means of environmental policies (Fischer 1990). Technocracy appears whenever government agencies rubber-stamp expert recommendations without independent consideration of other relevant input. Similarly, survivalists like William Ophuls and Garrett Hardin have argued that the urgency of environmental problems requires a technocratic approach (Dryzek 2013: 27–50). A more common conception of the political role of science appears in the *decisionist* approach associated with Max Weber. According to this view, experts are "on tap, not on top" (Barry 1999: 200). Politicians determine the ends of policy, while scientists determine the means. Climate change, for example, is often framed in terms of a division of labor between scientists who discern an acceptable threshold for atmospheric carbon-dioxide, such as 350 parts per million, and politicians who develop policies intended to reduce carbon-dioxide to that level (Hulme 2009a: 103).

Both the technocratic and decisionist approaches usually assume an outdated conception of value-free science. They tend to see attempts by non-scientists to shape scientific research as an unacceptable "politicization" of science. These approaches also tend to assume a *linear model* of the relation between science and politics, according to which technical expertise should both precede and compel political decisions. A linear conception of science advice may be appropriate in contexts characterized by consensus on both scientific knowledge and political values. But most environmental problems today involve irresolvable technical uncertainties and entrenched political conflicts. Such problems lack a single best solution that is best according to all relevant criteria. Policy scholars call these "ill-structured problems" or "wicked problems" (Fischer 2000: 127–9; Funtowicz and Ravetz 1993; Turner 2003: 52–4, 66–9).

In such contexts, when scientists or politicians adopt the linear model of science advice, they create an incentive for their opponents to criticize the relevant science. Science then becomes a proxy battleground for politics. Debate shifts from political, economic, or moral issues to questions of scientific credibility, which are generally less accessible to lay assessment and less amenable to compromise among competing views (Sarewitz 2004; Bocking 2006: 24; Pielke 2007). The reliance on climate science as the most prominent justification for policies to implement major social and economic changes, for example, creates an incentive for critics to challenge climate science (Demeritt 2001). And rather than simply acknowledging the uncertainties of climate science and offering moral reasons for precautionary, no-regrets policies, environmentalists have often allowed themselves to be drawn into debating the science. Ironically, the competing parties in such debates share the linear assumption that science drives policy, differing only in their views on whether the science is credible.

In such contexts, it seems more promising to pursue a *constructivist* approach that involves consultation among diverse experts and lay stakeholders (Jasanoff 1990). As the preceding discussion suggests, a constructivist approach to expert advice involves both an empirical conception of how science works (scientific knowledge is shaped but not entirely determined by society and politics) and a normative view of how scientific experts should relate to politics (experts should inform but not determine political decisions). Funtowicz and Ravetz (1993), for example, argue that in situations that combine high decision stakes with disagreement over both science and values, science advisory processes should involve an "extended peer community" that includes not only a wide range of disciplinary experts, but also lay people potentially affected by the issue.

Building on such considerations, Pielke (2007) identifies four acceptable roles for expert advisors. When the issue is characterized by consensus on both science and values, a linear conception of expertise is appropriate. Experts can adopt the role of a *pure scientist*, restricting themselves to summarizing the state of knowledge in their particular field. Or they can become *science arbiters* who respond to lay inquiries about specific technical matters. In situations where both science and values are in dispute, however, a constructivist approach is likely to be more effective. Experts might act as *issue advocates* who openly promote a political agenda, while being careful to specify that their political arguments do not follow directly from their scientific expertise. Or they might become *honest brokers of policy alternatives* who combine technical and political considerations to clarify existing policy options and identify new options. Given the hybrid nature of their task, honest brokers are usually interdisciplinary advisory committees rather than individual experts (Pielke 2007: 151, 154–6). Depending on the issue context and the personal preferences of the expert, Pielke argues, any of these four roles may be appropriate. Never acceptable, however, are *stealth issue advocates* who pretend that their political recommendations follow directly and necessarily from their scientific claims.

Public Understanding of Science

In addition to formal processes of expert advice, science also shapes environmental politics through its impact on public opinion. Surveys of public knowledge of science periodically lead commentators to fret over the appalling state of "science literacy" in wealthy democracies (Mooney and Kirschenbaum 2009; National Science Board 2012). Even more disturbing is that public knowledge of science often varies according to political affiliation. In the United States, surveys conducted since 2001 have found that 35–52 percent of Republicans agree that global warming is due mainly to human activities, while that view is held by 64–79 percent of Democrats (Saad 2014). Many commentators see the rejection of climate science among US conservatives as one manifestation of a much larger phenomenon of "denialism," loosely defined as the rejection of mainstream science for ideological purposes (Specter 2009; Brown 2014). Such rejection has often been justified with bogus studies funded by industry to "manufacture doubt" about mainstream science (Oreskes and Conway 2010; Jacques 2012). Environmentalists have tended to respond to such doubt with ever more insistent media campaigns, often resorting to sensational images. Such efforts apparently assume that the key problem is the public's failure to appreciate the reliability and importance of established scientific knowledge. As the eminent climate scientist Stephen Schneider put it, "If the public understood the basics of the real risks to nature and to themselves, their posterity, and their world, they would be much more likely to send strong signals to their representatives to act in a precautionary way" (Schneider 2009: 260). Similarly, political theorist John Barry expresses the hope that "agreement on the scientific nature of ecological problems can be useful in forging a politically workable normative agreement on social–environmental issues (Barry 1999: 30, but see 202–6).

Despite the best intentions, this approach mistakenly assumes a linear relation between scientific knowledge and public support for environmental policy. Several studies suggest that without clear and accessible possibilities for effective action, increased scientific knowledge induces political resignation rather than commitment, and sensational media campaigns actually lead people to become more skeptical toward science and less likely to support action on the relevant issues (Moser and Dilling 2011: 164–5). Studies also suggest that as people have come to better understand climate change, their expressed concern about it has actually decreased (Kellstedt et al. 2008). Moreover, in some respects, environmentalist disdain for conservatives who reject climate science amounts to the pot calling the kettle black, given that many environmentalists reject mainstream scientific assessments in other areas, such as genetically modified foods, homeopathy, and vaccines (Yearly 2010).

Most importantly, public rejection of environmental science is probably a less important cause of failures in environmental policy than industry lobbying and the dominance of economic elites in the policy process. Large majorities in the United States have long expressed support for energy research, carbon taxes, elimination of fossil fuel subsidies, and other climate-relevant policies, despite periodic fluctuations in public trust in climate science (Pielke 2010: 43–4; Leiserowitz et al. 2013). And while European countries enjoy broad societal acceptance of mainstream climate science, their efforts to reduce greenhouse gas emissions have not been much more successful than those in the United States. Moreover, the US government has frequently implemented major policies without scientific consensus on relevant matters, including ozone depletion, and more recently, health care and financial reform (Pielke 2007: 128; Sarewitz 2011).

This does not mean that public views on environmental science are unimportant. But efforts to inform public opinion need to go beyond a linear approach. Environmental issues like climate change need to be understood in light of the psychological dynamics of anxiety, resentment, and sense of powerlessness they often evoke (Lertzman 2008; Norgaard 2011). Research on "cultural cognition" suggests that those who reject climate science do so in part because they perceive a conflict between climate science and their cultural values. According to one study, those with hierarchical and individualist values tend to dismiss expert claims about environmental risks, because they assume that accepting such risks would lead to government regulation, which they reject. Those with egalitarian and communitarian values have the opposite response (Kahan 2010). One promising strategy for responding to this phenomenon is to reframe expert advice in a way that avoids direct links between expert claims and specific policies. For example, whereas the common "catastrophe" framing of climate change tends to suggest a need for a technocratic government response, thus inviting attacks on climate science, framing the issue in terms of "public accountability," "environmental stewardship," or "public health" may appeal across ideological lines (Nisbet 2009). To be sure, efforts to provide a less gloomy framing of environmental issues have been combined with both radical and reformist policy proposals, and the latter may not offer an adequate response to profound environmental challenges (Hall 2013). But radical policy proposals will have little chance of attracting public support unless they avoid creating incentives to debate environmental science rather than the policies themselves.

Scientists' Understanding of the Public

Several surveys have found that scientists generally think most ordinary citizens do not know very much about science and are uninterested in learning more. Scientists tend to view the public as non-rational and emotional, overly concerned about minor risks, and prone to rely on anecdotes rather than evidence. Scientists also tend to think that public presentations of science should be simple, visual, and entertaining. And one study found that less than a third of scientists thought that scientists themselves were responsible for shortcomings in the public understanding of science (Besley and Nisbet 2013: 647–8). These findings point toward a "deficit model" of science communication, which casts lay citizens as passive and ignorant recipients of expertise. This view has been widely debunked in sociological studies of science communication, which find that, when faced with a particular socio-technical controversy, lay citizens usually acquire the expertise they need to clarify and articulate their interests (Sturgis and Allum 2004; Bauer 2008).

An illustrative example of these issues appears in the "climategate" email scandal. In the fall of 2009, a few weeks before a major United Nations climate conference in Copenhagen, somebody leaked over 1,000 e-mails written over 15 years by climate scientists at the University of East Anglia and their colleagues. Among other things, the emails showed leading climate scientists evading Freedom of Information Act requests and discussing ways to prevent their critics from being published in leading journals (Tierney 2009; Muir Russell 2010; Pearce 2010; Randerson 2010; Grundmann 2013: 68–71). Conservatives seized on the emails to discredit the entire idea of global warming. Environmentalists replied, correctly, that the emails did not cast doubt on the basic conclusions of climate science. In accord with the environmentalist view, many scholars dismiss climategate as little more than a "manufactured" scandal (Dunlap and McCright 2011: 144). But even though the emails raised no serious questions about the scientific consensus on climate change, they did suggest a paternalistic view of the public and a linear conception of science advice (Hulme 2009b; Sarewitz 2010; Beck 2012; Grundmann 2013). In light of "pressure to present a nice tidy story" (Pearce 2010: 48), the scientists apparently concluded that maintaining public support for climate policy required downplaying uncertainties and disagreements in certain public presentations of climate science. For example, a key diagram was simplified to remove the poorly understood post-1960 "divergence" between tree-ring data and thermometer data. This diagram appeared on the cover of the World Meteorological Organization (WMO) report on the state of the global climate in 1999, and also in the IPCC Third Assessment Report of 2001 (Figure 2.21). Although the issue had long been openly discussed elsewhere, and was also mentioned within the reports themselves, the most prominent diagrams concealed it. An independent review established by the University of East Anglia found these diagrams "misleading" (Muir Russell 2010: 16, 60, 62). Ironically, there was arguably little need to downplay scientific uncertainties or establish a unified front against climate skeptics, given the previously mentioned public support for climate policy.

Multiple official inquiries into the climategate emails found no evidence of scientific fraud or misconduct, but they identified a bunker mentality and lack of public transparency among the scientists involved (Grundmann 2013). A review by the Inter-Academy Council (2010) recommended a series of reforms to the IPCC, including term limits for top officials, improved conflict-of-interest policies, and better procedures for responding to outside critics. Such reforms might be understood as contributing to the "democratization" of climate science.

Democratizing Environmental Expertise

The relation of science to democracy is no less ambiguous than its relation to environmentalism. Democracy takes different forms in different contexts and cultures, as do efforts to democratize environmental science. But there is clearly growing interest in applying democratic norms to environmental science (Bocking 2006: 207). Efforts to promote "public engagement" in science and technology have become a central feature of environmental politics around the world. Environmental justice activists, for example, while often relying on their own experiential knowledge of environmental risks, have long collaborated with sympathetic experts to produce scientific studies relevant to their concerns (Brown and Mikkelson 1990; Ottinger and Cohen 2011). The democratization of science also has the potential to ensure that government research priorities reflect public values. Surveys show strong public support for energy research, for example, but it remains one of the least funded areas in the US government's research portfolio. At the most basic level, public involvement potentially shapes problem definition and agenda setting, and thus the respective political roles of experts and non-experts.

Critics of democratization efforts often remark that it makes little sense to subject scientific methods or results to majority vote. But that objection reduces democracy to elections, and it reduces political legitimacy to empirical public acceptance. If we instead conceive democracy in terms of an ecology of institutions, some of which aim to improve the reasonableness or normative legitimacy of political decisions, then science becomes not only a threat to democracy but also a key part of it (Brown 2009). Established avenues for integrating expertise into democratic politics include expert advisory committees, science journalism, and expert testimony in public hearings, citizen juries, and other political processes. Scientific expertise is a potential source of normative political legitimacy, even if expertise only acquires empirical political legitimacy to the extent it becomes publicly accepted. According to a constructivist view of science and democracy, expertise is shaped (but not entirely determined) by politics, so it makes little sense to view expertise as an external force capable of either rescuing or destroying democracy, as do the rationalist and romantic approaches discussed previously. Instead, expertise can be seen as playing a key role in the tension between empirical and normative legitimacy, between public acceptance and public justification, that is central to democratic politics. From this perspective, rather than seeking to prevent the politicization of environmental science, it seems more promising to find ways to institutionalize and legitimize it.

References

Barry, J. (1999). *Rethinking Green Politics* (London: Sage).

Bauer, M. (2008). "Survey Research and the Public Understanding of Science." In *Handbook of Public Communication on Science and Technology*, edited by M. Bucchi and B. Trench (London: Routledge), 111–30.

Beck, S. (2012). "From Truth to Trust: Lessons Learned from 'Climategate.'" In *Environmental Governance: The Challenge of Legitimacy and Effectiveness*, edited by K. Hogl, E. Kvarda, R. Nordbeck, and M. Pregernig (Cheltenham, UK: Edward Elgar), 220–41.

Beck, U. (1992). *Risk Society: Towards a New Modernity*. Translated by Mark Ritter (Newbury Park, CA: Sage Publications).

Besley, J. C. and Nisbet, M. (2013). "How Scientists View the Public, the Media and the Political Process." *Public Understanding of Science* 22: 644–59.

Bocking, S. (2006). *Nature's Experts: Science, Politics, and the Environment* (New Brunswick, NJ: Rutgers University Press).

Brown, M. B. (2009). *Science in Democracy: Expertise, Institutions, and Representation* (Cambridge, MA: MIT Press).

Brown, M. B. (2014). "Climate Science, Populism, and the Democracy of Rejection." In *Culture, Politics and Climate Change: How Information Shapes our Common Future*, edited by D. A. Crow and M. T. Boykoff (London and New York: Routledge Earthscan), 50–68.

Brown, P. and Mikkelson, E. J. (1990). *No Safe Place: Toxic Waste, Leukemia, and Community Action* (Berkeley: University of California Press).

Carson, R. (1962). *Silent Spring* (Boston and New York: Houghton Mifflin Harcourt).

Cronon, W. (1996). "The Trouble With Wilderness; Or Getting Back to the Wrong Nature." In *Uncommon Ground: Rethinking the Human Place in Nature*, edited by W. Cronon (New York: W. W. Norton), 69–90.

Demeritt, D. (2001). The Construction of Global Warming and the Politics of Science. *Annals of the Association of American Geographers* 91: 307–37.

Desmond, A. and Moore, J. (2009). *Darwin's Sacred Cause: Race, Slavery, and the Quest for Human Origins* (London: Penguin).

Douglas H. E. (2009). *Science, Policy, and the Value-Free Ideal* (Pittsburgh, PA: University of Pittsburgh Press).

Dunlap, R. E. and McCright, A. (2011). "Organized Climate Change Denial." In *The Oxford Handbook of Climate Change and Society*, edited by D. Schlosberg, J. Dryzek, and R. Norgaard (London: Oxford University Press), 144–60.

Dryzek, J. (2013). *The Politics of the Earth: Environmental Discourses*, 3rd edn. (Oxford and New York: Oxford University Press).

Fischer, F. (1990). *Technocracy and the Politics of Expertise* (London: Sage).

Fischer, F. (2000). *Citizens, Experts, and the Environment: The Politics of Local Knowledge* (Durham, NC: Duke University Press).

Funtowicz, S. O. and Ravetz, J. R. (1993). "Science for the Post-normal Age." *Futures* 25(7): 739–55.

Grundmann, R. (2013). "'Climategate' and the Scientific Ethos." *Science, Technology, and Human Values* 38(1): 67–93.

Guston, D. H. (2000). *Between Politics and Science: Assuring the Integrity and Productivity of Research* (New York: Cambridge University Press).

Habermas, J. (1970). *Toward a Rational Society: Student Protest, Science, and Politics*. Translated by J. J. Shapiro (Boston: Beacon Press).

Hall, C. (2013). "What Will It Mean to Be Green? Envisioning Possibilities Without Dismissing Loss." *Ethics, Policy, and Environment* 16(2): 125–41.

Hay, P. (2002). *Main Currents in Western Environmental Thought* (Bloomington and Indianapolis: Indiana University Press).

Hays, S. P. (1959). *Conservation and the Gospel of Efficiency: The Progressive Conservation Movement, 1890–1920* (Cambridge, MA: Harvard University Press).

Hulme, M. (2009a). *Why We Disagree about Climate Change: Understanding Controversy, Inaction and Opportunity* (Cambridge: Cambridge University Press).

Hulme, M. (2009b). "The Science and Politics of Climate Change." *Wall Street Journal*. http://online.wsj.com/article/SB10001424052748704107104574571613215771336.html

Inter-Academy Council, Committee to Review the Intergovernmental Panel on Climate Change. (2010). *Climate Change Assessments, Review of the Processes & Procedures of the IPCC* (October). http://reviewipcc.interacademycouncil.net/report.html

Jacques, P. J. (2012). "A General Theory of Climate Denial." *Global Environmental Politics* 12(2): 9–17.

Jasanoff. J. (1990). *The Fifth Branch: Science Advisers as Policymakers* (Cambridge, MA: Harvard University Press).

Jasanoff, S., Markle, G. E., Petersen, J. C., and Pinch, T., eds. (1995). *Handbook of Science and Technology Studies* (Thousand Oaks, CA: Sage Publications).

Kahan, D. M. (2010). "Fixing the Communications Failure." *Nature* 463 (January 21): 296–7.

Kellstedt, P. M., Zahran, S., and Vedlitz, A. (2008). "Personal Efficacy, the Information Environment, and Attitudes toward Global Warming and Climate Change in the USA." *Risk Analysis* 28(1):113–26.

Latour, B. (2004). *Politics of Nature: How to Bring the Sciences into Democracy*. Translated by Catherine Porter (Cambridge, MA: Harvard University Press).

Leiserowitz, A., Maibach, E., Roser-Renouf, C., Feinberg, G., Marlon, J., and Howe, P. (2013). "Public support for climate and energy policies in April 2013." Yale University and George

Mason University. New Haven, CT: Yale Project on Climate Change Communication. http://environment.yale.edu/climate-communication/article/Climate-Policy-Support-April-2013

Lertzman, Renee. (2008). "The Myth of Apathy." *Ecologist* 19(6): 16–17.

Luke, T. W. (2011). "Environmentality." In *The Oxford Handbook of Climate Change and Society*, edited by D. Schlosberg, J. Dryzek, and R. Norgaard (London, UK: Oxford University Press), 96–109.

Marcuse, H. (1964). *One Dimensional Man: Studies in the Ideology of Advanced Industrial Society* (Boston: Beacon Press).

Merchant, C. (1980). *The Death of Nature: Women, Ecology, and the Scientific Revolution* (New York: Harper Collins).

Miller, C. A. (2004). "Climate Science and the Making of a Global Political Order." In *States of Knowledge: The Co-Production of Science and Social Order*, edited by Sheila Jasanoff (London: Routledge), 46–66.

Mooney, C. (2005). *The Republican War on Science* (New York: Basic Books).

Mooney, C. and Kirshenbaum, S. (2009). *Unscientific America: How Scientific Illiteracy Threatens our Future* (New York: Basic Books).

Moser, S. C. and Dilling, L. (2011). "Communicating Climate Change: Closing the Science–Action Gap." In *The Oxford Handbook of Climate Change and Society*, edited by D. Schlosberg, J. Dryzek, and R. Norgaard (London, UK: Oxford University Press), 161–74.

National Science Board. (2012). "Science and Technology: Public Attitudes and Understanding." In *Science and Engineering Indicators 2012* (Arlington, VA: National Science Foundation (NSB 12-01)). http://www.nsf.gov/statistics/seind12/c7/c7h.htm

Nisbet, M. C. (2009). "Communicating Climate Change: Why Frames Matter to Public Engagement." *Environment* 51: 12–23.

Norgaard, K. M. (2011). *Living in Denial: Climate Change, Emotions, and Everyday Life* (Cambridge, MA: MIT Press).

Ottinger, G. and Cohen, B. R., eds. (2011). *Technoscience and Environmental Justice: Expert Cultures in a Grassroots Movement* (Cambridge, MA: MIT Press).

Oreskes, N. and Conway, E. M. (2010). *Merchants of Doubt: How a Handful of Scientists Obscured the Truth on Issues from Tobacco Smoke to Global Warming* (New York: Bloomsbury Press).

Pielke, R. A., Jr. (2007). *The Honest Broker: Making Sense of Science in Policy and Politics* (Cambridge, New York: Cambridge University Press).

Pielke, R. A., Jr. (2010). *The Climate Fix: What Scientists and Politicians Won't Tell You about Global Warming* (New York: Basic Books).

Pearce, F. (2010). *The Climate Files: The Battle for the Truth About Global Warming* (London: Guardian Books).

Proctor. R. N. (1991). *Value-Free Science? Purity and Power in Modern Knowledge* (Cambridge, MA: Harvard University Press).

Randerson, J. (2010). "Climate Researchers 'Secrecy' Criticised—But MPs Say Science Remains Intact." *The Guardian*. (March 31). http://www.guardian.co.uk/environment/2010/mar/31/climate-mails-inquiry-jones-cleared

Saad, L. (2014). "A Steady 57% in U.S. Blame Humans for Global Warming: Even As More Americans Say They're Informed, Blame on Humans Hasn't Grown." Gallup (March 18). http://www.gallup.com/poll/167972/steady-blame-humans-global-warming.aspx

Sarewitz, D. (2004). "How Science Makes Environmental Controversies Worse." *Environmental Science and Policy* 7: 385–403.

Sarewitz, D. (2010). "Curing Climate Backlash." *Nature* 464(4): 28.

Sarewitz, D. (2011). "Does Climate Change Knowledge Really Matter?" *Wiley Interdisciplinary Reviews: Climate Change* 2: 475–81.

Schneider, S. (2009). *Science as a Contact Sport: Inside the Battle to Save the Earth's Climate* (Washington, DC: National Geographic).

Scott, J. C. (1998). *Seeing Like a State: How Certain Schemes to Improve the Human Condition Have Failed* (New Haven, CT: Yale University Press).

Shellenberger, M. and Nordhaus, T. (2007). *Break Through: Why We Can't Leave Saving the Planet to Environmentalists* (Boston and New York: Houghton Mifflin Harcourt).

Shiva, Vandana. (1991). *The Violence of the Green Revolution: Third World Agriculture, Ecology, and Politics* (London and New York: Zed Books).

Specter, M. (2009). *Denialism: How Irrational Thinking Hinders Scientific Progress, Harms the Planet, and Threatens Our Lives* (New York: Penguin).

Sturgis, P. and Allum, N. (2004). "Science in Society: Re-evaluating the Deficit Model of Public Attitudes." *Public Understanding of Science* 13(1): 55–74.

Tierney, J. (2009). "E-mail Fracas Shows Peril of Trying to Spin Science." *New York Times* (November 30). http://www.nytimes.com/2009/12/01/science/01tier.html?_r=3&n=Top/News/Science/Columns/Findings

Turner, Stephen P. (2003). *Liberal Democracy 3.0: Civil Society in an Age of Experts* (London and Thousand Oaks, CA: Sage Publications).

Wapner, P. (2010). *Living through the End of Nature: The Future of American Environmentalism* (Cambridge, MA: MIT Press).

Weingart, P. (1999). "Scientific Expertise and Political Accountability: Paradoxes of Science in Politics." *Science and Public Policy* 26(3): 151–61.

Yearly, S. (2010). "Science and the Environment in the Twenty-first Century." In *The New International Handbook of Environmental Sociology*, edited by M. Redclift and G. Woodgate (Cheltenham: Edward Elgar), 212–25.

CHAPTER 33

DEMOCRACY AS CONSTRAINT AND POSSIBILITY FOR ENVIRONMENTAL ACTION

ELISABETH ELLIS

PROBLEMS raised for democracy by environmental politics throw conventional democratic theory's inherent tensions into sharp relief. Traditional theories of democratic representation are unsettled by questions of intergenerational justice, the instability of the demos, and the fact that environmental problems do not respect political borders; more generally, traditional accounts of democratic agency are undermined by difficulties in incorporating environmentally appropriate time and space horizons, and by uniquely irreversible policy dynamics that place democratic agency out of reach. Thus while democratic means are essential for environmental action, the peculiar dynamics of environmental issues force us to revise existing democratic theory.

Both abstract formalizations of democratic decision-making in environmental policy and concrete case studies of them lead to troubling conclusions. Democratic theory depends upon suppositions exploded by environmental issues: on a discrete identifiable citizenry making decisions for itself, for example, or on the revisability of policy decisions. As we shall see in the first half of this chapter, democracy constrains environmental action while environmental challenges constrain democracy itself. The answer, however, is not less democracy, either for environmental issues or in general. There is no alternative to democracy if we seek justice in a plural world. Simple democratic assumptions are the best candidates for general adjudication of differences. Rather than turn away from democratic theory, we must return to its essence, which will also make it useful for a large fraction if not all environmental issues.

In the second half of this chapter I sketch a democratic approach that enables rather than constrains environmental possibilities. I refocus democratic theory on protecting majority interests and reframe environmental issues in terms of protecting majority interest in sustainability from minority interests in extraction.[1] In environmental political theory only the literature on environmental justice has understood that we must attend to real conflicts of interest among groups of human beings; building on work in environmental justice we can revise democratic theory to reflect people's interests in justice. Along the way I argue that the idea of a general conflict between human and non-human interests with regard to environmental issues has been unfortunate for democracy in environmental theory. Real as this conflict may be from some *ethical* standpoints, the *politically* relevant conflict is among human groups with different interests in environmental policies.

Democratic Constraints

Environmental politics presents democratic theory with three crucial challenges: paternalism, irreversibility, and scope problems. Given the gravity of the challenges it should not surprise us that some environmental thinkers have rejected democracy (Heilbroner 1974; Ophuls 1977; Shearman and Smith 2007). Other environmental theorists have turned away from democratic politics without rejecting its political legitimacy, convinced that work in social movements, public opinion, or environmental ethics—work, that is, aimed at transforming mass preferences rather than facilitating their representation—will contribute more over the long run. In the second half of this chapter, I pursue a third alternative, revising conventional democratic theory in light of the challenges presented by environmental politics. First, let me review each of the three challenges in turn.

Paternalism

Democratic decisionmakers faced with environmental decisions seem to confront "right answers" they can either accept or ignore, rather than the real choice among policy alternatives democratic theory requires. Normally democratic theory deals with these apparent "right answers" in one of two ways: either the policy is in fact a condition of possible democracy and may thus be required of would-be democratic decisionmakers, or the rightness of the policy must be affirmed by a majority of the demos to whom the decisionmakers are accountable. Policies of the former type are commonly enshrined in constitutions or otherwise protected from everyday democratic policy flux (incidentally, this is why constitutional protections are not necessarily antidemocratic); they include things like the freedoms of speech and association without which democracy cannot function. Policies of the latter type are justified without reference to democracy, but by some other idea that happens to be accepted by the relevant demos; they include things like road maintenance and postal service, neither of which is essential to democracy but both of which have widely accepted arguments legitimating them. If a theory is to be democratic and not paternalistic, there can be no "right answers" except for these two types. As Michael Walzer has written, "it is a feature of democratic government that the people have a right to act wrongly" (Walzer 1981: 385).

Unfortunately, environmental policies seem to have "right answers" that are neither constitutive of democracy nor accepted by the relevant demos. For example, decision-makers accountable to democratic publics are perfectly capable of supporting extractive industries that contribute to climate change without regard for the long-term harms done to that same public, so long as those harms occur in the future or are otherwise invisible. In cases like these, majority interest in things like food security and clean air are indeed vindicated by the "right answer" policy, though the present system fails to represent those interests.[2]

Other kinds of environmental policies seem paternalistic because the consensus best choice among environmentalists conflicts with the views of the relevant demos (barring new development, banning incandescent lighting, or replacing roads with bike lanes are three of many possible examples). In these cases, it would indeed be paternalistic from a democratic point of view to insist on the rightness of the policy in the face of public rejection: "democratic" is not a synonym for "good."

These, however, are the easy cases. Other environmental policies are even more stubbornly paternalistic and thus even more challenging for democratic theory because in these cases, the very structure of the issue seems to determine the outcome regardless of people's democratic preferences. Take, for example, a policy to protect some fragile habitat-dependent species whose medium-term conservation is technically possible but politically costly. Over time, democratic policy flux will effectively reduce the available policy choices to one: extinction. This is so because the normal policy flux that follows from alternation in power will drive a ratchet effect in which each win for the development side is permanent, while each win for the conservation side is temporary (Ellis 2008). In cases like this one, democratic decision-making seems constrained to reach a single outcome: if office-holders alternate as they should in a democracy, then sometimes development interests will prevail over those who would prevent development of land currently supporting fragile, habitat-dependent species. Each loss of viable habitat is permanent, and each instance of habitat preservation is temporary. Thus almost regardless of the series of choices made by the demos, over the medium term there is only one possible policy outcome: extinction. This limit to democratic agency found in species conservation policy arises from structural incompatibility between democratic self-government and the dynamics of the policy itself.

This species conservation policy example points to the fact that there are some kinds of decisions that we simply cannot make for ourselves no matter how technically feasible or politically popular those decisions might be. As long as biodiversity policy is framed in terms of prevention of extinction of individual species, and as long as there is alternation in power and thus in policy as we should have in a democracy, then over time we seem limited to the single policy outcome of (eventual) extinction. There is an important debate among democratic theorists about the significance of the fact of limits to democratic self-rule: some take the view that despite the normative stories we tell ourselves about obeying laws of our own making, what democracy really accomplishes is something less—exchanges of ruling elites, for example, or constraint of oligarchy (Schumpeter 1942; Przeworski 1999, 2010). But we need not resign ourselves to accepting that democratic ideals are merely legitimating myth just because some kinds of environmental action seem beyond the reach of democratic policy making. Structural incompatibilities are not even unique to environmental issues. Phillip Pettit worries about something similar in his study of the policy resilience of harsh criminal sentencing, which seems to persist for structural reasons independent of political will or the common good (2007). Whether it is criminal justice or species conservation, democratic theorists should worry about this kind of result. Processes that lead to a single outcome no matter what the distribution of preferences do not look democratically legitimate. As we shall see in the second half of this chapter, however, a reframing of democratic theory's approach to these kinds of environmental policies may help us retrieve the possibility of agency even for these seemingly paternalistic outcomes.

Irreversibility

Closely related to paternalism is the challenge of irreversibility. Both problems challenge democracy at its most fundamental level, since both seem to undermine the possibility of democratic self-rule. In a democracy the demos must make choices, and for choice to be real there must be genuine alternatives. In his 1784 essay on enlightenment, Immanuel Kant argues that it is illegitimate for any generation to try to constrain future generations' choices (in this case, about religious doctrine). In our own time, Adam Przeworski argues that an "essential feature of democracy is that nothing is decided definitively" (1999). Each demos must be free to make decisions as it sees fit, subject to the caveat noted earlier that democracy itself must continue to be possible. Thus in general democratic policies must be reversible. This is easy to understand: if democracy is fundamentally about self-rule, and there are some policies that other people made that affect us, but that we cannot change, this strikes us as undemocratic. Exactly what kinds of inherited policies should be fair game for democratic politics is a matter of ongoing contestation. The most generally endorsed rule for deciding this matter is Kantian in spirit: everything that doesn't violate the conditions of possible democracy should be open to democratic decision-making. Thus as I have already noted most theorists place basics like rule of law and freedom of expression under constitutional protection, with everything else subject to ongoing debate. If you take for example one of the simplest glosses on what democracy means—having a say in the policies that affect you—we can see that even for this simplest of democratic theories, democratic legitimacy depends upon the right to reverse existing policies.

Environmental policies are not the only irreversible policies, of course. Settlement of disputed territory aims at irreversibility, and nuclear war and other scorched-earth war efforts are particularly terrible because they cause permanent damage.[3] But these policies strike us as undemocratic in virtue of their irreversibility. If I am negotiating about the boundaries of a disputed area of territory with you, and I send settlers into this area without your permission, you will rightly complain that you were not consulted. You are affected by a policy in which you had no say; you are constrained by someone else's choice in an undemocratic manner. Environmental politics contains a great many examples of the kind of irreversible action that offends democracy. Exhaustion of non-renewable resources, extinction of species, pollution and salinization of groundwater, ocean acidification, desertification . . . over time spans relevant to anthropocentric democratic theory, none of these policies is reversible (de-Shalit 1995; Callon et al. 2011).

Even more troubling for democratic theory is that rejection of a policy on grounds of irreversibility often entails severe reduction of the scope of remaining democratic decision space (but see Humphrey 2001). For example, one could argue that allowing pollution while taxing it is essentially selling the right to destroy nature; one might conclude after accepting such an argument that in this arena there exists but a single legitimate policy choice: zero emissions (Goodin 1994). So the flip side of the democratic argument that we may not make irreversible decisions for others (including those outside our demos now and future generations) is that our own decisions are constrained by this very dynamic. How democratic can it be for the demos to be told what decisions it must make regarding use of non-renewable resources, species conservation, groundwater, atmospheric and oceanic conditions, and agricultural policy (to return to our earlier list)? It certainly strikes one as paternalistic, and this is how such messages have often been received in the public sphere. Apparent paternalism rooted in irreversibility problems contributes to the structural difficulties faced by environmental interests in democratic political contests; those with interests in sustainability can seem constrained to argue that democracies face choices that are quite limited in scope.

Scope Problems

There are two types of scope problem connected with democracy and environmental policy, having to do with time and space, respectively: first, there is the problem that democratic theory suggests we should maintain the largest possible scope for future decision-making while simultaneously suggesting that there is often only one appropriate policy; and second, the decision-making body must have authority appropriate to the geographic scope of the policy if it is to be held accountable. I shall discuss each of these types of problem in turn.

First, we have democratic theory demanding x and not-x at once. As I noted earlier, democratic theory suggests *both* that there can be only one legitimate decision regarding irreversible policies, *and* that every democratic decision that does not undermine democracy procedurally must involve at least two options. For example, we must conserve species for future decision-making, especially because we are operating under conditions of uncertainty regarding the value of the species; but we ought not to face paternalistically predetermined policy outcomes unless these directly undermine the practice of democracy itself. Democratic theorists may complain, for example, when people vote against their economic self-interest, but they cannot rule it out as illegitimate. It would be a paternalistic mistake to replace the legitimate judgment of the demos with the judgment of the theorist, however reasonable she might be. In the case of environmental policy, then, we frequently confront the following result: democratic theory prescribes *both* a single determined policy outcome (preservation of an endangered species, for example, so as not to reduce the scope of future decision-making), *and* substantive choice among two or more outcomes.

A democratic people should under normal circumstances be empowered to weigh values against each other: do we prefer guns or butter? investment or consumption? preservation or development? Democracies may choose to ignore arguments for the intrinsic value of unique and irreplaceable species, for example, as well as arguments for the rights of non-human animals or for the interconnectedness of all being on the planet. The only values that democracies must in principle preserve are those that provide the conditions of possibility for democratic decision-making. To continue with the endangered species example, once we allow a species to go extinct, no further policy decision can be made about it. But since we cannot substitute our theoretical judgment about the policy for that of the demos, shouldn't we respect a people's determination that the species has less value to them than the value that would accrue to them without it? The problem is that the demos *qua* demos is an entity that persists over time, and we cannot know the value of the species for the demos over time. Of course it is possible that the anthropocentric value of a given species may not exceed the value achieved by its extinction, and in such a case there is no democratic argument for preservation. But species extinction is irreversible, and we almost never have enough certainty even to make a good guess about the value of a species for the demos over time.

I turn now to the second kind of scope problem facing democratic environmental policy, namely, that the decision-making body must have authority across space appropriate to the scope of the policy if it is to be held accountable. Conventional democratic theory presumes that a clearly delineated demos has interests within a clearly demarcated territory; decisions are made and decisionmakers held accountable as the results of those decisions are experienced and judged by that same demos. In most decisions about environmental policy, none of these presumptions holds. The case of acid rain caused by industrial pollution in one region affecting forests in another region first brought the problem of geographic scope to the attention of environmental theory. The age-old issue of decisions in one region foreclosing opportunities in another becomes particularly fraught in environmental cases, whether the policy in question is dam-building, fisheries management, or overuse of the global atmospheric sink. In this era of adaptation to climate change, the adjudication of decisions to employ geoengineering to cool the planet is an extreme example of a problem of geographic scope; just as no one in the Maldives was consulted about the fossil fuel energy regime that is endangering their way of life by raising sea levels, no system is currently in place to require governments considering geoengineering efforts to gain the consent of people living in regions that might be disproportionately affected. Conventional democratic theory presumes a bounded demos, while environmental policy reveals this premise to be nearly always counter-factual.

Democratic decisions can be made across borders (see Dryzek, this volume), though the most powerful of our present array of international institutions are also the least democratic (the World Trade Organization (WTO), the European Commission, even the United Nations Framework Convention on Climate Change (UNFCCC)). However, the consequences of geographic scope difficulties go deeper even than the problem I have just raised, of a mismatch between the decision-making and policy-affected bodies. If the scope of authority of a decision-making body does not allow it to address the environmental problem confronting it, then the question of accountability necessarily arises (see also Eckersley 2002: 57). Scope problems systematically advantage the interests of extraction against the interests of sustainability. Take, for example, the mandate of the US Endangered Species Act (ESA), which is to prevent extinctions and promote recovery of endangered and threatened species. Fulfilling this mandate is difficult enough when the authority responsible is the US Fish and Wildlife Service or some other agency of the federal government in the United States, especially since many species are threatened by consequences of global climate change. However, when authority for fulfilling the mandate of the ESA is devolved to the city council level, as is often the case for protection of species covered by regional habitat conservation plans (HCPs), the link between decision-making and accountability for outcomes is severed. City planners and members of habitat conservation planning committees recognize that they lack the authority to preserve species whose territory transcends local boundaries and whose fate is determined by a welter of factors, only some of which are under the control of the local city council. Of course there are steps local authorities can take to preserve endangered species under their care, such as preventing development of pristine habitat or requiring mitigation for permitted development. However, conditions of fragmented authority, lack of accountability, and scientific complexity and uncertainty make it structurally difficult for local city councils to justify the high costs of fulfilling the mandate of the ESA. Instead, local planners will rely on other bodies to take action to protect endangered species existing across boundaries (Ellis 2008).[4]

Geographic scope problems play havoc with the decision-making–accountability link so essential to democratic rule (Dryzek 2011: 49). Moreover, these problems systematically privilege players on the extraction side of environmental conflicts. To take another example, consider the recent debate in southern New Zealand over exploratory deep-sea drilling. Two cities in the region, Dunedin and Invercargill, were competing to become the onshore base for offshore oil exploration (Morris 2014). As the mayors and chamber of commerce officials readily pointed out, they had no authority to determine the global or even the regional energy regime going forward. They could choose to reject offshore oil drilling, but in the absence of broad collective action such a city-level choice would have overwhelmingly large local costs and vanishingly small local benefits. The fragmented structure of democratic authority systematically benefits the extraction side of the policy debate, because the benefits of extraction are potentially excludable goods like jobs and hotel stays, while the benefits of sustainable policy are non-excludable goods like spill-free environments and slightly delayed global warming. In fact, for the more mobile side of the globalized economy (manufacture of consumer goods, say, as opposed to necessarily local sectors like food service or construction), scope problems regularly disable democratic decision and systematically advantage extraction over sustainability because would-be extractors are able to select the demos most favorable to their interests, while would-be sustainers have difficulty assembling coalitions large enough to contain them. As summarized in the news media, the leaked draft of the fifth IPCC working group III (mitigation) report implied that drops in rich countries' carbon emissions should be considered illusory since those countries have taken advantage of globalization to outsource much of their manufacturing to places where carbon emissions are rising fast (Gillis 2014). The report itself speaks more blandly of "carbon leakage" and differences in national carbon accounting according to whether the carbon is measured at the site of production or the site of consumption (IPCC 2014).

But if the 2014 IPCC reports give us reason to worry about democratic scope problems, they also give us reasons to return to democratic theory for answers to our environmental problems. True, the three problems of paternalism, irreversibility, and scope present quite serious barriers to the resolution of our environmental problems by democratic means. It can seem as if the legitimating structure of democratic self-rule was invented for another world in which small, isolated groups of people made choices together about the self-regarding actions they would take. However, democratic theory is in fact more nimble (and less dispensable) than such a narrowly historical view might imply. The IPCC puts the current state of climate policy in stark terms that necessitate a democratic response: we face a choice between costly action now and ruinously costly and possibly futile action later (IPCC 2014). Current policy is essentially a lien on future generations that funds present-day fossil fuel consumption (the report adds that governments today spend more subsidizing fossil fuels than adapting to climate change or shifting to renewable energy sources). Unless we make drastic reductions in our emissions now, we will have to find a way to remove greenhouse gases from the atmosphere (Gillis 2014). Though there are of course many ways to construct the landscape of interests in extraction and sustainability, the IPCC reports confirm that the benefits of "business as usual" accrue to a minority of all affected (whom Kant would call "rogues"), while the costs of business as usual (adaptation to rising sea levels, having to use expensive and as yet untried technology to remove other people's carbon emissions from the atmosphere, to name just two) are borne by quite a large majority.[5]

Climate change policy, like most environmental policy, involves a conflict between a relatively small group interested in extraction, and a relatively large group interested in sustainability. Of all political theoretical perspectives, democratic theory should be equipped to tell us how to redress injustice against a large majority.

Democratic Possibilities

The literature on environmental justice provides a clear picture of the diversity of interests at stake in environmental action. Originally focused narrowly on the injustice of the disproportionate distribution of environmental bads like pollution to minority communities, the environmental justice perspective has kept its lens turned toward inequality as it broadened the scope of analysis to include new issues and disadvantaged groups. From the perspective of environmental justice, conflict is endemic to politics, and it must be addressed rather than wished away (Schlosberg 2013a; see also Schlosberg 2005). Rather than seeking ideal principles that prescribe right answers to us, the literature on environmental justice encompasses multiple meanings of justice while consistently arguing against clear injustices like exposing poor children to asthma-inducing pollution (Holland 2008; see also Sen 2009).

Environmental justice rightly focuses our attention on the structure of interests in environmental policy, asking who is being disproportionately harmed and identifying unjust practices. We cannot find our fully democratic solution within this literature, however, because the underlying logic of environmental justice is ethical rather than political; ethical positions within environmental justice can lead to democratic institutions like rights of participation, but their justification is different. Arguments from environmental justice, like arguments for intrinsic worth and other moral claims, have a crucial place in democratic theory: in the mouths, from the pens, on the posters and blogs of citizens themselves. As democratic theorists, however, we cannot replace the moral judgment of the demos with our own judgment lest we violate the stricture against paternalism. However, we can learn from the environmental justice literature that fighting injustice is more important than identifying some single ideal of justice, and that empowering people to be capable of acting in their own interests is more important than distributing to them some share of goods according to our own theoretical lights.

What is democratic about fighting injustice? After all, some views of justice fall into the category of ethical norms that I have been considering as appropriate for the democratic public sphere but not as building blocks of democratic right per se. The most important element of justice from a democratic point of view is that the demos rules. Democratic injustice occurs when the interests of most people are set aside in favor of the interests of some other group, whether it is comprised of Kantian rogues, Lockean polecats, or those I have been calling extractors (see Meyer 2008). Oppression of the many in the interests of the few offends democratic justice, whether the offenders are large landholders using private violence to repress their workforce, white South African governments using the police to repress black political action, or even plutocratically captured legislatures using market ideology to perpetuate gross inequality (see Wilmot 2014; Shapiro 1996; and Green 2013, respectively). Ian Shapiro argues that those "who fight for democracy often define their goals reactively. Sure as they are about the fine details of what they are against, they are less clear about the texture of what they hope to create" (Shapiro 1999: 1; see also Sen 2009). Analytically speaking, most environmental policies take this same form: a (usually small) number of extractors reap a short-term benefit for which a (usually much larger) number of sustainers is forced to pay. Environmental policy provides exceptionally clear examples of democratic injustice.

If, then, we are to understand the political world rightly, we need to see past ordinary conventions that mischaracterize its real basis and instead focus on the norms and power dynamics that structure actual political relationships among actors. In particular, in democratic (as opposed to moral) arguments, we should avoid characterizing environmental politics as conflict between human and non-human interests, lest we miss the real structure of conflict between the (usually small) number of human beings with short-run interests in extraction and the (usually large) number of human beings with interests in alternatives to extraction. Of course the structure of interests is always complicated, and individual human beings can have multiple and conflicting interests in any one dispute, but the general fact remains that most environmental conflict pits a minority of short-term "extractors" against a majority of "sustainers," or people with medium-term interests in the sustainable provision of things like clean air and water. By characterizing environmental conflicts as conflicts between human and non-human interests, we would unwittingly adopt the ideological lenses of an unrealistic minority position. A critical ancillary error is to presume unanimity among human interests, as if there were a natural general will shared by humankind regarding our relationship to the environment and the difficulty is just in finding and then abiding by it. Broadly presumed and widely unacknowledged, this error lies behind such disastrous institutions as the consensus rule among the Conference of the Parties (COP) in the UNFCCC process. By framing environmental issues as "how must humanity respond to challenge x?" we set up a system in which policy consensus is pursued ad infinitum, a system in which a determined minority can prevent concerted action on behalf of the great majority without explicitly violating any public norms. Instead, we ought to frame most environmental issues democratically, as "how can most of us protect our interests in sustainability against the few who would pursue unsustainable policies?"

Moreover, democratic arguments need not address the interests of beings outside the circle of enfranchised agents. When Peter Singer argues for the "expanding circle" of moral consideration, he is making an ethical argument that might well sway large numbers of people, but only has democratic force if they are in fact so swayed. The democratic commitment to antipaternalism dictates that democrats must be suspicious of any theory that would pre-judge the policy decisions rightly made (and continually remade) by the demos. The only acceptable exceptions to the democratic bias against paternalism are decisions that would undermine the possibility of democratic decision-making itself. The circle of enfranchised agents has of course expanded from time to time, and rightly so; but it expands in circumstances in which key players' strategic democratic interests are served by that expansion and in circumstances in which many people become convinced of the ethical argument for expansion—and especially in cases where both circumstances occur (Mansbridge 2005). Thus there is no *general* reason for democratic environmental theory to consider the interests of non-humans.

There are certainly a number of *particular* circumstances in which participants in democratic policy-making ought to consider the interests of non-humans. They figure indirectly, for example, in decisions about biodiversity and ecosystem management, where most human and non-human interests coincide. More fundamentally, members of a demos may come to the ethical conclusion that non-human animals ought to be treated with respect. The most critical environmental problems for which democratic action is needed today—climate change and biodiversity loss—cannot be resolved by presuming an ever greater circle of common interest when what must urgently be recognized is the radical division of interests among groups of human beings. The proposals, therefore, to reconcile environmental and democratic impulses by representing non-human interests fundamentally miss the mark, even as an environmental democratic theorist can easily sympathize with the motivation behind the effort (see, in particular, Dobson, but also the recent work by Donaldson and Kymlicka). A realistic democratic argument would not seek to enfranchise non-human interest, but to identify the environmentally relevant conditions of possible democratic decision-making, to characterize the distribution of interests among enfranchised agents, and to interpret public rhetorics (arguments made by enfranchised agents) that are relevant to environmental politics.

What applies in general to environmental politics applies in particular to species conservation policy. Much of the public rhetoric around species conservation, for example, accepts a simple dichotomy of human versus non-human interests. For example, when it turned out that land deeded to the city for a school by the developer of a subdivision in San Diego contained some of the last remaining habitat of an endangered aquatic invertebrate, neighborhood people complained that the state cares more about shrimp than children. The real distribution of interests around fairy shrimp conservation is hard to specify, of course, but certainly the rhetoric of conflict with non-human interests distracted citizens from the moment in which the developer chose to locate a school in an area already occupied by a federally protected ecosystem (Ellis 2008; see also Schlosberg 2013b).

Recognizing the real structure of interest distribution in environmental conflicts should not only shift discourses like this one back to reality, but might also help ameliorate the three challenges to democratic theory presented by environmental policy itself. The problem of paternalism might be reduced by the application of a perspective that identifies the real conflict between extractors and sustainers, for example. As we saw in the first half of the chapter, uncertainty about the anthropocentric value for the demos of the persistence of particular species seemed to dictate the single outcome of a policy for preservation, while the democratic structure of decision-making seemed to contradict that by always reaching the extinction outcome over the medium term. Identifying the extractor/sustainer conflict in the case of species preservation would ameliorate the problem of alternations in power leading to medium-term extinctions because alternations in power would be less likely to lead to policies benefitting extractors exclusively. Instead, a range of representative options for sustainers would mean that what looked like a single option of preserving a single species at all costs might in fact be a basket of sustainer-promoting options, not all of which treat species independently. The realistic democratic perspective might similarly lessen our difficulties with irreversibility and scope, as an empowered larger demos including all potentially affected sustainers would naturally pursue their interests in preventing irreversible harm. Switching from a "common human challenge" perspective to a realistic democratic view that recognizes the division of interests among human groups might help us move, for example, from the unproductive consensus-based procedure used at the COP level in international climate-change negotiations toward the majoritarian system that would be better able to handle climate conflict.

Thus we see that democratic theory can in fact rise to the challenges posed for it by environmental policy. Reframed from the erroneous image of an elite pursuing arcane ethical commitments and love of the "big outside" at the expense of the working many, environmental activists can rightly position themselves as the representatives of the enormous majority with interests in sustainability (Cronon 1995; Meyer 2008; Schlosberg 2013a). As Nadia Urbinati has recently argued, representative democracy need not necessarily be captured by elites who seek to constrain the many; it need not stay "frozen in the non-democratic choices made by its founders" (Urbinati 2006: 1). Instead, democracy can return to its essence by orienting itself against injustice, which in environmental policy means fighting for the interests of the overwhelming majority in the sustainable provision of things like sufficient food, pure air, and clean water.

Acknowledgments

I would like to thank the editors for very helpful exchanges on drafts of this chapter. Early versions of these ideas were presented at meetings of the Association for Political Theory, the Western Political Science Association, and at gatherings of political theorists at Princeton University, Tulane University, and the University of Toronto. Thanks to my former colleagues and students at Texas A&M University and my new colleagues and students at the University of Otago for talking with me about these ideas in seminars and elsewhere.

Notes

1. In this chapter I use "extraction" and "extractors" as shorthand to refer to those activities and interests that are environmentally unsustainable, including, e.g., direct extraction of resources from the earth, indirect use of non-renewable energy to produce consumer goods, and other practices that conflict with the long-run interests of the vast majority of people in the sustainable use of things like clean air and water, food security, and so forth.
2. As Robyn Eckersley has argued, it is a mistake to confuse the failure of present-day liberal democracies to represent these kinds of interests with the non-existence of those interests. See Eckersley 2004.

3. Thanks to Gerry Mackie and his students for an enlightening conversation on this point at UC-San Diego.
4. The structure of this conservation problem can be seen as a tragedy of the commons: the disunited local players deplete a common resource (in this case, the "resource" is US federal permission to grant development permits on land occupied by endangered species) because none is willing to take independent action to conserve species if they have no reason to expect others to follow suit (for the classic discussion, see Hardin 1968). Authorities in the state of Texas seem to have recognized the threat that species listing under the ESA poses to the common "resource" of unregulated development: when it looked as though fragmented oil extractors and ranchers would be unable to take enough action on their own to prevent the federal government from listing local vulnerable species (which would have effectively taken the "commons" of permitted prospecting and grazing), the state granted itself unprecedented authority to represent localities and organize measures to prevent a listing decision. At the time of writing (early 2014), the species in question have not been listed as endangered, and thus central action on the part of the state of Texas preserved a common "resource" for the use of previously disorganized ranchers and oil companies.
5. Kant glosses the motto *fiat iustitia, pereat mundus* as "let justice reign even if all the rogues in the world perish because of it." See the discussion of his gloss and its meaning in Ellis 2008: 10–15 and 153–6.

References

Callon, Michael, Lascoumes, Pierre, and Barthe, Yannick. (2011). *Acting in an Uncertain World: An Essay on Technical Democracy*. Translated by Graham Burchell (Cambridge, MA: MIT Press).

Cronon, William. (1995). "The Trouble With Wilderness; or, Getting Back to the Wrong Nature." In *Uncommon Ground: Rethinking the Human Place in Nature*, edited by W. Cronon. (New York: W. W. Norton), 69–90.

de-Shalit, Avner. (1995). *Why Posterity Matters: Environmental Policies and Future Generations* (London: Routledge).

Dobson, Andrew. (1996). "Representative Democracy and the Environment." In *Democracy and the Environment: Problems and Prospects*, edited by W. Lafferty and J. Meadowcroft (Cheltenham: Edward Elgar), 124–39.

Dobson, Andrew. (2007). *Green Political Thought*. 4th edn. (New York: Routledge).

Dobson, Andrew and Eckersley, Robyn, eds. (2006). *Political Theory and the Ecological Challenge* (Cambridge: Cambridge University Press).

Donaldson, Sue and Kymlicka, Will. (2011). *Zoopolis: A Political Theory of Animal Rights* (Oxford: Oxford University Press).

Dryzek, John S. (1996). "Strategies of Ecological Democratization." In *Democracy and the Environment: Problems and Prospects*, edited by W. Lafferty and J. Meadowcroft (Cheltenham: Edward Elgar), 108–23.

Dryzek, John S. (2011). *Foundations and Frontiers of Deliberative Governance* (Oxford: Oxford University Press).

Dryzek, John S., Goodin, Robert E., Tucker, Aviezer, and Reber, Bernard. (2009). "Promethean Elites Encounter Precautionary Publics: The Case of GM Foods." *Science, Technology, and Human Values* 34(3): 263–88.

Eckersley, Robyn. (2002). "Environmental Pragmatism, Ecocentrism, and Deliberative Democracy: Between Problem-Solving and Fundamental Critique." In *Democracy and the Claims of Nature: Critical Perspectives for a New Century*, edited by Ben A. Minteer and Bob Pepperman Taylor (Lanham, Md.: Rowman & Littlefield), 49–70.

Eckersley, Robyn. (2004). *The Green State: Rethinking Democracy and Sovereignty* (Cambridge, MA: MIT Press).

Eckersley, Robyn. (2007). "Ecological Intervention: Prospects and Limits." *Ethics and International Affairs* 21(3): 293–317.

Ellis, Elisabeth. (2008). *Provisional Politics: Kantian Arguments in Policy Context* (New Haven, CT: Yale University Press).

Gillis, Justin. (2014). "U.N. Says Lag in Confronting Climate Woes Will Be Costly." *New York Times* (January 17), A8.

Goodin, Robert E. (1994). "Selling Environmental Indulgences." *Kyklos* 47(4): 573–96.

Green, Jeffrey Edward. (2013). "Rawls and the Forgotten Figure of the Most Advantaged: In Defense of Reasonable Envy toward the Superrich." *American Political Science Review* 107(1): 123–38.

Hardin, Garrett. (1968). "The Tragedy of the Commons." *Science* 162(3859): 1243–48.

Heilbroner, Robert L. (1974). *An Inquiry into the Human Prospect* (New York: W. W. Norton and Co).

Holland, Breena. (2008). "Ecology and the Limits of Justice: Establishing Capability Ceilings in Nussbaum's Capabilities Approach." *Journal of Human Development* 9(3): 401–25.

Humphrey, Matthew, ed. (2001). *Political Theory and the Environment: A Reassessment* (London: Frank Cass).

Humphrey, Matthew. (2001). "Three Conceptions of Irreversibility and Environmental Ethics: Some Problems." In *Political Theory and the Environment: A Reassessment*, edited by Matthew Humphrey (London: Frank Cass), 138–54.

IPCC, 2014: Climate Change 2014: Mitigation of Climate Change. *Contribution of Working Group III to the Fifth Assessment Report of the Intergovernmental Panel on Climate Change* [Edenhofer, O., R. Pichs-Madruga, Y. Sokona, E. Farahani, S. Kadner, K. Seyboth, A. Adler, I. Baum, S. Brunner, P. Eickemeier, B. Kriemann, J. Savolainen, S. Schlömer, C. von Stechow, T. Zwickel and J.C. Minx, eds.]. (Cambridge; New York: Cambridge University Press).

Mansbridge, Jane. (2005). "Cracking through Hegemonic Ideology: The Logic of Formal Justice." *Social Justice Research* 18(3): 335–47.

Mansbridge et al. (2010). "The Place of Self-Interest and the Role of Power in Deliberative Democracy." *The Journal of Political Philosophy*18(1): 64–100.

Meadowcroft, James. (2004). "Deliberative Democracy." In *Environmental Governance Reconsidered: Challenges, Choices, and Opportunities*, edited by Robert F. Durant, Daniel J. Fiorino, and Rosemary O'Leary (Cambridge, MA: MIT Press), 183–218.

Meyer, John M. (2008). "Populism, Paternalism, and the State of Environmentalism in the U.S." *Environmental Politics* 17(2): 219–36.

Minteer, Ben A. and Taylor, Bob Pepperman. (2002). *Democracy and the Claims of Nature: Critical Perspectives for a New Century* (Lanham, Md.: Rowman & Littlefield).

Morris, Chris. (2014). "Race to Host Oil and Gas Supply Base." *The Otago Daily Times* (Thursday January 9). Available at: http://www.odt.co.nz/news/dunedin/287660/city-race-host-supply-base Accessed June 16, 2015.

Ophuls, William. (1977). *Ecology and the Politics of Scarcity: Prologue to a Political Theory of the Steady State* (San Francisco: W. H. Freeman and Co).

Pettit, Phillip. (2007). "Resilience as the Explanandum of Social Theory." In *Contingency in the Study of Politics*, edited by Ian Shapiro and Sonu Bedi (New York and London: New York University Press), 79–96.
Przeworski, Adam. (1999). "Minimalist Conception of Democracy: A Defense." In *Democracy's Value*, edited by Ian Shapiro and Casiano Hacker-Cordón (New York: Cambridge University Press), 23–55.
Przeworski, Adam. (2010). *Democracy and the Limits of Self-Government* (New York: Cambridge University Press).
Schlosberg, David. (2005). "Environmental and Ecological Justice: Theory and Practice in the United States." In *The State and the Global Ecological Crisis*, edited by John Barry and Robyn Eckersley (Cambridge, MA: MIT Press), 97–116.
Schlosberg, David. (2007). *Defining Environmental Justice: Theories, Movements, Nature* (Oxford: Oxford University Press).
Schlosberg, David. (2013a). "Theorising Environmental Justice: The Expanding Sphere of a Discourse." *Environmental Politics* 22(1): 37–55.
Schlosberg, David. (2013b). "Political Challenges of the Climate-Challenged Society." *PS: Political Science and Politics* January 2013: 13–18.
Schlosberg, David and Carruthers, David. (2010). "Indigenous Struggles, Environmental Justice, and Community Capabilities." *Global Environmental Politics* 10(4): 12–35.
Schumpeter, Joseph A. (1942). *Capitalism, Socialism, and Democracy* (New York: Harper).
Sen, Amartya. (1999). *Development as Freedom* (Oxford: Oxford University Press).
Sen, Amartya. (2009). *The Idea of Justice* (Cambridge, MA: Belknap).
Shapiro, Ian. (1989). "Gross Concepts in Political Argument." *Political Theory* 17(1): 51–76.
Shapiro, Ian. (1996). *Democracy's Place* (Ithaca, New York: Cornell University Press).
Shapiro, Ian. (1999). *Democratic Justice* (New Haven: Yale University Press).
Shapiro, Ian. (2012). "On Non-domination." *University of Toronto Law Journal* 62(3): 293–336.
Shearman, David and Smith, Joseph Wayne. (2007). *The Climate Change Challenge and the Failure of Democracy* (Westport, CT: Praeger).
Singer, Peter. (2011). *The Expanding Circle: Ethics, Evolution, and Moral Progress* (Princeton: Princeton University Press).
Urbinati, Nadia. (2006). *Representative Democracy: Principles and Genealogy* (Chicago: University of Chicago Press).
Walzer, Michael. (1981). "Philosophy and Democracy." *Political Theory* 9(August 1981): 379–99.
Wilmot, Fiona Coralie. (2014). "Making Mangroves: Ecologies of Mangrove Restoration in El Salvador, 2011–2013." PhD Dissertation, Texas A&M University.

CHAPTER 34

ENVIRONMENTAL AUTHORITARIANISM AND CHINA

MARK BEESON

If only things were different. If there is one thing upon which we can probably all agree, it is this. Environmentalists, policymakers, (most) businesspeople, and a general public no doubt sick of a debate that is formidably technical and contentious, might all concur that the world would be a more agreeable place if we didn't have to worry (and disagree) about climate change. Unfortunately we do. Or we do if—as I do—we take the claims of the overwhelming majority of climate scientists seriously when they tell us that climate change is real, likely to have profound, quite literally life-changing effects, and that we are collectively responsible for it.

Different states respond to the challenge of climate change in different ways, not least because of the domestic political forces that shape policy. In many liberal democracies debate over climate change has become highly politicized as powerful lobby groups and vested interests have taken advantage of competitive, pluralistic political systems to push particular agendas in ways that advance and reflect their interests (Orsekes and Conway 2010; Dunlap and McRight 2011). This has made the development of a consensus about possible mitigation, much less effective action to remedy climate change's well known impacts, very difficult to achieve in places such as the United States.

China provides the quintessential example and test of a potentially very different response to dealing with climate change and environmental degradation. China's non-democratic approach to public policy is increasingly associated with a form of "environmental authoritarianism" (Beeson 2010), or what Gilley (2012: 288) calls "a public policy model that concentrates authority in a few executive agencies manned by capable and uncorrupt elites seeking to improve environmental outcomes." This chapter considers how closely the Chinese experience corresponds to this model, and how effectively the Chinese state is responding to the challenge of climate change and environmental degradation. At issue is whether an authoritarian state is potentially better able to make the potentially difficult decisions that may be required to address such problems in a way in which many of their democratic counterparts have thus far failed. Before doing so, however, I situate the discussion in the context of some long-standing debates about authoritarianism, and the political and economic contexts within which environmental policy emerges.

Environmental Policy in Context

It is frequently observed that we need two planets rather than one to support "Western" lifestyles (WWF 2012). There is, in short, a widely recognized fundamental disjuncture between the carrying capacity of the natural environment and the impact of human activities on the biosphere. The nature of this impact has been extensively detailed elsewhere and needs little repetition here. The key point to emphasize at the outset, however, is that there is a potentially unsustainable, incompatible tension between the goals of rapid economic development and a livable environment. In this regard, China's experience highlights what Marxists might aptly describe as a profound "contradiction," which the leaders of the People's Republic must address if they wish to maintain social stability and their place at the apex of China's authoritarian political system.

It might be supposed that China's unaccountable, electorally-unresponsive, top-down political system is especially ill-suited to respond to environmental concerns. There is, after all, a rich and influential literature that stresses the potential importance of market forces and/or democracy—especially the deliberative variety—in responding to climate change and environmental degradation (see Bohman 1998; Newell 2012). And yet there is another long-standing strand of environmentally-oriented political theory which argues that authoritarian regimes may have particular advantages over their democratic counterparts, especially when ecological pressures become increasingly severe.

As far back as the 1970s, Robert Heilbroner suggested that environmentally-constrained "limits to growth" would undermine capitalism with disastrous political consequences. For Heilbroner (1974: 47), there was "an ultimate certitude about the problem of environmental deterioration" that set it apart from all other problems. At its heart was an expansionary capitalist system, which needed reforming and reining in. In Heilbroner's view, however, the required transformation of the capitalist mode of production "will be likely to exceed the capabilities of representative democracies" (Heilbroner 1974: 90). In the long run, Heilbroner concluded, only socialism seemed capable of bringing human behavior and the natural environment into some sort of harmony. William Ophuls (1997: 276–7) took an equally pessimistic view, and came to similar sorts of conclusions: to avoid ecological calamity, Ophuls argued, "we must learn once again to govern—controlling, guiding, directing, and restraining individuals who would otherwise behave selfishly and destructively, so that they respect the interests and needs of the larger human and natural community of which they are a part."

Timing is everything in these debates, and the failure of some of these predictions to materialize in the short term did much to undermine their credibility. And yet it is important to remember that when the Club of Rome published its landmark study on the possible limits to growth (Meadows et al. 1974), with the notable exception of Japan, industrialization and rapid economic growth were still largely Western phenomena and the world population was "only" four billion. Now, however, with the rise of the so-called BRICs (Brazil, Russia, India and China) generally and China in particular, the picture looks very different and some of the earlier concerns appear prescient rather than alarmist. As a consequence, a number of observers have considered the possibility that authoritarian responses to the challenge of climate change might either prove more effective (Shearman and Smith 2007), or more likely as the environment deteriorates and the need to respond or at least control the social fall-out becomes ever greater (Beeson 2010). Before considering how effective or otherwise China can be in addressing such challenges, it is important to spell out the political and economic constraints it must grapple with if it is to have any impact. Ironically enough, many of these constraints have been identified most clearly by broadly Marxist scholars.

The Political-Economy of Climate Policy

Although China is still nominally a "socialist" country, it has become one of the world's most successful examples of capitalist development. Two caveats are in order here, however. First, and most immediately, the definition of success in this case is a somewhat limited one and revolves around the remarkable expansion of economic activity in China and the consequent rise in living standards this has underpinned. It is a success story that has given China's authoritarian "communist" leaders an authority and even a legitimacy they would not otherwise have had, of course. The second caveat flows from this point: "Chinese capitalism" is very different from the sort of liberal, market-oriented model that prevails in much of the West, a reality that has major consequences for economics *and* politics in China.

For all its undoubted "efficiencies" and capacity to generate growth, capitalism of any sort generates a complex array of economic, social, and political relations that is unprecedented in scale and in the concomitant impact it is having on the natural environment. True, industrialized "socialist" societies have inflicted a similar toll—China under Mao certainly did (Shapiro 2001)—but capitalism creates incentive structures and lifestyles that seem especially incompatible with sustainable ecological outcomes, particularly when market-oriented production has become the default model of economic organization across the world.

The potential incompatibility between capitalism's internal, expansionary logic and a sustainable environment that many contemporary radical scholars emphasize is difficult to gainsay (Foster et al. 2010). In a world of finite resources an economic order that is based on ever greater levels of production and consumption—for those in the "developed" world, at least—is by definition unsustainable. As Wolfgang Streek points, out, "The long-known fact that capitalism flourishes, not by covering existing needs but by eliciting new ones—that capitalist growth requires permanent demand-management not just in a quantitative but also in a qualitative sense—should be recognized as increasingly critical" (Streeck 2012: 13). This is a new problem with which China's leaders are beginning to grapple. It has been given particular urgency by the rising expectations of the Chinese people and the equally insistent demands of disgruntled trade partners who are demanding that China "rebalance" its development model to prioritize domestic consumption (Vermiren 2013; Anderlini 2014).

Capitalism may come in many varieties, but its essential underlying profit-driven, consumption-oriented internal dynamic presents an institutionalized obstacle to reform. Discussions of climate change are not only affected by the sorts of direct, politicized interventions noted at the outset, but because some actors enjoy far more enduring "structural power" than others (Bell 2012). This is a widely recognized phenomenon in much Western scholarship (Lindblom 1977), but has had little impact in China, where the study of political economy remains comparatively underdeveloped, not least because of acute sensitivities about the role of the state (Zhu and Pearson 2013). Nevertheless, the "varieties of capitalism" literature's distinction between "coordinated" and "liberal" market economies highlights an important institutionalized reality that—in theory, at least—holds out the prospect that China's state-dominated form of capitalism might actually be better able to implement major reforms of the sort that Heilbroner and Ophuls thought necessary but unlikely in liberal democracies (see Hall and Soskice 2001).

However, China is not immune from precisely the same sort of powerful vested interests that have made addressing climate change so problematic in much of the West. In China's case, as we shall see, many actors, ranging from ordinary citizens and local governments, to strategically important state-owned enterprises (SOEs), are dependent on a continuing growth paradigm that makes any retreat from high speed growth politically difficult. Ironically enough, therefore, having embarked so successfully and surprisingly on the once reviled "capitalist road," China's leaders find themselves having to deal with precisely the same sorts of problems and dilemmas as their counterparts in the West. There is one crucial difference, of course: unlike the leaders of liberal democracies, China's ruling elite is not directly accountable to the general population, nor as potentially constrained in its actions. The question is, therefore, does this different authoritarian mode of governance actually offer a better prospect for addressing China's growing list of environmental problems?

China and the Evolving Politics of Climate Change

No country more vividly highlights the tension between unconstrained economic development and implacable ecological constraints than China, as the growing social unrest in Beijing and other heavily polluted cities demonstrates (Hornby 2014). The key question for China and the world is whether an industrialization paradigm pioneered in the West is any longer environmentally feasible and sustainable on the scale and at the speed that China is currently developing. Even more fundamentally, perhaps, can China's political system cope with the combined ecological and social challenges its developmental model is generating?

The domestic and international impact of China's economic expansion on the environment are widely recognized and understood, but it is worth repeating what is at stake and its historically unprecedented nature. As Liu and Diamond (2005: 1185) put it,

> China's achievement of developed-world consumption standards will approximately double the world's human resource use and environmental impact. But it is doubtful whether even the current human resource use and impact on the world can be sustained. Something has to give, or change. That is why China's environmental problems are the world's.

There is a sobering litany of statistics that bear witness to this claim, which detail both China's voracious appetite for natural resources such as coal, as well as the increasingly dramatic declines in air, water, and soil quality—the very stuff of life, in fact (Economy 2004; Cooper 2008). But it is evident that China's material rise also has the potential to underpin significant changes in the way international politics is conducted and the goals to which international collaborative efforts are directed. Indeed, the abortive negotiations conducted at the recent United Nations' sponsored climate change conference in Copenhagen vividly illustrated that while China may not be able to provide leadership (Beeson 2013), it has the capacity to stop agreement from being reached (Christoff 2010). As we shall see, China's domestic politics provided a powerful constraining influence on what its foreign policy officials could contemplate, much less achieve.

But before we attempt to explain the complex dynamics of Chinese policy-making, however, it is important to emphasize one thing at the outset, which ought to be self-evident but often isn't considered: China has a unique history and distinctive political context that means its developmental trajectory is unlike that of any other state. Perhaps the same claim could be made about any country, but not only is much of the theorization of the politics of climate change often ahistorical, it is also generally predicated on a limited range of "Western" experiences. An unfortunate Eurocentricism still pervades much of the literature that deals with international development, politics, and climate change—despite the unambiguously global nature of all of these issues (Hobson 2012). Unless we take account of the very different basis of national politics in countries such as China, we shall fail to recognize some of the fundamental obstacles to international cooperation and mitigation or the possibility that current and future patterns of climate politics will not necessarily replicate what is in any case often an idealized Western experience.

The Domestic Context

The interconnected significance of politics and economics is especially pertinent in a Chinese context. Not only has the "uneven development" of capitalism within the world and China itself created major problems and contradictions (Wang and Hu 1999; Smith 2008), but China's historical developmental experience means that political and economic forces are tightly enmeshed in ways that shape environmental politics, too. Indeed, the central comparative point to emphasize in this context is that China's history has been quite unlike that of the West and shows no sign of converging on any sort of Western template in the foreseeable future. On the contrary, one of the most striking contradictions and paradoxes to emerge in China's recent history is that despite what is essentially a highly successful capitalist class coming to dominate economic activity in the "People's Republic," the reality is that they have shown little collective inclination to push for the sort of political liberalism that was the hallmark of Europe's transition to capitalism some 200 years or so earlier (Tsai 2007).

China's unique historical experience merits emphasis for two further reasons. First, one of the reasons that China's expanding capitalist class has played little part in pushing for political liberalization is—in part, at least—because China has subscribed to East Asia's state-led tradition of economic development. Powerful "interventionist" states have been the norm, especially in northeast Asia, and they have often enjoyed a good deal of "performance legitimacy" as a consequence (Beeson 2014). It is striking that such surveys of popular opinion as do exist in China routinely show higher levels of satisfaction among the general population than exist in the United States or Western Europe (Tang et al. 2013). It is also evident that many people are broadly satisfied with their standard of living and seemingly willing to make the implicit trade-off between economic development and political emancipation (Han 2012). Plainly, environmental pressures could change this picture, but even if they do, it is far from clear that this will presage a shift to democracy or a more inclusive attitude to public policy. Indeed, a second reason for stressing China's distinctive developmental trajectory is that there is no history of democracy in mainland China and civil society remains relatively under-developed and closely controlled. Lo (2010: 1016) claims that "Chinese discourse on climate change is highly pragmatic and dominated by governmental actors... Opposition social forces are perhaps even less influential in China than in other major developing countries."

Of course, things could change—perhaps abruptly. Many observers have questioned whether the Chinese Communist Party (CCP) can maintain its grip on power when its ideological raison d'être has long since disappeared and its primary function has been to oversee the management of the economy and the constellation of elite level economic and political interests that effectively constitute it (Brødsgaard 2012; Li 2012). It is in this context that environmental issues generally represent a profound threat to the extant order—as they do everywhere, for that matter. What gives the issues a particular immediacy in China is both the well documented deterioration in the environment itself, and the potential impact this could have on economic activity (*The Economist* 2013). The key concern here is that China's environmental problems are becoming so severe, that they "have the potential to bring the country to its knees economically" (Economy 2004: 25).

China's environmental problems are, like everything else about the country, on an epic scale. The recent much-publicized problems with Beijing's air quality are but the latest in a series of problems revolving around water shortages, soil erosion, and pollution which are quite literally taking years off the lives of its citizens (Silk 2013). What makes the Chinese case especially significant in this regard, however, is not simply the size of the problem, but the response this has triggered on the part of the state. One of the great paradoxes of authoritarian rule in China is what has been described as its "fragmented" nature (Lieberthal 1992). While China's political system may appear monolithic this conceals inter-agency rivalries, factional politics, and intense competition over the nature of policy. As in much of the world, "the failure of environmental policies is related to the dominance of economic policy institutions over environmental policy institutions" (He et al. 2012: 35). As a consequence, environmental policies can seem rather schizophrenic and contradictory at times. On the one hand, China has become the world's largest investor in renewable energy (Crooks 2011). On the other hand, however, policy continues to be heavily influenced by power companies, the oil industry, and powerful state-owned industries who are opposed to reform. These companies have either ignored the directives of government or used their positions on various committees to water down the reforms themselves (Wong 2013).

Recent events have made China's elites acutely conscious of the potential the environment has to create social unrest, especially given the growing importance of social media (Hille 2013). Premier Li Keqiang's (2014: 29–30) address to the Twelfth National People's Congress acknowledged that "environmental pollution has become a major problem, which is nature's red-light warning against the model of inefficient and blind development." Not only is China's leadership apparently increasingly willing to acknowledge the extent of the problem, but Xi Jinping is widely regarded as the most powerful president since Deng Xiaoping (Sheridan 2014). Xi consequently has the potential to act in ways that may have eluded some of his more factionally constrained predecessors, but this is no guarantee that this power will be used in constructive ways. On the contrary, not only do China's leaders seem preoccupied with pursuing territorial claims and historical grudges with neighbors (Chan 2014), but one of the main responses to pollution along the densely-populated Eastern seaboard is to shift the offending industries to the far west (Scott 2014).

It is also important to note the contradictory role China's increasingly influential civil society and social media are playing in shaping public and foreign policy. While social media may have played an important role in highlighting the extent of China's environmental problems (Hook 2013), they are also piling pressure on Chinese leaders to stand up for what they see as China's interests in regional disputes. In such circumstances nationalist forces may be difficult to control and feed into international relations in unpredictable and potentially destabilizing ways (Weiss 2013). China's increasingly influential international role may become more rather than less important as a consequence.

China's International Impact

The contrast with much of much of the rest of the world—especially Western democracies where powerful vested interests either frustrate a shift to a more sustainable economy (Lyoyd 2012), or where the failure of market-based mechanisms is encouraging a wholesale retreat from renewable energy (Peiser 2013)—is noteworthy and instructive. At the very least, it raises important and troubling questions about which political system is actually more capable of addressing climate change in the limited time frame available. At one level, for example, Chinese officials can justifiably claim that the "one child policy" that has attracted so much negative commentary in the West actually represents a profoundly important, unsurpassed contribution to global climate change mitigation (Goodenough 2009). Without it, China's population might be more than 400 million larger, and its domestic and international impact would be even more significant than it is.

At another level, of course, China's impact has been very different, and it has been noteworthy primarily for its obstructive role in climate change negotiations. China became the focus of much criticism in the aftermath of the unsuccessful climate change summit at Copenhagen. Whatever the comparative merits of such criticisms it is important to recognize how constrained China's foreign policy is and just how recently China has become a significant actor in multilateral forums of this sort. In part China's inability to act effectively is a reflection of long-standing problems associated with fragmented authoritarianism noted earlier, and the more recent, growing proliferation of influences on the foreign policy-making process in particular (Jakobson and Knox 2010). Ironically enough, the influence of various groups such as provincial governments, SOEs, and the People's Liberation Army is making China's policy less coherent and predictable and—in the case of China's unresolved regional territorial claims, at least—altogether more dangerous as nationalist forces and energy companies urge a more assertive line (ICG 2012). As far as climate change negotiations in particular are concerned, however, the rather cumbersome top-down decision-making processes in the Chinese state means that there is simply no capacity for its diplomats to make policy up on the spot (Conrad 2012).

Nevertheless, it is clear that China now has the capacity, by intent or inadvertence, to shape policy outcomes of concern to the "international community." The inverted commas are merited because it is questionable whether such a grouping actually exists in this or any other policy domain (Ellis 2009). The reality, of course, is that even in less challenging policy areas, such as financial sector reform, where the problems seem clear and the remedies are feasible, agreements are made difficult by clashing national interests, influential lobbies, and the unwillingness of established states to cede authority and influence to newcomers (Wade 2011). The great hope held by many outside China has been that China's elites and diplomats will be socialized into the ways of Western diplomacy and adjust their behavior accordingly. Although there is clear evidence that this has happened to some extent (Johnston 2008)—China is plainly not the destabilizing revolutionary force it once was—the technical and political impediments to international agreements over complex, contested issues remain formidable.

It is often assumed that it will continue to be "the West" that is in the vanguard of shaping the international order in the future. Great expectations were held about the EU's capacity to play a leadership role in climate change politics in particular (Patterson 2009), before economic crises, but the failure of its carbon trading scheme, and the renaissance of the coal industry effectively put paid to such hopes (Peiser 2013). Now however, it is authoritarian China rather than the EU or the United States that is making the biggest contribution to both creating and addressing some of the most fundamental environmental challenges of our time. Significantly, however, it is primarily domestic rather than international pressure that is forcing the Chinese government to act as it is compelled to address the reality of a degraded environment that represents a failure of its developmental model and the leaders who guide it. While the ability of domestic NGOs to influence government policy is still comparatively limited and evolving (Zhan and Tang 2013), there is no doubt that what Economy (2014) describes as "the environmental awakening of the Chinese people" is now an entrenched and growing part of national life to which the government is scrambling to respond.

Although we cannot know how successful China's people and its leaders will be in dealing with these monumental and unprecedented challenges, it is possible that non-democratic responses to dealing with environmental problems are likely to become more common rather than less. If China is even moderately successful this could add to the relative standing of the so-called "China model" in particular and of the attraction of top-down, state-led responses to environmental problems more generally (Zhang and Sun 2012). According to one high profile report, at least, the net result may well be that, "Among political systems, authoritarian ideologies would certainly be the 'winners.' One way or the other, severe climate change will weaken the capacity of liberal democratic systems to maintain public confidence" (Campbell et al. 2007: 77).

Concluding Remarks

Democracy is a remarkable invention, but as recent events in the Middle East and even parts of Europe remind us, it is fragile and susceptible to "rollbacks" (Diamond 2008). In the absence of the right sort of economic and social conditions it is difficult to achieve and sustain. Many observers have drawn attention to the potential impact a deteriorating environment may have on social and political life (Homer-Dixon 1999; Dyer 2010). Such implacable material forces may prove a challenge for established democracies, let alone those with no history of such practices. Much will depend on the scale and severity of the changes triggered by climate change and the ability of governments of any sort to counter them. Unfortunately, the likes of Ophuls and Heilbroner may ultimately prove to be alarmingly prescient, but not quite in the way they imagined, perhaps. Ironically, the fate of the remarkably resilient and now universal capitalist system may ultimately rest with the leaders of a notionally "communist" and still authoritarian state.

While it is not clear that authoritarian regimes will prove any more capable of dealing with the sorts of unprecedented challenges governments of all sorts confront in dealing with environmental problems, there are a number of reasons for believing that authoritarian responses are increasingly possible, even likely in places such as China. First, China already is an authoritarian regime and political change has been limited even in comparatively favorable circumstances. Second, the sorts of massive, rapid shifts in energy and infrastructure provision needed to address environmental degradation seem more feasible in China given its extant track record. This is no guarantee of success, of course, which leads to a third consideration. If China's leaders are unable to engineer a massive change in the health and sustainability of the natural environment then existing patterns of social unrest are likely to intensify. To judge from China's history and the absence of any democratic tradition, social instability is more likely to trigger a Tiananmen-style authoritarian crack down, than it is a democratic revolution.

The best hope, perhaps, is that the Chinese leadership will have the political space and time to institute reforms that will make a difference to the way the country is governed, the way the economy works, and the way the natural environment is managed. It has been suggested that China is uniquely placed to develop some sort of middle way between Asian-style technocratic rule and the market-oriented democracies of the West. The hope is that this will result in a form of "intelligent governance that will reconcile knowledgeable democracy with accountable meritocracy" (Berggruen and Gardels 2013: 13). It may prove to be wishful thinking, but it is important to recognize how astounding and unprecedented China's experience has already been. As even the liberal, pro-market *Economist* (2013: 18), points out, "If China cannot do it, no one can."

Acknowledgments

Thanks to Bruce Gilley and Matt McDonald for commenting on an earlier version of this chapter. The usual caveats apply.

References

Anderlini, J. (2014) "China's Rebalancing Requires More Investment of the Right Kind." *Financial Times* (January 23).

Beeson, M. (2014). *Regionalism and Globalization in East Asia: Politics, Security, and Economic Development*, 2nd edn. (Basingstoke: Palgrave Macmillan).

Beeson, Mark. (2010). "The Coming of Environmental Authoritarianism." *Environmental Politics* 19(2): 276–94.

Beeson, M. (2013). "Can China Lead?" *Third World Quarterly* 34(2): 235–52.

Bell, S. (2012). "The Power of Ideas: The Ideational Shaping of the Structural Power of Business." *International Studies Quarterly* 56(4): 661–73.

Berggruen, N. and Gardels, N. (2013). *Intelligent Governance for the 21st Century: A Middle Way Between West and East* (Cambridge: Polity).

Bohman, J. (1998). "Survey Article: The Coming of Age of Deliberative Democracy." *Journal of Political Philosophy* 6(4): 400–25.

Brødsgaard, K. E. (2012), "Politics and Business Group Formation in China: The Party in Control?" *The China Quarterly* 211: 624–48.

Campbell, K. M., Gulledge, J., McNeill, J. R., Podesta, J., Ogden, P., Fuerth, L., Woolsey, R. J., Lennon, A. T., Smith, J., and Weitz, R. (2007). *The Age of Consequences: The Foreign Policy and National Security Implications of Global Climate Change* (Washington: Centre for Strategic & International Studies).

Chan, M. (2014). "Will 'Strongman' Xi Jinping Lead China into Armed Conflicts With Rival Neighbours?" *South China Morning Post* (January 13).

Christoff, P. (2010). "Cold Climate in Copenhagen: China and the United States at COP15." *Environmental Politics* 19(4): 637–56.

Conrad, Bjorn. (2012). "China in Copenhagen: Reconciling the "Beijing Climate Revolution" and the "Copenhagen Climate Obstinacy." *The China Quarterly* 210: 435–55.

Cooper, R. N. (2008). "China's Coming Demand for Energy." In *China, Asia, and the World Economy*, edited by B. Eichengreen, C. Wyplosz, and Y. C. Park (Oxford: Oxford University Press), 1–17.

Hook, L. and Crooks, E. (2011). "China's Rush into Renewables: The Way the World Turns." *Financial Times* (November 28).

Diamond, L. (2008). "The Democratic Rollback." *Foreign Affairs* 87(2): 36–48.

Dunlap, R. E. and McRight, A. M. (2011). "Organized Climate Change Denial." In *The Oxford Handbook of Climate Change and Society*, edited by J. S. Dryzek, R. B. Norgaard, and D. Schlosberg (Oxford: Oxford University Press), 144–60.

Dyer, G. (2010). *Climate Wars: The Fight for Survival as the World Overheats* (Oxford: Oneworld).

Economy, E. C. (2004). *The River Runs Black: The Environmental Challenge to China's Future* (Ithaca: Cornell University Press).

Economy, E. (2014). "China Wakes Up to Its Environmental Catastrophe." *Bloomberg Business Week* (March 13).

Ellis, David, C. (2009). "On the Possibility of 'International Community.' " *International Studies Review* 11(1): 1–26.

Foster, J. B., Clark, B., and York, R. (2010). *The Ecological Rift: Capitalism's War on the Earth* (New York: Monthly Review Press).

Gilley, Bruce. (2012). "Authoritarian Environmentalism and China's Response to Climate Change." *Environmental Politics* 21(2): 287–307.

Goodenough, P. (2009). "Chinese Minister Links 'One-Child' Policy to Emissions Reduction at Climate Conference." *CNSnews* (December 11).

Hall, P. A. and Soskice, D. (2001). "An Introduction to the Varieties of Capitalism." In *Varieties of Capitalism: The Institutional Foundations of Comparative Advantage*, edited by P. A. Hall and D. Soskice (Oxford: Oxford University Press), 1–68.

Han, C. (2012). "Satisfaction With the Standard of Living in Reform-era China." *The China Quarterly* 212: 919–40.

Hille, K. (2013). "China: Citizens United." *Financial Times* (July 29).

Heilbroner, Robert. L. (1974). *An Inquiry into the Human Prospect*, vol. 74 (New York: Norton).

Hobson, J. M. (2012). *The Eurocentric Conception of World Politics: Western International Theory, 1760–2010* (Cambridge: Cambridge University Press).

Homer-Dixon, T. F. (1999). *Environment, Scarcity, and Violence* (Princeton: Princeton University Press).

Hook, L. (2013). "Weibo Alters China's Environmental Debate." *Financial Times* (March 4).

Hook, L. and Crooks, E. (2011). "China's Rush into Renewables: The Way the World Turns." *Financial Times* (November 28).

Hornby, L. (2014). "China Pollution: Trouble in the Air." *Financial Times* (February 26).

ICG. (2012). *Stirring Up the South China Sea (I)* (Brussels: International Crisis Group).

Jakobson, L. and Knox, D. (2010). "New Foreign Policy Actors in China." *SIPRI Policy Paper* 26 (September).

Johnston, Alastair Iain. (2008). *Social States: China in International Relations, 1980–2000* (Princeton: Princeton University Press).

Li, C. (2012). "The End of the CCP's Resilient Authoritarianism? A Tripartite Assessment of Shifting Power in China." *The China Quarterly* 211: 595–623.

Li, K. (2014). Report on the Work of Government, speech to the Second Session of the Twelfth National Peoples Congress on March 5, 2014. Available at: http://online.wsj.com/public/resources/documents/2014GovtWorkReport_Eng.pdf

Lieberthal, K. G. (1992). "Introduction: The 'Fragmented Authoritarianism' Model and its Limitations." In *Bureaucracy, Politics, and Decision Making in Post-Mao China*, edited by K. G. Lieberthal and D. M. Lampton (Berkeley: University of California Press), 1–30.

Lindblom, C. E. (1977). *Politics and Markets: The World's Political-Economic Systems* (New York: Basic Books).

Liu, J. and Diamond, J. (2005). "China's Environment in a Globalizing World." *Nature* 435: 1179–86.

Lo, A. Y. (2010). "Active Conflict or Passive Coherence? The Political Economy of Climate Change in China." *Environmental Politics* 19(6): 1012–17.

Lyoyd, G. (2012). "King Coal Still Reigns." *The Australian* (April 28).

Meadows, D. H., Randers, J., and Meadows, D. (1974). *The Limits to Growth: A Report for the Club of Rome's Project on the Predicament of Mankind* (New York: Universe Books).

Newell, P. (2012). *Globalization and the Environment: Capitalism, Ecology and Power* (Cambridge: Polity).

Ophuls, W. (1997). *Requiem for Modern Politics: The Tragedy of the Enlightenment and the Challenge of the New Millennium* (Boulder: Westview Press).

Oreskes, N. and Conway, E. M. (2010). *Merchants of Doubt: How a Handful of Scientists Obscured the Truth on Issues from Tobacco Smoke to Global Warming* (New York: Bloomsbury Press).

Paterson, M. (2009). "Post-hegemonic Climate Politics?" *British Journal of Politics and International Relations* 11: 140–58.

Peiser, B. (2013). "Europe Pulls the Plug on its Green Future." *The Australian* (August 10).

Shapiro, J. (2001). *Mao's War Against Nature: Politics and the Environment in Revolutionary China* (Cambridge: Cambridge University Press).

Sheridan, M. (2014). "Xi Outwits Foes to Wield Absolute Power." *The Australian* (March 10).

Silk, R. (2013). "Air Pollution from Coal Use Cuts Lifespans in China, Study Shows." *Wall Street Journal* (July 8).

Smith, N. (2008). *Uneven Development: Nature, Capital, and the Production of Space*, 3rd edn. (London: Verso).

Tang, W., Lewis-Beck, M. S., and Martini, N. F. (2013). "Government for the People in China?" *The Diplomat* (June 17).
The Economist. (2013). "The East is Grey" (August 10): 15–18.
Tsai, K. S. (2007). *Capitalism Without Democracy: The Private Sector in Contemporary China* (Ithaca: Cornell University Press).
Vermeiren, M. (2013). "Foreign Exchange Accumulation and the Entrapment of Chinese Monetary Power: Towards a Balanced Growth Regime?" *New Political Economy* 18(5): 680–714.
Wade, Robert H. (2011). "Emerging World Order? From Multipolarity to Multilateralism in the G20, the World Bank, and the IMF." *Politics & Society* 39(3), 347–78.
Wang, S. and Hu, A. (1999). *The Political Economy of Uneven Development: The Case of China* (Armonk: ME Sharpe).
Weiss, J. C. (2013). "Authoritarian Signaling, Mass Audiences, and Nationalist Protest in China." *International Organization* 67(01): 1–35.
Wong, E. (2013). "As Pollution Worsens in China, Solutions Succumb to Infighting." *New York Times* (March 21).
WWF. (2012). *Living Planet Report: Biodiversity, Biocapacity, and Better Choices* (Geneva: WWF International).
Zalasiewicz, J., Williams, M., Steffen, W., and Crutzen, P. (2010). "The New World of the Anthropocene." *Environmental Science & Technology* 44(7): 2228–31.
Zhan, X. and Tang, S.-Y. (2013). "Political Opportunities, Resource Constraints and Policy Advocacy of Environmental NGOs in China." *Public Administration* 91(2): 381–99.
Zhang, W. and Sun, F. (2012). "Resurrection Through Adaptation: The Dynamics of China's 'Comcapitalism' Model." *The Journal of Comparative Asian Development* 11(2): 349–78.
Zhu, T. and Pearson, M. (2013). "Globalization and the Role of the State: Reflections on Chinese International and Comparative Political Economy Scholarship." *Review of International Political Economy* 20(6): 1189–1214.

CHAPTER 35

GLOBAL ENVIRONMENTAL GOVERNANCE

JOHN S. DRYZEK

The Condition of Global Environmental Governance

The challenges presented by global environmental problems have yet to receive effective global governance response (for details, see Christoff and Eckersley 2013: 163–89). The 1987 Montreal Protocol for protection of the ozone layer remains the high point of effective multilateral treaty making on any significant global ecological issue. The 20 years that followed the landmark 1992 United Nations Conference on Environment and Development in Rio saw retreat in global ambitions. The sort of stirring language that could find its way into the 1992 Declaration proved too controversial 20 years later at the 2012 United Nations Conference on Sustainable Development (Rio+20). Compared to global economic governance, global environmental governance is under-developed and weak. There is no World Environment Organization, while there is a very powerful World Trade Organization (WTO). While the institutions of global economic governance (notably the International Monetary Fund (IMF), World Bank, and WTO) do notionally incorporate some degree of environmental concern, that is normally swamped by economic considerations. Meanwhile the national governments that threw trillions of dollars at the global financial crisis after 2008 have been reluctant to throw anything at all comparable in the direction of the global environmental crisis. Climate change represents the most obvious failure of global environmental governance, as the multilateral negotiations that began with the establishment of the United Nations Framework Convention on Climate Change (UNFCCC) in 1992 have fallen far short of the aspiration for a comprehensive global treaty to curb greenhouse gas emissions. In climate change and other areas, international relations scholars now speak of regime complexes rather than regimes (Keohane and Victor 2011). A regime complex is a multiplicity of loosely coupled institutional arrangements in no clear hierarchical relationship with each other, and can include efforts sponsored by the UN and other global institutions (including economic ones), more limited initiatives (such as those under the auspices of the G20 group of large economies), regional forums, unilateral actions, and bilateral agreements. While this devolution might provide one route beyond impasse in the peak multilateral negotiations, to date that seems to have done nothing to affect the trajectory of global greenhouse gas emissions.

Aside from its ineffectiveness in generating effective collective solutions to problems like climate change, disruption of nitrogen and phosphorus cycles, biodiversity loss, ocean acidification, and other threats to the planetary life support system, global environmental governance is also problematic from the viewpoint of justice and democracy. Of course justice can be defined in different ways. Yet those who suffer the most from environmental degradation are rarely those primarily responsible for causing it. Those suffering might be future generations, or vulnerable populations in developing countries subject to drought, storms, and floods. Democracy, though a key legitimating principle for collective action in much of today's world, is not at home in actually existing global governance. While a problem for global governance in general, this democratic deficit is a particularly acute issue for environmental governance to the degree claims about the environmental efficacy of democracy (for example, Lafferty and Meadowcroft 1996) can be sustained. Though there are plenty of ideas about how to remedy the global democratic deficit, most are currently a long way from realization.

How might environmental political theory speak to this condition? I will argue that environmental political theory can assist in the *critique of shortcomings* in global environmental governance, provide an important *lens for scrutinizing reform proposals*, and *generate insight into what qualities we should be looking for* in global environmental governance (which may also be adopted at other levels). Some of the contributions (notably, concerning legitimacy and justice) travel from political theory via environmental political theory to global environmental governance; some (notably, concerning questions of resilience and reflexivity) start from environmental political theory (with an assist from earth science). In all three of the tasks just identified, environmental political theory can help compensate for some of the failings of international relations theory, which has a hard time with concepts like democracy and justice as they pertain to the international system itself, let alone ideas such as resilience that are basic to the earth science vocabulary.

A caveat is in order. The contributions of environmental political theory to the analysis of global environmental governance will rarely stand alone. Sometimes they work in conjunction with other sorts of political theory, social theory, and international relations theory. Sometimes they inform, and can be informed by, empirical inquiry. Sometimes they can work with earth science. Such synergies will appear in the discussions that follow.

Critique of Global Governance

Diagnosis of the ills of global environmental governance can (and does) proceed without reference to environmental political theory. But environmental political theory can sharpen the critique in several useful ways.

To begin—and perhaps most fundamentally—existing global governance arrangements along with just about all analyses of these arrangements do not recognize the earth system itself as a key player. They proceed for the most part as though the environment is simply a medium through which some humans inflict harms or confer benefits on other humans. So long as human impacts on that system did not affect its basic parameters then perhaps little was lost by proceeding in this manner (though environmental ethicists would rightly bemoan the inattention to intrinsic value in the non-human world). But all that changes with the arrival of what earth scientists call the Anthropocene, the epoch in which human influences are decisive in driving the entire earth system (Crutzen and Stoermer 2000). The Anthropocene is the successor to the preceding Holocene, an epoch of around 10,000 years featuring highly unusual climatic stability. Human influences now threaten to re-introduce the kind of instability that was common in the preceding late Pleistocene (Steffen et al. 2011: 747). This instability enters most immediately and prominently with climate change resulting from climbing concentrations of greenhouse gases, but loss of biodiversity and disruption of nitrogen and phosphorus cycles are among the other profound anthropogenic effects. The response of earth scientists themselves has been to insist that the guideline for global action should be to respect the "planetary boundaries" that define "a safe operating space for humanity" (Rockström et al. 2009). Prominent scientists supported by environmental activists tried and failed to get recognition of planetary boundaries inserted in the declaration of the 2012 UN Summit on Sustainable Development (Rio+20). Yet the planetary boundaries concept tells us only to avoid the Anthropocene and try to maintain Holocene conditions, not what we should do once we are in the Anthropocene. Given that the boundaries associated with climate change, biodiversity, and the nitrogen cycle have already been exceeded, it is not obvious that return is possible. As I write, the concentration of carbon dioxide in the atmosphere has just passed 400 parts per million; there is no obvious way it can be reduced to the boundary of 350 parts per million. Thus we have to figure out what to do in this changed and changing world. Working with a dynamic and unstable earth system is going to require new kinds of governance arrangements, which thinking geared to the production of treaties that fix obligations for particular actions on particular categories of countries barely begins to comprehend. Later I will try to be more constructive about what the Anthropocene requires of global institutions.

The idea of the Anthropocene drives home the limitations of a system of global governance that prioritizes economic and security concerns above environmental ones. Environmental political theory can criticize this domination (though we cannot read off any alternative forms of governance from the critique). The critique can be extended to limited attempts to reconfigure economic and security priorities in environmental directions. The whole idea of sustainable development (and its successors such as ecological modernization and green growth) is an attempt to render economic growth environmentally friendly. Security for its part can be redefined from national security to human security—and human security can then be shown to require particular environmental attributes, such as security in the face of environmental threats (Barnett 2011). More radical green theorists would resist both the lure of sustainable development and the securitization of environmental concern. But whatever one thinks about the possibility of sustainable development or green growth, it is important to criticize how compromised their real-world uses are when it comes to global governance (and elsewhere). So for example von Frantzius (2004: 469) criticizes the "privatization of sustainable development" that was so evident at the 2002 United Nations Summit on Sustainable Development in Johannesburg. If environmental security for its part is seen as an aspect of conventional national security then it may ultimately reinforce the core priorities of the entrenched global order. If on the other hand environmental security is conceptualized in terms of amelioration of the insecurities of vulnerable people, the more it may contribute to an overhaul of that order (McDonald 2012). Now, sustainable development and securitization are concepts that can apply at any level, from the local to the global. However, it is at the global level that sustainable development has been so dominant as a discourse in environmental affairs, so that is where critique needs to operate. Environmental security has been far less prominent as a discourse at all levels, but has been making some inroads globally.

Security may be one component of justice (inasmuch as it involves reducing the level of risk to vulnerable people), but other aspects of justice prove particularly problematic in global environmental governance. Justice arguments are actually quite prominent in global environmental negotiations in particular. Yet they can do little to make that governance more tractable so long as they are articulated in terms of fairness across nations. Different national governments (and negotiating blocks) deploy different views of what such fairness entails—most of them self-serving. So India will argue that it has little obligation to reduce greenhouse gas emissions in comparison to countries that have built their prosperity on a long history of fossil fuel use—enabling its own substantial population of rich consumers to "hide behind the poor" (Ananthapadmanabhan, Srinivas, and Gopal 2007). The United States sees justice in terms of fair terms of trade, and does not want to be disadvantaged by being held to more stringent emissions standards than its competitors such as China. One logical way through this impasse would be to think of climate justice in more cosmopolitan terms, in which the units of obligation and concern are individuals, irrespective of where they happen to live (Vanderheiden 2008); or even which generation they happen to live in. The problem here may be that there is no mechanism or incentive for nation-states to adopt a cosmopolitan view, though Harris (2009) argues that if, say, China were to admit to global obligations in proportion to the size of its own large and growing number of rich, fossil fuel-using consumers, that would enhance the credibility and moral authority of the Chinese position. One can even imagine that the United States would recognize the moral force of this Chinese move, and in response even accept that the goods and services it produces should not be more emissions-intensive than those produced in similar economies in the European Union.

Global environmental governance suffers from a democratic deficit, and a related legitimacy deficit. While that does not matter to most international relations theorists, it should matter to those political theorists who believe that all public authority, at whatever level, needs to be legitimated in democratic terms. It should matter still more to those green political theorists who believe that democracy in general and deliberative democracy in particular are especially conducive to the effective resolution of environmental problems and promotion of environmental values, at the global level no less than elsewhere (Baber and Bartlett 2009). The content of the deficit can be further illuminated by environmental political theorists who insist on the need to listen to the non-human world in (democratic) political arrangements (for example, Dobson 2010), though that concern is not shared by most of those who worry about democratic deficits, and it applies at every level, from the local to the global. Of course there are some particular problems in pursuing any democratic agenda at the global level, but they are not insuperable. Support can be drawn here from the burgeoning literature on global democratic theory (Scholte 2011).

Contemplating Reform

Aside from contributing to the critique of actually existing institutions and practices, environmental political theory can both scrutinize and inform the numerous proposals that have been put forward to render global environmental governance more effective.

One of the more coherent and prominent packages for reform has been advanced by Biermann et al. (2012), summarizing a vast amount of work done under the auspices of the Earth System Governance project, a 10-year multi-national research project that began in 2009. Biermann et al. prescribe strengthening the United Nations Environment Program, creating a powerful United Nations Sustainable Development Council in conjunction with an enhanced role for the G20 large economies forum, global institutions to regulate emerging technologies, integrating global environmental concerns into economic governance, qualified majority voting to replace unanimity requirements in international negotiations, enhanced consultation with civil society organizations, and a mechanism for financial redistribution to poorer countries. The impetus of this summary statement (though not necessarily all the work on which it draws) is in the direction of formalization and coherence in central global institutions. They pin their hopes on a "constitutional moment" in global affairs that would enable all or at least some of this to happen.

There is plenty of grist in this reform package for environmental political theory analysis. While applauding the intent of bringing environmental concerns to the commanding heights of global governance, the more centralizing aspects might be criticized by those who believe that the lessons of social–ecological systems point to multiple loci for institutional innovation and experimentation. The emphasis on a constitutional moment might likewise worry those who believe effective innovation in environmental affairs requires continual experimentation and reflexivity, rather than a once-and-for all institutional leap. The role of the G20 might be scrutinized in light of concerns with legitimacy and procedural justice. Critiques of administrative rationalism might be brought to bear, if nothing else to warn how strengthened global institutions might go wrong, and how they might undermine the simultaneous appeal for enhanced participation for civil society.

Very different reform agendas are advanced by those who believe that peak-level attempts have either failed or reached the limit of their utility or gone downhill irrevocably since their 1987 Montreal high point. So Ostrom (2009) recommends a polycentric approach, building on her work on self-organizing social systems for the management of local common pool resources such as fisheries and irrigation systems. This approach recommends multiple self-organizing governance initiatives at different levels, from the local to the national to the regional to the global, but with a de-emphasis on the global. Critics might wonder what guarantees that multiple initiatives will somehow add up to a globally adequate response. Because of the grounding of her analysis in rational choice theory, Ostrom may miss the insights provided by a more communicative theory of politics and democracy—which might (for example) draw on Habermas's account of communicative action, as well as deliberative democratic theory, to inform thinking about how coordination might be constructed across numerous initiatives at different levels in the absence of formal central control. And at any level, in the absence of the social capital that Ostrom believes is one necessary condition for such initiatives to succeed, this sort of communicative action may be capable of generating joint commitments by engaging multiple actors accessing common resources in productive deliberative relationships with each other, and even in effective communicative relationships with non-human entities.

Polycentrism is given additional flesh by Hoffmann (2011), who believes multilateral governance failure can be countered by an "experimental system" of multiple, more limited initiatives. Hoffmann argues that promising initiatives are united by their recognition of economic growth and environmental conservation as potentially supportive of each other, their commitment to markets, and their voluntary nature. Hoffmann lists 58 experiments, ranging from voluntary carbon trading to transnational networks of cities. In an environmental political theory light, there are some clear problems related to the legitimacy of networks, especially those involving private governance and private–public partnerships. Moreover, as low-visibility, collaborative enterprises, networks are lacking in the moments of contestation required in any vibrant democracy—without which they are likely to institutionalize and reinforce decidedly moderate discourses of environmental concern and correspondingly limited kinds of collective actions (Dryzek, Norgaard, and Schlosberg 2013: 143–4).

Another alternative to apparently failed multilateralism is minilateralism, as advocated by Victor (2006) and others. The idea here is to seek a comprehensive agreement on key global issues such as climate change between 12 and 20 major players: notably, the United States, China, India, the EU, and a few other large emitters. Eckersley (2012) argues that such proposals fail on both legitimacy and justice grounds. She argues that the remedy is not to dispense with minilateralism, but to make it more inclusive. Inclusion would extend to representatives of the "most vulnerable" states normally ignored in minilateral proposals: when it comes to climate change, the African Union and Association of Small Island States. Representatives of the most vulnerable would join states that are the most responsible (for past damage) and most capable (of doing something) in a relatively small group. The legitimacy problem can then be overcome by requiring that any minilateral agreement be submitted to the multilateral Conference of the Parties for ratification. Eckersley's analysis is an exemplary constructive critique grounded in environmental political theory.

For Eckersley, inclusion extends only to different kinds of states. But there are other sorts of actors clamoring for inclusion, often grouped under the heading of global civil society. Numerous organizations are active on global environmental issues. What are we to make of their claims? Critics can and do claim that nobody elected global civil society and so these organizations and activists have no legitimate representation claim (though an electoral test would of course also rule out a fair number of states). A more sophisticated approach to representation would recognize that electoral representation is just one kind: there are others. Self-appointed and unelected representatives broaden the range of concerns that can be brought to the table; but they should not be accepted without passing some critical tests, concerning for example the freedom of the representative from strategic benefit and the existence of a constituency that could validate the representative's claim (Saward 2009). Especially important in environmental affairs are claims to represent the non-human world, which is not easily done in electoral terms (or indeed in Saward's terms, because it is hard to see the non-human world as a constituency). It is possible to think of global civil society as a pattern of discursive representation (Dryzek 2012: 114–15). Mainstream discourses such as business-friendly sustainable development and environmental marketization (through for example biodiversity offsets and emissions trading) are well-represented. Discourses such as environmental justice (at least to the degree it is something more than the self-serving fairness arguments that pervade multilateral negotiations) and various sorts of green radicalism have a harder time getting heard. At any rate, environmental political theory can help sort out the validity of various representation claims, point to the imbalances across different sorts of claims, and help figure out how the representation of different sorts of discourses might profitably be incorporated in governance arrangements—so for example Eckersley's inclusive minilateralism could be accompanied by an explicitly deliberative role for civil society representatives of particular discourses.

Civil society representatives may however prove to be problematic deliberators, their partisan commitments precluding much in the way of the reflection and openness to changing positions that is one of the defining features of deliberation. We know from experiments with citizen forums that lay citizens are less problematic in these terms—though they are more problematic in terms of their ability to justify the positions they take, which suggests that effective deliberation needs both partisans and lay citizens. No less than at local and national levels, it is possible to think about the insertion of deliberative mini-publics composed of lay citizens into global governance. The most ambitious attempts so far have involved the World Wide Views processes carried out in connection with climate change in 2009 (Rask, Worthington, and Lammi 2012) and biodiversity in 2012. In each case, the exercise involved 100 citizens in a large number of countries (38 for climate change, 25 for biodiversity) deliberating on the same day in the same way about a common set of questions, then responding to a questionnaire on the issues. While the results of the 2009 exercise were presented at the Conferences of the Parties of the UNFCCC later that year in Copenhagen, they were largely ignored by negotiators. The reception at the Conference of the Parties of the United Nations Convention on Biological Diversity in Hyderabad in 2012 was more positive, with the final decision text supporting further such deliberations. Thinking ahead, it is even possible to imagine global citizens' assemblies that combine participants from different—perhaps all—nations.

Reworking Governance for the Anthropocene

Beyond contemplation of specific and limited reform practices and proposals of the sort just discussed, some very fundamental questions exist about the qualities we should be looking for in global governance—especially if we take seriously the idea that we have now entered the Anthropocene in a major way. Given that existing governance arrangements (at all levels) enabled the world to begin to stumble into the Anthropocene, and then once warning signs became apparent to put on blindfolds so warnings could be ignored, governance presumably needs to look very different from what we have now. I have already noted the limitations of the planetary boundaries concept, so simply specifying that global governance should respect planetary boundaries is not enough. Existing dominant global institutions were designed with economic and national security priorities in mind, and there is little likelihood of them changing their ways in order to either respect planetary boundaries or figure out other ways of "navigating the Anthropocene," as Biermann et al. (2012) put it. Many of those who contemplate the reform of global governance see the problem in terms of the absence of the kind of authority that states can exercise in their internal affairs, and so the solution in terms of the adoption of state-like structures. But if no state looks remotely capable of meeting the challenge of the Anthropocene, that extrapolation becomes dubious.

The Anthropocene connotes a highly unstable earth system with a concomitant loss of fixed reference points (such as any baseline "natural" condition of an ecosystem) for collective action. Existing institutions—including states—evolved in the late Holocene, and as such could afford to devote minimal attention to the condition of the earth system. The Anthropocene promises to be a highly dynamic era, which means that the analysis of global governance arrangements cannot proceed in static terms. For example, it is common to see global environmental cooperation as mainly a matter of overcoming free rider problems and so securing effective collective action through coordination. But that implies the problem itself is a fixed one: such as excessive emissions of greenhouse gases or ozone-depleting chemicals that need to be curbed, or excessive depletion of ocean fisheries. Correspondingly, solutions are seen in static terms: notably, securing mutual commitments on the part of states through a treaty, or mutual commitments that may encompass corporations as well as states and cities in networked governance arrangements.

Environmental political theory can contribute to the search for more dynamic criteria for global environmental governance. Candidates here might include resilience, advocated very prominently by the global network of scholars in the Resilience Alliance. They define resilience as "the ability to absorb disturbances, to be changed and then to re-organize and still have the same identity (retain the same basic structure and ways of functioning)."[1] Resilience is a concept with its origins in ecology, and many of the members of the Resilience Alliance are natural scientists, though they have also involved some social scientists in their endeavors. A lot of conceptual work needs to be done in figuring out how to apply resilience to human institutions, while leaving open the possibility that the limitations of the concept as currently defined may require rethinking. The task here is largely theoretical (though it can be informed by analysis of empirical practice) because there are no good examples of resilient social–ecological systems in industrial or post-industrial societies. There are plenty of examples in long-lived local agro-ecosystems but we cannot extrapolate directly from those to the contemporary global level. An early theoretical task is to figure out the degree to which resilience can accommodate transformation of social–ecological systems; Folke et al. (2010) insist that it can, but then what happens to the idea of "retain the same basic structure" that appears in the Resilience Alliance definition just quoted? The reaction of those such as Catney and Doyle (2011: 190) who see resilience as essentially conservative and a way of suppressing challenges to the dominant order points to the need to think long and hard about the place of transformation. And such transformation might need to extend to (global) society's core values, including commitment to economic growth.

There does, then, seem to be a lot of conceptual stretching going on in the vicinity of resilience. Insistently analytical theorists might seek to refine the definition to better defend it against critics; others would be happy treating resilience as a discourse rather than a concept, joining discourses like democracy or sustainable development, which similarly resist precise definition. As a discourse, resilience highlights the importance of thinking in terms of social–ecological systems, and the idea that non-human aspects of these systems can play very active roles in how history (including global history) unfolds—for better or for worse.

In short, while resilience discourse highlights some crucial factors, by itself it seems it cannot guide global institutional reconfiguration, for three reasons. The first is that, as I have already noted, empirical examples of social–ecological resilience can only be located locally and are hard to extrapolate to the global level. The second is that as a discourse, resilience cannot give us precise criteria for institutions and governance. The third is that as soon as we incorporate transformability as an aspect of resilience, the search for fixed structures is off; instead, it is much more appropriate to think in terms of open-ended processes of reconstruction, starting from where we are now. My own feeling is that it is more productive to think in terms of reflexivity rather than resilience. Reflexivity is the critical capacity to change structure, ways of thinking, or processes in the light of reflection on success and failure (Beck, Giddens, and Lash 1994). Ecological reflexivity would also need to involve the development in human systems of an enhanced capability to listen to signals coming from ecological systems (Dobson 2010) and a capacity to reconsider what core social values should be in light of an earth system that is active and unstable.

It is very easy to point to the shortcomings of global institutions, structures, and practices in light of their lack of reflexivity (particularly acute given the painstaking way in which multilateral deals in particular have to be negotiated), more difficult to say what more reflexive alternatives would look like. But recognizing ecological reflexivity as the key quality actually eliminates the need to think in terms of any fully elaborated institutional architecture. It is more productive to think of global governance as an open-ended experimental system, in which the main task is to search for points of leverage to render the system more (ecologically) reflexive. Deliberative reforms can contribute to this task. So for example Stevenson and Dryzek (2014) interpret the global governance of climate change as a potentially deliberative system, and suggest a number of innovations that would move it in this direction. These include procedures for promoting more effective engagement across different discourses (especially moderate and radical ones) in the global public sphere; inserting citizen mini-publics more effectively into public discussion; more reflective and reciprocal ways to introduce climate science into public debate; attention to the rhetoric that accompanies particular policy proposals (following Litfin's 1994 identification of the importance of rhetorical moves in enabling the 1987 Montreal Protocol); conducting multilateral negotiations through standard deliberative principles (with a facilitator, rather than a chair as at present); a deliberative civil society addition to Eckersley's inclusive minilateralism; more systematic discursive representation; attention to the creation of contestatory public space in connection with emerging governance networks; a rethinking of the role of the UNFCCC as one of overseeing multiple governance arrangements (as opposed to trying to produce a global treaty); and the constructing of deliberative accountability chains linking different institutional locations.

These sorts of proposals would still only go part of the way, for one of the implications of the Anthropocene is the need to think about the system of global governance in its entirety—not just the parts that are conventionally recognized as environmental. As things stand, the institutions of global economic governance have far more environmental implications, for better or (mostly) worse than do the weak institutions of global environmental governance. In the Anthropocene, ecosystemic reflexivity should be the first virtue of global institutions in their entirety. Just how that might be pursued is going to be a task for many hands (including those of earth scientists, civil society, global governance analysts, and practitioners), not just those of environmental political theorists.

Note

1. Available at http://www.resalliance.org/index.php/key_concepts

References

Ananthapadmanabhan, G., Srinivas, K., and Gopal, V. (2007). *Hiding Behind the Poor: A Report by Greenpeace on Climate Injustice* (Bangalore: Greenpeace India).

Baber, W. F. and Bartlett, R. V. (2009). *Global Democracy and Sustainable Jurisprudence: Deliberative Environmental Law* (Cambridge, MA: MIT Press).

Barnett, J. (2011). "Human Security." In *The Oxford Handbook of Climate Change and Society*, edited by J. S. Dryzek, R. B. Norgaard, and D. Schlosberg (Oxford: Oxford University Press), 267–77.

Beck, U., Giddens, A., and Lash, S. (1994). *Reflexive Modernization: Politics, Tradition and Aesthetics in the Modern Social Order* (Cambridge: Polity).

Biermann, F. et al. (2012). "Navigating the Anthropocene: Improving Earth System Governance." *Science* 335: 1306–07.

Catney, P. and Doyle, T. (2011). "The Welfare of Now and the Green (Post) Politics of the Future." *Critical Social Policy* 31(2): 174–93.

Christoff, P. and Eckersely, R. (2013). *Globalization and the Environment* (Lanham, MD: Rowman and Littlefield).

Crutzen, P. and Stoermer, E. F. (2000). "The Anthropocene." *Global Change Newsletter* 41: 17–18.

Dobson, A. (2010). "Democracy and Nature: Speaking and Listening." *Political Studies* 58(4): 752–68.

Dryzek, J. S. (2012). "Global Civil Society: The Progress of Post-Westphalian Politics." *Annual Review of Political Science* 15: 101–19.

Dryzek, J. S., Norgaard, R. B., and Schlosberg, D. (2013). *Climate-Challenged Society* (Oxford: Oxford University Press).

Eckersley, R. (2012). "Moving Forward in the Climate Negotiations: Multilateralism or Minilateralism?" *Global Environmental Politics* 12(2): 24–42.

Folke, C., Carpenter, S. R., Walker, B., Scheffer, M., Chapin, T., and Rockström, J. (2010). "Resilience Thinking: Integrating Resilience, Adaptability, and Transformability." *Ecology and Society* 15(4): article 20.

Harris, P. G. (2009). *World Ethics and Climate Change: From International to Global Justice* (Edinburgh: Edinburgh University Press).

Hoffmann, M. J. (2011). *Climate Governance at the Crossroads: Experimenting with a Global Response after Kyoto* (Oxford: Oxford University Press).

Keohane, R. O. and Victor, D. G. (2011). "The Regime Complex for Climate Change." *Perspectives on Politics* 9(1): 7–23.

Lafferty, W. M. and Meadowcroft, J., eds. (1996). *Democracy and the Environment: Problems and Prospects* (Cheltenham: Edward Elgar).

Litfin, K. T. (1994). *Ozone Discourses: Science and Politics in Global Environmental Cooperation* (New York: Columbia University Press).
McDonald, M. (2012). *Security, the Environment and Emancipation: Contestation over Environmental Change* (Abingdon: Routledge).
Ostrom, E. (2009). "A Polycentric Approach for Coping with Climate Change." World Bank Policy Research Working Paper 5095.
Rask, M., Worthington, R., and Lammi, M. (2012). *Citizen Participation in Global Environmental Governance* (London: Earthscan).
Rockström, J. et al. (2009). "A Safe Operating Space for Humanity." *Nature* 461 (September 24): 472–5.
Saward, M. (2009). "Authorisation and Authenticity: Representation and the Unelected." *Journal of Political Philosophy* 17: 1–22.
Scholte, J. A., ed. (2011). *Building Global Democracy? Civil Society and Accountable Global Governance* (Cambridge: Cambridge University Press).
Steffen, W. et al. (2011). "The Anthropocene: From Global Change to Planetary Stewardship." *Ambio* 40: 739–61.
Stevenson, H. and Dryzek, J. S. (2014). *Democratizing Global Climate Governance* (Cambridge: Cambridge University Press).
Vanderheiden, S. (2008). *Atmospheric Justice* (Oxford: Oxford University Press).
Victor, D. G. (2006). "Toward Effective International Cooperation on Climate Change: Numbers, Interests and Institutions." *Global Environmental Politics* 6(3): 90–103.
Von Frantzius, I. (2004). "World Summit on Sustainable Development Johannesburg 2002: A Critical Assessment of the Outcomes." *Environmental Politics* 13: 467–73.

THEORIZING CITIZENSHIP, MOVEMENTS, AND ACTION

CHAPTER 36

GLOBAL ENVIRONMENTAL JUSTICE AND THE ENVIRONMENTALISM OF THE POOR

JOAN MARTINEZ-ALIER

THE fundamental clash between economy and the environment comes from two main drivers. First, population growth. Second, the changing social metabolism, or flows of energy and materials, of industrial economies, which causes environmental conflicts (Fischer-Kowalski and Haberl 1997; Steinberger et al. 2010; Muradian et al. 2012; Martinez-Alier, Temper, and Demaria 2014). Energy cannot be recycled. Therefore, the energy from the fossil fuels is used only once, and new supplies of coal, oil, and gas must be obtained from the "commodity frontiers" (Moore 2000). Similarly, materials are recycled only in part, and therefore, even an economy that would not grow would need fresh supplies of iron ore, bauxite, copper, and paper pulp. The economy is not circular, it is entropic (Haas et al. 2015). Meanwhile, renewable resources such as aquifers, timber, and fisheries are overexploited, and the fertility of the soil is jeopardized. Thus, the social metabolism of industrial economies gives rise to growing numbers of resource extraction conflicts and also waste disposal conflicts (including on a global scale that arising from the production of an excessive amount of carbon dioxide). Such ecological distribution conflicts sometimes overlap with other social conflicts on class, ethnicity or indigenous identity, gender, caste, or territorial rights.

The perception of such injustices (particularly regarding waste disposal) gave rise to a widespread social movement in the United States in the early 1980s with roots in the civil rights movement. The words "environmental justice" (EJ) began to be used in a sociological sense in the United States in struggles against the disproportionate dumping of toxic waste in urban or periurban African–American areas. Environmental justice is a powerful lens through which to make sense of many struggles over the negative impacts that the increasing metabolism imposes on human livelihoods and nature conservation worldwide (Gottlieb 2005). As early as 1991, at the Washington DC multinational "People of Color Environmental Leadership Summit" broader ties were forged so as "to begin to build a national and international movement of all peoples of color to fight the destruction and taking of our lands and communities." The principles developed at the summit spoke to the world, and not to a minority. Participants wanted to establish humans' spiritual interdependence to the sacredness of our Mother Earth; to respect and celebrate each of our cultures, languages, and beliefs about the natural world and our roles in healing ourselves; to ensure EJ; to promote economic alternatives which would contribute to the development of environmentally safe livelihoods; and, to secure political, economic, and cultural liberation that had been denied for over 500 years of colonization and oppression, resulting in the poisoning of communities and land and the genocide of peoples.

The related concept of the "environmentalism of the poor" (applied to rural and sometimes indigenous populations in India and Latin America) was introduced by activists and academics in the late 1980s contributing to a global EJ movement which was in full swing and aware of itself by the 1990s. Academic work has been published since the mid-1990s, if not before, making explicit connections between the EJ movement in the United States and manifestations of the environmentalism of the poor in Latin America, Africa, and Asia (Guha and Martinez-Alier 1997, 1999; Varga et al. 2002). This connection was obvious after the deaths of Chico Mendes in Brazil in 1988 fighting deforestation and of Ken Saro-Wiwa and his Ogoni comrades in Nigeria in 1995 fighting against Shell. Classic books analyzing EJ movements against dams (McCully 1996) and against tree plantations (Carrere and Lohman 1996) were published by activists working outside academia.

Critical to the development of global EJ networks and activist movements has been the conceptual language that has arisen from particular conflicts. In conjunction with work on the Environmental Justice Organizations, Liabilities and Trade (EJOLT) research project (http://www.ejolt.org 2011–15), in this chapter we present a set of concepts with origins outside academia and which are used by the global EJ movement (Sikor and Newell 2014). On their own or sometimes with the help of sympathetic academics the environmental justice organizations (EJOs) have produced a series of powerful concepts linked to practice or what Charles Tilly called "repertoires of collective action" (Tilly and Tilly 1981; Martinez-Alier et al. 2014). Short definitions and the dates of origin of such concepts are provided in Table 36.1. While there are some concepts of academic origin (such as "working class environmentalism" (Barca 2012), "ecologically unequal trade" or "strong sustainability") that are also used or could be used by the global EJ movement, we focus on concepts of non-academic origin.

The first concept in the list is "environmental justice," born in the United States in struggles against waste dumping in North Carolina in 1982. Activist authors such as Robert Bullard, but also civil rights activists with no academic affiliation and members of Christian churches, saw themselves as militants of EJ (Bullard1999; Bryant and Mohai1992). Brilliant research has been done in this field of which only a small sample can be given here (Pellow 2000, 2002; Agyeman et al. 2003). The fight against the

Table 36.1 The Vocabulary of the Global Environmental Justice Movement

	EJOs, authors promoting it	Short description
Environmental justice (EJ)	USA Civil Rights Movement, North Carolina 1982 against environmental injustices (Bullard 1990, 1999).	"People of color" and low-income populations suffer disproportionate harm from waste sites, refineries and incinerators, and transport infrastructures.
Environmental racism	Rev Benjamin Chavis c. 1982	The fight for EJ, against pollution in black, Hispanic, and indigenous areas, was seen as a fight against *environmental racism.*
Ecological debt	Instituto Ecología Política, Chile 1992, Acción Ecológica 1997	Rich countries' liability for resource plunder and disproportionate use of space for waste dumping (e.g. GHG).
Popular epidemiology	Brown 1992, 1997	"Lay" local knowledge of illnesses from pollution may be more valid than official knowledge (sometimes absent).
Environmentalism of the poor	Agarwal/Narain (CSE, Delhi) c. 1989; Blanco 1991.	Struggles by poor/indigenous peoples against deforestation, dams, mining, etc.; proactive collective projects for water harvesting, and forest conservation.
Food sovereignty	Via Campesina c. 1996	People's right to healthy, culturally appropriate, sustainably produced food. Right to define own food and agriculture systems.
Biopiracy	RAFI (Pat Mooney) 1993, popularized by Vandana Shiva	Appropriation of genetic resources (in medicinal or agricultural plants) without recognition of knowledge and property rights of indigenous peoples
Climate justice	CES (Delhi) 1991, Durban Alliance, CorpWatch 1999–2002	Radically reduce excessive per capita emissions of carbon dioxide and other GHG. "Subsistence emissions vs. luxury emissions."
Water justice, hydric justice	Rutgerd Boelens, EJOs in Latin America (e.g. CENSAT) 2011.	Water should not run toward money, or toward power. It should go to those needing it for livelihood.
Water as human right	Pablo Solon (Bolivian envoy to UN), Maud Barlow (Council of Canadians) 2001	Human right to water recognized at UN level in 2011, as an independent human right.
"Green deserts"	Brazil, network against eucalyptus plantations, *Rede Alerta contra o Deserto Verde*, 1999	Brazilian local term for eucalyptus plantations, used by networked CSO and communities, also by researchers and activists for any tree plantation.
Tree plantations are not forests	*Pulping the South* by Carrere and Lohman, World Rainforest Movement, 1996	The WRM collects and spreads information on tree plantation conflicts. It proposes a change in the FAO definition of forest, to exclude tree monocultures.

(continued)

Table 36.1 (Continued)

	EJOs, authors promoting it	Short description
Land grabbing	GRAIN (small pro-peasant EJO) 2008	The wave of land acquisitions in Southern countries for plantations for exports, leading to first statistics on land-grabbing.
Resource caps	Resource Cap Coalition, RCC Europe, c. 2010	It advocates reduction in global resource use and in poverty. It calls for a *European energy quota scheme* and the ratification of the *Rimini protocol*.
To Ogonize/Yasunize	ERA Nigeria, Acción Ecológica, Oilwatch 1997–2007	Leave oil in the soil to prevent damage to human rights and biodiversity, and against climate change. Adopted by anti shale gas fracking, tar sands, and coal mining movements.
Rights of nature	Ecuador, Constitutional Assembly 2008	In Constitution of Ecuador 2008, art 71, promoted by Acción Ecológica and Alberto Acosta. Actionable in court.
Corporate accountability	Friends of the Earth International 1992–2002	At UN Johannesburg summit in 2002, FoE proposed the adoption of a Corporate Accountability Convention, against lukewarm CSR principles.
"Critical mass," cyclists rights	San Francisco 1992 (Chris Carlsson)	International movement reclaiming the streets with cyclists marching to impose cyclists' rights.
Urban waste-recyclers movements	c. 2005, GAIA against incineration and "energy valorization" of urban waste.	Unions or cooperatives of urban waste gatherers, emphasizing positive environmental impact, including climate change (in Delhi, Pune, Bogota, etc.).
Urban "guerrilla food gardening"	c. 2000, started by "food justice" networks	Vacant lot food growing, permaculture, community gardening movements in cities around the world.
Toxic colonialism, toxic imperialism	BAN, Basel Action Network, c. 2000, Greenpeace	Fighting the long-distance export of waste from rich to poor countries, forbidden by the Basel Treaty. e.g. ship-breaking in India or Bangladesh, chemical residues or nuclear waste, electronic waste.
Post-extractivism	Latin America 2007, Eduardo Gudynas (CLAES), Alberto Acosta, Maristella Svampa	Against the reprimarization of Latin American economies. Transition to a sustainable economy based on solar energy and renewable materials. Impose quotas and taxes on raw materials exports.
Buen Vivir, Sumak Kawsay	Ecuador and Bolivia 2008	Adopted in constitutions of both countries, inspired by indigenous traditions and by the "post-development" approach.
Indigenous territorial rights, and prior consultation	Convention 169 of ILO, 1989; adivasi forest rights in India . . .	In conflicts on mining, oil exploitation, dams, etc., communities campaign for legislation defending indigenous rights.

Table 36.1 (Continued)

	EJOs, authors promoting it	Short description
"Sand mafias"	Name given c. 2005 by environmental movement, journalists	The illegal "mining" of sand and gravel in India in many rivers, driven by the growing building and public works industry.
"Cancer villages"	In China, popular name adopted by academics, officials (Lora-Wainright 2013)	Rural villages where industry has caused pollution (e.g. heavy metals), where lay knowledge of illness is relevant, and subdued protests take place.

indigenous was also seen as a fight against "environmental racism," a concept that in the EJOs' language means to treat badly other people in pollution or resource extraction injustices on grounds of membership of particular ethnic groups, social class or caste. In the EJOLT inventory of environmental conflicts (http://www.ejatlas.org), we find that in many countries indigenous populations are involved in ecological distribution conflicts much more than one would expect by their share of population in the country as a whole. All of these populations have responded to being made more vulnerable to the social metabolic demands and processes of industrial economies.

In EJ conflicts, evidence of disproportionate incidence of morbidity or mortality sometimes cannot be proven from official statistics because of the lack of doctors or hospitals in the areas concerned. Hence the rise of so-called "popular epidemiology" (Brown 1992, 1997), a concept of relevance in many struggles inside and outside the United States—think for instance of the attempts by the plaintiffs in the Chevron-Texaco case in Ecuador to gather information in the 2000s related to the 1970s and 1980s of the incidence of cancer in the Sucumbios region of the Amazon by resorting to the memories of the local populations, proving that such memories concentrated around areas with wells and pools for disposal of extraction water (Martin Beristain et al. 2009). Popular epidemiology implies that "lay" knowledge of pollution illnesses is as valid or more valid than official knowledge. In the academic discussion it is a concept that fits into the "post-normal science" theory (Funtowicz and Ravetz 1993) and "street science" (Corburn 2005).

Reflecting the specific environmental challenges and distributional inequities of the global South, some EJOs adopted the term "environmentalism of the poor." It is very close to the notion of EJ born in the United States but it applies less to urban than to rural peoples in the global South involved in extractive conflicts, similar to the Navajo in New Mexico who suffered from uranium mining. Although academics (Ramachandra Guha and the present author) started to use this term in 1988–89 (drawing on research on India and Latin America), it is clear that the idea and perhaps the very words had been used by Anil Agarwal, the founder of the Centre for Science and Environment (CSE) in Delhi, and editor of the first "citizens' reports" on the state of India's environment. His successor, Sunita Narain, often uses the term "environmentalism of the poor" to refer to the struggles in India against dams, deforestation, mining projects, and nuclear power stations (Narain 2008). The concept goes back to the 1980s in the activist tradition of the CSE and other EJOs in India to refer to the many struggles by poor and/or indigenous peoples against resource extraction and for nature conservation. Shrivastava and Kothari (2012) have compiled many socio-environmental struggles and successes in India ending with a proposal for a radical ecology democracy. The concept was also used by the well-known Peruvian peasant activist Hugo Blanco in 1991 who gave a list of conflicts some of which are still active (Blanco 1991).

The "environmentalism of the poor" (and of the indigenous) is a concept opposed to the "post-materialist" interpretation of environmentalism (and other new social movements) by Ronald Inglehart (Inglehart 1995). It neither essentializes environmentalism with poor or indigenous populations (see Godrej, this volume), nor envisions environmental preservation as a luxury good as does Inglehart. In contrast to Ulrich Beck's view of environmental risks as being impartial to social class (as might have been the case for a nuclear accident such as Chernobyl but which is not true in general—for example, for hurricane Katrina in New Orleans) (Beck 1992), the environmental movements of the poor and indigenous are place-based struggles for their own material livelihoods (Nixon 2011). In many resource extraction and waste disposal conflicts in history and today, the poor are often on the side of preservation of nature against business firms and the state. This behavior is consistent with their interests and their values, including the defense of indigenous territorial rights and claims regarding the sacredness of particular elements of nature (a mountain, a forest, or even a tree). It is also consistent with concerns for social justice, including claims to recognition and participation, and builds on the premise that the fights for human rights and environment are inseparable. When livelihood and values are threatened, those affected will be motivated to act provided that there is a sufficient degree of democracy and they are not suffocated by fear or violently repressed, as is often the case. In the EJOLT inventory (n. 1354, April 2015) in 12 percent of conflicts one of the outcomes is "deaths."

One of the primary environmental challenges faced by populations of the global South stems from an economic system that produces "ecologically unequal trade," an academic concept (Bunker 1985; Hornborg 1998, 2005; Hornborg et al. 2007). One aspect of such unequal trade was given the name of biopiracy (by Pat Mooney of RAFI in 1993, Shiva 1997). Biopiracy denotes the appropriation of genetic resources (in medicinal or agricultural plants) without any recognition of the original knowledge and "property rights" of indigenous peoples. The examples of such robbery are indeed numerous. The word "biopiracy" has been used in many complaints by EJOs. Even state authorities in countries like Brazil and India have started to use this term. Academics writing in scientific journals and doctoral students in their theses also use it (Robinson 2010).

There are a number of other EJO concepts and policies that stem from conflicts over biomass. The complaints against tree plantations of eucalyptus, acacia, or gmelina, grown for wood or paper pulp, depriving local people of land and water, gave rise 20 years ago to the slogan and movement "Plantations are not forests." In Brazil, "green deserts" was the spontaneous, bottom up name for eucalyptus plantations in Espiritu Santo and other regions, opposed by local peasants and indigenous peoples. This was certainly a form of enclosure of forest commons. The driving force was the export of paper pulp and cellulose.

Relatedly, the concept "food sovereignty" was introduced in the early 1990s by Via Campesina, an international movement of farmers, peasants, and landless workers. Food sovereignty means the right of rural people (including women in particular) to grow their own food for themselves and for local markets, against corporate agriculture, particularly against agrofuel and tree plantations (Schutter 2012; GRAIN 2005). A small organization called GRAIN (a partner of RAFI in the 1980s and 1990s in the fights against agricultural "biopiracy") introduced the term and the first statistics for "land-grabbing" in 2008 for the new wave of land acquisitions often by force in Southern countries, for new plantations for exports. The term was then taken up by the *Journal of Peasant Studies* in special issues under Jun Borras' editorship.

A term from the EJOs that has been very successful in the fights against ecologically unequal trade and climate change is that of the "ecological debt" (Robleto and Marcelo 1992; Borrero 1994). There was an alternative treaty in Rio de Janeiro in 1992 on the ecological debt from North to South, and Acción Ecológica of Ecuador took the term and the struggle up in 1997, with several publications which included a definition and many examples. The ecological debt arises from the plunder of resources and also from the occupation of disproportionate environmental space by the rich countries (for example, to deposit excessive amounts of carbon dioxide in the oceans and the atmosphere, which belong to all humans equally). Some governments from countries of the South have deployed the concept of "ecological debt" (or one part of it, the "climate debt") in international negotiations on climate change (Bond 2010). In the 2009 Copenhagen Climate Change Conference of the Parties (COP), perhaps over 30 heads of government or ministers talked about the ecological debt awakening the fury of the US Ambassador, Todd Stern (Reuters 2009). The origin of the concept and many of the theoretical developments are mainly due to Latin American EJOs, and to some extent also to the international Friends of the Earth (FoE) and Jubilee South (Friends of the Earth 2005). Academics joined in later doing some calculations (Roberts and Parks 2007, 2009; Paredis et al. 2008; Srinivasan et al. 2008; Rice 2009). Pope Francis' encyclical *Laudato si* of June 2015 devotes two paragraphs (51 and 52) to the ecological debt from North to South.

Unsurprisingly, it was also EJOs that introduced and developed the concept of "climate justice." An influential role in its introduction and dissemination was played by the CSE (Delhi) booklet of 1991, *Global Warming: A Case of Environmental Colonialism*, authored by Anil Agarwal and Sunita Narain (1991) pointing out that there were subsistence carbon dioxide emissions vs. luxury carbon dioxide emissions (an idea taken up by Shue 1994, 1999). Then in the late 1990s came the Jubilee campaign against Northern financial bullying of the South, comparing the large ecological debt from North to South to the financial debt from South to North (Simms et al. 1999; Simms 2005). The concept of climate debt was supported by the World Council of Churches (Peralta 2006) and other groups including the Third World Network, Action Aid, and Christian Aid.

Turning specifically to climate justice (Bond 2013), a 2000 event in The Hague sponsored by the New York group CorpWatch was the first known conference based on this term. CorpWatch had published a document in November 1999 authored by Bruno, Karliner, and Brotsky:

> Climate Justice means, first of all, removing the causes of global warming and allowing the Earth to continue to nourish our lives and those of all living beings. This entails radically reducing emissions of carbon dioxide and other greenhouse gases. Climate Justice means opposing destruction wreaked by the Greenhouse Gangsters at every step of the production and distribution process—from a moratorium on new oil exploration, to stopping the poisoning of communities by refinery emissions—from drastic domestic reductions in auto emissions, to the promotion of efficient and effective public transportation. (Bruno et al. 1999)

Four years later, the Durban Group for Climate Justice was launched. It has made itself well-known by its campaigns against fake Clean Development Mechanism projects.

The concept of water justice or hydric justice is associated with a university professor, Rutgerd Boelens (Wageningen University) but he has been working so closely with activists for many years that he himself would no doubt like water justice or hydric justice to be seen as concept of the EJOs (Boelens et al. 2011; Isch et al. 2012). Their favorite slogans are "water runs towards power," and "water runs towards money" unless stopped by civil society movements. The World Commission on Dams (WCD) was a civil society initiative that reported its conclusions in 2000 (WCD 2000). Among its members were representatives of business and of the World Bank, and also of conservationist organizations. It arose because of the strength of resistance movements against dams, the most visible at the time being the Narmada Bachao Andolan in India where Medha Patkar's campaigns had been influential (McCully 1996). The WCD's conclusions went directly against much of the previous literature in favor of dams, and also against the cost–benefit analysis procedures for deciding on dam building. The WCD report recommendations have not been implemented. Anti-dam movements continue to denounce water enclosures along with forced acquisition of land, diversion of rivers, and dispossession and displacement of rural and indigenous communities inhabiting territories rich in biodiversity and water sources. They include the Brazilian MAB (Movement of People Affected by Dams) and the MAPDER network in Mexico.

Meanwhile, another new term has been appearing with greater regularity in recent years in EJ struggles: the commons movement. This sees the commons as a crucial sector of the economy which must be defended to preserve decommodified access to food, water, forests, and clean air (Di Chiro 1998). Influenced by Karl Polanyi, the movement fights against old and new enclosures. Since the late 1980s, as a reaction against Garrett Hardin's misnamed "tragedy of the commons" that mistook "open access" for "commons," authors like John Kurien have defended small scale fisheries against large scale industry, using the term "modern enclosures" or "the tragedy of enclosures" (Martinez-Alier 1991). In municipal water management, paradigmatic movements against privatization of urban water services as in Cochabamba, Bolivia, are seen internationally as sources of inspiration for the defense of the commons in general (including access to information) and also for the defense of the human right to water.

Proposals to "leave oil in the soil," also in defense of the commons, were first put forward in 1997. We now call them *Yasunizing* or *Ogonizing* and they come from Acción Ecológica Ecuador, ERA of Nigeria, and the Oilwatch network founded in 1995.The proposals apply also to tar sands, to coal ("leave coal in the hole"), and shale gas. They are meant for areas of great biodiversity value and where human rights are threatened. To such local reasons, climate change reasons are added, based on the thesis that there are "unburnable fuels," if we want to stop increasing the concentration of carbon dioxide in the atmosphere (Temper et al. 2013) Also in the field of energy policy, the civil society movements against nuclear energy since the 1970s gave rise to their own concepts. One of them, in Germany, was *Energiewende* (energy turnaround, born in Wheyl, c. 1980) which is now used in official public policy. Germans are using a parallel term, *Wachstumwende* (growth turnaround), to translate the French *décroissance* or English "degrowth," a movement in some Northern countries, not born in EJOs but rather in alternative urban or rural movements (Hess 2009; Chatterton and Pickerell 2010; Conill et al. 2012) that disengage mentally and practically from the growth economy. In Germany, post-Wachstum is also used. The degrowth movement might enter into an alliance with EJOs, for instance in its support for resource caps, meaning a policy to reduce extraction of materials. Resource caps have been used since the 1990s (Spangenberg 1995) in terms of calculations of "fair shares" in the use of limited resources and limited environmental space. Degrowth is also very sympathetic to claims of an ecological debt from the South. This "degrowth" movement has different sources (Martinez-Alier et al. 2010; Demaria et al. 2013) including the proto-ecological economist Georgescu-Roegen (1971) but also the "post-development" movement of the 1980s of Ashish Nandy, Gustavo Esteva, Arturo Escobar, Wolfgang Sachs, Serge Latouche, and Vandana Shiva (Sachs 1992). An alliance between the degrowth (or steady-state economy or *postWachstum*) movements in the North and the global EJ movement was proposed by (Martinez-Alier 2012) while in South America there are calls for a "post-extractivist" economy (Gudynas 2012) leading to *buen vivir* instead of economic growth.

Other new concepts that are growing among the EJOs are "ecocide" (Zierler 2011) and the call for an international environmental crimes tribunal (complementary to demands for civil liabilities). The CSO Global Witness provides statistics on the hundreds of environmentalists killed in many countries of the South. Refusing to participate in the game of corporate social responsibility, the EJOs have asked for corporate accountability (Broad and Cavanagh 1999; Broad 2002; Utting 2008). The new provision on the rights of nature (introduced in Ecuador's Constitution 2008, article 71, after an original idea from Acción Ecológica) is also popular among the EJOs that see themselves as fighting against crimes against humanity and crimes against nature.

The movement in Southern Italy known as the eco-mafia campaigns against waste dumping, complaining about "biocide" (Armiero and D'Alisa 2012). There must also be many other national or regional terms of EJ. Thus, we know that one of the main materials flows in the metabolism of growing economies is sand and gravel for the building industries. These are non-toxic materials. Nevertheless, they give rise to some ecological distribution conflicts. In India, conflicts on sand and gravel mining from rivers or beaches are particularly acute (with people getting killed in different states), and a new label "sand mafias" was given to this phenomenon. Similarly in China, in the complaints against pollution not only in urban areas but also in rural areas, the term "cancer villages" has begun to be used in the last ten years or so (Lora-Wainright 2013). Researchers of such complaints in China appeal to the notion of "popular epidemiology" born in the 1980s in the United States' EJ movement. In a country like Argentina there is a movement against glyphosate (used in large scale transgenic soy cultivation introduced by Monsanto), under the name *paremos de fumigar* ("stop fumigating"). This links up with the many EJ campaigns by the Pesticide Action Network (Harrison 2011). In Brazil there are terms born from local conflicts such as *justiça nos trilhos*, from the movement for "justice in the railways" against the loss of life in accidents caused by massive iron ore transport from Carajás to the export harbours (Porto et al. 2013, for other examples).

The social metabolism of cities has also produced an international vocabulary of EJ. The US movement of the 1980s, with urban roots, insisted on the importance of the social distribution of urban space for a good life. Environment, as defined by the 1991 People of Color Environmental Leadership conference in Washington DC, was a safe, non-polluted place for living and making a living—environment is where we "live, work, and play." Most of the world population is now urban. Inside cities, there are movements introducing new concepts for a less unsustainable economy, such as "food justice" (Aikon and Agyeman 2011), "transit justice" (Lucas 2004), cyclist and pedestrian rights (with cyclists' "critical mass" movements in many cities) (Carlsson 2008), and fights against gentrification (Mitchell 2003). Such urban movements know and use the metrics of the "ecological footprint" and other environmental indicators. They give a political meaning to squatting (Cattaneo 2011), they remake place for groups in danger of being displaced, re-assert traditional or new practices of land use and water harvesting, and try to protect territory from contamination, land grabbing, gentrification, and real estate speculation (Gottlieb 2009; Gottlieb and Joshi 2010; Anguelovski 2014).

Conclusion

The benefits and costs of the use of the environment are often unjustly distributed not only as regards other species or future generations of humans but also among humans living today.

But social mobilizations over resource extraction, environmental degradation, or waste disposal are not only about the distribution of environmental benefits and costs (expressed in economic or non-economic valuation languages); they are also about participation in decision-making and recognition of group identities (Schlosberg 2007; Urkidi and Walter 2011; Walker 2012; Sikor and Newell 2014). EJ research encompasses issues of exclusion (Agarwal 2001) but also, crucially, of the potential of new leadership of environmental movements by different social actors. For example, in the environmentalism of the poor as in EJ movements in general, it is crucial to recognize the contribution women make in poor communities both rural and urban. Women not only provide cheap or unpaid domestic work, they more often collect water, gather wood, look for medicinal plants, tend to domestic animals, and grow crops, and therefore they have greater knowledge and awareness of their community's direct dependence on the natural environment. This does not imply that women have an empathy with nature denied to men for biological reasons. The argument is based on social roles (Agarwal 1992) as emphasized by eco-feminist economics (Waring 1988; Mellor 2006; Perkins 2007; O'Hara 2009). In an urban setting, it is women who often take leading positions in EJ conflicts (in contrast to labor union struggles) as regards complaints against waste dumping, or air or water pollution. This is just one example of how both EJ movements, and their study, goes beyond simple distributional issues—and one example of how a conception of justice ties together a wide range of issues across the EJ spectrum.

As this chapter suggests, since the 1980s, EJOs and their networks have reinforced their battles by introducing several concepts to political ecology that have also been taken up by academics and policy makers. It has provided definitions of a wide array of concepts and slogans related to environmental inequities and sustainability, and explored the connections between them in the last 30 years. Thus, demands for "food sovereignty" from the Via Campesina fit in with climate change issues, as in the slogan "traditional peasant agriculture cooled down the Earth" (Martinez-Alier 2011). While the protests of the World Trade Organization in Seattle in 1999 and the World Social Forums of the 2000s certainly pushed forward the globalization of EJ, the analysis in this chapter shows its earlier underpinnings in the alternative "treaties" signed at Rio de Janeiro in 1992 and in the 1991 People of Color Environmental Justice Leadership Summit. EJ spread through organizations like FoE, which, while born in California as a "white" conservationist movement, became international bringing in EJOs which had existed since the 1980s, like CENSAT in Colombia and WHALI in Indonesia. Many other important environmental organizations in a range of countries, such as the Centre for Science and Environment in Delhi, continued to link the idea of environmentalism of the poor with wider notions of EJ and climate justice.

With these activist and social movement roots, the concepts of EJ were then taken up in academic research. Focusing on case studies, the field of political ecology has, since the 1980s, studied many environmental conflicts in Southern countries. Going beyond case studies, researchers now generate statistics of conflicts on resource extraction and waste disposal (Ozkaynak and Rodriguez-Labajos 2012, Latorre et al. 2015). The social sustainability sciences (human ecology, ecological economics, political ecology, environmental law, environmental sociology, ecological anthropology, environmental history, environmental politics, urban ecology, agroecology, industrial ecology, and more) have an academic origin, with international societies, academic journals and handbooks, and professorships that go under such names. Many concepts and theories have been produced by these booming fields of science in the last 30 years. There are also grassroots concepts for sustainability introduced by EJOs which have been discussed here. Concepts like EJ, the environmentalism of the poor, ecological debt, land grabbing, biopiracy, corporate accountability, climate justice, food sovereignty, and many others, became keywords of the EJOs and their networks in the global EJ movement before becoming also objects of academic research. Such concepts support the global EJ movement, at the same time they also support local rural and urban movements protecting territory and defending place-based interests and values (Escobar 2008; Anguelovski and Martinez-Alier 2014).

References

Agarwal, A. and Narain, S. (1991). *Global Warming in an Unequal World: A Case of Environmental Colonialism* (New Delhi: Centre for Science and Environment).

Agarwal, B. (1992). "The Gender and Environment Debate: Lessons from India." *Feminist Studies* 18(1): 119–58.

Agarwal, B. (2001). "Participation Exclusion, Community Forestry, and Gender: An Analysis for South Asia and a Conceptual Framework." *World Development* 29(10): 1623–48.

Agyeman, J., Bullard, R., and Evans, B. (2003) *Just Sustainabilities: Development in an Unequal World* (Cambridge, MA: MIT Press).

Anguelovski, I. (2014). *Neighborhood as Refuge: Environmental Justice, Community Reconstruction, and Place-remaking in the City* (Cambridge, MA: MIT Press).

Anguelovski, I. and J. Martinez-Alier. (2014). "The 'Environmentalism of the Poor' Revisited: Territory and Place in Disconnected Global Struggles." *Ecol. Econ.* 102: 167–76.

Armiero, M. and D'Alisa, G. (2012)., "Rights of Resistance: The Garbage Struggles for Environmental Justice in Campania, Italy." *Capitalism, Nature, Socialism* 23(4): 52–68.

Barca, S. (2012). "On Working-class Environmentalism. An Historical and Transnational Overview." *Interface. A Journal for and about Social Movements* 2: 61–80.

Beck, U. (1992). *Risk Society. Towards a New Modernity* (London: Sage).

Blanco,H.(1991)."Elecologismodelospobres,LaRepública."April6,1991.http://hugoblancogaldos.blogspot.com.es/2008/12/el-ecologismo-de-los-pobres.html

Boelens, R., Cremers, L., and Zwarteveen, M., eds. (2011), *Justicia Hídrica. Acumulación, conflicto y acción social* (Lima: Instituto de Estudios Peruanos).

Bond, P. (2010). "Repaying Africa for Climate Crisis. 'Ecological Debt' as a Development Finance Alternative to Emissions Trading." In *Upsetting the Offset. The Political Economy of Carbon Trading*, edited by Steffen Böhm and Siddhartha Dabhi (London: MayFlyBooks), 275–91. http://mayflybooks.org/wpcontent/uploads/2010/07/9781906948078UpsettingtheOffset.pdf

Bond, P. (2013). "Climate Justice." In *Critical Environmental Politics*, edited by C. Death (London: Routledge), 133–45.

Borrero, J. M. (1994). *La Deuda Ecológica. Testimonio de una reflexión* (Cali: FIPMA).

Broad, R., ed. (2002). *Global Backlash: Citizen Initiatives for a Just World Economy.* (New York: Rowman and Littlefield).

Broad, R. and Cavanagh, J. (1999). "The Corporate Accountability Movement: Lessons and Opportunities." *The Fletscher Forum of World Affairs* 23(2): 151–69.

Brown, P. (1992). "Popular Epidemiology and Toxic Waste Contamination: Lay and Professional Ways of Knowing." *Journal of Health and Social Behavior* 33: 267–81.
Brown, P. (1997). "Popular Epidemiology Revisited." *Current Sociology* 45: 137–56.
Bryant B. I. and Mohai, P. (1992) *Race and the Incidence of Environmental Hazards: A Time for Discourse* (Boulder: Westview Press).
Bruno, K., Karliner, J., and Brotsky, C. (1999)., "Greenhouse Gangsters vs. Climate Justice." CorpWatch. http://www.corpwatch.org/article.php?id=1048
Bullard, R., ed. (1999). *Confronting Environmental Racism: Voices from the Grassroots*. Foreword by Benjamin F. Chavis, Jr. (Boston: South End Press).
Bunker, S. (1985). *Underdeveloping the Amazon. Extraction, Unequal Exchange, and the Failure of the Modern State* (Chicago: University of Chicago Press).
Carlsson, C. (2008). *Nowtopia: How Pirate Programmers, Outlaw Bicyclists and Vacant-lot Gardeners Are Inventing the Future Today* (Oakland, CA: AK Press).
Carrere, R. and Lohman, L. (1996). *Pulping the South: Industrial Tree Plantations and the World Paper Economy* (London: Zed Books).
Cattaneo, C. (2011). "The Money-free Life of Spanish Squatters." In *Life Without Money*, edited by Anitra Nelson (London: Pluto Press), ch. 10.
Chatterton, P. and Pickerell, J. (2010). "Everyday Activism and Transitions Towards Post-capitalist Worlds." *Transactions of the Institute of British Geographers* 35: 475–90.
Conill, J., Castells, M., Cardenas, A., and Servon, L. (2012). "Beyond the Crisis: The Emergence of Alternative Economic Practices." In *Aftermath: The Cultures of the Economic Crisis*, edited by M. Castells, J. Caraça, and G. Cardoso (Oxford: Oxford University Press), ch. 9.
Corburn J. (2005). *Street Science: Community Knowledge and Environmental Health Justice* (Cambridge, MA: MIT Press).
Demaria, F., Schneider, F., Sekulova, F., and Martinez-Alier, J. (2013). "What is Degrowth? From an Activist Slogan to a Social Movement." *Environmental Values* 22(2): 191–215.
Di Chiro, G. (1998). "Nature as Community. The Convergence of Social and Environmental Justice." In *Privatizing Nature: Political struggles for the Global Commons*, edited by M. Goldman (London: Pluto).
Escobar, A. (2008). *Territories of Difference: Place, Movements, Life, Redes* (Durham: Duke University Press).
Fischer-Kowalski, M. and Haberl, H. (1997). "Tons, Joules and Money: Modes of Production and their Sustainability Problems." *Society and Natural Resources* 10(1): 61–85.
Friends of the Earth International (FOEI). (2005). *Climate Debt. Making Historical Responsibility Part of the Solution*. http://www.foei.org/en/resources/publications/climate-justiceand-energy/2000-2007/climatedebt.pdf/at_download/file
Funtowicz S. and Ravetz J. R. (1993). "Science for the Post-Normal Age." *Futures* 25: 735–55.
Georgescu-Roegen, N. (1971). *The Entropy Law and the Economic Process* (Cambridge: Harvard University Press).
Gottlieb R. (2005). *Forcing the Spring: The Transformation of the American Environmental Movement* (Washington, DC: Island Press).
Gottlieb R. (2009). Where We Live, Work, Play ... and Eat: Expanding the Environmental Justice Agenda. *Environmental Justice* 2: 7–8.
Gottlieb, R. and Joshi, A. (2010). *Food Justice* (Cambridge, MA: MIT Press).
GRAIN. (2005). "Food Sovereignty: Turning the Global Food System Upside Down." *Seedling*. http://www.grain.org/article/entries/491-food-sovereignty-turning-the-global-food-system-upside-down (accessed March 28, 2013).

Gudynas, E. (2012). "Estado compensador y nuevos extractivismos. Las ambivalencias del progresismo sudamericano." *Nueva Sociedad* 237: 128–46.
Guha, R. and Martinez-Alier, J. (1997). *Varieties of Environmentalism. Essays North and South* (London: Earthscan).
Guha, R. and Martinez-Alier, J. (1999). "Political Ecology, the Environmentalism of the Poor and the Global Movement for Environmental Justice." *Kurswechsel* (Vienna) 3: 27–40.
Haas, W., Krausmann, F., Widenkofer, D. and Heinz, M. (2015). "How Circular is the Global Economy?: An Assessment of Material Flows, Waste Production, and Recycling in the European Union and the World in 2005." *Journal of Industrial Ecology*. doi: 10.1111/jiec.12244
Harrison, J. L. (2011). *Pesticide Drift and the Pursuit of Environmental Justice* (Cambridge, MA: MIT Press).
Hess, D. J. (2009). *Localist Movements in a Global Economy: Sustainability, Justice, and Urban Development in the United States* (Cambridge, MA: MIT Press).
Hornborg, Alf. (1998). "Towards an Ecological Theory of Unequal Exchange. Articulating World System Theory and Ecological Economics." *Ecological Economics* 25: 127–36.
Hornborg, Alf. (2005). "Footprints in the Cotton Fields: The Industrial Revolution as Time–Space Appropriation and Environmental Load Displacement." *Ecological Economics* 59: 74–81.
Hornborg, A., McNeill, J. R., and Martinez-Alier, J., eds. (2007). *Rethinking Environmental History, World-system History and Global Environmental Change* (Lanham MD: Atamira Press).
Inglehart, R. (1995). "Public Support for Environmental Protection: Objective Problems and Subjective Values in 43 Countries." *Political Science and Politics* 28(1): 57–72.
Isch, E., Boelens, R., and Peña, F. eds. (2012). *Agua, Injusticia y Conflictos* (Lima: Instituto de Estudios Peruanos).
Latorre, S., Farrell, K., and Martinez-Alier, J. (2015). "The Commodification of Nature and Socio-Environmental Resistance in Ecuador: An Inventory of Accumulation by Dispossession Cases, 1980–2013." *Ecological Economics* 116: 58–69.
Lora-Wainright, Anna. (2013). *Fighting for Breath: Living Morally and Dying of Cancer in a Chinese Village* (Honolulu: University of Hawai Press).
Lucas, K. (2004) *Running On Empty: Transport, Social Exclusion and Environmental Justice* (Bristol: The Policy Press).
Martinez-Alier, J. (1991)., "Ecology and the Poor: A Neglected Dimension of Latin American History." *Journal of Latin American Studies* 23(3): 621–39.
Martin Beristain, C., Paez, D., and Fernandez, I. (2009)., *Las palabras de la selva: Estudio psicosocial del impacto de las explotaciones petroleras de Texaco en las comunidades amazónicas de Ecuador* (Bilbao: Hegoa).
Martinez-Alier, J. (2011). "The EROI of Agriculture and Its Use by the Via Campesina." *Journal of Peasant Studies* 38(1): 145–60.
Martínez-Alier, J. (2012). "Environmental Justice and Economic Degrowth: An Alliance Between Two Movements." *Capitalism, Nature, Socialism* 23(1): 51–73.
Martinez-Alier, J., Pascual, U., Vivien, F., and Zaccai, E. (2010). "Sustainable De-growth: Mapping the Context, Criticisms and Future Prospects of an Emergent Paradigm." *Ecological Economics* 69(9): 1741–7.
Martinez-Alier, J., Temper, L., and Demaria, F. (2014). "Social Metabolism and Environmental Conflicts in India." *Indialogs* 1: 51–83.
Martinez-Alier, J., Anguelovski, I., Bond, P., Del Bene, D., Demaria, F., Gerber, J.-F., Greyl, L., Haas, W., Healy, H., Marín-Burgos, V., Ojo, G., Firpo Porto, M., Rijnhout, L.,

Rodríguez-Labajos, B., Spangenberg, J., Temper, L., Warlenius, R., and Yánez, I. (2014). "Between Activism and Science: Grassroots Concepts for Sustainability Coined by Environmental Justice Organizations." *Journal of Political Ecology* 21: 19–60.

McCully, P. (1996). *Silenced Rivers. The Ecology and Politics of Large Dams* (London: Zed Books).

Mellor, M. (2006). "Ecofeminist Political Economy." *International Journal of Green Economy* 1: 139–50.

Mitchell D. (2003). *The Right to the City: Social Justice and the Fight for Public Space* (New York and London: The Guilford Press).

Moore, J. (2000). "Sugar and the Expansion of the Early Modern World Economy: Commodity Frontiers, Ecological Transformation, and Industrialization." *Review (Fernand Braudel Center)* 23(3): 409–33.

Muradian, R., Martinez-Alier, J., Walter, M. (2012). "Hegemonic Transitions and Global Shifts in Social Metabolism: Implications for Resource-rich Countries." *Global Environmental Change* 22: 559–67.

Narain, S. (2008). "Learn to Walk Lightly." *Business Standard* (August 1, 2008).

Nixon, R. (2011). *Slow Violence and the Environmentalism of the Poor* (Cambridge: Harvard University Press).

O'Hara, S. (2009). "Feminist Ecological Economics: Theory and Practice." In *Eco-Sufficiency and Global Justice*, edited by A. Salleh (New York: Pluto Press), 152–75.

Ozkaynak, B., Rodriguez-Labajos, B., et al. (2012). "Mining Conflicts Around the World: Common Grounds from an Environmental Justice Perspective." EJOLT Report n. 7, 198.

Paredis, E., Goeminne, G., Vanhove, W., Maes, F., and Lambrecht, J. (2008): *The Concept of Ecological Debt: its Meaning and Applicability in International Policy* (Gent: Academia Press).

Pellow D. N. (2000). "Environmental Inequality Formation: Toward a Theory of Environmental Justice." *American Behavioral Scientist* 43: 581–601.

Pellow D. N. (2002). *Garbage Wars: The Struggle for Environmental Justice in Chicago* (Cambridge, MA: MIT Press).

Peralta, A. K., ed. (c. 2007). *Ecological Debt. The Peoples of the South are the Creditors. Cases from Ecuador, Mozambique, Brazil and India* (Geneva: World Council of Churches), 145.

Perkins, E. (2007). "Feminist Ecological Economics and Sustainability." *Journal of Bioeconomy* 9: 227–44.

Porto, M. F., Pacheco, T., Leroy, J. P.,eds. (2013). *Injustiça ambiental e saúde no Brasil. O mapa de conflitos* (Rio de Janeiro: Fiocruz).

Reuters. (2009). "U.S. Will Pay into Climate Fund, but Not Reparations: Todd Stern." http://www.reuters.com/article/2009/12/09/us-climate-copenhagen-sternidUSTRE5B82R220091209

Rice, J. (2009). "North South Relations and the Ecological Debt: Asserting a Counter-Hegemonic Discourse." *Critical Sociology* 35: 225–52.

Roberts, J. T. and Parks, B. C. (2007). *A Climate of Injustice: Global Inequality, North- South Politics, and Climate Policy* (Cambridge, MA: MIT Press).

Roberts, J. T. and Parks, B. C. Parks (2009). "Ecologically Unequal Exchange, Ecological Debt, and Climate Justice. The History and Implications of Three Related Ideas for a New Social Movement." *International Journal of Comparative Sociology* 50: 385–409.

Robinson, D. F. (2010). *Confronting Biopiracy. Challenges, Cases and International Debates* (London: Earthscan).

Robleto, M. L. and Marcelo, W. (1992). *Deuda ecológica* (Santiago de Chile: Instituto de Ecologia Politica).

Sachs, W. ed. (1992). *The Development Dictionary: A Guide to Knowledge as Power* (London: Zed Books).

Schlosberg, D. (2007). *Defining Environmental Justice. Theories, Movements and Nature* (Oxford: Oxford University Press).

Schutter, O. de. (2012). *From Food Security to Food Sovereignty*. http://www.eesc.europa.eu/resources/docs/de-schutter.pdf (accessed March 28, 2013).

Shrivastava, A. and Kothari, A. (2012). *Churning the Earth. The Making of Modern India* (New Delhi: Penguin Viking).

Shiva, V. (1997). *Biopiracy: The Plunder of Nature and Knowledge* (Boston: South End).

Shue, H. (1994). "Subsistence Emissions, Luxury Emissions." *Law & Policy* 15: 39–59.

Shue, H. (1999). "Global Environment and International Inequality." *International Affairs* 75: 531–45.

Sikor, T. and Newell, P. (2014). "Globalizing Environmental Justice?" *Geoforum* 54: 151–7.

Simms, A. (2005). *Ecological Debt. The Health of the Planet and the Wealth of Nations* (London: Pluto Press).

Simms, A., Meyer, A., and Robins, N. (1999). *Who Owes Who? Climate Change, Debt, Equity and Survival* (London: Christian Aid). http://www.ecologicaldebt.org/Whoowes-Who/Who-owes-who-Climate-change-dept-equity-and-survival.html

Spangenberg, J., ed. (1995). *Towards Sustainable Europe. A Study from the Wuppertal Institute for Friends of the Earth Europe* (Luton/Brussels: FoE Publications Ltd).

Srinivasan, U. T., Carey, S. P., Hallstein, E., Higgins, P. A. T., Kerr, A. C., Koteen, L. E., Smith, A. B., Watson, R., Harte, J., and Norgaard, R. B. (2008). "The Debt of Nations and the Distribution of Ecological Impacts from Human Activities." *PNAS* 5: 1768–73.

Steinberger, J. K., Krausmann, F., Eisenmenger, N. (2010). "Global Patterns of Materials Use: A Socioeconomic and Geophysical Analysis." *Ecol. Econ*. 69: 1148–58.

Temper, L., Yánez, I., Sharife, K., Ojo, G., Martinez-Alier, J., CANA, Combes, M., Cornelissen, K., Lerkelund, H., Louw, M., Martínez, E., Minnaar, J., Molina, P., Murcia, D., Oriola, T., Osuoka, A., Pérez, M. M., Roa Avendaño, T.,Urkidi, L., Valdés, M., Wadzah, N., and Wykes, S. (2013). *Towards a Post-Oil Civilization: Yasunization and Other Initiatives to Leave Fossil Fuels in the Soil* (EJOLT Report No. 6), 204.

Tilly, L. and Tilly, C., eds. (1981). "Class Conflict and Collective Action." (Beverly Hills: Sage).

Urkidi, L. and Walter, M. (2011). "Dimensions of Environmental Justice in Anti-gold Mining Movements in Latin America." *Geoforum* 42: 683–95.

Utting, P. (2008). "Social and Environmental Liabilities of Transnational Corporations. New Directions, Opportunities and Constraints." In *Corporate Accountability and Sustainable Development*, edited by J. Clapp and P. Utting (Delhi: Oxford University Press).

Varga, C., Kiss, I., and Ember I. (2002). "The Lack of Environmental Justice in Central and Eastern Europe." *Environmental Health Perspectives* 110: 662–3.

Walker, G. (2012). *Environmental Justice: Concepts, Evidence and Politics* (London: Routledge).

Waring, M. (1988). *If Women Counted: A New Feminist Economics* (San Francisco: Harper & Row).

Zierler, D. (2011). *The Invention of Ecocide: Agent Orange, Vietnam, and the Scientists Who Changed the Way We Think About the Environment* (Athens: University of Georgia Press).

CHAPTER 37

INDIGENOUS ENVIRONMENTAL MOVEMENTS AND THE FUNCTION OF GOVERNANCE INSTITUTIONS

KYLE WHYTE

INTRODUCTION

I understand indigenous peoples to encompass the roughly 370 million persons whose communities governed themselves before a period of invasion, colonization or settlement and who live within territories where nations, such as New Zealand or Canada, are more widely recognized internationally as sovereigns. Groups identifying as indigenous typically exercise political and cultural self-determination through their own laws, rights, and governing capacities—often having to navigate ongoing forms of colonialism, such as settler colonialism, colonial legacies, and numerous legal, political, bureaucratic, and social barriers imposed by nations, international organizations, subnational and municipal governments, corporations, and groups of private citizens (Sanders 1977; Niezen 2003; Anaya 2004; Cadena and Starn 2007; Larson et al. 2008). The United Nations Declaration on the Rights of Indigenous Peoples (UNDRIP) articulates political and cultural self-determination as indigenous peoples' being able to "freely determine their political status ... and economic, social and cultural development" (article 3), exercise "autonomy or self-government" (article 4), and "strengthen their distinct political, legal, economic, social and cultural institutions ..." (article 5) (United Nations General Assembly 2007). These articles express indigenous renditions of self-determination and cultural integrity in international human rights law.

A significant part of indigenous political and cultural self-determination involves the operation of indigenous *environmental governance institutions*, which refer to systems ranging from customs to social orderings to decision-making processes that coordinate the achievement of environmental outcomes such as clean air and water, sustainable crop yields, and upkeep of culturally meaningful places. UNDRIP also enshrines such institutions by protecting "traditional subsistence economies" (article 20), "traditional plants, animals and minerals" (article 24), and "spiritual relationships with . . . traditionally owned or otherwise occupied and used lands, territories, waters, and coastal seas and other resources" (article 25) (United Nations General Assembly 2007). These institutions are often seen as the practical embodiments of indigenous cosmologies expressing webs of mutual responsibilities shared across human and non-human beings, entities, and collectives.

As major architects of environmental movements, indigenous environmentalists advance important arguments about what the function, or purpose, of environmental governance institutions should be. Different from functions discussed by people of other nations and heritages—like creating trading markets that incentivize pollution abatement or synthesizing diverse scientific sources for climate change planning—many indigenous environmentalists argue that institutions should be structured to function as *conveners*, or orchestrators, of relationships that connect diverse parties (from humans to forests) as *relatives* with reciprocal *responsibilities* to one another.

To make this case, I will provide an overview in the following section of indigenous environmentalism and the theory of institutions. Then, in the third section, I will identify a set of themes about the function of institutions in the communications of indigenous environmentalists. In the fourth section, I will analyze these themes as a framework of indigenous conceptions of the function of institutions. In the fifth section, I will describe in more detail two cases of how indigenous environmentalists have structured institutions that function in this way. I will conclude with some remarks on why indigenous institutional frameworks are important dimensions of political and cultural self-determination and should be at the table in academic and policy spheres.

Indigenous Environmentalists and Institutions

As a citizen of an indigenous nation, activist, and scholar, I have participated in and am aware of diverse indigenous environmental movements. The collective actions of these movements include declarations, public performances, direct actions, reformation of law and policy, court victories, and grassroots institution building. Numerous indigenous-led organizations spark these actions, such as networks, clubs, coalitions, nongovernmental organizations, governmental agencies and committees, intergovernmental or multiparty organizations, and research centers. Moreover, diverse persons in wide-ranging walks of life and professions are involved, including elders and youth, people of all genders, indigenous knowledge keepers and scientists, employees of indigenous governments, and indigenous activists/advocates, among many others. While certain literatures on indigenous environmentalism tend to focus on the appropriation of romantic or false conceptions of indigenous peoples' cultures as rhetorical tools (Churchill and Jaimes 1992; van Ginkel 2004; Harkin and Lewis 2007), I emphasize instead how indigenous peoples have taken on substantial intellectual and organizational leadership.

Indigenous environmental movements have achieved too many outcomes to document here. For example, international activists shaped the environmental dimensions of UNDRIP, such as articles 23 to 25 (United Nations General Assembly 2007), and succeeded in ensuring the United Nations Framework Convention on Climate Change (UNFCCC) would include an International Indigenous Peoples' Forum on Climate Change and support the Indigenous Peoples Biocultural Climate Change Assessment (2014). Indigenous environmentalists have pressed scientists to recognize indigenous peoples in assessment reports such as the Intergovernmental Panel on Climate Change reports, Arctic Climate Change Assessment, and US National Climate Assessment (McLean et al. 2011; Smith and Sharp 2012; Maldonado et al. 2013; Bennett et al. 2014). Idle No More, the Midwest Treaty Network, and the Indigenous Environmental Network have solidified both greater awareness of and concerted actions on significant environmental issues such as pollution, mining and extraction, deforestation, and removal (Gedicks 1993; Goldtooth 1995; Grinde and Johansen 1995, 2014; Idle No More Berry and Camacho 1998; LaDuke 1999; Clark 2002; Igoe 2004; Schlosberg and Carruthers 2010).

Māori organizing, including the Waitangi Tribunal and its report on the river claim, spurred New Zealand's government to recognize the legal voice and rights of the Whanganui River (Te Aho 2010). Indigenous organizing in Ecuador motivated the government to recognize legal rights of tropical forests, islands, rivers, and air in its new constitution (Postel 2012; Pachamama Alliance 2008). Court victories, such as the *Saramaka People v. Suriname* in the Inter-American Court in 2009, or the *Voigt* decision in the Great Lakes region in 1983 by the US Court of Appeals, have served to protect, in certain respects, indigenous ways of life (Carlson and Coulter 2012). Western Shoshone grandmothers, Mary and Carrie Dann engaged in legal and direct actions at the US federal and international levels to resist gold mining and land seizure, achieving victories such as a 2006 review of their case by the United Nations Committee on the Elimination of Racial Discrimination, which decided against the United States (Fishel 2006, 2007). Indigenous peoples have repurposed (*indigenized*) non-indigenous legal and policy mechanisms by creating conservation easements (Middleton 2011), tribal national parks in the United States (Carroll 2014) and protected conservation zones (Corntassel 2008).

In all these collective actions, indigenous environmentalists actively criticize, reform, envision, create, and participate in many environmental governance institutions. Specifically, environmental governance institutions refer to any systems of customs, norms, conventions, social orderings, and decision-making processes that function to coordinate various aspects of a society toward achieving certain environmental outcomes, such as pollution abatement or biodiversity conservation (Borrows 2002; Richardson 2008; Shockley 2012; Napoleon 2013). Institutions range from massive state actors such as the US Environmental Protection Agency (EPA) or Michigan Department of Environmental Quality, to networks such as Idle No More or the Coalition Against Tarsands, to civil society organizations such as the Sierra Club, to widely practiced cultural norms in some societies such as frugality or respect for nonhuman life. Theoretical debate in many academic, public, and private sectors occurs over what functions institutions should serve. I understand an institution's function to refer to the *purpose* it should be structured to accomplish for achieving targeted outcomes such as safe air quality or forest conservation. The structure is made up of the specific ways in which customs, norms, conventions, social orderings, or decision-making processes are designed, articulated, and arranged strategically to carry out the function.

Possible functions of environmental governance institutions range widely, and I can only account for several here. They can integrate individual decisions through market-based mechanisms, such as carbon trading in the Kyoto Protocol or credits for conserving forests in the UN Reducing Emissions through Deforestation and Forest Degradation (REDD+) program. Institutions can function to gather and synthesize critical sources of knowledge, such as the Intergovernmental Panel on Climate Change, US National Climate Assessment, and the Transnational Environmental Law Clinic in Detroit, Michigan. Institutions can function to establish decision-making processes or engage political leverage points that ensure all affected parties can influence policy equally, such as the Michigan Environmental Justice Coalition, Tarsands Solutions Network, and EPA's Plan Environmental Justice 2014 and the Sierra Club's environmental justice program. Other institutions function to work with or appeal to the predictable psychological biases and "irrational" tendencies of individuals and groups, such as the United Kingdom's Behavioral Insight Team (the *Nudge Unit*) or the social advertising of the International Union for Conservation of Nature.

Each of these ideas represents a function, or conception of how institutions should be structured to coordinate various aspects of a society to achieve outcomes. The actual structures derive from number of strategic choices, such as whether to appeal to human emotions instead of tendencies toward irrationality, or whether knowledge synthesis should only include peer-reviewed research, or what metric should be used to equate forest conservation and monetary value. Institutions may also be complex, integrating different functions, such as REDD+, which seeks to achieve equitable decision-making through mandating UNDRIP as forest-carbon markets are being established by different nations. Institutional functions also vary greatly in scale, from county level conservation programs to earth governance systems. The question of what functions and structures are best for achieving environmental outcomes is actively discussed in academic, public, and private spheres. There are plenty of arguments on whether, for example, market mechanisms or social advertising, and so on, are ethically appropriate functions.

Responsibility and Institutional Function

I know of few indigenous environmental movements that fail to discuss ideas about what functions institutions ought to serve. I am drawn to a particular set of themes about institutions and mutual responsibilities. While I am sure that these themes resonate with or even support the claims found in a host of scholarly literatures, from actor–network theory to coupled human and natural systems, I seek to engage with these themes without depending on references to these literatures, many of which are discussed and cited in this volume. For the intellectual landscapes of indigenous environmental movements are often strongly rooted in indigenous people's cultures, intellectual traditions, and insights from their experiences negotiating various forms of colonialism and oppression. Here, I will highlight themes in indigenous environmentalist communications about how the function of institutions should concern mutual *responsibility*, which I hope to suggest is different than other functions such as creating market mechanisms or synthesizing peer reviewed research. By highlighting, I will hold off on extensive analysis until later. To begin with, though, a few definitions are in order.

Indigenous environmentalists' recent communications share concerns with other groups about their communities suffering exploitation at the hands of nations, corporations, and powerful institutions, such as scientific organizations (Clark 2002; Doolittle 2010; Schlosberg and Carruthers 2010). Indigenous environmentalists go further and claim that institutions fail when they undermine the conditions that parties such as humans and non-human entities (for example, water) require to carry out the mutual responsibilities they have to one another. Here, mutual responsibilities will be understood as the reciprocal (though not necessarily equal) attitudes and patterns of behavior that are expected by and of various parties by virtue of the different contributory roles each has within a system of relationships (Whyte 2013). Attitudes refer to enduring dispositions such as empathy, sensitivity and trust, among others, that we can expect to express in roles such as a parental guardian, steward of a fishery, or caretaker of the elderly, among others. Patterns of behavior refer to the range of actions we can expect to discharge in such roles; what actions are appropriate can vary depending on the particular circumstances we may encounter. Our roles refer to how we are supposed to contribute to the continuance of the relationships as parties to those relationships. For example, in a parental relationship the parent may have the role as guardian, a fish harvester, as a steward, a young adult, as a caretaker, and so on. In this essay, parties have these roles because they see themselves as having special qualities, traits, and personalities that can interact systematically with those of the other parties toward achieving outcomes such as pollution abatement or community resilience to extreme weather. Responsibilities, then, are types of attitudes and patterns of behavior that facilitate the interactions needed for systems of relationships to be able to underwrite important outcomes. The notion of responsibility is closely tied to notions of interdependence, caring, sharing, reciprocity, and stewardship.

Consider, to begin with, the Indigenous Peoples Kyoto Declaration written by participants at the 2003 Third World Water Forum. The Declaration challenges institutions such as international agreements to support "Indigenous elders, women and youth to protect water" and to strengthen indigenous peoples' "role as caretakers with rights and responsibilities to defend and ensure the protection, availability and purity of water [in accordance with] traditional laws" (Third World Water Forum 2003). The statement highlights themes related to responsibility including caretaking and respect for different kinds of relations, from elders to youth, as well as indigenous systems of relationships for achieving important environmental outcomes ("traditional laws").

In 2004, a group of 17 indigenous organizations came together during the seventh Conference of the Parties (COP 7) to the UN Convention on Biological Diversity in Kuala Lumpur Malaysia, and created The Manukan Declaration of the Indigenous Women's Biodiversity Network. The Declaration seeks to address concerns about the Convention on Biological Diversity as an institution, and claims that the Convention must respect that

> We, Indigenous women, continue to affirm our cultures, histories, perspectives on creation and ancestry, our views of life and the world, and ways of being. These ways of life are essential for the perpetuation, promotion and development of the world's biodiversity. We, Indigenous women, secure the health of our Peoples and our environment. We maintain a reciprocal relationship with Mother Earth because she sustains our lives... Our right to self-determination is fundamental to the freedom to carry out our responsibilities in accordance with our cultural values and our customary laws... (Indigenous Women's Biodiversity Network 2004)

The Declaration argues that institutions such as the Convention on Biodiversity should support indigenous political and cultural self-determination, both of which are tied to systems of relationships. A collective, "Mother Earth," is also assigned a role as "sustaining our lives." Roles and responsibilities are not only for humans.

Other declarations and statements reiterate similar language. The Rural and Indigenous Women's Statement on Climate Change, submitted to the Parties to the United Nations Framework Convention on Climate Change in 2009, is critical of the institutions associated with the Kyoto protocol because they are based on markets or trading schemes for emissions, such as the Clean Development Mechanism and Joint-Implementation. The statement criticizes the "market-based" functions of these institutions because they fail to address "exploitation [by]... northern countries and transnational corporations in the name of development." The statement also argues that, at the same time, these institutions affect indigenous women's responsibilities because they "undermine rural and Indigenous women's roles and contributions to sustainable livelihoods, ecological health and human security including food sovereignty"

(Asia Pacific Forum on Women, Law and Development et al. 2009). This sentence is supported by a growing literature that seeks to acknowledge and respect the often invisible contributions of indigenous women as "crucial biodiversity managers, custodians of seeds, keepers of sophisticated water management systems and agricultural technology (Fincke and Oviedo 2009), long term observers and recorders of cyclical environmental change (Glazebrook 2011: 769), protectors of water (McGregor 2012), among many other contributions (Arora-Jonsson 2011; Mandaluyong Declaration 2011; Whyte 2014).

The Mystic Lake Declaration of 2009 takes similar positions. The Declaration integrates the voices of a small gathering of community members, youth and elders, spiritual and traditional leaders, indigenous organizations, and supporters of indigenous peoples, who gathered in the Shakopee Mdewakanton Dakota Oyate. The Declaration criticizes market-based institutions by claiming:

> We are concerned with how international carbon markets set up a framework for dealing with greenhouse gases that secure the property rights of heavy Northern fossil fuel users over the world's carbon-absorbing capacity while creating new opportunities for corporate profit through trade . . . the largest number of rights is granted (mostly for free) to those who have been most responsible for pollution in the first place.

The statement states, as an alternative,

> We choose to work together to fulfill our sacred duties, listening to the teachings of our elders and the voices of our youth, to act wisely to carry out our responsibilities to enhance the health and respect the sacredness of Mother Earth, and to demand Climate Justice now . . . We hereby declare, affirm, and assert our inalienable rights as well as responsibilities as members of sovereign Native Nations . . . Mother Earth's health and that of our Indigenous Peoples are intrinsically intertwined . . . This inseparable relationship must be respected for the sake of our future generations . . .

This Declaration, as with others, emphasizes the contributions of different roles within a society, from elders to youth, interdependence, and responsibility. Rights and responsibilities are also distinguished. Corntassell, a Cherokee scholar, argues that rights are "political/legal entitlements" that "[deemphasize] the cultural responsibilities and relationships that Indigenous peoples have with their families and the natural world (homelands, plant life, animal life, etc.) that are critical for their well-being and the well-being of future generations . . ." (Corntassel 2008: 107–8). Though both are important, rights and responsibilities differ. As an entitlement, a right can secure access to a resource, but it cannot necessarily motivate a responsibility to care for that resource as part of a system of relationships.

In the Rio Earth Summits in 1992 and more recently in 2012, large gatherings of up to 500 indigenous persons took place, resulting in two declarations, the Indigenous People's Earth Charter from the Kari-Oca Conference in 1992, and the Kari-Oca 2

Declaration of the Indigenous Peoples Global Conference on RIO+20 and Mother Earth in 2012. On institutions, the 2012 Declaration invites

> civil society to protect and promote [Indigenous] rights and worldviews and respect natural law, our spiritualties and cultures and our values of reciprocity, harmony with nature, solidarity, and collectivity. Caring and sharing, among other values, are crucial in bringing about a more just, equitable and sustainable world. In this context, we call for the inclusion of culture as the fourth pillar of sustainable development. (Kari-Oca 2 Declaration 2012)

In this declaration, culture is equated with entire systems of relationships that are tied to responsibilities. These values are viewed as part of the fundamental function of institutions.

In the Water Declaration of the Anishinaabek, Mushkegowuk and Onkwehonwe from the 2008 First Nations Water Policy Forum convened by the Chiefs of Ontario, it is stated that these peoples "have a direct relationships with all waters . . . that must be taken care of to ensure that waters provide for humans . . . for all living things . . . forests, land, plants, marine life, air, fish, insects, birds, animals . . ." (Chiefs of Ontario 2008). Water, then, has responsibilities to humans and other forms of life as a party within a system of relationships. McGregor, an Anishinaabe scholar and activist who participated in the events leading to this Declaration, argues for the importance of institutions to facilitate "the life that water supports (plants/medicines, animals, people, birds, etc.) and the life that supports water (e.g., the earth, the rain, the fish). Water has a role and a responsibility to fulfill, just as people do. We do not have the right to interfere with water's duties to the rest of Creation . . . water itself is considered a living entity with just as much right to live as we have" (McGregor 2009: 37–8).

The declarations and statements of indigenous environmentalists just referenced are not meant to be part of an exhaustive list. Yet, from looking at just these examples, indigenous environmentalists have made a number of arguments connecting the function of institutions to concepts associated with responsibility, such as interdependence, caring, reciprocity, and the roles involved in particular kinds of relationships. In the next section, I will offer my interpretation about what these communications are saying about what function many institutions ought to have. In the fifth section, I will provide specific examples of how institutions can be structured to perform this function.

Institutions as Conveners of Responsibilities

The communications referenced in the previous section are philosophically complex. I will interpret the communications discussed in the previous section as establishing a theoretical framework of the function of environmental governance institutions. The framework differs from the market-based or knowledge synthesis functions described earlier because it is grounded in the connection between institutions and mutual responsibilities. Again, I understand an institution's function to refer to the purpose it should be structured to accomplish for achieving environmental outcomes. The structure, then, is made up of the specific ways in which customs, norms, conventions, social orderings, or decision-making processes are designed, articulated, and arranged strategically to carry out the function.

To begin with, the communications just discussed are adamant that institutions should function to endorse systematic interactions among parties who are seen as having different roles in relation to one another. Institutions must function to acknowledge and elicit these various roles. That is, institutions should be structured to support the different parties in their recognizing and (or) acting as *relatives* of one another. As parties, when we see ourselves or act as relatives, we can exercise our responsibilities (attitudes and patterns of behavior) to other parties as contributions to ensuring that the system of relationships achieves the needed outcomes. More specifically, though, as relatives, our responsibilities must aim to do their part in supporting the conditions needed for each relative to exercise its role. For example, as humans, we may be responsible for being careful with what we do in relation to water (damming, recreational activities, pollution, and so on) because we can affect the conditions required for water to perform its role in serving to provide life for the plants and animals that depend on a certain water quality. Water, in turn, can be seen as having a responsibility to attend to the conditions that plants, animals, and humans require to perform all the responsibilities they may have to one another. So, here, relatives have responsibilities to support the conditions needed for other relatives to practice their roles within a system of relationships that produces important environmental outcomes. My interpretation of the communications in the previous section rests on the idea that institutions function in ways that respect and elicit systems of relationships in which the parties recognize themselves and (or) act as relatives of one another.

The indigenous environmental framework I am exploring, then, suggests that institutions must be structured to function as conveners of processes that renew or initiate systems of relationships that form the basis of reciprocal responsibilities among *relatives*. In short, institutions should function to convene *relatives and responsibilities*. Here, convening involves *facilitating* or *orchestrating* and sorts of processes, or protocols, that can help the different parties to see themselves and act as relatives with responsibilities. There are examples of this outside the environmental activism sphere that concern primarily humans, such as the Navajo Peacemaker Court. The process of the Peacemaker Court, an alternative to Western punitive justice, "focuses on establishing communication between the participants by encouraging them to address each other in the process. Each person may bring family members and friends to the court, and their opinions and support are encouraged by the system because all acts, according to Navajo tradition, affect the community" (Yazzie 1994; Wall 2001: 541). The Peacemaker Court brings together a process by which the parties associated with some wrong have to come to see themselves as relatives of each other who are part of a larger system of relationships that serve certain outcomes such as community tranquility and accountability.

Convening, then, is a kind of facilitation for ensuring that parties recognize in themselves and others that they are relatives with mutual responsibilities. A key aspect of this framework is that it is open to a pluralism of different and changing roles of relatives. These roles need not favor one culture's worldview about animal or plant agency or about whether earth or bodies of water have personalities. Rather, there is an appreciation of the evolving, adaptive and creative qualities of these roles. Some of the unquoted passages of the declarations referred to earlier appreciate the special contributions of scientists, even though the profession and work of the particular kinds of scientists being referenced do not originate in indigenous cultures and have often oppressed. The Mystic Lake Declaration, for example, claims that "Science can urgently work with traditional knowledge keepers to restore the health and well-being of Mother and Grandmother earth." So there is a need to continue to find ways of seeing parties who may not have typically interacted as relatives.

Convening also involves processes for moving on and ending certain relationships, such as mourning. Willox writes that

> at the 2009 Conference of the Parties [UNFCCC] . . . the Tuvalu Delegation publicly shared their grief, sadness, and distress about the destruction of their coastlines and the rapid disappearance of parts of their island due to rising water levels. Ian Fry, one of the lead negotiators for Tuvalu, wept during his public speech, and this emotional outpouring of grief . . . served to disrupt the conversations momentarily, and to cause discomfort throughout the delegation. (2012)

Indeed, the emotion expressed by the Tuvalu delegation disrupted the COP and mobilized NGOs and others to support stronger responsibilities to address climate justice (Farbotko and McGregor 2010).

Convening relatives and responsibilities is a function of institutions that differs from some of the functions described earlier, such as those based on markets, equity, and appeals to human psychology. Convening involves bringing us to an awareness of the special qualities we have as relatives. This is different from functions that see humans as irrational choosers, voters, and profit maximizers, and non-humans as inert objects, goods, resources, and flows. Convening casts parties in terms of their contributor potential as sources of action. Again, processes and protocols of convening are not limited to one cosmology's conceptions of contributory potential. Convening also places tremendous importance on culture in several senses. Indigenous cultures are seen ideally as ones in which parties are supposed to *acknowledge* (instead of ignoring or being unaware of) their roles within systems of relationships connecting humans, non-human beings and entities, and collectives. More broadly, indigenous environmentalists see achieving environmental outcomes as requiring no less than bonds across many parties that are as rich and systematic as cultural relationships. Culture, then, is foundational for motivating people to engage in environmentally responsible behavior; this emphasis on culture can be contrasted with the foundations of other functions that posit markets, regulation of people's choices, and democratic structures as tools toward motivating environmentally responsible behavior.

I understand many indigenous environmentalists, then, as positing a framework of institutional function that has aspects such as a theory of agency through the idea of roles and relatives; and a theory of the morality and justice of the appraisal of institutions through the idea that institutions ought to convene mutual responsibilities and systems of relationships modeled on the richness of cultural systems. These aspects of the framework are important for non-indigenous parties to understand because they reflect indigenous expectations of how to respect the political and cultural self-determination enshrined by UNDRIP. Since I am introducing an outline of this framework to readers in this essay, in the next section I will discuss in more detail some of the structures that indigenous environmentalists have designed to convene relatives and responsibilities.

The Mother Earth Water Walk and the Nmé Stewardship Program

In this section, I describe two examples of *Anishinaabe* environmental movements in the Great Lakes basin, the first involves Anishinaabe Grandmothers, the second, the Natural Resources Department of the Little River Band of Ottawa Indians. I select these two examples because they arise from different ends of the spectrum of indigenous environmentalism; the first is a direct action, viral movement; the second is an initiative by a US recognized indigenous governmental agency. Both illustrate structures of how to convene relatives and responsibilities.

The Mother Earth Water Walk was initiated by two Anishinaabe Grandmothers along with a group of women and men in response to concerns about water quality outcomes in the Great Lakes due to pollution from industrial facilities such as factories and large farms, as well as activities such as commercial fishing, tourism, and vacationing, and climate change. In terms of the structure of the institution, the walkers, including Grandmother Josephine Mandamin, started walking first around Lake Superior in the Spring of 2003, and then, year after year, around other large lakes. The springtime walks include an Anishinaabe water ceremony, feast, and celebration, and the participating Grandmothers take turns carrying a water vessel and eagle staff.

The structure arises from the Anishinaabe cosmology that understands water as acting as a source and supporter of life, which enables the supported life forms to contribute to each other in unique ways. Water is a considered a relative with responsibilities to life (Chiefs of Ontario 2008). Humans, in turn, have responsibilities to care for and respect water as relatives too; they must especially do things that encourage water's life giving force. Ceremonies are structured to remind people of their connections to water and bodies of water are considered to have their own unique personalities. Anishinaabe women, in particular, have responsibilities to attend to the quality of water, responsibilities to develop and pass on knowledge of water and its stewardship to younger generations. They also have responsibilities to take action to protect water when its quality is compromised (Lavalley 2006; Foushee and Gurneau 2010; McGregor 2012). The Water Walk calls out people of other nations and heritages to focus on and learn about their responsibilities to water, developing new relationships with water as a relative.

The Water Walk has important achievements for supporting greater convening of relatives and responsibilities. The Anishinabek Nation, an indigenous multi-party organization that plays an important role in Canadian politics, created the Women's Water Commission for bringing women's voices into Ontario and Great Lakes water issues. The explicit goal of the commission includes fostering "the traditional role of the Women in caring for water." The Commission seeks to encourage recognition of traditional responsibilities along with the need to include women as part of the decision-making processes (McGregor 2012: 12–13). The Walk has also spread across North America, becoming a regional form of action that includes more people each year, not just Anishinaabek alone (McGregor 2012; Mother Earth Water Walk 2013). The Mother Earth Water Walk is an institution structured to function as a convener of relatives and responsibilities, and facilitates responsibility based attitudes and patterns of behavior toward water.

The Little River Band of Ottawa Indians is located in the Western part of the lower peninsula of what is now called the state of Michigan by most people. The band is Anishinaabe, and the government includes a Natural Resources Department staffed by band members, along with indigenous and non-indigenous persons. The community has a cultural system called *Baamaadziwin*, which translates into " 'living in a good and respectful way' " (Mitchell 2013: 21). Director Jimmie Mitchell describes the Baamaadziwin as motivating people to do more than only be "good and just," but "to being servants, devoting ourselves to making a difference in all that has occurred and may still be occurring within our respective communities and environment . . . [which] includes restoring the balance of our shared natural environment and of all inhabitants who are dependent upon a robust ecosystem" (Mitchell 2013: 22). One example is the Nmé (Sturgeon) Stewardship Program, which seeks to restore nmé populations in the Big Manistee River. Nmé are on the decline from historic overharvesting from newcomers, dams, stocking rivers with other species for tourists and sport fishing, and environmental change. Nmé is an important species for Anishinaabe as it figures as a source of food but also as an integral part of clan identity. An elder, Jay Sam, refers to sturgeon as "The grandfather fish (sturgeon)," and that it would "sacrifice" itself "so the people would have food until the other crops were available." Sturgeon is a clan spirit and leaders would sign their names in treaties with the images of the clan spirits, such as sturgeon (Holtgren 2013: 135).

To re-connect Anishinaabe and Nmé, the Department sought to renew Nmé as a relative and encouraging in humans responsible attitudes and patterns of behavior. The Department started a cultural context group made up of a diverse range of tribal members and biologists that would develop goals and objectives for restoration. Biologist

Marty Holtgren describes the cultural context group as facilitating "a voice" that "was an amalgamation of cultural, biological, political, and social elements, all being important and often indistinguishable" (135). Holtgren discusses how the goal was to "restore the harmony and connectivity between Nmé and the Anishinaabek and bring them both back to the river... Bringing the sturgeon back to the river was an obvious biological element, however, restoring harmony and connectively between sturgeon and people was steeped in the cultural and social realm. Each meeting began with a ceremony, and the conversation was held over a feast" (Holtgren 2013: 136). Ultimately, the Department established a riverside rearing system for protecting young sturgeon before they can be released each fall. The program is based on relationships with government, non-profit, and community partners in the watershed, and the integration of scientific and indigenous knowledges of nmé.

Every September, a public release ceremony occurs involving a pipe ceremony and feast. Each attendee guides a young sturgeon to its release. Today, the event can garner hundreds of attendees. The new relationships become stronger as the members of the relationships realize their own responsibilities to Nmé. This was evidenced at the last annual and public sturgeon release ceremony, which I attended. Participants, including many children, according to their own ways, are beginning to feel a sense of responsibility to Nmé or sturgeon. Moreover, many commented that they had come to realize that it is people who also depend on Nmé. The fish have the power to reconcile and create new relationships among people. This is a major development in a watershed where settler colonialism strains people's relationships. Importantly, the participants need not take on the exact Anishinaabe way of thinking and living, but they are embracing a sense of themselves as relatives and a mutual responsibility that respects Nmé as a relative. It is too soon to be certain, but current evidence suggests that the program is headed for success in restoring Nmé populations (Holtgren et al. 2014).

Environmental governance institutions such as the Mother Earth Water Walk and Nmé Stewardship Program are structured to facilitate a convening of relatives and responsibilities. Importantly, both emphasize the roles of relatives in terms of their contributory potential within systems of relationships and are inclusive of culture. They show signs of being successful in their outcomes in terms of improving how people understand interdependence with non-human beings and entities and collectives. They also are set up to succeed in terms of more typical management aims such as clean water or the recovery of sturgeon populations.

Conclusion

There are many reasons why indigenous ideas about institutions as conveners of relatives and reciprocal responsibilities should be at the table in the policy sphere when different functions and structures of institutions are debated, planned and put in motion. They form a key dimension of how indigenous peoples exercise political and cultural self-determination as it is understood in UNDRIP. They also offer important institutional tools for achieving outcomes such as pollution abatement or forest conversation, and have unique niches in terms of their emphases on culture and responsibility, which are often absent in other frameworks of the function of institutions. In academic circles, indigenous environmentalists should be at the table in conversations about the morality and justice of market-based and other institutions commonly asserted as potential solutions for global earth governance institutions. If indigenous peoples are involved from the beginning, discussions aiming for cross-pollination should continue to occur between indigenous ideas and emerging trends in institutional scholarship such as ecosystem fit (Folke et al. 2007), ecosystem stewardship (Chapin et al. 2010), coupled human–natural systems (Liu et al. 2007) and actor–network theory (Latour 2004), among others.

References

Anaya, J. (2004). *Indigenous Peoples in International Law* (New York: Oxford University Press).

Arora-Jonsson, S. (2011). "Virtue and Vulnerability: Discourses on Women, Gender and Climate Change." *Global Environmental Change* 21: 744–51.

Asia Pacific Forum on Women, Law and Development (APWLD), Asian Rural Women's Coalition (ARWC),Asian Peasant Women's Network (APWN), Asian Indigenous Women's Network (AIWN), Asia Indigenous Peoples Pact (AIPP), People's Action on Climate Change (PACC). (2009). *Rural and Indigenous Women's Statement on Climate Change.* Available at http://www.madre.org/page/madre-news-125/news/rural-and-indigenous-womens-statement-on-climate-change-229.html Accessed June 21, 2015.

Bennett, T. Bull, M., Maynard, Nancy G., Cochran, Patricia, Gough, Robert, Lynn, Kathy, Maldonado, Julie, Voggesser, Garrit, Wotkyns, Susan, and Cozzetto, Karen. (2014). "Indigenous Peoples, Lands, and Resources." In *Climate Change Impacts in the United States: The Third National Climate Assessment*, edited by J. M. Melillo, T. Richmond, and G. W. Yohe (Washington, DC: U.S. Global Change Research Program), 397–13.

Berry, K. and Camacho, D. (1998). "Race for Water? Native Americans, Eurocentrism, and Western Water Policy." In *Environmental Injustices, Political Struggles*, edited by D. Camacho (Durham, NC: Duke University Press), 101–24.

Borrows, J. (2002). *Recovering Canada: The Resurgence of Indigenous Law* (Toronto: University of Toronto Press).

de la Cadena, M. and Starn, O. (2007). *Indigenous Experience Today* (New York, NY: Berg).

Carlson, K. M. and Coulter, R. T. (2012). "Natural Allies: Conservationists, Indian Tribes, and Protecting Native North America." In *Tribes, Land, and the Environment*, edited by S. A. Krakoff and E. Rosser (Burlington, VT: Ashgate Publishing Company), 195–214.

Carroll, C. (2014). "Native Enclosures: Tribal National Parks and the Progressive Politics of Environmental Stewardship in Indian Country." *Geoforum* 53: 31–40.

Chapin, F. S., Carpenter, S. R., Kofinas, G. P., Folke C., Abel, N., Clark, W. C., Olsson, P., Smith, D., Walker, B. and Young, O. R. (2010). "Ecosystem Stewardship: Sustainability Strategies for a Rapidly Changing Planet." *Trends in Ecology & Evolution* 25: 241–9.

Chiefs of Ontario. (2008). "Water Declaration of the Anishinaabek, Mushkegowuk and Onkwehonwe." Toronto, Ontario: 1–6. Available at http://www.chiefs-of-ontario.org/node/76 Accessed June 21, 2015.

Churchill, W. and Jaimes, M. A. (1992). *Fantasies of the Master Race: Literature, Cinema and the Colonization of American Indians* (Monroe, ME: Common Courage Press).

Clark, B. (2002). "The Indigenous Environmental Movement in the United States Transcending Borders in Struggles against Mining, Manufacturing, and the Capitalist State." *Organization & Environment* 15: 410–42.

Corntassel, J. (2008). "Toward Sustainable Self-Determination: Rethinking the Contemporary Indigenous-Rights Discourse." *Alternatives: Global, Local, Political* 33: 105–32.

Doolittle, A. A. (2010). "The Politics of Indigeneity: Indigenous Strategies for Inclusion in Climate Change Negotiations." *Conservation and Society* 8: 286–91.

Farbotko, C. and McGregor, H. V. (2010). "Copenhagen, Climate Science and the Emotional Geographies of Climate Change." *Australian Geographer* 41: 159–66.

Fincke, A. and Oviedo, G. (2009) "Indigenous Women: Most Vulnerable to Climate Change But Key Agents of Change." International Union for Conservation of Nature News Stories. International Union for Conservation of Nature, Gland, Switzerland.

Fishel, J. A. (2006). "United States Called to Task on Indigenous Rights: The Western Shoshone Struggle and Success at the International Level." *American Indian Law Review* 31: 619–50.

Fishel, J. A. (2007). "The Western Shoshone Struggle: Opening Doors for Indigenous Rights." *Part of Symposium: Sovereignty and Sustainable Development of Indigenous Peoples* 2: 41–91.

Folke, C., Pritchard, L., Jr., Berkes, F., Colding, J., and Svedin, U. (2007). "The Problem of Fit Between Ecosystems and Institutions: Ten Years Later." *Ecology & Society* 12: 1–38.

Foushee, L. and Gurneau, R., eds. (2010). *Sacred Water: Water for Life* (Lake Elmo, MN: North American Water Office).

Gedicks, A. (1993). *The New Resource Wars: Native and Environmental Struggles Against Multinational Corporations* (Boston, MA: South End Press).

Glazebrook, T. (2011). "Women and Climate Change: A Case-Study from Northeast Ghana." *Hypatia* 26: 762–82.

Goldtooth, T. (1995). "Indigenous Nations: Summary of Sovereignty and Its Implications for Environmental Protection." In *Environmental Justice: Issues, Policies, and Solutions*, edited by B. Bryant (Washington, DC: Island Press), 138–48.

Grinde, D. A. and Johansen, B. E. (1995). *Ecocide of Native America: environmental destruction of Indian lands and peoples* (Santa Fe, New Mexico: Clear Light).

Harkin, M. E. and Lewis, D. R. (2007). *Native Americans and the Environment: Perspectives on the Ecological Indian* (Lincoln, NE: University of Nebraska Press).

Holtgren, M. (2013). "Bringing Us Back to the River." In *The Great Lake Sturgeon*, edited by N. Auer and D. Dempsey (East Lansing, MI: Michigan State University Press), 133–47.

Holtgren M., Ogren S., and Whyte K. P. (2014). "Renewing Relatives: Nmé Stewardship in a Shared Watershed." Publication forthcoming on *Tales of Hope and Caution in Environmental Justice*. Available at https://www.academia.edu/9009937/Renewing_Relatives_Nm%C3%A9_Sturgeon_Stewardship_in_a_Shared_Watershed

Idle No More. (2014) *The Manifesto*. Available at http://www.idlenomore.ca/manifesto Accessed June 21, 2015.

Igoe, J. (2004). *Conservation And Globalization: A Study Of The National Parks And Indigenous Communities from East Africa to South Dakota* (Belmont, CA: Thomson/Wadsworth).
"Indigenous Peoples Biocultural Climate Change Assessment Initiative." (2014). http://ipcca.info/
Kari-Oca 2 Declaration Indigenous Peoples Global Conference on RIO+20 and Mother Earth. (2012). Rio de Janiero, Brazil. http://www.iwgia.org/iwgia_files_news_files/0535_DECLARATION-of-KARI-OCA-2-Eng.pdf Accessed June 21, 2015.
LaDuke, W. (1999) *All Our Relations: Native Struggles for Land and Life* (Cambridge, MA: South End Press).
Larson, E., Johnson, Z., and Murphy, M. (2008). "Emerging Indigenous Governance: Ainu Rights at the Intersection of Global Norms and Domestic Institutions." *Alternatives: Global, Local, Political* 33: 53–82.
Latour, B. (2004). *Politics of Nature: How to Bring the Sciences into Democracy* (Cambridge, MA: Harvard University Press).
Lavalley, G. (2006). *Aboriginal Traditional Knoweldge and Source Water protection: First Nations' Views on Taking Care of Water* (Toronto, Canada: Chiefs of Ontario and Environment Canada). Available at http://www.chiefs-of-ontario.org/node/111 Accessed June 21, 2015.
Liu, J., Dietz, T., Carpenter, S. R., C arl Folke, M. A., Redman, C. L., Schneider, S. H., Ostrom E., Pell, A. N., Lubchenco, J., Taylor, W. W., Ouyang, Z., Deadman, P., Kratz, T., and Provencher, W. (2007). "Coupled Human and Natural Systems." *AMBIO: A Journal of the Human Environment* 36: 639–49.
Maldonado, J. K., Pandya, R. E., Colombi, B. J. (2013). "Climate Change and Indigenous Peoples in the United States: Impacts, Experiences, and Actions." *Climatic Change* 120: 509–682.
Mandaluyong Declaration. (2011). "Mandaluyong Declaration of the Global Conference on Indigenous Women, Climate Change and REDD Plus." In *Indigenous Women, Climate Change & Forests*, edited by Tebtebba (Baguio City, Philippines: Tebtebba Foundation).
McGregor, D. (2012). "Traditional Knowledge: Considerations for Protecting Water in Ontario." *The International Indigenous Policy Journal* 3: 11.
McLean, K. G., Ramos-Castillo, A., and Rubis, J. (2011). "Indigenous Peoples, Marginalized Populations and Climate Change: Vulnerability, Adaptation and Traditional Knowledge." In *Expert Workshop on Indigenous Peoples, Marginalized Populations and Climate Change* (Mexico City, Mexico: United Nations University).1–48.
Middleton, B. R. (2011). *Trust in the Land: New Directions in Tribal Conservation* (Tucson, AZ: University of Arizona Press).
Mitchell, J. (2013). "N'me." In *The Great Lake Sturgeon*, edited by N. Auer and D. Dempsey (East Lansing, MI: Michigan State University Press), 21–6.
Napoleon, V. (2013). *Thinking about Indigenous Legal Orders* (Dordrecht, Netherlands: Springer).
Indigenous Women's Biodiversity Network. (2004). "The Manukan Declaration of the Indigenous Women's Biodiversity Network." Tebtebba Foundation: Baguio City, Phillipines.
Niezen, R. (2003). *The Origins of Indigenism: Human Rights and the Politics of Identity* (Berkeley, CA: University of California Press).
Pachamama Alliance. (2008). "Pachamama Addresses Ecuadorian Constitutional Assembly on Ecosystem Rights." Available at http://www.pachamama.org/news/pachamama-addresses-ecuadorian-constitutional-assembly-on-ecosystem-rights Accessed June 21, 2015.

Postel, S. (2012). “A River in New Zealand Gets a Legal Voice.” *National Geographic* Blog. Available at http://voices.nationalgeographic.com/2012/09/04/a-river-in-new-zealand-gets-a-legal-voice/ Accessed June 21, 2015.
Richardson, B. (2008). “The Ties that Bind: Indigenous Peoples and Environmental Governance.” CLPE Research Paper.
Sanders, D. E. (1977). “The Formation of the World Council of Indigenous Peoples.” The International Secretariat of International Work Group for Indigenous Affairs, Copenhagen, Denmark.
Schlosberg, D. and Carruthers, D. (2010). “Indigenous Struggles, Environmental Justice, and Community Capabilities.” *Global Environmental Politics* 10: 12–35.
Shockley, K. (2012). “Human Values and Institutional Responses to Climate Change.” In *Ethical Adaptation to Climate Change: Human Virtues of the Future*, edited by A. Thompson and J. Bendik-Keymer (Cambridge, MA: MIT Press), 281–98.
Smith, H. A. and Sharp, K. (2012). “Indigenous Climate Knowledges.” *Wiley Interdisciplinary Reviews: Climate Change* 3: 467–76.
Te Aho, L. (2010). “Indigenous challenges to enhance freshwater governance and management in Aotearoa New Zealand—The Waikato river settlement.” *Water Law* 20: 285-292.
Third World Water Forum. (2003). “Indigenous Peoples Kyoto Water Declaration.” Kyoto, Japan. Availabe at http://portal.unesco.org/science/en/ev.php-URL_ID=3886&URL_DO=DO_TOPIC&URL_SECTION=201.html Accessed June 21, 2015.
United Nations General Assembly. (2007). “United Nations Declaration on the Rights of Indigenous Peoples.” United Nations: G.A. Res. 61/295, U.N. Doc. A/RES/61/295 (September 13, 2007), 46 I.L.M. 1013.
van Ginkel, R. (2004). “The Makah Whale Hunt and Leviathan’s Death: Reinventing Tradition and Disputing Authenticity in the Age of Modernity.” *ETNOFOOR* XVII: 58–89.
Wall, B. E. (2001). “Navajo Conceptions of Justice in the Peacemaker Court.” *Journal of Social Philosophy* 32: 532–46.
Whyte, K. P. (2013). “Justice Forward: Tribes, Climate Adaptation and Responsibility.” *Climatic Change* 120: 117–30.
Whyte, K. P. (2014). “Indigenous Women, Climate Change Impacts and Collective Action.” *Hypatia: a Journal of Feminist Philosophy* 29: 599–616.
Willox, A. C. (2012). “Climate Change as the Work of Mourning.” *Ethics & the Environment* 17: 137–64.
Yazzie, R. (1994). “Life Comes From It: Navajo Justice Concepts.” *New Mexico Law Review* 24: 175–90.

CHAPTER 38

REIMAGINING RADICAL ENVIRONMENTALISM

EMILY RAY AND SEAN PARSON

IN March of 1981, activists from the newly formed direct action group, Earth First! dropped a black banner down the side of the Glen Canyon Dam, which visually created a fake crack. In doing so, the group highlighted their opposition to the dam and brought to life the fictional desires of the protagonists in Edward Abbey's influential book *The Monkey Wrench Gang* (1975)—George Hayduke, Bonnie Abbzug, "Seldom Seen" Smith, and Doc Sarvis—who planned and failed to destroy the dam. Since the 1970s, activists and academics have been wrestling with this and other manifestations of radical environmentalism, particularly the range of approaches to contentious topics like population control, women's rights, approaches to activism, and the place of humans in nature. In the subsequent decades the radical environmental movement has seen changes as more voices and perspectives have been included in the dialogue. The inclusion of people of color, women, trans and queer individuals, indigenous voices, and labor activists, however controversial or resisted, has forever altered radical environmentalism.

Since the 1970s, we see three major philosophic perspectives that have shaped radical environmental thought: spiritual ecologies, which are best illustrated by deep ecology; humanist ecologies, such as social ecology and eco-Marxism; and luddite ecologies, such as primitivism. On the ground, activism has often embraced a fusion of these perspectives as most Western radical environmentalism brought together a secular sacred regard for all living things with a materialist critique of Western civilization, particularly developments in technology and consumerism. In this chapter we introduce and examine these three major theoretical threads of radical environmentalism and provide an analysis of their philosophic strengths and weaknesses. We then argue that activists tend to fuse different aspects of these philosophies together, sometimes intentionally and sometimes unintentionally.

Spiritual Environmentalism: Deep Ecology and Biocentrism

In the 1970s and 1980s, Norwegian philosopher Arne Naess promoted a way of rethinking the relationship between humans and nature. Naess (1993) looked to the anthropocentrism, or human centered ethic, of Western philosophy and civilization as being the primary barrier to humans living sustainably on the planet. Anthropocentrism is a worldview that emphasizes how humans experience reality, and prioritizes shaping the world—from public policy to ethical orientation—to suit the needs of humans. According to Naess, by placing humans at the center of the ethical world, Western philosophy denigrated the non-human and created a "break" between humans and the natural world. He argued that humans have no philosophic basis for privileging themselves above other living beings and that we need to radically change our ethical foundations and find a way to incorporate non-human nature into our ethical calculations.

This idea, which he called biocentrism, contends that all life on the planet—from mosquitoes to whales—are deserving of ethical consideration. This ethical value is not rooted in their value to humans, what is called extrinsic value, but in the fact that they have intrinsic value, or value in themselves. By pursuing an ethical system that de-centers the human, Naess and deep ecologists provided a powerful critique of human anthropocentrism that provided a unique way of understanding environmental concerns. For instance, a tree, for an anthropocentrist, has economic value if pulped into paper products, as well as spiritual/aesthetic value for those humans who gain pleasure from hiking and nature sojourns. To a deep ecologist that tree has value regardless of the value humans gain from it. To argue for protection of that tree from these anthropocentrist views would simply reinforce the destructive Western ethical view that has dominated for centuries. By contrast to what Naess called shallow ecology, deep ecology looked toward root problems with Western philosophy that cause humans to perceive nature as something outside of themselves. Supporters of deep ecology argue that changes in public policy need to reflect an integrated view of humans and ecology. As such, a capitalist, growth-based economy is contrary to a "deep" relationship with other species that respects the right of other beings to exist and to thrive.

The version of deep ecology that has influenced radical environmentalism iterates the need to engage with the wild and to individually and socially reclaim the capacity to communicate with nature with less mediation. In discussing this point, philosopher David Abram (1996) argues that we need to open our eyes and ears to the world; to embrace the magic of shamans; to actively listen to the birds in the forests; and to accept the limits of human understanding. By changing ourselves, we change the world. Bron Taylor (2008: 28) described practicing this deep connection:

> This can be facilitated in a number of ways... by spending time in nature with a receptive heart, for the central spiritual episteme among radical environmentalists

> is that people can learn to "listen to the land" and discern its sacred voices. Other means activists employ to evoke and deepen a proper spiritual perception include visual and performance art, music, dancing, and drumming... Such ritualization is believed capable of eroding that everyday sense of ego and independence in favor of belonging to the universe... and evoking one's intuitive sense of the sacredness of intact ecosystems.

As expressed in this quote, deep ecology does not view the human as atomistic and self-sufficient and instead sees us all as connected in a web of life. For this reason, to save the rainforest we must come to see the rainforest as part of ourselves (Taylor 2008; Duvall 2008).

To foster this deep connection, humans are encouraged to seek individual practices, even if done in a group setting, to strengthen their personal bond with nature, and to reimagine their identity as one with the cosmos. In our analysis there is nothing wrong with these practices if they suit an individual but they do not constitute political action. Cultivating a sense of belonging to the universe as practice emphasizes the importance of creating a right human–nature relationship, instead of directing attention toward the material conditions that produce environmental and social crises. Deep ecology here overemphasizes the importance of ideology in the radical environmental movement and limits its revolutionary potential.

To further complicate translating deep ecology into political action, the assertions of the proper human–nature relationship are problematic. To "only take what is socially necessary" assumes that an individual's consumption choices are sufficient to confront the scale of production in a globalized capitalist economy, and that the principles of deep ecology will be universally accepted in time for us to reimagine the socially necessary. This position does not adequately understand the dialectical relationship between humans and the more-than-human world, and even though deep ecology views the world as an interconnected web, when it comes to humans the philosophy asserts that humans are separate from the natural world. In reality, humans are part of the natural world, and as such, viewing human action as only a "taking" from the world obfuscates that we also give back. While deep ecologists are right to critique the general lack of reciprocity between humans and the natural world under capitalism, this is largely a systemic issue and not an individual consumptive problem.

As an extension to deep ecologists' focus on consumption, many activists have turned their attention toward population growth, especially third world population growth. The preoccupation with reducing population growth—a key issue elevated by Naess himself—does not adequately examine the unequal nature of consumption and turns the blame away from capitalism, the state, or civilization and instead places the blame on women's bodies. As such the campaigns and policy recommendations that emerged from this current of deep ecological thought, such as opposing AIDS research and promoting restrictivist immigration policies, were fraught with undercurrents of racism, misogyny, and misanthropy that has dogged radical environmentalism ever since (Bookchin 1987; Luke 1997).

Deep ecology often encourages individual level, not collective, change and reinforces the primacy of negative freedoms and the importance of individual choice. The influence of liberalism in radical environmentalisms such as deep ecology enables individuals to address the ecological crisis by tidying up their personal lifestyle while sidestepping political engagement and collective responsibility. Although deep ecology does not avoid discussing large-scale change, like finding a new economic model different from capitalism, the actual practices of deep ecology tend to take place on an individual level. The emphasis on individualism is evident in the rise of green consumerism (Szasz 2007), schemes to become "carbon neutral," and the fact that more people give money to environmental non-profits than participate in environmental movements (Putnam 2001). The energy needed to address environmental issues is easily channeled into the marketplace of products, offsets, pledges, home design, and food consumption. While a personal environmental ethics does not preclude collective political action, it is convenient and socially encourages one to make their lifestyle a demonstration of both ethics and politics. These characteristics of individualized environmentalism are increasingly found in radical environmentalism influenced by deep ecology. In addition to lifestyle activism, radical environmentalism struggles with calls to balance social and political change with the political realities they face.

Across mainstream and radical environmental movements, individuals are asked to audit their lifestyles and look for opportunities to act differently, from choosing greener energy to composting. These actions suggest individuals have a consumer choice that enables them to live within specific ethical ideas of the human–nature relationship, without acknowledging the relative political futility of these actions. Even some of the most militant environmental activists seem to see their consumption habits as being central to their ethical positionality. The extent of political responsibility is often limited by the presumed extent of an individual's capacity to promote change through their actions. One of the problems with this emphasis on individualized action is that it weakens collective action as a political alternative. Individual action tends to focus on momentary disruptions, and in the case of environmental activism, fighting to stop a particular environmentally destructive act with an urgent action.

Jodi Dean (2012) levels a similar critique at new left politics that eschews a party-centric approach to abolishing capitalism. Dean provides valuable insight that liberal–leftist activism displaces politics to something performed and consumed as a spectacle. In other words, as long as radical environmentalism focuses on cultivating the correct idealism, action will appear individualized and unable to alter political institutions. The focus within the radical environmental movements becomes justifying the right ideological disposition, which reinforces the individual, rather than engaging in collective action and responsibility that moves us beyond contemporary political limits. Deep ecology has placed undue focus on finding a correct ideology—and then getting others to adopt it—rather than emphasizing its utility for creating an action-oriented way of addressing environmental and social justice issues. Because of the liberal ethical orientation to deep ecology, humanistic radical environmentalism promotes a more politically oriented approach than deep ecology, and in some instances, acts as a counter-approach to deep ecology.

Humanistic Radical Environmentalism: Social Ecology and Eco-Marxism

Humanist ecologies, unlike deep ecology, look to understand the environmental crisis as largely the result of human behavior and primarily impacting human society. By centering on humans, ethically and politically, humanist approaches are anthropocentric and tend to look to institutional cases of the ecological crisis over individual accounts. The two most dominant humanist approaches are social ecology and eco-Marxism.

Social ecology is a philosophy developed by activist and scholar Murray Bookchin beginning in the 1960s. Bookchin (2005) argued that destruction of the natural world is not rooted in our disconnection from nature, but in our disconnection from each other. Central to this disconnect are human created hierarchical institutions—such as the state—which create relationships of domination. To social ecologists, institutions like the state, religion, and capitalist economic systems create divisions between people and privilege certain people while justifying the exploitation of others; once people are seen as exploitable, humans inevitably start to treat the natural world as a resource to be exploited as well.

Since to Bookchin, and other social ecologists, the focus of environmental thinking was the human world, Bookchin fought to create a direct democratic political system, one where everyone was actively involved in deciding and regulating the political institutions that govern their life. This re-empowering of local democratic institutions did not just end with formal political institutions, as many social ecologists promote a participatory society in which economic decisions as also governed democratically, through things like workers' councils and democratically run businesses. This idea, which Jeff Shantz (2012) calls Green Syndicalism, argues that the best way to protect the natural world is for people to collectively and democratically meet. Shantz argues that workers, when not forced into a politics of fear through scarcity and political manipulation, would be the best stewards of the environment because environmental destruction impacts and hurts them. By building local, egalitarian, and democratic institutions, social ecologists argue that the natural world would invariably be protected, as only an unequal, non-democratic political system would be willing to harm certain members of its community for the economic benefit of the few.

Social ecology can be seen as a humanist attempt to understand the ecocide of modern society, thus, central to social ecology is a rejection of the spiritualism and biocentrism of deep ecology. According to Bookchin, these practices end up re-mystifying the world in a way that rejects rationalism and scientific pursuits. Social ecologists criticize the tendency of deep ecologists to blend all of human experience into general statements. This practice blurs differences between people and distorts the way we view responsibility. Bookchin (2007), after viewing a museum exhibit writes:

> I shall not easily forget an "environmental" presentation staged by the New York Museum of Natural History . . . exhibits, each depicting examples of pollution and ecological disruption. The exhibit . . . carried a startling sign, "The Most Dangerous Animal on Earth," and it consisted simply of a huge mirror which reflected back the human viewer who stood before it. I clearly recall a black child standing before the mirror while a white school teacher tried to explain the message . . . There were no exhibits of corporate boards or directors planning to deforest a mountainside or government officials acting in collusion with them. The exhibit primarily conveyed one, basically misanthropic, message: people *as such*, not a rapacious society and its wealthy beneficiaries, are responsible for environmental dislocations—the poor no less than the personally wealthy, people of colour no less than privileged whites, women no less than men, the oppressed no less than the oppressor. A mythical human "species" had replaced classes; individuals had replaced hierarchies . . .

He had previously argued that the spiritual environmental approach, at its heart, is xenophobic, racist, and proto-fascist (Bookchin 1987). His critique comes from an historical and materialist understanding of the environmental crisis: instead of embracing the spiritualism of deep ecology, the humanism of Bookchin is concerned with systems of hierarchy and domination which allow us to treat fellow humans as objects. He contends that in dehumanizing humans these institutions make it nearly impossible for us to care about the natural world.

Similar to Bookchin, eco-Marxism looks to scientific rationalism and an historical analysis to develop a modern, green paradigm. For Marx and Engels, nature is understood in the conceptual framework of historical materialism. Foster (2000) argued that, "from the start, Marx's notion of the alienation of human labor was connected to an understanding of the alienation of human beings from nature" (8). Marx and Engels considered our relationship with nature to be both fundamental to human existence, and also something that we alter and produce through our political actions and economic history. When humans engage in an exploitative relationship with the environment, people fall out of synch with nature.

Marx recognized that the transport of nutrients from the country to the town was a unidirectional movement that left soil depleted and urban spaces polluted. The growth and density of urban populations drove the industrialization of agriculture, which in turn "produces conditions that provoke an irreparable rift in the interdependent process of social metabolism, a metabolism prescribed by the natural laws of life itself" (Foster 2006: 155). Through the metabolic rift theory, eco-Marxists argue that capitalism is inherently incompatible with a healthy human–nature relationship because capitalism cannot self-regulate or consider other values of nature besides exchange value. This connects with James O'Connor's (1998) argument that capitalism destroys the means of its own survival, and in the process the means of survival for all species. Toward this concern, eco-Marxism speaks to the industrial scale of environmental harms and of economic activities that produce and reproduce these damages. Eco-Marxism is not preoccupied with the role of the individual as a consumer or as an element of the environment. Instead, the problems and solutions are scaled to that of political organization and formations. To change an individual's metabolic relationship, for instance through an activity like gardening, is not on a scale appropriate to the critiques leveled by eco-Marxists. Humanist ecologies do not require the individual to reshape their ontological and epistemological positions toward nature in order to realize significant change, just their position toward others humans and human constructed institutions.

While humanist environmentalism is strongly committed to historical analysis and philosophic materialism, and includes radical systemic critiques of capitalism, both eco-Marxism and social ecology propose political projects that come far short of addressing the problems they describe. Foster, Clark, and York (2011) look to the ecological politics of Venezuela, a petro-state that uses its oil resources to accumulate capital, and to urban redesign as solutions to the ecological crisis. These policies, while perhaps pragmatic, do not address the problems of global neoliberal capitalism. Similarly, Bookchin (1990) promoted a form of agorism, or local direct democratic republicanism, which in practice looked more like pluralist liberalism then a radical alternative. While Bookchin's agorism required an anti-capitalist ethos, it falls short of addressing the larger ecological crisis, and does not adequately address the historical problems of rational scientific discourse in protecting racist, colonial, and sexist discourses and practices. Much like spiritual ecologies, humanist ecologies do not adequately connect their ontology with their political practice. In both cases, the recommended changes exist comfortably within the present political and economic formations and do not tackle the deeper causes of the crises.

Luddite Environmentalism: Primitivism and the Critique of Civilization

While spiritual ecology is primarily concerned with the relationship between humans and the natural world, and humanist ecology focuses on human institutions, luddite ideologies focus specifically on the human institution of civilization and the ways it separates people from the natural world. To primitivists, the development of complex social, political, and technological systems represent a threat to human freedom, community, and ecological wellness. These complex systems require oppressive and exploitative social and economic systems that the world would be better off without. In place of complex systems, primitivism calls for locally based institutions—such as those found in hunter–gatherer or village societies. Primitivism differs from the previous two approaches as it is intimately connected with both deep ecology and social ecology. In practice, the primitivist approach adds an expanded scope and militancy to the previous ideologies.

The connection between primitivism and deep ecology is most clearly seen by those who argue that civilization has distorted humans' ability to understand and communicate with the more-than-human world. Derrick Jensen (2000) argues that civilization has made us deaf to the world, which is always trying to communicate with us. While the world tries to speak, we, much like Jensen's abusive father, military generals, corporate CEOs, and politicians, refuse to listen (Jensen 2000). Jensen calls for us to listen to the world around us and hear the cries of the earth being cannibalized by civilization. This analysis puts the emphasis on comparing civilization to individual personalities: serial killer, torturer, abuser, narcissist, insane, and psychopath (McBay, Keith, and Jensen 2011). According to Jensen, the root problem is a certain mindset. Just as systems like industrialization and capitalism are given the attributes of individual humans, the approach to unsettling these systems similarly lies in the capacity of individuals to live radically by connecting with nature and rewilding.

Taking up the social ecological strand, Fredy Perlman (1983) argues that civilizations emerged with the founding of hierarchies and divisions of labor and spread throughout the world by force. Building on the work of Perlman, Dave Watson (1998) argues that the "mega-machine" of the modern world is inconsistent with human freedom and liberty and that it hides the coercive nature of modern life. For example, the computer is embedded in a large web of harmful power relationships: raw materials are extracted by underpaid miners in the developing world; the carcinogenic computer chips are produced by women working in sweatshops in Indonesia; and the components are shipped across thousands of miles, sold in stores, and later thrown away, where the chemicals seep into water supplies and poison the poor communities that surround e-waste dumping zones. For Watson, modern civilization needs these hidden webs of relationships to exist; it needs cheap goods that demand the exploitation of people and the environment. In addition, the complex technologies that industrialized societies are dependent on, from power plants to the Internet, require a strict division of labor and political centralization, which is inconsistent with human emancipation and freedom. To Watson, this means that a social ecologist must also be a primitivist.

Both strands of primitivism tend to embrace spiritual ecological critiques of population and consumption, which were critiqued earlier. Because of this an unnerving racial and gendered subtext runs just below the surface of these deep green changes. Likewise, primitivism tends to embrace a civilizational reductionism, in which all problems, from sexism to colonialism, are the byproducts of industrial civilization. Much like Marxism, this reductionism obfuscates differences between people and is problematically teleological.

Good and Bad Ideological Syncretism: Judi Bari and the ELF

The earlier sections explain the ideologies that form the ontological basis for a wide range of contemporary radical environmental movements. On-the-ground contemporary activism, however, is not committed to ideological and philosophical purity. Instead, in the pages of the *Earth First!* journal or at the campfire discussions at activist action camps, what emerge are syncretic ideologies that combine aspects of the three main approaches. This is often done either overtly, as in the case of Judi Bari and Redwood Summer, or less intentionally, as is the case with the ideology that emerges from the Earth Liberation Front (ELF) communiqués. Regardless, the fusing of ideologies across the spectrum of radical environmental theories ends up having profound impacts on a movement's tactics, strategies, and their overall political projects. This impact can be either positive or negative, the outcome of which largely depends upon the attention movements give to understanding the implications of adopting particular perspectives and ideologies. The two examples below offer a view of the successful integration of radical ideologies, and a view of the hazards that come along with cherry picking from various ideologies without considering the complications that emerge when these ideologies lead toward different political realities. In this section we will first look at the philosophic work of Judi Bari and follow that with an analysis of the ELF.

In the summer of 1990 Judi Bari, an environmental activist and labor organizer, coordinated a summer-long series of actions and protests to stop timber logging in the redwood forests of Northern California. In constructing this campaign, Bari intentionally looked to develop an inclusive and movement-oriented radical environmentalism, working both with members of Earth First! and with loggers and community members to create a powerful coalition of stakeholders who are typically at odds. According to Shantz (2001, 2012), her syncretic ideology combined the spiritual ecologies with materialist critique of capitalism. She leveraged this to create a theory that understood that capitalist economic relations deny people their fair economic share of production as well as a spiritual connection to a more-than-human world. In constructing this view, Bari did not reject the biocentrism of older Earth First! activists but she critiqued their piecemeal wilderness-centered approach, which typically excluded the working class who engaged in land-based labor. Instead of just saving wilderness areas and building one's personal connection to the land, Bari called for social revolution and the abolition of capitalism. Her analysis intentionally sought to build a link between humanist and spiritual ecologies in a productive way. According to Shantz, she thought, "Only when workers are in a position to refuse to engage in destructive practices or produce destructive goods could any realistic hope for lasting ecological change emerge" (Shantz 2001). This is a hybrid ideology where different philosophic components complement each other. There is no tension between this political worldview and the attendant actions, and Bari's work attempted to confront the negative qualities of the primary ideologies she borrowed from. She did not embrace the misanthropic and sexist tendencies of spiritual ecologies nor did she embrace the reductionist tenets of the humanist approaches. She provides a good example of how radical environmental theories can be drawn together into a new, consistent ideology with useable and effective political strategies.

Bari's experience can be contrasted with that of the ELF, which has not been as successful in constructing their political ideology. The ELF formed, at least in part, as a response to the influence of Bari on the tactics and strategies of Earth First!. Prior to Bari's influence, Earth First! embraced ecotage, or environmental sabotage, as a means of stopping ecological destruction. Bari, in an attempt to build linkages with timber workers, pressured activists to reject the most controversial ecotage tactic of the time, tree spiking, due to timber workers' fears that the action would cause harm to mill workers. Her request asked activists to respect logging industry workers, even though activists and loggers had a long-standing adversarial relationship. In response to the shift away from property damage promoted by Bari and others, radical activists formed the ELF, a covert, leaderless organization that destroys property in protection of the natural world.

Because of the history of the ELF many of the analyses of the group argue that they hold onto a radical deep ecology perspective but, as one of the present authors has argued previously, this view is incomplete (Parson 2008). In reality the communiqués of ELF activists highlight not a singular deep ecology ideology, but a complex and syncretic ideology that combines aspects of spiritual, humanist, and luddite ecologies. For instance, nearly all ELF communiqués promote a biocentric view and an understanding that the natural world has value outside of its use to humans, while a sizable number of ELF activists also note the materialist basis of capitalism and the role of global capitalism in the creation of racism, sexism, and colonial practices (Parson 2008). Finally, communiqués that discuss genetic modification all highlight the need to fight domestication and fight for the "wildness" of nature.

Unlike Bari's work to coherently theorize and organize across multiple radical ideologies, there is little evidence that the activists involved with the ELF have intentionally created this syncretic belief; even if they did, due to the secretive nature of the group, that discussion has not happened in public. As such there are contradictions and problems within the ideologies of the ELF that emerge from this uncritical application of beliefs. One such problem is the way that individualized ethical values have been smuggled in through their reliance on deep ecology and individualist strands of primitivism. This is expressed by the individual and isolated nature of ELF actions. One such example was the 2003 arson of a suburban housing development in San Diego in order to draw attention to development in the nearby canyon (Green and Hughes 2003). Despite generating media attention from the action, the arson was not directly tied to a larger campaign to stop the canyon development, and the ELF affinity group did not conduct any follow-up actions to stop the building. Not all radical environmental direct action has to follow this particular, highly individualized ideological and tactical approach. The action to protest canyon development can be compared to the Animal Liberation Front, ELF's sister organization. The ALF, which is more influenced by work on animal rights, rather than deep ecology, has a deeper focus on collective political action and responsibility. ALF activists have been central in the campaign entitled "Stop Huntingdon Life Science." Huntingdon Life Science is the largest producer of animals for medical experimentation, and the ALF has waged a multi-year campaign against mink farming that has created massive economic hardships for the industry and forced many of the largest mink farms to shutter their doors (Goodwin 1996). This particular approach to direct action maintains a politically useful strategy of working on multiple fronts, from juridical justice to civil disobedience, while connecting their core concern for the intrinsic value of animal life to collective political action. The ELF struggles to move beyond individualized ethics and actions, and as such produces a momentarily powerful but politically weak resistance to environmentally degrading activities.

As the two examples above highlight, ideological hybridity can have either positive or negative consequences for a movement or organization. The three dominant radical environmental views have all emerged from different philosophic traditions and have different worldviews, and understandings of the ecological crisis. As such, without critical analysis and intentional thought, there is a good chance that poorly conceived assumptions can be smuggled into a movement's politics. For instance many Earth First! activists end up having difficulty untangling their anti-racist feminism with their critique of population. In this case, their deep ecological and social ecologic views come into conflict, leading to internal contradictions. That said, there are ways to combine ideological views in a way that produces internally consistent and political positive results.

Conclusion

Radical environmental theory and practice have helped shape modern environmentalism, and have acted as critiques and checks on the ideological assumptions bound up in mainstream environmental writing and practice. All three theoretical perspectives discussed in this chapter call into question the value of non-human life, and have encouraged looking toward a dramatically different relationship between humans and the environment; one mediated by economic, social, and political relations that emerge from a sense of responsibility, respect, and care. However, these various approaches to radical environmentalism present different philosophic traditions that, when applied as political strategy, produce different visions of the human–nature relationship of the future.

While all three of the forms of radical environmental thought discussed here challenge late modern capitalism and the imposition of extrinsic value on the more-than-human, each of these fall into tension with one another, particularly over who the agent(s) of change should be, and how change should be manifested. Because these different traditions generate so many different approaches to radical politics, activists who seek to draw on these systems of radical thought tend to pick the most desirable perspectives of each, and recombine them to create a new basis for political engagement. However, because these ideologies are not always in line with one another, radical environmentalism tends to have ideologically inconsistent theoretical frameworks, which leads to internal dissent within organizations, and lends itself to disjointed and short-term political action that does not always create successful and sustained change in the relations between humans and non-humans. If the radical environmental movement wishes to take seriously the opportunity to create significant change, then it needs also to take seriously the charge to wisely choose from among the radical environmental philosophic tradition. In doing so, activists and theorists can build an ideologically consistent movement, which has a better chance at producing meaningful change and offering a robust and intelligent counter-balance to industry and mainstream environmentalism alike.

References

Abbey, E. (2006). *The Monkeywrench Gang* (New York: Harper Perennial).

Abrams, D. (1996). *Spell of the Sensuous: Perceptions and Language in a More-Than-Human World* (New York City: Vintage Press).

Bookchin, M. (1990). *Remaking Societies: Pathways to a Green Future* (Boston, MA: South End Press).

Bookchin, M. (1995). *Re-enchanting Humanity: A Defense of the Human Spirit Against Antihumanism, Misanthropy, Mysticism, and Primitivism* (London; New York: Cassell).

Bookchin, M. (2005). *Ecology of Freedom: The Emergence and Dissolution of Hierarchy* (Oakland, CA: AK Press).

Bookchin, M. (2007). "Society and Ecology," retrieved July 2014 from http://theanarchistlibrary.org/library/murray-bookchin-society-and-ecology

Cascadia Forest Defenders. (n.d.). "Who Are We?" Retrieved from http://www.forestdefensenow.com/p/what-is-cfd.html

Cullman, S. and Curry, M. (Producers), and Cullman, S. and Curry, M. (Directors). (2011). *If a Tree Falls* [Motion picture]. USA: Marshall Curry Productions, LLC.

Dean, J. (2012). *The Communist Horizon* (New York: Verso Books).

Devall, B. (2008). "Deep Ecology and Radical Environmentalism." *Society and Natural Resources* 4: 247–58.

Diamond, S. (1981). *In Search of the Primitive* (New Brunswick, NJ: Transaction Publishers.) Earth First! http://www.earthfirst.org/about.htm/

Earth First! Journal Collective. (2013, May 15). "Deep Green Transphobia: A statement from the *Earth First! Journal* Collective." *Earth First! Newswire*. Retrieved February 26, 2014 from http://earthfirstjournal.org/newswire/2013/05/15/deep-green-transphobia/

Foster, J. B., Clark, B., and York, R. (2010). *The Ecological Rift* (New York: Monthly Review Press).

Foundation for Deep Ecology. (2014). "Our Mission." Retrieved from: http://www.deepecology.org/mission.htm

Fox, W. (1995). "The Deep Ecology—Ecofeminism Debate and its Parallels." In *Deep Ecology for the Twenty-first Century*, edited by G. Sessions (Boston and London: Shambala).

Goodwin, J. (1996). "Fur Wars Heat Up: ALF is on the Warpath!" from *No Compromise* issue 4 retrieved September 4, 2014 from http://www.nocompromise.org/issues/04furwar.html

Greed, K. and Hughes, J. (2003). "Damage in University City Blaze May Top $20 Million." *San Diego Union Tribune*, August 2, 2003. Retrieved September 6, 2014 at http://legacy.utsandiego.com/news/metro/20030802-9999_1n2condos.html

Hajer, M. and Wagaaner, H. (2003). *Deliberative Policy Analysis* (Cambridge: Cambridge University Press).

Jensen, D. (2000). *A Language Older Than Words* (New York City: Chelsea Green Publishing).

Lavin, C. (2008). *The Politics of Responsibility* (Champaign: University of Illinois Press).

Leopold, A. (1986). *A Sand County Almanac* (New York: Ballantine Books).

McBay, A., Keith, L., and Jensen, D. (2011). *Deep Green Resistance* (New York: Seven Stories Press).

Naess, A. (1993). *Ecology, Community, and Lifestyle* (Cambridge, UK: Cambridge University Press).
O'Connor, J. (1998). *Natural Causes: Essays in Ecological Marxism* (New York: The Guilford Press).
Parson, S. (2008). "Understanding the Ideology of the ELF." *Green Theory and Praxis* 4(2): 50–66.
Shantz, J. (2001). "Syndicalism, Ecology, and Feminism: Judi Bari's Vision" found on September 4, 2014 at http://theanarchistlibrary.org/library/jeff-shantz-syndicalism-ecology-and-feminism-judi-bari-s-vision
Shantz, J. (2012). *Green Syndicalism: An Alternative Red/Green Vision* (Syracuse, NY: Syracuse University Press).
Potok, M. (2010). "Greenwash: Nativists, Environmentalism, and the Hypocrisy of Hate." *SouthernPoverty Law Center*. Retrieved from: http://www.splcenter.org/getinformed/publications/greenwash-nativists-environmentalism-and-the-hypocrisy-of-hate
Smith, N. (2008). *Uneven Development* (Athens: University of Georgia Press).
Szasz, A. (2009). *Shopping Our Way to Safety: How We Changed from Protecting Our Environment to Protecting Ourselves* (Minnesota: University of Minnesota Press).
The Nature Conservancy. (n.d.) "What's My Carbon Footprint?" Retrieved from http://www.nature.org/greenliving/carboncalculator/index.htm
The Sierra Club. (n.d.). "Stand with the Planet: Take Action!" Retrieved from http://www.standwiththeplanet.com/#news
Taylor, B. (2008). "The Tributaries of Radical Environmentalism." *Journal for the Study of Radicalism* 2(1): 27–61.
The Sierra Club. (n.d.). "Weclome to the Sierra Club." Retrieved from: http://action.sierraclub.org/site/MessageViewer?em_id=275045.0&dlv_id=231579
Watson, D. (1998). *Against the Megamachine: Essays on Empire & Its Enemies* (New York: Autonomedia).

CHAPTER 39

FRAMING AND NUDGING FOR A GREENER FUTURE

CHERYL HALL

INTRODUCTION

IN light of various environmental threats—especially long-term, wide-scale threats such as those posed by climate change and biodiversity loss—the first key question to ask is: what is the source of the problem? Fundamentally, what human institutions, systems, practices, and values are degrading earth's ecosystems? Closely linked to this investigation, the second question to ask is: what is to be done? What changes in these human institutions, systems, practices, and values are necessary to minimize the threats? The third question to ask is: how can we bring about these necessary changes? In this chapter I largely set aside the first two questions in order to focus on the third. Answers to the question of how to bring about change may include, among other things, governmental regulations requiring or prohibiting certain actions, market mechanisms that use economic incentives to motivate certain behaviors, and individual choices to engage in or refrain from certain practices. But each of these particular methods has its limitations, from popular resistance to restrictive government actions to difficulties in modifying the driving logic of capitalist economies to the insufficiencies of individual changes unless they are widespread and help to modify larger structures. In response to these limitations, a number of environmentalists have turned to framing and nudging as tools to facilitate change. These strategies are neither governmental regulations, nor market mechanisms, nor personal choices in themselves; rather they exist in the interstices of some or all of these sources of change. Framing and nudging both entail investigating how various symbolic and material contexts interact with human perceptions, thought-patterns, feelings, habits, and practices to shape the way that we live, individually and collectively, and so how we might change the way that we live through changing these contexts. While the literature on these activities as tools for change extends far beyond environmental issues, in recent years a broad range of scholars, advocates, and policy makers have begun to investigate how framing shapes (or could shape) people's relationship to environmental issues and how nudging shapes (or could shape) choices that have environmental significance.

The chapter begins with a discussion of the activities of framing and nudging, particularly as applied to environmental cases. I argue that they are profoundly similar in that both involve context design. Next I discuss a number of concerns about these practices of context design: in particular, worries that they are manipulative, paternalistic, privatizing, individualizing, and superficial. Finally, I suggest that the best response to these worries is not to attempt to reject framing and nudging, since this is effectively not possible, but rather to frame and nudge in democratic and environmentally transformative ways.

Framing

George Lakoff describes frames as "mental structures that shape the way we see the world" (Lakoff 2004: xv).[1] According to Lakoff, these structures occur in the "cognitive unconscious," so we cannot access them directly. We can, however, access them indirectly through noticing the language we use, the way we reason, and what we consider to be common sense. In turn, by changing the language we use, we can eventually change our mental structures. The reason frames are so crucial is because they act as filters through which information is evaluated and processed; information that does not fit our frames is simply ignored or otherwise disregarded. Frames thus "shape the goals we seek, the plans we make, the way we act, and what counts as a good or bad outcome of actions" (2004: xv). Not everyone accepts Lakoff's argument about the cognitive unconscious, but many echo his ultimate conception of frames. As one summary of the literature puts it, "frames are generally conceived as organizing principles that enable a particular interpretation of a phenomenon" (de Boer, Wardekker, and van der Sluijs 2010: 502). Emphasizing the shared nature of these organizing principles, Clark Miller describes frames as "the perceptual lenses, worldviews or underlying assumptions that guide *communal* interpretation and definition of particular issues" (Miller 2000: 211, emphasis added). The key to organizing the interpretation of information, as many point out, is selectivity: "A frame allows complex issues to be pared down and for some aspects of that issue to be given greater emphasis than others in order that particular audiences can rapidly identify why an issue may be relevant to them" (Spence and Pidgeon 2010: 657, citing Nisbet and Mooney 2007). Finally, some authors link frames to narratives: "Frames are interpretive storylines that set a specific train of thought in motion, communicating why an issue might be a problem, who or what might be responsible for it, and what should be done about it" (Nisbet 2009: 4). In other words, by highlighting certain aspects of a situation and leaving other elements out of the storyline, frames convey an analysis of a problem and its solution in a condensed format.

Several points about frames are important to stress. First, they are necessarily partial. If one could include everything within a frame, it would no longer be a "frame." Second, although they are necessarily partial, they are not thereby necessarily untrue, or at least not any more so than language in general, which also inevitably condenses, interprets, organizes, and otherwise shapes reality. To be sure, it is possible to frame an issue in a way that violates essential realities of the situation—but this does not mean that all frames of an issue violate essential realities. Finally, frames are unavoidable, particularly in communication. As Nisbet puts it, "there is no such thing as unframed information" (2009: 4). The question, then, is not whether to frame, but how.

To see how frames play a role in the interpretation and valuation of environmental problems, consider the case of "climate change." Clark Miller provides an historical perspective on the issue by analyzing how "the CO_2 problem" was viewed within the United States' scientific policy community in the 1970s. He identifies several different frames of the problem that emerged during this time, each of which corresponded to a different societal narrative and invoked a different response strategy. For example, the "global warming" frame saw carbon emissions in terms of "pollution" and led to calls for "end-of-pipe" technology to curb that pollution. In contrast, the "weather extremes" frame focused on the narrative of natural disasters and led to calls to reduce vulnerability to such disasters, while the "energy planning" frame saw carbon emissions in terms of the debates over limits to growth, and led to arguments for de-carbonization and the transition to a low energy economy (Miller 2000: 216). Looking ahead instead of behind and broadening the scope to the general public, Nisbet provides a typology of possible ways to frame climate change in media coverage. He considers three of these frames to be particularly promising for encouraging broad-based support for mitigation: the "economic development" frame, the "morality and ethics" frame (especially as linked to a faith-based notion of responsible stewardship), and the "public health" frame (Nisbet 2009; Maibach et al. 2010). Of course climate change may also be framed, as is evident in US Pentagon reports among others, as a "national security" issue, particularly given potential conflicts over resources and the possibility of mass migrations (Davenport 2014).[2] Each of these perspectives on climate change emphasizes a different facet of how to understand the problem and, accordingly, different conceptions of what can or should be done about it, and by whom. Each frame also potentially fuels or dampens different sources of motivation for addressing the problem among different people.[3]

Nudging

In their influential book, *Nudge: Improving Decisions About Health, Wealth, and Happiness*, Richard Thaler and Cass Sunstein define a nudge as "any aspect of choice architecture that alters people's behavior in a predictable way without forbidding any options or significantly changing their economic incentives" (Thaler and Sunstein 2009: 6). A nudge, then, is a kind of "choice architecture." Like building architecture, choice architecture is the design of contexts in which people live—in this case, the design of the various informational, symbolic, and material contexts in which people make choices. It is the structure of the "background against which choices are made" (Sunstein 2014: 14). Thaler and Sunstein use the example of a school cafeteria to explain. The food in the cafeteria is necessarily presented to the children in a particular order and fashion. Significantly, the way in which the food is presented will likely influence how much of each kind of food the children will "choose" to put on their trays, even if—perhaps especially if—the children are unaware of this influence. Furthermore, since there is no way to avoid arranging the presentation of food in some manner or another, there is no way to avoid influencing the children's choices in some manner or another. (Notice, though, that this influence need not be intentional. To avoid glossing over this difference, I follow Hansen and Jespersen in using the term nudging to refer only to *deliberate* acts of choice architecture (Hansen and Jespersen 2013).) Not surprisingly, Thaler and Sunstein argue that, in these circumstances, the food should be arranged in whatever way will encourage the children to eat as nutritiously as possible. To *not* do so would be perverse. That is to say, it would be perverse to abdicate the potential of choice architecture to increase the welfare of the people whose choices it will influence. Or to characterize their argument more precisely: because choice architecture in general is unavoidable, choice architects can and should intentionally design that architecture to nudge people for their own and society's good.

As the example of the school cafeteria immediately makes clear, nudging is paternalistic. The reason it seems so obvious (to adults) that the food should be arranged to serve the children's nutritional needs is because we (adults) believe that children are not yet consistently able to choose food that will be good for their health. So it seems indisputable that we should guide their choices. The difficulty comes in making an argument that "we" (we who?) should guide the choices of adults who are in full possession of their faculties. One of Thaler and Sunstein's responses to this issue is to limit their argument to "soft" paternalism (or, in their words, "libertarian paternalism") as opposed to "hard" paternalism. The characteristic feature of soft/libertarian paternalism is that it preserves "liberty of choice." Recall that Thaler and Sunstein defined a nudge as "any aspect of choice architecture that alters people's behavior in a predictable way *without forbidding any options or significantly changing their economic incentives*" (emphasis added). They immediately add: "To count as a mere nudge, the intervention must be easy and cheap to avoid. Putting the fruit at eye level counts as a nudge. Banning junk food does not" (Thaler and Sunstein 2009: 6).[4]

But why any kind of paternalism at all? Although choice architecture in general is unavoidable, nudging, as I have characterized it, is not. When the design of a particular choice context is inadvertent (for example, when cafeteria designers pay no attention to how their design will influence the food that people put on their trays), then the context's choice architects are not intentionally trying to nudge people in any particular way. So the deliberate paternalism entailed in nudging still requires a defense. The key argument for nudging adults as well as children is that adults are not as different from children as is often assumed. Like children, adults frequently make decisions and act in ways that are not in our own interests. This is because in a sense we're actually *not* in full possession of our faculties, or at least not all of the time in the way that is usually meant by that term. This claim depends on research in the field of behavioral economics, which in turn builds upon work in the fields of neuroscience and psychology. As Thaler and Sunstein report, many people in those fields have come to see the brain as operating with two different kinds of systems (Thaler and Sunstein 2009: 19). What Thaler and Sunstein call the "Automatic System" refers to the largely subconscious, fast, automatic, and habitual neurological processes that function to enable us to do many of the things we do and make many of the decisions we make. For example, after some practice, most of us are able to ride a bicycle, drive a car, or type on a keyboard without much conscious effort or even attention, in spite of the complex coordination and constant decisions such activities require. On the other hand, the "Reflective System" refers to the relatively conscious, slow, rational, and deliberative processes that enable others of our actions and choices, such as writing a letter or deciding between job offers.[5]

It might seem that the Automatic System is the source of all our problems and the Reflective System the solution, but this is not the case. If we had to consciously deliberate about everything we do, we would get very little done—and would have never survived as a species. Still, behavioral economics emphasizes that we are all "running on automatic" much more than we realize, and prone to certain kinds of errors as a result. We use heuristics or "rules of thumb" to quickly assess situations in the absence of full knowledge, often leading to misjudgments and biases. For example, we often automatically estimate how likely it is that an event such as an accident or natural disaster will occur in the future based on whether it has happened in the recent past, rather than on a complete historical survey (Thaler and Sunstein 2009: 24–6). We then make decisions about what is safe and how much we need to prepare for threats using these incomplete estimates. In addition, many of us have an "optimism bias" that leads us to overestimate how quickly, easily, or well something will go. And we often tend to prefer short-term over long-term goals, the status quo over change, and avoiding loss over obtaining gain (Thaler and Sunstein 2009: 31–5). Such unexamined preferences can lead to any number of decisions that are not in our own interest, such as waiting to save for retirement when it is far more cost effective to start saving sooner. The purpose of, and justification for, nudging is thus to counteract the kind of errors we're prone to as human beings.

Needless to say, many of these errors play a role in environmental degradation; consequently, there are many types of nudges that may potentially help to foster greener practices. Some kinds of nudges rely on the design of physical space, the use of material objects, or the ordering of choices in time (Jones, Pykett, and Whitehead 2011; Yeung 2012). Environmental examples of these kinds of nudges include the relative placement, sizing, and labeling of bins for recyclables and garbage (including labeling the latter bins "landfill" instead of "garbage"), as well as technologies specifically developed to encourage energy efficiency by providing immediate feedback on energy use (including smart energy meters in homes and fuel consumption gauges in hybrid cars). A second way to nudge relies on establishing defaults that can be changed but often aren't—such as printers set up to print double-sided—or providing "anchors" or focal points that encourage people to make particular kinds of comparisons—such as ecolabels on products for sale that clearly rank the carbon emissions involved in their production or the fuel economy involved in their use. Whereas the primary mechanism of the nudges mentioned so far is to shape people's cognitive processing, the mechanism of other kinds of nudges is to influence the social meaning (Jones, Pykett, and Whitehead 2011: 487–8; John et al. 2013: 14–17; Moseley and Stoker 2013: 8; Sunstein 2014: 60).[6] Nudges of this sort attempt to elicit and/or encourage specific norms or values in their intended audience. One environmental example of this kind of nudging is adding smiling or frowning faces to household utility bills, depending on whether the residents' energy use is greater or lesser than that of their neighbors (Thaler and Sunstein 2009: 69–70). Another example is "social marketing," which uses marketing tools (such as understanding "the customer" and analyzing "the competition") in order to promote "pro-social behavior change" (Corner and Randall 2011: 1006–7). Finally, some forms of nudging can be characterized as "deliberation tools" because they "facilitate more informed, thoughtful decision-making" by helping people to understand the options better and, in some cases, to discuss them with others (Yeung 2012: 132–3). Environmental examples here would again include ecolabels, as well as environmental information campaigns and mandatory disclosures of environmental risks.

As should be clear by now, framing and nudging overlap significantly. Peter John and his co-authors explain that nudging is effectively a matter of "framing choices" (John et al. 2013: 2). By the same token, framing is effectively a matter of nudging interpretations. Both are ways to design contexts, whether for understanding an issue or acting on it. To highlight the commonality, in what follows I will sometimes speak of framing and nudging together as context design.

Context Design as Anti-democratic and Anti-political

It is not hard to raise concerns about framing and nudging as methods for effecting change. While there have been any number of criticisms, though, most can be grouped into two general categories: first, worries that these activities are manipulative and paternalistic, and second, worries that they are privatizing, individualizing, and superficial—that is, limited to trying to change the attention and "behavior" of people as private individuals or consumers within the neo-liberal capitalist state. Clearly these two concerns overlap, but the first emphasizes the charge that context design is anti-democratic while the second emphasizes the charge that it is anti-political. In either case, however, the worry is that context design positions people as passive objects rather than active political subjects.

Let me address the concern that context design is anti-democratic first. Although both framing and nudging have been accused of being manipulative and paternalistic,

I limit my discussion here to the charges that framing is manipulative and nudging is paternalistic. Interestingly, the specter of manipulation is raised by advocates of framing as much as by critics, as evidenced by the pains advocates take to distinguish framing from "spin" and "propaganda." Lakoff, for example, specifically defines spin as "the manipulative use of a frame... an attempt to put an innocent frame on [an embarrassing occurrence]," and "propaganda" as "an attempt to get the public to adopt a frame that is not true and is known not to be true, for the purpose of gaining or maintaining political control" (Lakoff 2004: 100). Similarly, Nisbet differentiates framing from "placing a false spin on an issue" (Nisbet 2009: 4). Finally, Miller identifies a common model of framing as "a tactical choice in communication. Spinning information to comport with culturally embedded narratives purportedly raises its credibility with target audiences. This model presumes an ignorant and uninformed public with all the dangers that implies for democracy" (Miller 2009). Along with Lakoff and Nisbet, Miller rejects this model, preferring a second model of framing as "an ineradicable element of reasoning" that does not "exploit" this element "for political gain." Such rejections notwithstanding, the conceptual distinctions these advocates draw between framing, spin, and propaganda serve to highlight the point that spin and propaganda are still forms of framing—and, moreover, forms that in practice may prove hard to differentiate from those that are not manipulative. These distinctions turn on whether or not a given frame goes beyond selectively presenting reality to truly misrepresenting it, as well as whether or not its purpose is to promote interests that are selfish or partisan. Needless to say, the answers to these questions are matters of judgment about which people will likely disagree. Robert Brulle would add that it is characteristic of spin to define the "public interest" *for* people, rather than encouraging them to discuss it themselves (Brulle 2010: 89). Insofar as framing is used for "one-way communication," then, he argues that it is indistinguishable from spin and inherently functions to treat citizens "as objects of manipulation and control" (2010: 89).

The concern that nudging is paternalistic is also directly addressed by its advocates. As already indicated, Thaler and Sunstein claim "libertarian paternalism" as another term for "soft" nudging. According to Sunstein, governments or other actors are paternalistic when they "[do] not believe that people's choices will promote their welfare, and... [take] steps to influence or alter people's choices for their own good" (Sunstein 2014: 54). Given this definition, he argues that some nudges are unquestionably paternalistic; others, however, are not. In his words, "paternalism does not include government efforts to prevent people from harming others—as, for example, in the case of assault, or theft, or air pollution. There is nothing paternalistic about preventing people from beating you up, stealing your car, or making the air hazardous for you to breathe" (2014: 80). Now, following this view, it might seem that nudging for environmental purposes is rarely paternalistic, since in these cases people's choices usually harm the welfare of other people, beings, and ecosystems as much as (if not more so than) their own welfare. Yet paternalism need not be limited to individuals.[7] If the collected choices of a community are not promoting the welfare of that community (for example, if they are not supporting the ecological systems upon which that community depends), then nudges that attempt to influence the community as a whole to act for the benefit of the community as a whole are arguably still paternalistic. They are still interventions intended to help people not engage in "self-harm," even if the "self" in this case is larger than a single human being.

Of course, many questions can be raised about the legitimacy and effectiveness of paternalism, particularly when directed at adults. The most obvious question is whether choice architects have the necessary *knowledge* to nudge other adults well. Even in the case of experts, can they possibly know more than people do themselves about how to promote their own welfare? Especially when a problem is as complex and multi-layered as some of the biggest environmental problems are? Another question is whether choice architects have the *integrity* to nudge well. How can we be sure they won't be biased or corrupt? A third question is whether paternalism is *effective* over the long term. By preventing people from making mistakes, doesn't it prevent people from learning to make good choices on their own? Critics of nudging—and some of its advocates, too—express these concerns and more about the paternalism entailed in this form of context design (Selinger and Whyte 2011; Gill and Gill 2012; Goodwin 2012; Moseley and Stoker 2013; Sunstein 2014).

I turn now to the concern that context design is an anti-political response to environmental problems: privatizing, individualizing, and superficial. Again, there are two main aspects to this concern. The first is that, when used as methods to effect change, framing and nudging situate people as individuals and consumers rather than citizens. From a green perspective, insofar as these strategies focus on encouraging what is often called "pro-environmental behavior," they hold people responsible for their personal energy use or carbon emissions or consumption of resources with little attention to the larger structures (energy grids, transportation systems, capitalist economies) within which these "individual choices" are made. This criticism is quite similar to that levied against some models of green citizenship: that these approaches function to "[promote] sustainability through changing individuals *rather than* structures" (MacGregor, this volume, p. 613, emphasis added, citing Gabrielson 2008: 430). As Sherilyn MacGregor argues, "buying, washing, collecting, and transporting one's plastic bottles to a privately-contracted recycling bank are not citizenly acts. Instead, a citizenly act is demanding free, curbside recyclable waste collection for all, or pressing governments to pass laws against unnecessary and wasteful packaging thus reducing the need to recycle in the first place" (MacGregor, this volume, p. 618). Building on this example, to the extent that recycling is framed solely in terms of individual responsibility and people are nudged only to recycle on their own, the context that necessitates so much personal recycling is left unexamined and unchanged. At its worst, then, an approach that merely encourages individuals to behave differently is not only insufficient to solve the problem, it actually prevents a full solution by drawing attention away from the fundamental structures causing the problem and the political engagement necessary to address them.

The second aspect to the concern that context design is superficial and privatizing stems from the prospect that it takes people's values as fixed individual preferences, seeking only to frame information or nudge behavior in ways that better "fit" what people already believe and care about. In this case, individuals as well as structures remain essentially unchanged. Consider Lakoff's explanation of how reframing an issue works. Lakoff distinguishes between "deep" frames and "surface" frames—a distinction that parallels the one he draws between unconscious mental structures that cannot be accessed directly and language that can be. Deep frames are fundamental but unconscious worldviews about what is good, right, and true, while surface frames are words or phrases (what might be considered slogans). Again, only surface frames can be explicitly changed. But for a new surface frame to change a person's conscious orientation toward an issue, it must resonate with an existing deep frame: otherwise there is nothing for it to hook onto (Lakoff 2006: 29). "Reframing is not just about words and language. Reframing is about ideas. The ideas have to be in place in people's brains before the sound bite can make any sense" (Lakoff 2004: 105). The goal, then, is to "activate" the right [deep] frame. "Framing is about getting language that fits [a person's] worldview" (2004: 4). The key point here is that the deep frame, the worldview, is already present in that person's mind. It is not introduced, produced, investigated, or changed in this process; it is merely "activated."

Again, some framing advocates specifically endorse Lakoff's deep vs. surface model and some do not, but either way, most operate with the same aim of finding "language that fits [a person's] worldview." In discussions about ways to encourage support for climate change action, for example, it is common to note that people generally support addressing the problem, but not at the expense of addressing other problems that hit closer to home (usually everyday economic and security concerns). This means that the values for taking action on climate change exist; they just get "crowded out" or "shouted down," so to speak, within people's interior dialogues, and correspondingly in their political dialogues with other people. So the task becomes figuring out how to help people make the connections between climate change and these other daily concerns—or, we might say, figuring out how to see that the values (or voices) are really harmonious rather than conflicting. Although not specifically discussing framing, John Meyer provides an example of this when he references work by Michael Shellenberger and Ted Nordhaus showing that "popular support can deepen if the concerns for global warming are persuasively tied to the everyday concerns of citizens and to their hopes for a better future" (Meyer 2005: A7). Meyer is clear that "this is not an effort to change public attitudes. Instead, it is a change intended to bring the progressive agenda into closer contact with public attitudes that are already sympathetic, yet tepid" (2005: A6).

Tying climate change to people's everyday concerns is crucial work. At the same time, it may not be entirely possible. To the extent that this approach assumes that the different things people care about (such as economic security and climate change mitigation) only appear to be in conflict, it fails to account for cases where the tension between values is real.[8] But this is common in life. Even people who are committed to a comprehensive progressive agenda value incompatible things, both within and between themselves. For instance, they may well value many things that a low-carbon lifestyle can offer, from the ethical satisfaction of preserving the planet's ecosystems to the more bodily rewards of, say, getting more exercise and sunshine while biking to work. At the same time, they also likely value the ability to easily travel long distances by plane, and for good reason, since it can enable them to maintain ties with far-flung family and friends and experience different landscapes and cultures first-hand. Unfortunately this ability to travel easily comes at the cost of significant greenhouse gas emissions.[9] Barring some massive technological advance, the value of plane travel and the value of mitigating climate change truly do conflict. If this is the case—if living more sustainably really does jeopardize some of the things many people currently value—then the task at hand requires something more than just connecting to people's existing values. It requires changing some of their existing values.

Notice, though, that the structure of the last sentence still situates people as objects of transformation, not subjects. "People's values must be changed," not "people must change their values." This point returns us to the fundamental concern about context design: that it positions people as passive private individuals rather than active political subjects. Manipulation, paternalism, privatization, and individualization: where is democratic politics here? Where is collective action? Where is deliberation? Where is change substantial enough to meet our substantial environmental threats?

Designing Contexts Democratically

These questions have important democratic and environmental implications. The concerns that critics raise about framing and nudging are real possibilities. At the same time, completely rejecting these activities is not an option. Communities and their members may refuse to purposely frame or nudge, but they cannot escape structuring and reinforcing—however inadvertently—the ways that information and choices are presented within their community, and thus establishing and maintaining contexts that shape the community's thinking and behavior. Anyone in a position to communicate and/or make background decisions that affect other people (in government, industry, and elsewhere) will inevitably be influencing people's interpretations and choices, one way or another, deliberately or not, toward one kind of end or another. Recall Nisbet's point that "there is no such thing as unframed information" (2009: 4). The same point applies to choices: there is no such thing as unframed choices. In other words, there is no choice that exists outside of some kind of choice architecture. As Sunstein notes, "People make only a very small fraction of the decisions that actually affect them" (2014: 105). The rest of the decisions are made by multitudes of other people, past and present, who have thereby created the contexts that circumscribe the small fraction of decisions people do make. This holds true not just for individuals but for entire communities. For example, most people in the United States did not decide (or, at least, certainly not on their own) to build communities that lack the transportation infrastructure, geographical layout, and culture that would foster other forms of transportation besides automobiles. Background decisions about infrastructure, space, and values all set the context for the "choice" people make to use cars to get around. Moreover, as this example illustrates, the design of contexts is not only unavoidable but powerful. When it comes to encouraging more environmentally sustainable modes of life (as with many other possible goals), context design has the potential to be very helpful—or not. Consequently, I think Thaler and Sunstein are right that we should not abdicate the potential of context design to increase the welfare of those whom that design will influence.

How, then, to respond to the concerns raised above? From a green perspective, the best option is to frame and nudge in ways that are as deliberative, democratic, transparent, and environmentally transformative as possible—in other words, for people (and the "voices" of other beings) to be as involved in the process as possible, and for the process to include as much questioning of ends and means as possible. Context design should be something that people pay attention to and engage in themselves, as political subjects capable of collective action to shape their future. It should not be something that is done to them as objects of manipulation by experts.

Surely this is a challenging goal, but communities can at least move in this direction. Let me briefly sketch some possibilities for more democratic, political, environmentalist forms of both framing and nudging. In the case of framing, it is important to note that there is no *necessary* self-interest, partisanship, whitewashing, or misrepresentation—no *necessary* spin or propaganda—built into the concept. Frames may well provide candid, broad-based perspectives that advocate for inclusive and just aims. Furthermore, frames may be used to foster exploration and discussion. Will Friedman offers a helpful distinction between framing-to-persuade ("defining an issue to one's advantage in the hopes of getting an audience to do what you want it to do") and framing-for-deliberation ("clarifying the range of positions surrounding an issue so that citizens can better decide what they want to do") (Friedman 2007: 2). Friedman does not imagine that framing-to-persuade will or should disappear, but he argues that framing-for-deliberation can provide a way to help citizens assess and respond to persuasive frames more productively (2007: 5). He notes that some nonpartisan organizations already approximate framing-for-deliberation by providing guides that sort through and compare various approaches to a particular issue of public debate (2007: 2). The key point for my purposes is that framing-for-deliberation does not position us as passive objects to be acted upon by experts. Nor does it take our values as set individual preferences. On the contrary, by fostering deliberation, it encourages us to actively examine our values, identify where they conflict, and consider how and why they might be understood or prioritized differently. Among environmental advocates, much scholarly and political effort has been put into finding ways to frame climate change so that people will be persuaded to believe it is a serious problem worthy of attention and action. I argue that advocates should put more effort into finding ways to frame it as a situation worthy of serious and sustained public investigation and debate—including investigation and debate about what contributes to the situation and what is to be done about it. More broadly, I argue that we should all put more effort into finding ways to frame our lives as situated within, and in relationship to, the ecosystems of this planet.

In the case of nudging, the more that citizens and not just "experts" or leaders are involved in the process, the less paternalistic the activity is. To the extent that a broad range of people are involved in determining the structure of the choice architecture in their lives, concerns about whether choice architects have the knowledge or integrity to nudge other adults well or whether nudging prevents people from learning from their mistakes diminish. In effect, choice architecture becomes a practice of people nudging themselves. This is actually not unusual at the individual level: many of us nudge ourselves by (literally or metaphorically) "putting the fruit at eye level" in our own homes. It is less common on a political level, but not entirely absent, and not implausible to pursue as a goal. More democratic forms of nudging could begin with citizens being nudged to participate in political processes, processes through which they would then decide how to nudge themselves as a community.[10] As Jones, Pykett, and Whitehead put it, we need "*deliberative* choice architecture" (2011: 494, emphasis added). It could also involve citizens nudging leaders, for example by using social marketing techniques (John et al. 2013: 139).[11] Beyond this, more environmentally transformative forms of nudging could begin with citizens being nudged to expand their awareness, experience, and knowledge of the environment in which they live, including their impact on it and its impact on them. Such expansion could in turn enable them to contribute to designing more environmentally conscious nudges for their communities.[12] Together, these suggestions sketch nudging as an activity that could incorporate multiple human and non-human voices in designing frameworks for human choices.

Taken seriously, attention to context design points to a deeper examination of values, practices, structures, and systems than critics fear. While framing and nudging may be used to influence superficial beliefs and behaviors within existing value systems and institutions, they are not inherently limited to operating at superficial levels. On the contrary, these activities have the potential to draw our attention to the foundational contexts that shape our views, actions, and ways of life—and thereby to enable us to begin to change them. Unless and until we come to recognize how much is "built in" to the conceptual and material contexts surrounding us, we will not be able to make fundamental changes. For this reason, environmentalists who believe that fundamental changes are necessary in order to address substantial environmental problems such as climate change and biodiversity loss should not reject framing and nudging as methods for effecting change; rather, they should use them in democratic and transformative ways.

Acknowledgments

I am especially grateful to my co-editors, Teena Gabrielson, John M. Meyer, and David Schlosberg, for their contributions to the development of this chapter.

Notes

1. Lakoff is a cognitive scientist and linguist who has been leading the charge that progressives of all stripes need to make better use of framing.

2. This list does not exhaust the different possible ways that climate change can be framed. Other possibilities include framing the issue in terms of what will be gained from mitigation vs. what will be lost without it, or in terms of local impacts vs. distant ones, and so forth (Spence and Pidgeon 2010).
3. For a more in-depth discussion of a central debate over how to frame environmental problems in general, see my article "What Will it Mean to Be Green? Envisioning Positive Possibilities without Dismissing Loss" (Hall 2013).
4. Here is another distinction between choice architecture and nudging: where the latter is limited to soft paternalism, the former is not. Just as a building may be constructed with only one door, choice architecture may be constructed to allow only one real "choice."
5. The two systems are often referred to more generally as System 1 and System 2.
6. Of course, some forms of nudging attempt to do both. See Jones, Pykett, and Whitehead (2011), Yeung (2012), and Mosely and Stoker (2013) for more categorizations of types of nudging.
7. Nudges need not be limited to human beings, either, but I leave that point aside here.
8. To be clear, Meyer does not assume that people's values only appear to conflict. In his book, *Engaging the Everyday: Environmental Social Criticism and the Resonance Dilemma* (2015), he does not contend that tying climate change or other environmental issues to people's everyday concerns will "resolve tensions or result in consistency." Rather, he argues that it will "politicize these aspects of life that often can seem disconnected from concerns like climate change" (personal correspondence). Other authors, however, do appear to assume inherent consistency in values.
9. Of course airplanes are not the only mode of transportation with significant environmental costs. I choose this example because planes are both carbon intensive and, in industrialized countries, often used for leisure travel. As such, the carbon emissions from this kind of travel surely count as luxury emissions, not subsistence emissions (see Henry Shue's distinction in "Subsistence Emissions and Luxury Emissions" (2010)).
10. For further discussion of this reciprocal process, see Peter John et al. *Nudge, Nudge, Think, Think: Experimenting with Ways to Change Civic Behaviour*. While the authors initially distinguish between nudge strategies and "think" strategies (strategies that involve collective deliberation), they ultimately argue for integrating the two by nudging citizens to be involved in deliberation about the design of nudge strategies (2013: 152).
11. John et al. acknowledge that constraints in existing government structures and procedures may limit citizens' effectiveness in nudging representatives (2013: 141–2).
12. I thank David Schlosberg for this suggestion.

References

Brulle, R. J. (2010). "From Environmental Campaigns to Advancing the Public Dialog: Environmental Communication for Civic Engagement." *Environmental Communication: A Journal of Nature and Culture* 4(1): 82–98. doi:10.1080/17524030903522397.

Corner, A. and Randall, A. (2011). "Selling Climate Change? The Limitations of Social Marketing as a Strategy for Climate Change Public Engagement." *Global Environmental Change* 21(3): 1005–14. doi:10.1016/j.gloenvcha.2011.05.002.

Davenport, C. (2014). "Pentagon Signals Security Risks of Climate Change." *The New York Times*, October 13. http://www.nytimes.com/2014/10/14/us/pentagon-says-global-warming-presents-immediate-security-threat.html

De Boer, J., Arjan Wardekker, J., and van der Sluijs, J. (2010). "Frame-Based Guide to Situated Decision-Making on Climate Change." *Global Environmental Change* 20(3): 502–10. doi:10.1016/j.gloenvcha.2010.03.003.

Friedman, W. (2007). *Reframing "Framing."* Occasional Paper 1. Public Agenda Center for Advances in Public Engagement. https://apha.confex.com/recording/apha/138am/pdf/free/4db77adf5df9fff0d3caf5cafe28f496/paper227186_3.pdf

Gabrielson, T. (2008). "Green Citizenship: A Review and Critique." *Citizenship Studies* 12(4): 429–46.

Gill, N. and Gill, M. (2012). "The Limits to Libertarian Paternalism: Two New Critiques and Seven Best-Practice Imperatives." *Environment and Planning C: Government and Policy* 30(5): 924–40. doi:10.1068/c11149r.

Goodwin, T. (2012). "Why We Should Reject 'Nudge.'" *Politics* 32(2): 85–92. doi:10.1111/j.1467-9256.2012.01430.x.

Hansen, P. G. and Jespersen, A. (2013). "Nudge and the Manipulation of Choice. A Framework for the Responsible Use of Nudge Approach to Behaviour Change in Public Policy." SSRN Scholarly Paper ID 2555337. Social Science Research Network. http://papers.ssrn.com/abstract=2555337 (Rochester, New York).

John, P., Cotterill, S., Richardson, L., Moseley, A., Stoker, G., Wales, C., Smith, G., Liu, H., and Nomura, H. (2013). *Nudge, Nudge, Think, Think: Experimenting with Ways to Change Civic Behaviour* (London: Bloomsbury Academic).

Jones, R., Pykett, J., and Whitehead, M. (2011). "Governing Temptation: Changing Behaviour in an Age of Libertarian Paternalism." *Progress in Human Geography* 35(4): 483–501. doi:10.1177/0309132510385741.

Lakoff, G. (2004). *Don't Think of an Elephant! Know Your Values and Frame the Debate*, 1st edn. (White River Junction, Vermont: Chelsea Green).

Lakoff, G. (2006). *Thinking Points: Communicating Our American Values and Vision.* (New York: Farrar, Straus and Giroux).

MacGregor, S. (2015). "Citizenship: Radical, Feminist, and Green." In *The Oxford Handbook of Environmental Political Theory*, edited by T. Gabrielson, C. Hall, J. M. Meyer, and D. Schlosberg (Oxford; New York: Oxford University Press), 608–23.

Maibach, E., Nisbet, M., Baldwin, P., Akerlof, K., and Diao, G. (2010). "Reframing Climate Change as a Public Health Issue: An Exploratory Study of Public Reactions." *BMC Public Health* 10(299): 1–11.

Meyer, J. M. (2005). "The Afterlife of Environmentalism: Can We Tie Big Global Concerns to the Everyday Lives of Americans?" *The American Prospect* 16(10), September. Available at http://www.prospect.org/article/afterlife-environmentalism

Meyer, J. M. (2015). *Engaging the Everyday: Environmental Social Criticism and the Resonance Dilemma* (Cambridge, MA: MIT Press).

Miller, C. (2000). "The Dynamics of Framing Environmental Values and Policy: Four Models of Societal Processes." *Environmental Values* 9(2): 211–34.

Miller, C. (2009). "Why Only One Framing?" In "Is There a Better Word for Doom?" *SeedMagazine.com.* http://seedmagazine.com/content/article/is_there_a_better_word_for_doom/

Moseley, A. and Stoker, G. (2013). "Nudging Citizens? Prospects and Pitfalls Confronting a New Heuristic." *Resources, Conservation and Recycling* 79 (October): 4–10. doi:10.1016/j.resconrec.2013.04.008.

Nisbet, M. and Mooney, C. (2007). "Framing Science." *Science* 316(5821): 56.

Nisbet, M. (2009). "Communicating Climate Change: Why Frames Matter for Public Engagement." *Environment Magazine: Science and Policy for Sustainable Development*, April. http://www.environmentmagazine.org/Archives/Back%20Issues/March-April%202009/Nisbet-full.html

Selinger, E. and Whyte, K. (2011). "Is There a Right Way to Nudge? The Practice and Ethics of Choice Architecture." *Sociology Compass* 5(10): 923.

Shue, H. "Subsistence Emissions and Luxury Emissions." In *Climate Ethics: Essential Readings*, edited by S. M. Gardiner, S. Caney, D. Jamieson, H. Shue, and R. K. Pachauri (Oxford: Oxford University Press): 200–14.

Spence, A. and Pidgeon, N. (2010). "Framing and Communicating Climate Change: The Effects of Distance and Outcome Frame Manipulations." *Global Environmental Change* 20(4): 656–67. doi:10.1016/j.gloenvcha.2010.07.002.

Sunstein, C. R. (2014). *Why Nudge?: The Politics of Libertarian Paternalism*. (New Haven and London: Yale University Press).

Thaler, R. H. and Sunstein, C.R. (2009). *Nudge: Improving Decisions About Health, Wealth, and Happiness*. Updated. (New York: Penguin).

Yeung, K. (2012). "Nudge as Fudge." *The Modern Law Review* 75(1): 122–48. doi:10.1111/j.1468-2230.2012.00893.x.

CHAPTER 40

CITIZENSHIP

Radical, Feminist, and Green

SHERILYN MACGREGOR

INTRODUCTION

ALTHOUGH it is regarded as a promising new development in environmental political theory, ecological, environmental or, what I will call, "green citizenship," is also one of the most enervating. This is because, as a concept that expresses a complicated relationship between the state and the people, citizenship must be approached as a double edged sword: "an institution of domination and empowerment" (Isin 2009: 376). Citizens might be empowered to participate in deliberative forms of governance on one edge of it, while being drawn into a technology of neo-liberal governing on the other. Theoretical analyses should address both the political promise and the political danger that the concept of citizenship entails; one needs to proceed with caution. And yet a review of the environmental political literature over the past two decades suggests that this necessary caution and *ambivalence* have rarely been practiced. Instead, green citizenship has been embraced as a promising means of promoting a more sustainable society without concern for the risks of cooptation into the dominant neo-liberal order. A growing number of critics point to the exclusivity and instrumentalism of green citizenship, but without offering detailed alternatives for how it might be rehabilitated—if it should be rehabilitated at all.

If we view this situation against a backdrop of the vexing debate over the state of democratic eco-politics in the early twenty-first century, then it might be reasonable to conclude that green citizenship theory has run its course. For what place is there for green citizens in a post-political, post-democratic, and *post-ecological* world? Contrary to some declarations, the life of neo-liberalism as a mode of governance has not ended; it has become so deeply embedded in the spheres of politics and everyday life that "its potency can easily be missed" (Thompson 2007). In fact, in the contemporary context of fiscal austerity, climate threats, and the "hegemonic grip that neoliberal ideas have over public affairs" (Catney and Doyle 2010: 178), it is easy to see symptoms of a post-political turn within environmentalism in the global North. The post-political thesis holds that a depoliticization process, driven by the economic reasoning of neo-liberalism, has reduced governance to the promotion of consensus so that policy processes can be left to experts and bureaucrats (Mouffe 2005; Swyngedouw 2010). While citizens may be invited into environmental decision-making processes via participatory mechanisms, these simply manufacture popular consent to decisions which serve the interests of a powerful elite rather than promote democracy. When the aim of management is to avoid making decisions that cause social unrest, compromise and expert administration are central, resulting in "the end of politics" (Rancière 2001).

In a similar vein, Blühdorn's post-democracy and post-ecologist politics thesis contends that environmental movements have failed fundamentally "to alter the developmental trajectory of advanced modern societies" (2013: 17) and that there is nothing citizens can do but engage in a form of politics that simulates democracy. "Simulative democracy," suggests Blühdorn, is about cultivating the (false) impression that governments are responding to the needs and wishes of the masses; it is "about reassuring citizens that despite the overwhelming power of global corporations, credit rating agencies and systemic imperatives, democratically elected governments are still in control of the social order and societal development" (2013: 28). In such a context, citizen efforts to defend the interests of the environment against the interests of the market are delusional. What is more, these actions are self-deceptive in that, according to Blühdorn's claim that we are now in a post-ecologist era, the majority of ordinary people in advanced consumer societies accept *simultaneously* the green cause and the non-negotiable right to over-consume. They may talk the green talk, but fail—en masse—to walk the walk, thereby "sustaining the unsustainable" neo-liberal democratic capitalist order (Blühdorn 2013). In these scenarios, the day of the green citizen ostensibly has passed.

While I share the discomfort that these "post" analyses provoke (see, for example, Smith 2002; Barry 2004), I argue that theorists of green citizenship ought to do a better job of facing the vicissitudes of neo-liberalism head on. Insufficient attention in the literature to the ways that green citizenship dovetails into the dominant neo-liberal agenda is cause for concern. As Gabrielson (2008: 441) observes, mainstream approaches to green citizenship are unfortunately narrow and instrumental such that "its democratic potential" has been "blunted." My aim in this chapter is to consider some possibilities for sharpening the blade. After a brief discussion of the dominant state of affairs in the literature, I discuss three inter-related ideas that might serve as theoretical whetstones. Found at the margins of environmental political theory, or at least from outside the dominant "tent" (Dobson 2006) of green citizenship theory, they are un-ignorable contributions from (eco-)feminist, postcolonial/environmental justice and radical democratic theorists. In my view these are ideas that have inspired some of the most insightful critical commentaries on green citizenship to date. They are similar in offering necessary—but of course not sufficient—correctives/possibilities for transforming green citizenship into a mode of political subjectivity that can re-politicize environmental politics. I bring these ideas together here because, while being suitably cautious and ambivalent, I still want to argue that the citizen *qua* political being is necessary for political action and resistance and is "the basis on which can be built a human community resourceful and thoughtful enough to cope with the present challenges" (Bauman 1994: 45, quoted in Smith 2005: 61).

Citizenship in Environmental Political Theory

The emergence of the concept of green citizenship in the 1990s was part of green political critique and revision of all institutions of liberal democracy. Early contributors argued that the global and transboundary nature of environmental problems make traditional understandings of citizenship insufficient (Steward 1991: van Steenbegen 1994). This analysis led them to rethink the spatial and temporal constructions of citizenship as being confined to people living in the here and now in nation-states. There is now a substantial body of literature on citizenship that transforms the traditional state-based meaning of citizenship to accommodate green concerns. Since the early 2000s, there has been an explosion of publications on ecological and environmental citizenship, mostly notably with the publication of Andrew Dobson's *Citizenship and the Environment* in 2003 and the edited collection *Environmental Citizenship* (Dobson and Bell, eds. 2006), which have become the most widely-cited volumes to date. The *Environmental Politics* journal has been a forum for discussion and development of the concept, with a special issue on the topic in 2005 (edited by Dobson and Valencia Sáiz) and over 30 articles published on the topic since then.

Some theorists have pursued a liberal version of green citizenship, which can be explained as a response to the illiberal eco-authoritarianism of the 1970s and '80s. The main issue that interests liberals is the environmental rights that individuals are owed by virtue of having the status of a citizen, as conferred by the state (Wissenburg 1998; Bell 2005). Few offer much beyond a minimal definition of environmental citizenship that provides maximum scope for individual freedom. The reason for this is that to be loyal to the meaning of political liberalism, it is necessary to maintain state neutrality and to avoid a substantive definition of the environment or the good life. Although Arias-Maldonado (2012) suggests that rights-based liberal environmental citizenship may be the most practical in the face of contemporary socio-political realities, there remains a reluctance to accept this position on the part of many green political theorists.

The majority of green citizenship theorists are not content to reform existing liberal institutions to include environmental concerns. Both a more fundamental reorganization of the state and changes to individual citizens' values and actions are necessary. Mark J. Smith (1998: 281) defines the green citizen as "an individual who recognizes their duties in relation to the environment and takes responsibility to act in line with those duties." Consistent with the civic republican tradition, the emphasis here is on deliberative democracy and the cultivation of individual virtues of responsibility and stewardship among the participants in this system (Barry 1999, 2006). The focus on duties is a response to the dominance of rights in theories of citizenship over the past two centuries. Scholars such as Smith and Pangsapa (2008) have noted that too many rights and entitlements and not enough responsibilities arguably have led to a crisis of social and ecological unsustainability. This is to say that because people in affluent countries have been socialized into prioritizing their material interests and claiming their just deserts from the state, they are less inclined to consider how their actions contribute to, or detract from, the common good. If we are to move toward a more sustainable society, the argument goes, then there needs to be a dramatic change in the way people understand their relationships to the state and to fellow inhabitants of the planet.

Environmental political theorists have turned to citizenship because they are skeptical of the idea that the liberal democratic state will ever lead societies toward sustainability (Eckersley 2004). Although environmental regulation has resulted in important incremental changes, most theorists place greater emphasis on citizens' adoption of more environmentally-friendly lifestyles. For example, Dobson and Bell (2006) suggest that government "carrot and stick" policies (such as subsidies and taxes) will not be as effective at influencing people's behavior as the idea of green citizenship. If people do things because they are compelled by the state, then the prospects for long-term, fundamental social change are minimal. What is needed are voluntary "shifts in attitudes at a deep level" (Dobson and Valencia Sáiz 2005: 157). Proponents share the view that people need to adopt the kinds of "pro-environmental" values and virtues that promote sustainability by making the exploitation of nature unacceptable. Among the key virtues listed are self-reliance and self-restraint (Barry 1999) and justice (Dobson 2003).

For Dobson (2003), who has developed an influential post-cosmopolitan version of (what he calls) ecological citizenship, justice is the primary virtue. When citizens recognize that they have taken more than their fair share of ecological space, justice demands that they reduce and redistribute resources so that others have a chance of a decent quality of life. According to Dobson, the obligations of the citizen are asymmetrical and non-reciprocal: those who occupy more than their fair share of ecological space have a greater duty to care than those whose labor and land have been exploited. In his conception, being a good green citizen entails the responsibility to take responsibility both for one's causal role in environmental injustice and for ensuring a more just distribution of ecological space. And the pursuit of justice can involve actions in both the public and private spheres of life, as long as they are actions that help to define and realize a more sustainable society. In his most recent publication on the topic, Dobson gives the following definition of ecological citizenship: "pro-environmental practice, in public and in private, driven by a belief in fairness of the distribution of environmental goods, in participation, and in the co-creating of sustainability policy" (Dobson 2012: 522).

For the majority of theorists working on this topic, green citizens do not simply hold green values and participate in deliberative processes aimed at policy change, they also "do their bit" for their environment in everyday lives. The kinds of responsibilities that are commonly listed under the banner of ecological citizenship include a range of practices that reduce environmental impact and improve the quality of degraded ecosystems such as reducing energy consumption and growing one's own food. Breaking with the traditional understanding of politics, many green citizenship theorists contend that it is in the private sphere of the household that the most meaningful changes can take place. This move fundamentally changes the notion of citizenship as strictly related to the public sphere. As Dobson and Bell (2006: 7) write:

> [O]ne key environmental point has always been that "private" actions can have important public consequences. Decisions . . . as to how we heat or cool our homes, or how and what we choose to consume in them, are decisions that have public consequences in terms of [their] environmental impact.

In sum, although there are differences and debates among green political theorists of different shades, most agree that the concept of green citizenship is a distinct form of citizenship that challenges traditional citizenships by being non-territorial, non-reciprocal, and not confined to the public–political domain. It is more about individual values and duties than about rights, and it challenges the traditional emphasis on the individual by locating citizens in a larger community that is global, unequal and dependent on the natural world.

What's Wrong With Green Citizenship?

That green citizenship theory has developed in, and in response to, particular historical and cultural contexts is important to note. It is a product of its time (late 1900s/early 2000s) and place (affluent liberal democracies) and of its producers (mostly white, male eco-political theorists). Arguably, these particularities have led to its near-exhaustion as a useful figure in contemporary green thought. As I explain in this section, a growing number of green scholars find the dominant versions of green citizenship problematic for a variety of reasons.

For the sake of brevity, I shall summarize what I think are the two most important criticisms found in the literature. These are long-standing criticisms that appear to take on new contours when considered in light of the post-political challenges noted earlier. The first major criticism is that dominant conceptions of green citizenship are narrow and exclusionary. They suffer from being products of intellectual discussions in the affluent global North, from being produced by people with privileged lives. This exclusivity problem has a number of dimensions that stem from the false universalism that is endemic to all scholarly writing on citizenship. Based as they are on mainstream political theory, both liberal and civic republican versions are problematic because they fail to include "minority subject positions, dissenting visions of nature and divergent understandings of dialogue" (Latta 2007: 383). As in non-green political theory, deliberative democracy is promoted as an ideal without sufficient acknowledgement that not all citizens are able to participate equally due to structural asymmetries and misrecognition. That green citizenship theory has been blind to gender hierarchies and inequalities (MacGregor 2006a, 2006b), as well as those stemming from class, race, sexuality, and geographical location has led critics to dismiss its potential as a means of achieving environmental justice (Agyeman and Evans 2006). It is also largely blind to political struggles and emerging forms of citizenship elsewhere in the world (Latta and Whitman 2012). These blind spots arguably reduce the relevance and resonance of green citizenship to a diverse global population, thereby making it ineffective as a concept that might ignite political resistance to neo-liberal developments and discourses.

A less-developed, but equally persuasive critique points to the narrow and exclusionary way in which the natural environment appears in green citizenship theory. The idealized construction of nature that appears in this work is related to the issue of the false universalism of the citizen as a liberal subject. As Gabrielson and Parady (2010: 378, 383) argue, models of green citizenship that are based on morally-loaded notions of stewardship, or an ecological footprint, tend to privilege a "particularly Western and pristine" conception of the natural world that excludes a range of other types of environment (for example, urban, degraded, domestic/ated). Consequently, the types of human–nature relationships, and related forms of knowledge about nature, that are included in these conceptions are limited to those held by elites—as land owners and (over)consumers of resources. What makes this problem particularly serious is that there is reduced scope for contesting the meaning of "the green" in green citizenship. In light of the post-political consensus on all matters ecological (climate change is the obvious example), it seems more important than ever to engage in discussion about "how nature can be politicized as part of the politics of citizenship and vice versa" (Latta 2007: 382).

The second important criticism of ecological citizenship theory is the emphasis it places on individual responsibility in the private sphere. There have been critics of the individualizing nature of environmentalism stretching at least as far back as Bookchin's 1992 book *Urbanization without Cities: The Rise and Decline of Citizenship*. Individualization has been seen as symptomatic of environmentalism's "flight from politics" (Maniates 2001). The instrumental use of citizenship as a tool for promoting sustainability through changing individuals rather than structures, it has been argued, effectively depoliticizes environmentalism and "dampen[s] citizenship's democratic potential" (Gabrielson 2008: 430). It is instructive to note the extent to which the green citizen has become synonymous with the "sustainable consumer" in the "pro-environmental behaviour change" discourse. As a product of its time/place, green citizenship theory has responded to the common view that consumers have more power to change the system than citizens do. This is a shame, however, because as Meyer (2015: 155) notes:

> [the] incorporation of the home within a conception of citizenship ... appears to have morphed into a presumption that private individualism and green consumerism is a—perhaps the—primary manifestation of citizenship itself. Rather than

publicizing private household practices, this appears as a privatization and individualization of the concept of citizenship.

In an era when many people see their consumption choices as akin to voting, and when collaborative forms of consumption are promoted by governments (for example, collective switching of energy providers), this embrace of the consumer-citizen has diminished the potential for citizenship to be a positive force in counter-hegemonic green politics. Conceiving citizenship as being primarily about personal responsibility can be criticized as part of the "responsibilization" (Rose 1999) that is central to neo-liberal governmentality (Webb 2012; Hobson 2013). This means that it is complicit with—rather than being a challenge to—the dominant socio-economic paradigm. There is very little difference between green citizenship-as behavior-change and neo-liberal social psychological—"nudge"—approaches to government environmental policy that are increasingly being used in affluent countries (Felli and Castree 2012; see also Hall, this volume). Self-reliance and self-governance can be read as similar tools in the neo-liberal project of "governing at a distance." As such, there seems to be a growing number of critics who would agree that green citizenship is now hopelessly apolitical and has little to offer an already floundering movement for socio-ecological transformation.

Re-sharpening Green Citizenship: Insights from Feminist, Postcolonial, and Radical Democratic Theories

These criticisms might well be viewed as nails in the coffin of what started out in the 1990s as a reasonably radical eco-political project. Exclusivity and instrumentalism are commonly noted problems that look even more serious when set against the backdrop of "the posts" I mentioned at the start. Not only have we moved beyond a meaningful search for sustainability, but citizenship itself arguably has been reduced to mere simulation and self-deception (Blühdorn 2013). Green citizenship falls into post-political/post-ecological traps by promoting lifestyle and behavior change, failing to appreciate social and geopolitical differences, and by giving scant attention to the diversity of the other-than-human natural world. Is there a way out of these traps or is it time to call it quits?

Rather than calling it quits, I am drawn to the writings of political theorists such as Hannah Arendt who faced similar crises in even darker times and saw citizenship as a way out rather than a dead end (Smith 2005). For Arendt, and for contemporary radical democrats such as Chantal Mouffe (2005), citizenship is a mode of human political subjectivity that we relinquish at our peril. In this final section, therefore, I consolidate what I think are important insights from outside the mainstream green citizenship tent into a coherent project that is better suited for this post political/post-ecological age. These are insights not only from radical democratic but also from (eco-)feminist and postcolonial theories that thus far have not found their way in to the green political canon. What is promising about them is that they offer possibilities for resistance to the dominant neo-liberal frame as well as challenges to the dismal pictures of the current state of eco-politics that have been painted by Blühdorn and Swyngedouw.

Corporeality: Material Intersections

The dominant figure of the green citizen is exclusionary because it is modeled after the abstract and disembodied individual. If it were modeled after specific bodies, and if it were accepted that all bodies share certain traits, then "the citizen" would look very different indeed. (Eco-)feminist theorists have contributed an approach to environmentalism that is useful here; one that recognizes both the embodied nature of all life and the inter-connections and blurred boundaries between human bodies and the non-human natural-material world. This approach is a product of long-standing eco-feminist work (Plumwood 1993) that more recently has been theorized as *corporeality* (Alaimo 2009; Lykke 2009). It is an approach that calls attention to difference and sameness: starting at the level of bodies reminds us that we are differently-situated while simultaneously demanding we see the similarities between humans, animals, and the rest of the natural-material world. These similarities disturb the tendency to see all living beings as objects for consumption and exploitation. It is an approach that promotes the inestimable value, significance, and force of ecosystems and living beings; not as mere resources for human use, but valuable in and of themselves (Alaimo 2009: 30–1).

These insights are useful to the task of theorizing green citizenship because they provide a needed corrective to the exclusivity that I explained earlier. Gabrielson and Parady (2010) have given this remedy as a reason for their application of the concept of corporeality to green citizenship. They argue that starting with bodies and the material is a way to broaden the scope of who/what counts, as well as what gets labeled "environmental," in environmental political theory. They write that corporeal citizenship enables the advancement of "an understanding of citizenship that is not only embodied and attentive to the particularities of human difference but also one that recognizes humans' *inescapable* embeddedness in differing social and natural contexts that shape subjectivity and condition our collective agency" (Gabrielson and Parady 2010: 76, emphasis in the original). Another important advantage of this approach is that because citizens are always-already embodied and embedded in the natural-material world, the concept of citizenship is "*inherently* rather than *instrumentally* green" (2010: 381, emphasis in the original). To this I would add the point that inserting a sense of corporeality into green citizenship enables it better to become a position from which to resist constructions of the neo-liberal, self-reliant subject. For example, in response to increasingly popular discourse of "resilience"—the idea that humans should be able (read: should be *responsible* enough) to survive and thrive after extreme disruptions of climate change—it makes sense to argue that all embodied life on the planet is dependent and vulnerable: always precarious and exposed to the material world. Here we might consider the merits of Alaimo's concept of "insurgent vulnerability"[1] for inspiring a more humble notion of green citizenship as well as greater solidarity across contexts, peoples and species.

(Eco-)feminist and postcolonial theorists have argued that citizenship should not be seen as an abstract and homogenous concept but rather as an embodied category that includes "concrete people who are differentially situated in terms of gender, class, ethnicity, sexuality, ability, state in the life cycle, etc." (Yuval-Davis 2007: 562). A focus on bodies and the interconnections between/across bodies is inextricably linked to the feminist concept of "*intersectionality*" that is also useful for rethinking the concept of the green citizen. Intersectionality offers a way of theorizing the intersections of power and the social categories that shape identities. It points to the importance of starting from local contexts, or "embedded localization" (Lykke 2009: 38). Seen in this way, intersectionality provides an alternative to the one-size-fits-all approach that has so far dominated the green citizenship literature which rarely includes discussion/theorizing of social difference. Part of what makes a corporeal approach so attractive to Gabrielson and Parady (2010) is that its attendant intersectionality provides a foundation for greater solidarity and collaboration across diverse movements for environmental justice. Rob Nixon (2011: 138–42) demonstrates the role that intersectionality already plays in environmental movements by showing how women activists in the Kenyan Greenbelt Movement use a deliberate strategy of integrating the intersecting issues of soil quality, food security, political violence women's, and human rights (and more) into their internationally recognized struggle for environmental and gender justice. Although he does not mention citizenship specifically, Nixon presents this as a case where "*intersectional environmentalism*" (2011: 138; my emphasis) is possible and simply makes more sense as a way of articulating claims against the state than do single-issue green campaigns. This example (and Nixon's sensitive analysis of it) should serve as a reminder that, although the view from within affluent consumerist societies is important, it is also partial: all environmental political theorists ought to consider how citizens make their claims and enact their political identities, including citizens in "other" parts of the world.

Social Reproduction: Politicizing Private Practices

The second insight that is useful to my re-sharpening efforts also comes from (eco-) feminist theory and offers a way to address the criticisms of the emphasis on private sphere behaviors in green citizenship literature. Although there are scholars who are critical of the hyphenated consumer-citizen, there are many more who view sustainable consumption as a key practice of green citizenship and who thus see the blurring of the traditional boundary between public and private as a positive move (see, for example, Jagers et al. 2014). Many of the problems that plague green citizenship stem from this boundary blurring. I have argued elsewhere that the way the private sphere is treated in theories of green citizenship is problematic from an (eco-)feminist perspective (MacGregor 2006b). There are two points to make here: first, that consumption needs to be politicized by being defined and valued as *practices of social reproduction*, and, second, that consumption should not be seen as an act of green citizenship.

(Eco-)feminist scholars have theorized work performed in the private or domestic sphere as a feminized form of labor called social reproduction (di Chiro 2008). Social reproduction involves the provision of services upon which the economy, the state, and individuals depend for survival. Those who do provisioning work make it possible for individuals to act as citizens in much the way that the functions provided by material-natural environments/ecosystems do (Langley and Mellor 2002). Although provisioning activities ensure the ongoing reproduction and maintenance of life, they have traditionally been "ignored or trivialized in mainstream political, economic and environmental analyses" (di Chiro 2008: 281). On this view it is a good thing that green citizenship theorists have brought these activities into the frame of what counts as citizenship. However, the problem is that they tend to describe the private sphere as primarily a place of consumption and give almost no consideration to the gendered division of labor within it. A feminist approach, on the other hand, regards consumption and other provisioning work as being embedded in particular contexts and performed by embodied people (with different personal and institutional capacities) under conditions that are not entirely of their choosing (Middlemiss 2010: 163). This means that responsibility for unpaid, domestic practices (disproportionately borne by women) should be understood as socially determined, a product of unequal social structures, and therefore as deeply political. The deliberate use of the words "practices" and "work" in place of the word "behavior" resonates with a growing body of literature that criticizes the take-over of green citizenship by economic and behavioral psychology and argues for a more contextual and politically sensitive approach (Evans 2011).

Seen from this angle, there is a need to stop seeing private acts like buying organic food or recycling one's plastic bottles as acts of citizenship. I want to argue that it is time to kill off the figure of the "consumer-citizen." Following the long-standing critiques of environmentalism's flight from politics, if green citizenship is to survive, it must be theorized in a way that resists privatization. As Maniates (2001: 34) argued in the early days of green citizenship thinking, people ought to "understand themselves as citizens in a participatory democracy first, working together to change broader policy and larger social institutions." In light of the extent to which being a consumer has surpassed being a citizen as a meaningful identity in affluent capitalist societies, the citizen has all but been erased in the "consumer-citizen" construction. Therefore perhaps there is *a strategic need* to reestablish the line between the private and the public and thereby restore the specificity of citizenship in green citizenship theory. It is important to argue that even though private sphere acts and consumption choices are undeniably important (connected to the feminist arguments about corporeality and the value of social reproduction), they do not count as acts of citizenship (MacGregor 2006b). They are part of relationships between household members and between consumer and sellers;

they may be political but they are not citizenly acts in the specific sense of the word. So rather than promoting private (unpaid, feminized) pro-environmental behaviors as acts of citizenship, green citizenship should be seen as a position from which to contest these practices as part of a challenge to the relationship between green citizens and the state. For example, it should be seen as a position from which to claim the right to state-delivered environmental services and regulations that reduce the need for individuals to conduct them. Buying, washing, collecting, and transporting one's plastic bottles to a privately-contracted recycling bank are not citizenly acts. Instead, a citizenly act is demanding free, curbside recyclable waste collection for all, or pressing governments to pass laws against unnecessary and wasteful packaging thus reducing the need to recycle in the first place. Collectivized environmental services redistribute time and resources in efficient and sustainable ways that have greater potential to break down the gendered division of labor than does the so-called "greening the household." The fact that one rarely hears of citizen movements for "sustainable homeservices" (Halme et al. 2004) is symptomatic of the way that the concept of green consumerism as citizenship has depoliticized environmentalism. As Eckersley puts it, citizenship must be seen as "shared activity, united around collective problems" (2004: 184). Whether ecological citizens are active in a "green public sphere" (Torgerson 1999) or a "green state" (Eckersley 2004), what is important is that they are acting collectively and publicly to bring about changes to existing power structures, rather than acting alone to green their lifestyles. It is unlikely that the most pressing collective problem of all—global climate change—stands a chance of being solved unless citizens can see beyond their immediate, everyday concerns.

Being Political: Performativity and the Right to Claim Rights

The third insight that offers hope for revitalizing green citizenship comes from radical democratic theory and provides ideas for reformulating it in a properly political way. Here we start from a position that citizenship is a deliberate, *political performance* rather than a tool for promoting a narrowly-defined and imposed consensus. There are several critics of green citizenship who have looked to the work of Arendt (Sandilands 1999; Torgerson 1999; Smith 2005) and Mouffe (Machin 2013; MacGregor 2014) for help in constructing more politically robust alternatives. Mick Smith (2005: 61), for example, advocates an "Arendtian environmental citizenship" that is a site of contestation and struggle rather than a meek acceptance of green obligations. Machin (2012: 847) builds on Smith's and Gabrielson and Parady's (2010) models to create a Mouffian account of "agonal green citizenship" that celebrates politics as constituted by the "irreducible disagreement arising from differently embodied citizens" and that offers an alternative to the post-political consensus-seeking tendencies in liberal environmentalism. Gilbert and Phillips (2003) draw on Henri Lefebvre's conception of "right to the city" to bring a notion of performativity (referring to "self-actualization in the presence of others," in Arendt's terms [Smith 2005: 54]) together with a desire to defend, (re)appropriate, and expand the rights of citizens. They, along with Isin (2009), emphasize the activist and insurgent nature of performative citizenship as a mode of political subjectivity: it is about "stepping outside or pushing the boundaries of the [established neo-liberal governance] system" (Gilbert and Phillips 2003: 327). For them, an example of this performative citizenship is Toronto's homeless people politicizing government inaction on homelessness by illegally occupying derelict land (that was ear-marked as a potential Olympic site) in a Tent City. They actively claimed their rights to the city, to home and belonging, as part of their being citizens. For me, an example of insurgent, performative green citizenship might be refusing to cooperate with domestic recycling by publicly dumping plastic bottles at the headquarters of drinks manufacturers (as Friends of the Earth did in the UK over 40 years ago (Secrett 2011)) as a way of politicizing neo-liberal government inaction and hypocrisy on waste.

Citizenship for each of these scholars, and for me, is defined not as a legal, territorially-determined status but as a practice driven by commitment to the ethico-political values of democracy, publicity, equality, and liberty. This understanding draws on Mouffe's radical democratic vision of citizenship as a political identity that can unite social movements in common resistance to neo-liberalism and post-politics (Mouffe 2005). In addition to this approach, it is also worth reconsidering the place of rights in the theory of green citizenship. As noted earlier, the liberal focus on rights has been overshadowed by the civic republican concern for duties in the mainstream literature. If this was a needed corrective to the perceived imbalance between rights and duties back then, there is a need for the pendulum to swing back toward rights at a time when states are downloading ever more responsibilities to individuals and communities while eroding all manner of rights—to privacy, sovereignty, healthy environments, to socialized care. Just as we need to reassert the specificity of citizenship as a public practice at a time when the public is under threat and disappearing, so too do we need to restore balance between duties and rights at a time when rights are being eroded. Reclaiming these rights, which were once taken for granted, would be part of restoring the definition of citizen as "the subject of rights" and assertions of the "right to claim rights" as an enactment of citizenship—of *being political* (Gilbert and Phillips 2003; Isin 2009). Of course this argument applies to contexts where rights have already been won and lost; there are many places in the world where rights to the city and rights to nature are part of struggles for basic services, for recognition, and for democracy—the kind of life "we" take for granted in the global North (see for example, Cornwall et al. 2011). Green theorists of citizenship—and their critics—have much to learn from these struggles.

Rather than being resigned to an assessment that we are now "post-democracy" and that environmentalism is dead, I argue for a turning back to the promise of the citizen. This requires seeing performances of green citizenship as being above all about speaking and acting against neo-liberal responsibilization and exploitative human–nature relations as "historical inevitability" (Smith 2005: 60). I am in agreement with Swyngedouw (2010) that in the face of the depoliticizing forces of neo-liberalism, techno-scientific certainty, and environmental managerialism, there is a need to reclaim political space for debate. Reasserting the specificity of the political is necessary before we can even begin to imagine alternative futures that challenge the neo-liberal frame (Swyngedouw 2010). But Swyngedouw does not tell us who is the subject of this re-politicizing move; "the citizen" is largely absent from his analysis. In Blühdorn's analysis, where the words "ordinary citizens" appear one could easily put the word "people" in their place—he shows no explicit concern for the meaning of citizenship. This is unfortunate because by neglecting the role of the citizen, these "post" analyses can be paralyzing to a movement whose future is already in question.

Conclusion

Should environmental political theorists continue to include citizenship as a key part of their vision for political change? It may have made sense in the dying days of the last century, but does it make sense in these post-political, post-ecological times? I have argued that if it is to play any meaningful role in the future of environmentalism, citizenship must be reclaimed from the managers and re-sharpened by a set of new concerns for materiality/corporeality, intersectionality, social difference, and political resistance. It should be seen as a position from which to resist neo-liberalism's presentation of human self-interest as natural and inevitable. This move requires an opening up of political space that has been shut down by the post-political rhetoric of crisis and a return to genuine collectivism and public spiritedness. There is a desperate need for public spaces that enable citizens to act *qua* citizen, where they enact *being a citizen* as something distinct from being a parent, worker, and consumer. Rejecting the conflation of citizen and consumer seems necessary in order to reclaim the democratic impulse within environmentalism and to understand citizenship as a site of political contest. Perhaps we might consider how understanding embodiment and embeddedness and "an agency that starts from insurgent vulnerability" (Lykke 2009: 42; Alaimo 2009) can change the way we think about citizenship. It seems important, moreover, to open up discussion about "how nature can be politicized as part of the politics of citizenship and vice versa" (Latta 2007: 382). Only if those inside the main tent of green political theory are willing to incorporate these insights from feminist, postcolonial, and radical democratic theories will the concept of green citizenship be sharp enough to cut through the hardened crust of neo-liberal hegemony.

Note

1. Stacey Alaimo (2009: 26) defines "insurgent vulnerability" as "a recognition of our material interconnection with the wider environment that impels ethical and political responses." Although it requires further theoretical development, this concept should be understood as an eco-feminist response to—or rebellion against—the denial of human vulnerability that has deep roots in dominant Western cultures. Contemporary efforts to

"combat" climate change through techno-science and to foster "resilience" through environmental management can be seen as symptomatic of delusional human exceptionalism. Arguably it is this exceptionalism, and the desire to become invulnerable to natural processes, that have led to socio-environmental crises. Acceptance of the inescapable facts of human fragility and dependence, on the other hand, can be a common starting point for a transformative ecological politics.

REFERENCES

Agyeman, J. and Evans, B. (2006). "Justice, Governance, and Sustainability: Perspectives on Environmental Citizenship from North America and Europe." In *Environmental Citizenship*, edited by Andrew Dobson and Derek Bell (Cambridge, MA: MIT Press), 185–206.

Alaimo, S. (2009). "Insurgent Vulnerability and the Carbon Footprint of Gender." Special Issue on Gender and Climate Change—*Kvinder, Køn & Forskning* NR 3–4: 22–33.

Arendt, H. (1958). *The Human Condition* (Chicago: University of Chicago Press).

Arias-Maldonado, M. (2012). *Real Green: Sustainability after the End of Nature* (London: Ashgate).

Barry, J. (1999). *Rethinking Green Politics* (London: Sage).

Barry, J. (2004). "From Environmental Politics to the Politics of the Environment." In *Liberal Democracy and the Environment*, edited by M. Wissenburg and Y. Levy (London: Routledge), 179–92.

Barry, J. (2006). "Resistance is Fertile: From Environmental to Sustainability Citizenship." In *Environmental Citizenship*, edited by Andrew Dobson and Derek Bell (Cambridge, MA: MIT Press), 21–48.

Bell, D. (2005). "Liberal Environmental Citizenship." *Environmental Politics* 14(2): 179–94.

Blühdorn, I. (2013). "The Governance of Unsustainability: Ecology and Democracy after the Post-democratic Turn." *Environmental Politics* 22(1): 16–36.

Bookchin, M. (1992). *Urbanization without Cities: The Rise and Decline of Citizenship* (Montreal: Black Rose Books).

Catney, P. and Doyle. T. (2010). "The Welfare of Now and the Green (Post) Politics of the Future." *Critical Social Policy* 31(2): 174–93.

Cornwall, A., Robins, S., and Von Lieres, B. (2011). "States of Citizenship: Contexts and Cultures of Public Engagement and Citizen Action." IDS Working Paper 363. University of Sussex-Brighton, UK.

Di Chiro, G. (2008). "Living Environmentalisms: Coalition Politics, Social Reproduction and Environmental Justice." *Environmental Politics* 17(2): 276–98.

Dobson, A. (2003). *Citizenship and the Environment* (Oxford: Oxford University Press).

Dobson, A. (2006)."Citizenship." In *Political Theory and the Ecological Challenge*, edited by Andrew Dobson and Robyn Eckersley (Cambridge: Cambridge University Press), 216–31.

Dobson, A. (2012). "Ecological Citizenship Revisited," in *Handbook of Global Environmental Politics*, 2nd edn., edited by Peter Dauvergne (Cheltenham, UK and Northampton, USA: Edward Elgar), 520–9.

Dobson, A. and Bell, D., eds. (2006). *Environmental Citizenship* (Cambridge, MA: MIT Press).

Dobson, A. and Valencia Sáiz, A. (2005). "Introduction." *Environmental Politics* 14(2): 157–62.

Gilbert, L. and Phillips, C. (2003). "Practices of Urban Environmental Citizenship: Rights to the City and Rights to Nature in Toronto." *Citizenship Studies* 7(3): 313–30.

Eckersley, R. (2004). *The Green State: Rethinking Democracy and Sovereignty* (Cambridge, MA: MIT Press).
Evans, D. (2011). "Consuming Conventions: Sustainable Consumption, Ecological Citizenship and the Worlds of Worth." *Journal of Rural Studies* 27: 109–15.
Felli, R. and Castree, N. (2012). "Neoliberalising Adaptation to Environmental Change: Foresight or Foreclosure?" *Environment and Planning A* 44(1): 1–4.
Gabrielson, T. (2008). "Green Citizenship: A Review and Critique." *Citizenship Studies* 12(4): 429–46.
Gabrielson, T. and Parady, K. (2010). "Corporeal Citizenship: Rethinking Green Citizenship through the Body." *Environmental Politics* 19(3): 374–91.
Halme, M., Jasch, C., and Scharp, M. (2004). "Sustainable Homeservices? Toward Household Services that Enhance Ecological, Social and Economic Sustainability." *Ecological Economics* 51: 125–38.
Hobson, K. (2013). "On the Making of the Environmental Citizen." *Environmental Politics* 22(1): 56–72.
Isin, E. (2009). "Citizenship in Flux: The Figure of the Activist Citizen." *Subjectivity* 29: 367–88.
Jagers, S., Martinson, J., and Matti, S. (2014). "Ecological Citizenship: A Driver of Pro-environmental Behaviour?" *Environmental Politics* 23(3): 434–53.
Langley, P. and Mellor, M. (2002). "Economy, Sustainability and Sites of Transformative Space." *New Political Economy* 7(1): 49–65.
Latta, A. (2007). "Locating Democratic Politics in Ecological Citizenship." *Environmental Politics* 16(3): 377–93.
Latta, A. and Wittman, H., eds. (2012). *Environment and Citizenship in Latin America: Natures, Subjects and Struggles* (New York: Berghahn Books).
Lykke, N. (2009). "Non-innocent Intersections of Feminism and Environmentalism." *Kvinder, Køn & Forskning* NR 3–4: 36–44.
MacGregor, S. (2006a). "No Sustainability without Justice: A Feminist Critique of Environmental Citizenship." In *Environmental Citizenship*, edited by Andrew Dobson and Derek Bell (Cambridge, MA: MIT Press), 106–26.
MacGregor, S. (2006b). *Beyond Mothering Earth: Ecological Citizenship and the Politics of Care* (Vancouver: University of British Columbia Press).
MacGregor, S. (2014). "Only Resist: Feminist Ecological Citizenship and the Post-politics of Climate Change." *Hypatia* 29(3): 617–33.
Machin, A. (2012). "Decisions, Disagreement and Responsibility: Towards an Agonistic Green Citizenship." *Environmental Politics* 21(6): 847–63.
Maniates, M. (2001). "Individualization: Plant a Tree, Ride a Bike, Save the World?" *Global Environmental Politics* 1(3): 31–52.
Meyer, J. M. (2015). *Engaging the Everyday: Environmental Social Criticism and the Resonance Dilemma* (Cambridge MA: MIT Press).
Middlemiss, L. (2010). "Reframing Individual Responsibility for Sustainable Consumption: Lessons from Environmental Justice and Ecological Citizenship." *Environmental Values* 19(2): 147–67.
Mouffe, C. (2005). *On the Political* (New York: Routledge).
Nixon, R. (2011). *Slow Violence and the Environmentalism of the Poor* (Cambridge, MA: Harvard University Press).
Plumwood, V. (1993). *Feminism and the Mastery of Nature* (London: Routledge).
Rancière, J. 2001. "Ten Theses on Politics." *Theory & Event* 5(3): 17–34.

Rose, N. (1999). *Powers of Freedom: Reframing Political Thought* (Cambridge: Cambridge University Press).

Sandilands, C. (1999). *The Good-Natured Feminist* (Minneapolis: University of Minnesota Press).

Secrett, C. "Environmental Activism Needs its Own Revolution to Regain its Teeth." *The Guardian*, June 13, 2011. Online: http://www.theguardian.com/environment/2011/jun/13/environmental-activism-needs-revolution (accessed April 28, 2014).

Smith, M. J. (2005). "Obligation and Ecological Citizenship." *Environments* 33(3): 9–23.

Smith, M. J. and Pangsapa, P. (2008). *Environment and Citizenship: Integrating Justice, Responsibility and Civic Engagement* (London: Zed Books).

Smith, M. (2002). "Review Article—Negotiating Nature: Social Theory at its Limits?" *Environmental Politics* 11(2): 181–6.

Smith, M. (2005). "Ecological Citizenship and Ethical Responsibility: Arendt, Benjamin and Political Activism." *Environments* 33(3): 51–63.

Steward, F. (1991). "Citizens of Planet Earth." In *Citizenship*, edited by G. Andrews (London: Lawrence and Wishart), 65–75.

Swyngedouw, E. (2010). "Apocalypse Forever? Post-political Populism and the Spectre of Climate Change." *Theory, Culture and Society* 27(2): 213–32.

Thompson, G. "Responsibility and Neoliberalism." *Open Democracy* July 31, 2007. Online: http://www.opendemocracy.net/article/responsibility_and_neo_liberalism (accessed March 14, 2014).

Torgerson, D. (1999). *The Promise of Green Politics: Environmentalism and the Public Sphere* (Durham and London: Duke University Press).

Van Steenbergen, B. (1994). *The Condition of Citizenship* (London: Sage).

Webb, J. (2012). "Climate Change and Society: The Chimera of Behaviour Change Technologies." *Sociology* 46(1): 109–25.

Wissenburg, M. (1998). *Green Liberalism: The Free and the Green Society* (London: UCL Press).

Yuval-Davis, N. (2007). "Intersectionality, Citizenship and Contemporary Politics of Belonging." *Critical Review of International Social and Political Philosophy* 10 (4): 561–74.

CHAPTER 41

ECOLOGICAL DEMOCRACY AND THE CO-PARTICIPATION OF THINGS

LISA DISCH

Introduction

Is ecological democracy possible? Influential academic and popular writers have painted an authoritarian future for the ecologically compromised world, casting authoritarian politics either as the outcome of ecological crisis or as the only way to forestall it (Hardin 1968; Kaplan 1994; Ophuls 1977).[1] Deliberative democratic theorists have been valiant in resisting such eco-political doomsday scenarios (Sagoff 1998; Wilson and Howarth 2002). Yet deliberative democracy, with its ideal of public decision-making by unconstrained discursive exchange, has had an uneasy relationship to green environmental politics. Dryzek (1995: 19-20; citing Alford 1985: 77 and Eckersley 1992: 109–17) argues that insofar as deliberation is understood in Habermasian terms as a distinctively inter*subjective* (that is, human-to-human) mode of interaction and is juxtaposed against the instrumental (that is, subject–object) rationality of science, economics, and other technical disciplines, it necessarily reaffirms the fundamental anthropocentrism of democratic politics. As a remedy to this problem, Dryzek (1995: 20) has proposed to "rescue communicative rationality from Habermas" and, thereby, defend it as both empirically and normatively applicable to ecological democracy. He argues that the ideal of deliberative public exchange describes the green movement, which has relied on non-governmental actors to speak for constituencies that escape representation by official state institutions. More importantly, it characterizes the "regulatory ideal" of ecological democracy: "effectiveness in communication that transcends the boundary of the human world" (Dryzek 1995: 24).

This rescue mission will involve a proposal that Dryzek expects to be controversial. He argues that environmental political theorists need to recognize "communicative rationality" in non-humans, that is, in those "entities that can act as agents, even though they lack the self-awareness that connotes subjectivity" (Dryzek 1995: 20). Doing so challenges what Dryzek (1995: 23) terms "perhaps the biggest political boundary of them all: that between the human and the non-human world." As Dryzek conceives it, this boundary crossing would occur by communicative means. Humans would pay "attention to feedback signals emanating from natural systems," treating "signals emanating from the natural world with the same respect we accord signals emanating from human subjects, and as requiring equally careful interpretation" (Dryzek 1995: 2, 21). Simply put, Dryzek (1995: 23) proposes to extend the deliberative model to "accommodate non-human communication," including non-humans in deliberation by the mediation of their human advocates.

This idea of humans acting as proxy representatives for natural systems (and future generations) has become a standard way for environmental political theorists to conceive of ecological democracy (for example, Goodin 1996; Eckersley 2000; Ball 2006). It rests on two presuppositions that ought not to go unquestioned. The first, which they state explicitly, is that non-human entities and natural systems can have interests, in an "objective" sense, as conditions that are "necessary for and/or conducive to [their] functioning and/or flourishing" (Ball 2006: 137). The second, which is only implicit, is that science delivers the factual certainties from which these putatively objective interests derive, and on which the possibility of proxy representation rests. Those environmental political theorists who make these assumptions pair a fairly conventional notion of empirical research, as a transparent and unidirectional process of attending to "signals" from nature, with an equally conventional notion of political representation as a similarly transparent and "unidirectional" process that "proceeds from the assumed given character of the represented to the adequacy of the representative's perception of that character" (Saward 2006: 188). It is not quite, as Marres (2012: 1. emphasis original) has argued, an attempt to extend the "*existing* machinery of politics, morality and ethics... to include [non-human] entities." The interest-group politics of existing liberal democracies is far from deliberative. But it does unquestioningly make "communicative competence" a prerequisite for participation in politics, and conceive representation as the remedy for those who cannot speak (Eckersley 2000: 119).

This chapter presents an alternative line of environmental political thinking, descended from the strand of science and technology studies (STS) known as actor-network theory (ANT), that is known (or notorious) for two moves.[2] The first is overturning the representationalist model of science as a transparent medium that supplies the "matters of fact" from which representative democracy takes its bearings (Latour 2004: 237). The second is for the "claim that things have politics" which has sought to dismantle the fiction (originating with Aristotle but intensifying with the theorists of the social contract), that politics is uniquely a work of humans and distinctly a domain of speech (Marres 2013: 418).

There is no question that this approach undermines the possibility of ecological democracy if it is to be defined as environmental political theorists have done, as the "unidirectional" representation of non-humans by humans (Saward 2006: 188). This, however, is all the more reason for environmental political theorists to read this work and take it seriously. It offers a provocative shift of focus from the responsibility of humans to represent nature to the agency of things in representing humans.

This essay treats three distinct initiatives within ANT and ANT-inspired theories of politics. First is the ANT critique of scientific objectivity, which I argue reframes the problem of ecological democracy by arguing that as non-humans are already active co-participants in forging social ties, there is no need to bridge a grand "boundary" between them. Second is "object-oriented democracy" (Latour 2005: 14), which I argue contributes to environmental political theory and democratic theory more generally by drawing attention to the agenda-setting capacity of objects and their effects on constituency formation. Third is "material participation" (Marres 2012), or "material politics" (Barry 2013), which, with its focus on the "capacities of things to facilitate, inform and organize citizenship and engagement," radically redefines the environmental political theory problematic (Marres 2012: 7). It recasts non-humans from mute (and potentially injured) objects in need of human advocates to mediators of environmentally responsible action in their own right.

The Critique of Scientific Objectivity

Actor-network theory (ANT) emerged around 1980 with the publication of Bruno Latour and Steve Woolgar's *Laboratory Life* (1979), Michel Callon's "Some Elements of a Sociological Theory of Translation" (1986), and Bruno Latour's *Science in Action* (1987) and *The Pasteurization of France* (1988), works that initiated an ontological turn (Marres 2013) in STS. These scholars give "ontology" a specialized meaning as conceptualizing not the stable, transhistorical nature of matter but, rather, its dynamic, contingent "variability" (Marres 2013: 432). It signals their break from an epistemological orientation that treats science as a means of representing the world, to an "ontological" orientation toward science as an intervention that "change[s] the world materially, socially, technologically, morally and politically" (Marres 2013: 420; cf. Hacking 1983). De Vries (2007: 803) calls ANT "a philosophical technique to describe what presents itself as a given, unproblematic object . . . as the outcome of . . . the chains of mediations that align a scientific text to the world."

Latour (1999) tells the story of a particularly ingenious mediator in his account of a pedology (soil science) expedition to Brazil in which scientists wrung from clods of dirt a surprising testimony: savannah was transforming into forest (that is, desertification was working in reverse). They gathered this testimony by means of a "pedocomparateur," a drawer-like box, fitted with a grid of square cubes, and equipped with a handle. This "cunning . . . hybrid," a briefcase-drawer-grid, is exemplary as a mediator that translates matter into "sign" (Latour 1999: 47–8). Introduced into an area of land that has itself been translated (by the mediation of survey instruments) into a grid, it enables the pedologist to extract lumps of soil, collect them systematically, subject them to various coding operations, and then render them as a diagram that affords an "implausible vista"—a vantage point for which an "observer could never exist" (Latour 1999: 54, 66). As Latour (1999: 66) explains, to "see" what the diagram discloses, the "observer would have not only to reside under the earth like a mole but also be able to cut the soil as if with a blade hundreds of meters long and replace the confusing variation of forms with homogeneous hatchings." The diagram does not resemble the landscape because "no step—except one—resembles the one that precedes it," yet because each step articulates to the next, the sequence adds up to a statement that "truly speaks of the world" (Latour 1999: 61).

This is one of most profound insights to come from ANT: in addition to the mediation of knowledge by language there is also the mediation of language by "inscription" devices that translate phenomena into symbol (Latour and Woolgar 1986). Stories like the pedology expedition elaborate what I will call a "political theory of scientific representation," an account that aims to reframe the "normative distinction between truth and falsity" from a question of accuracy to one of alliance (Latour 1999: 149). It demonstrates that ascertaining whether a claim is more or less representative does not turn on assessing its correspondence to (pre-existing) reality but on distinguishing "between well-articulated and inarticulate propositions" (Latour 1999: 149). By "articulation," these scholars mean something similar to Laclau and Mouffe (1985: 58, 65, 85): an intervention that at once specifies the properties of an entity and transforms it by bringing it into a new alliance. But ANT differs in being what Law (1999: 4) calls a "semiotics of materiality," which emphasizes that the identities of material entities are, like the meanings of words, "relational." Things, like words, are performative in the sense that knowing what an entity is depends on knowing what it can *do* not what it *is* in the abstract. What it can do depends, in turn, on whether and how it is allied to other actors.

By their emphasis on intervention and mediation, these works set out to challenge precisely that divide "between the human and the non-human world" that Dryzek imagines to pose so daunting a challenge to ecological democracy. But ANT does not problematize that divide as a gap to be bridged, as environmental political theorists typically do. Instead, it conducts empirical work to painstakingly document how hybrids—experimental apparatuses, vaccines, genetically engineered mice—confound the distinction between the natural and the social, and engages in argumentation to historicize this ontology as a construct specific to modernity.

Latour (1993: ch. 2, 2004: 236–7) dates the nature/society split, which he dubs the "Modern Constitution," to the advent of experimental science in the seventeenth century, with the "sudden and somewhat miraculous appearance of matters of fact." The fact, in its uniquely modern incarnation as autonomous and indisputable, made an ontological and epistemological revolution. It separated nature from society, assigned science and politics to separate realms, and perpetuated a separation and asymmetry between political representation, as (merely) speaking for, and scientific representation, as (actually) knowing.

Plenty of scholars, political theorists especially, have taken aim at this "absurdly unrealistic epistemology" (Latour 2005: 21). The ANT version of this critique is unique for arguing that it is disabling to humans and non-humans alike. For the Modern Constitution to privilege scientific representation as objective, it must cast non-humans as mute and passive "objects" of investigation. It strips things of their politics so as to grant human subjects a monopoly on politics—as speech and action. This, too, comes at a price. It renders political representation irreducibly uncertain, being based on the opinions and preferences of beings who can be moved to change their minds. The Modern Constitution sets politics at a double disadvantage: not only is political argumentation of lesser epistemological value than scientific findings but the "objects" of science limit by their obdurate facticity what the "subjects" of politics can move by the power of argument.

To be sure, deliberative democrats have powerfully challenged any simple opposition between fact and value by proposing that representations of the common good need not be "objective" to be valid: they may be *intersubjectively* valid if they are secured by public reason through deliberative exchange. Nonetheless, their vision of environmental democracy, where humans act as proxy representatives for nature's interests, remains grounded in the epistemology of the Modern Constitution whenever it treats those interests as "matters of fact."

ANT sets out to abrogate the Modern Constitution altogether by proposing the "new generalized principle of symmetry": the requirement that analysts treat humans and non-humans alike with respect to the capacity for action (Latour 1992: 283). General symmetry did not aim, as some critics have asserted (Schaffer 1991: 182; cf. Shapin 1988), to attribute human agency—"purpose, will and life"—to things. It is "a methodological principle of empirical research" that aims to render visible the active participation of things as varied as facts and theories, plants and microbes, machines and institutions in composing society and social relations (Brown 2009: 180). Without aiming to be a critique of anthropocentrism, it effectively displaces the human subject from its position of pride with respect to action by acknowledging the co-participation of material actors in human performances. The message, simple (but radical), is that action is a capacity that resides in associations between human and non-human actors; it is neither the property of any one individual nor of humans in isolation from their material entourages.

Pasteur's anthrax research, as famously retold in Latour's (1988) *The Pasteurization of France*, is a striking example of co-participation. Latour painstakingly narrates Pasteur's scientific practice as involving the creation of alliances of human and non-human actors: microbes, urine, vaccination in the laboratory and in the field, hygienists, scientists, farmers, and veterinarians. The result is nothing less than a materialist retelling of the emergence of biopolitics in which the *microbe* features centrally as a "new social link" and Pasteur's laboratories as a quietly governmental force (Latour 1992: 284). Pasteur's researchers and the microbe together transformed the "very composition of society," intervening in the "daily details of life—spitting, boiling milk, washing hands—and at the macroscale—rebuilding sewage systems, colonizing countries, rebuilding hospitals—without ever being clearly seen as a stated political power" (Latour 1983: 158). As Callon and his co-authors (2009: 68) have observed, "this is the meaning of Latour's claim that science is the continuation of politics by other means": not that "science is reducible to just politics" but that successful laboratory science achieves (and even sometimes aims to achieve) the "reconfiguration of the worlds in which we decide to live."

Such work challenges the very terms of the problem that Dryzek has posed for the would-be environmental discursive democrat. It is not a matter of bridging a grand, timeless human–non-human divide by means of cross-species communication but, rather, one of recognizing that non-human entities of various kinds—from microbes to technological innovations—are already actively forging so-called "social" ties. Dryzek (1995: 24) overlooks that activity when he poses connection as the problem; when he frames connection as a matter of paying "attention to feedback signals emanating from natural systems," he glosses over the "mediators" that Latour (2005: 39) and his colleagues take such pains to render visible.

On the one hand, then, ANT would insist that natural systems do not "signal": signals have to be articulated (in the sense of translated from phenomenon to text) by apparatuses like the pedocomparator and procedures like the bioassay. On the other hand, ANT would insist that non-human entities do much more than signal. Like the microbe, which lent credence to new ways of governing milk production, the municipal water supply, and even the simple practice of spitting, they forge new associations that bring into being new social relations and social needs, thereby recomposing our ways of life.

General symmetry achieved what Dryzek called for: it challenged the human–non-human divide. Yet it did so in service of a project that struck many as contrary to the very ethos of environmentalism (Demeritt 2006: 472). ANT set out explicitly to call scientific authority into question as a source for "indisputable knowledge about nature" (Marres 2012: 112) and to question scientific evidence as "a firm foundation or 'rational solution' on which political decisions can then be made" (Barry 2013: 8). Emphasizing the "diverse practical activities and material and cultural resources involved in creating representations of nature," ANT scholarship made it clear that mimesis is no better a model for what science does than it is for what politicians do. It abrogated the "Modern Constitution" to establish that the "representation of nonhumans involves no less doubt, work and mediation than the representation of humans" (Brown 2009: 177).

Does this serve ecological democracy? Does it not, rather, make ANT complicit with ecological bad faith in its most dangerous forms?[3] Climate skepticism, for example, seems to rest on a similar conviction that science cannot offer incontrovertible proof regarding the outcomes and trajectory of climate change. Or consider Republican electoral strategists in 2002. Did they not lay bare the political uses of the constructivist account of fact when they "counseled candidates "to 'challenge the science' because if 'the public came to believe that the scientific issues are settled, their views about global warming [would] change accordingly'" (Demeritt 2006: 454)?

For his part, Latour (1999: 114) has always insisted that he believes that science *does* make it possible to "talk truthfully about a state of affairs." He steadfastly maintains that his approach never aimed "to get *away* from facts but *closer* to them" by challenging the way they are constructed—as objective, obdurate, mute—by the Modern Constitution

(Latour 2004a: 231). This is the focus of their critique, not facts in general but the specifically modern, objectified "matter of fact," which, as a "disfigured version of the scientific referent," has pernicious effects on science and democratic politics alike (Latour 2003: 143). Not only does it fuel skepticism about science by creating misconceptions about the kind of certainty that scientific research can provide, but once the laboratory came to be seen as the domain of "indisputable matters of fact" it was juxtaposed against Parliament (or the legislature), as the domain of "endless discussion" (Latour 2004b: 223). The result: talk-based politics was doomed at virtually the moment of its inception. In short, the project that originated as ANT and has become infamous as an attack on scientific objectivity has set itself the task of defending the practice of discursive politics.

Object-oriented Democracy

That defense begins with a move that deliberative theorists of politics may well perceive as an attack. ANT-inspired political theory proposes to bring the notion of alliance, the premise that "actors never act alone," back to politics (where they imported it from in the first place) to challenge the autonomy of the deliberative subject (Marres 2013: 421). The idea is to extend from scientific to political representation ANT's attention to the "masses of intermediaries [that are] necessary to represent anything" (Latour 2005: 29). They propose to develop the concept and practice of "*object-oriented* democracy," by focusing on the relationship between the constitution of objects and the creation of political constituencies, which means attending to the mediation of that relationship by the apparatuses of knowledge production (Latour 2005: 14).

One could argue that democracy has *always* been object-oriented. The very notion of a public politics rested on the belief in the power of seventeenth-century experimental science to provide the common body of fact that would constitute autonomous, independent individuals as a public (Ezrahi 1996: 74). Not only by delivering up matters of fact, but also by modeling reasoned exchange, scientific practice was supposed to make it possible to achieve "consensus among individuals of diverse social and religious affiliations *taken as equals*" (Ezrahi 1996: 83, emphasis added). The social contract version of object-oriented democracy was clearly premised on the Modern Constitution. The question is whether public politics remains practicable *outside* the terms of that ontological fiction? Can democracy survive in an era where, as Latour (2005: 19) contends "transparent, unmediated, undisputable facts have . . . become rarer and rarer" and, at the same time, indisputability has become a standard partisan weapon, to be claimed irrespective of evidence for initiatives that one wants to pursue and denied for those that one does not. If we can no longer count on public proofs to orient public discussion, but must fear facts as political weapons, are we simply to "despair of politics" (Latour 2005: 19)? Or might we rather trade "the worn-out cliché of incontrovertible matters of fact" for a paradox: a politics in which disputes would "conclude with 'disputable' assertions" (Latour 2005: 19)?

ANT-inspired political theory chooses the paradox, aiming for an account of object-oriented democracy that accords with this "sea change" in our understanding of science: as an institution existing not to secure "matters of fact" but to generate "matters of concern" (Latour 2004b: 66). Matters of concern, which Marres (2007: 762) characterizes as "troubling, partially unknown entanglements of humans and non-humans, which are often introduced to the world by science and technology, and which endanger society (from 'BSE' [Mad Cow Disease] to 'GM Food')," provoke "perplexity" on two counts (Latour 2004b: 66): 1) Shall we count them as real? 2) If so, how we will live with them? The modernist would assign this first "perplexity" to science and the second to politics. To the object-oriented democrat, by contrast, both the epistemological task of determining what such entities are and the critical theoretic task of assessing the ways of life to which they (in concert with us) give rise are equally matters of experiment and testing (science), and persuasion and alliance-building (politics).

Put differently, facts and subjects are "co-constructed" (Marres 2007: 771). Moreover, as both Callon (1998: 259) and Barry (2001) have demonstrated, they are called forth by "metrological frameworks." Callon (1998: 258) focuses on what might be termed the surreptitious publicity of negative externalities, detailing how the formation of affected publics depends on the existence of measurement devices that make the externalities visible. By contrast to Callon, Barry (2001: 68) focuses on the explicit publicity of entitles such as the European Union, whose formation "entails not just the development of European laws, markets and regulations, but also the formation of European objects and practices." Take the example of water quality near bathing beaches throughout Europe. Achieving a common standard for European beaches was not simply a matter of reaching agreement and issuing a directive. It required the various laboratories engaged in water quality monitoring to agree to adhere to the same experimental protocols. Lacking commonality of protocol and instrumentation, Europe's beaches would not be properly "European" in anything other than a rhetorical sense. Barry (2001: 83) reaffirms, "if we are to understand Europe today, we need to think of it as an entity which is being united as much by instruments, lines and devices as by more conventional political associations."

Callon (1980: 210–11) has also emphasized that experimental scientists influence constituency formation by the research questions they pose. He proposes the concept "socio-logic of translation" to capture how defining a research program is at once a cognitive move and "an attempt to mobilise social groups." Callon (2009: 543) likens issues to stem cells: they could become anything and take particular shape only as they are problematized by this socio-logic. Climate change, for example, can take shape as anything from a problem of "market efficiencies, [to] negative externalities, [to] developing countries' right to development"; these various "socio-logics," in turn, will solicit quite different political constituencies (Callon 2009: 543).

The concept "socio-logic" recalls what Schattschneider (1975: ch. 1) aims to capture with the notions "scope" and "bias" of conflict. Against those who imagine that political participation is spontaneous wherever interests are at stake, Schattschneider argues that conflict draws people into politics. Depending on how the stakes are defined and the arena in which it is played out (for Schattschneider the relevant distinction is that between party competition and interest competition), conflict can be more or less inclusive. In addition—and this is key—conflict can be framed to favor the "exploitation of some kinds of conflict and the suppression of others" thereby mobilizing some actors while suppressing the participation of others (Schattschneider 1975: 69).

Schattschneider's work is radical and interesting precisely because his emphasis on alternate framings of conflict as both mobilizing and de-mobilizing constituencies recognizes an aspect of the "ontological politics" of conflict (Mol 1999: 75). But whereas Schattschneider focuses on subject-formation, object-oriented democrats focus on object-formation. They make the symmetrical (and counter-intuitive) claim that "objects come into being—and disappear—with the practices in which they are manipulated" (Mol 2002: 5).[4] The object-oriented democrats also emphasize that agenda setting is not merely a human capacity that takes place in the medium of ideology. It is also a property of things that de Vries (2007: 782) terms "sub-politics": decisions and actions that have an impact on society but are beyond democratic control.

To illustrate, de Vries (2007: 787, 802) cites an instance of Dutch university researchers effectively making public policy when a prenatal blood screening test, which the researchers offered "to large numbers of women" in the experimental phase, took hold "as a way to aim at public health" before the results were in. Although the Dutch government ultimately decided neither to endorse the blood test, nor to pay for it as a matter of routine, women continued to request and pay for the test. They had accepted it as "a *praxis* that aims at a political object," in this case, public health. The research protocol, which mandated that it be widely diffused, together with the fact that it was "widely discussed in newspapers, in women's magazines and on television," made the test a "*political* fait accompli" entirely apart from government decision-making (de Vries 2007: 785–6, emphasis original). "Sub-political" actors (the test, its publicists, and its university imprimatur) created a constituency for prenatal blood screening that official political actors (that is, elected political representatives) could not disband.

In a related but distinct line of argument, Wynne (2008: 28) exposes the "unstated politics [that operates] in the name of 'science'" wherever putatively participatory forums reduce public concerns about techno-scientific innovation (such as GMOs) to "scientific questions" regarding the risks such innovations pose. Legitimate public concerns regarding how reliably science can project risk, or whether—regardless of risk—we want to live with such innovations become impossible to raise (Wynne 2001: 457). This, too, is agenda-setting power, "pursued *unaccountably* through 'science'" as the Modern Constitution defines it: unframed and exercising no power to frame (Wynne 2007: 103, emphasis added). Wynne's (2008: 23) argument suggests that whenever environmental political theorists conceive science as the requisite empirical base for representing nature's putatively objective interests, they make its "unaccountable normative commitments" more difficult to contest. Far from establishing ecological democracy on a firm footing, this sets it at odds with democratic structures and processes, which are distinctive, as Warren (1999: 214) has argued, for removing barriers to the contestation of power.

It is easy to see how this ANT-inspired political turn, with its shift from matters of fact to matters of concern and its attention to the capacities of objects to participate in agenda-setting and constituency formation, opens new avenues for the critique of power. When it comes to offering an innovative account of democratic practice, critics have argued that such theorists of object-oriented democracy as Latour and Callon and his co-authors fall short. De Vries (2007: 806) charges them with falling back on an "off-the-shelf conception of politics" as public deliberation. Wainwright (2005: 118–19; citing Latour 2004b: 89, emphasis original) has observed that Latour's vision of a " 'politics of nature' " where it is the common work of politics and the sciences to " '*make [entities] speak*'," simply "translates Habermas's principle of discourse ethics... [to] include[e] non-humans." This is no small irony. Despite their "ontological" innovations, ANT-inspired accounts of democratic practice fall back on the most basic version of proxy representation.

Material Participation/ Material Politics

This criticism has provoked studies of "material politics" (Barry 2013) and "material participation" (Marres 2012), ANT-inspired accounts of democratic politics that its proponents tout as being "quite different from how politics is normally understood: as a distinctive activity that depends on specific institutions and requires particular procedures" (Marres 2013: 420). Material politics and material participation aim to "foreground the role of objects, technologies and settings in the organization of publics" (Marres 2012: 60), and, thereby, to bring to light a capacity in non-humans that has gone unrecognized by theorists of discursive participation in conventional political institutions: their capacity to solicit human action and cast it in explicitly moral and political terms. Analysts of material participation aim to extend the concept of the public beyond the "narrowly confined" spaces of "bourgeois debate" to "include the spaces of everyday living" (Marres 2012: 49). In their accounts, devices such as the tea light or smart electricity meter, settings such as the eco-show home, procedures such as prenatal blood screening, and even everyday objects such as plastic bags "turn everyday material activities into forms of engagement with the environment" (Marres 2012: 64).[5]

Marres's (2012: 64–5) work focuses on "domestic environments," examining various devices—carbon accounting, sustainable living experiments, and eco-show homes—which index the environmental cost of everyday activities. Such devices render these activities public in an unaccustomed way: by registering their effects on distant others and thereby implicating our ways of living here and now in lives that are lived elsewhere or may be lived tomorrow. The tea light, a sphere roughly the size of a softball that sits next to the electric kettle, monitors the electricity grid so as to glow red when demand for energy is high, green when it is low. It sends a blunt message, prompting the tea drinker to prioritize her cup of tea in relation to other anonymous but potentially more urgent uses of current. The smart electricity meter illustrates the "capacity of electricity to engage users" in even more sophisticated ways (Marres 2012: 24). Displaying "three measures simultaneously—kilowatts, Pounds Sterling, and CO_2 emitted," it "co-articulates" three different registers on which electricity consumption acts: resource depletion, household expense, and depletion of sink capacity (Marres 2012: 69).

Material participation makes an especially provocative contribution to environmental political theory by radically redefining its problematic. To the materialist, participation is decidedly not a discursive process that requires "communicative competence" as its requisite (Eckersley 2000: 119). Material participation, like ANT generally, treats non-humans and humans symmetrically with respect to the capacity for action. Far from presuming that non-human objects need human agents to represent them, Marres (2013: 426) emphasizes how accounts of material participation foreground the "capacity of domestic environments to do normative work . . ., to engage people, to encourage them to act in moral, political and economical ways on environmental issues." Accounts of material participation do not position non-humans as "affected" (in the sense of injured) by ecological harms but, rather, aim to demonstrate how things acquire "normative capacities . . . to activate and mobilize publics" Marres (2012: 33).

The use of the term "public" in this context is unconventional, to say the least. Whereas it is easy to see how an eco-show home itself is public in the sense of being on display (as a "show home"), how might those who engage with its many devices be said to form a public? Theirs are individual actions, taken in a domestic setting. They are neither commonly visible, as the Arendtian conception of publicity would have it, nor subject to deliberation, as in the Habermasian version. Moreover, individuals' engagement with the devices is not necessarily reflexive, as engaging in collective action or deliberation tends to be. The devices seek to move rather than to persuade. The red glow of the tea light, the mounting costs (or energy savings) registered on the smart meter, these are coded to provoke a sense of emergency (the light) and tap an aversion to waste (the meter).

An important political element is missing from the "device-centered" (Marres and Lezaun 2011; Marres 2012: ch. 3) accounts of material participation: organizing. Its importance and centrality, even in a materialist account of participation, is illustrated by Sze's (2007) study of a citizen coalition that mobilized against the Bronx-Lebanon Medical Waste Incinerator in New York City in 1991. In this case, garbage and publics were co-constituting. Specifically, "increased exposure to pollution" gave local citizens' groups a way to transform the "symbolic meaning of garbage," (Sze 2007: 56) so as to frame a demand for environmental justice. Sze tells the story of how organizers built the Clean Air Coalition, using the discourse of environmental justice and dramatizing the everyday reality of asthma (wearing gas masks to a political protest, among other things) so that "rather than representing disease and health in the 19th-century sense, garbage now represent[ed] political neglect, broadly defined" (2007: 56). Although Sze does not use this vocabulary, her story testifies to how an association of humans and non-humans—schools, churches, neighborhood groups, garbage, pollution, and asthma—nominated a proposed incinerator to represent environmental justice in multiple senses: by standing for injustice, advocating for remedy, and as a mobilizing force for grassroots organizing.[6]

Conclusion

This essay has traced an alternative approach to ecological democracy from its beginnings in STS through the two ANT-inspired approaches to political theory, "object-oriented democracy" and "material politics/participation." I have demonstrated that *because of* and not *in spite of* its critique of scientific objectivity, this approach has the potential to resolve some of the conundrums associated with ecological democracy. Specifically, it shows that an environmental politics that believes it cannot do without "matters of fact" as an empirical base is at cross-purposes with democratic epistemology and practice in two ways. First, it reinstates the Modern Constitution's separation of nature from society and its privileging of scientific over political representation, which serves only to foster skepticism about science and cynicism about politics. Second, it affirms the unaccountability of the normative commitments of science, thereby narrowing the agenda for public disputes over technological innovation and giving free rein to the presumption that such innovations inevitably bring progress.

Whereas this work has important contributions to make to environmental political theory, it is neither as radical a departure from politics as it is "normally understood," nor as *political* as its proponents claim. First, whereas object-oriented democrats tend to emphasize that they break new ground in studying politics outside the institutions of government, it has been rare to find even political scientists (let alone political theorists) equating "politics with government decision-making" since the 1970s (Warren 1999: 213). The object-oriented democrats, like ANT more generally, are actually behind the curve insofar as they work with a "juridical" or substitution model of political representation that many democratic theorists would consider to be outmoded (Brown 2009: 172). Scholars of democratic political representation have made a "constructivist turn" (Disch 2011) that, as Brown (2009: 7) has argued, parallels the "ontological turn" in science studies: both are engaged in depicting "political and scientific representation as practices of mediation that engage and transform what they represent."

Second, it is simply not the case that contemporary political theorists consider it "taboo" for people to engage democratic practice to achieve "concrete results" (Marres 2005: 217). Environmental political theorists are analyzing examples of "object-oriented" democratic practices around food justice movements, new energy collectives, and crafting (Schlosberg and Coles N.D.). Sze's (2007) case study is a particularly noteworthy example, which suggests that the device-centered approach may overstate the point. With its emphasis on the "normative capacities of *things* to activate and mobilize publics," its attention to features of design and setting, and its repudiation of speaking in public as participation, the device-centered approach tends to overstate the agency of devices in themselves and to overlook the discourses and practices (such as organizing) that lend them political force (Marres 2012: 3, emphasis added). In Sze's account a thing (the incinerator) was combined with a discourse (environmental justice) by the hard work of coalition building. It was this combination, no thing alone, that moved New York City's waste management policy.

Acknowledgments

I thank *Handbook* editors David Schlosberg and Cheryl Hall for their astute feedback on this essay. Mark Brown and Noortje Marres each gave me excellent comments, and Justin Williams gave the essay an exceptionally generous, constructive, and insightful reading.

Notes

1. For a thoughtful discussion of some of this literature, see Paehlke (2004).
2. This approach has some uptake among environmental political theorists. See Gabrielson and Parady (2010: 376) for an "ontological shift" to conceptualize green citizenship as "corporal citizenship."
3. For an insightful discussion and critical analysis of this position, see Demeritt (2006).
4. Mol (2002: 35), e.g., has argued that "clinical" and "pathological" atherosclerosis are two different diseases, the one enacted in the outpatient clinic by questioning a patient about her leg pain, the other enacted in a pathology lab by examining tissue samples from the arteries of an amputated leg under a microscope.
5. For prenatal blood screening, see de Vries (2007). On plastic bags, see Hawkins (2006: ch. 2).
6. See Di Chiro (2008) for additional examples of coalition politics. For an altogether different approach to garbage, as a source of enchantment rather than hazards, see Bennett (2010).

References

Alford, C. Fred. (1985). *Science and the Revenge of Nature: Marcuse and Habermas* (Gainsville, FL: University Press of Florida).

Ball, Terence. (2006). "Democracy." In *Political Theory and the Ecological Challenge*, edited by Michael Saward and Robyn Eckersley (Cambridge: Cambridge University Press), 131–47.

Barry, Andrew. (2001). *Political Machines: Governing a Technological Society* (London, England: The Athlone Press).

Barry, Andrew. (2013). *Material Politics: Disputes Along the Pipeline* (Chichester, West Sussex: John Wiley and Sons).

Bennett, Jane. (2010). *Vibrant Matter: A Political Ecology of Things* (Durham, NC: Duke University Press).

Brown, Mark. (2009). *Science In Democracy: Expertise, Institutions, and Representation* (Cambridge, MA: MIT Press).
Callon, Michel. (1980). "Struggles and Negotiations to Define What is Problematic and What is Not. The Socio-Logics of Translation." In *The Social Process of Scientific Investigation, Sociology of the Sciences Yearbook*, Vol. 4, edited by K. D. Knorr-Cetina, Roger Krohn, and Richard Whitley (Boston, Dordrecht D. Reidel), 197–219.
Callon, Michel. (1986). "Some elements of a Sociology of Translation: Domestication of the Scallops and the Fishermen of St. Brieuc Bay." In *Power, Action and Belief: A New Sociology of Knowledge?*, edited by John Law (London: Routledge), 196–223.
Callon, Michel. (1998). "An Essay on Framing and Overflowing: Economic Externalities Revisited by Sociology." *The Sociological Review* 46(S1): 244–69.
Callon, Michel. (2009). "Civilizing Markets: Carbon Trading Between *in vitro* and *in vivo* Experiments." *Accounting, Organizations and Society* 34(3–4): 535–48.
Callon, Michel and Latour, Bruno. (1992). "Don't Throw the Baby Out With the Bath School! A Reply to Collins and Yearley." In *Science as Practice and Culture*, edited by Andrew Pickering (Chicago, IL: University of Chicago Press), 343–68.
Callon, Michel, Lascoumes, Pierre, and Barthe, Yannick (2009 [2001]). *Acting in an Uncertain World: An Essay on Technical Democracy*. Translated by Graham Burchell (Cambridge, MA: MIT Press).
Demeritt, David. (2006). "Science Studies, Climate Change and the Prospects for Constructivist Critique." *Economics and Society* 35(3): 453–79.
Di Chiro, Giovanna. (2008). "Living Environmentalisms: Coalition Politics, Social Reproduction, and Environmental Justice." *Environmental Politics* 17(2): 276–98.
Disch, Lisa. (2011). "Toward a Mobilization Conception of Democratic Representation." *American Political Science Review* 105(1): 100–14.
Dryzek, John. (1995). "Political and Ecological Communication." *Environmental Politics* 4(4): 13–30.
Eckersley, Robyn. (1992). *Environmentalism and Political Theory: Toward an Ecocentric Approach* (Albany, NY: State University of New York Press).
Eckersley, Robyn. (2000). "Deliberative Democracy, Ecological Representation and Risk: Towards a Democracy of the Affected." In *Democratic Innovation: Deliberation, Representation and Association*, edited by Michael Saward (London and New York: Routledge), 117–32.
Ezrahi, Yaron. (1996). "Modes of Reasoning and the Politics of Authority in the Modern State." In *Modes of Thought: Explorations in Culture and Cognition*, edited by David R. Olson and Nancy Torrance (Cambridge, UK: Cambridge University Press), 72–89.
Gabrielson, Teena and Parady, Katelyn. (2010). "Corporeal Citizenship: Rethinking Green Citizenship Through the Body." *Environmental Politics* 19(3): 374–91.
Goodin, Robert E. (2006). "Enfranchising the Earth, and Its Alternatives." *Political Studies* 44: 835–49.
Hardin, G. (1968). "The Tragedy of the Commons." *Science* 162(1): 1243–8.
Hawkins, Gay. (2006). *The Ethics of Waste: How We Relate to Rubbish* (New York: Rowman and Littlefield).
Kaplan, Robert D. (1994). "The Coming Anarchy." *The Atlantic Monthly*, February: 1–18.
Laclau, Ernesto and Mouffe, Chantal. (1985). *Hegemony and Socialist Strategy: Towards a Radical Democratic Politics* (New York: Verso).

Latour, Bruno. (1983). "Give me a Laboratory and I Will Raise the World." In *Science Observed*, edited by K. Knorr-Cetina and M. Mulkay (London: Sage), 141–70.

Latour, Bruno. (1987). *Science in Action: How to Follow Scientists and Engineers through Society* (Cambridge, MA: Harvard University Press).

Latour, Bruno. (1988). *The Pasteurization of France* (Cambridge, MA: Harvard University Press).

Latour, Bruno. (1992). "One More Turn After the Social Turn..." In *The Social Dimension of Science*, edited by E. McMullin (Notre Dame: Indiana University of Notre Dame Press), 272–94.

Latour, Bruno. (1993). *We Have Never Been Modern*. Translated by Catherine Porter (Boston, MA: Harvard University Press).

Latour, Bruno. (1999). *Pandora's Hope: Essays on the Reality of Science Studies* (Cambridge, MA: Harvard University Press).

Latour, Bruno. (2003). "What if we *Talked* Politics a Little?" *Contemporary Political Theory* 2: 143–64.

Latour, Bruno. (2004a). "Why has Critique Run out of Steam? From Matters of Fact to Matters of Concern" *Critical Inquiry* 30 (Winter): 225–48.

Latour, Bruno. (2004b). *Politics of Nature*. Translated by Catherine Porter (Cambridge, MA: Harvard University Press).

Latour, Bruno. (2005). *Reassembling the Social: An Introduction to Actor-Network Theory* (Oxford: Oxford University Press).

Latour, Bruno and Callon, Michel. (1981). "Unscrewing the Big Leviathan: How Actors Macro-structure Reality and How Sociologists Help Them To Do So." In *Advances in Social Theory and Methodology: Toward an Integration of Micro and Macro-sociologies*, edited by K. D. Knorr-Cetina and A. V. Cicourel (Boston, MA: Routledge and Kegan Paul), 277–303.

Latour, Bruno and Woolgar, Steve. (1986 [1979]). *Laboratory Life: The Construction of Scientific Facts* (Princeton, NJ: Princeton University Press).

Law, John. (1999). "After ANT: Complexity, Naming and Topology." In *Actor Network Theory and After*, edited by John Law and John Hassard (Oxford and Malden, MA: Blackwell), 1–14.

Marres, Noortje. (2005). "Issue Spark a Public into Being: A Key but Often Forgotten Point of the Lippmann-Dewey Debate." In *Making Things Public*, edited by Peter Weibel and Bruno Latour (Cambridge, MA: MIT Press), 208–17.

Marres, Noortje. (2007). "The Issues Deserve More Credit: Pragmatist Contributions to the Study of Public Involvement in Controversy." *Social Studies of Science* 37(5): 759–80.

Marres, Noortje. (2012). *Material Participation: Technology, the Environment and Everyday Publics* (Houndmills, Basingstoke, Hampshire: Palgrave Macmillan).

Marres, Noortje. (2013). "Why Political Ontology Must Be Experimentalized: On Eco-Show Homes as Devices of Participation." *Social Studies of Science* 43(3): 417–43.

Marres, Noortje and Lezaun, Javier. (2011). "Materials and Devices of the Public: An Introduction." *Economy and Society* 40(4): 489–509.

Mol, Annemarie. (1999). "Ontological Politics." In *Actor Network Theory and After*, edited by John Law and John Hassard (Oxford and Malden, MA: Blackwell), 74–89.

Mol, Annemarie. (2002). *The Body Multiple: Ontology in Medical Practice* (Durham and London: Duke University Press).

Ophuls, William. (1977). *Ecology and the Politics of Scarcity* (San Francisco: W.H. Freeman).

Paehlke, Robert. (2004). "Democracy and Environmentalism: Opening a Door to the Administrative State." In *Managing Leviathan*, edited by Robert Paehlke and Douglas Torgerson (Peterborough, Ontario: Broadview), 25–44.

Sagoff, M. (1998). "Aggregation and Deliberation in Valuing Environmental Public Goods: A Look Beyond Contingent Pricing." *Ecological Economics* 24: 312–30.

Saward, Michael. (2006). "Representation." In *Political Theory and the Ecological Challenge*, edited by Michael Saward and Robyn Eckersley (Cambridge: Cambridge University Press), 183–99.

Schaffer, Simon. (1991). "The Eighteenth Brumaire of Bruno Latour." *Studies in History and Philosophy of Science* 22(1): 174–92.

Schattschneider, E. E. (1975 [1960]). *The Semisovereign People: A Realist's View of Democracy in America*. Revised edn. (Fort Worth, TX: Harcourt Brace Jovanovich).

Schlosberg, David and Coles, Romand. N.D. "The New Environmentalism of Everyday Life: Sustainability, Material Flows, and Movements." Unpublished manuscript.

Shapin, Steven. (1988). "Review: Following Scientists Around." *Social Studies of Science* 18(3): 533–50.

de Vries, Gerard. (2007). "What is Political in Sub-Politics: How Aristotle Might Help STS." *Social Studies of Science* 37(5): 781–809.

Wainwright, Joel. (2005). "Politics of Nature: A Review of Three Recent Works by Bruno Latour." *Capitalism Nation Society* 16(1): 115–22.

Warren, Mark E. (1999). "What is Political?" *Journal of Theoretical Politics* 11(2): 207–31.

Wilson, M. A. and Howarth, R. B. (2002). "Discourse-Based Valuation of Ecosystem Services: Establishing Fair Outcomes through Group Deliberation." *Ecological Economics* 41: 431–43.

Wynne, Brian. (2001). "Creating Public Alienation: Expert Cultures of Risk and Ethics on GMOs." *Science as Culture* 10(4): 445–81.

Wynne, Brian. (2007). "Public Participation in Science and Technology: Performing and Obscuring a Conceptual—Category Mistake." *East Asian Science, Technology and Society* 1: 99–110.

Wynne, Brian. (2008). "Elephants in the Rooms Where Publics Encounter 'Science'?: A Response to Darrin Durant, 'Accounting For Expertise: Wynne and the Autonomy of the Lay Public." *Public Understanding of Science* 17: 21–33.

Index

n = endnote. *t* = table/diagram.

Lightning Source UK Ltd.
Milton Keynes UK
UKHW050326290519
343510UK00002B/3/P

9 780198 823865